PERSONAL MONEY MANAGEMENT

PERSONAL MONEY MANAGEMENT

THOMAS E. BAILARD
DAVID L. BIEHL
RONALD W. KAISER

SCIENCE RESEARCH ASSOCIATES, INC.
Chicago, Palo Alto, Toronto, Henley-on-Thames, Sydney, Paris
A Subsidiary of IBM

We wish to acknowledge the following for permission to reprint or adapt material.

George Katona, Lewis Mandell, and Jay Schmiedeskamp. *1970 Survey of Consumer Finances.* Copyright © by The University of Michigan 1971. Used by permission of the Survey Research Center of the Institute for Social Research, University of Michigan.

1972 Life Rates and Data. Copyright, 1972, by The National Underwriter Company. Used by permission.

FundScope. Allen Silver, ed. Copyright © FundScope, Inc. 1972. Used by permission.

3-Trend Cycli-Graphs. © 1972 by Securities Research Company. Used by permission.

CONTENTS

PREFACE

This text is designed to enable the student to analyze and direct his own or his family's financial affairs. Most texts in this field are highly descriptive: they offer the reader a wealth of descriptive material, facts, and impersonal data without providing him with an insight into their effective application to his own needs. In this text we have worked to provide not only the necessary subject material but also the tools needed to relate that material to individual situations. As financial consultants and educators, we believe that such a prescriptive approach is necessary and justifiable.

There are four aspects of this text that help implement this how-to approach: (1) the Chuck and Nancy Anderson case problem series and other case problems; (2) step-by-step procedures for making important financial decisions; (3) discussions of the appropriateness of various financial alternatives; and (4) the organization of the text topics around major financial strategies.

The Chuck and Nancy case problems at the end of each chapter offer the student the opportunity to apply his newly learned skills to types of financial decisions that are made by "typical" American families. As he works through these cases, the reader can see how financial decisions interrelate and through this understanding he can proceed to build his own financial programs. (Problem cases commonly used in texts on personal money management do not relate to each other in this way and so do not give the student this essential overview.) In addition to the Chuck and Nancy cases, we have attempted to provide problem cases that deal with financial questions more immediately related to the life of a college student. These are designed to help students using this text develop skills for today, not merely for some hazily defined tomorrow.

The step-by-step procedures provide the student with readily understandable, clearly structured methods that he can use to resolve specific financial problems. They are designed to enable him to work with the relevant information and translate it into answers for himself. Although developed around sophisticated present-value-of-the-dollar methods, these relatively simple procedures enable the financial manager to design a personal income statement and balance sheet, determine accurately his needs for all types of insurance, set up and operate a monthly budget, develop an effective investment portfolio strategy, and plan for his retirement.

In our experience as personal financial consultants, we have found that individuals often lack the information necessary to choose wisely between financial alternatives. They cannot decide whether to buy term or cash-value life insurance. They wonder how long a maturity to get on a home mortgage and how large that mortgage should be. They do not know how to decide when to borrow money or how much to borrow. They have no good idea of how to select a stockbroker. We have attempted to portray clearly the issues involved and to isolate financial considerations from emotional or social concerns. By learning to compare the financial and nonfinancial ramifications of certain decisions the student will acquire the judgment needed to make sound decisions. Although we may have sometimes failed to satisfy proponents on one side or the other of these issues, we believe that we have been as financially correct as possible in arriving at our conclusions.

Finally, we have attempted to place a rational structure on subject matter that is typically presented as merely a series of related topics. Unit I helps the student *get started*: to establish his goals and determine his present financial position. Unit II shows him how to *protect what he has* in order to provide for the financial security necessary to proceed confidently to other financial matters. Unit III helps him *get more out of his income*: to budget, to reduce his taxes, to save interest costs in borrowing, to buy and finance his housing efficiently. In short, it helps him to streamline his cash flow so he can have money available for his goals. Unit IV shows him how to apply the savings of unit III to *increase his total income* through various common investment alternatives. Unit V wraps up with some important issues for *retirement planning and estate transfer.*

In conclusion, we believe that this text offers a directly useful approach to solving the increasingly difficult and very real problems faced by today's family financial manager. We trust that it will serve your needs in this regard.

We would like to acknowledge the efforts of those who helped to create this text. Osborne Bethea, Jr., our sponsoring editor, provided considerable impetus to the project through his continued enthusiasm and encouragement. Gretchen Hargis is to be commended for editorial labors above and beyond normal expectations. We also thank Sandra Sailer for her attention to detail, and Paul Kelly, as well as our manuscript reviewers, Professor Helen Potter (Purdue University), Professor John C. Ritchie, Jr., (Temple University), Professor Henry C. Hatcher (City College of San Francisco), and especially Professor Helen F. McHugh (Oregon State University) for her constructive suggestions on several phases of revision. Additional appreciation goes to Kathy McEldowney, Lelana Jo Randall, M. Kathleen Hunt, Jody Adair, Fran Randolph, Thomas R. Rudd and many others who helped in one way or another. Our many class students helped us develop the teaching methods that evolved through several preliminary versions of the text. And, of course, this whole work might never have come about without the understanding and encouragement of our wives and other members of our families.

I. GETTING STARTED

The opening unit of this book deals with the beginning concerns of money management: establishing what one's financial goals and resources are. As a financial manager, you must first determine what you want to do with your resources and how personal financial strategies can be used to achieve these goals. Chapter 1 discusses these issues. The second chapter will help you determine your financial starting point. You will learn how to set up a record-keeping system and examine your income and expenses, assets and liabilities. The remainder of the text will help you design strategies for moving from your present financial situation to the achievement of your goals. However, it is important to realize that financial strategies in and of themselves can be meaningless without a good understanding of the material in unit I.

1
INTRODUCTION

Some of us may consider money of supreme importance, whereas others may consider it only a minor necessity. Each must decide for himself how important money is, and that decision will probably reflect how much we value the things money can buy. To get some idea of how important money and the things it can provide are to you, consider the amount of time you either devote or anticipate devoting to making money. If you are a breadwinner, this commitment is probably considerable.

No matter how you feel about money, it can seldom be ignored. To gain satisfaction from money, you must be able not only to earn it but also to manage it. Through managing your money you can best obtain the things money can buy. Although most of your energies may be directed at developing your money-making skills, it is equally important to be competent in managing money. The purpose of this book is to help you develop money management skills.

WHERE MONEY FITS IN

Everyone has personal assets, financial resources, and goals. Personal assets include God-given talents and abilities—such as intelligence, muscle coordination, and creativity—as well as skills and knowledge acquired through education and experience. Financial resources, (which result from using personal assets) include both income (salary, interest, dividends, rents, royalties) and assets (savings, stocks and bonds, real estate, business interests, mutual funds). Goals are (what a person wants for himself and for his family) By this definition, a person can have among his goals the provision of necessities such as food and shelter. Some goals can be achieved mainly through personal efforts: respect for himself and for others, a happy family life, job advancement. Other goals require the use of both money and personal efforts: food, shelter, clothing, education, leisure time, certain luxuries. Figure 1-1 shows how personal assets, financial resources, and goals are related to each other.

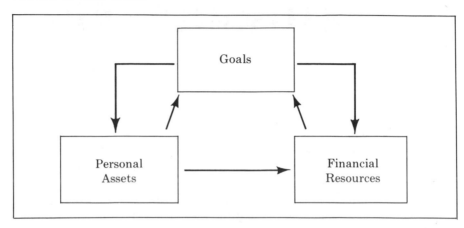

Fig. 1-1. Relationships between personal assets, financial resources, and goals

A person can use his personal assets to achieve his goals. For example, someone who wants an outlet for his singing ability might join a local singing group. Personal assets can also be used to earn income at a job and thus to create financial resources, which can in turn be used to reach goals. This application of financial resources to goal achievement is known as money management and will be of primary concern in this text. Personal assets and financial resources do not simply end in the fulfillment of goals, however. Out of that fulfillment may come a recycling back to personal assets and financial resources. For example, a person who applies his personal assets to win a job promotion will probably increase his financial resources through a pay increase. The higher level of skills acquired through the promotion will probably enhance his personal assets as well.

Good
EXAMPle →

An extended example should help make the framework in figure 1-1 meaningful to you. Gary has excellent muscle coordination and strength, and he enjoys playing football. While in college, he decided to become a professional football quarterback, but he also worked at being a good student. Gary's personal assets would therefore include better than average muscle control and intelligence as well as the acquired skills of a quarterback and a student. Gary signed with a pro team and thus achieved one of his goals. Gary also went to work as an insurance agent in his spare time. He hoped eventually to set up his own agency so that he would have an income long after he retired from professional football.

In these ways Gary used his personal assets to create an income and increase his financial resources. When Gary accumulated substantial cash, he had to decide how best to distribute it to achieve his goals. His football goals could be achieved through practice, but many of his other goals (a house, car, insurance, travel, investments) could be achieved only through effective utilization of his financial resources—through money management.

MONEY MANAGEMENT

The objective of money management is to achieve those goals that can best be satisfied with money. If you are to know what you want and how to get it with what you have, you must know how to set financial goals and how to apply money management strategies to achieve them.

Setting Financial Goals

People work and earn money in order to have food, shelter, and clothing. These are basic, easily recognizable goals; however, because they are so ordinary, they may be overlooked in a plan for good money management. Some goals are not easily identified, perhaps because they are bound up in personal values and philosophies that are not easy to explain. Nevertheless, you should think about both your financial and nonfinancial goals and put them in perspective. This is very important. Personal financial development will probably remain aimless and awkward until a person decides what his goals are.

Take some time to express your goals. Consider your spouse's also. If you have children who are old enough to help plan family goals, ask them to consider theirs. Organize your goals according to those that can be achieved through the use of personal assets only, and those that require the use of financial resources. They will, of course, vary according to the person's age, sex, status, values, and so on. You may want to develop new skills, have more time for leisure and travel, acquire certain household goods, or continue your education. Figure 1-2 (p. 6) shows some goals that a family might plan to reach through the use of financial resources. The cost of reaching each goal has been projected, as well as the year in which it is expected to be reached.

You might find it helpful to go through a similar exercise. Be as specific as possible, but do not try at this time to decide what you want most. As you read this text, you may find that some goals are easier or harder to achieve than you thought. After you learn about the methods for reaching them, you will be ready to arrange them in order of realistic preference.

As a result of this exercise, you will probably become more aware of those things you have long wanted. You may also discover some new goals. With these in mind, you are ready to find out what your financial

Goal	Projected Expenditures By Year							
	1973	1974	1975	1976	1977	1978	1979	1980
Emergency Fund		$2000						
New Furniture					$2000			
Washer and Dryer	$400							
Home Down Payment				$5000				
European Vacation							$3000	
TOTAL	$400	$2000		$5000	$2000		$3000	

Fig. 1-2.
Sample financial goals and projected expenditures by year

resources are. In the next chapter, you will learn how to assess these resources. This assessment is necessary so that, as you read further in this text, you will see what financial resources can be used (and how) to help you achieve your goals.

Strategies of Money Management

Besides planning for what you want and determining what your financial resources are, you must develop strategies to achieve your financial goals. These may be grouped into three categories: protecting what you have, getting the most out of your income, and increasing your total income.

To protect what you have, you must insure against financial calamities such as losing the dollar value of your property, having to pay big medical bills or liability suits, and being unable to provide for your family because of a disability or death. The basic insurance principles that should be considered by the prospective purchaser will be discussed in chapter 3. In the four chapters after that, property, liability, auto, health, and life insurance will be specifically treated. After reading these chapters you should be able to outline your own insurance strategies.

To get the most out of your income, you must direct it to cover your expenses and avoid unnecessary drains. The first of these strategies, budgeting, will be discussed in chapter 8. You will analyze how you are using your income and learn methods of controlling your expenditures. The four succeeding chapters concern four common drains on your income: income taxes, consumer loans, consumer credit, and housing.

To increase your total income, you must make investments that accord with your goals. Chapter 13 will further discuss setting goals and treat the fundamentals of investing. Chapters 14 through 19 will discuss various investment strategies you might use to achieve financial goals.

At the end of the text are a chapter on retirement financial planning and one on estate transfer. Although parts of these subjects could have been treated within the three categories of financial strategies, they will be discussed in toto by themselves.

THE MONEY MANAGER

As a financial manager, you should be concerned with achieving those goals that can be reached primarily through money management. Figure 1-3 illustrates the process of money management: using financial resources to reach goals. The money manager receives funds most commonly from his job and his investments. He then decides how much of this income should be allocated to normal living expenses, how much to the accumulation of fixed assets, and how much to savings for future goals (investment assets). This last use is simply a temporary diversion of some financial resources so that they will increase the total inflow and be available to reach a goal at a later time.

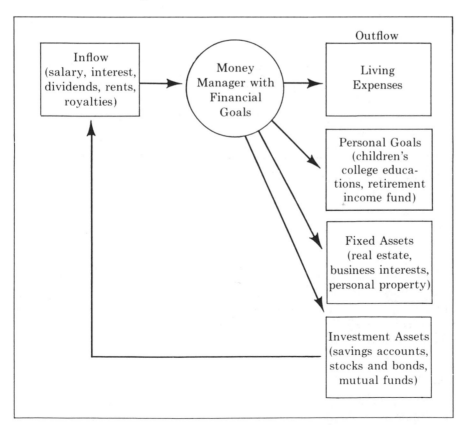

Fig. 1-3.
The money
management process

A money manager is distinguished from a money spender by the manner in which his goals are reached. The money manager, on the one hand, carefully plans and forecasts his goals and then controls both the inflow and the outflow of financial resources to achieve them. In other words, he budgets his expenses and income needs. A money spender, on the other hand, spends his paycheck until it is used up. When faced with a major goal, he has no way to satisfy it except by borrowing money at high interest rates. He has not planned ahead to achieve his goals.

The money spender's philosophy toward spending is "How much can I buy with the income I have?" The money manager's philosophy is "How much income, whether from investments or earnings, do I need to buy what I really want?" This distinction is crucial to personal money management. As a money manager, you control your economic environment rather than being controlled by it. The actual abilities you must develop to be an effective money manager are planning, directing, and controlling.

Planning

The primary responsibility of the money manager is to plan. He varies the size of his financial resources according to his goals rather than varying his goals according to the size of his financial resources. The money manager must first determine his goals, as you have begun to do. To achieve these (Goals) he must determine how much of his financial resources should be routed to living expenses, how much to fixed assets, and how much to investments. He can then plan investment strategies to provide the proper inflow of financial resources to reach these goals when they occur. There are two steps to the planning function: planning the amount and direction of the outflow and planning the source and timing of the inflow.

Planning the outflow of financial resources involves goal setting. You have already begun to think about the types of goals you want to achieve with your financial resources and to list those that are possible. Planning the inflow calls for far-sighted money management. To be financially successful over the years, you have to manage your money during the weeks and months. This can best be accomplished through budgeting.

The objective of planning is to match your total outflow with your total inflow while protecting the safety of your financial resources and preserving the security of your economic environment. If you carefully follow the strategies outlined in this text, you should be successful in meeting this objective.

Directing

Once you, the money manager, have planned your strategies, you must determine who should help you carry them out. If you are initiating an insurance program, you must select an insurance agent and company. If you are planning to borrow money, you must seek out the proper lending source. If you are beginning an investment program, you must choose the most appropriate broker, lawyer, or banker. In other words, to direct as a money manager you must be able to communicate effectively your goals and strategies to the most appropriate individual or organization that will help put them into effect.

The following chapters will help you decide what you want before approaching the people you need, identify which people can help you get what you want, learn the language and the concepts you need to communicate your needs effectively, and evaluate the performance of the professionals you hire. We will discuss the duties and responsibilities commonly rendered by various business services. We will advise you of the qualities you should look for in a stockbroker, insurance man, lender, creditor, and real estate agent. The basic background you will gain from this book should enable you to evaluate the performance of those selling you their services.

Controlling

No one has the foresight to be able to plan his entire life's financial future at one sitting. The money manager who is in control knows when to rethink old plans and prepare new ones. The control function should link past financial decisions to current desires and ambitions. As a money manager, you should beware of executing plans to achieve goals that no longer exist. For example, the life insurance you bought fifteen years ago may have become either unnecessary or inadequate. Make it a habit to review and revise your financial programs. Perhaps you should review your insurance program prior to each renewal date and your investment portfolio every month.

Your ability to control depends also on the currentness of your information. Insurance companies are constantly issuing more comprehensive policies and developing more sophisticated rating schemes. Investment yields are always in flux. Federal and local regulations are becoming stronger in many areas; this growing strength signals changes both good and bad. You must keep on top of a continuous information stream. This course should help you assimilate information in a usable form. You should seek information from the people serving you. Develop meaningful relationships of confidence and trust with them and let them know about changes in your financial condition.

CONCLUSION

The purpose of this chapter has been to prompt you to think about how important money is to you and where it fits into your life. You should also have come to appreciate the importance of setting financial goals and learning money management strategies. Instead of working entirely within the superficial constraints of your economic environment, you can develop the ability to control and expand it. The idea of money management need not intimidate and confuse you. It can become a powerful and effective tool in helping you achieve the things you really want and freeing you from the daily worries and problems of mismanaged money.

VOCABULARY

financial resources
money management
living expenses
investment assets

CASE PROBLEM

Develop lists of your goals, your personal assets, and your financial resources. Identify the goals that can be achieved by financial means. Develop a chart showing when major financial goals will occur and how much they are likely to cost. How can you use your personal assets to increase your financial resources?

CHUCK AND NANCY ANDERSON

INTRODUCTION

Chuck Anderson is thirty-five years old and works as a salesman. His wife Nancy is also thirty-five. She works part-time as a school librarian. They were married twelve years ago, shortly after Chuck took his present job. Three years later he received a promotion and was transferred. Soon after the move they bought a $26,000 two-bedroom home six miles from the office. Within a year they had a son named Jim and three years later a daughter named Melissa.

Since their move, the Andersons have bought much of the furniture for their house, some of it on installment. They have also purchased the necessary insurance policies in addition to the life insurance Chuck bought at the time of their marriage. To celebrate Chuck's second promotion last year, they traded in their six-year-old car and took out a $4000 loan to buy a high-horsepower car for Chuck. Nancy still drives a five-year-old compact.

The Andersons would like to have more money for things such as a family vacation abroad and a motorboat. They would also like to begin a savings or investment program so that they will have enough money for a college education for each of their children. Nancy's car should probably be replaced soon. In addition, Chuck and Nancy want to be assured of having a comfortable retirement when that time comes. These are the financial goals the Andersons have set for themselves.

2

YOUR FINANCIAL STARTING POINT

Have you ever devoted an evening to financial planning? If so, you probably spent much of the evening gathering together the data you needed: checkbook, savings passbook, current bills, cancelled checks, last year's tax return, life insurance policies, recent paycheck stubs, and so on. Even when you got all the information together, you probably could not decide how to relate the various pieces to each other.

Financial planning would be a lot easier if you could gather the necessary records together in a few minutes and then review a summary of the important relationships within your entire financial picture. In this chapter we will discuss a simple but adequate system of record keeping and the use of an income statement and a balance sheet.

RECORD KEEPING

The problem of locating your financial records can be solved by keeping them in a series of loose-leaf folders in a single box, preferably fireproof. As you can see in table 2-1 (pp. 12–15), the file system is composed of a general file, a budgeting file, a housing file, several insurance files, several investment files, and a tax file. An appropriate heading should be written on each one along with a list of the contents and a notation about where original documents can be found—whether in a safety deposit box, at

an attorney's office, or at a broker's office) In addition, the appropriate operational checklist should be written on each file. It is a good idea to leave space in which to record the date when each task was last performed. The meaning of the checklists will become clear as you proceed through the text. In all cases, however, useless and outdated information should continually be weeded out, lest the files become unmanageable. Those files that accumulate bulky loads (tax files, for example) may require separate storage boxes. You will not be able to complete all the forms for the various files at this time since only the personal information sheet (fig. 2-1), income statement (fig. 2-2), and balance sheet (fig. 2-3) will be dealt with in this chapter.

For now, simply assemble as much of the file as you can. Make sure that documents such as deeds and wills are in their proper places. Not only will this file system be convenient; it could also save you money if you regularly update the information.

TABLE 2-1

CONTENTS AND OPERATIONAL CHECKLIST
FOR EACH FILE OF FINANCIAL RECORDS

HEADING	CONTENTS	OPERATIONAL CHECKLIST
General	Personal information sheet (p. 16) List of items in safety deposit box Letter of last instructions (chapter 21) Copy of will (chapter 21) [The original should be kept with your attorney or in a safety deposit box.]	Update personal information sheet to reflect any changes. Update safety deposit box list as new items are added or old ones eliminated.
Budgeting	Lists of goals Income statement (chapter 2) Forecasts of income and expenses (chapter 8) Forecasts for short-term and long-term goals (chapter 8) Old budget control sheets (chapter 8)	Review budget planning sheets. Revise goals, if necessary.

TABLE 2-1 (cont.)

HEADING	CONTENTS	OPERATIONAL CHECKLIST
Housing	Purchase contract and receipt [deed in safety deposit box] Mortgage papers Title insurance policy Home improvement receipts (including landscaping expenses) Property tax receipts Termite inspection and policy Warranties/guarantees on appliances or services rendered Copy of lease or rental agreement	Keep records of all permanent home improvements so that you can establish an accurate cost basis if you ever sell your home.
Property Insurance	Details of property insurance coverage [Insurance policies should be kept *away* from the house, in a safety deposit box.] Personal property inventory (chapter 4) [copy in safety deposit box] Pictures of highly valued items [negatives in safety deposit box]	Change insurance limits on property insurance policy annually to reflect changes in personal property holdings and/or changes in replacement costs of all structures. Update personal property inventory once a year: add new items; revalue old items; eliminate items sold, lost, or condemned; take more pictures if necessary. Shop for rates. Get a minimum of three quotes before each renewal date.
Auto Insurance	Details of auto insurance coverage held [insurance policies in safety deposit box] Record of traffic violations and accidents Auto registration receipts [ownership certificate in safety deposit box]	Update auto insurance fact sheet annually by adding new cars to be insured, amending coverages, and increasing drivers' ages. Update traffic violation and accident records. Note which violations or accidents occurred over three years ago and stop including them in computing your insurance rates.

TABLE 2-1 (cont.)

HEADING	CONTENTS	OPERATIONAL CHECKLIST
Auto Insurance (cont.)		Shop for rates. Get a minimum of three rate quotes before each renewal date.
Health Insurance	Details of present health coverage, including employee plans [insurance policies in safety deposit box] Current medical history for each family member List of drugs to which each family member is allergic	Update health insurance fact sheet to reflect changes in limits, coverage, and so on. Update medical histories to reflect new ailments or diseases.
Life Insurance	Details of insurance policies owned, including employee group plans [insurance policies in safety deposit box] Results of eleven-step procedure (chapter 7) for determining life insurance needs	Recompute insurance needs using eleven-step procedure every five years—sooner if new financial assets are acquired, you have a new child or a child leaves home, or your spouse gets a job or acquires a job skill. Update life insurance fact sheet to reflect changes in needs and coverage increases in employee policies. Shop for at least three rate quotes before each change in policy or coverage limits.
Investments— General	Goal planning sheet (twelve-step procedure, chapter 13) Annual balance sheets (chapter 2) List of bank accounts	Replan goals using twelve-step procedure. Plot your progress using annual balance sheet.
Investments— Stocks and Bonds	Records of purchase and sale of common stocks and bonds [All stock certificates and bonds should be kept either with broker or in safety deposit box]	Update records to reflect purchases and sales evidenced by transaction slips.

TABLE 2-1 (cont.)

HEADING	CONTENTS	OPERATIONAL CHECKLIST
Investments— Stocks and Bonds (cont.)	Records of stock dividends and bond interest List of stock certificate numbers and dates of issue (if you keep certificates in safety deposit box rather than with broker) Transaction slips and monthly statements (annual envelopes for each)	Add new stock numbers and dates of issue to list (if certificates are sent to you). Place each year's transaction and monthly statements in an envelope.
Investments— Mutual Funds	Records of purchase and sale of mutual funds [Keep mutual fund shares with broker, with the mutual fund transfer agent, or in safety deposit box.]	Use transaction slips and statements to update records of purchases, sales, and stocks accrued through reinvested dividends and capital gains. Place each year's transaction slips and monthly statements in an envelope.
Tax	Purchase receipts, interest payment records, charitable gift confirmations, medical expense records, and so on Tax forms, schedules, and supporting data for past ten years Quarterly estimated tax forms W–2 forms, 1099 forms, and so on All cancelled checks for last seven years	File all receipts required to substantiate type I and type II deductions. After your annual tax form is filed, place all receipts and other substantiating records in an envelope and file either here or in extra storage boxes.

NAME(S) _____

DATE _____

PERSONAL INFORMATION SHEET

	ACCOUNT NUMBER	INSTITUTION NAME
Checking accounts	_____	_____
	_____	_____
Savings accounts	_____	_____
	_____	_____
Safety deposit box (Location of keys)	_____	_____
Brokerage account	_____	_____

Location of stock certificates _____

Location of deeds _____

Location of other securities _____

Location of will _____

Name of executor(s) _____

Lawyer's name _____ Phone _____

   Address _____

Broker's name _____ Phone _____

   Address _____

Accountant's name _____ Phone _____

   Address _____

Insurance agents, other brokers, etc. _____

_____

_____

This sheet should be kept in your general file. Other members of your family should know where it is.

Fig. 2-1.
Personal
information sheet
for general file

FINANCIAL STATEMENTS

Locating your financial data is only the first step in preparing for your tasks as money manager. The second step is to review your present financial situation and see how assets and liabilities and income and expenses interrelate. You can do this by periodically drawing up an income statement and a balance sheet. The income statement shows where the family's money has come from and where it has gone over the past year. The balance sheet lists financial assets and debts and shows the difference between them—financial net worth. This is a distinction you should keep in mind: the income statement describes your recent financial history, whereas the balance sheet describes your financial situation at one point in time.

The Income Statement

The income statement is actually an income and expense statement. It summarizes where your income for the past year came from, where you spent your money, and how much you added to (or subtracted from) your savings and investments by the end of the year.

How do you construct an income statement? To show you, we have provided a sample income statement (fig. 2-2, p. 18) and a set of instructions. The numbered steps in the instructions correspond to the numbers in the sample. The sample has been filled out for a fictitious couple, George and Sybil Barnes. Sybil is working while George finishes graduate school. Note how they arrive at the numbers on their income statement, and then construct your own.

Instructions

1 *Income. List the dollar amounts of income received from all sources during the past year.*

   Sybil made $8000 working at a law firm. George made $1800 working in a bank during the summer. Both of these figures represent gross income—what the employer paid, not the actual take-home salary. (Income taxes and Social Security and disability taxes will be subtracted in step 3.) The Barneses received $15 interest from a savings account at the local savings and loan and $50 from a mutual fund. George also sold his 1963 car for $200. He marked this gain under "other."

2 *Total Income. Add all income items.*

   George and Sybil accumulated $10,065 last year.

3 *Taxes. Enter the combined total of federal and state income taxes paid last year and the amount paid in Social Security taxes.* If you have a state disability tax, this should also be included here.

NAME(S) *George and Sybil Barnes*

FOR THE YEAR BEGINNING JAN. 1, *1972* AND ENDING DEC. 31, *1972*

INCOME STATEMENT

1 *Income*

Wages or salary

Husband *(summer job)*	$	1800
Wife *("full"-time job)*		8000
Dividends and interest		65
Capital gains and losses (e.g., from sale of stock)		_____
Rents, annuities, pensions, and such		_____
Other *sale of old car*		200

2 *TOTAL INCOME* $ 10,065

3 *Taxes*

Personal income taxes	1380
Social Security and disability taxes	540

4 *TOTAL TAXES*   1920

5 *Amount Remaining for Living Expenses and Investment*   8145

6 *Living Expenses*

	Fixed	Variable
Housing		
Utilities	200	_____
Repairs	_____	_____
Insurance	_____	_____
Taxes		_____
Rent or mortgage payments	2200	_____
Other _____	_____	_____
Food	_____	1200
Clothing (including laundry, dry cleaning, repair, and personal effects)	_____	460
Transportation		
Gas	_____	200
Repairs	_____	70
Licenses	_____	30
Insurance	220	_____
Auto payments or purchase	720	
Recreation, entertainment, and vacations	_____	500
Medical		
Doctor	_____	20
Dentist	_____	20
Medicines	_____	60
Insurance		
Personal	1400	140
Life insurance	100	
Outlays for fixed assets	_____	300
Other expenses _____	_____	200
SUBTOTAL	4840	3200

7 *TOTAL ANNUAL LIVING EXPENSES* $ 8040

8 *Amount Remaining for Savings and Investment* $ 105

9 *TOTAL OF STEPS 4, 7, AND 8* (should equal total in step 2) $ 10,065

**Fig. 2-2.
Sample income
statement**

George and Sybil paid $1380 in income taxes and $540 in Social Security taxes.

4 *Total Taxes. Add all tax items.*
The total for George and Sybil is $1920.

5 *Amount Remaining for Living Expenses and Investment. Subtract total taxes (step 4) from total income (step 3).*
George and Sybil arrived at $8145.

6 *Living Expenses. List those expenses that were reasonably fixed and those over which you had some control (variable).* Only by knowing which outlays you are committed to (i.e., fixed expenses) will you be able to decide how much flexibility you will lose by undertaking additional fixed expenses.

To complete these blanks, George and Sybil looked back through their checkbooks and old receipts but had to make some guesses as well. In order of entry, their expenses were: $200 for utilities; $2200 for rent; $1200 for food; $460 for clothing, repair, and personal effects; $300 for gas and car expenses; $220 for auto insurance; $720 for monthly payments on their car; $500 for entertainment; $100 for medicine and medical miscellany (Sybil's employer provides health insurance coverage); $1400 for tuition; $140 for books, newspapers, and magazines; $100 for life insurance premium; $300 for a television and a chair; $200 for miscellany such as gifts, charitable donations, and unaccounted-for items.

7 *Total Annual Living Expenses. Add the subtotals of the fixed and variable expenses.*
George and Sybil spent $8040 last year.

8 *Amount Remaining for Savings and Investment. Subtract living expenses (step 7) from the total amount remaining for living expenses (step 5).* This amount represents the profit realized from financial activities of the past year.
The Barneses had $105, which they added to their savings account.

9 *Total of Steps 4, 7, and 8. Recheck your computations.* The total of lines 4, 7, and 8 should equal the total in line 2. If not, a mistake somewhere in addition or subtraction should be corrected.

Now that you have completed your income statement, you may want to get a perspective on it. Let's review a typical American family's income and expenses. Table 2-2 illustrates typical expense patterns for urban American families of four—parents in their thirties, one family breadwinner, two grade-school children—with incomes ranging from $7000 to $15,500. As you can see from table 2-3, roughly half of all American households are within that range of income. For the four-person households, this figure is probably higher since the income distribution table

TABLE 2-2
TYPICAL EXPENSES FOR A FOUR-PERSON URBAN AMERICAN FAMILY
(Annual budget as estimated in Spring 1970)

CATEGORY	LOWER BUDGET		INTERMEDIATE BUDGET		HIGHER BUDGET	
	Cash Amount	Percent of Total Budget	Cash Amount	Percent of Total Budget	Cash Amount	Percent of Total Budget
Housing	$1,429	20	$ 2,501	23	$ 3,772	24
Food	1,905	27	2,452	23	3,092	20
Clothing and Personal Care	807	12	1,137	11	1,655	11
Transportation	505	7	912	8	1,185	8
Medical Care	562	8	564	5	588	4
Other Consumption[b]	345	5	639	6	1,056	7
Other Expenses[c]	343	5	539	5	905	6
Total Living Expenses	$5,926	85	$ 8,744	82	$12,245	79
Social Security and Disability Insurance	345	5	387	4	387	2
Income Taxes	719	10	1,533	14	2,875	19
Total Taxes	$1,064	15	$ 1,920	18	$ 3,262	21
Total Budget	$6,690	100	$10,664	100	$15,511	100

SOURCE: U.S. Bureau of Labor Statistics, *1971 Labor Statistics Handbook* (Bulletin 1705).

[a] By 1972, these figures were approximately 10 percent higher because of inflation.
[b] Includes recreation and entertainment, books and magazines.
[c] Includes gifts, charitable contributions, life insurance, and job-related expenses.

TABLE 2-3

PERCENT DISTRIBUTION OF AMERICAN FAMILY INCOME
By Years of School Completed For 1969

FAMILY INCOME FOR 1969	TOTAL	YEARS OF SCHOOL COMPLETED BY HEAD OF HOUSEHOLD				
		Elementry School or Less	High School 1–3 years	High School 4 years	College 1–3 years	College 4 or more years
Under $3,000	9.0%	19.3%	9.1%	4.5%	4.5%	2.1%
$ 3,000–5,999	15.7%	27.9%	17.4%	11.6%	8.4%	4.9%
$ 6,000–8,999	20.4%	21.9%	24.2%	22.5%	16.9%	10.3%
$ 9,000–11,999	20.2%	15.3%	21.0%	24.6%	22.4%	17.2%
$12,000–14,999	14.2%	8.2%	13.8%	16.9%	18.2%	17.4%
$15,000–24,999	16.6%	6.7%	12.9%	17.3%	23.8%	33.5%
$25,000 and over	4.0%	0.9%	1.4%	2.7%	6.2%	14.5%
Median Income of Group[a]	$9,721	$6,386	$8,893	$10,390	$11,760	$14,654

SOURCE: U.S. Bureau of Labor Statistics, *1971 Labor Statistics Handbook* (Bulletin 1705).

NOTE: The percentages in each column total 100 percent.

[a]Inflation boosted these figures approximately 15 percent by 1972.

includes all households, even those as small as one person, which probably include a higher proportion of sub-$7000 earners. It should also be noted that families in certain high-cost northeastern or western metropolitan areas had to spend about 10 percent more than the figures in table 2-2 to achieve the standard of living shown, whereas lower-cost southern cities allowed budgets as much as 10 percent lower. Family income also tended to vary in proportion to regional living cost differences.

The figures in these two tables and the research behind them show the following differences in spending and income between lower- and higher-income families:

1. Lower-income families tend to rent housing while higher-income families tend to own their housing.
2. A higher proportion of lower-income families travel on mass transit systems rather than own their own cars.
3. Actual dollars spent for medical care (including insurance) are about the same for both lower- and higher-income families.
4. Discretionary "other consumption" (largely recreation) tends to rise relatively rapidly as budgets increase.
5. Higher levels of educational attainment correlate with higher-income levels.
6. The percentage of the total budget spent on food decreases as income increases.

How does an income statement differ from a budget? An income statement is a report on the *past;* a budget is a plan for the *future.* Before you can construct a budget, you must have some idea of how you have spent your money in the past. When you budget, you can assign priorities to various expense categories. Further discussion of the budget will be deferred to chapter 8. It will be easier to construct a precise budget for your household once you understand how much you should allocate for proper (or at least minimum) insurance protection. After you have carefully considered how to protect what you have (chapters 3 through 7), you will be ready to consider creating a budget.

2 The Balance Sheet

The balance sheet lets you know your present financial position, which is the result of your past financial activities. The balance sheet is composed of assets and liabilities, balanced against each other. The difference between assets and liabilities is *net worth.* Fill out a balance sheet for yourself by completing steps one through seventeen as in the sample (fig. 2-3) for George and Sybil Barnes.

Instructions

1 *Cash. List total cash by noting cash on hand, checking account balance, and money in savings accounts.*

George and Sybil have on hand $15 cash. Their checking account balance reads $50 and they have $300 in a savings account at the local savings and loan. Therefore, their total cash is $365.

2 *Money Loaned. Estimate the return you can reasonably expect on money loaned.*

The Barneses loaned Sybil's brother $100 a year ago and as yet have not been repaid. They decide that there is a 25 percent chance of being repaid, and so they put $25 (25 percent of $100) on their balance sheet.

3 *Investments. List total investments by noting the values of savings bonds, stocks and bonds, mutual funds, life insurance, and annuities.* If you have savings bonds or bank bonds, determine how many years you have had them and read the current cash value off the table on the bond. To find the total value of your stock market investments, use the values in stock and bond tables in today's newspaper. Call your broker if a stock is not listed and use the bid price for over-the-counter stocks. To find the current market value of mutual funds, use the bid price, not the asked. If a fund is not listed in your local newspaper, check the *Wall Street Journal* at your library for a complete daily listing. To find the current guaranteed cash value of a life insurance policy, turn to the table printed in the policy itself. Figures in the table are for each $1000

NAME(S) *George and Sybil Barnes*

DATE *January 10, 1973*

BALANCE SHEET

	ASSETS		LIABILITIES		
MONETARY ASSETS			12 *Unpaid Bills*		
			Taxes	_____	
1 *Cash*			Insurance		
On hand	$ 15		premiums	210	
Checking account	50		Rent	_____	
Savings account	300		Utilities	12	
TOTAL CASH		365	Charge accounts	23	
2 *Money loaned to others*			Other _____	_____	
(repayment expected)		25	TOTAL UNPAID BILLS		245
3 *Investments*			13 *Installment Loans* (balance due)		
Savings bonds	_____		Automobile	1280	
Stocks and bonds	_____		Other *television*	150	
Mutual funds	150		TOTAL		1430
Cash value of					
life insurance	50		14 *Loans* (balance due)		
Cash value of			Bank	_____	
annuities	_____		Educational	5000	
TOTAL INVESTMENTS		200	Other _____	_____	
4 TOTAL MONETARY ASSETS		590	TOTAL		5000
FIXED ASSETS			15 *Mortgage Loans* (balance due)		
5 *Home and property*	_____		Home	_____	
6 *Other real estate*			Other _____	_____	
investments	_____		TOTAL		
7 *Automobiles*	2000		16 TOTAL LIABILITIES		$ 6675
8 *Ownership interests*			17 *Net Worth of Family*		($2585)
in small businesses	_____				
9 *Personal property*	1500				
10 TOTAL FIXED ASSETS		$ 3590			
11 TOTAL ASSETS OF FAMILY		$ 4090			

Fig. 2-3.
Sample balance sheet

worth of face amount (total amount of insurance) for each year of the policy's age. The cash value of annuities can be determined in the same way. However, if you have started taking payments from your annuity policy, deduct the total payments received to date from the total amount you invested.

George invested $100 in a mutual fund two years ago. Checking the stock market quotations, he finds that his investment is now worth $150. The Barneses' only other investment is a $10,000 life insurance policy that is three years old. George looks down the "years" column on the table to 3 and reads across the "cash values" column to $5. Since the stated cash value applies to each $1000 of coverage, he has a current cash value of $50 ($5 per $1000 × 10 thousands). He has no accumulated dividends or interest, and so he puts $50 on his balance sheet under "cash value." George and Sybil have a total of $200 in investments.

4 *Total Monetary Assets. Add total cash (step 1), money loaned (step 2), and investment assets (step 3).* These assets can be quickly converted to cash if necessary.

George and Sybil have $590 in monetary assets.

5 *Home and Property. Estimate what your house and land would sell for if you were to sell them today.* Check the newspaper listings, call a local realtor, or compare the price a similar house on your block sold for recently.

The Barneses are renting and so enter nothing here.

6 *Other Real Estate Investments. Compute the current market value as you did in step 5.* If you are in a partnership or syndicate, enter the current value of your proportionate share.

The Barneses own no real estate and so enter nothing here.

7 *Automobiles. Compare the blue book value of your car with the prices in the classified ads for similar cars and estimate the car's worth.*

George and Sybil bought a car a year ago for $2800. They put $800 down and borrowed the rest at 14 percent interest per year. They estimate the car's present worth at $2000.

8 *Small Business Interests. Use the current book value (total assets minus total liabilities) to determine your ownership interest in a small business.*

The Barneses have no such investments.

9 *Personal Property. Estimate the market value of salable possessions.*

The Barneses have some dishes, books, clothing, a new color television, and a diamond wedding ring. They estimate that if they were to sell these, they would get $1500.

10 *Total Fixed Assets. Add the figures in steps 5, 6, 7, 8, and 9.*
George and Sybil have total fixed assets of $3500.

11 *Total Assets of the Family. Add the figures in steps 4 and 10.*
The Barneses have total assets valued at $4090.

12 *Unpaid Bills. Add the total amounts of bills that you have received but have not yet paid.* Bills that you know you will have to pay

several months from now but have not yet come due should not be included.

George and Sybil have a $210 insurance premium, $12 utility bill, and $23 charge account balance—a total of $245 in unpaid bills.

13 *Installment Loans. Add the balance due on installment loans.*

George and Sybil have a total balance of $1280 due on their automobile (a total loan of $2000 minus total repayments to date of $720) and a balance of $150 due on their television—a total installment loan balance of $1430.

14 *Loans. Add the balance due on loans from bank, government, or other sources.*

George and Sybil owe $5000 on educational loans they took out to finance their undergraduate educations. They have not yet started to repay the loans.

15 *Mortgage Loans. Enter the principal balance due.*

The Barneses do not own a home and therefore have no mortgage.

16 *Total Liabilities. Add unpaid bills (step 12) and balance due on installment loans (step 13), loans (step 14), and mortgage loans (step 15).*

The Barneses have $6675 in debts.

17 *Net Worth. Subtract liabilities (step 16) from assets (step 11).*

The Barneses have a negative net worth of $2585. They do not have enough assets to cover all their debts. Although this is not a healthy financial position, it is fairly typical among college students today. One very important asset that does not appear on the Barneses' balance sheet is their educational attainment. This education may have little monetary value now, but probably represents hundreds of thousands of dollars in future income.

Now that you have computed your balance sheet, look at the figures. Are there any surprises? What questions do the figures raise? Why is your money used the way it is? Consider your assets. Where have you put most of your money—into fixed assets or monetary assets? Have you been accumulating monetary assets in anticipation of investment income or large purchases? What purpose does each of your assets serve? Look at your liabilities. Compare your total amount of cash with your total bills due and with your monthly fixed expenses. Is your emergency cash reserve large enough to carry you for a few months if you were unable to work? Look at the loan liabilities you have incurred. Which assets did these loans finance? In other words, were these liabilities assumed for any visible use, or did they merely cover ordinary living expenses? In general, how healthy is your financial condition? These are some of the questions we will help you answer in the following chapters.

3. Using Financial Statements

Financial statements are probably most useful in helping you with your budget. Once you have constructed your income statement and balance sheet, you need not refer directly to the original data. With the income statement, you can plan next year's budget. You can see what you must spend, and you can allocate the remainder according to the goals you set in chapter 1, whether for current consumption or for savings. With the balance sheet, you can reallocate assets according to your investment goals (which will be discussed in chapter 13). Or you can consider which debts to pay off first (generally those with the highest interest costs, as we shall see in chapters 10 and 11).

In your directing function as money manager, you will probably rely more on personal judgment than on financial statements to help you select the best people or proper financial instruments. There are times, however, when you will need these statements even in this function. For example, you might go to a bank for a loan and have to present your financial statements.

To control your financial resources, you will again rely on these financial statements. With the income statement you know where your money went and can therefore make adjustments in the future. The balance sheet helps you see how well you have achieved your objectives. Only by creating a new balance sheet each year (more often if you prefer) can you monitor your progress.

CONCLUSION

In the first chapter you learned about setting financial goals and about the functions of a money manager. This second chapter offers the tools necessary to begin managing. Only by first getting your financial records in order and by using your financial statements to know your present financial position can you establish a financial starting point from which to begin implementing the three primary strategies that will be discussed in the next three units.

VOCABULARY

balance sheet
fixed assets
income statement
liabilities
monetary assets
net worth

Richard is just finishing his senior year in college. He carried a heavy course load that allowed him no time for a job during the school year. Last summer he went to a science camp, and so he has earned no money in the past twelve months. His only support for the year was $2400 that his parents gave him and $2000 that he borrowed through the college loan program. He will have to begin repaying this loan when he finishes school. His expenses for the year were $900 for tuition, $1600 for room and board, $200 for books and supplies, $550 for gas and maintenance on his car, $250 for car insurance, and $900 for miscellaneous.

Richard's assets consist of his two-year-old car ($2500 new, $1400 after two years' use), his checking account ($180), and his personal belongings ($2400). Liabilities include his college loan, a bookstore bill of $40, and the auto insurance annual premium that will come due next month.

Draw up Richard's income statement and compute his net income or loss for the past twelve months. Also, draw up his balance sheet as of today and compute his net worth.

Cohen, Jerome B., and Hansen, Arthur W. *Personal Finance: Principles and Case Problems*. Homewood, Ill.: Irwin, 1972.

> Chapter one provides a good, in-depth discourse on the distribution, source, and trends of family income.

Katona, George; Mandell, Lewis; and Schmiedeskamp, Jay. *1970 Survey of Consumer Finances*. Ann Arbor: University of Michigan, 1971.

> This survey describes many aspects of families as consumers, including income, expenses, assets, liabilities, and attitudes. Although this source offers more detail than do census bureau statistics, the results pertaining to income and expense are biased slightly upward largely because of nonresponse problems and a different definition of the family unit.

THEIR BALANCE SHEET AND INCOME STATEMENT

As you try to help Chuck and Nancy reach their financial goals in succeeding chapters, you will need to use their balance sheet and income statement. Be sure to update items as they are changed by the financial decisions you make for the Andersons.

As you can see from the income statement (p. 29), Chuck and Nancy together have a good income. They did incur a capital loss, however, on the sale of some common stock.

Fixed expense items include auto payments of $133 a month ($1600 a year) and furniture financing payments of $46 a month ($550 a year). In later chapters, some of these expense items will be examined in greater detail.

The balances outstanding on these loans show up on their balance sheet (p. 30) as liabilities. The balance due on the $4000 automobile loan is $3192 ($133 monthly payment multiplied by the twenty-four remaining payments). This loan could be repaid with a single $2850 cash payment against the principal. The additional $342 is the 12 percent interest that is due over the remainder of the loan period. The balance due on the $2000 furniture loan is $1300. This five-year loan is two years old and carries a 15 percent annual interest cost.

Other loans on which they owe money are a $1500 margin loan and a $21,000 first mortgage (6 percent interest for twenty years—$150 a month). The margin loan is money that Chuck's broker loaned him at 7 percent, with interest-only payments, to help him purchase stock. Without this loan, Chuck's common stock value would total $5600. The home mortgage has an actual principal balance due of $14,500.

On the assets side of their balance sheet, however, their house shows up as worth $35,000. It has appreciated in value $9000 since they bought it nine years ago.

As you can see, the Andersons have a net worth that is similar to that of other American families of their age, income level, and family status.

QUESTIONS

1. Judging by their income statement, what general financial concerns do you think the Andersons probably have? How important is each? What recent purchases helped to create a problem? Are all of the problems you see recurring ones?
2. With regard to the balance sheet, what factors appear to have contributed most to their positive financial position?

NAME(S) *Chuck and Nancy Anderson*

FOR THE YEAR BEGINNING JAN. 1, *1972* AND ENDING DEC. 31, *1972*

INCOME STATEMENT

1 *Income*

Wages or salary		
Husband	$12,500	
Wife *(part-time job)*	4000	
Dividends and interest	330	
Capital gains and losses (e.g., sale of stock)		
Rents, annuities, pensions, and such	(1100)	
Other _____	_____	

2 **TOTAL INCOME** $15,730

3 *Taxes*

Personal income taxes	2230
Social Security and disability taxes	700

4 **TOTAL TAXES** $ 2930

5 *Amount Remaining for*
  Living Expenses and Investments $12,800

6 *Living Expenses*

	Fixed	Variable
Housing		
Utilities		600
Repairs		250
Insurance	80	
Taxes	770	
Rent or mortgage payments	1800	
Other _gardening_		100
Food		2300
Clothing (including laundry, dry cleaning, repair, and personal effects)		1500
Transportation		
Gas		506
Repairs		500
Licenses	100	
Insurance	694	
Auto payments or purchase	1600	
Recreation, entertainment, and vacations		660
Medical		
Doctor		194
Dentist		250
Medicines		25
Insurance	481	
Personal		550
Life insurance	570	
Outlays for fixed assets *(furniture)*	550	70
Other expenses _allowances for children_		70
SUBTOTAL	6645	7575

7 **TOTAL ANNUAL LIVING EXPENSES** $14,220

8 *Amount Remaining for Savings and Investment* (1420)

9 *TOTAL OF STEPS 4, 7, AND 8* (should equal total in step 2) $ 15,730

NAME(S) Chuck and Nancy Anderson

DATE January 16, 1973

BALANCE SHEET

	ASSETS		LIABILITIES

MONETARY ASSETS

1 *Cash*

On hand $ 50

Checking account 150

Savings account 600

TOTAL CASH $ 800

2 *Money loaned to others*
(repayment expected) 100

3 *Investments*

Savings bonds 1500

Stocks and bonds 7100

Mutual funds 1400

Cash value of
life insurance 4800

Cash value of
annuities _____

TOTAL INVESTMENTS $14,800

4 TOTAL MONETARY ASSETS $15,700

FIXED ASSETS

5 *Home and property* 35,000

6 *Other real estate
investments* _____

7 *Automobiles* 4600

8 *Ownership interests
in small businesses* _____

9 *Personal property* 10,000

10 TOTAL FIXED ASSETS $49,600

11 TOTAL ASSETS OF FAMILY $65,300

12 *Unpaid Bills*

Taxes _____

Insurance
premiums _____

Rent _____

Utilities _____

Charge accounts $ 100

Other_____ _____

TOTAL UNPAID BILLS $100

13 *Installment Loans* (balance due)

Automobile 3192

Other *furniture* 1656

TOTAL 4848

14 *Loans* (balance due)

Bank _____

Educational _____

Other *margin account* 1500

TOTAL 1500

15 *Mortgage Loans* (balance due)

Home 14,500

Other_____ _____

TOTAL $14,500

16 TOTAL LIABILITIES $20,948

17 *Net Worth of Family* $44,352

II. PROTECTING WHAT YOU HAVE

In chapter 3 we present an overall view of insurance, including the various methods of insuring one's assets. In chapters 4 through 7, we devote a chapter to each type of insurance available to the individual: property insurance, comprehensive liability and automobile insurance, health insurance, and life insurance. Each chapter covers the purpose of the particular type of insurance under discussion, ways of determining one's insurance needs, the various policy alternatives available as well as other alternatives for fulfilling these needs, and the costs of fulfilling them.

3

INSURANCE PRINCIPLES

The purpose of insurance is to restore financial well-being after a financial calamity. It can take the form of an insurance policy or a self-established reserve. Insurance does not promise to return your $2000 automobile if it is destroyed in an accident; it simply promises to return $2000. In short, insurance is money.

INSURABLE RISKS

Every day you encounter many risks, or possibilities of loss. In the morning you run the risk that you will oversleep. As you dress, you run the risk that what you want to wear will not be clean. On your way to class or to work, you run the risk that you will have an accident. Every step of your life can involve some sort of risk.

Insurance, however, is concerned only with fortuitous risks that result in financial loss and are personal in origin. Fortuitous risks occur because of chance, not because of deliberate action on the part of the insured. The chance that lightning may start a fire at your summer cabin is a fortuitous risk, but the possibility that you may intentionally set fire to the cabin is not. Insurance companies spend much time and money determining causes of financial losses before settling claims.

To qualify as an insurable risk, a risk must also produce a reduction in monetary value. The theft of your car would constitute a financial loss. To restore your financial well-

being, if your car were stolen, you would probably need money not only to buy a new car but also to replace property left in the stolen car and to provide transportation until you buy a new car or the old one is recovered. In contrast, if you do not prepare for a class and therefore are unable to answer a professor's question properly, your grade and self-esteem may go down, but there will probably be no immediate monetary effect: such a situation would not qualify as an insurable risk. Nor are wagers, bets, or investment risks insurable, since they carry with them the chance for profit. Some people think that insurance, like gambling, is an opportunity for gain as well as for loss. On the contrary, insurance is a way of restoring value, not enhancing it. You cannot profit from insurance.

The last qualification for an insurable risk is that it must be personal in origin. An auto accident, for example, is an isolated loss affecting only a few people. It can be spread over a large number of exposures to reduce the odds that every insured will experience a loss at the same time. It also produces a definite, measurable loss that is small compared to losses from large-scale disasters such as flood or war.

A person is said to have an insurable interest in assets that are vulnerable to insurable risks. The risk of a significant financial loss may seem remote to you if you have not yet accumulated many assets. Several years from now, however, if you are married and own a home and are making a good salary, the potential financial loss may appear very large.

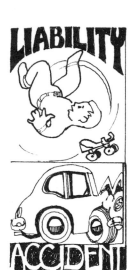

There are three ways to deal with insurable risks: take preventive measures to reduce or eliminate risk, retain the risk and assume financial responsibility for absorbing the loss yourself, or transfer the risk and potential financial burden to someone else. Sound insurance planning utilizes all three methods of dealing with insurable risks.

Minimizing Risks

You can minimize risks by not engaging in activities likely to cause accidents or loss. For example, the risk of accidental injury or death is increased if you ride motorcycles, fly small private aircraft, or engage in certain hazardous occupations. In other words, you can reduce risks by being cautious.

Insurance rates are set according to the magnitude of risk. The greater the risk, the higher the premium you must pay to obtain coverage for that risk. Conversely, the smaller the risk, the lower the premium. By watching your behavior patterns and tempering your more dangerous inclinations, you will not only reduce risk but also minimize the price you pay for insurance coverage.

Government at all levels is active in reducing risk and preventing financial loss. Police departments and fire departments, for example, are loss preventive agencies. They contribute much to the reduction of the risks we face and the premiums we have to pay for insurance. National, state, and local health and safety agencies have printed hundreds of brochures and booklets describing precautionary measures you can take around the home, in your car, and concerning your health. A list of these agencies and their addresses is given at the end of this chapter. Since the cheapest insurance is careful behavior, you would do well to read some of the pamphlets and follow the advice given.

Retaining Risks

Along with trying to prevent financial loss by reducing risk, you must decide whether to retain the risk of financial burden or transfer it to an insurance company. Since this decision will be made in favor of the most financially attractive alternative, you must use your personal loss experience and your financial statements to help you decide. Your *personal loss experience* is a record of how much money or monetary value you have lost because of insurable risks. If you have never had any loss for which a claim was filed, then you have a good loss record. If you have had three accidents in the last three years costing you a total of $5000, then you have a poor loss record. Your personal loss record can be used in all areas of insurance underwriting to determine whether you are a good risk. The better risk you are, the less will be your insurance costs, whether you decide to retain the risk yourself or to transfer the risk to an insurance company.

Your balance sheet and income statement can be used to determine where the risks are, the size of the financial burden to be assumed, and whether you have the financial strength to assume all the risk of a financial burden. What would happen if your assets were reduced? If your liabilities increased? If your income were reduced? If your expenses increased? Will you need $2000 or $7000 to replace your car if it is stolen? Will your family need $500 or $1500 a month to live on if you die or become disabled? Where is the most value on your balance sheet and income statement? Car? Home? Income? Your asset of greatest value constitutes your largest exposure to financial loss and therefore probably also your greatest insurance problem. How great is your financial capacity to assume risk? Do you have enough in your savings account, for example, to replace your automobile if it is damaged beyond repair? If you have enough monetary assets to equal the fixed assets that pose financial risks, then you can afford to *self-insure* those assets—to set aside adequate funds to protect yourself against possible losses.

To determine whether it is financially sound for you to self-insure, first compute the annual premium you would have to pay if you were to obtain insurance coverage from an insurance company. Then arrive at an average dollar loss per year by looking over your loss history and dividing the total amount of dollars lost by the number of years in which

the financial burden has been assumed. If the average loss per year is less than the required annual premium and if you can reasonably expect that your loss experience will not worsen and if you have enough monetary assets to cover the loss in case your experience does worsen, then consider retaining the risk.

Suppose you have a car worth $500. Your insurance agent says it will cost you $100 a year to insure it against collision damage. Suppose as well that you have incurred $250 worth of damage costs over the last five years because of collisions. This would mean that your average annual loss was $50—half the annual premium. If you can expect that your loss experience will not worsen, the financially sound alternative would be to put $500 (an amount equal to the value of the car) into a reserve savings account and not purchase collision insurance. You thereby have enough money to cover a total loss. You also have interest income on the $500, and you have saved the $100 annual premium.

Regarding health risks, you use the same self-insurance procedure to determine not the maximum potential loss, but the size of the deductible you can afford. For example, you may have been spending $280 a year to buy a health insurance policy with no deductible, although your total annual medical bills have averaged only $120. For $100 you might purchase a health insurance policy with a $200 deductible (i.e., the insurance company would assume any loss over $200) and save an average of $60 a year since you would be paying only a $100 premium and an average of $120 in medical bills rather than a $280 premium. (Deductibles will be further discussed later in the chapter.)

When determining the financial effects of your premature death, examine the financial statements of your beneficiaries. These may or may not be the same as your own. You need to know both how much money they will need to support themselves after your death and how many of your financial assets can be used to satisfy their needs. Previous loss experience plays no part in this planning. Building a life insurance reserve on your own rather than transferring the risk to an insurance company could save you tens of thousands of dollars in your lifetime.

Transferring Risks

The third method of dealing with financial risks is to transfer the responsibility for the potential financial burden to someone else, usually an insurance company. Such a company pools risks and uses statistics to calculate probabilities of loss. A fee called a *premium* is charged on the basis of the risk involved, the size of the financial loss the company might be required to absorb, and the number of individual risks the company can gather together. To arrive at a fee that will both cover the expected loss and render a profit, the company follows generally the same procedure as you would use to determine whether to self-insure. Instead of using data on just one individual, however, the company pools

information about the loss experience of thousands of policyholders throughout the country. Mathematicians, called actuaries, use probability theory to calculate the degree of risk in each potential loss situation. For each type of risk, they divide the total expected loss by the number of loss exposures and arrive at a base premium (the price insurers may charge their customers in exchange for insurance coverage). Insurers then add a sum to cover administration costs and profit to the base premium to arrive at the premium charged the policyholder.

For example, if you wanted to determine the base premium for fire damage coverage in an area of 10,000 homes, you would first determine the total expected loss due to fire based on the history of fire damage in that area. If this figure turned out to be $320,000, the base charge to each homeowner would be $32 ($320,000 expected loss ÷ 10,000 exposures) to cover the risk of fire. The cost of premiums will rise if the expected loss due to bad loss experience increases or if the number of good risks over which to spread the total expected loss decreases.

Now that you know how premiums are set, you can see that if your loss experience is better than the average experience of the group to which you are assigned by an insurance company, self-insurance may be more economical, provided you have assets sufficient to cover the largest potential loss. If your experience is worse than the average of the group to which you are assigned, consider yourself lucky to be able to transfer financial responsibility for your actions to someone else.

There is another thing you should consider before you decide whether to transfer an insurable risk. If there is a great probability that a loss will occur to nearly all potential policyholders, it is useless to insure against it: the price you pay will closely approximate the loss itself. For example, almost everyone has a physical examination from a doctor at least once a year. So if you plan to have one physical or less each year, the price you pay the doctor will probably be less than the price you pay the insurance company for a general medical policy (pp. 104–105), including administrative costs, commissions, and profit.

It is generally best to retain those risks that involve relatively small financial losses and have a high probability of occurrence. The risks that are best transferred involve relatively large financial losses and have a low probability of occurrence.

BUYING INSURANCE

In this section we will discuss insurance companies, insurance policies, and insurance agents as they relate to the buying process.

The Insurance Company

The insurance company offers financial responsibility through pooling risks and providing for losses out of its reserves. You contract for this service by paying a premium. You thereby absorb a small but certain loss (the premium) to avoid the burden of a much larger potential loss (theft of your car, for example).

The insurance company normally makes a profit through underwriting (assuming a risk by means of insurance) and investing. An insurance company earns an *underwriting profit* when actual losses stay below expected losses. Such a profit indicates that the company is either attracting more good risks than bad, performing efficiently, or charging too high a premium. An insurance company earns an *investment profit* when its invested reserves earn a yield in excess of investment costs. This profit indicates that the company is selecting good investment instruments.

There are five types of insurers: stock insurance companies, mutual insurance companies, health expense associations, reciprocals, and Lloyds of London. All insurance companies, whatever the type, are regulated by the states in which they operate. Laws governing the types of policies that may be sold and the business practices of each licensed insurer differ from state to state. Historically, New York and California have been the most progressive in championing better insurance protection. State departments of insurance enforce the laws and regulate the insurance industry. Offices of the state department of insurance are usually located in major cities throughout the state and serve to test and license insurance sales representatives, investigate policyholder complaints, disburse financial information on all insurers licensed to do business in the state, and much more. Sometimes the federal government steps in to deal with insurance problems that are too big for each state to handle. National crime insurance and Medicare have resulted from such intervention.

stock insurance companies Stock insurance companies are owned by the stockholders. All profits belong to the stockholders in the form of dividends or retained earnings. Stock companies offer two types of policies. The first is called a participating policy (par policy). It returns a portion of the premium to the policyholder at the end of the policy period. This portion is called a dividend; but it is actually a refund of premium, not a payment of earnings. The other type of policy is called a nonparticipating policy (nonpar policy). It does not refund any portion of the premium at the end of the policy period. Be sure to compare the costs of these two types of policies. Many times, the difference in price between the two is the amount of the proposed premium refund or dividend, the size of which cannot be guaranteed. Most property and casualty policies are written by stock companies.

mutual insurance companies Mutual insurance companies are owned by the policyholders, not by stockholders. In other words, the policyholders share in the profit of the company. As in the participating policies issued by stock companies, the profits are distributed through dividends attached to the policies. Theoretically, the greater the profits, the greater the dividends received by each policyholder. Most life and health policies are written by mutual companies.

There has long been controversy as to whether stock insurance companies or mutual insurance companies offer the least expensive product. Proponents of the former maintain that, because of the profit motive, stock companies have to be efficient and offer products at the best rate. Proponents of the latter argue that, because mutual companies do not have to make a profit, they can offer the least expensive coverage and pass on any gains to the policyholders as premium refunds. In reality, nothing conclusive can be proven one way or the other. The potential policyholder must shop both stock and mutual companies to determine which offers the best policy at the cheapest rate for a specific situation.

health expense associations   Health expense associations are insurance organizations formed by hospitals and physicians' groups to disburse medical services. Unlike stock or mutual insurance companies that pay to injured parties whatever money is required, health expense associations pay physicians according to a specific fee structure. The associations make money by offering medical services at the lowest cost. In contrast, corporate insurers have no control over cost and make money by selecting good risks.

There are two types of plans offered by these associations: closed-end plans, which stipulate that services must be rendered only at certain contracted hospitals, and open-end plans, which enable the insured to obtain medical care from any hospital. The two largest health expense associations are Blue Cross and Blue Shield.

reciprocals   Reciprocals (often termed interinsurance exchanges) are composed of individual insureds who normally assume their proportionate share of losses incurred by everyone other than themselves. An attorney-in-fact usually performs the underwriting functions. Reciprocals are found in certain business insurance risk situations.

Lloyds of London   Lloyds of London is an insurance group composed of many subgroups or syndicates. Each syndicate is made up of from ten to a hundred individuals who invest in insurance risks. Unlike other insurers, who specialize in certain risks and pool only similar exposures, Lloyds gathers different types of risk exposures together in the same syndicate, thereby balancing certain risk exposures against the experiences of other risks. Normally these syndicates insure very large risks to which there may be only one or two exposures. Insuring a concert pianist's fingers or the overland shipment of millions of dollars by armored car are examples of such risks. Lloyds of London, however, is licensed to sell their services in only a few states in this country.

The Insurance Policy

An insurance policy is a legal contract. It spells out what the insurance company will or will not do in certain loss situations. There are basically two types of provisions in an insurance policy: jacket provisions and coverage provisions. Jacket provisions set forth the insurance company's commitment to the policyholder. There are usually five such provisions:

1. the general insuring agreement, whereby the company agrees to pay any sum of money that the contract directs as settlement against a coverage claim;
2. supplementary payments, whereby the company outlines the expenses, if any, it will pay in addition to the settlement expense (provision 1);
3. definitions, whereby the company defines some common terms relating to the conditions of their coverage;
4. conditions, whereby the company details those conditions under which the contract will be considered valid; and
5. declarations, whereby the company identifies who is to be covered against what (as determined by the coverage provisions that the policyholder selects).

The coverage provisions are the policyholder's instructions to the insurance company. By choosing one or more coverage provisions, the policyholder tells the insurance company who is to be covered, what injury or property damage is to be covered, and what is not to be covered.

Policies are required to conform to state insurance statutes. Therefore, policies written by the same company in different states may cover the same insurable risks in different ways, depending on the state in which they are written. Amendments (endorsements) are often added to policies to restrict or expand coverage. Some endorsements may be required by state law or by the insurance company. Others may be automatically included unless specifically excluded by the policyholder. Still others may be added only if the policyholder so requests.

Policies can be paid for in various ways, although annual payment is usual. Paying premiums more frequently than annually is likely to result in a larger yearly premium because more administrative work is required. Premiums may be upgraded so that smaller than ordinary amounts are paid in earlier years and larger than ordinary amounts are paid in later years.

The Insurance Agent

Agents can be classified according to the type of insurance they sell. *Property/casualty agents* handle auto insurance, home insurance, personal property floaters, and such. These agents perform much, if not all, of the underwriting as well as the sales for an insurance company.

That is, they determine whether the applicant is a good risk and what he should be charged. They have the power to bind an insurance company to the coverage desired by the applicant before the policy is actually issued by the company. In this way a potential policyholder can become insured immediately. Since the property/casualty agent owns the policyholder's records, he has the power to transfer a policyholder's coverage from one insurance company to another. A release need not be first obtained from the present insurer. All in all, the property/casualty agent has a lot more underwriting and service responsibility than does the life/health agent. The *life/health agent* simply submits a potential policyholder's application to an insurance company, and the decision to accept or reject the application is up to the company itself.

Agents can also be classified according to their relation to insurance companies. Exclusive agents sell policies for just one company. They are salaried sales personnel, usually employed by very large insurance companies. Independent agents sell policies for several companies. Brokers are similar to independent agents in that they are licensed by more than one company; but, unlike agents, they can sell all lines of insurance, not simply one or two.

Insurance agents are usually compensated by commissions from the insurance companies for the policies they sell for them. The size of the commission depends on the type of insurance and the size of the premium. Some types of policies make more money for the agent than do other types. The buying process can be somewhat complicated by the fact that the agent profits from the advice he gives. You must determine for yourself which is the right insurance policy for your situation.

The Buying Process

Once you have decided to transfer the risks of a financial calamity to an insurance company, you have to determine exactly what your needs for insurance are and how to fulfill those needs with the least cost and effort. There are five major questions you should answer. What should I insure? What perils should I insure against? How much should I insure for? How long should I keep the insurance in force? How should I buy the policy? These five questions are applicable to all types of insurance policies and represent the only variables about which you as a policyholder need be concerned. Each of these questions will be dealt with in more detail in the next four chapters when the particular types of insurance are discussed.

what to insure   What you need to insure is not always easy to determine. Since insurance protects the pocketbook, you will want to insure only those things that, if lost or destroyed, would cause you or someone dependent upon you a monetary loss. Therefore, your first task is to identify the various assets you own and their respective values. Your

home, personal property, and income are all assets that, if lost, might cause financial hardship. Determine priorities. Which assets are most dear to you? Given that the cost of protection may be a constraint, separate your assets into those that must be insured, those that should be insured, and those that might be insured.

As you determine your insurance needs, make sure you are using insurance properly. Ask yourself if you are truly guarding against a financial calamity or merely making a prepayment for an anticipated loss that is likely to occur. As we saw earlier in the example using the general medical policy, if you buy insurance to cover small expenses that have a high probability of occurrence, you may be paying a cost for that coverage almost equal to the expected loss. In such a situation, it would be more prudent to invest an amount of money equal to the probable expense.

what perils to insure against Once you have decided what assets you want to insure, you must decide what hazards and perils pose a threat to their safety. This is a difficult decision because it is impossible to foresee all the calamities that might occur.

Most insurance companies separate perils into groups according to their probability of occurrence. To determine this, they look at past experience. Since as many cases of vandalism have occurred as theft, for example, vandalism and theft are considered to be of equal risk and are therefore grouped in the same peril category. Because of this practice of grouping perils, you often must buy policies that offer protection against events unlikely to occur in your circumstances. For example, you may live in the country and need insurance against windstorms or hail, but your policy might also cover damage due to riot or civil commotion. Naturally, the more perils you insure against, the greater will be the premium cost. Some policies offer all-risk coverage. These policies cover virtually all perils or hazards that might jeopardize what you are insuring. Because these policies offer the widest scope, they are more expensive.

how much to insure for In order to answer this question, you must be able to determine the value of what you are insuring. The value of personal property may not be difficult to determine. Determining the financial effect of your death, however, is a weighty task. In chapter 7 you will learn an effective way to do this.

You may not be able to retain the entire risk of financial loss, but you can retain a portion of it through the use of deductibles. The *deductible clause* in an insurance policy provides that you pay all expenses incurred in a loss up to a specified limit. The company will pay losses above that amount up to the maximum coverage of the policy. Naturally, the higher the limit you set on the deductible, the less risk and financial burden the insurance company has to assume. Your premiums are small because the insurance company reduces its operating costs by not having to settle many small claims and by reducing the payout on larger claims.

If you use deductibles, you should establish an *emergency fund* from which deductibles can be paid. Normally, this fund should be large enough to cover not only all deductibles but also the replacement value of items you are self-insuring as well as items that are not insurable. The financial consequences of losing one's job, however, probably pose the largest potential emergency cash drain, and your emergency fund should be large enough to withstand this drain for a reasonable length of time.

To determine the appropriate amount to handle a six-month job loss, you should take into account how much the family could cut back expenses in an emergency; sources of support you could count on (unemployment insurance, food stamps, sick pay allowances if ill, and so on); how much you could extend your credit on current credit cards and accounts; and other sources of support (investments not earmarked for important goals, family help, and so on). An easier, though sometimes less precise, method is to create a fund equal to two to three times your monthly pay minus income and Social Security taxes and amounts put into payroll investment plans. If your take-home pay is $600 a month, an appropriate emergency fund would be $1200 to $1800, depending on your current debts. This amount—combined with severance pay, unemployment insurance benefits, and frugality—would probably be enough to carry you through six months of unemployment. You should plan that after that time you would either have a new job or begin liquidating investments. Such an emergency fund would probably be large enough to pay any insurance deductible you might have as well.

Having decided what you want to insure, what you want to insure against, and what insurance benefits you need, you have automatically determined the type of insurance policy you need. All policies are simply combinations of these three variables.

how long to keep the insurance in force   Most property insurance is issued for either one- or three-year terms. Life insurance is issued for as long or as short a period as you want. Health and automobile policies are normally written for one-year terms. Consider the length of time appropriate for you. Keep insurance in force only as long as you have a need for it. If a policy has guaranteed renewable provisions, it is automatically continued until you give instructions to the contrary. Since your insurance needs are constantly changing, you should make certain that your protection period is neither too short nor too long nor too inflexible to allow you to make adjustments as your needs change.

how to buy the policy   Buying the insurance policy is important because the success of your plans depends largely on the people you choose

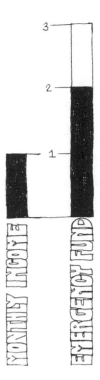

to carry them out. Your buying decision involves selecting the agent to sell you the policy, obtaining the best price for the coverage involved, and choosing the best insurance company among those offering the least expensive coverage. You will be evaluating primarily service and price.

One way to begin the selection process is to ask friends, attorneys, bankers, or accountants to recommend agents who have proven satisfactory. Another way is to check the yellow pages of your local telephone directory. You may want to call the largest independent agencies in town. Chances are that most insurance companies will want to license agents who can give their products the broadest market exposure and these agents will be found in the largest agencies.

Once you have gathered the names of recommended agents or of agents you wish to call from the phone directory, it is time to get rate quotes and find out where you can obtain coverage at the lowest cost. Remember that the agent is only a means to an end—good coverage at the lowest cost. You start the process of selecting the best policy with agent selection because a good agent should give you exposure to the best companies with the best rates, and the best rates are what you are looking for.

After you have obtained several rate quotes and found which agents seem to offer the best coverage at the lowest cost, look at the insurance company itself. If the insurance company offering the lowest rate is represented by a large agency with a good reputation, you can feel fairly confident that the company is a good one. Write the nearest department of insurance for information about the company's financial strength, length of registration to do business within the state, and so on. Check the company's background and rating in *Best's Insurance Guide* at your local library.

The only way to know whether you have the best insurance deal is to shop for rates both when you first buy the policy and when you renew. Be sure you read your policies so that you know exactly what you are paying for and the true cost of each increment of coverage you select. Compare costs before making a final choice. The cost savings will probably more than make up for the time and effort you spend.

CONCLUSION

Insurance is a way of protecting what you have by eliminating or easing the financial hardships resulting from a calamity. You can either minimize risk by taking precautionary measures to reduce the likelihood that a calamity will occur, retain the risk by providing a cash reserve, or transfer the risk to an insurance company by buying an insurance policy. Most likely you will use a combination of all three measures.

Through insurance policies, insurance companies offer a means of transferring the risk of calamity and the resulting financial losses to them. To select the policy most appropriate to your needs, you must decide what you want to insure, what perils you want to insure against, how much you want to insure for, how long you want to insure, and whom you want to insure with. You will pay a premium for this service based on the insurance company's past experience with similar insurance arrangements. Know how much each policy will cost before you buy.

VOCABULARY

deductible clause
emergency fund
health expense association
health/life agent
insurable risk
investment profit
Lloyds of London
mutual insurance company

personal loss experience
premium
property/casualty agent
reciprocal
self-insure
stock insurance company
underwriting profit

QUESTIONS

1. What are the major differences between investment risks and insurable risks?
2. Discuss the three ways insurable risks can be treated. How might you use all three ways to deal with the risk of fire damage to your personal property?
3. You pay $100 a year for collision coverage on your automobile. In the five years since you began driving, you have incurred only one minor fender dent that was your fault. You anticipate that you will continue to be a careful driver. Under what circumstances should you self-insure? Under what circumstances should you not?
4. You pay $35 a month for medical expense insurance that covers every dollar of medical expense you might incur. An insurance agent has offered you a medical expense policy covering all your costs above the first $100 for only $15 a month. Your medical expenses over the last five years have been $50, $75, $175, $100, and $0 respectively. Assuming both policies are of the same quality, which one would you buy? Why?

5. Which risks listed below might reasonably be retained? Which risks might reasonably be transferred? Why?

   Your home might burn down.

   Your bicycle may be stolen.

   You might die leaving no dependents.

   You might have a heart attack and need to be hospitalized.

   You might have to receive a shot of penicillin.

   A tree might fall on your car, crushing it.

   You might die leaving a wife and three children.

6. What would the base premium be for auto theft insurance in the following situation? Auto thefts of a certain make of car in Detroit next year are expected to result in $50,000 worth of losses. There are 2500 owners of this make of car in Detroit.

CASE PROBLEM

Bob and Julia Phillips are both thirty-one years old and have been married for eight years. They have decided to review their insurance programs for their house, car, and personal property in order to find out what assets they should insure, how much of the financial burden they should retain, and how much of it they should transfer. In the five years that they have owned their home, with a current market value of $35,000, they have incurred only $300 in losses due to natural perils. Their present home insurance policy costs them $180 a year. During the fifteen years that Bob and Julie have each been driving, they have incurred a total of $450 in car damages from collisions that were their fault. They now pay $85 a year for collision coverage on their car, which is worth $500. Since they have been married, Bob and Julie have lost $160 in stolen personal property. Their present property insurance costs them $15 a year to cover $10,000 worth of personal property.

What is the Phillipses' greatest financial risk? Their second greatest? Their third greatest? Which of these risks can be transferred to an insurance company? Which risk should be entirely transferred?

In trying to determine whether they would be able to self-insure, the Phillipses compare their assets and liabilities. They find that they have $4360 in monetary assets (cash, savings account, mutual funds, and savings bonds) and $45,500 in fixed assets (home, car, and personal property) for a total of $49,860. Their liabilities consist of $150 in unpaid bills, $4000 for an education loan, and $30,000 for a home mortgage, making their net worth $15,710.

Which risks might the Phillipses absorb either in part or in the entirety? Which might they retain? Use the following insurance rate information for their existing policies to determine how much money all your insurance recommendations would save the Phillipses each year.

HOME		AUTOMOBILE		PERSONAL PROPERTY	
Deductible	Annual Premium	Deductible	Annual Premium	Deductible	Annual Premium
none	$180	none	$85	none	$15
$ 50	170	$ 50	70	$ 50	13
100	150	100	52	100	8
1000	80	250	32		

Denenberg, Herbert S.; Eilers, Robert D.; Hoffman, G. Wright; Kline, Chester A.; Melone, Joseph J.; and Snider, H. Wayne, *Risk and Insurance.* Englewood Cliffs, N.J.: Prentice-Hall, 1964.

RECOMMENDED READING

The authors discuss the theory of risk management and differences in dealing with property, personal, and liability risks. Parts one, two, three and five are especially relevant to this chapter. Part four relates more to our chapters 4 through 7.

Organizations offering materials on preventive measures in dealing with risks:

Aetna Life and Casualty
Public Relations and Advertising Dept.
151 Farmington Avenue
Hartford, CT 06115
Free loan films (safety)

American Insurance Association
Engineering and Safety Dept.
85 John Street
New York, NY 10038
Leaflets, pamphlets, film catalog

Insurance Institute for Highway Safety
711 Watergate Office Building
2600 Virginia Avenue, N.W.
Washington, D.C. 20037
Detailed source list of companies and organizations that issue laymen's publications on traffic safety

Kemper Insurance
Public Relations Dept.
4750 N. Sheridan Road
Chicago, IL 60640
Pamphlets

Liberty Mutual Insurance Company
Public Relations Dept.
175 Berkeley Street
Boston, MA 02117
Pamphlets

National Safety Council
Director of Public Information
425 N. Michigan Avenue
Chicago, IL 60611
Films, pamphlets, posters

Public Health Servie
Inquiries Branch
U.S. Dept. of Health, Education and Welfare
Washington, D.C. 20201
Leaflets on farm and home safety, poisons, and so on

The Travelers Insurance Companies
Public Information and Advertising
One Tower Square
Hartford, CT 06115
Posters and booklets containing street and highway accident data

CHUCK AND NANCY ANDERSON

COMPUTING THE SIZE OF THEIR EMERGENCY FUND

The Andersons' emergency fund should cover deductibles on insurance policies, items not covered by insurance (such as unusual dental costs), and items for which they choose to self-insure (such as collision coverage on their five-year-old compact). However, all of these expenses are of limited consequence when compared with the possibility, no matter how remote, that Chuck might lose his job, even temporarily. Therefore, if Chuck's possible loss of job is the one item he provides for, he would also have sufficient funds to cover the family's other emergency needs.

QUESTIONS

1. If the Andersons' annual take-home pay is $13,200, what is an appropriate amount for their emergency fund? (Keep in mind that Chuck has financial assets he can call on in emergencies.)
2. How will the Andersons' balance sheet and income statement be affected if they decide to place their emergency fund in a passbook savings account?

4

PROPERTY INSURANCE

For insurance purposes, the term *property* refers to two categories: physical structures (most commonly a house) and personal property (one's belongings). Land is not considered insurable by the insurance industry. Therefore, when we refer in this text to property, we exclude land holdings.

Property probably represents your largest investment. Look at the assets side of your balance sheet, which you constructed in chapter 2. Are the figures representing your home and personal property greater than the figure representing your total monetary assets? Could you afford to replace all of your property with your monetary assets if your fixed assets were lost, stolen, or destroyed?

Look at the liabilities side of your balance sheet. What percent of your total fixed asset value is represented by items that are still being financed? If you were to lose some of your fixed assets that are not completely paid for, could you convert enough monetary assets not only to replace those you have lost but also to complete the payments on them?

Such questions may make you anxious about both the safety and the relative importance of your fixed assets. Property insurance is designed to relieve your anxieties by enabling you to replace your property if it is destroyed or damaged through fire or some other calamity. To appraise your property insurance needs, consider the following questions. What property can I insure? How do I value my property for insurance purposes? How do I choose the insurance coverage I need—at the lowest cost?

WHAT PROPERTY CAN I INSURE?

You can insure anything that belongs to you and has a determinable value except land. Insurance companies insure only property that, if damaged, will cause financial loss to the person actually holding the insurance policy. No matter how much you like your neighbor's home, for example, you are not permitted to buy property insurance on it, since your neighbor has the only true monetary interest in the property.

Even though your right to ownership may be unquestioned, the property itself may still be uninsurable by most insurance companies because of the difficulty involved in determining its value. Any items that are difficult to value, or appear to have value only to you—manuscripts, rare book collections, or old family heirlooms—may automatically be excluded from general property coverage. Instead, they will be itemized in your policy. The company will charge you a much higher premium to insure these articles and may pay you only a fraction of their value if they are damaged. Often, only insurers such as Lloyds of London will accept the risk of insuring such items.

Specifically, you can insure your home and attached structures (e.g., garage); detached structures (e.g., tool shed, separate garage); trees, plants, and shrubs around the house; personal property when on the premises; personal property when away from the premises; other people's property while on the premises; and additional living expenses, if you are forced to vacate your home.

The manner in which you value your property is extremely important. Let us look at the proper methods of evaluating your home and personal property so that you can tell how much insurance you really need.

HOW DO I VALUE MY PROPERTY
FOR INSURANCE PURPOSES?

What do you own? Larger items may be easy to identify—house, refrigerator, color television. You would readily remember items you use every day if they were destroyed or stolen. But what about things such as the wedding silver that may be packed away or the gold pin you gave your wife last Christmas? These may receive little use but may be of great value. You may own dishes, clothing, garden tools, furniture, and books that you wish to protect. In order to know what you do own, you must inventory your personal property.

Personal Property Inventory

If a fire were to start in a closet of your house and completely destroy that closet and the adjoining room, how easy would it be for you to identify all the items of personal property that were destroyed in those two places? If your estimate of loss appeared to be abnormally high because of a mink coat in the closet where the fire began, would your insurance company demand documented proof of the alleged contents of the closet? A room-by-room inventory of your personal property can be used not only to let you know what has been lost but also to substantiate your claim.

A personal property inventory—which is easy to update as personal property is acquired, given away, or moved from one room to another—facilitates matching the value of your insurance coverage with that of the property you have accumulated year by year. The inventory will also tell you how you have distributed value throughout your home. Many people have most items of value in one or two rooms. To reduce the magnitude of loss through any one incident, you might distribute them more evenly throughout the house.

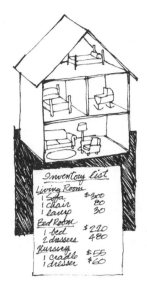

Market Value

As you take inventory room by room, you may have difficulty setting a value on certain items. How much is that green sofa really worth? Even though you may have spent a lot for it when it was new, you probably would receive only a fraction of that amount if you were to sell it today. What about your wardrobe? What value do you put on a four-year-old suit that is worn at the elbows? Insurance companies have an answer to this dilemma, and you should be aware of their solution and apply it to your personal property. Too many families have learned, only after fire has destroyed their belongings, that their insurance coverage is scarcely enough to replace many of them.

The market value of an item is the dollar value that you could realize if you were to sell that item. This value is considered by the insurance industry as the appropriate value to assign to personal property, since it best reflects the amount of money necessary to restore your financial position after a loss. Unlike the purchase price, market value reflects any changes in value. For example, the value of automobiles, furniture, and clothing normally declines with use. These items are said to *depreciate*. Homes, antiques, and real estate, however, will probably be worth more today than when they were purchased. These assets are said to *appreciate*. Because most insurable items depreciate, an old item's market value may bear no relation to the cost of replacing that item with a new one at current prices.

Insurance adjusters use depreciation schedules to determine the market value of goods lost or stolen. A sample depreciation schedule is provided in figure 4-1. Those articles with the largest annual depreciation percentages lose their value the fastest. Which types of articles are these? Which articles retain their value? This depreciation schedule will help you determine the amount of insurance you need; for by using these figures you can approximate the amount you could collect on a claim.

A sample personal property inventory is provided in figure 4-2 (p. 55). The instructions on page 54 tell you how to apply the personal property

Type of Article	Specific Articles	Annual Depreciation (%)
Appliances	Phonograph	10
	Tape recorder	10
	Refrigerator	7
	Television	10
	Automatic washer	12
	Automatic dryer	8
	Stove or range	7
	Minor appliances	10
Bedding	Blankets (cotton)	10
	Blankets (wool)	5
	Box springs	5
	Mattresses	5
	Sheets, pillowcases	20
	Bedspreads	10
Books	Reference	4
	Fiction or nonfiction	Use 60% of replacement cost
	Paperbacks	Use 75% of replacement cost
Carpets and Rugs	Under $5/yd.	20
	$5–$10/yd.	10
	Over $10/yd.	7
Clothes	Men's sport coats, suits, slacks, sweaters, and such	20
	Men's shirts, underwear, hose, shoes, and such	33
	Men's topcoats, raincoats	10
	Women's dresses, suits, skirts, leather hand-bags, evening gowns	20

Fig. 4-1.
Personal property depreciation schedule

Type of Article	Specific Articles	Annual Depreciation (%)
	Women's blouses, shoes, nightclothes	33
	Women's hats, fabric handbags	50
	Women's fur coats, jackets	7
Dishes and Glassware		Use 90% of replacement cost
Draperies and Curtains	Drapes	10
	Curtains	20
	Shades	10
	Venetian blinds	7
Foodstuffs		Use replacement cost
Furniture	Upholstered, chrome or plastic	10
	Wood	7
	Other	20
Lamps	Table or floor	7
	Shades	20
Linens		20
Silverware	Plated	4
	Sterling	Use 90% of replacement cost
Toys		10
Yard Equipment		20
Miscellaneous	Luggage	5
	Mirrors	5
	Picture frames	5
	Tools (power or hand)	5
	Ornaments, decorations	Use 75% of replacement cost

Fig. 4-1. *(cont.)*

SOURCE: Aetna Life & Casualty Company's Scheduled Guide, 1970.

depreciation schedule (fig. 4-1) to determine your property's market value. The first step in the instructions corresponds to the first column in the sample inventory (fig. 4-2), and so on for all nine columns. You may want to round your figures to the nearest ten, as has been done in the sample.

Instructions

1 *Within each room separate the articles of personal property into categories.*

2 *Indicate the number of articles in each category.*

3 *Write the original cost for the entire group of articles in each category.* This figure is often useful in claims adjustment. If you do not know the original cost of an article, estimate what you think it might have been.

4 *Estimate the collective age of the various articles in each category and mark down the average number of years of age.* In figure 4-2, for example, even though books may have been accumulated over several years, the average age is two years.

5 *Using the depreciation schedule (fig. 4-1), record the appropriate annual depreciation percentage for each category of articles.* The annual depreciation factor for wooden tables, for example, is 7 percent.

6 *Determine the total depreciation to date by multiplying the annual depreciation percentage (column 5) by the age (column 4).* For the two tables (fig. 4-2) that are two years old, the total depreciation to date is 14 percent (2 × 7%).

7 *Estimate what it would cost today to replace the old items with new ones.* Newspaper ads should give a good idea of current prices. According to figure 4-2, new end tables would cost about $35 each.

8 *Multiply the total depreciation percentage (column 6) by today's cost (column 7) to get the accumulated dollar depreciation.*

9 *Subtract the accumulated dollar depreciation (column 8) from today's cost (column 7) to compute the present market value.* This is the amount you could probably collect on a claim to the insurance company. For example, the total dollar depreciation to date for the two tables in figure 4-2 is $9.80 (14% × $70). Therefore, the tables' present market value is $60.20 ($70.00 – 9.80), or simply $60.

If, after taking your personal property inventory, you find that most of your furniture and belongings have negligible value because of their age but are still in good condition, take pictures of the various rooms in your home to use as evidence. Snapshots taken from opposite corners of a room should encompass most of what you have and give you bargaining power in adjusting your claim. Pictures help the claims adjuster determine not only the value but also the quantity of personal property in each room.

Article Category	Number of Articles	Total Original Cost ($)	Average Age (Years)	Annual Depreciation (%)	Total Depreciation (%)	Today's Cost ($)	Accumulated Dollar Depreciation ($)	Market Value ($)
Carpets	1	$ 250	4	10	40	$ 300	$120	$ 180
Chairs	2	100	2	10	20	150	30	120
Tables (wooden)	2	50	2	7	14	70	10	60
Couch	1	85	4	10	40	100	40	60
Record Player	1	60	6	10	60	100	60	40
Television	1	250	2	10	20	300	60	240
Mirrors	1	50	4	5	20	75	15	60
Lamps	3	60	2	7	14	70	10	60
Drapes	2	100	4	10	40	150	60	90
Window Shades	2	10	4	10	40	16	6	10
Picture Frames	2	25	2	5	10	33	3	30
Decorations	15	30	2	Use 75% of replacement cost	25	40	10	30
Bookcases	1	25	2	7	14	35	5	30
Books (fiction)	30	100	2	Use 60% of replacement cost	40	100	40	60
TOTAL	48	$1235				$1589	$499	$1090

Fig. 4-2.
Sample personal property inventory for living room

You may be thinking that you would not want to replace some articles if they were lost or destroyed. You should consider, however, what the insurance company would pay you if you lost only those items that really matter to you—probably nowhere near the amount of money you would need to buy them new today. The only way to have enough money available for items you care about is to insure everything. In practice, it may be wise to insure all of your personal property.

In addition to the problem of valuing your personal property, you face the problem of arriving at an accurate value for your home. Insurance companies allow you to insure your home for either its market value (what you could sell it for prior to a loss) or its replacement cost (the amount you would have to pay to replace it new at current prices).

Replacement Cost

Picture a wood frame garage constructed three years ago at a total cost of $2500. Because of damage from weathering, a heavy hailstorm, and daily use, the garage has an estimated current market value of only $1500. The garage can be said to have depreciated by $1000 or 40 percent. If inflation and other factors have raised the cost of new construction at an annual rate of about 8 percent for the past three years, then the cost of building a new garage just like the one constructed three years ago is $3100 ($2500 + 24% of $2500). The garage's replacement cost is $1600 higher than its market value. Since most insurance companies allow the policyholder to insure the home and other building structures (but *not* personal property) for replacement cost, the owner of the garage could have estimated that replacement costs were advancing approximately 8 percent each year and insured his garage for its true replacement value.

If you insure your home for replacement cost, you must not only determine its replacement value but also keep up with inflation's effect on construction costs. For an added premium, many insurance companies offer inflation guard policies that automatically adjust policy limits upward approximately 1 percent every four months. However, some of these policies base their adjustments on changes in the consumer price index (CPI) and, historically, construction costs have risen at over twice the rate of general inflation (CPI). Other policies use nationwide construction indices, which may not reflect local variations. You should compute your home's replacement cost annually on the basis of local construction cost information, rather than purchase a policy that automatically determines replacement cost. If your construction costs are rising more slowly than national averages, computing the replacement cost yourself will be more accurate and may save you money in insurance premiums. Conversely, if rates in your area are rising faster, you can keep from being underinsured by computing the replacement cost yourself.

The standard way of determining replacement cost for a house is to multiply the local construction costs per square foot by the number of square feet in the house. As a rule of thumb, multiply the square footage of your home by $15 to $20, depending upon your regional costs and the construction quality of your home. The resulting figure represents the replacement value of your home today according to current construction cost indices. For example, if you have a 2000-square-foot home of standard frame construction in an average cost area, multiply the 2000 square feet by $17 per square foot. The current replacement cost on the home is $34,000.

The penalty for not accurately gauging your home's replacement cost may be a reduction in the benefits available to you under your insurance contract. This penalty is spelled out in the policy's coinsurance clause.

the coinsurance clause According to the coinsurance clause, if you choose to value your home at replacement cost you must insure your property for a sum of money equal to at least 80 percent of the property's replacement cost. If your appraisal is lower than this, you will be paying premiums for coverage on which you cannot fully collect.

For example, five years ago Harry Simms insured his home for $20,000 replacement cost. This year a tornado did so much damage that his house had to be totally rebuilt. The insurance company and a contractor appraised the replacement cost at $30,000. In order to satisfy the coinsurance requirement, Harry should have carried $24,000 worth of insurance (80 percent of $30,000) instead of $20,000. The company paid only $16,665, even though he carried $20,000 coverage. How did the company arrive at $16,665 to settle the claim? The company computed the ratio of Harry's current coverage ($20,000) to the minimum required ($24,000). They then applied this ratio to the amount of his claim (five-sixths of $20,000).

Harry suffered a financial loss not only because he misguessed the replacement cost of his home but also because the coinsurance clause caused him to be paying premiums on coverage for which he could never collect. If Harry had maintained his coverage at a level that reflected the current replacement cost, the total extra cost in raised premiums over the five years from the time he took out the policy to when he needed to collect would have been $80 ($16 a year). By not doing so, Harry had to supply the remaining $13,335 to rebuild his home.

market value or replacement cost? Which method of valuation should you use in determining your property insurance needs? If you want to be certain that you will be able to rebuild any damaged structures at no out-of-pocket cost to yourself, choose the replacement cost option. Then be sure to estimate as accurately as you can what the replacement cost will be during the policy period. If you only want to be certain that you will be able to purchase a similar structure in the same condition at another location, insuring for market value will be sufficient. Under this option, of course, your premiums will probably provide less coverage and cost you less because either the house has not appreciated as fast as construction costs have risen or it has depreciated. However, if only a portion of your home is destroyed, your out-of-pocket costs could be quite large, since the insurance company would not pay enough to enable you to hire a carpenter to rebuild the damaged part with new lumber and new hardware (this would be the case if replacement cost were used) but would pay only a portion of the home's market value as determined by an insurance appraiser. Because of the large cost that may be incurred if market value is selected, many homeowners choose to insure their homes for replacement cost.

HOW DO I CHOOSE THE INSURANCE COVERAGE I NEED?

Now that you have decided what property you want protected, you must decide what you want to protect that property against. There are many possibilities, as shown in the key to perils in figure 4-3 (pp. 60–61). Using this list of perils commonly covered by property insurance contracts, decide which are dangerous to you because of the nature of the property you wish to insure, the area in which you live, or both. As explained in chapter 3, those risks that are seldom, if ever, covered include excessive heat or scorching (no flame), self-inflicted hazards (such as pouring gasoline around your home and lighting it), snowstorms, tidal waves, earthquakes, floods, and war. With your insurance needs in mind, you are ready to consider the kinds of property coverage available.

There are four groups of policies that cover your home or your personal property, or both: basic fire contract, dwelling and dwelling contents forms, homeowners forms, and floater policies. Basic fire contracts cover your home and other physical structures against damage due to fire. Because they cover only one peril, they are to be used cautiously. Dwelling and dwelling contents forms offer coverage for physical damage done by a burglar but do not cover the actual stolen property. They are used primarily by apartment owners to cover their rental property. Homeowners forms are the most popular contracts and are specifically designed to meet the needs of homeowners and renters. The standard homeowners contract is divided into two sections—one that offers property coverage against many perils and one that offers coverage over a wide range of potential liability situations. The latter section will be discussed in chapter 5 as part of general liability coverage. Floaters cover personal property (not physical structures) anywhere in the world. They are used to cover highly valued items such as furs and jewelry. Figure 4-3 shows the various types of coverage these policies offer.

Basic Fire Contract

The basic fire contract offers minimal protection. This policy covers damage only to your home or adjoining structures by fire, lightning, and chemicals used to extinguish fire. Your personal property is not included. Consequently, the premiums are the lowest of any policy. For an additional premium, an extended coverage endorsement (E.C.E.) can be attached to the basic fire contract. This endorsement adds coverage for hail, windstorm, explosion, riot and civil commotion, smoke, aircraft, and vehicles.

When considering a basic fire contract, be sure you understand exactly what is meant by the various terms used to describe the perils covered. Often "loss due to fire" means that you will be reimbursed only for damages caused by the fire itself, not for damages due to whatever caused the fire. Smoke coverage rarely covers smoke from fireplaces and other common sources of smoke damage. Even though basic fire protection is a component of all other types of policies, as a policy in itself it is rarely satisfactory because it leaves the home unprotected against all other perils.

Dwelling and Dwelling Contents Forms

There are three dwelling forms that offer property coverage: the dwelling building(s) special form, the dwelling building(s) and contents form, and the dwelling building(s) and contents broad form. Each of these forms offers more extensive coverage than does the basic fire contract.

dwelling building(s) special form   This form provides all-risk coverage. Unlike the basic fire contract, which states exactly what is covered, the dwelling building(s) special form lists only what is *not* covered by the policy. Common exclusions include losses caused by wear and tear; rust; mold; settling, cracking, or expansion of pavements, patios, foundations, walls, floors, roofs, and ceilings; earthquake or landslide (unless fire ensues, and then only the actual loss caused by the fire is covered); the freezing of plumbing, heating, or air conditioning systems if the building has been unoccupied for more than four consecutive days; war, nuclear explosion, and so on; smoke or fumes from industrial operations; and theft of auto stereo equipment plus tapes (unless covered by endorsement). Everything other than what is specifically excluded is covered.

As the name implies, the dwelling building(s) special form covers only building structures, not personal property. However, further coverage may be added as follows: up to 10 percent of the face amount of the policy can be applied to any detached structures on the premises (such as a garage or tool shed); up to 5 percent of the total policy face amount

COVERAGE	HOME ($20,000)		PERSONAL PROPERTY ($10,000)			HOME ($20,000) AND PERSONAL PROPERTY ($10,000)					
	Basic Fire Contract	Dwelling Building(s) Special Form	Personal Articles Floater	Personal Property Floater	Homeowners Form 4	Dwelling Building(s) and Contents Form	Dwelling Building(s) and Contents Broad Form	Homeowners Form 1	Homeowners Form 2	Homeowners Form 3	Homeowners Form 5
Perils[c]	1–3	All risks[a]	All risks[a]	All risks[a]	1–11, 13–19	1–10	1–10, 12–19	1–11	1–19	All risks[b]	All risks[a]
Home	Insured value of home	Insured value of home	No coverage	No coverage	No coverage	Insured value of home	Insured value of home	Insured value of home	Insured value of home	Insured value of home	Insured value of home
Detached buildings	10% of insured value of home	10% of insured value of home	No coverage	No coverage	No coverage	10% of insured value of home	10% of insured value of home	10% of insured value of home	10% of insured value of home	10% of insured value of home	10% of insured value of home
Trees, shrubs, plants	No coverage	5% of insured value of home	No coverage	No coverage	No coverage	No coverage	5% of insured value of home	5% of insured value of home	5% of insured value of home	5% of insured value of home	5% of insured value of home
Personal property on premises	No coverage	No coverage	Insured value of scheduled property	Insured value of any property	Face value of policy	Insured value of property	Insured value of property	50% (may be reduced or increased) of insured value of home	50% (may be reduced or increased) of insured value of home	50% (may be reduced or increased) of insured value of home	50% (may not be reduced but may be increased) of insured value of home
Personal property off premises	No coverage	No coverage	Insured value of scheduled property	Insured value of any property	10% of insured value of property	10% of insured value of property on premises	10% of insured value of property on premises	10% of insured value of property on premises	10% of insured value of property on premises	10% of insured value of property on premises	10% of insured value of property on premises

COVERAGE	HOME ($20,000)		PERSONAL PROPERTY ($10,000)			HOME ($20,000) AND PERSONAL PROPERTY ($10,000)					
	Basic Fire Contract	Dwelling Building(s) Special Form	Personal Articles Floater	Personal Property Floater	Homeowners Form 4	Dwelling Building(s) and Contents Form	Dwelling Building(s) and Contents Broad Form	Homeowners Form 1	Homeowners Form 2	Homeowners Form 3	Homeowners Form 5
Additional living expense	No coverage	10% of insured value of home	No coverage		20% of insured value of property	10% of insured value of home			20% of insured value of home		
Annual cost[d]	$34	$62	$150	$250	$80	$89	$111	$78	$95	$100	$220

[a] **All-risks** coverage protects against all perils except those specifically excluded (e.g., war, vermin). Therefore, perils 1 through 19 plus other imaginable perils are insured under all risks.

[b] Applies only to home. Personal property covered only against perils 1–19.

[c] Key to Perils

1. Fire and lightning
2. Damage to property removed from house (for a period of time not to exceed five days) if endangered by fire
3. Damage from water and chemicals used to extinguish fire
4. Windstorm and hail
5. Explosion
6. Riots and civil commotion
7. Damage by aircraft
8. Damage by vehicles other than those owned and operated by people covered in policy
9. Damage from smoke
10. Vandalism and malicious mischief
11. Theft
12. Window breakage
13. Damage from falling objects
14. Weight of snow, ice, sleet
15. Collapse of part or all of building
16. Damage from steam heating system or appliance for heating water
17. Water or steam leakage or overflow
18. Freezing of plumbing, heating, air conditioning
19. Short circuit injury to appliances and such

[d] Sample costs are for Santa Clara County, California, 1972.

Fig. 4-3.
Coverage of various policies for home ($20,000) or personal property ($10,000) or both ($30,000)

can be applied to any damaged trees, plants, or shrubs (up to $250 per plant); and up to 10 percent of the face amount can be used for living expenses while you and your family are displaced from your home.

For example, if you held a $20,000 dwelling building(s) special form policy on your home, you would be covered for up to $20,000 for the repair of your home; up to $2000 for the repair of any detached property; up to $2000 for living expenses while forced to vacate your home; and up to $1000 for the replacement of any trees, plants, or shrubs (with a limit of $250 per plant). In short, your potential claim for all items can total more than the face amount of the policy.

Remember that property insurance policy limits are per occurrence limits, not lifetime limits. In other words, you can receive benefits up to the face amount of your insurance policy each time your home is damaged or destroyed by a covered peril.

dwelling building(s) and contents form This form covers *personal property* in addition to physical structures, but it does not cover as many perils (only fire, explosion, windstorm and hail, riot and civil commotion, aircraft and vehicles, smoke, and vandalism) as does the dwelling building(s) special form. This form excludes coverage of damage caused by smoke escaping from a fireplace, damage due to rise or fall in temperature and/or humidity, breakage of glass, or theft of personal property. This last exclusion, personal property theft, is an important one; for you must purchase separate burglary, robbery, and theft insurance in order to be fully covered under the dwelling building(s) and contents form. This is not the case with the homeowners forms.

The dwelling building(s) and contents form covers detached structures and additional living expenses. However, unlike the dwelling building(s) special form, the dwelling building(s) and contents form limits the amount of additional living expense that can be paid each month. Only one-twelfth of the 10 percent face amount may be distributed each month until the benefits are used up. In addition, the dwelling building(s) and contents form enables the policyholder to cover his personal property, while away from the premises, for up to 10 percent of the insured value of his total personal property coverage. For example, if you insure your home for $20,000 and the personal property contained therein for $10,000, $1000 (10% × $10,000) will cover any personal property while it is away from your home.

dwelling building(s) and contents broad form This form, which extends coverage over more perils than does the dwelling building(s) and contents form, covers the same property plus landscaping. Unlike the dwelling building(s) and contents form, the broad form does cover damage to trees, plants, and shrubs (except if caused by wind or hail); damage caused by smoke escaping from the fireplace; damage due to a change of temperature if such loss results from physical damage to the building or contents caused by one of the insured perils; and breakage of glass (unless the building has been vacant for thirty consecutive days). This last provision may be especially worthwhile if your house has expensive picture windows.

The broad form does not cover loss due to theft. It covers only damage done to the building by the burglar as he entered and left (such as breaking a window or lock). Therefore, as with the regular dwelling building(s) and contents form, you must purchase separate burglary, robbery, and theft insurance to obtain coverage for such loss of personal property.

Homeowners Policy

The homeowners policy is a package policy or multiple-line insurance program. In other words, this policy contains a number of types of coverage (home, personal property, and personal liability). Homeowners policies normally have the following features.

1. They cover the dwelling; any detached structures located on the premises; unscheduled personal property (property not specifically defined on the face of the policy) on and off the premises; trees, plants, and shrubs; and additional living expenses.
2. They cover all personal property while in transit (up to 10 percent of the total insured value of all your property), and while at a new location for a maximum of thirty days (up to 50 percent of the total insured value of all your property).
3. They cover the cost of removing debris caused by a loss or damage covered by the policies.
4. They provide for the payment (up to $250) of any fire department service charge incurred.
5. They impose certain per occurrence limits on the following stolen valuables: money, bank notes, and bullion ($100 limit); securities, bills, deeds, letters of credit, passports, tickets, and stamps ($500 limit); manuscripts ($1000 limit); and jewelry, furs, watches, and precious and semiprecious stones ($500 limit).
6. They include personal liability and medical expense coverage arising out of personal liability suits. (These will be covered in chapter 5.) The basic maximum limits are $25,000 liability per occurrence, $500 in medical expenses per person, and $250 in property damages per occurrence. All of these limits can, of course, be raised by paying an additional premium.
7. They offer a choice of two deductible clauses. One clause provides a $100 deductible for damages done by a windstorm or hail. If the damage is between $100 and $500, the insurance company will pay 125 percent of those damages in excess of $100. In other words, if you incur $200 worth of damage because of a severe windstorm

or hail, your insurance company will pay you $125 (125 percent of $100) and you will have to pay only $75. When the damage exceeds $500, there is no deductible, and the insurance company pays for everything. Such a deductible arrangement is called a *declining deductible* because the deductible, or what you must pay, decreases as the amount of damage loss increases. The other clause merely provides for a $50 to $100 deductible to be applied to all perils.

There are five types of homeowners policies. They differ in the range and nature of perils covered, the maximum benefit allowable under each type of coverage (i.e., home, personal property, personal liability), and minimum coverages. Homeowners forms 1, 2, and 3 limit minimum coverage to $8000. Homeowners form 5 has a minimum coverage of $15,000 and homeowners form 4 has no minimum.

homeowners form 1 (HO-1) (homeowners basic form)   This covers only a limited range and nature of perils. For example, the fire coverage excludes loss resulting from sudden and accidental injury to or disturbance of electrical appliances, fixtures, or wiring, if that loss was caused by anything other than lightning. The smoke coverage excludes any damage from smoke escaping from a fireplace; and the explosion coverage excludes damage due to sonic booms, leakage from steam boilers and pipes, and bursting of water pipes. The breakage of glass coverage excludes any loss above $50 and is void if the residence is vacant for more than thirty days. The accidental collapse of a building is not covered.

homeowners form 2 (HO-2) (homeowners broad form)   This covers a wide range of perils, including all kinds of fire, smoke, and explosion damage. Unlike HO-1, HO-2 imposes no $50 ceiling for glass damage. Whereas HO-1 defines theft as any act of stealing or attempt thereat, HO-2 broadens the meaning to include mysterious disappearance—i.e., loss of property from a known place under circumstances when a probability of theft exists. The vehicle coverage is also broadened in HO-2. HO-1 excludes loss caused by any vehicle damaging fences, driveways, or walks, whereas HO-2 excludes only damages caused by vehicles owned or operated by any occupant of the premises.

homeowners form 3 (HO-3) (homeowners special form)   This combines broad form peril coverage for unscheduled personal property (as in HO-2) with all-risk coverage for the dwelling and detached structures. With regard to personal property, falling objects coverage is expanded to cover objects other than those falling from aircraft. Also, under HO-3, vehicle damage is unqualified. That is, any loss will be covered no matter who drives a vehicle into your house or other property.

HO-3 covers any loss or damage to television antennas, awnings, and outdoor equipment; whereas HO-2 specifically excludes these items from coverage. Because of its diversified coverage, HO-3 is now the most popular homeowners package, and many consider it the broadest coverage for the least cost.

homeowners form 4 (HO-4) (contents broad form)   This is a policy for renters. It covers unscheduled personal property on or away from the premises plus additional living expenses. As a broad form, it covers the same range of perils as HO-2. The only difference in the nature of the perils covered occurs under vandalism and malicious mischief. Unlike HO-2, all losses are covered against vandalism and malicious mischief even if the apartment is vacated for thirty days or longer. If you build any additions to or make alterations in your apartment at your expense, these additions can be covered for an amount not exceeding 10 percent of the face amount of the policy, even though they are actually a permanent part of the building.

homeowners form 5 (HO-5) (homeowners comprehensive form)
This form offers comprehensive coverage for your home and unscheduled personal property. It is the broadest coverage available under either the dwellings or the homeowners programs. Basically HO-5 extends all-risk coverage to your personal property as well as your home and detached structures. For example, your personal property is covered against earthquake damage, and glass breakage coverage is expanded to cover mirrors. However, in return for this all-risk coverage, you may have to pay twice as much in premiums as you would for any other policy.

Floater Policies

Floater policies are basically personal property policies. They cover property not just in your home but wherever you might transport it. Such policies may also be called by their original name, *inland marine*. There are two types of general property floater policies, both of which protect your property against all perils except war, radioactive contamination, insects or vermin, and normal wear.

personal articles floater   This policy provides all-risk protection for specified classes of personal property. Each article or class of articles to be insured must be listed on the face of the policy along with the conditions under which it is insured. For example, you might want to insure your golf clubs against theft when they are in your car. To keep the premiums low, the policy might state that the clubs are covered only if the car or compartment of the car from which they were stolen was locked at the time of theft and if there is clear physical evidence of forced entry. Obviously, the more articles you wish to insure and the more conditions you wish to guard against, the higher the premiums you will have to pay. Once you have recorded a class of articles such as golf clubs on your policy, you do not have to change your policy until you renew it even if you acquire new items in the same categories as those you have already insured. Coverage is applicable in Canada and the United States and all of its territories.

The personal articles floater is called a scheduled floater because each article of property must be listed on the face of the insurance contract itself. Details of sample floaters are provided in figure 4-4. The personal effects floater (see fig. 4-4) is basically an all-risk policy, but its use is quite limited. It covers only personal property worn or carried by travelers away from the insured premises. Because it offers such specialized coverage, it is usually attached to other property floater policies for periods often no longer than three months. The amount of coverage for jewelry, watches, and furs is limited to the lesser of 10 percent of the total coverage amount or $100 for each article lost or stolen.

personal property floater Unlike the personal articles floater, this policy offers protection on all articles, scheduled or not, on a worldwide basis. You have a choice of three types of policies, each with varying levels of coverage on high-value items. The first type limits coverage on the following items: jewelry, watches, and furs ($250 per occurrence of damage); money ($100 per occurrence); and securities ($500 per occurrence). The second type of coverage allows jewelry, watches, furs, and other property of extraordinary value to be scheduled on the face of the policy and insured separately for whatever price the policyholder wants. The third type of coverage is similar to the first except that jewelry, watches, and furs may be insured for an additional amount beyond the $250 limit against the perils of fire and lightning only. Because personal property floaters are expensive, they are seldom used.

Burglary, Robbery and Theft Insurance

If you rent an apartment and are not concerned about the threat of fire or if you wish to purchase any of the dwellings forms, you should consider a basic theft policy. The theft broad form covers any property, belonging either to you or to your guests, that is lost through theft or mysterious disappearance.

For protection against losses on the premises, you can obtain either of two types of coverage: blanket coverage, in which the full amount of coverage applies to all property; or divided coverage, in which coverage is divided between furs and jewelry and all other property. Blanket coverage costs approximately twice as much as divided coverage.

You can also protect your property away from the premises with an amount of coverage equal to that which applies to on-the-premises theft. The exclusions (theft committed by a relative or member of the insured's

Article or Class of Articles	Deductible or Special Conditions	Exclusions	Cost
Personal effects	$25 deductible (sometimes)	Money, passports, auto licenses, tickets, securities, baggage	$15 plus 1% of total insured value
Bicycle	$5 deductible	Damage from rust or mechanical breakdowns	$12.50 per $100 of coverage
Camera			$1.54 per $100 of coverage
Fine arts		Damage from restoration or breakage of fragile objects	58¢ per $100 of coverage
Furs		Damage caused by moths or vermin	70¢ per $100 of coverage
Jewelry			$1.50 per $100 of coverage
Musical instruments			Nonprofessional: 85¢ per $100 of coverage Professional: $4.50 per $100 of coverage
Silverware		Pencils, pens, articles of personal adornment, smoking implements	25¢ per $100 of coverage
Sporting equipment		Loss due to failure of people to return equipment you loaned to them	$1 per $100 of coverage
Stamp and coin collections	$250 limit on any one stamp or coin		Stamps: $1.45 per $100 of coverage Coins: $2 per $100 of coverage
Wedding presents	Covered before wedding and ninety days afterwards		55¢ per $100 of coverage
Food freezer	Food in family freezer covered if power goes off		$1 per $100 of food

Fig. 4-4. Personal articles floaters

household, and theft from auto, aircraft, and the like) and the limits ($100 for cash, $500 for securities, and so on) are the same as on similar policies.

Clauses to Be Aware Of

There are four clauses that may be appended to the dwelling, dwelling contents, and homeowners policies we have discussed: the other insurance clause, the mortgagee clause, the leasehold clause, and the apportionment clause.

other insurance clause This clause protects insurance companies against having to pay, collectively, an amount more than the damaged property is worth when the insured has similar policies with more than one company. With this clause, an insurance company limits its liability to that portion of the loss that is equal to the company's portion of the total insurance coverage. In other words, if you were to hold three policies with equal coverage benefits on your home, each insurance company would pay only one-third of the damages.

This clause clearly serves the interest of the insurance companies and is designed to prevent anyone from making a profit on his misfortunes. However, since this clause saves the companies the excess costs of undue claims, it also serves the interests of policyholders by keeping premiums at a reasonable level.

mortgage clause This clause covers the rights of the mortgagee (the issuer of the mortgage—usually a bank or savings and loan). Since the mortgagee, by virtue of the mortgage, can be said to have an insurable interest in your home, he may require that your property insurance policy contain a mortgage clause that promises to pay him an amount equal to the mortgage debt outstanding at the time your home is destroyed. As the debt is paid off, his interest in the property decreases. Once the mortgage is paid off, the clause becomes ineffective.

The insurance company requires that the mortgagee pay the premiums if you, the homeowner, fail to do so. It also requires that he inform the insurance company if there is either a change of ownership or an increased hazard that might alter the premium rate. If he complies with these two conditions, the insurance, as it concerns the mortgagee, cannot be invalidated through any fault or neglect of yours.

leasehold clause This clause covers a renter for damages to any leasehold improvements he may have made. For example, if you have just repainted at your own expense the apartment you are renting, you can be reimbursed for that expense in the event that fire or some other peril destroys the apartment.

apportionment clause This clause states that the maximum extended coverage for any peril covered by a fire insurance policy equals the ratio of that policy's fire coverage to the total amount of fire coverage on the property. For example, suppose you have two policies: a $10,000 basic fire policy and a $10,000 basic fire policy with extended coverage endorsement for your $20,000 home. If an airplane crashed into your home and caused damages of $10,000, your basic fire plus extended coverage policy would pay you only $5000, since that policy's fire protection is only 50 percent of the total fire protection on the home, even though the face amount of falling object protection is $10,000.

In addition, the apportionment clause states that the maximum extended coverage for any peril covered by a fire insurance policy equals the ratio of that policy's extended coverage to the total amount of extended coverage insurance covering the property. In other words, if you have two basic fire policies, each with an extended coverage endorsement, each would pay 50 percent of the damage caused by a covered peril. The primary purpose of the apportionment clause is to force the insured to purchase fire policies with coverage limits identical to those offered in extended coverage riders. The clause applies only to policies with such riders.

Relative Costs

Property insurance premiums are established on the basis of two separate sets of data: the number of fires and extent of fire damage in any one specific area and the number of thefts and extent of theft loss in any one specific area. The basic fire rate is determined from the former data, and the extended coverage rate is determined from the latter. In addition to these data, the prevalence of civil disorder in the area and the probability of perils other than fire and theft may be taken into account in your premium rate, depending upon the policy purchased.

You may be paying a higher premium for identical coverage from the same insurance company than someone else living in the same part of town. This happens because property insurance rate-making takes into consideration the relative vulnerability of many types of property toward many types of perils. For example, one person may live in a brick house while another lives in a frame house. One person may have fire extinguishers in his kitchen and garage, while another does not. Although both people will receive the same benefit payments if calamity strikes, the person who lives in a brick house, equipped with fire extinguishers, may be paying 20 percent less each year in premiums.

Here are ways that you can lower the cost of your property insurance.

1. Pay premiums computed on a three-year basis (if available), rather than on a one-year basis.
2. Increase the deductible.

3. Buy a house that is constructed of fire resistant materials.
4. Put fire extinguishers throughout your home.
5. Live in an area where theft activity and civil disorder are low.
6. Purchase package policies rather than separate policies for different perils.
7. Live in a house that is worth less than $50,000.

There are also conditions that may raise the cost of your property insurance: if you live over five miles from a fire department; if you live over 1000 feet from a fire hydrant; if your home is a wood structure; if the building is not satisfactorily maintained (broken plaster, broken windows); if there is an unsafe arrangement of cooking devices, heating devices, or wiring; if there is a hazardous accumulation of rubbish in the attic or basement; if your home is within several feet (usually ten feet) of another building; if the premises are occupied by three or more families; if the building is under construction. Check with your insurance agent to see how any of these factors might affect your policy.

CONCLUSION

Several questions must be answered by the potential property insurance policyholder.

1. What property can I insure? What property do I want to insure? (Be sure you keep a personal property inventory.)
2. Am I going to value what I own at market value or replacement cost?
3. Which policy covers my property against the most threatening perils at a cost I can afford?

If you can satisfactorily answer these questions, you are ready to deal intelligently with an insurance agent.

VOCABULARY

coinsurance clause
floater policies
homeowners forms
insurable interest
market value
personal property inventory
replacement cost
scheduled property coverage

1. Can you insure your neighbor's home? Why or why not?
2. Tim has two insurance policies on his $20,000 bungalow: a fire policy for $20,000 and a homeowners form 2 for $10,000. How much would each policy pay if Tim's bungalow were totally destroyed by fire?
3. What are the major reasons why you should prepare a personal property inventory?
4. Use the personal property depreciation schedule (fig. 4-1) to determine the market value for the following items: a four-year-old sofa that would cost $400 new today; a two-year-old wooden dinette set that would cost $150 new today; and a three-year-old television that would cost $200 new today.
5. What is the best way to take inflation into account when insuring your home?
6. The expected fire loss to single-family residences for next year in Middletown is $200,000. There are five thousand such residences. What would insurance companies have to charge each homeowner as a base premium to cover their expected losses?
7. Harry's home has a replacement cost of $40,000. For insurance purposes, Harry chooses to value his home at replacement cost and insures it for $20,000 with a homeowners form 3 policy. If his home suffers a fire loss of $10,000, how much will his insurance policy pay?
8. Which homeowners form offers the broadest coverage for the least cost? Why?
9. Which property insurance policies are best suited to apartment dwellers? Why?
10. What are the primary differences between floater policies and homeowners policies?

Jim and Janet Lewis got married in their last year of college and moved into a one-bedroom apartment near school. Items of furniture they purchased and their respective market values are: a new queen-sized bed ($250), a two-year-old dinette set ($150), two ten-year-old chairs ($50), a new bookcase ($20), a fifteen-year-old desk ($25), a new stereo ($200), and a four-year-old bureau ($80). In addition to these furnishings, they each had approximately $500 worth of clothes.

How large is the Lewises' risk exposure? How much of the potential loss could be covered by insurance? What type of property insurance (basic fire, dwelling and dwelling contents, homeowners, or floater) would you recommend for them? If you chose any of last three types, specify also the kind of policy. What policy limits would you recommend?

RECOMMENDED READING

Insurance Information Institute. *Sample Insurance Policies: Property/ Liability Coverages*. Advanced Book. New York: Insurance Information Institute, 1969.

> This book is intended to be used by college students. It provides policies and forms that are representative of property and liability policies in use in most states.

James S. Kemper Institute for Insurance Training. *Study Kit for Students of Insurance: Casualty, Fire, Marine, Life*. Chicago: American Mutual Insurance Alliance.

> This kit provides policies, forms, endorsements, and manual pages for all lines of insurance. These samples may be useful in understanding the language of insurance policies.

CHUCK AND NANCY ANDERSON

INSURING THEIR HOME AGAINST FINANCIAL CALAMITY

The Andersons bought a $25,000 basic fire insurance policy and a $10,000 homeowners form 1 policy on their 1250-square-foot home when they bought it for $26,000 ($21,000 for the house and $5000 for the land) nine years ago. They wanted the full replacement value of their home covered against fire because that seemed to be the peril most likely to destroy it, and so they bought the basic fire policy. The homeowners policy provides coverage against fire damage, too, but it also covers damage due to perils such as windstorm and hail, which are less likely to occur. The Andersons pay $42 a year for the basic fire policy and $40 a year for the homeowners form 1 policy.

The Andersons recently took a personal property inventory and found that their personal property has a current market value of $11,260. They also had an estimate made on the house and found out that it would cost $20 per square foot to replace it.

QUESTIONS

1. Do the Andersons have too little, too much, or just enough insurance coverage on their house?
2. Which of the following policies would you recommend: dwelling buildings(s) and contents form ($104 a year), homeowners form 3 ($130 a year), homeowners form 5 ($270 a year), or would you advise them to retain their present coverage? Why? What dollar limit would you suggest for the policies you are recommending?
3. What effect would your recommendations have on the Andersons' balance sheet and/or income statement?

5

COMPREHENSIVE LIABILITY AND AUTO INSURANCE

If you were sued, taken to court, and found guilty of a wrongdoing against someone or against his property, you might lose everything you own and have to declare bankruptcy in order to settle the final claim. Or you might have to pay as much as half of your income for several years to settle a large claim. Liability insurance protects the policyholder against claims arising from bodily injury and property damage.

The two kinds of liability insurance discussed in this chapter are comprehensive, which covers a wide range of potential liability situations, and automobile, which covers only one or two areas of exposure. Auto liability insurance is probably more important to you than comprehensive liability insurance because you are more exposed to liability risks when you are driving a car than at any other time. Two-thirds of the civil liability suits clogging our courts today involve bodily injury and property damage claims arising out of automobile accidents. Also, auto liability claims tend to be larger than other liability claims. Although automobile insurance may cover property damage to your car and its contents as well as the liability claims of others, we will treat both these types in their entirety in this chapter.

Unlike property insurance, liability insurance pays money to others, not to you. This also entails certain services such as investigating a claim, defending a policyholder, interviewing witnesses, and preparing a court case. The insurance company performs these services whether the claim against its client is just or fraudulent.

LIABILITY AND THE LAW

The law states that invasion of or interference with the rights of others is a legal wrong. Therefore, you may be liable for punishment under law for any interference with another person's rights as granted him by the Bill of Rights. In the United States there are two bodies of law that cover various types of legal wrongs: statutory law, the body of law written and enacted by legislatures; and common law, the body of unwritten law evolving from court decisions. Common law derives authority through usage, whereas statutory law derives authority through congressional approval. Each of these types of law contains both criminal law, which deals with crimes against the state (such as murder and grand larceny), and civil law, which deals with wrongs against individuals (such as destroying someone's property or breaking a contract). Within the civil law lies the greatest legal liability exposure.

There is a further subdivision of civil law into the law of contracts and the law of torts. The law of contracts is concerned with the enforcement of rights arising out of contracts. For example, under the law of contracts, a player who quits his team before the expiration of his contract may be sued by the owner of the team. The law of torts is concerned with the prosecution of those who commit a wrongful act or an omission, arising out of social relationships (as opposed to business relationships) other than contracts, which violates a person's legally protected right. This wrongful act, or tort, can be intentional (drowning a man's dog), unintentional (accidentally hitting a fellow golfer with a drive), or simply the result of carelessness (hitting another car at night because you did not have your headlights on).

Three Types of Liability

There are three types of liability exposure with which you should be familiar: negligence, absolute liability, and vicarious liability.

negligence The dictionary defines negligence as the failure to safeguard others from injury by using reasonable care in everything that you do, and to safeguard other people's property by taking care when using anything that belongs to someone else. In order to be able to measure negligence, the courts have altered this definition to read: the failure to use that degree of care required by law that a prudent man would in the same or similar circumstances. It becomes grounds for legal action when injury occurs to another as a direct result of such failure; injury must be a consequence of the negligent act.

By the legal definition, a person who is negligent might have exercised a proper degree of care; but, having failed to do so, the result of his failure can be clearly predicted. The proper degree of care varies according to the circumstances under which the injured party comes to be on your property. Basically, people who are invited to your home are owed the highest degree of care, while those who come unannounced (i.e., trespassers) are owed the lowest degree of care. The legal definition of negligence further suggests that there is a norm for human behavior and for moral standards, which a prudent man would follow. In a negligence suit, the injured party must prove that his injuries resulted directly from the defendant's negligence.

absolute liability   The second type of liability occurs when a person is responsible for the existence of conditions or activities that lead to injury or loss. For example, if your front step is loose and causes the postman to trip and break his leg, or—because of a frayed cord—a neighbor is electrocuted while plugging in your percolator, you would be liable. Such situations make you vulnerable to a liability suit in which negligence is not an issue.

vicarious liability   The third type of liability is vicarious liability. You may be liable for actions of people in your employ, particularly when you direct the manner and method of work they do. For example, if you direct the gardener to mow especially close to trees and the mower blade strikes a root and sends a splinter into the gardener's eye, you may be sued for bodily injury, because, theoretically, you directed him to subject himself to such a hazard.

Defenses Against Liability

There are three basic defenses you may use to protect yourself from being found guilty in these types of liability suits. First, you may prove that you have exercised a proper degree of care. Second, you may attempt to show contributory neglience—that the person suing you was in some degree responsible for the injury he incurred. If you have taken proper precautions, contributory negligence may be fairly easy to prove. For example, the milkman may have been careless in disregarding the "beware of dog" sign you posted on the gate. Third, you may charge that the injured person was aware of the risk or that he voluntarily exposed himself to that risk. For example, if your child's friend and his parents knew that a mountain climbing expedition would be dangerous and they consented to let their child accompany you in spite of the danger, you would not be liable for any accident that occurred.

LIABILITY AND YOU

Could any of the following situations happen to you?

> An elderly lady takes a shortcut across your yard, trips over a surfaced root from a large elm tree, and breaks her elbow. She sues you for negligence.

> You take your son and his friend on a camping trip and the friend falls into a patch of poison ivy. His parents sue you for damages.

> Your son pushes a friend into a drinking fountain at school, damaging the friend's front teeth. The friend's parents sue you for deliberate bodily injury.

> You slice your drive off the sixteenth tee at your local golf course and hit a woman on the fifteenth fairway. She sues you for carelessness.

> Your dog bites a visitor, and the visitor sues for damages.

> As you approach an intersection, the traffic signal turns yellow. You keep going; the light turns red before you are through the intersection and you hit a car that is pulling out from the cross-street. The driver sues you for carelessness.

> While you are away on vacation, some neighborhood children sneak into your swimming pool where they drown. Their parents sue you for negligence.

Anyone can be sued. Reports of lawsuits are common in newspapers. As we have seen, however, in the discussion of types of liability and defenses against them, a suit does not necessarily mean that the defendant is liable for the actions that prompted the suit. One thing you can do to reduce your liability is to look around your home for hazards and nuisances and check to see that you have taken appropriate precautions.

Determining Your Liability Exposure

Before you buy coverage for your liability exposure, you should know what that exposure is—the total amount of money or property for which someone might sue and attempt to collect damages. As we have seen in chapter 4, property coverage needs are rather easy to determine: you simply total the value of your personal property and insure the total amount against whatever perils you choose. Liability coverage, however, is not so easy to determine.

Selecting the proper amount of liability insurance depends on both the nature of the liability exposures you and your family face and the relative visibility of your family's wealth. The first factor requires an assessment of your family's activities. Do you or does any of your family members engage in activities that involve physical interaction with other people? Contact sports, for example, pose more opportunities for bodily injury or property damage caused by carelessness or negligence than do bird-watching or card-playing. Do you own property that contains attractive nuisances such as a swimming pool or a fruit tree? These offer opportunities for injuries to children, who might decide to take a swim or to steal some fruit. Do you own or operate any motor vehicles? Automobiles, snowmobiles, motorcycles, dune buggies, or motorboats can cause much damage and probably represent your greatest liability exposure. Do you own any pets? Dogs and cats, if unleashed or not fenced in, can easily provoke a lawsuit. In short, consider all your activities.

The second factor to consider in analyzing your liability exposure is your financial position and its visibility. Certain professions, for example, are known to offer high salaries. If you or your family are known or believed to have achieved relative financial wealth, your liability exposure is increased considerably. Therefore, even though the number of situations that might provoke a lawsuit may be limited, your potential loss per exposure might be great. Consider both factors—the number of exposures and visible wealth—when planning your liability insurance.

You will probably go through three or four phases of liability exposure in your lifetime. The first phase occurs when you are under twenty-one and are still covered by your parents' policy. The second phase stretches from the time you leave home to the time you either buy a house or accumulate a net worth of approximately $25,000 or both. Phase three occurs when you are making a good salary and your net worth is from $25,000 to $100,000. Phase four begins when your net worth exceeds $100,000. At this point, your salary may be quite high (over $40,000), and you would have become financially visible.

Figure 5-1 shows the four phases of liability exposure and the relative costs of purchasing the necessary coverage. Maybe none of these phases exactly reflects your situation; but you and your family will probably confront several phases of liability exposure, and you should analyze your needs in light of these changes.

| PHASE | POLICY LIMITS | | ANNUAL COST[a] |
	Comprehensive Liability	Umbrella	
1	[Parents' Policy]		
2	$ 25,000		$ 6
3	$100,000		$12
4	$ 50,000 (underlying limits)	$1,000,000	$70

[a]Sample costs are for Santa Clara County, California, 1972.

Fig. 5-1.
Four phases of liability exposure

Determining the Amount of Coverage You Need

You can put your liability insurance limits at whatever level you desire. Naturally, the limits you select will be determined, in part, by the number and nature of the liability exposures you have.

There are several methods for computing how much liability insurance to buy. One of these methods (the life value method) is to purchase enough comprehensive liability insurance to equal your present net worth (assets minus liabilities) plus the aggregate value of your future earnings. For example, if your net worth is $15,000 and you can expect to earn $12,000 a year for forty-five years, according to this method you should purchase $555,000 ($15,000 + [45 × $12,000]) worth of liability coverage. This is perhaps the most conservative approach to determining your liability needs because you can never be successfully sued for more than what you have now and will have in the future. Another method (the net worth method) is to purchase enough insurance to cover your present net worth. This method assumes that future income will not be attached to fulfill a claim. The last method we will mention (the jury awards method) is to purchase enough insurance to equal the maximum jury awards being assessed by your local courts. For example, if a local court recently awarded $300,000 in a bodily injury suit and this is the largest amount to be awarded for such a suit, according to this method you should insure yourself for $300,000.

Actually, the time and effort involved in trying to make an accurate assessment of your liability exposure may be incommensurate with the potential cost savings. For example, $25,000 worth of liability coverage attached to section II of a homeowners policy (p. 63) would add only $6 to the policy's annual premium; $50,000 worth of coverage would cost only $3 more than that. Raising your auto insurance liability limits from $50,000 to $100,000 per person might cost an extra 10 percent a year. As you can see from these examples, the cost of liability insurance (for people other than dentists and physicians) is relatively low because the likelihood of a lawsuit is not great. Nevertheless, the question of how much liability insurance to buy should not be avoided.

The comprehensive policy attached as section II of the homeowners form automatically gives $25,000 worth of liability coverage per occurrence, $250 for property damage, and medical expense limits of $500 per person. During phase two of your liability exposure, you can probably cover your comprehensive liability exposures adequately by maintaining this $25,000 coverage. During phase three you would do well to raise this coverage to $100,000. The best coverage if you are in phase four would probably be a $1,000,000 umbrella liability policy (p. 80) to supplement the liability coverage provided by section II of the homeowners and by auto liability insurance.

COMPREHENSIVE LIABILITY INSURANCE

There are two types of comprehensive liability insurance: general and umbrella.

General Liability Policies

General liability policies offer coverage over a variety of potential liability situations. Section II of the homeowners policy (p. 63) is such a policy. It covers activities in and around the home as well as away from the home. The only exposures it does not cover are situations involving slander or libel and activities involving motor vehicles. The first exception, however, may be covered by an umbrella policy (p. 80) and the second by an auto liability policy (pp. 80–84).

All general liability policies have jacket provisions, which define the insurance company's commitments to the policyholder, and coverage provisions, which state who is covered, what is covered, and what is not covered.

jacket provisions   Under these provisions, the insurance company will make supplementary payments on your behalf if you are sued. These payments usually include all expenses incurred while investigating claims and defending the insured; court bonds; bail bond expenses up to $250; expenses incurred by the insured; and any other reasonable expenses (including up to $25 a day for missed salary while the insured attends legal hearings). The jacket provisions also state that the insurance company reserves the right to inspect the insured's property at any time. The insurance company, however, is not obligated to make inspections and therefore cannot be held legally liable for an accident occurring on that property. The provisions also state that the insured must notify the company in writing of any occurrence that has led or might lead to a damage claim. Finally, as in property insurance policies, the jacket provisions state that, if two or more policies for the same coverage exist, the insurance companies will divide the loss expense in proportions equal to their share of the total coverage.

coverage provisions   Your comprehensive liability policy covers you and your spouse, any relatives living with you, and anyone under twenty-one years of age living in your care. Therefore, you need only one policy for your entire household. Comprehensive policies cover bodily injury and property damage on or around your premises if incurred by guests, visitors, resident employees, or deliverymen. They also cover bodily injury and property damage from the acts of members of your household; from the acts of animals; from the use of sport or recreational equipment (including owned or rented power boats under fifty horsepower or sailboats under twenty-six feet in length); and from fire, smoke, explosion, or smudge caused by household members to property not owned but in control of the insured (i.e., a borrowed lawn mower that explodes while you are cutting the grass). Bodily injury and property damage sustained at hotels or other temporary residences, at cemetery plots, at owned vacant land, or at rented dwellings are also covered. In addition, medical expenses due to accidents are covered. These policies do not cover intentional injury or damage; any business activities (these must be covered in a separate comprehensive business policy); the operation of automobiles, aircraft, and boats above the prescribed size limits; and injury to employees already covered by Workmen's Compensation (pp. 115, 117).

Umbrella Liability Policies

Umbrella liability policies (otherwise known as personal catastrophe insurance) were originally available only to doctors, lawyers, and other professionals, but in the last few years these policies have been made available to everyone. These policies not only extend your liability coverages but also broaden the definition of liability exposure to include more situations. Umbrella policies cover personal injury claims (i.e., slander, libel) as well as the standard comprehensive liability situations. They also enable the insured to buy $25,000 worth of excess major medical expense insurance (above a $10,000 deductible) for approximately $15. In order to purchase an umbrella policy, you must maintain underlying liability limits on your auto insurance of $100,000 per person and $300,000 per accident (p. 82) and $50,000 worth of comprehensive coverage on your homeowners policy. You can purchase from $1,000,000 to $3,000,000 worth of insurance.

AUTOMOBILE INSURANCE

Automobile insurance consists of liability coverage and physical damage coverage. The former includes bodily injury and property damage liability, uninsured motorist, and medical expenses. The latter includes comprehensive and collision. Like general liability policies, auto insurance policies have jacket and coverage provisions.

Jacket Provisions

Auto insurance has the same basic jacket provisions as other liability policies we have discussed. One important difference, however, is that auto insurance policies contain a *cancellation clause*. This clause gives the insurance company the right to cancel a policy for any reason during the first sixty days of the policy term. After sixty days, a policy can be cancelled only with thirty days' notice, and if the insured or any member of the insured's household has his driver's license suspended; becomes subject to heart attacks or epilepsy; has three traffic violations within an eighteen-month period; or is convicted of a felony, criminal negligence with regard to the operation of a motor vehicle, or drunken driving.

Insurance companies use the cancellation clause at their discretion. Some companies seek only preferred risks and therefore enforce the cancellation clause quite stringently. Other companies raise their rates, and the risk of cancellation with these companies is quite low.

Coverage Provisions

Like comprehensive liability policies, auto policies may be written to include bodily injury and property damage liability, and medical expense payments. Unlike other liability coverage, auto policies offer physical damage coverages that act in the same way as property insurance coverage. Some auto policies offer only property damage coverage and no liability coverage, while others offer only liability coverage. In addition, auto coverage may protect the policyholder against bodily injury and losses caused by a driver who carries no insurance. Figure 5-2 compares these various types of coverage.

Auto Insurance Coverage	Your Coverage			Other Driver's Coverage		
	Car and Property	Oneself	Others in Car	Car and Property	Oneself	Others in Car
Bodily injury liability			X[1]		X	X
Property damage liability				X		
Uninsured motorist		X	X			
Medical expense		X	X			
Comprehensive damage	X					
Collision damage	X					

[1]Only if you are convicted of drunk driving or if they complained of your driving habits prior to the accident can passengers in your car sue you and collect for damages under your bodily injury liability coverage. Passengers ordinarily are said to have assumed the risk by agreeing to be driven by you.

Fig. 5-2. Types of auto insurance and their coverage

bodily injury and property damage liability coverage This coverage protects you, your spouse, and anyone who claims your home as his primary residence against claims for bodily injury and property damage while driving your car and occasionally driving cars belonging to others. In addition, it covers anyone driving your car with your permission.

You have your choice of liability limits. Bodily injury limits are normally stated on a per individual and per occurrence basis. If your policy's bodily injury liability limits are $15,000/$30,000 (15/30), your insurance company will make $30,000 available to pay bodily injury claims arising from an accident in which you are at fault. However, only $15,000 of the $30,000 can be used for any one person. For example, if three people received like injuries, your policy could pay as much as $10,000 to each. If only one person were involved, your policy would only pay up to $15,000 on a claim. Some policies offer single limit liability coverage by which a maximum amount of money can be allocated to meet the injured parties' expenses in whatever manner necessary.

Liability limits, both minimum and maximum, vary from state to state. They may run up to 100/300 or higher. New York, Massachusetts, and North Carolina are the only states that require every motor vehicle owner to carry automobile liability insurance. All the other states have financial responsibility laws, which require the driver of a vehicle involved in an accident that was his fault and that involved bodily injury or property damage claims of more than $50 to $250 (depending on the state in which the accident occurs) to show proof of financial responsibility. Financial responsibility may be demonstrated by posting a bond, by depositing cash or securities with the state treasurer, or by purchasing an auto liability insurance policy for a specified amount (normally 10/20 or 15/30). This proof is required after an accident and may be required for one year following the accident. If a driver fails to show financial responsibility, his driver's license is suspended until his financial responsibility can be proven.

If you now carry only minimal coverage, you may want to consider raising your liability limits. As we have already mentioned, there is a greater chance for large medical bills and liability claims when automobiles are involved than in general home accidents. Furthermore, the people you injure on the highway will probably be strangers, whereas the people you injure in your home or at school are likely to be acquaintances. Someone who does not know you and does not expect to have to face you again may try to get all he can in a claim against you. One last consideration is that higher limits may help you get better service from the insurance company since the company would probably lose a lot of money by not vigorously defending you in a lawsuit. If, however, you maintain low liability limits, the insurance company stands to lose much less and may not be able to justify the costs of a good defense.

Property damage liability (injuries to the other party's car and personal property) is normally written in limits of $5000, $10,000, or $25,000 per accident. Once again, it may be wise to keep your limits high. The destruction of just one power pole with three or four different users (electric company, telephone company, cable television, for example) could cost you over $10,000. Since you can be charged for damages by the state department of highways, by municipal governments, and by private businesses who own property you destroy as well as by the owner of the automobile you run into, it is not hard to imagine $25,000 worth of claims arising out of one accident.

uninsured motorist coverage If you sustain bodily injury from a motorist who has no auto liability insurance, this coverage pays you the amount of money you would have been legally entitled to recover had the motorist carried insurance. Uninsured motorist coverage offers payments in excess of what you may collect either from medical expense coverage or from the uninsured motorist himself up to the amount to which you are legally entitled. This coverage also protects you from loss incurred because of an unapprehended hit-and-run driver. The maximum limits you may purchase (normally 10/20 or 15/30) are governed by the state. Remember that in most states damage to your automobile is not covered under uninsured motorist coverage; only bodily injury claims are.

medical expense coverage This coverage promises to pay any reasonable medical expenses incurred within one year from the date of an accident by any person riding in your car who sustained bodily injury as a direct result of that accident, regardless of fault. Benefits are also paid if you or a member of your family is a pedestrian injured by a motor vehicle. The expenses covered include medical supplies, surgery, X rays, hospital expenses, dental care, ambulance costs, professional nursing care, and funeral expenses. People not riding in your car are reimbursed through your bodily injury liability coverage, provided you were at fault.

If you and everyone who rides in your car own a health insurance policy, then you will never need medical expense coverage protection as a part of your auto policy. However, since you do not always know your passengers have adequate health expense coverage, it may be wise to include a couple of thousand dollars worth of medical expense coverage. The normal medical expense limits are $500, $750, $1000, $2000, or $5000 per person.

physical damage coverage This coverage provides payments for the repair and replacement of your automobile, its equipment, and its material contents. There are two major coverage options from which to choose: comprehensive coverage and collision coverage.

Comprehensive coverage insures your car against loss caused by theft and larceny, explosions, earthquakes, windstorm and hail, falling missiles, water and flood, vandalism and malicious mischief, and riot and civil commotion. It also insures your car's contents (and the car) against loss caused by fire and lightning. To be eligible for this coverage, the contents of the car—often referred to as robes, wearing apparel, and other personal effects—must be owned by the insured or by residents in his

household. (If your car burns with your neighbor's golf clubs in the trunk, for example, your auto insurance comprehensive coverage does not cover these golf clubs. The family auto policy (p. 86), however, will pay up to $100 per occurrence for contents damage, and your property insurance will cover losses to property in the car for up to 5 percent of the insured value of your home or 10 percent of your insured personal property.) Comprehensive does not cover your car against collision damage.

Collision coverage for the automobile you are driving is separate from comprehensive coverage because of the greater probability that an auto accident will happen. Since most physical damage claims arise from accidents involving collisions, the basic premiums for this type of coverage are as much as six times the premium for the same amount of comprehensive coverage. The high cost of collision coverage, however, can be reduced up to 50 percent or more through the use of a $50 or $100 deductible. Collision insurance covers impact with an object, another vehicle, or the earth (a turn-over).

The amount of the available physical damage insurance benefits depends on the current market value of your car. To determine whether to carry physical damage coverage, you must compare the out-of-pocket cost if your car were destroyed and you did not carry insurance with the cost of the premium if you did. You can estimate the current market value of your car by applying the following percentage depreciation factors to the car's original cost: first year, 25 percent; second year, 18 percent; third year, 14 percent; fourth year, 11 percent; and for every year after that until the car reaches a minimum value of $250, 10 percent. Subtract from your car's original cost the dollar depreciation figure for each year of your car's present age, and you have its current market value. For example, Bill has a four-year-old car that originally cost him $3000. Its market value over the last four years is indicated in table 5-1.

TABLE 5-1

THE MARKET VALUE OF BILL'S CAR
OVER THE LAST FOUR YEARS

Age	Depreciation Factor[a]	Dollar Depreciation (depreciation factor × original cost)	Market Value
New	0	0	$3000
1	25%	$750	2250
2	18%	540	1710
3	14%	420	1290
4	11%	330	960

[a]*Journal of American Insurance*, American Mutual Insurance Alliance.

Bill carries $50 deductible collision insurance on his car. The premium is $157. If he carried collision insurance and he had an accident in which his car was destroyed, his out-of-pocket cost would be $207 ($157 premium + $50 deductible). Theoretically, if his car is worth $960 and its value is declining by 10 percent of its original cost each year, he will be better off not buying collision coverage even if he wrecks his car every one and one-half years (see table 5-2).

TABLE 5-2

COMPARISON OF BILL'S POTENTIAL LOSS AND INSURANCE OUTLAYS
OVER THE NEXT FOUR YEARS

Time	Market Value	Annual Premium	Cumulative Premium Plus $50 Deductible	Difference in Potential Loss and Accumulated Insurance Outlay
Today	$960	$157	$207	$753
One year from now	$690	$157	$364	$326
Two years from now	$420	$157	$521	($99)
Three years from now	$250	$157	$678	($428)
Four years from now	$250	$157	$835	($585)

In Bill's situation it may be wise to self-insure. This option is appropriate if Bill has enough money in a ready cash reserve to replace his car this year if he has an accident and if his loss record indicates that he will probably not accumulate damage repair bills totaling more than the accumulated insurance premiums over the next one and one-half years.

This computation does not take into consideration the potential tax savings if Bill itemizes his deductions on his annual income tax. Since the nonreimbursable loss of an asset above the first $100 can be deducted from adjusted gross income, you can save taxes because your taxable income becomes less. The amount of taxes you save depends on your marginal tax bracket. If Bill makes $14,000 a year and is in the 20 percent tax bracket, his out-of-pocket loss next year would be $552 ($690 market value – $118 tax savings). These tax savings can make self-insurance more attractive. (Tax deductions will be fully explained in chapter 9.)

This procedure for determining what physical damage coverage you need is more applicable to collision insurance than to comprehensive insurance. To some extent you can control collisions that are your fault (the main type of collisions your insurance will cover). By driving safely, you can avoid these accidents and, therefore, reduce the need for collision coverage. Collision damage caused by an uninsured motorist, however, will probably have to be paid out of your own pocket, since this is not covered by uninsured motorist coverage and since a driver who does not have auto insurance may not be able to afford the cost of repairing your car if it is damaged in an accident that is his fault. Accidents covered by comprehensive insurance (i.e., damage caused by vandals, windstorm, and so on) are normally beyond your control. Your loss record in this respect is largely a function of luck. Therefore, comprehensive coverage is a worthwhile coverage to buy in most situations whereas collision coverage may not be.

Types of Automobile Insurance Contracts

There are two basic types of automobile insurance policies: the family auto policy (FAP) and the special auto policy (SAP). Even though insurance companies call their policies by different names (i.e., Challenger, Protecto-guard, Champion), these policies are all basically family auto policies, special auto policies, or a combination of the two, depending on the insurance company and state regulations. The FAP lets you choose the coverages and dollar liability limits you want. Coverage for newly acquired cars is automatically granted, and anyone living with you is covered if he drives your car.

The special auto policy is designed to make every car owner carry his own insurance and to avoid some of the coverage problems that commonly arise with the FAP. They are usually less expensive than FAPs because they reduce the insurance company's risk exposure by restricting the policyholder's choice of coverage provisions and limits. For example, although SAPs cover you in any car you drive, they never provide insurance coverage for the policyholder while riding a motorcycle or a motorscooter. They never cover a house trailer or vacation trailer or anyone in a non-owned vehicle if that person owns his own car (e.g., if your friend owns a car but borrows your car, he would not be covered by your policy). Furthermore, SAPs force the policyholder to deduct medical expenses paid by the medical expense payment portion of his own policy for any liability claims filed under the bodily injury and property damage liability provisions. Before the SAP will make any payments, other applicable medical insurance policies must pay their part.

Determining How Much You Should Pay

Auto insurance rate-making is based on the past driving experience of motorists in a given locality. Standard premium rates are established by a few national rating bureaus. These rates serve as a basis for each company's insurance policy pricing. If the insured is a preferred risk (one who, according to past experience, is least likely to have an accident), he may pay less than the standard rate. If the insured is in a class of motorists with a higher accident experience, he may pay more than the standard rate. Although each insurance company has its own formula for setting premium rates, they all rely on certain factors.

Liability and medical expense coverage rating is based on use of the auto, ownership of the auto, distance driven, age of driver, sex of driver, and territory in which the auto is driven. On the basis of these six factors, each motorist is classified into one of about twenty-five groups. Premium rates are then assigned to these groups. The other form of rating is termed collision rating. It applies if you carry collision coverage on your automobile. Collision rating is based on use, ownership, age of driver, sex of driver, occupation of driver, make of car, model of car, age of car, and territory in which the car is driven. A classification system, much like the liability classification system, is established for both liability and collision underwriting, and basic rates are attached to each class. The classification system used by the national rating bureaus for the two types of classes is outlined in figure 5-3 (p. 88).

safe driver plans   Safe driver plans were first introduced in the spring of 1959 in California, but they have since been instituted in almost every state. For the first time, insurance rate-makers began to consider each motorist's driving record in addition to general information about the individual that does not necessarily indicate driving expertise. The safe driver plan is a mandatory part of the rating program for the special auto policy, but it may be applied to the family auto policy at the discretion of the insurer. Rate decreases or increases may be applied to bodily injury and property damage liability coverage, medical expense coverage, and collision coverage. Safe driver plans do not affect comprehensive or uninsured motorist rates.

The safe driver plan involves a point system whereby points are allocated to certain types of automobile traffic violations. In a family with more than one motorist the points accumulated by each driver are added together to determine the rate adjustment. The total number of points each motorist accumulates (usually over two or three years) determines the amount of reduction or increase to be applied to his premium rate as determined from his liability and collision classification (fig. 5-3). Figure 5-4 (p. 89) shows how many points are assigned by the California safe driver plan to each violation. Figure 5-5 (p. 89) shows the effect various accumulations of points will have on your premium rates.

Safe driver plans may differ from state to state in the length of the experience period required, the number of points assigned to each violation, and the allowable credit for insureds with no points or only one point. To be certain of your state's point system, check with the State Department of Motor Vehicles.

Major Factors Determining Classification	Liability Class[a]			Collision Class[b]	
If insured is male driver over 25, or female driver	1A	1B (10% higher rates than 1A)	1C (45% higher rates than 1A)	1	
If male under 25 lives in insured's household	2A (90% higher rates than 1A)		2C (3 times higher rates than 1A)	2A (45% higher rates than 1)	2C (90% higher rates than 1)
If insured's auto is used for business purposes	3 (1½ times higher rates than 1A)			3 (25% higher rates than 1)	

[a] Liability Classes

1A The insured auto is owned by an individual and is used for personal reasons; there is no male operator under twenty-five living in the insured's household.

1B As in class 1A, but auto is used to drive to or from place of business, and the one-way mileage to or from work is less than ten miles. (Cars used in car pools or driven to and from the railroad station as part of commuter travel are included in class 1B, not 1C, no matter how many miles are driven.)

1C Same as class 1B, but mileage to or from work is ten miles or more.

2A The insured auto is owned by an individual with one or more male operators younger than twenty-five years old residing in the household. No under-twenty-five-year-old, however, is the owner of the car or its principal operator. (It makes no difference if the car is used for business or pleasure.) Underage (twenty-four years or less) males who are married and owners or principal operators fall into this class.

2C The owner or principal operator is unmarried and under twenty-five.

3 The insured's auto is used in business or owned by a corporation.

[b] Collision Classes

1 The insured car is owned by an individual, not customarily used in business, and not used by any underage male operator residing in the household. It makes no difference if the car is driven to or from work.

2A Same as class 1, but there is a male operator under twenty-five years of age residing in the household. If this male operator is the principal operator or owner, he must be married to qualify for this classification.

2C Same as class 2A, but the male owner or principal operator under twenty-five years of age is unmarried.

3 Same as class 3 liability rating.

Fig. 5-3. Liability and collision classification system for determining premium rates

Violation	Number of Points
Driving while intoxicated	5
Failure to stop and report an accident when involved	5
Manslaughter	5
Driving while your license has been suspended or revoked	5
Reckless driving	3
Any moving vehicle violation	1
Any accident resulting in property damage of more than $50	1
Illegal parking	0
If you are in an accident for which someone other than you is convicted	0
If your auto is damaged by a hit-and-run	0
If payments for an injury are handled by you, not your insurance company	0

Fig. 5-4.
Points for
each violation under
the California safe
driver plan

Total Number of Points	Premium Reduction or Increase
0	20% reduction
1	10% reduction
2	no change
3	20% increase
4	40% increase
5	70% increase
6 or more	100% increase

Fig. 5–5.
Effect of point
accumulation on
insurance premiums

assigned risks Sometimes insurance companies do not insure drivers who have poor driving records. Such drivers can still buy minimum insurance through state-regulated assigned-risk pools. When they apply for insurance, they are assigned to insurance companies who must then cover them for three years for the state-designated liability limits. Every insurance company licensed to sell insurance within the state must accept a certain percentage of the drivers in the assigned-risk pool. These drivers have no choice as to which insurance company underwrites their specific risk, nor do the insurance companies have a choice as to the assigned risks they accept.

Liability coverage limits for assigned risks range from $5000 per person, $10,000 per accident, and $5000 property damage per accident (in Louisiana, Massachusetts, Oklahoma, and Puerto Rico) to $20,000 per person, $40,000 per accident, and $10,000 property damage (in Maine). Most states, however, offer 15/30/5 or 10/20/5 coverage. No physical damage coverage is available, but uninsured motorist coverage is.

how much auto insurance costs Insurance companies consult the various classification systems, apply the appropriate discounts, and then set a premium rate. This rate is a composite of individual rates for liability, medical expense, and physical damage coverage. For example, Bill Morris is forty years old, married, and has no children of driving age. He owns a one-year-old car worth $2800 and he has a good driving record. His annual premium of $175 is composed of the following rates:

bodily injury liability ($50,000 per person, $100,000 per accident)	$56
property damage liability ($25,000 per accident)	$33
medical expense coverage ($5000 per person)	$13
uninsured motorist coverage (15/30/5)	$ 6
comprehensive physical damage coverage ($50 deductible)	$11
collision physical damage coverage ($100 deductible)	$56

With insurance premiums doubling every ten years because of rising medical care costs, more expensive automobile repairs, and more generous lawsuit settlements, you should consider ways to keep your rates low. In general, liability rates will be lower for the driver who has a good driving record over the two-to-three-year period before the policy begins. If an underage driver (younger than twenty-five years old) has taken an accredited driver education course, class 2 rates may be reduced by 10 percent. If more than one car is insured under the same policy, both liability and collision rates may be reduced by 25 percent on each additional car. If the insured is a farmer or uses his car primarily on a farm or ranch, both liability and collision rates may be reduced by 30 percent.

If you have no more than one point in the safe driver point system, you may be eligible for a safe driver discount of 10 to 20 percent (fig. 5-5). Furthermore, if you drive 6500 miles or less each year, you may be able to reduce your premiums by 10 percent. Perhaps your company offers a special group insurance plan with automatic deductions from your paycheck, which can save you 15 percent or more. If you are an underage driver and are away at school or in the armed services, or if you are a student whose grades average B or better, you may be eligible for a discount. It is also cheaper to insure a compact car than an expensive car. In addition, most insurance companies charge higher premiums for higher horsepower engines. Such a "hot car" surcharge may run as much as 50 percent higher. Another factor to remember in trying to lower your collison and liability rates is using a deductible.

You should also be aware that auto insurance rates vary from company to company depending upon both individual company loss experience with various types of drivers and the company's intended market. Since different companies hold different conditions important in their rate-making, it will be important for you to shop for rates whenever you renew your insurance policy. The company that thinks you are an excellent risk today, as a young married man or woman, may consider you a bad risk when you have a child of driving age.

Figure 5-6 shows how rates for the same risk vary among six insurance companies. Notice that the company with the least expensive policy changes as conditions change. In all examples the rates were based on 50/100 bodily injury liability or $100,000 single limit liability (depending on company format), $5000 property damage (or company minimum), $2000 medical payments, full comprehensive, $100 deductible collision, and coverage for uninsured motorists (included in single limit liability in some cases). Not all of the examples of potential policyholders would be acceptable as new business to the companies used in this comparison. These examples are used for information only.

Potential Policy-holder[a]	Home Ins. Co. (Gold Key)	St. Paul (Easy Auto)	Fireman's Fund (Economy Plus)	Central Mutual	Safeco Ins. Co.	Aetna Casualty & Surety (Auto-Rite)
1	$205.65	$254.80	$228.00	$240.00	$214.60	$226.00
2	205.65	341.80	306.00	324.00	214.60	304.00
3	375.48	461.20	410.00	437.00	323.60	412.00
4	375.48	548.00	494.00	521.00	323.60	490.00
5	169.88	211.40	188.00	202.00	187.00	186.00
6	169.88	298.40	266.00	283.00	187.00	264.00

[a] Key to potential policyholder

1. Man and wife, age forty-five, clean driving record, state job (Tucson, Arizona). Vehicle is a three-year-old, two-door sedan, small engine.
2. Same as 1 except for one chargeable accident.
3. Same as 1 except for one occasional male operator, age twenty.
4. Same as 3 except for one chargeable accident.
5. Over sixty-five driver in good physical condition as noted on recent physician's report, pleasure use only, clean driving record.
6. Same as 5 except for one chargeable accident.

Fig. 5-6. Variations in annual premiums (1971) among six insurance companies

What Happens if an Accident Is Not Your Fault

If you are involved in an automobile accident that is another person's fault, you will probably need to file a claim and test the strength and resources of the other person's policy. It is important that you know how to file a claim so that you can reach a satisfactory settlement with his insurance company.

meeting the claims adjuster   The claims adjuster is the link between you and the other driver's insurance company. He performs three tasks.

First, he determines what kind of person you are, the extent of your injury, your eagerness to get well, the extent of damage to your car, and so on. Then he estimates the amount of money that the insurance company will probably have to pay to come to a satisfactory settlement. This estimate is the reserve limit, the amount required to fulfill the insurance company's obligation under its insurance contract. Lastly, he settles the claim as quickly as possible by delivering a check to you, the claimant. Your acceptance of this check releases the insurance company from any future liability. Now that you know what the claims adjuster does, you should consider how you will deal with him during his performance of each of these three tasks.

Normally, the claims adjuster is one of the first people who will visit you while you are recuperating after an accident that is clearly someone else's fault. The adjuster may be a salaried employee of the insurance company used by the person responsible for the accident, but it is more likely that he will be an independent adjuster hired by the company to settle the claim. Usually, he will discuss the accident and ask questions about how it happened and who was at fault. He will also discuss your medical condition and ask questions about your injury, your doctor, and your probable length of stay in the hospital. He will also ask questions about your background such as who you work for, your age, and your medical history. In general, it is all right to talk to the claims adjuster as long as you do not say anything that might prejudice your case. Specifically, do not discuss your medical background. If the insurance company finds that you have had a similar injury before, they may claim that your present injury is merely a recurrence of an old medical problem. Do not discuss the accident. The insurance company may try to prove that you contributed to the accident by being careless or negligent. Instead of saying "I don't remember" to questions involving the accident, merely respond with "I do not care to answer that." Do not sign any statement or allow any tape recording of the discussion. In short, be pleasant and thank him for showing interest in your health and welfare, but be very uninformative. Remember that he represents the insurance company of the person at fault in the accident.

After visiting you, the adjuster will estimate the size of your claim. To do this, he will first estimate your total medical expenses including hospital or convalescent room and board, doctor's visits, X rays, lab tests, drugs, physical therapy, wheelchair and other special apparatus, and nursing care. Then, judging from your present salary level, he will estimate the amount of income lost because of your medical condition and inability to return to work. He will consider both overtime you might normally have received and your base wage. He will then estimate any miscellaneous expenses that you or your family incurred because of the accident: mileage expenses to and from the hospital or doctor's office, babysitting fees, damage to your clothes or other personal property, and the like. Finally, he will apply the pain and suffering multiplier to the total of medical expense, loss of income, and miscellaneous bills. Normally this multiplier is three. For example, if all other expenses are estimated at $2000, the amount of the claim that the adjuster figures will be made for pain and suffering will be $6000 (3 × $2000). In this instance then, the total claim would be projected at $8000 ($2000 expenses + $6000 pain and suffering).

This estimate of expenses expected to be incurred by you, the claimant, serves as the reserve limit that the insurance company allocates to your case. In other words, by notifying the insurance company that your case should have a reserve limit of $8000, the adjuster is saying, "I think we can eventually settle this claim for $8000 or less."

Naturally, by duplicating the process the claims adjuster uses, you can project what a reasonable claim might be. Realize that, if your claim is above the reserve limit, you will have more trouble settling with the insurance company. Since the skill of a claims adjuster is measured by how often he settles within the reserve limit he has stipulated, he will fight to keep your claim within that limit.

settling the claim   Since each dollar of medical expense can raise the eventual claim by $4 (through the pain and suffering multiplier), it is easy to understand why insurance companies want to settle quickly. Usually, they will make an initial settlement offer as soon after the accident as possible. You might think this offer is quite generous. Remember, however, that once you endorse an insurance settlement check, you are most likely releasing the insurance company from any future liability. Therefore, wait to file a claim until you know what all your expenses are going to be. You have one year from the date of the accident to file a valid claim. If your injury is a serious and expensive one, such as a back injury, it is wise to hire a good attorney. Too much money may be at stake for an amateur prosecutor such as yourself to deal with.

If you have filed a claim and have been waiting weeks or even months to receive compensation, often the mere threat of involving an attorney will bring a quick settlement. Insurance companies do not like to see attorneys involved because the attorney's fee (normally one-third of the eventual settlement) will automatically raise the claim settlement. For example, if an insurance company is balking at paying a $1000 claim and an attorney becomes involved and the company loses the case, the company will have to pay not only $1000 to the claimant but also $500 to the attorney. In addition, insurance companies do not like to go to court because of the expense of defending their client and the long court delays often involved. They realize that the longer they have to wait to get a court date, the higher the claim against them will be. Time, they feel, is never on their side, since time may bring more medical bills, more miscellaneous expenses, and more pain and suffering. Therefore, if you are at an impasse with an insurance company, it may help to tell the company that you will turn the case over to an attorney if just compensation is not received within a certain time.

In general, as soon as possible after you are in an accident, you should write down all the details you remember about it. You should also get the names and addresses of witnesses; but do not harass them or try to force them to see the accident your way. To substantiate future claims, take photographs of your injuries. File your claim with the insurance company of the person responsible for the accident before your statute of limitations runs out (normally one year from the date of the accident).

Most important, always notify your insurance agent of any accident, whether or not you were at fault and even if you decide to pay for the damage yourself. If you do not report an accident to the insurance agent within a reasonable amount of time following the accident (normally forty-eight hours), your insurance company can refuse to honor any claim that may be lodged against you. Remember that a person has up to one year from the date an injury was incurred to file such a claim. Reporting an accident will not cause your insurance premiums to be raised, and it is the best means of ensuring that the coverage you have paid for will be there when you need it.

No-Fault Insurance

Insurance companies are losing money on their auto insurance underwriting. Rates are steadily increasing. Policyholders are dissatisfied that only 42¢ of every $1 paid in premiums is paid out in claims. Both insurers and insureds admit that there are inadequacies in the system. These inadequacies are basically that few people involved in auto accidents are fully reimbursed for their losses; settlements are often uneven and the settlement process long and expensive; and insurance protection itself is expensive. Some find fault with the tort liability structure of the law, which gives an injured party the right to sue the negligent party for damages. Others find fault with trial lawyers who win huge jury awards for their clients. Many people feel that, if injured parties can be compensated without first having to determine who was at fault, a number of the problems within the current system would be solved.

No-fault insurance would reimburse injured parties for their economic losses from auto accidents (i.e., medical expenses and loss of income) without regard to fault. It would enable you to receive payments from your own insurance company without going through the settlement process. No-fault would also make pain and suffering claims available only to people who have suffered permanent impairments. Its proponents are the insurance commissioners and most insurance companies who are looking for a way to reduce their costs and improve their service. Those who disagree with the concept feel that no-fault insurance would deny a person his constitutional right to receive just compensation for his loss from the wrong doer himself. They are also afraid that the power to determine just compensation would lie with the insurance industry instead of with the insured through the aid of his attorney.

Forms of no-fault insurance have existed in Saskatchewan, Canada, since 1946 and have proven reasonably successful in reducing insurance costs. It has also been reasonably successful since its inception in Puerto Rico in 1969. The battle over no-fault still rages in this country, however, because states are unwilling to throw out the tort liability system. Hence, quasi-no-fault plans have appeared in Massachusetts, Delaware, and Illinois. These plans attempt to disburse money on a no-fault basis for small claims (under $2000, for example), and yet reserve the right to sue on large claims. It seems inevitable that all states will adopt some form of no-fault insurance. What form it will take remains to be argued in the courts, state legislatures, and even the U.S. Congress.

CONCLUSION

Comprehensive liability policies cover all liability exposures other than those surrounding the operation of motor vehicles and those involving slander and libel. They are inexpensive and should be purchased with limits that correspond to both your liability exposures and your visible wealth.

Auto liability represents probably your greatest liability exposure. Bodily injury and property damage liability, medical expense payments, uninsured motorist protection, and comprehensive physical damage coverage are all valuable coverages to have. The need for collision coverage depends upon the value of your car. The lower the value of the car, the less the need for this type of insurance.

Shop for auto insurance rates. Different companies favor different driver characteristics. If you have forgotten how to shop for rates, refer to pages 43–44. The best way to minimize your costs is to keep your driving record clean.

Know how to get just compensation from a claim if you are involved in an accident that is not your fault and therefore may not involve your insurance company. Remember always to notify your insurance company of any accident you are involved in.

absolute liability
assigned risks
claims adjuster
contributory negligence
FAP
financial responsibility
liability
negligence
no-fault insurance

pain and suffering multiplier
preferred risk
safe driver plan
SAP
tort
umbrella policy
uninsured motorist coverage
vicarious liability

QUESTIONS

1. What are three ways to defend against a liability claim without using a liability policy?
2. Larry has a current net worth of $10,000 and expects to earn $15,000 a year for the next forty years. Under the life value approach to determining comprehensive liability limits, how much comprehensive liability insurance should Larry purchase?
3. What coverage does an umbrella liability policy offer that a normal comprehensive liability policy does not?
4. How is an auto insurance policy different from a comprehensive liability policy?
5. Tom has auto bodily injury liability limits of 50/100. If three people sustain injuries because of Tom's careless driving and each injured person files a claim for the same dollar amount, what is the maximum amount of money Tom's insurance policy can pay each of them?
6. Under what conditions should a person self-insure rather than buy collision coverage for his car?
7. A claims adjuster estimates that your medical expenses will be $500, your loss of income $1000, and your miscellaneous expenses $100. How large a reserve limit will he probably set for your case?
8. What types of auto coverages are denied assigned risks?
9. Ron paid $200 a year for auto insurance before he was convicted of reckless driving. Under the California safe driver plan, how much will Ron's auto insurance rates increase?
10. What problems do proponents of no-fault auto insurance claim that it will solve? What problems do its opponents feel it will create?

CASE PROBLEM

Sally Bond is a junior in college. Last year she bought a six-year-old compact car for $300, so that she would be able to drive to classes and to a part-time job. Sally has few assets besides the car, which she has driven approximately 20,000 miles. She had a perfect driving record until this year when she was given three tickets for speeding.

Should Sally purchase auto insurance? If so, which types and what limits might be appropriate? Why? How much greater will her rates be because of her three speeding tickets than if she qualified for reduced rates under the safe driver plan? (Assume that she is a licensed California driver.) What can she do to reduce her rates?

Denenberg, Herbert S.; Eilers, Robert D.; Hoffman, G. Wright; Kline, Chester A.; Melone, Joseph J.; Snider, H. Wayne. *Risk and Insurance.* Englewood Cliffs, N.J.: Prentice-Hall, 1964.

> Chapter 24 covers the concepts of liability and negligence.

Insurance Information Institute. *Sample Insurance Policies.* New York: Insurance Information Institute, 1969.

> Provides a good way to understand what is and what is not covered by insurance policies.

RECOMMENDED READING

CHUCK AND NANCY ANDERSON

INSURING AGAINST THE FINANCIAL CALAMITY OF A GENERAL LIABILITY SUIT

For $3 a year, Chuck and Nancy's homeowners policy provides $25,000 personal liability coverage, $500 for medical expenses, and $250 for damage to others' property. They can either retain this coverage, raise the liability limit to $100,000 for an extra $6 a year, or buy an umbrella liability policy with $1,000,000 worth of coverage for an extra $61 a year.

QUESTIONS

1. Which of the three alternatives would you recommend that they select? Why?
2. What effect would this recommendation have on the Andersons' balance sheet and/or income statement?

INSURING AGAINST THE FINANCIAL CALAMITY OF AN AUTO LIABILITY CLAIM

Chuck holds separate policies on his two cars for bodily injury and property damage liability (15/30/5), medical expense coverage ($1000), and physical damage coverage—comprehensive (full value) and collision ($50 deductible). The annual premiums are as follows:

Coverage	High Horsepower Car	Compact Car
Liability (15/30/5)	$ 91	$ 91
Medical expenses ($1000)	13	13
Comprehensive (full)	78	36
Collision ($50 deductible)	158	102
TOTAL	$340	$242
"Hot car" surcharge (33%)	112	
Annual premium	$452	$242
TOTAL PREMIUM $694		

While shopping for better coverage at reduced rates Chuck and Nancy learned what various coverages would cost on an annual basis for several limits.

Coverage	High Horsepower Car	Compact Car
Liability		
15/30	$ 91	$ 91
50/100	107	107
100/300	135	135
Medical expenses		
$1000	$ 13	$ 13
$3000	17	17
$5000	21	21
Comprehensive		
full	$ 78	$ 36
$50 deductible	35	16
Collision		
$50 deductible	$158	$102
$100 deductible	131	75
Uninsured motorist (15/30)	$ 14	$ 14

In addition, they learned that if they put both cars on the same policy, they would save 25 percent of the total premium on the cheaper car. The insurance agent also told them that, since they had not had any moving violations in the last three years, their premiums can be decreased by 20 percent.

QUESTIONS

1. Which coverage limits would you raise? Which would you reduce or eliminate? Why?
2. How much would the coverage you recommend cost? (Assume that their driving records improve.)
3. What effect would your recommendation have on the Andersons' balance sheet and/or income statement?

6

HEALTH INSURANCE

Many people carefully protect their physical assets but not their most important possessions—the lives and health of themselves and their families. If you were to become sick or disabled, you and your family might lose a significant portion of the income that produced the material assets you enjoy. In addition, a prolonged illness could severely drain the financial resources your family has built up. Health insurance is designed to minimize the effect of these drains.

DETERMINING YOUR MEDICAL EXPENSE INSURANCE NEEDS

As with every type of insurance, you must plan for peril protection before the peril strikes. Even though you may rarely be sick, you should consider buying health insurance. If you became ill or disabled when you were uninsured, you would probably be ineligible for health insurance and, therefore, unprotected when you and your family most needed protection. Furthermore, as you get older you will likely become more susceptible to sickness and poor health and less able to meet the rising costs of medical care.

It is difficult to determine medical expense insurance needs. Unlike planning for property insurance coverage, you cannot determine the extent of your potential loss. In other words, it is nearly impossible to establish with accuracy the economic value of your family's health or

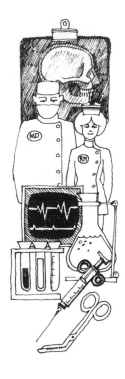

the potential costs of medical care or disability should their health become impaired.

Even though you cannot put a maximum value on the medical costs that you might face, you can identify the types of expenses that could occur. Because the people who serve you medically are highly trained and use sophisticated equipment, their services tend to be expensive. Also, because precision and accuracy are a necessity, there are many checks and counter-checks (i.e., lab tests, consultations with specialists, and round-the-clock nursing care) to ensure that the quality of service is high. These checks are also expensive. Figure 6-1 shows some of the services that doctors, nurses, laboratory technicians, and pharmacists may perform for you if you require medical treatment. Whenever possible, the probable cost of these services is given. These fees may be considered typical for metropolitan areas in the Far West and Northeast. Generally, the cost of medical treatment varies with the skill, the time, and the nature of the medicines and machines required to administer treatment.

Home	Doctor's Office	Hospital	Pharmacy
Examination and treatment ($35/visit)	Examination and treatment ($25/visit)	Examination and treatment ($25 and up)	Drugs and medicines ($5 and up)
Dressings	Minor surgery ($100 to $1000)	Surgery ($100 to $10,000)	Crutches, splints, braces, bandages
Nursing	Dressings	Dressings ($25/visit)	
	X ray ($20 each)	X ray ($20 each)	
	Physiotherapy	Physiotherapy	
	Prosthetics	Prosthetics	
	Lab tests	Lab tests ($5/test)	
		Room and board ($70 to $90/day)	
		Nursing	
		Blood	
		Rental of equipment	
		Maternity expenses ($900)	
		Ambulance service	

Fig. 6-1. Medical services that may be given by doctors, nurses, laboratory technicians, and pharmacists

PLANNING TO ABSORB MEDICAL COSTS

Look at your balance sheet. How much could you reasonably afford to spend on medical expenses before incurring a financial hardship? Which types of medical expenses (such as doctor bills for periodic family check-ups) occur with relative certainty and regularity? Which types of expenses are impossible to predict? The larger the financial burden you are able to assume, the smaller the burden you have to pass on and the smaller the premium you have to pay.

Self-Insuring Through Deductibles

The key to using deductibles in purchasing medical expense policies is to self-insure as much as you can afford (i.e., eliminate "first-dollar" coverage) and buy higher coverage maximums with the premium dollars saved. Figure 6-2 shows how annual premiums decrease as the deductibles increase on a major medical expense policy.

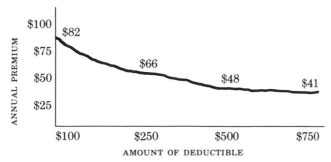

NOTE: Rates from General American Life Insurance Co. policy, 1972.

Fig. 6-2. Decrease in premiums as deductibles increase ($10,000 major medical expense policy for a male, age twenty-one)

Determine the extent to which you can use deductibles by evaluating your financial capacity to assume risk. Often you will find it wise to use your cash reserves to raise your deductibles; this will lower your health insurance premiums and/or increase the maximum benefits you can buy. Of course, the decrease in premium caused by raising the deductible must justify taking on a greater risk.

Because of the great uncertainties surrounding a potential financial calamity caused by poor health, you will need to transfer much of the risk to the insurance industry.

Transferring Health Risk to the Insurance Industry

When looking at health insurance policies, be sure to distinguish between those types of protection that are truly insurance plans and those that are merely prepayment plans. True insurance protection requires the payment of a small premium for possible benefits exceeding the total amount of the premiums paid. By paying a premium, you are accepting a small loss today to prevent a potentially larger loss in the future.

Prepayment insurance gives you coverage for an event that is almost certain to occur (i.e., an annual physical). In this case, the insurance company requires you to pay enough money to cover such an occurrence. There are two major disadvantages inherent in such a plan. First, you must assume the cost of commissions, claim servicing, and so on. As a consequence, your total premiums will probably be higher than the actual cost of the certain-to-occur event. You do not have this extra expense if you pay for your own medical services. Second, if you do not buy the insurance you can regularly invest the amount of the premiums and have even more money when the bills come. A possible advantage, however, is that prepayment insurance plans represent a form of forced savings.

Types of Medical Expense Coverage

Planning to meet your needs for medical expense coverage is really a matter of understanding what is available and then purchasing the maximum limits you can afford. Basically, there are six types of medical plans: hospital expense, surgical expense, general medical expense, major medical, comprehensive expense, and independent associations. Figure 6-3 outlines the major features of each type of coverage.

hospital expense insurance   This type of insurance is held by more people in the United States than any other type of coverage. Most individual policies are guaranteed to be renewed each year until the insured reaches age sixty-five. Premium rates, however, may change from year to year depending upon the insured's age and health. It is becoming popular to include a deductible clause of $25 to $50 in the policy to reduce high premiums caused by small claim costs.

The policy may be written to cover your dependents including your spouse; unmarried children under eighteen (sometimes under twenty-one); children under twenty-three who are full-time students; and, under certain group policies, adopted children, foster children, and stepchildren living in your home. There are four basic benefit provisions under hospital coverage: room and board charges, hospital extra-service charges, maternity charges, and nursing charges.

Room and board charges include the housing and feeding of a hospital in-patient. The insurance company may handle these charges on a valued basis or a reimbursement basis. The valued basis pays a set sum for each day (such as $70/day) no matter what expenses have been incurred. The more popular reimbursement basis pays the actual costs incurred

Type of Coverage	Items Covered[1]	Items Not Covered[1]	Range of Benefits (per occurrence)		Deductible	Remarks
			Time	Money		
Hospital expense	1–10	23–29	30 days to 2 years	$10 and up per day room and board; $10,000 expenses	$25 to $50	Most popular plan
Surgical expense	11	Anything not stated on schedule of operations		$300 to unlimited per operation	At discretion of insured	Usually attached to hospital expense coverage as rider
General medical	12–14	23–24	50 to 100 days	$5 to unlimited per day; total limit $250 to $500	At discretion of insured	Little more than a prepayment plan
Major medical	1–22	23–33	1 to 3 years	$5000 to $50,000	$100 to $1000	10 to 25% of all expenses to be paid by the insured in addition to deductible of his choice
Comprehensive (group plan)	All expenses	23–28	1 to 3 years	$10,000 to $50,000	$25 to $50	10 to 25% of all expenses to be paid by insured in addition to a deductible
Independent associations	All expenses	23–28	Indefinite	Usually no stated maximum	$1 to $5 per visit	Emphasis on preventive care; offers most coverage for premium dollars

[1]Key to Expense Coverage

1. Hospital room and board
2. X rays
3. Drugs
4. Laboratory examinations
5. Dressings
6. Physiotherapy
7. Maternity (including complications)
8. Mental disorders
9. Nursing expenses, in hospital
10. Nursing expenses, outside hospital
11. Operations
12. Doctor's home visits
13. Doctor's office visits
14. Doctor's hospital visits
15. Crutches
16. Splints
17. Blood and blood plasma
18. Braces
19. Prosthetics
20. Oxygen
21. Radiology
22. Rental of oxygen equipment, wheel chairs, hospital beds, and iron lungs.
23. Anything not recommended or approved by a legally qualified physician.
24. Injury sustained before the initial date of policy
25. Injury or illness due to war, declared or undeclared
26. Injury sustained while on active duty
27. Self-inflicted injury
28. Dental work
29. Eye examinations
30. Cosmetic surgery
31. Illness due to narcotic addiction
32. Illness due to alcoholism
33. Health examinations
34. Travel expenses (not ambulance)

Fig. 6-3.
Medical expense coverage

by the patient as long as those costs are "usual, customary, and reasonable." These policies usually stipulate that you must accept a double or triple bedroom unless a contagious disease requires a private room. Most policies cover room and board expenses for a maximum period of 70 to 120 days. Some policies cover periods as short as 30 days or as long as two years. To be eligible for benefits, the patient must be admitted to a hospital (not a nursing home or convalescent center) upon the recommendation of a medical doctor licensed to practice in the state.

Hospital extra-service charges include such costs as X rays, drugs, laboratory examinations, dressings, and physical therapy. Instead of instituting a maximum expense limit for each service, most insurance companies apply a blanket limit (usually five to twenty times the daily room and board benefit) to all types of charges. However, some companies reimburse the patient for the full amount of his extra-service expense up to a certain dollar limit and then pay only a percentage of the remaining expense.

Maternity charges usually provide a lump-sum benefit that may be applied to room and board charges and/or hospital extras. This amount, which is almost always only a fraction of actual maternity costs, is limited to about ten times the daily room and board benefit. Maternity benefits usually begin after the policyholder has been covered for nine to twelve months. If bought as part of an individual (not group) policy, these benefits are very expensive.

Nursing charges vary from policy to policy. Some policies cover nursing expenses only while the patient is in the hospital; others cover them outside the hospital as well. Normally there is a separate coverage limit for each type of disease or accident. Such limits may be as short as 5 days or as long as 180 days.

surgical expense insurance   This is the second most popular type of health insurance coverage. Most policies contain a schedule of operations that specifically indicates what operations are covered by the policy and what the dollar limits are for each operation. The most serious normally have a maximum dollar limit of $300 to $2500, depending on the policy. All operations must be performed by a legally qualified surgeon. In most policies, a portion of the dollar limit for an operation may be applied to the cost of services rendered by either a second surgeon or an anesthesiologist. Maternity benefits are provided only after the policy has been in effect for nine to twelve months. Individual health insurance policies normally contain surgical expense coverage in the form of a rider attached to the basic hospital coverage.

general medical expense insurance   This type of insurance covers little more than the expense of a doctor's visit. It usually provides a benefit of $5 for each day of hospitalization for in-hospital medical coverage, more than $5 a day for home visits, and less than $5 a day for office visits. Group general expense policies normally impose an aggregate dollar limit that cannot be exceeded. For example, if the daily rate is $5 a day and you are hospitalized for 100 days, the benefit payable will be $500. However, if the insurance company imposes an aggregate limit of $300 for the same time period, you can collect only $300. Coverage exclusions under this type of policy include pregnancy, childbirth, miscarriage, dental work, eye examinations, X rays, drugs, dressings, medicines, and equipment. Since this type of policy covers only the doctor's hourly visiting fee plus routine items involved in such a visit (such as blood tests) up to the maximum specified limit, its limits are small in relation to the premium charged. You should consider the advantages and disadvantages to see if this type of plan is financially appropriate for you.

major medical insurance   This insurance covers expenditures on nearly all types of medical care and equipment: hospital room and board; treatment by physicians and surgeons; psychiatric care for mental disorders; administration of anesthesia; radiology, physiotherapy, nursing care, and laboratory examinations; drugs, medicines, and blood and plasma; casts, splints, braces, crutches, and artificial limbs; and rental of oxygen and oxygen equipment, wheel chairs, hospital beds, and iron lungs.

Rather than having a schedule of limits for each of these expenses, major medical covers a fixed percentage of all expenses. Some limits are imposed for room and board, extended care, private nursing, and out-patient psychiatric treatment. Group contracts normally contain a single lifetime maximum figure covering all types of injuries. Upper limits for most individual contracts range from $5000 to $50,000 per injury, the most common being $10,000. Most insurance companies also impose time limits within which expenses must be incurred. In other words, if your leg is broken in a motorcycle accident, the insurance company will probably cover only those medical expenses accumulated within one to three years from the date of injury.

Deductibles are an important way to reduce the costs of major medical coverage. They should be used not only to eliminate costs of small claim handling but also to eliminate duplication of coverage. The most popular form of deductible is the initial deductible whereby the insured pays for an initial specified amount. The most common deductibles are $500, $750, and $1000, although they can be as low as $50.

In addition to deductibles, insurance companies require the insured to pay from 10 to 25 percent of all the eligible expenses in excess of the chosen deductible amounts. For example, if a person who is covered by a policy that pays 80 percent of all extra costs above a $500 initial deductible incurs medical costs of $1000, he must pay 20 percent ($100) of the expense above his $500 deductible (or a total of $600). The purpose of this percentage participation procedure is to encourage the insured to keep costs to a minimum. This procedure is called a coinsurance feature. It should not be confused with the coinsurance requirements of property insurance policies.

comprehensive medical expense insurance There are two types of comprehensive insurance. A pure comprehensive insurance policy is merely an extension downward of major medical insurance. By lowering the deductible and thereby raising the percentage of the total medical expenses the insurance company must pay, comprehensive insurance eliminates almost all of the financial headaches of illness and injury. Most comprehensive plans are written on a group, rather than an individual basis. A typical plan might include 80 percent reimbursement of covered medical expenses in excess of a $25 to $50 deductible per accident or illness up to a maximum limit of $20,000 per occasion.

Modified comprehensive insurance is a further extension of major medical insurance in that it covers 100 percent of all medical costs. No deductibles are permitted. Naturally, this first-dollar coverage costs much more than any other type of health insurance.

independent association insurance Instead of reimbursing you for the cost of medical treatment, independent associations offer actual medical treatment that is as broad as that covered by modified comprehensive expense insurance. Normally there is no benefit period associated with the treatment and no limit to the amount of treatment you can receive. Independent associations will be discussed later in this chapter (pp. 119–20) when we discuss the organizations that offer insurance.

DETERMINING YOUR DISABILITY INCOME NEEDS

In addition to the costs of medical services, health insurance covers loss of income caused by disability due to accident or illness. Although your medical expense needs can be estimated only roughly, you can determine how much disability income you might need by using the following procedure. Of course, this procedure will have to be repeated whenever your needs or your assets substantially increase or decrease.

To illustrate the procedure, we will use the example of a fictitious couple, Judy and Art, who are schoolteachers. Their statement of disability income needs as calculated for Art is shown in figure 6-4. The same procedure would be used to determine how much disability insurance Judy would need if she were disabled.

Instructions

1   *Annual Living Expenses. Determine your current level of annual living expenses,* based on the figures you computed for your income statement in chapter 2.

Judy and Art's living expenses amount to $12,000.

NAME _Art_

DATE _December 1972_

STATEMENT OF INCOME DISABILITY NEEDS

1 _Annual Living Expenses_ $12,000

2 _Adjusted Annual Living Expenses_

    Tax $2000

    Insurance   1000

    Other _____

3 _Spouse's Income_   4000

4 _Social Security Benefits_   3500

5 _Net Annual Disability Income Needs_   1500

6 _Average Annual Inflated_
Disability Income Needs   3825

    Age 85 Minus Present Age   60

    Inflation Factor   153

TOTAL INFLATED NET DISABILITY INCOME NEEDS   229,500

7 _Annual Income from Investment_   400

    Assets for Investment   7500

    Annuity Factor   18.7

8 _Annual Disability Income Insurance Need_ $3425

Fig. 6-4.
Sample statement
of income
disability needs

2   *Adjusted Annual Living Expenses. Make adjustments in categories that would be affected if you were to become disabled.* Since disability income payments are not taxed, you need not allocate money for income taxes. Take into account also that some expense categories such as transportation and entertainment may be reduced if you become disabled. Furthermore, if your insurance policies have waiver of premium clauses that enable you to retain insurance coverage without paying premiums while disabled, subtract the amount of the annual premiums from your living expense needs.

Taxes for Judy and Art average $2000 annually. Their health and life insurance policies have waiver of premium clauses and together cost $1000 in annual premiums.

3   *Spouse's Income. Determine how much income your spouse would earn if you became disabled and he or she continued working or returned to work.*

Since Judy is working as a substitute teacher and probably would continue to do so if Art were disabled, she would have an annual income of $4000.

4   *Social Security Benefits. Check the Social Security Addendum (pp. 493–97) to determine the level of benefits you would be entitled to if you have worked long enough to qualify for Social Security.* As you will learn (p. 115), Social Security benefits are paid only if you are unable to perform any gainful employment and the disability is expected to last at least twelve months. They will begin after you have been disabled six months.

Art's average countable earnings for Social Security purposes have been $6600. Therefore, Art figures that his annual benefits from Social Security would be approximately $3500.

5   *Net Annual Disability Income Needs. Subtract the items (steps 2, 3, and 4) that may reduce your living expense needs if you become disabled to arrive at your net annual disability income needs.* These are the needs that must be met with income from other sources.

Judy and Art have net annual disability income needs amounting to $1500.

6   *Average Annual Inflated Disability Income Needs. Adjust your net needs to allow for the effects of inflation.* Your spouse's income and your Social Security benefits can probably be assumed to rise at about the same rate as inflation. Your remaining needs, however, will probably be met by fixed income sources (i.e., insurance policies that promise to pay a certain number of dollars each month, regardless of the purchasing power of those dollars). You must therefore "inflate" your needs to see how much money you will need if the general cost of living, as measured by the consumer price index,

continues to rise at about 3 percent a year. For example, if you need $1000 a month to live on this year, you will need $1030 a month next year to buy the same things.

Figure the number of years between your current age and age eighty-five—the average age when you are expected to die. For example, if you are twenty-two years old, there will be sixty-three years until you turn age eighty-five. If you have reason to think that you will live beyond age eighty-five, add a couple of years to this difference.

Select the inflation factor (table 6-1) that corresponds to the number of years between your current age and age eighty-five. Table 6-1 gives inflation factors that represent the effect of 3 percent inflation on the purchasing power of the dollar. (Factors for intermediate years can be found in the 3 percent column of compound interest table B, page 500.) Multiply this factor by your net disability income need (step 5) to arrive at your inflated disability income needs for the rest of your life.

Divide this total by the total number of years between your present age and age eighty-five to determine your average annual inflated need. This annual figure will be greater than your present annual needs because it accounts for rising needs in future years. For example, if you needed $1000 a year for forty years, you would actually need $75,000, or $1875 a year as derived from table 6-1.

TABLE 6-1
INFLATION FACTORS

Years	10	20	30	40	50	60	70
Inflation factor	12	27	41	75	113	153	200

Judy and Art are twenty-five years old and therefore have sixty years before they reach age eighty-five. Art multiplied his net annual need ($1500) by the inflation factor for sixty years (153) to arrive at an aggregate inflated need of $229,500, or a net annual inflated need of $3825.

7 *Annual Income from Investment. Divide the total asset figure you would like to invest by the annuity factor (table 6-2).* The years in table 6-2, as in table 6-1, represent the number of years between your current age and age eighty-five. The result will be the annual income your investments will produce if invested either in a 5 percent savings account or in securities yielding 7 percent.

You may be able to use your assets to meet some of your disability needs. For example, if you were disabled, would you still want

TABLE 6-2
ANNUITY FACTORS

Years	10	20	30	40	50	60	70
Annuity factor for 5 percent savings account	7.7	12.5	15.4	17.2	18.2	18.7	19.0
Annuity factor for 7 percent investment	7.0	10.6	12.5	13.4	14.0	14.2	14.3

to save for a European vacation? Would you still need a second car? If you converted your assets into cash and invested them, they could produce a yield that would help meet your expenses. For example, $10,000 invested at 5 percent could help defray annual living expenses by $500. If, however, you were willing to dip into the principal of your investment as well as the interest, you could establish an annuity that would pay you a certain sum each year for the rest of your life. Used this way, $10,000 invested at five percent would produce $582 a year for forty years. Of course, if you annuitize your investment, you will have nothing left when the annuity runs out. You will have more money to use each year, however, than if you took the investment's income yield only.

Instead of using all your assets to cover a portion of your annual expense needs each year, you may find it more economically sound to use up some or all of your investment assets before relying on a disability income policy. For example, if your assets would cover your living expenses for the first six months, you could purchase a disability income policy with a six-month waiting period and thus save money on premiums.

Art has investment assets of $10,000. He decided to use $2500 to meet the six-month waiting period for Social Security and cover all his disability income needs during that time. The rest he decided to invest in a 5 percent passbook savings account. This investment would provide him with $400 extra income a year, were he to annuitize the remaining $7500 and thereby exhaust all principal and income by the end of the sixty-year period ($7500 ÷ 18.7, the annuity factor for 5 percent for sixty years).

8 *Annual Disability Income Insurance Need. Subtract the annual income from your investments (step 7) from your annual inflated disability income needs (step 6) to see how much insurance you will need to cover the remaining needs.*

Judy and Art need a disability income policy for $3425 a year ($3825 − $400), or less than $300 a month with payments to begin after six months of disability. (The annual premium for such a policy is approximately $120.)

PLANNING TO ABSORB LOSS OF INCOME

As we have seen in the procedure for determining disability income needs, it is a little easier to plan for these needs than for medical expense needs because you can make some assumption about your future life style based upon your present life style. Of course, as your standard of living increases and/or inflation causes prices to increase, satisfying your monthly needs will cost more.

Self-Insuring Through Waiting Periods

How long could you support yourself with your present assets? If you need $600 a month and you have saved $1200 in an emergency fund, you could theoretically support yourself for two months. Hence, an appropriate policy would begin to pay you $600 a month after sixty days. This waiting period serves as a deductible in time rather than in money. It forestalls income payments until they are required. Other things being equal, the longer the waiting period you can afford, the lower your premium will be. This relationship between waiting period and premium is expressed in figure 6-5. Sick leave benefits (p. 118) may help you determine how long your waiting period should be since they can be used to bridge the gap between the time when you are disabled and the time when your employer's long-term disability benefits begin.

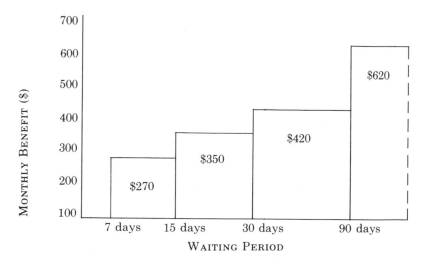

Fig. 6-5.
Amount of disability income that can be purchased for a $100 annual premium for a male, age twenty-one

NOTE: Rates and monthly benefits from Paul Revere Life Insurance Company, preferred 35 disability income policy, 1972.

Income Loss Coverage

Under the broadest definition of disability, income loss coverage provides payments to the policyholder as long as he is unable to perform any or all functions of his occupation. Under a strict definition of disability, income loss coverage provides payments only if the insured can perform no gainful employment whatsoever. If the disability occurred because of accidental injury, payments may be made for life; in the case of a disabling illness, payments may be made only to age sixty-five. The maximum possible limits on payments are $3500 a month or, normally, 66 2/3 percent of the disabled person's salary, whichever is smaller. Also, there can be a waiting period of up to one year before payments begin. You should consider your own needs in relation to these limits.

Women are often discriminated against in health insurance underwriting, especially in disability income policies. A woman may be able to purchase disability income coverage for a maximum of five years, but not for a lifetime unless she is deemed to hold an executive position. Dollar limits are restricted as well. Often a woman cannot buy more than $500 a month in disability payments.

basic contract   Basic contracts (also called commercial contracts) are the most popular form of disability income coverage. The policy may be written to cover total or partial disability due to accident or illness. It may provide income benefits if you become totally disabled and unable to perform either your regular job or any other job. The most common contracts cover you for two years if you are unable to perform your previous job. Then, if you cannot perform your own job, but can perform another one, benefits stop even if the income from the new job is insufficient to cover your needs. The most liberal policies cover you until age sixty-five, if you are unable to work at your own job, and then revert to the strict definition of disability. If you are totally disabled because of an accident, income benefits may last for your lifetime. However, if you are totally disabled because of disease, few policies pay benefits beyond age sixty-five. Payments may begin the day of the accident or 7, 15, 30, 90, 180, or 365 days after the accident. However, if you are stricken with a disease, most policies impose at least a one-week waiting period before beginning benefit payments. The length of the policy term is important in determining the premium. Policy terms can be short (26 weeks to 3 years), intermediate (37 to 99 months), long (100 months to 10 years), or extra-long (over 10 years or to age sixty-five).

There are three types of clauses that may be part of basic contracts: presumptive disability, double indemnity, and prorating. *Presumptive disability clauses,* contained in many basic contracts, define the conditions under which the insured will be deemed disabled. In these clauses, the policy states what accidents are covered—virtually all accidents except such normal exclusions as war, military service, maternity, childbirth, or miscarriage. Loss of a member (such as an arm or leg) may be defined in terms of actual severance or loss of use. These clauses also tell the amount of payments that will be made as a result of each accident. Lump-sum payments are offered for the loss of various body members and may be paid in addition to regular monthly income payments.

Double indemnity clauses often receive a lot of attention, particularly from insurance salesmen; but they are nothing more than a sales gimmick. This type of clause provides that you will receive twice the normal benefit payment if you suffer certain accidents. For example, if you lose both legs in an auto accident, you might receive double the amount of benefits. However, if you lose both legs in some sort of accident not specified in this clause, you would receive only the normal benefit amount. It seems illogical that you would need more money (double benefits) because of the nature of the accident rather than the nature of the injury.

Prorating clauses are provisions for altering the cost of your insurance. Here are four of them that you should recognize.

1. If you change your occupation, your rate may change. If your new job is in any way more hazardous than your old one, your rate will go up.
2. If you falsify information regarding your age, the insurance company can adjust your rate to match the rate appropriate for your real age, with no further penalty imposed.
3. Your basic contract will not duplicate benefits paid by other forms of insurance such as Social Security and Workmen's Compensation.
4. The insurance policies covering the insured will never pay, either individually or collectively, monthly benefits totaling more than the current monthly salary of the insured or his average monthly salary over the past few years, whichever is greater.

life insurance riders   A disability income rider can be attached to your life insurance policy if you choose. This extra-cost rider generally offers a $10 a month disability income benefit for each $1000 face amount of your life insurance policy. Only one-third of the insurance companies offer such an option.

limited contracts   Limited disability income contracts impose restrictions and exclusions beyond those in basic contract policies. The most common limitation concerns the type of accident or disease covered and the length of the coverage period. Aviation ticket policies are the most popular type of limited contract. These policies are sold through coin-operated machines in airport terminals. Coverage includes injuries sustained as a result of accidents while one is a passenger on a scheduled U.S. common carrier airline, in transit to the airport on an airport bus or limousine (not taxi), or on the airport premises waiting for a flight. Benefits from $20,000 to $100,000 may be purchased for 25¢ per $10,000 of insurance benefit. You will be paid the full value of the face amount if you suffer loss of sight, double dismemberment (i.e., loss of one arm and one leg), or death; one-half of the face amount for single dismemberment; and one-fourth of the amount for loss of one eye. If you really believe, however, that you and your family need $100,000 to live on in case you are totally disabled, you would do better to insure yourself for this amount against all accidents.

industrial policies Industrial policies are similar in coverage to basic contracts except in the amount and duration of the benefits provided. These policies, which have nothing to do with company sponsored group plans, are sold and issued individually. The amount of protection is generally less than basic contract coverage, and the premiums are payable weekly or monthly to an agent who calls at the home of the insured. To keep costs down, a minimum waiting period of five weeks is usually imposed and there are few extras. The benefits, typically $10 to $20 a week, are paid in lump sums daily or weekly.

The major advantage of such a policy is that it provides a means for a person of low income and/or poor savings habits to obtain a minimum amount of short-term disability protection at a cost within his weekly budget. No physical examination is required. Since the insured is billed weekly, he need make only a small commitment each time. For these reasons, industrial insurance may be the only type of health insurance available to housewives, the unemployed, students, or welfare recipients. The major disadvantage is long-term cost. The carrying, collection, and commission costs are so high that the benefits are smaller per premium dollar than for most other types of policies.

WHAT YOU MAY ALREADY BE PROVIDED WITH

If you work now, or have ever worked, you may be entitled to medical and disability benefits under the federal Social Security system and your state's Workmen's Compensation program. These benefits can form a base on which to build the coverage limits you desire, but rarely will they satisfy your needs for health insurance. For example, the maximum allowable monthly income for a disabled worker under Social Security is a little over $350. Under Workmen's Compensation, the monthly maximum is rarely over $350. These levels of support are probably not sufficient to meet the living expense requirements of either an individual or a family. In addition to federally supported medical coverage, some states have medical care programs for individuals earning less than $2000 to $3000 a year.

Social Security Health Benefits

Social Security provides disability income benefits and health expense benefits. In order to qualify for disability income payments, you must have a severe mental or physical condition that prevents you from doing not only your present job but also any other substantial work. This condition must be expected to last at least twelve months or until death. After you have been disabled for six months, Social Security benefits can begin if you are under twenty-four years of age and have Social Security credit for one and one-half of the three years preceding disability; if you are between twenty-four and thirty-one years old, have worked at least half the time between your twenty-first birthday and the date of disablement, and have earned a minimum of $50 a quarter year; or if you are over thirty-one years of age and have worked five of the ten years prior to disablement. The size of the benefit payments you receive is a percentage of your earnings over a period of years. To see what the monthly payment might be, if you were to qualify, look at the Social Security addendum (pp. 493–97).

In order to qualify under Social Security for medical expense coverage (Medicare), you have to be age sixty-five or over and have accumulated forty quarters of credits (p. 493). The benefits available include coverage for hospitalization and medical expenses. Hospitalization benefits (fig. 6-6, p. 116) are automatic. Medical expense benefits are optional and must be applied for within three months before or after your sixty-fifth, sixty-sixth, sixty-seventh, or sixty-eighth birthday. If you are more than three months past age sixty-eight and have failed to apply for benefits, medical expense insurance is unavailable to you.

Medicare benefits include physician's and surgeon's services, no matter where you receive them (at home, hospital, doctor's office); home health care (e.g., nursing care)—even if you have not visited a hospital—up to 100 home visits per calendar year; diagnostic tests, surgical dressings and splints, and rental or purchase of medical equipment; and outpatient physical therapy service, and the like. Under this coverage, you pay a yearly deductible of $50, and Medicare pays 80 percent of every expense above the first $50. Because the federal government matches your premium payment, dollar for dollar under this plan, Medicare is probably the least expensive insurance available for persons over age sixty-five.

Workmen's Compensation Benefits

Workmen's Compensation covers accidental (not self-inflicted) injuries and illness arising from one's employment. Unlike Social Security, Work-

Place	Limits Within Benefit Period[1]		Lifetime Reserve		Home Health Visits	Remarks
	Time	Money	Time	Money		
Hospital	90 days	Total expenses over $72 (first 60 days); expenses over $18/day (last 30 days)	60 days	Expenses over $34/day		Lifetime limit of 190 days of care in mental hospital
Nursing home	100 days	All covered expenses (first 20 days); expenses over $9/day (last 80 days)				Coverage applicable only if hospitalized for at least 3 days and then admitted to extended care facility within 14 days
Home					Up to 100 (by health workers, such as nurses, therapists, and aides, from participating agency)	Must be within 365 days following at least a 3-day hospital stay, or release from extended care facility

Source: U.S. Department of Health, Education, and Welfare, "Your Medicare Handbook," SSI-50 (Washington, D.C.: Government Printing Office, January 1973).

[1] A benefit period begins the first time you enter a hospital after your hospital insurance starts. It ends after you have not been an in-patient for sixty continuous days in any hospital or facility that mainly provides skilled nursing care.

Fig. 6-6.
Hospitalization benefits under Medicare

men's Compensation programs are mostly state controlled and funds are provided by employer contributions.

The majority of states allow full coverage of any accident or illness arising from one's job. One-third of the states, however, list diseases that are occupational in origin and therefore should be covered. In either situation, the burden of showing that a disease or accident resulted from his occupation rests with the employee. If you are now employed, check with your employer to find out what Workmen's Compensation offers in your state. Some states (e.g., California) offer state disability indemnity insurance to cover monthly needs for up to six months (when Social Security begins) on non-work-oriented disabilities.

There are five benefit provisions in the Workmen's Compensation laws: medical expense, disability income, second injury, rehabilitation, and death and survivor. Death and survivor benefits will be discussed in the next chapter.

medical expense benefits   Surgical, hospital, medical, and nursing expenses are normally covered in full. Some states, however, impose limitations on either the time over which the medical treatment is administered or the total amount of expenses to be paid.

disability income benefits   These are provided in weekly installments to the injured employee. The amount and duration of these payments depend on whether the disability is partial or total, the employee's average weekly wage level, the maximum duration of benefits stated in the law, the maximum dollar limits under the law (normally 66 2/3 percent—but sometimes as high as 90 percent and as low as 50 percent—of the weekly wage), and the waiting period after which payments can begin (normally one week).

second injury benefits   These simply protect the employer from having to pay the total amount due if a partially disabled employee becomes permanently disabled. The employer need pay only the new disability expense. For example, if he hires someone who is blind in one eye and that employee is then blinded in the other eye through an accident on the job, the employer is responsible for compensating only for loss of the second eye, not for the total cost of permanent disability. The state covers the remaining necessary compensation. This provision was included in the law so that employers would not be discouraged from hiring the handicapped for fear that they might be charged with the full cost of total disability.

rehabilitation benefits   These are provided by only half the states. Through state established funds, employees who have been disabled can be given weekly allowances while being trained in a new skill.

Group Insurance Plans

In addition to fulfilling his obligations under the Workmen's Compensation laws, an employer may provide group health insurance coverage for his employees. Normally, such health coverage is made available both to the employee and his family. The employer may pay the complete cost of the insurance, a portion of that cost, or none at all. If you leave your job, you usually have thirty days in which to switch your group coverage to an individual policy with the same company. If you fail to do so within thirty days, you must show proof of insurability (i.e., pass a physical examination) before a new policy will be issued. Five types of group insurance may be offered.

group health expense coverage This coverage is usually made available in equal amounts to all members of a general class of employees (e.g., managers, clerks, supervisors). There may be a short waiting period before a new employee is eligible to join the plan. If you have such coverage at work, you should know both the major medical maximum to which you are entitled under your plan and the amount of any deductible required.

short-term disability benefits Sick leave is the time an employer allots an employee for absence from work because of sickness or accident. If it can be proven satisfactorily that the absence occurred for legitimate reasons, the employee will be paid his normal salary. Sick leave credits are usually allocated according to length of employment—the longer a person has worked, the more days of sick leave he is allotted. Sick leave benefits are important because they bridge the gap between the time a person becomes disabled and his employer's long-term disability benefits begin. The longer the sick leave, the less the employee has to worry about financing his disablement needs.

long-term disability plans These plans are coordinated with Social Security and Workmen's Compensation payments. They generally offer monthly benefits proportionate to the employee's salary (often 66 2/3 percent). Benefits begin after waiting periods of from one to twenty-four months, depending on the plan. As an employee, you should find out from your employer what the maximum benefits are, when they start, and when they end. When benefits end depends on the plan's definition of disability. Many plans stop benefit payments after two years if it can be proven that you are capable of working at any gainful employment, not merely the job you held prior to the disability.

accidental death and dismemberment This coverage is normally offered on a voluntary basis and enables the employee to receive a lump-sum payment if he dies or loses a bodily member in an accident. The shortcomings of this double indemnity type of coverage have already been discussed (p. 113). You should buy enough coverage to insure you properly, no matter how you become disabled or die.

dental insurance Some group plans (primarily those offered through labor unions) are beginning to offer dental insurance, which covers such expenses as examinations, fillings, and extractions. There are three types of dental insurance: basic, comprehensive, and combination. Basic covers most expenses except for orthodontics to a maximum of $500 within a certain period. Comprehensive requires a $25 to $50 deductible per family each year. For a single individual, a $25 deductible is required the first year and a $10 deductible in the successive years. The maximum benefits per family are $500 the first year, $750 the second, and $1000 thereafter. The maximum benefits for an individual are $200, $300, and $400, respectively. The insured is also required to pay 20 percent of the cost of examinations, for any care in excess of his limit, and 40 percent of the cost of denture replacement and orthodontics. Combination coverage offers full reimbursement for basic expenses such as examinations and fillings, and partial reimbursement for more expensive or voluntary treatment such as oral surgery or orthodontics.

WHERE TO OBTAIN ADDITIONAL INSURANCE COVERAGE

There are three types of organizations from which health insurance is available: Blue Cross and Blue Shield, independent health expense associations, and commercial insurance companies.

Blue Cross and Blue Shield

Blue Cross (founded in 1929) and Blue Shield (founded in 1946) are the largest single health expense plans in the nation. Blue Cross offers primarily hospitalization coverage, whereas Blue Shield provides surgical and general medical insurance. Often these nonprofit associations cooperate in issuing joint plans for comprehensive medical care. To receive medical treatment, you go to any doctor's office or any hospital (except an independent association) and show proof of membership in the plan.

Independent Associations

There are many independent medical service groups, sometimes called health maintenance organizations, that render treatment in return for monthly dues. These associations are composed of doctors and medical service personnel. They own their own facilities and provide medical care at a reasonable cost. The monthly dues are kept low so that people will seek out medical care before major treatment is required. Normally, there is no limit to the amount of care provided, and only nominal charges are made for laboratory work and medicines. The primary disadvantage of such a plan is that it is often difficult to see any doctor on a regular basis.

The Kaiser Foundation Health Plan in California is one of the most successful independent association plans in the country. If a national health plan is ever implemented in the United States, it will probably take the form of the plans offered by the independent associations.

Commercial Insurance Companies

Commercial insurance companies specialize in policies that conform to individual needs and desires. A policyholder can receive medical care wherever he chooses. He does not have to be admitted to certain member hospitals or doctor's offices. For those who wish to have one doctor in particular rather than go to a clinic, individually issued health policies (with a commercial insurance company, Blue Cross, or Blue Shield) may be the best answer. However, the costs are generally higher than similar coverage provided in group plans or through independent associations.

COST CONSIDERATIONS

The four major factors, other than age and health, that determine the cost of premiums for health insurance are size of deductible, length of policy term, type and amount of coverage (major medical, for example), and provisions covering renewal of the policy. The cost relationships of deductibles and policy terms are fairly simple. The bigger the deductible the smaller the premium. The shorter the term, the smaller the premium.

Type of Coverage

The type and amount of coverage you purchase is the major determinant of policy costs. For medical expense coverage, modified comprehensive and independent association plans are the most expensive. Regular comprehensive is next most expensive. Hospital and surgical policies are the least expensive but offer the least coverage. General medical is really a prepayment plan. Major medical protects against catastrophic risks at a cost below most hospital expense policies. Under such a plan, however, you must normally pay 10 to 25 percent of expenses. If you anticipate using your health insurance coverage because you have a large family or because you are accident prone, independent association plans represent the greatest value. If you seldom go to the doctor and yet want to be covered in case of a major illness or accident, major medical probably represents the greatest value.

For income coverage, industrial policies are the most expensive. Limited contract policies cost the least. Basic contract policies have the best combination of cost and breadth of benefit coverage. In general, group policies offer the best coverage for the premium dollar, since operating costs are minimized. Moreover, if the policy is for an employee group, the employer may shoulder part of the cost.

Renewability Provisions

Renewability provisions determine who has the right to cancel your coverage once the policy terms are completed—you or the insurance company. Such provisions affect the premium rate.

Optionally renewable policies can be renewed only at the option of the company. If your health deteriorates during the policy term, you may be unable to renew your policy except at much higher rates. Guaranteed renewable policies must be renewed by the company at their expiration, if you so request. The premiums may be changed only if they are altered for your whole classification group, as they may be if medical costs rise or risk experience changes. The guaranteed renewable policy costs more than an optionally renewable one but less than the noncancellable policy. Noncancellable guaranteed renewable policies must be renewed, with no change in premium, at the end of the policy term, if you so request. For this privilege you pay a higher premium from the beginning, but the security may be worth the extra cost. Find out the difference in premiums before you decide.

CONCLUSION

If you can afford only one type of insurance, health insurance is the most important to have. As long as you can work and earn an income, you can replace personal property, rebuild an estate, or build a new home. If, however, you were sick for a long time or became totally disabled, you would face big medical bills at a time when you have lost your income-producing capability. Gauge your needs carefully. If you can purchase only one type of health insurance, consider major medical. This policy prevents sizeable losses due to the expense of serious illness or accident. Social Security would provide a minimum income if you were totally disabled. Be sure you understand where you are protected and where you are not. Avoid excess premium costs by eliminating duplication of coverage and by setting your deductibles as high as your emergency financial resources allow.

VOCABULARY

coinsurance feature
disability
double indemnity
guaranteed renewable

Medicare
prepayment plan
sick leave
waiting period

QUESTIONS

1. Why is it difficult to determine medical expense insurance needs?
2. What purpose do deductibles serve in purchasing a health insurance policy?
3. For $350 Lucy can buy a hospital and surgical expense policy that would cover her medical bills in their entirety up to $10,000. For $225 a year she can also purchase a $10,000 major medical policy with a $200 deductible. Over the last ten years, Lucy has had medical expenses totaling $800. Which policy would you recommend that Lucy purchase and why?
4. What is the difference between a true insurance plan and a prepayment plan?
5. Jerry contracted hepatitis and ran up the following medical expenses: $800 for hospital room and board, $400 for X rays and lab work, $500 for physician's fees, and $150 for medicines. How much of these expenses will Jerry have to pay if he carries a major medical policy with a $100 deductible and an 80 percent coinsurance feature?
6. What factors should govern your decision concerning the length of the waiting period to select when purchasing a disability income policy?
7. An employee earned $600 a month prior to his disablement. Under his employee plan, his long-term disability coverage pays two-thirds of his former monthly salary. How much would the employee receive in total benefits each month?
8. Which renewability provision offers the most safety to the policyholder? Why?
9. What is the major difference between a health insurance medical expense policy and an independent association plan?
10. Define *double indemnity*. What value does it have? Why?

CASE PROBLEM

Jeff Mapson graduated from college last June and began earning $700 a month as an auto salesman. He uses only $500 of his monthly earnings to live on since he pays $100 a month in income taxes and adds $100 each month to his savings account, which now amounts to $3000. Jeff's company provides him with a long-term disability policy that would pay, after three months, benefits equal to 50 percent of his salary at the time of the disability.

How much would Jeff's company pay him if he were to be disabled now? Does Jeff need more disability income insurance? If he were to buy a policy on his own, what benefits and how long a waiting period would you recommend? Disregard any potential Social Security or Workmen's Compensation.

RECOMMENDED READING

Social Security and Medicare Simplified: What You Get for Your Money. Washington, D.C.: Books Division of U.S. News and World Report, 1969.

> A clear explanation of the benefits offered under Social Security and their history. Good charts and graphs.

Time Saver for Health Insurance, 1971. Cincinnati: National Underwriter Co. Published annually.

> Describes the various policies available by company. Provides coverage limit and rate information.

Personal finance texts that provide statistical data on amount of health insurance purchased, average medical expense payments, and so on:

> Cohen, Jerome B., and Hanson, Arthur W. *Personal Finance: Principles and Case Problems.* Homewood, Ill.: Irwin, 1972.

> Donaldson, Elvin, and Pfahl, John. *Personal Finance.* New York: Ronald Press, 1971.

CHUCK AND NANCY ANDERSON

INSURING AGAINST A FINANCIAL CALAMITY DUE TO MEDICAL EXPENSES

Chuck and Nancy carry a hospital, medical, and surgical expense policy, which costs them $309 a year. The policy benefits include $30/day for a maximum of 120 days of hospitalization, $5/day for in-hospital doctor visits, up to $100 for X rays and diagnostic services, and up to $600 for surgery. The policy benefits extend to the entire family. Through his company Chuck and the family have a $30,000 major medical policy that covers 80 percent of the expenses not covered by other insurance above a $100 deductible. Chuck pays $172 toward the cost of this policy.

QUESTIONS

1. Chuck was in the hospital for ten days and incurred the following expenses: $70/day for room and board, $150 for X rays, and $10/day for doctor visits. How much of these expenses will his major medical policy cover? How much will he have to pay?

2. During the past ten years Chuck and Nancy have incurred $3500 of medical expenses, not including pregnancy expenses. On the basis of their loss record, would you advise them to cancel both health policies and purchase no insurance; cancel the hospital, medical, and surgical expense policy but keep the major medical policy; or keep both policies as they are? Why?

INSURING AGAINST A FINANCIAL CALAMITY DUE TO LOSS OF INCOME

If Chuck were disabled, his company's long-term disability plan would pay him 60 percent of his salary, or $625 a month, beginning six months after the date of disability. This plan costs him $100 a year. Chuck figures that, if he were disabled, Nancy would continue earning her same salary and he would receive Social Security benefits (based on $6600 of average annual earnings) as well as the benefits from his company's disability plan. He also plans to annuitize $15,000 of investable assets at 7 percent, and he can take advantage of waiver of premium clauses on his health and life insurance policies.

QUESTION

1. How much extra disability income insurance should Chuck buy? (Consider the benefits from his company's disability plan only after you have inflated the Andersons' annual needs.)

7

LIFE INSURANCE

Life insurance is really death insurance, for it assumes the financial responsibilities of the family's breadwinner at his death. If people (e.g., wife, children, parents) are dependent upon you, you must consider how they will be cared for after you die. Perhaps, those who are in good health and have a marketable skill can get a job and provide for themselves. Perhaps, they can turn to an alternate source of income, such as dividends or interest from investments. In most cases, however, the only way a breadwinner can provide for his dependents after his death is through life insurance. By paying a relatively small sum each year (an annual insurance premium), he ensures that his family will be paid a larger sum if he dies prematurely. The size of the annual premium depends upon his probability of death.

If you are thinking of buying life insurance, you should ask yourself several questions. What purpose does life insurance serve for you? Is there anyone you want to protect after you die? If so, who? If not, do you really need life insurance? If you are married and die, would your widow be likely to remarry or live with her parents or other family? If so, do you really need life insurance? How much of the responsibility for her support after your death would your widow be willing or able to shoulder? Could she get a job or adjust to a lower standard of living? If so, how should this affect your life insurance needs?

By answering these questions, you are to some extent envisioning your family's life style without you. Look at the ramifications of your death with candor and honesty. Talk over the alternatives with your family. The premiums you now pay will, to a degree, influence your family's current life style. The death benefit you plan for will determine their life style after you die.

Determining whether you need life insurance is not as difficult as deciding how much life insurance you should have.

DETERMINING THE RIGHT AMOUNT OF LIFE INSURANCE

Before choosing an insurance policy, it is important to identify what your needs are and when they will arise. Since death may come at any time, consider what your dependents' needs would be if you were to die now, not ten or twenty years from now. Reevaluate your program periodically. What may be adequate to meet your needs today may well be inadequate five years from now. If inflation continues to rise at its current rate of 3 percent a year, the dollar's purchasing power will be reduced 15 percent in five years. Furthermore, the younger you are the more difficult it is to predict accurately what your needs will become. New goals arise to replace old ones. You may not have children for a couple of years, and yet twenty years from now your children may be living away from home. As your family grows, your needs may increase, then decrease. They will probably at least change with time.

An Eleven-Step Procedure for Determining Life Insurance Needs

To compute your life insurance needs, use the following eleven-step procedure. With this procedure, you can determine your family's financial needs after your death and the sources of income to meet those needs. You can then plan to use insurance to make up the difference between these two.

To illustrate the procedure, we will use the example of a fictitious family, Leroy and Thelma Jackson (each twenty-two) and their two-year-old son Jerry. Figure 7-1 shows the needs and income the Jacksons predicted for themselves if Leroy were to die now.

Instructions

1 *Funeral, Administrative, and Estate Tax Expenses. Estimate these expenses on the basis of your gross estate (net worth plus existing life insurance proceeds). If your gross estate is below $20,000, you can estimate your funeral, administrative, and estate tax expenses to be $2200. If your gross estate is between $20,000 and $40,000, use a $4400 estimate. If it is over $40,000 estimate $6600.*

NAME(S) _Leroy and Thelma Jackson_

DATE _December 1972_

ELEVEN-STEP PROCEDURE

1 *Funeral, Administrative, and Estate Tax Expenses* — $2200

2 *Debt Resolution* — 1075

3 *Contingency Fund* — 1250

4 *College Education Fund* — 21,000

5 *Annual Living Expenses* (by period) — 6000 4800 4800

6 *Annual Sources of Income* (by period) — 3800 4800 4600

7 *Net Annual Income Needs* (by period) — 2200 ____ 200

Number of Years in Period — 20 23 19

TOTAL NET INCOME NEEDS (by period) — 44,000 ____ 3800

TOTAL NET INCOME NEEDS — 47,800

8 **TOTAL DISCOUNTED INCOME NEEDS** — 41,540

Discount Factor (by period) — 18 16.8 9.7

Discounted Income Needs (by period) — 39,600 ____ 1940

9 **TOTAL MONETARY NEEDS** — 67,065

10 **TOTAL INVESTMENT ASSETS** — 900

11 *Your Life Insurance Needs* — $66,165

Fig. 7-1.
Sample eleven-step procedure

The Jacksons' gross estate is $5000, and so they estimate expenses to be $2200.

2   *Debt Resolution. Determine the amount of money in debts to be paid off at your death.* Look at the current debts (liabilities) on your balance sheet. All of these debts (with one possible exception) should be resolved at your death so that your family does not have to worry about maintaining credit relationships. The home mortgage can be considered a separate debt and handled differently. You can either buy a mortgage term policy to pay off this debt if you die or include the annual mortgage payment in an assessment of your family's annual living expense needs (step 5).

Leroy and Thelma Jackson have $1075 in nonmortgage debts outstanding.

3   *Contingency Fund. Estimate the amount of money your family will need for immediate daily use if you die.* With all the other worries they will have upon your death, you do not want them immediately to have to worry about money. Also, you probably cannot predict all the expenses that might surround your death. Normally a contingency fund equal to twice your current monthly take-home pay is sufficient to tide the family over until they have adjusted to your absence.

Leroy earns $625 (take-home wage) each month, and so his contingency fund should be $1250.

4   *College Education Fund. Estimate how much it will cost to send your children to college.* By this method, a lump sum covering all four years is planned to be available when the child first starts college. Of course, what is not needed each of the first three years may be invested to keep pace with the rising cost of education.

State-supported colleges cost approximately $2500 a year for tuition, room and board, and books. Private colleges average $4000 a year. Table 7-1 estimates the probable annual cost of education five, ten, fifteen, and twenty years from now for both private and state-supported schools, assuming these costs grow at 5 percent a year.

TABLE 7-1

ANNUAL COST OF UNDERGRADUATE EDUCATION

| School | Year | | | | |
	1972	1977	1982	1987	1992
State-supported	$2500	$3250	$4000	$5250	$6500
Private	4000	5200	6400	8400	10,400

If you have other goals that would not change because of the death of your family's breadwinner, you will have to allow for their expense in a similar way.

The Jacksons figure that Jerry will start college in sixteen years. According to table 7-1, sixteen years from now (1987) the annual cost for a state-supported school will be $5250 and, for a private school, $8400. They decide to plan to have $21,000 in sixteen years to provide for four years of state-supported schooling. What is not needed each year will be invested at 5 percent.

5 *Annual Living Expenses. Estimate the amount of money your family will need for the various periods in your family's life cycle.* Consider both whether your spouse will work after your death and the length of time between now and when your children will be on their own. Your family's income needs will probably change, as figure 7-2 demonstrates. Ignore for now the effect of inflation.

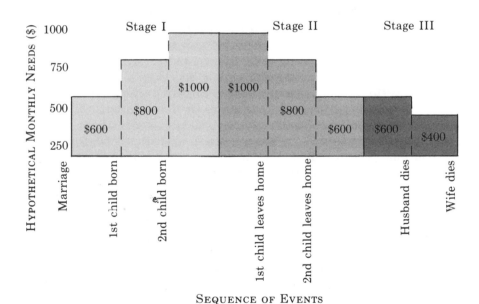

Fig. 7-2.
Stages in the family life cycle

Leroy and Thelma Jackson are in stage I of their family's life cycle. They must determine how their living expense needs will change if Leroy dies now. The Jacksons looked at their income statement to find out how much it costs the three of them to live. Then they subtracted those expenses that were incurred by Leroy. In so doing, they arrived at an estimate of Thelma and Jerry's living expense needs from the time of Leroy's death until Jerry finishes college ($500 a month or $6000 a year) and from then until Thelma dies ($400 a month or $4800 a year).

6   *Annual Sources of Income. Estimate income your family will receive from Social Security (pp. 493–96), corporate pension or profit sharing plans, and surviving spouse's income.*

Thelma and Leroy determined that, since Leroy has average earnings of $4200, Thelma and Jerry would receive about $3800 a year until Jerry graduated from college. Thelma would receive nothing until age sixty, and after that she would receive from Leroy's Social Security $1800 a year until she died. Thelma had some sales experience and thought that she could return to work after Jerry finished college twenty years from now. She figured that she could make $4800 a year—enough to support herself until she retired at age sixty-five, twenty-three years later. Then she would have, in addition to Leroy's survivor benefits of $1800, $2800 a year in retirement benefits because of a pension from her own job for a total of $4600.

7   *Net Annual Income Needs. Subtract the income (step 6) from the expenses (step 5) to get a net annual need for each period in your family's projected life cycle. Multiply the net annual need by the number of years in each period.* To determine the length of the period ending in the death of the surviving spouse, look at table 7-2. For example, a female age twenty-two can expect to live to age seventy-nine. Add five years to the figure you find in table 7-2 and use this number as the final period.

For the first period (from Leroy's death to when Jerry finishes college), the Jacksons subtracted their expenses ($6000) from their income ($3800) and found their projected annual net income needs to be $2200. Since they expect this period to last twenty years, their net income needs for the first period are projected to be $44,000. During the second period (from the time Thelma begins work until she retires), Thelma's income and expenses are expected to equal each other, and so for twenty-three years there would be no net income need. In fact, if at age 60 she started receiving her widow Social Security benefits, she could either raise her standard of living the last five years or save for the future. From the time Thelma retires to when she dies, a nineteen-year period, Thelma's projected income of $4600 will not cover her expenses of $4800. The net income need for that period would be $3800. The total net income need for all periods would be $47,800.

8   *Total Discounted Income Needs. Determine the after-tax-and-inflation yield you feel is achievable, and then determine the discount factors (Table 7-3) to apply to each period's net income needs. Multiply these factors by the net annual income needs for the various periods to arrive at the discounted need for each period. Then total these discounted needs.* Since your family will not have

TABLE 7-2

AVERAGE FUTURE LIFETIME IN UNITED STATES

AGE INTERVAL	AVERAGE REMAINING LIFETIME	
	Male	Female
0–1	67.8	75.1
1–5	68.3	75.3
5–10	64 6	71.5
10–15	59.7	66.7
15–20	54.9	61.7
20–25	50.2	56.9
25–30	45.7	52.1
30–35	41.0	47.2
35–40	36.4	42.5
40–45	31.8	37.8
45–50	27.4	33.2
50–55	23.3	28.7
55–60	19.5	24.5
60–65	16.1	20.4
65–70	13.0	16.5
70–75	10.4	13.0
75–80	8.2	9.9
80–85	6.2	7.1
85 and over	4.5	4.8

SOURCE: National Center for Health Statistics, U.S. Dept. of Health, Education, and Welfare, 1967.

to use all of the money represented by their total net income needs during the first day, month, or year after you die, much of the money can be invested and withdrawn in increments as needed. The more money your investments earn, the more money can be used to meet your family's needs. Therefore, the amount of money your family really requires is equal to the amount of money that, when invested at a certain yield, will supply the amount of income your family needs over your wife's expected life span and while your children are dependents.

Suppose you determine that your family needs an average of $5000 a year for thirty years—a net income need (step 7) of $150,000. If your family invested the proceeds from a life insurance policy in a 5 percent passbook savings account and allowed 4 percent of that yield to cover increased prices due to inflation and taxes, all your family would need would be $129,000 in proceeds. In other words, this $129,000 invested at 5 percent would provide $150,000 over the thirty-year period, counting both interest income and principal withdrawals. (Compound interest will be explained in chapter 14, as will the various investments you might select for this purpose.)

Table 7-3 presents discount factors for two types of investments: savings, and securities and real estate. These factors are already adjusted to allot 4 percent of the investment yield to cover inflation and taxes. If the first period of need is twenty years, the discount factor for a 1 percent rate of growth would be 18. For the next twenty-year period the discount factor would be 14.8, the difference between the factor for twenty years (18) and the factor for forty years (32.8). The factor for the next ten years after that would be 6.4, the difference between the discount factor for forty years (32.8) and the factor for fifty years (39.2). The discount factors for securities and real estate are related in the same way.

TABLE 7-3

DISCOUNT FACTORS FOR TWO TYPES OF INVESTMENTS

	DISCOUNT FACTORS	
YEARS	Savings Account 1% rate of growth (5% − 4%)	Securities and Real Estate 3% rate of growth (7% − 4%)
5	4.8	4.6
10	9.5	8.5
15	14.0	11.9
20	18.0	14.9
25	22.0	17.4
30	25.8	19.6
35	29.4	21.5
40	32.8	23.1
45	36.1	24.5
50	39.2	25.7
55	42.1	26.7
60	43.9	27.5
65	45.5	28.2

Thelma and Leroy felt that a savings account would be a good investment for them, and so they calculated the appropriate discount factors: 18 for the first period, 16.8 for the second, and 9.7 for the third. The last two factors fell between the year designations in table 7-3 and so were interpolated. For example, the second period ends in forty-three years, three-fifths of the way between forty and forty-five. Three-fifths of the difference between 32.8 and 36.1, the factors for forty and forty-five years respectively, is 2. So the factor for forty-three years would be 34.8. The factor for twenty years (18.0) is then subtracted from the interpolated factor to arrive at 16.8 for the second period.

The Jacksons multiplied these factors by their net income needs for each period and totaled the results to get a total discounted income need of $41,540. Notice that the difference between investing the proceeds (step 8) and not investing the proceeds (step 7) is $6260. The Jacksons can save premiums by purchasing $6260 less insurance, but they can satisfy the same needs by investing the proceeds from the insurance they do buy in a savings account.

9 *Total Monetary Needs. Add the results from steps 1, 2, 3, 4, and 8 to determine your family's total monetary needs.*
   The Jacksons' total monetary needs are $67,065.

10 *Total Investment Assets. Determine what investment assets may be used to help alleviate your family's needs.* These assets include all monetary assets and real estate (non-income), as shown on your balance sheet.
   The Jacksons have $900 in a savings account that can be used to cover the family's needs.

11 *Your Life Insurance Needs. Subtract your family's monetary assets (step 10) from your family's total monetary needs (step 9).* The result indicates the amount of insurance you should own.
   The Jacksons need $66,165 worth of life insurance.

Decreasing Needs and Increasing Benefits

In designing an insurance program, it is helpful to understand how needs change during your lifetime. With time, your total insurance needs decrease, largely because your beneficiary has an increasingly shorter life expectancy and living expenses are by far the largest needs. When your spouse dies or your dependents reach adulthood, their living expense needs end. Although, in the aggregate, needs seem to decrease in a uniform manner, individual needs do not. Funeral and administrative expenses as well as federal and state estate taxes increase as your estate grows larger. Liabilities (large purchases involving debts) usually come at the middle of one's life and can be expected to decrease. The need for a contingency fund remains constant because it is a need that occurs at death. However, the size of the fund needed may increase slightly as your standard of living increases. College education funds represent needs that have a fixed lifetime. A child's education fund will be needed only when he reaches college. Such a need tends to remain constant for a fixed period of time, and then disappears entirely. Of course, providing a college education may not be among your goals, or your child may help provide it for himself through his own earnings.

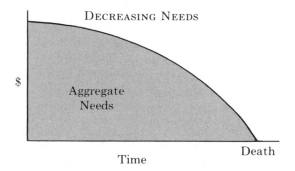

Whereas, over all, needs decrease, assets increase. If your monetary assets are invested in savings accounts, mutual funds, real estate, or common stock, they should grow. If you add to these investments in order to meet specific goals, this additional investment will make your total investments become larger.

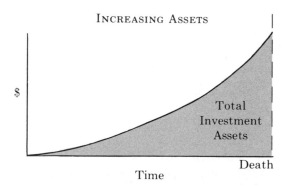

The total Social Security benefits you can expect decline as the years pass. The earlier you die the greater the total amount your family will receive from Social Security. However, once your youngest child reaches his eighteenth birthday, your widow receives nothing from Social Security until she reaches age sixty.

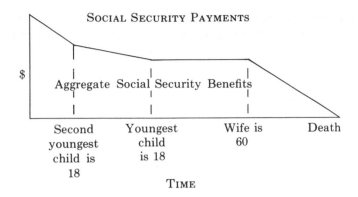

SOCIAL SECURITY PAYMENTS

Aggregate Social Security Benefits

Second youngest child is 18 | Youngest child is 18 | Wife is 60 | Death

TIME

Although your aggregate living needs decrease over time, the resources available to fulfill them (i.e., assets and Social Security) eventually become large enough to cover them and continue to grow after that.

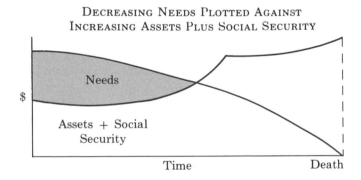

DECREASING NEEDS PLOTTED AGAINST
INCREASING ASSETS PLUS SOCIAL SECURITY

Needs

Assets + Social
Security

Time   Death

Life insurance is most important while your needs exceed your assets. The pattern of the difference between these two factors over the years shows the need for life insurance first increasing and then decreasing.

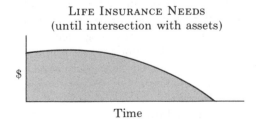

LIFE INSURANCE NEEDS
(until intersection with assets)

Time

Life insurance needs can be reduced in three ways. If you reduce your family's expected standard of living, your life insurance requirements are lowered. If you devote more money to investments, your assets become larger and come closer to covering your needs. If you can make your investments earn a higher yield, your assets rise more sharply.

Your life insurance program should be reevaluated (by means of the eleven-step procedure) every five years. You may be paying premiums on insurance you no longer need. This money could be used for living expenses and investments. Or, your needs may have increased since you last bought insurance, and financial disaster could strike your family if you died.

LIFE INSURANCE POLICIES

There are hundreds of different life insurance policies. But they vary primarily in only five areas: policy period, premium, face amount, savings, and protection.

The policy period may be for a specific number of years or for the rest of your life. If you choose a policy period that ends before age sixty-five, you should consider renewability provisions. For example, if you purchase a five-year renewable term insurance policy (pp. 137–139), you can renew the policy at the end of five years without showing proof of insurability. Although this costs a few dollars more each year in premiums, it assures you that, if you suffer some accident or illness that renders you uninsurable, you can still protect your family.

Premiums may be paid for the duration of the policy or for shorter periods. They may be paid annually in equal amounts (level premiums) or in decreasing or increasing amounts. The size of the premium depends on the other four policy variables (period, face amount, savings, and protection) and on your age and health.

Over the life of the policy, the face amount payable at death may increase, decrease, or remain constant.

The savings pattern in a cash-value insurance policy (pp. 140–42) represents the cash from the premium that is not used to buy insurance but is stored by the insurance company as a reserve. It may increase at varying rates over the life of the policy. A term insurance policy, however, provides only protection and does not contain any savings element. This protection may increase, decrease, or remain constant.

The protection pattern is merely the reciprocal of the savings pattern. Assuming the face amount of the policy remains constant, the protection element decreases, as the savings element increases. When premiums are first paid on cash-value policies, most of the money is used to provide protection (the death benefits). As the years go by, more and more of your annual premium goes to building up a reserve (the savings element).

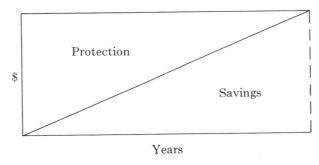

PROTECTION AND SAVINGS IN A
CASH-VALUE POLICY

Face Amount

Protection

$

Savings

Years

Figure 7-3 (p. 138) shows how these variables change depending on the type of policy.

Term Insurance

Term insurance is pure insurance issued for a set period of time. You can purchase term insurance to cover yourself through age 70 or, in some cases, age 100. Because term insurance has no savings element or cash value, it requires the smallest cash premiums. The insurance company will pay money only if you die, and then that money is received by your beneficiary. Since relatively few people die before most term policies terminate (age 65), the insurance company will experience a very low level of losses. Term insurance follows the same principle as auto, property, and health insurance and pays only if there is a loss.

renewable term insurance There are two types of renewable term insurance. One can be renewed every year; the other can be renewed every five, ten, fifteen, or twenty years.

Annual renewable term insurance offers pure protection for periods of one year. If you purchase an annual term policy with a guaranteed renewable feature, you may renew the policy each year, even though your health may have rendered you uninsurable. At each renewal date you can lower the level of coverage or keep it the same. You cannot raise it without demonstrating to the insurance company that you are insurable. The premium per $1000 worth of coverage will increase each year as you get older. If you reduce your total coverage level, the premium may be the same or less, even though the cost per $1000 has risen. Normally the annual premium rises very slowly in the early years and then quite rapidly as you near age 65. Most term policies stop coverage at age 65 or 70, but some go on even to age 100. Figure 7-4 (p. 139) shows

$20,000 Policy	Period	Annual Premiums At Age				Savings and Protection	Remarks
		25	35	45	55		
Level term	Any number of years but seldom past age 70	$88	$106	$185	$398 (5 year term[a])	All protection	True insurance; premiums increased at renewal
Decreasing term	Any number of years but seldom past age 70	$82	$98	$189	Cannot be purchased (20 year term[b])	All protection	Level of insurance decreases; premiums remain level
Straight life	Whole life	$262	$368	$545	$828	Protection and savings	Half investment, half insurance; cash-value build-up; premiums remain level
20-payment life	Whole life	$537[c]	$648	$814	$1056	Medium protection and high savings	Premiums paid within 20 year; cash-value rises rapidly; premiums remain level
Life-paid up-at-65	Whole life	$334[c]	$486	$814	$1750	Medium protection and medium savings	Premiums paid before retirement; cash value rises rapidly; premiums remain level
Year (20) endowment	20 years	$914[c]	$930	$989	$1141	Little protection and rapid savings accumulation	Best investment but worst protection for premium dollar; premiums remain level

NOTE: Rates quoted from Equitable Life Insurance Co. of Iowa.

[a]Such policies are usually guaranteed renewable to age sixty-five or seventy.
[b]Premium paid only for the first sixteen years.
[c]A participating policy. Dividends have been subtracted for the annual premiums to make the policy comparable.

Fig. 7-3.
Comparison of life insurance policies

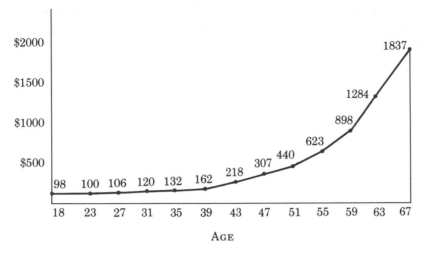

Fig. 7-4.
Annual
$50,000 worth of
annual renewable
term coverage

NOTE: Rates from Jackson National Life Insurance Company.

how the cost of annual renewable term insurance increases over time. Its prime advantages are that it requires a small cash outlay and that it is flexible. However, if you will need insurance beyond age 65 or 70, it may not be appropriate.

Five-, ten-, fifteen-, and twenty-year renewable term resembles annual renewable term except that the coverage stays level for longer periods between renewal dates. The premiums stay level during these periods as well, but this usually represents no real advantage. The level premium on a five-year renewable policy, for instance, is simply the average of the five separate annual renewable rates for that five-year period. Therefore, in the first half you would be paying more for five-year renewal than you would for annual renewable term, and in the last half you would be paying less.

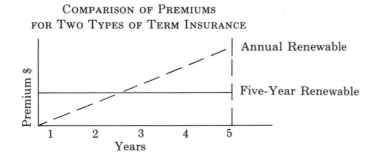

If you might cancel a term policy before the term period is over, it is better to buy annual renewable term.

level term to age sixty-five   This type of insurance offers protection at the same premium year in and year out. It provides the longest term of unrenewed protection of any term policy. The premiums are higher than those of renewable term policies in the early years, but lower in the later years. Most corporation group life insurance plans utilize this form of insurance.

decreasing term insurance   *Uniform decreasing term insurance* provides coverage that decreases by the same dollar amount each year the policy is in force. Therefore, if you purchase a $20,000 decreasing term policy for twenty years, the coverage level would drop $1000 each year ($20,000 ÷ 20). *Mortgage term insurance* decreases in uneven dollar amounts, which keep pace with the reduction of the principal balance due on a mortgage loan. Since in the early years of a home mortgage a large portion of each mortgage payment goes to pay interest, reduction in the amount of principal due on the loan is slight, and the reduction in coverage of your mortgage term insurance is correspondingly slight. In the later years, the principal balance is reduced quickly because most of the interest has been paid, and your mortgage term insurance coverage decreases equally quickly. (Chapter 12 will explain the home mortgage in greater detail.) If you expect your needs to decrease less in the early years of the term (perhaps while your family is growing up) than in the later years (after your children leave home), decreasing mortgage term might make sense.

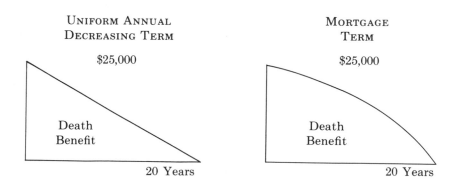

Cash-Value Insurance

This type of insurance has a savings element and is issued for a set period of time or for life. This savings element, or cash value, is not refunded when you die; it is included in the face amount benefits payable to your beneficiary. He receives only the face amount of the policy, no matter what the level of cash value is.

A cash-value policy is nothing more than a decreasing term policy and a savings plan put together. (The investment aspects of cash-value insurance will be discussed in chapter 15.) As your investment increases, your protection decreases. Both the savings element gain and protection loss, however, are so timed that the face amount remains the same.

straight, ordinary, and whole life   Straight, ordinary, and whole life are different names for the same policy. Premiums are the same each year and continue for life, or until you cash in the policy. It has the smallest cash-value accumulation for your premium dollar. Hence, it offers more protection for the same amount of premium. The total premiums paid always exceed the cash value. This policy is the least desirable from a strict investment viewpoint because your return (i.e., cash value) is less than your cost. However, the lower premiums, relative to other cash-value policies, make this coverage the most popular of its type.

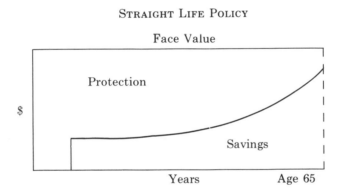

STRAIGHT LIFE POLICY

Face Value

Protection

$

Savings

Years   Age 65

limited payment life   This type of insurance is like straight life, except that it becomes paid up within ten to twenty years and no more money is required to keep it in force. The shorter the premium period, the greater each premium payment is. However, the shorter the premium period, the faster the cash-value build-up. For younger people, twenty-payment life yields a guaranteed cash value at age sixty-five that exceeds total premiums paid. This type of policy enables the policyholder to meet the cost of the insurance during his income-producing years. Life-paid-up-at-sixty-five is another example of this type of insurance.

endowment   These are generally designed for those who wish to build up a significant investment, while obtaining a certain amount of insurance protection. Endowment policies build up cash value at such a rate that at maturity there is no term insurance protection left. The death benefit is entirely covered by the cash paid in.

ENDOWMENT POLICY

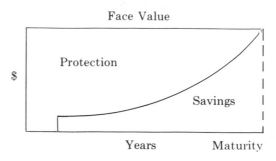

The maturity term of the policy is equal to the premium paying period. Policies are written to mature in ten, twenty, or thirty years, or at age sixty, sixty-five, seventy, and so on. Your guaranteed cash value will exceed your total paid-in premiums if you purchase the policy at a young enough age. Since these policies are written for terms as short as ten years, you can use them to accumulate funds for fairly short-term goals, provided you can meet the higher annual premiums.

Retirement endowment policies are designed to accumulate funds for retirement income. They are a special form of endowment policy in that you continue to pay premiums until age sixty-five—beyond the point at which the cash value reaches the face amount, which is usually at fifty-five. In the event of death between the ages of fifty-five and sixty-five, the beneficiary receives the face amount plus the excess cash value. Thus, after fifty-five all of your premium goes toward the investment portion of your policy. This type of policy yields an average of $10 monthly retirement income for each $1000 face amount. Or you may take the lump sum at age sixty-five.

RETIREMENT ENDOWMENT POLICY

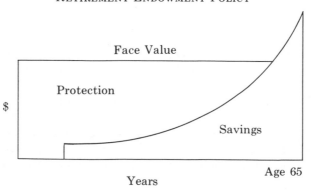

The Contract Itself

Most life insurance contracts contain eight clauses. Each of them involves decisions that determine the effectiveness of your policy in accomplishing your goals. You must decide not only how much insurance you need but also who is to receive the benefits upon your death; how the benefits are to be paid (lump-sum, installments, and so on); whether to borrow on your policy; whether to pay your premiums annually, semiannually, or monthly; how to receive dividends from your policy; how to provide for cancellation of your policy and still receive your cash value; how to provide for reinstatement of your policy's five variables (period, premium, face amount, savings—if any—and protection) if you fail to pay the premium and policy coverage lapses; and how to change your policy from cash value to term or vice versa.

beneficiary clause   This clause provides for two classes of beneficiaries: the primary beneficiary and the contingent beneficiaries. The primary beneficiary is the person you designate to receive your policy death benefits. If he dies before the benefits have been completely distributed, the remainder of your policy's benefits will go to the contingent beneficiaries you name in the policy. For example, you may choose your wife as your primary beneficiary and, in the event of her death, your children as contingent beneficiaries.

settlement options   The insurance company allows you to choose how your policy's death benefits will be distributed to your beneficiaries or how the cash value of your policy will be distributed to yourself. If you surrender the cash value of your policy, you also have your choice of nonforfeiture options (p. 146). There are four ways in which the proceeds can be received. First, the benefits can be withdrawn in installments of any fixed amounts you choose until all the benefits are distributed or in equal installments over a specified period of time (installment option). Second, the beneficiary may leave the proceeds with the company and receive the interest on them annually, semiannually, quarterly, or monthly (interest option). Third, the benefits may be paid to the beneficiary for as long as he lives (life annuity option). Fourth, the benefits can be withdrawn in one lump sum (lump-sum option).

The last option offers the most flexibility because it makes it possible to consider settlement option alternatives not offered by the policy. One might put his benefits into an investment medium that earns a higher return (interest rate) than is offered by insurance companies. Used this way, the option also offers the greatest opportunity to reduce insurance costs because the initial amount of benefits needed, or the policy's face amount, can be lowered. For example, a $100,000 policy might earn $3000 interest a year at 3 percent. However, that same $3000 can be gained from only a $60,000 investment in a savings account at 5 percent.

There is one serious disadvantage to the lump-sum settlement option. Persons who receive large sums of money are often easily tempted to overspend and dissipate the funds within a few years. This defeats a primary purpose of life insurance—to provide financial security for one's family long after one's death. To avoid this problem, you may want to arrange with your banker and lawyer, before your death, to set up a trust to protect the funds from your life insurance and invest them at a reasonably high yield. (Chapter 21 gives more information on trusts.)

Of course, monthly-income type settlements (options 1–3) also prevent dissipation of life insurance proceeds. The insurance company will make regular payments in interest, in principal, or both and sometimes also in dividends. (Life annuities will be discussed in chapter 15 when we consider life insurance strictly as an investment.)

The settlement options can be changed at will. However, if an option other than lump-sum withdrawal is chosen by the insured before his death, it cannot be changed by the beneficiary, unless an option was signed by the insured leaving complete discretion to the beneficiary.

loan clause   This clause details those provisions under which you can borrow from your cash-value policy, in which you have built up an equity. Your loan limit at any one time is the amount of cash value plus dividends and interest that your policy has accumulated up to that time. When you borrow, the face amount of the policy (your death benefit) is reduced by the amount of the loan during the period for which the money is borrowed. When the money is repaid, your policy returns to full force. There are advantages to borrowing from your policy if you need to borrow: the interest rates are often lower than those available from other financial institutions, since you are really borrowing your own money; no fees or carrying charges are imposed; and you may repay the loan in full whenever you can.

premium payment clause   This clause arranges for premium payments to be made on an annual, semiannual, or some other basis. The insurance company charges an additional administration fee if the premium is paid other than annually. This fee may be as much as 16 percent of the annual premium. If you pay your premiums annually rather than monthly or quarterly, you can obtain significant cost savings on your insurance.

dividend clause   This clause provides for the distribution of dividends, the monetary rewards paid to an insurance policyholder at the end of the year. They mean different things depending on whether they are issued by mutual companies or stock companies. Mutual companies are nonprofit organizations established for the benefit of the policyholders, who are the owners. Any time a mutual company anticipates more deaths than actually occur and consequently charges a higher premium than necessary, it passes this saving on to the policyholders as a dividend. A mutual company dividend, then, is a refund of premium.

A stock company pays dividends to its shareholders (not policyholders) as a return on their investments. The shareholders are the owners of the company; they may or may not be policyholders. In recent years, stock companies have begun to offer participating policies (par policies), which compete with mutual policies by offering a dividend to their policyholders. This dividend, like a mutual company's dividend, is a refund of premium. However, these stock company par policy dividends are made available by intentionally charging a higher premium than necessary so that there will be something left at the end of the year to return to the policyholders. In addition to this premium refund, stock companies continue to pay true dividends to their stockholders.

The important thing to consider in buying a life insurance policy is not whether the company you are buying from is mutual or stock nor whether there are dividends but rather what the policy offers and what it actually costs. To find this cost, compare the net prices (premiums minus dividend, if there is one) offered by the companies you are considering. Investigate a number of companies before you decide because prices of various policies differ significantly from company to company, depending on the company's management skill, profit mark-up, preferred-risk selection criteria, and so forth.

There are six dividend options from which you must choose if you decide to buy a participating policy from a mutual or stock company. First, you can take the dividends in the form of a check to do with as you please. Second, you can apply the dividends to premium payments (i.e., partially pay your premiums with your dividends). Third, you can leave the dividend with the insurance company, as you leave money in a bank, to accumulate interest at 3 or 4 percent. Fourth, you can buy paid-up additions, which are nothing more than prepaid cash-value insurance. In other words, each dividend can be used to purchase additional coverage. The face amount of a paid-up addition depends on the age of the policyholder, the duration of the additional coverage, and the cost charged by the company. The higher the cost, the lower the amount of protection one dividend can buy. The main advantage of paid-up additions is that they are issued without evidence of insurability. The main disadvantage is that, since they are single-premium policies (paid before coverage starts), they are the most expensive form of life insurance. Fifth, you can buy term additions, which provide additional term insurance coverage, with your dividends. Unlike paid-up additions, term additions have no cash value, and therefore each dividend dollar buys protection only, not savings. You can get much more protection for your dividend dollar through term additions than through paid-up additions. Sixth, you can use some of your dividend dollars to buy term insurance and leave the rest to accumulate interest with the insurance company.

nonforfeiture clause This clause declares what the insurance company must do if you default on your policy. Only cash-value policies contain such a clause. There are three nonforfeiture options for you to consider. First, you can withdraw the cash value of your policy (the cash surrender value). Second, you can trade your policy's cash surrender value for a fully paid-up policy of the same duration as your previous policy. However, because its cash value in no way equals the sum of the annual premiums you would have to pay to keep the policy in force for the rest of your life, the face amount of the policy will be less than that of your previous policy. The face amount will be further reduced because the company will charge you the current rate, not the rate at which you purchased your first policy. Third, you can trade your policy's cash surrender value for a fully paid-up term policy with a shorter duration than your previous policy but with the same face amount.

If you do not choose a specific nonforfeiture option, your policy, if discontinued, will automatically be transferred to a term policy (third option). The details and current status of these options are printed in tables on the policy.

reinstatement clause This clause gives the policyholder who has discontinued his policy the opportunity to put it in force again. He may do this if he has not already redeemed the policy's cash surrender value; if he pays all unpaid premiums, plus accumulated interest, in cash; if he still qualifies for insurance protection; and if he requests reinstatement within a specified time after his policy has been discontinued.

change of policy clause This clause may be provided in both cash-value and term policies. It enables the policyholder to make changes in his policy after he buys it. For example, if you have a straight-life policy and wish to change it to a twenty-payment life policy, you are moving to a coverage that has a higher annual price since the total premium payments are spread over only twenty years instead of your whole life, which may be very much longer. In this case the insurance company would charge you either the difference in cash values between the two policies plus a carrying charge or the difference in back premiums plus interest. When converting a term policy to a cash-value policy, no evidence of insurability need be shown. However, when changing from a higher-priced policy to a lower-priced one, evidence of insurability is normally required.

HOW LIFE INSURANCE RATES ARE DETERMINED

Life insurance premiums are based on mortality tables—sets of statistics showing how many people die at various ages. Insurance companies use these tables to determine how much total insurance coverage will be needed and how much money they have to charge each policyholder in order to have enough income to cover their needs.

For example, according to mortality tables, at age forty there will be 353 deaths for every 100,000 people. If each of these 353 people carried $20,000 life insurance coverage, the insurance companies would need $7,060,000 to meet all the required payments. In order to collect $7,060,000, the companies must charge each of the 100,000 people a premium of $70.60 plus charges for administration cost, commissions, and profit (or dividends). If the policyholder is over forty, the probability of death increases and the total amount of money needed increases. If the policyholder is younger, the opposite is true.

Always shop for rates before buying a life insurance policy. The rate for a given type of policy can vary as much as 100 percent between the highest and lowest premium. Check with the agents of several major companies, as well as with several independent agents, before making your decision. Sometimes a company will offer an unusually low rate on a certain type of policy in the hope of selling you a different policy or obtaining further business from you.

Most companies realize that some of their expenses do not vary in direct proportion to the amount of benefits carried. As their coverages increase, their costs do not. Therefore, they have started to pass this savings on to the policyholder by way of quantity discounts (i.e., the more you buy, the less the cost per $1000 worth of insurance). Discounts can also be realized through the purchase of group policies because in this situation insurance companies save on administrative expenses and can better predict their risk exposure.

CONCLUSION

Many people buy life insurance because they think it is the thing to do. They feel they must have life insurance, even though there may be no one to protect. Many purchase life insurance in response to their emotional needs—not the financial needs of the individuals who will receive the actual benefits. Remember that your plans should include only those who will be financially disadvantaged when you die. Often the opposite approach is taken: "Why should I leave any money behind, if it is not going to do me any good?" This attitude is selfish and inappropriate when determining one's life insurance needs.

It is important to realize that, no matter what financial hardship results from your death, you are not going to be the one to experience it. Unlike property, liability, and health insurance, life insurance provides financial protection solely for someone other than yourself.

If you are now in the market for life insurance or think you may be soon, you should proceed carefully through these five steps.

1. Keep your emotions under control.
2. Buy the right amount of insurance. If you buy too much, you will limit your family's current purchasing power. If you buy too little, you will leave them inadequately protected. Use the eleven-step procedure to determine your needs.
3. Consider choosing the lump-sum settlement option. You can set up a trust to receive the amount and have it invested at a higher rate of return than the insurance policy will provide, thus reducing the face amount you have to purchase.
4. Tailor the policy period, premium pattern, face amount, savings, and protection to fit your needs.
5. Be sure you understand all clauses and options. This understanding will enable you to choose what is right for you.

VOCABULARY

beneficiary
cash surrender value
cash-value insurance
endowment policy
face amount
inflation
life expectancy
limited payment policy

nonforfeiture option
nonparticipating policy
paid-up addition
participating policy
settlement option
straight life policy
term insurance

QUESTIONS

1. Discuss the methods by which you can reduce your needs for life insurance coverage. Given your situation, which methods make the most sense?
2. Bill has a life insurance policy for a stated face amount of $10,000. Currently, it has $3000 in accumulated cash value. How much can Bill borrow from his policy? If Bill borrows the maximum from his policy, how much insurance will remain in force?
3. Jim and Louise (both age thirty) determined that, if Jim died today, Louise and their daughter would need $6000 a year to live on in addition to what Louise would receive from Social Security. After the daughter leaves home at age twenty-two, ten years from now, Louise's net needs are projected to be $4000 a year until her expected death at age eighty-five. If Louise could achieve a 3 percent rate of growth after taxes and inflation, by investing the benefits from Jim's life insurance, how much life insurance would the family need to buy today? (Assume that their present investments are sufficient to pay funeral, administrative, and estate expenses; resolve all debts; provide a contingency fund; and send their daughter to college.)
4. Which type of term insurance is the most flexible? Why?

5. What are the major advantages of the lump-sum settlement option? What are the disadvantages?
6. Everyone needs life insurance. From what you have learned in this chapter, do you agree or disagree? Why?
7. "Life insurance is love." Does this advertising slogan help the buyer determine how much life insurance he needs?

CASE PROBLEM

Jason and Heather Bell were married during their senior year in college. Soon after they graduated, a life insurance salesman talked with them about buying a life insurance policy. He emphasized their need for permanent protection. He said that if Jason bought a $10,000 endowment policy and paid $200 in level premiums every year for forty years, he could then cash in his policy for $8000 (40 × $200). The salesman said that the policy would actually cost Jason nothing.

A friend of the Bells, who was also in the life insurance business, told them they could buy $10,000 worth of term coverage for $20 the first year. The premium would increase each year they held the policy, and forty years from now the premium would be $100. The average premium over the forty years would be $60. Jason figured that if each year he invested at 5 percent the $140 difference between the average term premium and the endowment premium, over the forty years his investment would grow to $16,800.

Under what circumstances might it be more appropriate for Jason to buy the endowment policy? Under what circumstances might it be more advantageous to buy the term insurance? Why is there such a difference in the return from these two investment alternatives?

RECOMMENDED READING

The Consumers Union Report on Life Insurance, by the editors of Consumer Reports. Mount Vernon, New York: Consumers Union, 1967.

> This book offers a method for determining one's life insurance needs, and explains the agent/customer role and the advantages and disadvantages of the various policies.

Institute of Life Insurance. *Life Insurance Fact Book.* New York: Institute of Life Insurance, 1971. Published annually.

> This paperback is filled with statistics regarding the life insurance industry.

Smith, Carlton; Pratt, Richard P; and editors of *Time-Life. The Time-Life Book of Family Finance.* New York: Time-Life Books, 1969.

> The chapter on life insurance compares term insurance with cash-value insurance.

CHUCK AND
NANCY ANDERSON

INSURING CHUCK'S LIFE

Chuck and Nancy have a whole life policy with a face amount of $20,000 payable to Nancy upon Chuck's death. The dividends from the whole life policy are applied to the purchase of paid-up additions. The Andersons also have a mortgage term policy to cover the amount of the mortgage payments due on their home if Chuck dies before the mortgage is paid off. The face amount of this term policy decreases each year by the amount that the total balance due on their mortgage has decreased.

The Andersons have total benefits of $34,500 that could be received now. The whole life policy costs them $360 a year in premiums; the mortgage term costs $65 a year; and the paid-up additions cost $145 in dividends from the whole life policy. The annual total amount the Andersons are paying for life insurance is $570.

Now that his children are growing up, Chuck feels that he needs more life insurance. Even with Nancy working he figures that, if he dies, his family will need $9000 a year in addition to Nancy's earnings until his son graduates from college fourteen years from now. At that time, his wife and daughter would need only $7000 a year in addition to what Nancy could earn. When his daughter graduates, Nancy alone could get by on a $5000 yearly addition to her earnings in today's dollars, until she died, approximately fifty years from now. Chuck's average earnings (credited for Social Security purposes) have been $6600 a year. He also wishes to provide for a four-year state college education for each of his children. Since Chuck is considering buying annual renewable term insurance, he found out that for a male age thirty-five such a policy costs $4 per $1000 worth of coverage for the first year, whereas whole life costs $18 per $1000.

QUESTIONS

1. How much life insurance does Chuck need? Use the eleven-step procedure and the balance sheet for Chuck and Nancy (chapter 2). Assume that Chuck has no present coverage and that Nancy would invest the proceeds from his life insurance in a 5 percent savings account.
2. If Chuck buys term insurance, how much will it cost him the first year to cover his family's needs? How much will it cost him the first year if he buys whole life? Under what circumstances would term be more appropriate than whole life? Under what circumstances would whole life be more appropriate than term? Under what circumstances might Chuck want to surrender his present whole life policy and buy only term insurance?

III. GETTING THE MOST OUT OF YOUR INCOME

In chapters 3 through 7 you learned how to protect your home, property, health, income-producing ability, and life from many common perils. You learned how to do this with minimum cost and without duplicating your insurance coverage.

The strategy for getting the most out of your income will be dealt with in chapters 8 through 12. The first aspect of this strategy is to direct your income to cover your expenses. This problem may be solved by the budgeting techniques discussed in chapter 8. The second aspect of this strategy is to avoid such unnecessary drains on your income as overpaid income taxes, excessive consumer credit costs, an improperly made decision to rent or buy, or an improperly purchased home. Chapters 9 through 12 discuss these and similar problems. You will learn how to minimize your income taxes; how to analyze the costs, dangers, and benefits of credit; and when and how to buy a home. This strategy for getting the most out of your income should enable you to free more money for use in increasing your total income, the strategy discussed in unit four.

BUDGETING

Budgeting is simply allocating one's income to cover one's expenses. Some people realize that they need to budget when they cannot write a check to cover the price of something they want or need. For example, if you and your wife find a $200 dishwasher you want, but you have only $100 in the bank, you are forced either not to buy it or to buy it on credit and pay an interest cost of 18 percent a year. Some people do not realize that they need to budget until their lack of financial management frequently has more serious consequences: they often run out of money before the next paycheck comes, they cannot pay their bills and keep incurring new ones, or they are unable to save any money.

Budgeting requires that you set goals. When a budget provides a means for you to improve or maintain your life style in the ways you and your family select, it is worthwhile. In general, budgeting will help you achieve your goals by allowing you to consider all your spending alternatives within a single framework. Specifically, budgeting will help you save for the things you want (reducing the need for consumer credit) live within your income, and know where your money is going. Since it also involves a system of record keeping, it can help you keep an annual record of all tax deductions for income tax purposes.

If you recognize far enough in advance that you will need something, you can save money each month so that you can buy it when the time comes. Anyone who dreads trying to save should realize that when he buys something

on credit he is, in effect, enrolling in a forced savings plan. Each month, instead of investing the amount of his payment and *earning* interest on it, he is giving that money to his creditor and *paying* interest. The price of buying on credit is the monetary difference between the interest you would receive from a savings account and the interest you must pay for using credit.

You probably think a lot about vacations because you are forced to plan for them. Your school tells you months in advance when vacations begin and end. When you begin a full-time job, you probably are required to schedule your vacation months ahead. By planning for a vacation, you prepare to get the most out of it so that when it finally comes you are ready for it. This same technique of planning for things in advance can make you financially prepared to enjoy them. It gives you something to look forward to, some reason for saving money or waiting until you can get the best.

Budgeting can mean a lot to couples who frequently accuse each other of spending too much money. It enables you to spend money without guilt. By deciding jointly how much money to spend on what before the money is spent, you can make planned purchases knowing that your spouse agrees with your spending. Budgeting, then, can be a means of keeping peace in the family by uniting family members to achieve pre-planned and selected goals. This is all the reason most families need to give budgeting a try.

Budgeting, as described in this chapter, is meant to be a tool for you to use to get what you want with money. It can help you plan expenditures, record them, and control them. If it becomes merely tedious book-keeping, then it is not serving its purpose.

HOW TO SET UP A SUCCESSFUL BUDGET: THE PLANNING STAGE

It is not enough merely to decide to try budgeting. To develop a good, workable budget requires careful planning.

The Objectives of Budgeting

Budgeting has two objectives, both of which must be accomplished if a budget is to be successful. The first objective is to implement a system of disciplined spending. Instead of spending money each month until the checkbook balance reads zero, you and your family must learn to spend each month only as much as is allotted for various expense categories. For example, if the money allotted for entertainment has been used up, none of the extra $100 in the checkbook can be spent on entertainment since that money has been allotted for something else (perhaps, the insurance premium that is due next month).

The second objective is to reduce the amount of money wasted through needless expenditures in each budgeted expense category. This objective can be reached only after the first objective has been mastered. Do not try to do everything at once. First become comfortable with living on a budget. Then try to reduce expenditures in the various budget areas.

Step I: Becoming Aware of Expenditure Patterns

The first step in planning a successful budget is to become aware of how your money has been spent in the past and how it is being spent now. Check your income statement (chapter 2) for past expenditures. To get an up-to-date, detailed breakdown of current expenditures, keep a trial budget. We suggest you decide on a manageable budget period of, perhaps, a month during which to study your family's spending habits. Then, for one period simply record what you and your family are doing with the money you receive. Keep a pad of paper and a pencil in a place where it will be convenient for every member of the family to jot down daily how much he spent that day and what he bought. Round the amounts to the nearest dollar and keep a running total for each day. Of course, if you spend small amounts daily (such as 25¢ for coffee), add these together on a weekly basis and round the total amount. Do not attempt at this time to separate expenses into categories.

Step II: The Planning Session

During the planning session you and your family will meet to decide what you want to spend your money on and set priorities for your goals. Each family member should be involved in giving direction to your family's life. If all have a say in the goals represented by the budget, everyone will probably try to help make the system work.

Before the actual meeting, you must find out what your average income will be for the next year and decide on appropriate expense categories for your budget. After the meeting during which family members make known their goals, you can determine the monthly cost of reaching these goals. Then you can also determine your fixed and variable expenses and set further priorities.

sources of income for the coming year Let us assume that you have chosen to use a month as the budget period. To help yourself forecast your average income over the next year, design a worksheet like that shown in figure 8-1 (p. 156), which has been filled out for a ficitious young couple, Alexander and Karen.

First, estimate your annual after-tax income in each of the categories. Enter the amount of your after-tax paycheck in the appropriate salary category for each month in the next year. Then divide the annual total for each category by twelve to get the average estimated income per month. Total the monthly figures to get the amount that is to be distributed for monthly expenditures (your total average monthly expenditures

NAME(S) *Alexander and Karen*

DATE *December 1972*

FORECASTING INCOME

Source	Jan.	Feb.	Mar.	Apr.	May	June	July	Aug.	Sept.	Oct.	Nov.	Dec.	Estimated Twelve-Month Total	Average Per Month	Actual Year's Income
Husband's take-home wages or salary	675	665	705	675	665	705	675	665	705	665	675	665	$7980	$665	
Wife's take-home wages or salary															
Bonuses or commissions												520	520	43⅓	
Interest	10			10			10			10			40	3⅓	
Dividends			40			40			40			40	160	13⅓	
Rents															
Annuities, pensions															
Other															
TOTAL	675	665	705	675	665	705	675	665	695	675	675	1225	$8700	$725	

Fig. 8-1.
Sample worksheet for estimating next year's income

allowed), and enter that figure in the box at the bottom of the "average per month" column. It is a useful practice to make forecasted entries in pencil and then enter them in ink as they become actual. Then, at the end of the year, you can total the year's actual income in the last column.

From your income you will need to set aside a minimum cash reserve of probably about $300. This checkbook working capital can be used to allow for intermediate fluctuations in expenses such as will occur with large lump-sum fixed expenses that come due before enough money has been accumulated to cover them.

grouping expenses   It is easier to budget and plan your expenditures if you group expenses. Break down your recorded expenditures for the past budget period into several general categories such as food, clothing care, personal grooming, entertainment, transportation, and shelter. Examples of expense groupings compiled from several successful budgets are given in figure 8-2 (p. 158). You may want to make some changes such as having a separate category for vacations, or putting all clothing-related expenses into one classification that includes laundry and dry cleaning expenses. Of course, some categories may not pertain to you at all. Tax, for example, should be included only if you usually pay more than is withheld from your paycheck. Then this category will help you plan for the excess amount.

Note that the suggested classifications also include a savings and investment category. If you do not budget for savings and actually deposit the amounts budgeted, you probably will find it difficult to save for things you want such as a new rug or your children's college educations. Instead, you may have to do without or borrow the money at 18 percent and make interest payments that cut into what you can spend on other things.

Note also the "mad money" category. This is designed to keep your family from resenting your budget scheme. It minimizes the chances that the budget will become too restrictive. Every member of the family should have a certain amount of money he can spend on impulse or save for something special without having to account for it.

No matter how you classify your expenses, you should observe a few logical rules.

1. Keep similar expenses in the same category.
2. Set up enough different categories so that you have a meaningful record of your expenses. Do not lump too many different expenses into catchall categories.
3. Keep the number of categories small enough to make bookkeeping simple.

Housing
  Rent
  Mortgage payments
  Repairs and improvements
  Property insurance
  Property taxes

Utilities
  Gas and electricity
  Waste disposal
  Water
  Telephone

Food
  All food items
  Meals taken out
  Pet food

Recreation and Entertainment
  Admissions
  Games and hobbies
  Club dues
  Alcoholic beverages
  Tobacco
  Photographic supplies
  Musical supplies
  Sporting goods
  Vacations

Automobile and Transportation
  Purchase or installment
    payments
  Gas and oil
  Insurance and license fees
  Repairs, parking, and tolls
  Rental, taxi, and bus fare

Medical
  Insurance
  Drugs and medicines
  Hospital bills

Doctor bills
Dentist bills

Family Necessities
  Laundry and dry cleaning
  Toiletries and cosmetics
  Barber and hairdresser
  Postage and stationery
  Minor home furnishings

Clothing
  All clothing purchases
  Alterations
  Repairs (shoes and so on)

Personal Improvement
  Books
  Magazines and newspapers
  Tuition and course fees

Savings and Investment

Gifts

Church and Charity

Life Insurance

Outlays for Fixed Assets
  Major purchases or installment
    payments on appliances,
    garden equipment, and
    furniture
  Repairs (appliance and
    television)

Taxes

Contingency
  Legal services
  Unspecified debt repayments
  Union dues

Mad Money

Fig. 8-2.
Suggested
budget expense
classifications

family meeting The first order of business should be to inform your family what they are currently spending their money on. Identify the areas and the totals. Do not be critical of how money was spent or chastise any member of the family for seemingly spendthrift ways. Simply inform. The second order of business should be to discuss goals—the areas in which each member would like to see money spent. Ask each family member to write on a slip of paper what he would like to see money spent on, how much, and when. Then ask them to number their goals in order of importance. (See chapter 1 for goal planning.) The third order of business should be to collect the slips of paper and transcribe each person's goals onto a goal forecasting sheet. Use the short-term goal sheet (fig. 8-3, p. 160) for goals that can be reached during the next twelve months. For long-term goals, use the long-term goal sheet (fig. 8-4, p. 161). In chapter 13 we will see how to use investment planning and monthly investment commitments to reach these goals.

goals   Divide the cost of each goal that can be reached within five years by the number of months you have in which to achieve it, and place the total monthly figure in your savings and investment category. (We are not yet ready to consider goals that will be reached after more than five years. For these we must take into account inflation, taxes, and investment yield, which will be dealt with in chapter 13.) Karen and Alex had to allocate $55 a month ($2000 ÷ 36) for the car they will want to buy three years from now and $33 ($2000 ÷ 60) for the European trip they expect to take in five years. To this $88 sum they added the $25 a month for short-term goals to arrive at a total of $113 they must allocate each month for the savings and investment category for next year (fig. 8-5, pp. 162–63).

expenses   Forecast the rest of your expenses by using your month-long expense record and your checkbook.

First, determine the cost of fixed expenses such as rent or mortgage, insurance premiums, and installment payments. Enter these amounts under the months when the expenses will be incurred. (See figure 8-5 for an example.) This breakdown will let you know when your major bills are due and will enable you to plan to pay them without having to borrow. Take careful note of the fixed expenses that will come due within the next few months. If you do not have a large enough cash reserve, temporarily cut back your spending in other categories to make sure you can meet these early obligations without borrowing.

Second, estimate amounts for the remaining expense and investment categories. If you wish to keep the same life style as in previous months (at least in some categories), look back over your past expenditures. From them you can estimate what amounts to enter in your budget plan. Do not become too involved in deciding exactly how many dollars to allocate to each category. After you use your budget for a couple of months, you can revise the amounts (especially for regular expenses such as food, laundry, and commuting) to reflect more closely your actual expenses.

Figure 8-6 (p. 164) shows approximately what portion of the total living expenses major categories are likely to require for a typical family of four. This may help you get some idea whether your estimates are grossly

NAME(S): _Alexander and Karen_

DATE: _December 1972_

FORECASTING SHORT-TERM GOALS

Goals	Jan.	Feb.	Mar.	Apr.	May	June	July	Aug.	Sept.	Oct.	Nov.	Dec.	Total	Average by Month
New rug										96			96	8
Ski trips	36	36											72	6
Build barbeque					84								84	7
New puppy					48								48	4
TOTAL	36	36			132					96			300	25

Fig. 8-3.
Sample forecast for short-term goals

FORECASTING LONG-TERM GOALS

Goals	Years From Now					Beyond 5 Years
	1	2	3	4	5	
European vacation					2000	
Summer home						10,000 (uncertain)
Replace car			2000			
Son's education						8000 (yr. 16)
TOTAL			2000		2000	18,000

Fig. 8-4.
Sample forecast for
long-term goals

over or under what might be expected under usual conditions. Of course, there may be variations that you should take into consideration because of differences not only in personal experience but also in family size.

Total each category for the twelve-month projection and divide by twelve to arrive at monthly allowable expense limits. Now total the monthly averages.

priorities   Can the total monthly average be accommodated by your average monthly income? If not, start making some priority decisions. Where can you make changes? What goals can be postponed? Let the family set some priorities. Do they want several magazines each month or more steak dinners? Do they want a camping trailer or more clothes? A long summer trip or weekend activities? An expensive new car or a compact? Because your income is limited, your family cannot have everything they want all at once. They must learn to use money to buy only those things they really want. Most of the decisions can be reached by family consensus, but the specific implementation of decisions regarding insurance and investments require knowledge and objectivity. The planning process will require sacrifices and compromises, but it is best to resolve these issues before the money is spent.

NAME(S) _Alexander and Karen_

DATE _December 1972_

FORECASTING

Expense Category	Fixed and Variable Subcategories	Jan.	Feb.
Housing	Rent, mortgage payments, insurance, and taxes	$160	$160
	Repairs and improvements		
Utilities		25	25
Food		110	110
Recreation and entertainment	General	25	25
	Vacation		
Clothing		50	50
Automobile	Purchase payments, insurance, and license fees		30
	Gas, oil, repairs, parking, tolls, and so on	45	45
Medical	Insurance		
	Doctor, dentist, drugs, and hospital	15	15
Family necessities		30	30
Personal improvement	Magazines and newspapers	12	12
	Books and tuition	20	
Savings and investment	For short-term and long-term goals	113	113
Gifts		5	5
Church and charity		20	20
Life insurance			
Taxes			
Contingency	Legal services, debt repayments, union dues	10	10
Outlays for fixed assets	Repairs	5	5
	Purchases and installments	15	15
Mad money		20	20
TOTAL BY MONTH		680	690

Fig. 8-5.
Sample forecast
of expenses

Mar.	Apr.	May	June	July	Aug.	Sept.	Oct.	Nov.	Dec.	Twelve-Month Total	Average by Month
$160	$160	$160	$160	$160	$160	$160	$160	$160	$160	$1920	$160
24	23	21	18	16	16	15	16	19	22	240	20
110	110	110	110	110	110	110	110	110	110	1320	110
25	25	25	25	25	10	25	25	25	40	300	25
					180					180	15
50	50	50	50	50	50	50	50	50	50	600	50
			150							180	15
45	45	45	45	45	45	45	45	45	45	540	45
paid by employer											
15	15	15	15	15	15	15	15	15	15	180	15
30	30	30	30	30	30	30	30	30	30	360	30
12	12	12	12	12	12	12	12	12	12	144	12
	20					20				60	5
113	113	113	113	113	113	113	113	113	113	1356	113
5	5	5	5	5	5	5	5	5	185	240	20
20	20	20	20	20	20	20	20	20	20	240	20
					240					240	20
covered by withholding											
10	10	10	10	10	10	10	10	10	10	120	10
5	5	5	5	5	5	5	5	5	5	60	5
15	15	15	15	15	15	15	15	15	15	180	15
20	20	20	20	20	20	20	20	20	20	240	20
659	678	656	653	801	1056	670	651	654	852	8700	725

Expense Category	Percentage
Housing and utilities	24–31
Food	25–32
Automobile and transportation	8–10
Medical	5–9
Clothing and family necessities	10–14

Fig. 8-6. Percentage of total living expenses for typical family of four

SOURCE: Adapted from *1971 Labor Statistics Handbook* (Bulletin 1705), U.S. Bureau of Labor Statistics.

HOW TO SET UP A SUCCESSFUL BUDGET: RECORDING EXPENDITURES

The success of a budget depends partly on how often each family member records his expenditures. Expenditures should be recorded often enough that none are forgotten, but not so often that the procedure becomes a nuisance. Perhaps recording expenditures could be done when the entire family is together. If each member sees other family members trying to make the budget work, he will be motivated to participate. Since most families are together at dinner time, it might be wise for everyone to record his expenditures for the day just before dinner. If the family tends to congregate in the kitchen, you might keep the budget book there. The idea is to make the recording function as automatic as possible.

A Recommended System

To make it easy to record expenses, the record-keeping system should be simple—with the budget categories easy to find and the arithmetic easy. Here is one system that meets these specifications.

1) Keep budget category sheets in a loose-leaf binder. Set aside plenty of pages for each category and mark each category section with a paper clip, tab, or colored sheet of paper to make it easy to find.
2) Use a bankbook type of entry system for each category. For example, if you spend $30 of the monthly $150 food allotment, enter the date of the expenditure, the item purchased, and the amount spent, and then subtract the amount ($30) from the previous balance ($150). Subtract the next food expenditure from the remaining balance ($120). This system lets you see how much money you have left in a category at any time.

Date	Item	Amount	Balance	Tax Check (✔)
1/2/73			$150	
1/5/73	groceries	$30	120	✔ Boy Scout picnic
1/8/73	lunch	5	115	

3.) In the last column put a check by expenses that qualify as tax deductions and therefore might help you determine your taxable income. If, for example, you bought the $30 worth of groceries for a Boy Scout picnic, you can deduct the expense as a charitable gift. To determine your total annual deductions, you need only consult the tax column of your budget sheets. (Chapter 9 will cover the expense categories that might have tax ramifications).

4.) To make the arithmetic quick and easy, round each expense entry to the nearest dollar.

Recording Transactions and Monthly Statements

If you make purchases on a charge account or with a credit card, it is better to record each transaction as you make it than to wait until the monthly statement arrives and enter all the purchases at one time. Although the latter method is easier, it may let you run over your budget while the former method lets you keep track of your expenses and control them before you have spent too much. Only for regular expenses such as gasoline, perhaps, can you safely use the monthly statement method.

When accounting for a cash loan in your budget, enter the loan repayments as an expense each month. Do not enter either the loan income or the initial purchase. In other words, you fit the monthly loan repayments (including interest)—not the actual purchase—into the appropriate budget category. Similarly, in accounting for the savings and investment category, enter an expense only when you actually spend money for a goal, not when you put money in a savings account or other investment. The savings and investment category should build up large surpluses that will be spent for major goals. As these goals are reached, subtract the amount from the accumulated surplus.

HOW TO SET UP A SUCCESSFUL BUDGET: CONTROLLING EXPENDITURES

At the end of the month when you try to see how well the budget has worked, remember that you want to make your family comfortable with the budget system. Remind yourself not to get upset if the money spent that month bears no resemblance to the amount you budgeted. Nothing will damage a budget's chances for success more than a premature indictment of the family's spending habits.

If you have kept your budget up to date, the control function can be accomplished in three steps.

1. Add all the expenditures for the budget period, category by category, and enter these figures on the budget control sheet (fig. 8-7, p. 167) under "actual." If you have been using the outstanding balance approach described in the sample record-keeping system, just subtract the final outstanding balance for each category from the original balance to arrive at your monthly expenditures.

2. Subtract the actual expenses in each category from the budgeted expenses and enter these figures on your control sheet under "plus or minus." (At this point you may want to have someone check the arithmetic to make sure that the figures are correct.) You will then be able to see how much you have left over or how much you overspent in each category. For example, in January Alex and Karen overspent on food by $5 but spent only $15 of their $20 gift allotment (fig. 8-7). In later months you will be subtracting actual expenses from the figure in the balance forward column to get the amount of money you have overspent or underspent. The balance forward equals the plus or minus amount added to the monthly budgeted amount.
3. Consider those expense categories that exceeded the budget limits and those that fell short. Was too little money budgeted for the former categories and too much for the latter? Or did you simply overspend in some categories because of carelessness or unusual circumstances? In other words, did the discrepancy actually occur in planning the budget or in implementing it?

At this time, it is very important to determine how realistic your planning actually was. A budget must be realistic before a family can feel comfortable with it and be concerned about reducing expenditures in various categories. Carefully analyze which categories were so far underestimated that they carried forward large deficits and which were so liberally funded that they carried forward large surpluses. Once you have determined why there were deficits and surpluses, you can control your budget either by decreasing spending or by reallocating your income to allow for smaller or larger expenses.

As you go over your budget and update it after your first month's experience, remember that some categories, such as insurance premiums and taxes, will develop large plus balances since they are built up during the year to provide enough money for a lump-sum payment. For example, Karen and Alex have a March surplus in gifts because they plan to use most of the allotment to buy Christmas presents later (fig. 8-7).

There are two methods that can help you control expenses: the fail-safe budget and the flexible budget.

Control Method I: the Fail-Safe Budget

The fail-safe budget is designed to make sure that you meet your budgeted goals. With this method you should try never to spend more than the current amount in any budget classification, but do be sure that your classification limits are realistic. There should not be any negative numbers in the plus or minus columns of the budget control sheet, except for categories involving disbursements that are made only once a year (e.g., insurance premiums).

NAME(S) _Alexander and Karen_

DATE _May 1973_

BUDGET CONTROL SHEET

Expense Category	Budgeted Monthly Average	January Actual	January Plus or Minus	February Balance Forward	February Actual	February Plus or Minus	Revised Monthly Average	March Balance Forward	March Actual	March Plus or Minus	April Balance Forward	April Actual	April Plus or Minus
Housing	$160	$160		$160	$160			$160	$160		$160	$160	
Utilities	20	16	+4	24	17	+7		27	19	+8	28	23	
Food	110	115	−5	105	108	−3		107	114	−7	103	116	
Recreation and entertainment	40	20	+20	60	26	+34		74	32	+42	82	31	
Clothing	50	120	−70	−20	15	−35		15	30	−15	35	45	
Automobile	60	25	+35	95	80	+15		75	55	+20	80	85	
Medical	15	20	−5	10	12	−2		13	8	+5	20	26	
Family necessities	30	35	−5	25	36	−11	35	24	28	−4	31	34	
Personal improvement	17	23	−6	11	7	+4		21	19	+2	19	12	
Savings and investment	113	36	+77	190	40	+150		263		+263	376		
Gifts	20	15	+5	25		+25		45	6	+39	59	11	
Church and charity	20	15	+5	25	15	+10	15	25	15	+10	25	33	
Life insurance	20		+20	40		+40		60		+60	80		
Taxes													
Contingency	10		+10	20	10	+10		20		+20	30	5	
Allowances	20	20		20	20			20	20		20	20	
Outlays for fixed assets	20	60	−40	−20		−20					20		
Other													
TOTAL	725	680	+45	770	546	+224		949	506	+443	1168	601	

Fig. 8-7.
Sample budget control sheet

You may, however, have a surplus in certain budget categories. For example, you may budget $50 a month for clothes and spend $30 the first month so that you will have $70 to spend in that category for the next month. If you do this for several consecutive months, you will have saved enough to buy a major clothing article such as a new suit. If you had bought the suit earlier, you would have had either to cut back in some other category, to use some of your savings, or to buy it on credit. By using the fail-safe budget, you have forced yourself to save for a major purchase.

You should observe two cautions, however, in using the fail-safe budget. First, do not let this method rule with too tight a fist! It may put an unnecessary strain on you or some member of your family (for example, if it kept your wife from getting a new iron when she really needed it). Second, do not pay for such things as life insurance on a monthly basis just to keep the "plus or minus" figure from being negative or you will be paying unnecessary service charges. If you pay $360 a year for such an item, simply budget $30 a month. If the premium is due next month and you have to pay it out of your minimum cash reserve, the budget category will go minus, but it will come out even in the long run. In such cases, negative numbers are compatible with the fail-safe budget.

Control Method II: the Flexible Budget

The flexible budget is designed to allow for natural variations in month-to-month expenditures. Negative or positive accumulations may occur within categories. For example, as we can see in figure 8-7 (p. 167), in January Alex and Karen spent $70 more than their monthly allotment of $50 for clothing. In February the minus carried forward was reduced to minus $20 (as it appears in the balance forward column) because of the $50 budgeted monthly average. Recognizing that the clothing category was already minus $20, Alex and Karen spent only $15 on clothing in February, making their "plus or minus" figure minus $35 . In March the $50 budgeted monthly average combined with the minus $35 carried forward to create a balance forward of plus $15. Anytime a budget category has a negative balance forward, purchases of items in that category should be held back as much as possible until the balance is positive enough to begin more normal spending. Otherwise, you will overspend your budget.

Look at the monthly totals along the bottom of the budget control sheet (fig. 8-7). Karen and Alex's budget allows spending and investment of $725 a month. In January they spent $680, leaving them plus $45. However, since savings and investment was plus $77 instead of plus $113 (because of the $36 they spent on a ski trip), they were obviously negative in the aggregate for the other categories. So in February they had to keep their total expenditures under control. To do this, they cut back everywhere they could and spent only $546. You can see that going into April they have built up a surplus of $443. Of course, they would not spend $443 on something frivolous, because this surplus has been built up for future outlays. One of the strengths of a successful budget scheme is that it helps prevent you from spending the extra money you have today if you know you will need it in the future.

There are two cautions that should be observed if you choose to use the flexible budget control method. First, your family should have enough self-restraint to avoid overspending in a category that has gone into the red. You must refrain from saying, "Oh well, it won't hurt if I let that category go a little more minus for one more month." Otherwise, your budget is no longer a control device. It only tells you where the money went. Budgeting does take a certain amount of personal discipline in order to make it work! Second, do not let too many of the categories go negative at the same time. You may far overspend your income for one month and have either to borrow at high interest rates to cover the expenditures or to draw down your investments. Your budget will have failed in its control function if this happens.

If you observe these two cautions, the flexible budget can provide for successful control of your family's finances. In addition, it should be more acceptable to the other members of the family because it can be temporarily modified to allow for unanticipated expenses or decisions.

RETHINKING THE BUDGET PROCESS

After you have been on a budget system for a couple of months, you will be able to predict pretty accurately what size each budget category should be. At this time you should begin to consider whether you are getting full satisfaction out of the money you are spending. Even though your family may be spending precisely the amount available in each category, they may not be happy with what they are achieving. A budget must be continually updated to reflect the changing needs and wants of the family. Perhaps every three months your family should reconsider what they want from money. Going to a movie every weekend may have been an important family goal three months ago, but now they might want to spend more money on records or tapes. Once you have rethought your goals, you can adjust your budget categories by eliminating some, adding some, or expanding or reducing already existing categories to reflect your changing needs. A budget is good only as long as it is relevant to the family using it.

CONCLUSION

Some people feel that budgeting takes the fun out of spending money; yet spending too much money can take the fun out of life by creating needless worry. Budgeting need not be a straitjacket if done as described in this chapter.

Budgeting lets you know where the money goes, allowing you to eliminate unnecessary spending and get what you really want; it also helps you save. Through budgeting you can avoid needless drains on your income. These drains will be discussed in the next four chapters.

VOCABULARY

after-tax income
budget
budget period
fail-safe budget
flexible budget

QUESTIONS

1. Using the information on Karen and Alex's budget control sheet (fig. 8-7), compute their April plus or minus and May balance forward.
2. At the end of June, Karen and Alex will make their six-month review of their budget. In light of their experience to date, which expense categories, if any, should probably be revised upward (have greater expense limits)? Which categories, if any, could be revised downward to allow for the upward revision of other budget categories? Why?
3. Describe at least three distinct advantages to being on a budget.
4. What is probably the best method for recording charge account purchases? Why?
5. Should you always select a budget period equal to your pay period? Why, or why not?
6. Under what circumstances can an expense category be given a little flexibility in the fail-safe budget?
7. Is it possible for a student with a full-time summer job, a full-time Christmas job, and a part-time school job to set up a budget? If so, how?

CASE PROBLEM

Janet is a freshman at State University. She has several sources of income to provide for her education and living expenses. Her parents will give her $150 a month during the nine months she goes to school and also pay her expenses during the summer when she lives at home. The state provides a $1000 annual scholarship. Janet expects to earn $1200 (net) on a summer job and $50 a month during the school year.

Janet's expenses fluctuate widely. Tuition of $40 is due at the beginning of each of the three terms, as are room and board fees of $450. Books will probably cost $180 for the year. Transportation and personal expenses are expected to total $110 a month during the school year and $220 a month for the three-month summer vacation because of a trip she plans to take.

Janet thinks that, because of this irregular pattern of income and expenses, a monthly budget would be useless, and so she plans just to keep a tight watch on her expenses.

Do you agree with Janet that a monthly budget would not work for her? Why or why not? If she were to use a monthly budget, what should her budgeted monthly average income be? Compute her monthly average expense total. Is there any discrepancy between this and her average income? What probably will happen if Janet does not set up a budget and stick to it—provided that her monthly income and expenses do not change?

RECOMMENDED READING

Cohen, Jerome, and Hanson, Arthur. *Personal Finance: Principles and Case Problems.* Homewood, Ill.: Irwin, 1972.

> Chapter 2 deals with budgeting techniques.

Donaldson, Elvin, and Pfahl, John. *Personal Finance.* New York: Ronald Press, 1971.

> Chapter 2 discusses budgeting techniques.

Unger, Maurice, and Wolf, Harold. *Personal Finance.* Boston: Allyn and Bacon, 1972.

> Chapter 1 provides a good overview of earning opportunities and how they relate to the satisfaction of budgeting goals. Chapter 2 offers various budgeting techniques.

Changing Times, published monthly by the Kiplinger Washington Editors, Editors Park, Maryland, provides insights into the expenditure patterns of typical American families, ways to stretch budgets and beat inflation, and so on.

CHUCK AND NANCY ANDERSON

SETTING UP A BUDGET

Chuck and Nancy do not have a budget. As a result, their income seems to be slipping away without their getting the most out of it. In preparing to set up a budget, they looked at their balance sheet and income statement to find out how much money they have and where it is likely to be spent.

QUESTIONS

1. What is the average income per month, after taxes and Social Security, that the Andersons should use in setting up their budget? (Do not include in your computations their capital loss on the sale of stock.)
2. What net effect will the insurance revisions the Andersons made in chapters 3 through 7 have on their annual expenses?
3. If they spend money this year as they did last year—except on insurance—will there be a budgeted deficit for the year?
4. If they want to eliminate a deficit and/or expand the surplus for savings and investment, what categories of income and/or expenses should they reevaluate?
5. How should Chuck and Nancy structure their budget to avert quarrels over the amounts each of them spends on personal expenses?

9

FEDERAL INCOME TAXES ON INDIVIDUALS

Federal taxation of personal income is ever changing. It probably represents one of the most complex bodies of laws, rules, and regulations in history. There are three reasons for this. First, the sources and nature of personal income are so complex that any attempt to tax that income is bound to become complex itself. Second, income taxation is used not only to raise revenues for the federal government, but also to benefit certain forms of economic activity. For example, certain industries that Congress deems to be of vital interest to the nation (e.g., oil and gas production) enjoy preferential tax treatment that enhances their profitability for investors. Third, there is a large and divergent group of special interests that lobby to have personal income tax laws written in their favor or, more commonly, to have some of the more stringent applications of tax laws softened for them. The end result of all this is the complex nature of the tax system.

Probably the single most important feature of the federal income tax system is that it is progressive as opposed to regressive. The more income you make, the higher the percentage that is taken from it in taxes. For example, on $8000 of taxable income the tax for a married couple filing a joint return is $1380. For every dollar of the next $4000 of taxable income, 22¢ must be paid to the federal government. Between $12,000 and $16,000 of taxable income, 25¢ of every dollar must be paid in income taxes.

This $12,000 to $16,000 is also an example of a tax bracket, which represents the spread of income that is subject to a certain percentage of taxation, or tax rate. This tax system is unlike the Social Security tax, which is regressive, i.e., the tax rate is the same for all people.

From this brief description of our federal income tax system two things should be evident. First, by reducing the amount of your taxable income (especially if that reduction results in a lower tax bracket), you lower the amount of tax you must pay. Second, the better understanding you have of the income tax system, the better prepared you will be to reduce your income tax liability. This reduction would not be possible with other forms of personal taxation. Social Security is the same for all. Property taxes vary with the value of property. Sales taxes always represent a fixed percentage of the value of items purchased. The only other two taxes that warrant some effort at tax savings are gift and estate taxes, which will be discussed in chapter 21.

If you know how to plan your income taxes and prepare your tax return, you may be able to avoid unnecessary tax expenditures. This chapter offers some common methods of tax planning that should enable you both to reduce your income taxes and to assess the tax effect of various financial actions. This information should help you both in making financial decisions with an awareness of their tax implications and in tax preparation (filing a correct return). Subsequent chapters treat the tax aspects of particular subjects as part of the general discussion of those subjects.

WITHHOLDING

One of the most common ways of paying the federal income tax (as well as the Social Security tax) is for an employer to withhold a portion of each employee's income and send it to the Internal Revenue Service (IRS) every fifteen days to three months, depending on the amount. For income tax, the portion withheld depends on the level of job income and the number of withholding exemptions claimed. For example, Jose Martinez will make $8000 this year from his job at a hospital. His income tax on that amount will be withheld by his employer and sent to the federal government, and at the end of the year Jose will have paid all the necessary tax on his income from that job. The hospital will summarize Jose's tax record for the year and send the summary to him on a W-2 Form some time in January. This form gives Jose figures to use in filling out his tax return. The hospital also sends a copy to the IRS for them to use in checking his tax return.

GROSS INCOME

Gross income serves as the starting point for all income tax computations. As defined by the IRS, it includes all income in the form of money, property, and services that is not, by law, expressly exempt from tax. Income that must be included consists of wages, salary, tips, rent, interest, dividends, alimony, bonuses, commissions, gambling winnings, and even buried treasure. Among items not considered income for income tax purposes are:

- accident, health, and term life insurance premiums paid by employer
- accident and health insurance proceeds
- Armed Forces trailer-moving allowance
- amounts received for expenses incident to education
- annuity payments that are a return of original investment
- benefit payments from general welfare fund in interest of general public
- bequests
- campaign contributions received by candidates
- capital contributions to a corporation
- car-pool receipts by automobile owner
- child care reimbursement payments to foster parents
- clergyman's rental allowance
- combat service pay
- damage payments received for injury or illness
- death payments to survivors of Armed Forces personnel who died on active duty
- disability pensions (including Workmen's Compensation)
- dividends from U.S. corporations (up to $100 tax free annually on separate return, $200 on joint return)
- employee death proceeds up to $5000
- gain on sale of residence for individuals sixty-five and over
- gifts and inheritances
- income tax refunds
- interest on debt obligations of states and municipalities
- life insurance proceeds
- Peace Corps travel and living allowances
- Peace Corps allowance for basic necessities
- portion of certain pension or annuity payments attributable to taxpayer's contributions
- Pulitzer Prize
- Railroad Unemployment Insurance Act benefits
- scholarships and fellowship grants
- school board allowance for transporting children to and from school
- sick pay (within certain limits)
- Social Security benefits (both disability and retirement)
- stock rights and stock dividends
- strike benefits in the form of food or rent
- veterans' allowance benefits for education, subsistence, training
- veterans' disability compensation benefits

- veterans' insurance proceeds and dividends paid either to veterans or their beneficiaries
- veterans' pension paid either to veterans or their families

This list of tax-exempt income is partial and does not indicate qualifications or limitations that may accompany certain items. Therefore, when considering items that you may be able to exclude from gross income, be sure to check a more extensive list, which may be found in *Your Federal Income Tax—for Individuals*. (This publication is revised annually by the Internal Revenue Service and published by the Government Printing Office.) None of the exclusions from gross income need be listed on your tax return.

DEDUCTIONS

Deductions are expenses that may be subtracted from one's gross income. No item may be considered a deduction unless a specific provision in the tax law or regulations makes it one. Deductions show up in two places on your tax return. Some deductions are subtracted from gross income to arrive at *adjusted gross income*. These deductions are generally derived from business expenses and must always be itemized—that is, listed on the tax return. Here is a partial list.

- business expenses—depreciation, employee benefits, entertainment, gifts, loan interest, property rents and repairs, salaries, travel and transportation
- capital losses
- convention expenses
- depletion
- education expenses required by employer
- expenses of travelling salesman
- lobbying expenses
- moving expenses due to job transfers
- payments by self-employed person to retirement fund
- expenses ordinary and necessary for the performance of employment

Other deductions are subtracted from adjusted gross income to give *income before exemptions*. These deductions usually cover nonbusiness expenses. Because the limitations and qualifications that surround them are not given here, you should seek professional advice, perhaps at an IRS office, when attempting to determine which of these deductions apply to you.

- alimony and separate maintenance payments
- attorney's fee in tax consultation

- certain nonbusiness automobile expenses (e.g., use of car for charitable work)
- child care expenses up to $900
- contributions to qualified charitable and nonprofit organizations
- employee's tools (one-year life or less)
- fees for bond interest collection
- finance charge on installment payments and charge account credit and on small loans
- gambling losses to the extent of gambling winnings
- gasoline tax (state and local)
- general sales tax (state and local)
- interest on home mortgage, including points (p. 265)
- investment advisory fees, expenses for investor advisory services, and the like
- margin account interest
- medical and dental expenses, drug expenses (under certain circumstances) in excess of 3 percent of adjusted gross income
- medical insurance premiums (one-half of premiums up to $150) including medical insurance portion of auto insurance premium (The remaining portion of health insurance premiums is added to medical, dental, and drug expenses in the calculation of expenses that may be used as a deduction.)
- obtaining employment (fees paid)
- personal casualty losses in excess of $100
- personal property tax (state and local), including auto license fees above a certain figure (varies by state)
- professional publications used by employees
- professional societies' dues paid by employees
- property casualty losses over $100
- real property taxes (state, local, and foreign)
- safety deposit box fees (for boxes used to hold documents related to the production of income, such as stocks and bonds)
- state disability income taxes
- state income taxes (those actually paid or withheld during the taxable year)
- tax preparation fees
- theft loss in excess of $100
- union dues paid by employees

For the sake of clarity, in this text deductions that are subtracted from gross income are called type one deductions, and deductions that are subtracted from adjusted gross income are called type two deductions.

The taxpayer may either itemize type two deductions or take a *standard deduction*. Obviously, you would use the standard deduction when it represents a larger deduction than would be available if you itemized your type two deductions. The standard deduction may be taken in the form of either a percentage standard deduction or a low income allowance. The percentage standard deduction allows you to deduct 15 percent of your adjusted gross income up to a dollar maximum of $2000. For example, if your adjusted gross income were $10,000, by this method the deduction would be $1500. If your adjusted gross income were $21,000, the deduction would be limited to $2000. The low income allowance is intended to provide tax relief for taxpayers with very modest incomes. To avail yourself of this deduction, which is a flat $1300, your adjusted gross income must be less than $10,000. To determine whether low income allowance or percentage standard deduction will give the largest deduction, you should compute your taxes both ways.

How will you know whether to itemize or to take the standard deduction? First, know the major categories of type two deductions that can be itemized: contributions to qualified charities; interest on indebtedness; nonfederal taxes; dental, hospital, and medical expenses; net losses because of casualties or theft; care of children and other dependents; alimony payments; ordinary and necessary expenses incurred for employer's benefit; expenses of earning nonbusiness income. Second, keep records throughout the year of those expenditures that are type two deductions. Certain expenditures (most commonly property and sales taxes and state taxes on gasoline and income) can be estimated at the end of the year from tables in the tax booklet in which Form 1040 comes. Last, figure your type two deductions both by itemizing and by taking the standard deduction. Take the alternative that represents the largest deduction from adjusted gross income to determine income before exemptions.

To get maximum value from itemized type two deductions, you may want either to prepay them or to postpone your payment on them so that they all occur in one year and thus exceed the percentage standard deduction in aggregate value. In the preceding or succeeding year in which you have minimal itemized deductions, you can use the standard deduction. For example, let us assume that if you were to itemize your type two deductions in each of two years, you would be able to subtract $1700 from your adjusted gross income each time—$300 less than the maximum standard deduction, assuming an adjusted gross income greater than $13,333. Obviously, it would reduce your taxable income more to take the standard deduction both years. A more profitable method, however, would be to prepay as much of the second year's $1700 in the first year as possible (prepay property taxes and interest on loans, for example) so that your itemized type two deductions would be greater than $2000. Then it would be to your advantage to itemize your deductions the first year and take the standard deduction the second year.

Some expenses cannot be used as either type one or type two deductions. Among these are:

- adoption fees
- commuting costs
- estate taxes
- food
- FICA employee taxes
- funeral expenses
- gift taxes
- life insurance premiums
- passport fees
- rent
- self-employment tax
- Social Security tax paid for domestic help
- tax penalty payments
- traffic tickets or fines
- uniforms for military personnel
- upkeep on pleasure car

EXEMPTIONS

Exemptions represent specific, stated amounts that, under certain circumstances, you can deduct from your *income before exemptions* to arrive at *taxable income*. The most commonly applied exemptions are for oneself, for a spouse when filing a joint return, and for each dependent. To qualify as an exemption, the dependent must be recognized as a dependent by law (as are most close relatives and adopted or foster children), have over 50 percent of his support furnished by the taxpayer who wants to take this additional exemption, and have a gross annual income that is lower than the level at which he would be required to file a return ($750 for taxable year 1972). A child under nineteen or a full-time student (no age limit) may be claimed as an exemption, no matter what his gross income, as long as the support condition is met and he is your child. You may qualify for additional exemptions when you reach the age of sixty-five, when your spouse reaches sixty-five (when filing a joint return), if you are blind at the end of the taxable year, or if your spouse is blind at the end of the taxable year (when filing a joint return)—other blind dependents do not qualify as exemptions. The amount allowed for each of these exemptions is $750.

TAX COMPUTATION

Figuring your tax can be done by one of three methods.

1. The IRS will compute your tax for you if your adjusted gross income is $20,000 or less; if your income consists only of wages, salaries, tips, pensions, annuities, dividends and/or interest; and if you do not itemize your type two deductions.

2. If your adjusted gross income is less than $10,000 and you do not itemize your type two deductions, you have the option of computing your tax from one of the thirteen tax tables provided in the tax booklet. (There is a different table for each number of exemptions claimed.) If one of these tables is used, you need not concern yourself with the type two standard deduction since it is reflected in the tables themselves. Deductions for exemptions have also been taken into account in determining the taxes shown in the tables.

3. If you itemize your type two deductions or have an adjusted gross income of $10,000 or more, you use a set of rate tables called Tax Rate Schedules, which are part of the tax booklet in which Form 1040 comes. Do not confuse these with the schedules that may be appended to the basic tax form. The Tax Rate Schedules provide tax rates for a particular group of taxpayers, whereas the other schedules are forms to be filled out by taxpayers who have particular kinds of financial information to report.

The Tax Act of 1969 instituted new Tax Rate Schedules, which went into effect for the taxable year 1971. The new schedules contain tax rates for single individuals that are only 20 percent higher than those for married individuals filing joint returns. Previously the rates for single taxpayers were as much as 40 percent higher. The rates for heads-of-household are structured halfway between the rates for single and married taxpayers. To qualify as a head-of-household, you must furnish more than half of the cost of maintaining a household for at least one qualified dependent. You do not have to be married.

Who Must Pay

All U.S. citizens, including minors, and all aliens residing in this country must file tax returns by April fifteenth each year if their gross income the previous year exceeds certain limits. U.S. citizens living abroad and nonresident aliens who have earned money in the United States are required to file returns by June fifteenth each year if their incomes for the preceding year have exceeded these limits. Figure 9-1 shows the general categories of taxpayers and the limits their gross incomes must exceed before the filing requirements come into effect.

Joint and Separate Returns

If you are married, you and your spouse may elect to file either a joint return or separate returns. (A married individual may not be entitled to file a joint return if either spouse uses a different taxable year or at any time of the year is a nonresident alien.) In most instances, especially those in which one spouse has little or no income, filing a joint return results in a lower tax. Surviving spouses may elect to file either a joint or a separate return for the year in which their spouse dies. Since this

Characteristics of Taxpayers	If Gross Income Exceeds
Single person, unmarried head-of-household, or surviving spouse with dependent child	$2050
65 or older	2800
Married persons filing a joint return	2800
One spouse 65 or older	3550
Both spouses 65 or older	4300
Married persons filing separate returns	750

Fig. 9-1.

Filing requirements for taxpayers

decision may be closely related to the settlement of the deceased's estate, you should consult your attorney and the executor of the estate before deciding how to file.

Form 1040, Schedules, and Other Forms

All individual taxpayers file their tax returns on Form 1040. Taxpayers whose income sources and expense items are fairly standard need use only this basic two-page form. Some taxpayers may have to include certain schedules to give details about the year's financial transactions. Most of these schedules are included in the tax booklet in which Form 1040 comes. Schedules not included in the booklet can be obtained at a bank or savings and loan association or at an IRS office. The information asked for in these schedules is shown in figure 9-2. If you need to include one or more of them with your next return, you may want to consult either the local IRS office or a private tax consulting firm for advice.

Schedule	Contents
A	Itemized type two deductions
B	Dividend and interest income that cannot be included on Form 1040
C	Profits or losses from one's business or profession
D	Gains and losses on sales or exchanges of property
E	Income from pensions, annuities, rents, royalties, partnerships, estates, trusts, small business corporations, and miscellaneous sources
F	Farm income and expenses
G	Income averaging computations
R	Retirement income credit
SE	Self-employment tax

Fig. 9-2. Contents of tax schedules

From time to time you may have other contacts with the Internal Revenue Service. Figure 9-3 shows the various forms that may be used. All of these forms except the W-2 and the 1099 are for individual use.

Form	Purpose
SS-5	To obtain a Social Security number, replace a lost card, or obtain a Federal Taxpayer Identification number
W-2	To indicate total wages subject to withholding, the amount of income tax withheld by an employer, and the total amount withheld for Social Security taxes (FICA)
W-4	To file with an employer the number of dependent exemptions
W-4E	To obtain an exemption from withholding if no tax liability is foreseen
843	To apply for a refund of FICA taxes
935	To grant power of attorney to another individual for a tax return
1040ES	To declare an estimated tax
1040X	To amend an already filed return
1099	To inform the IRS how much income was made on accounts (filed by banks, savings and loan associations, brokerage houses, and similar institutions)
2119	To declare the sale or exchange of a residence
2333	To request blank income tax forms
2688	To apply for an extension of time in which to file a return
4070	To report tips
4506	To request a copy of a previously filed return

Fig. 9-3.
Purpose of IRS forms

An Example

An analysis of the tax computations for the Martinezes' 1972 income may be helpful. Their gross income includes $12,000 ($8000 salary for Jose and $4000 for part-time work by Mrs. Martinez), $175 (interest from their savings account), and $75 (raffle prize). The $500 they received in health insurance payments is not included in the total gross income of $12,250. Jose changed jobs, and so the Martinez family moved in early 1972. The deductible (type one) expenses related to moving were $750. From his gross income ($12,250) Mr. Martinez takes a type one deduction of $750 to arrive at his adjusted gross income of $11,500.

Mr. Martinez and his wife plan to file a joint return and take the standard deduction. The low income allowance will not apply here because their adjusted gross income is more than $10,000. They must take the percentage standard deduction, which in this example is 15 percent of $11,500, or $1725. Therefore, from his adjusted gross income ($11,500) Mr. Martinez subtracts the appropriate type two deduction ($1725) to arrive at his income before exemptions, or $9775. From this amount, three $750 exemptions (for Jose, his wife, and their son) are taken to arrive at the taxable income. On this final amount of $7525 Mr. Martinez computes his tax using the Tax Rate Schedules.

Mr. and Mrs. Martinez decide to compare what their tax would be if they filed separate returns with what it would be if they filed a joint return. Figure 9-4 gives the figures they arrived at. As you can see, filing separate returns would result in a $1460 tax whereas the tax on a joint return would be $1290.

Elements of Tax Computation	Separate Returns		Joint Return
	Mr.	Mrs.	
Gross Income	$8,250	$4,000	$12,250
Type One Deductions	750		750
Adjusted Gross Income	7,500	4,000	11,500
Standard Deduction			1,725
Income Before Exemptions	7,500		9,775
Exemptions[a]			2,250
Taxable Income	7,500	4,000	7,525
Tax	1,004[b]	467[b]	1,290

[a]Because he has the largest income and is, therefore, in a higher tax bracket, Mr. Martinez takes both himself and his son as exemptions.

[b]Tax computed from rate tables that take into account the standard deduction and deductions for exemptions.

Fig. 9-4. Comparison of tax computation for separate returns and joint return

ESTIMATED TAX

In spite of the withholding tax, many taxpayers with sources of income other than wages would incur a large tax liability on their annual income tax return were they not required to estimate their tax and make quarterly payments. The estimated tax gives the federal government a means of quickly collecting taxes on income not subject to withholding. If it were not for the estimated tax and withholding, the Treasury would have to wait until April fifteenth of each year to collect taxes on income made during the previous taxable year. Because of its revenue needs, our federal government is compelled to collect income taxes as quickly as possible after income is earned.

Filing Requirements

Estimated tax is filed on Form 1040ES. This form is composed of instructions for filing, a worksheet for your computations, four vouchers (one to accompany each of your installment payments), and four addressed envelopes in which your vouchers and payments are to be sent. In general, you must submit 1040ES by April fifteenth of the current taxable year if you can reasonably expect that your total income tax (including self-employment tax) will be $100 or more greater than the amount to be withheld by your employer. Specifically, a declaration must be filed if your gross income can reasonably be expected to consist of wages subject to withholding exceeding (1) $20,000 and you are an unmarried individual, a surviving spouse entitled to special tax rates, a head-of-household, or a married individual whose spouse has no earned income; (2) $10,000 and you are a married individual whose spouse has an earned income; (3) $5000 and you are a married individual not entitled to file a joint declaration. The last condition on which you must file a declaration is if you can reasonably expect that more than $500 income will come from sources other than wage earnings.

Computation Procedure

The estimated tax is computed on Form 1040ES as follows:

1. Estimate your adjusted gross income for the current taxable year.
2. Estimate your type two deductions (itemized or standard).
3. Compute the amount of exemptions available to you this year.
4. Subtract steps 2 and 3 from step 1. This is your estimated taxable income.
5. Compute your tax on this amount from the table that suits your circumstances and comes with the form.
6. Add any self-employment tax (p. 188) to this amount.
7. Deduct the amount expected to be withheld by your employer (ask him for an estimate) plus any tax credits (credits against future taxes because of past overpayments) from the amount derived in step 6.
8. The remaining amount is your estimated tax. If it is less than $100, you are not required to file Form 1040ES. If it is $100 or over, your estimated tax should be divided into four equal amounts and paid in installments on April fifteenth, June fifteenth, and September fifteenth of the current year and on January fifteenth of the following year. The IRS will not bill you for each installment; you will have to remember to make your payments on time.

Avoiding underpayments is important because a 6 percent annual penalty is assessed against delinquent amounts. Delinquent amounts are computed by the IRS as the difference between 80 percent of the amount that should have been paid and the amount, if any, actually paid. This penalty will not be applied, however, even in the case of an underpayment if, for example, the estimated tax paid is equal to or more than the combined income and self-employment taxes paid for the previous taxable year.

TAXES ON CAPITAL GAINS

Taxes are levied against income received from the sale of a capital asset such as real estate, stocks and bonds, jewelry, and furs. A capital gain is the gain, after commissions and brokerage fees, resulting from the sale or exchange of a capital asset. Of course, a capital loss, rather than a capital gain, may result from such a sale. A long-term capital gain or loss occurs when an asset was owned for more than six months before the sale. A short-term capital gain or loss occurs when an asset was held for six months or less prior to the sale. A tax rate advantage applies to long-term capital gains. At the end of the required holding period, the tax rate on capital gains is one-half the regular income tax rates and has a maximum rate of 25 percent for the first $50,000 of capital gains income. Above this amount the maximum rate for individuals, as set down in the Tax Act of 1969, is 35 percent.

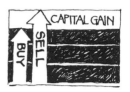

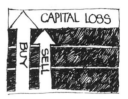

In general, long-term capital gains income is equal to the amount of one or more years' ordinary income received in one lump sum. If you paid regular income tax on all of it, you would be paying more tax than if average amounts of the capital gain were taxed each year that it accumulated. Let us assume that you bought a piece of real estate for $10,000 and sold it ten years later realizing $20,000 after subtracting your expenses from the actual selling price—a taxable gain of $10,000. Theoretically, this is equivalent to $1000 income for each year of the ten years you held the property. However, you could not pay income tax on that $1000 each year because the capital appreciation did not occur regularly or in easily determined amounts. If the gain were to be taxed at the progressive rates that apply to ordinary income for the year during which you sold the property, the $10,000 added to your regular income for the year would place you in a much higher tax bracket and the resulting tax bill would be substantially more than if taxes had been paid on an extra $1000 each year. The capital gains tax was created to protect people against unnecessarily high tax rates where capital appreciation has occurred over an extended period of time. Another reason for a capital gains tax is to encourage people to invest in capital assets since profits they make because of long-term appreciation will be taxed at rates that are lower than for regular income.

Computation Procedure

Computing your capital gains tax can seem rather complicated since there may be many gains and losses, both long-term and short-term, in any one year. We recommend that you use the five-step procedure below and the eight guidelines that follow it to ensure that you accomplish this task correctly. The first three steps must be done for each gain and loss, whether long-term or short-term, so that in steps 4 and 5 you can determine your net short- and long-term gains or losses. The guidelines tell how to use these net gains and losses in determining your gross income and thus your capital gains tax. (The guidelines apply only to the first $50,000 of net capital gains.)

1. Determine whether the gain or loss qualifies for tax treatment. All gains from the sale or exchange of capital assets must be included in gross income. All capital losses, except those due to the sale of your house or personal effects, may be deducted from gross income. (Depending on the amount, this deduction may have to be taken over a period of years.)
2. Determine the amount of the gain or loss by first calculating the original value or purchase price of the capital asset involved. (Remember to include any expenses you incurred in acquiring this asset, the cost of any capital improvements you made to it, and any expenses incurred in selling or exchanging it.) Then subtract the adjusted original value or purchase price from the final exchange value or sale price.
3. Determine whether the transaction qualifies as a short-term or long-term gain or loss.
4. Determine the net short-term capital gain or loss by subtracting your short-term capital losses from your short-term capital gains. For example, if your short-term capital gains for the taxable year are $1500 and your short-term capital losses are $1000, then your net short-term capital gain is $500.
5. Determine the net long-term capital gain or loss by using the same procedure as in step 4.

Eight Guidelines

1. When a net short-term gain is greater than a net long-term loss, all of the excess should be included in gross income on your tax return.
2. When there is a net short-term gain and no net long-term loss, the entire gain is included in gross income.
3. When a net short-term loss is greater than a net long-term gain, the excess (up to $1000) is deducted from gross income. Any remaining excess is carried forward to the next year when it is offset first against net short-term gains, then against net long-term gains, then against $1000 of gross income. This is done each year until the excess is exhausted. (The excesses carried forward each year must be shown on schedule D, which you use to compute your capital gains.)

4. When there is a net short-term loss and no net long-term gain, the amount of the loss up to $1000 is deducted from gross income. Any excess is carried forward as described in guideline 3.
5. When a net long-term gain is greater than a net short-term loss, only 50 percent of the excess is included in gross income. (This procedure has the same effect as reducing the tax rate on the gain by one-half.) However, if you are in a tax bracket greater than 50 percent, do not include this excess in your gross income. Instead, determine a 25 percent tax on it, and on Form 1040 add this to the tax you will pay on the rest of your income.
6. When there is a net long-term gain and no net short-term loss, include only 50 percent of the gain in your gross income. For individuals in tax brackets greater than 50 percent, the practice is the same as described in guideline 5.
7. When there is a net long-term loss greater than a net short-term gain, 50 percent of this excess up to $1000 is deducted from gross income. Any remaining portion of the excess is carried forward to the next year when it is offset against first net long-term gains, then net short-term gains, then up to $1000 of gross income, and so on for the remaining years until it is exhausted.
8. Where there is a net long-term loss and no net short-term gain, 50 percent of the loss is offset against $1000 of gross income and then carried forward as described in guideline 7.

Capital Gains Taxes and Selling a Home

Capital gains taxes on the sale of your home receive special consideration. If you sell your principal place of residence at a profit, you do not have to pay a capital gains tax if you buy or build another home with the proceeds within the two-year period extending from one year before to one year after the sale. If you do not use all the proceeds to buy or build another home, you will be taxed on the portion not used. Also, if you are age sixty-five or over when the sale occurs, and the price of the house is under $20,000, there is no capital gains tax. If it sells for more than $20,000, only a portion of the gain is tax-free.

SOCIAL SECURITY TAXES

There are essentially three Social Security taxes that are of interest to the individual. These taxes are not deductible for federal income tax purposes.

Federal Insurance Contributions Act

The Federal Insurance Contributions Act (FICA) combined all old-age, survivors, disability, and hospital insurance taxes into a single tax. The

rate is the same for both you and your employer. In other words, you each pay half of the amount that goes toward this federal insurance program. The tax is applied to your annual income and is deducted from your paycheck up to a certain income limit each year as determined by federal law. If you change jobs in the middle of the year, each employer will take the total FICA tax out of your paycheck as he has been instructed to. This may result in your paying the tax on more income than is required for that year. If you consult the IRS and find out that you have paid too much FICA tax, you can use the excess taxes paid as a credit against your personal income taxes. For example, if you paid $43 too much FICA tax in a year, you could pay $43 less on your federal income tax. Or you may use Form 843 to apply for a refund. However, you must take the initiative within three years to establish the overpayment and keep all your records of taxes paid (paycheck stubs and W-2 Forms). Otherwise, the extra taxes paid are lost.

The standard age at which you may begin to receive retirement benefits from this tax is sixty-five. (See chapters 6, 7, and 20 and the Social Security Addendum on pages 493–97 for a more complete discussion of Social Security benefits.)

Federal Unemployment Tax Act

The Federal Unemployment Tax Act (FUTA) created the unemployment insurance tax. This tax is imposed on your employer only. Up to a certain limit specified by federal law, he must pay taxes at a rate (also specified by federal law) on wages he pays you each year. The proceeds from this tax are used to finance federal-state unemployment compensation programs that are administered by the state. When you receive unemployment benefit payments, they are paid by your state. Some states levy additional unemployment taxes on employers.

Self-Employment Tax Act

The Self-Employment Tax Act (SETA) created the self-employment and hospital insurance tax. This tax is levied against self-employed individuals whose income from their work is $400 or more a year (with certain exceptions for religious activities). It is computed as a fixed percentage of a certain amount of earnings above $400 and is paid along with the regular income tax. This tax provides the same benefits for self-employed individuals as the FICA tax provides for employed persons.

THE MINIMUM INCOME TAX

The minimum income tax was created by the Tax Act of 1969 to prevent wealthy individuals and corporations from escaping taxation by investing in situations that enjoy special tax treatment. Congress identified the following specific tax preferential situations and made them subject to the minimum income tax: accelerated depreciation on real or personal property, amortization of certified pollution control facilities, amortization of railroad rolling stock, depletion, stock options, and certain untaxed capital gains. A minimum income tax of 10 percent is levied on the value of these tax preference items where they exceed a $30,000 annual exemption and a deduction in the amount of regular income taxes already paid for that year. For example, if you had $100,000 of tax preference items and had regular income taxes of $20,000, your minimum income tax would be $5000, or 10 percent of $50,000 ($100,000 minus $30,000 minus $20,000). If you are required to pay a minimum income tax, you should seek the advice of a professional tax authority.

MARGINAL TAX RATES

When making certain financial decisions, it is important to take into account the tax effect of various alternatives. One of the simplest ways to determine the tax effect of additional income or deductible expense items is to use the marginal tax rate.

An example of the progressive structure of our tax system is shown in figure 9-5. Increasing amounts of income are taxed at increasing rates.

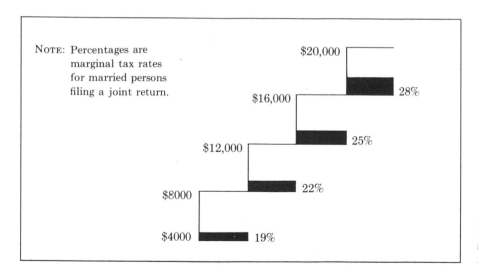

Fig. 9-5. Progressive structure of income tax

The marginal tax rate is the final one at which, given your level of income, your income is taxed. Your marginal tax rate is different from your aggregate income tax rate since the latter is the average of the rates for all the preceding levels of income. For example, on $14,000 of taxable income, the marginal tax rate is 25 percent. The aggregate income tax rate is derived by dividing the total taxes paid ($2760) by the total taxable income ($14,000); the result is approximately 19.5 percent.

To understand how the marginal tax rate works, let us take as an example the difference in tax on taxable income between $12,000 and $16,000.

Taxable Income	Tax
$16,000	$3,260
12,000	2,260
$ 4,000	$1,000

As you can see, the marginal tax rate in the $12,000 to $16,000 tax bracket is 25 percent. A quarter of every dollar of taxable income between $12,000 and $16,000 goes to the federal government in income tax. Conversely, every dollar of deductible expense that reduces one's taxable income between $12,000 and $16,000 represents twenty-five cents in taxes saved. With our progressive tax structure, in lower-income brackets the percentage rate is less than 25 percent and in higher-income brackets it is more. This can readily be seen by examining the IRS tax rate schedules.

Assume that Jose Martinez receives a $400 bonus from his employer. If he knows that his taxable income places him in a bracket with a 19 percent marginal tax rate, he can determine that the additional tax he owes as a result of the bonus will be $76 (19% × $400). As a further example, assume that the Martinezes are planning to itemize their type two deductions. If they buy a home, property taxes and the interest on the mortgage ($1500 in sum) will qualify as deductions. Provided that these deductions do not change the tax bracket the Martinezes are in, the taxes saved as a result of the additional deductions would be $285 (19% × $1500).

COMMON METHODS OF TAX REDUCTION

There are several methods by which you may be able legally to reduce the amount of tax you must pay. Among these are income averaging and income splitting. Another method, holding assets for more than six months in order to obtain the capital gains tax advantage, has already been discussed. A further method, depreciation used in real estate investments, is discussed on page 437 under tax shelter benefits.

Income Averaging

Taxpayers who experience radical fluctuations in their incomes from year to year are at a disadvantage because of the progressive structure of income tax rates. In high income years, they pay a larger tax than they would pay on an average of their incomes for each year. In low income years they lose the full effect of deductions and exemptions. Income averaging gives these taxpayers a way to spread their income evenly over a period of five years and thus avoid these problems.

Even though the computational procedure for income averaging has been simplified somewhat, it is still too extensive to allow full treatment in this chapter. The following formula, however, will serve as a quick guide in helping you determine, once you have computed your taxable income for the current year, whether income averaging could save you tax dollars.

1. Take the sum of your taxable incomes for the previous four years, not including the current year.
2. Multiply this sum by 30 percent (.3).
3. Add $3000 to this amount.

If your current year's taxable income is larger than the amount computed using the formula, then income averaging may be appropriate for you and you should seek more information or assistance, perhaps at an IRS office. (In calculating your current year's taxable income, be sure to include salaries; dividends; commissions; bonuses; fees; interest; long-term capital gains; and income from wagering, gifts, inheritances, and bequests.)

Income Splitting

Income splitting allows income to be shifted from an individual in a high tax bracket to one in a lower tax bracket. For example, if you build up a college fund for your son, you may set it up so that the income from the fund goes to him. He will pay a lower tax rate than you do (or maybe no taxes), thus saving tax dollars and making it easier to increase the eventual size of the investment. Custodial gifts can often be used to accomplish such an end.

Let us assume that your current year's taxable income is projected to be $14,000. As a married person filing a joint return, your projected federal tax should be $2760. Let us also assume that $600 of your taxable income represents interest earned on a 6 percent savings certificate of $10,000. You have earmarked this investment to provide funds to put your eight-year-old child through college. It is possible to make a gift to your child of the $10,000 savings certificate without incurring federal gift taxes. (How this can be accomplished and why it is possible will be treated in chapter 21.) By doing this, you will effect two tax savings. First, your projected taxable income will be reduced to $13,400 ($14,000 − $600) and your recomputed tax will be $2610, a tax savings of $150. Over the ten-year period before your child enters college, your savings could be $1500 or more. Second, assuming that your child does not make more than $2050 income in any one year (p. 181), the interest earned on the certificate should go untaxed each year. Because of compounding (to be discussed in chapter 13), by the tenth year this investment should have grown to $18,000, tax-free. If you had not made the custodial gift, the after-tax value would be $15,400. By income splitting, your tax savings have caused your child's college fund to increase by an additional $2600 over a ten-year period.

YOUR RELATIONS WITH THE IRS

A taxpayer cannot legally evade payment of taxes, but he can avoid paying too much. Evasion means an unlawful escape from taxation, whereas avoidance refers to legal reduction of the amount of tax that must be paid. We have tried in this chapter to give you the information and perspective that will enable you legally to avoid paying unnecessary taxes.

You have the primary responsibility for determining your lawful tax. You carry out this responsibility when you compute your tax return. If you have a question when filling out your tax form, contact your local IRS office. Around tax payment time each year, these offices are staffed with extra, trained personnel ready to help you solve both simple and complex tax problems.

Dates to Remember

Depending on your circumstances, you are obliged to observe certain dates in each taxable year. To the extent that you meet these deadlines, your relations with the tax authorities should remain on good terms. Here are some of the more common and important dates.

January 15   Final day to pay remaining estimated tax for the previous year's income.

January 31   Final day for employer to mail W-2 Forms to employees.

April 15   Income tax returns for the previous year are required of individuals (self-employed or otherwise) and partnerships, and for decedents who died in previous year. If necessary, individuals must also file estimated tax Form 1040ES for the current year and pay the first installment tax due.

June 15   Income tax returns for previous year are required of nonresident aliens and citizens living abroad. Second installment of estimated tax must be filed by individuals.

September 15   Third installment of estimated tax due.

Penalties

Penalties may be levied against you if you fail to comply with these due dates or other filing requirements. For late filing, the penalty is

5 percent of the tax due for each month that your return is outstanding, up to a maximum of 25 percent of the unpaid tax. For underpaying your tax, the penalty is 6 percent (of the unpaid tax due) a year plus 0.5 percent a month for each month the tax due is outstanding, up to a maximum of 25 percent of the unpaid tax, until you pay it. For negligence, or intentional disregard of rules and regulations but without intent to defraud, the penalty is 5 percent of the tax due. For fraud, the penalty is 50 percent of the tax due and possible criminal proceedings against you by the IRS.

Auditing of Returns

The IRS audits, or carefully checks, many tax returns each year, and it is possible that you and the IRS may not agree on certain issues. The IRS may view as unlawful evasion what you honestly regard as lawful avoidance of paying unnecessary taxes.

If your tax return is audited and some questions are raised by the IRS, an agent will contact you. You should attempt to resolve the disputed issues informally with this agent. It is important to keep in mind, however, that not all agents are of equal ability and that he may have made a mistake. The agent also has a bias: his job is to collect taxes, not to rule on the legality of certain tax strategies. If you are unable to negotiate a satisfactory settlement with the agent and you genuinely believe you are right, ask for a hearing with other IRS personnel. The individuals at the hearing might have different views than your agent on the matter under contention. If you are still unsuccessful at this level, you can take your case to the IRS appellate division.

Small tax cases involve disputes between you and the IRS for amounts up to $1000 (either income or estate taxes). The Tax Reform Act of 1969 authorized four tax commissioners to handle these cases under the supervision of a tax court judge. These commissioners are in various cities at certain times of the year to hear cases. To petition the IRS Small Case Tax Court for a hearing before the commissioners, write the U.S. Tax Court (Box 70, Washington, D.C. 20044) and ask for its Form A-S. Answer the five questions on this form and submit it according to the instructions thereon. You will be notified when your case is to be heard. You have the option of seeking legal assistance if desired, but, because of the size of these claims, the hearing procedures have been set up so that you may represent yourself. Decisions of the court for small tax cases may not be appealed.

If you want a hearing before an independent body, you must turn to the federal courts. Before you venture into these courts, engage a good tax attorney. He should be willing to give you, in advance, an opinion on your chances of winning your case and an estimate of his fee for representing you. It probably would be best to solicit opinions and fee estimates from several tax attorneys before deciding on one. Consider this alternative only if the amount under contention is quite large in relation to the potential fee costs, as it may be necessary to follow the appeals process all the way to the Supreme Court.

Tax Return Preparation Services

Tax return preparation services are one means of possibly avoiding legal difficulties with the IRS. Certain attorneys and all certified public accountants can help you determine what taxes you legally must pay. There are also tax practitioners who must be certified by the IRS before they are permitted to offer this service.

Some preparation services are not subject to federal qualifications or regulations. If you engage an unregulated tax practitioner, you should require him to give you an accurate estimate of his fee in advance; to guarantee your return's accuracy (given correct information); to agree to pay any penalty or interest charge leveled against your return by the IRS, should he file a faulty return (you must pay any tax deficiencies, however); to double-check for mathematical correctness; and to prepare the form in your presence.

Liability for filing incorrect, misleading, or false information is somewhat unsettled where tax preparation agents (attorneys, CPAs, regulated or unregulated agents) are involved. In general, these individuals are responsible for filing an accurate, complete, and true return based upon the information you supply them. If your tax consultant finds an error, omission, or irregularity in the work he has done for you, he must promptly inform you. It is then your responsibility to see that the problem is rectified with the IRS.

CONCLUSION

Rather than merely show you how to fill out the forms, we have presented a framework for many of the considerations about the federal income tax. It is our hope that from this discussion you will be able to see how different elements of income, deductions, and exemptions relate to each other. With this insight, you will be able to file your return correctly. In addition, you will be better prepared to make financial decisions for the best tax advantage.

VOCABULARY

adjusted gross income   capital loss
avoidance of tax   deduction
capital gain   estimated tax

evasion of tax
exemption
Form 1040
gross income
marginal tax rate
progressive tax

regressive tax
taxable income
tax bracket
tax exempt
withholding

1. Your current taxable income is $13,000, and your marginal tax rate is 25 percent. You are informed that unexpected dividends will increase your income by $800. What will be the tax effect?
2. Your current taxable income is $15,500, on which your marginal tax rate is 25 percent. The bank suddenly informs you that you owe an additional $2600 in interest on your newly written home mortgage. How will your taxes be affected by this added deductible expense, and in what amount?
3. Under what circumstances might too much be paid in Social Security taxes? How could you correct this overpayment?
4. List five sources of income that can be excluded from gross income for tax purposes.
5. What is the primary purpose of tax planning and how does it differ from tax preparation?
6. Describe the three options you have in terms of type two deductions. How would you determine which option offers you the best tax break? Under what circumstances might you be restricted from using one of the options? Which one?
7. What alternative is available to you if you and the IRS cannot settle a disputed tax return?

John and Marsha Howard's taxable income for the current year is $18,500. Their taxable incomes for the four previous years were $8000, $12,000, $6000, and $15,000. Do the Howards qualify for income averaging this year? Would they qualify if their current taxable income were to drop to $15,000?

The Howards derive $2500 of their $18,500 income from an investment with John's three married brothers. The total income from this investment is $10,000, which is split evenly among the four brothers. If each of the other brothers has a taxable income of approximately $18,000, what is each brother's marginal tax rate? What will be the total amount of tax paid on the $10,000 of investment income? How much would be saved in taxes on each of the brother's returns if this investment provided $200 of depreciation deductions for each of them?

RECOMMENDED READING

MAGAZINES AND NEWSPAPER

"How Tax Bills Compare, City by City." *Changing Times,* June 1971, pp. 14–15.

> Article with tables showing state and local tax burden at various income levels for twenty-five major U.S. cities.

Sonderling, Sterling E. "Whose Tax Burden Is Heaviest." *Wall Street Journal.* May 9, 1972.

> A discussion of the individual taxpayers' burden as revealed in the Herriott-Miller studies.

"What the New Tax Law Does for You." *Changing Times,* June 1970, pp. 41–44.

> A brief summary of the Tax Reform Act of 1969 as it affects individual taxpayers.

"What the Tax People Don't Tell You." *Changing Times,* March 1970, pp. 17–20.

> This discussion of the individual's relations with tax authorities emphasizes a few generally unknown benefits in the taxpayer's favor.

BOOKS

Commerce Clearing House. *Federal Tax Course.* Published annually.

> A complete and accurate overview of federal taxation.

Internal Revenue Service. *Your Federal Income Tax—for Individuals.* Washington, D.C.: Government Printing Office. Published annually.

> An authoritative source of information on filing your tax return. It may be bought at post offices for a small charge.

CHUCK AND NANCY ANDERSON

COMPUTING THEIR INCOME TAXES

Chuck and Nancy have asked you to help them fill out their Form 1040. You decide to calculate their taxable income first using the standard deduction and then using itemized type two deductions to determine which method results in the smallest tax liability.

The Andersons give you the following list of items that they say represents their tax lives for the past year.

charitable contributions	$ 130
Widget Salesman subscription fee	5
salaries	16,500
two auto licenses	100
nonreimbursed auto expenses related to employment	125
interest paid	
furniture loan	182
car loan	445
home mortgage	940
margin loan	55
dividends received	310
health insurance premiums	86
medical insurance portion of auto insurance	42
interest received	20
medical and dental expenses	
doctor	194
dentist	250
medicines	25
employee tools (briefcase)	55
long-term capital loss	1,100
taxes	
previous year's state income taxes	175
sales taxes (table value from IRS tax booklet)	191
gasoline taxes (table value from IRS tax booklet)	62
property taxes	770
health insurance settlement proceeds	675

Your first task is to make some order out of this list. After perusing the IRS tax booklet, you find the following regulations that seem to apply.

Only medical expenses in excess of 3 percent of adjusted gross income may be used as a type two deduction. Medicines may be used in the calculation of medical expenses only to the extent that they exceed 1 percent of adjusted gross income. Only 50 percent of health insurance premiums paid may be deducted up to a dollar maximum of $150, but in this calculation the portion of auto insurance premiums used for medical expense coverage may be included. That portion of health insurance premiums not allowable as a health insurance deductible, however, may be included in the calculation of total medical and dental deductible expenses.

The $200 sales tax on the Andersons' car purchase may be added to the sales tax deduction value allowed in the IRS tax booklet for a family of four with the Andersons' gross income. The first $11 paid on each auto license is not deductible.

Only 50 percent of long-term capital losses may be used as a type one deduction.

QUESTIONS

1. What item on the Andersons' list should not be included in gross income?
2. How should the Andersons' dividends be treated for federal tax purposes?
3. What are the two type one deductions on the Andersons' list?
4. How much of their long-term capital loss can be offset against their gross income?
5. What is the current standard deduction allowed by the IRS? What is the amount of the Andersons' standard deduction?

6. What is the current exemption level allowed by the IRS per person? What is the total amount of the Andersons' exemptions?
7. Does the Andersons' expense for medicines qualify as a type two deduction?
8. How much of the Andersons' health insurance premiums may be used as deductions? What can be done with the remaining amount?
9. What is the Andersons' taxable income using the standard deduction? Using itemized deductions?

10

BORROWING: CONSUMER LOANS

Chapters 10 and 11 deal with borrowing money. The principal reason for treating this subject in two chapters is that we felt there was too much information to cover in one chapter. Chapter 10 deals with basic considerations about borrowing and consumer loans. Chapter 11 covers consumer credit transactions. The distinction between consumer loans and consumer credit is subtle. A borrower who takes out a consumer loan goes to one party (the lender) to obtain funds that he then gives to a second party (the seller) to purchase something from that party. When a borrower uses consumer credit, however, the lender and the seller are the same.

THE CONCEPT OF BORROWING

When you borrow money, you obtain the use of someone else's money for a certain period of time in order to expand your immediate purchasing power. In exchange for the use of this money, you pay a fee, often called a *finance charge*. This fee is comprised of two elements: interest, the amount you pay for the opportunity to borrow money; and carrying costs, the costs the lender incurs by loaning you money (e.g., bookkeeping, collection, insurance, and so on). Interest rates have legal ceilings that are established by state usury laws.

Here is an example of how a borrowing arrangement might work. Assume that you want to build a patio but cannot pay cash for it. In shopping for a loan that would enable you to purchase the patio materials, you obtain quotes from three different lenders.

Lender	Amount of Loan ($)	Repayment Period (Months)	Monthly Payments ($)	Finance Charges ($)[a] (%)		Total ($)
1	400	12	35.00	20	10	420
2	400	24	18.34	40	10	440
3	400	12	35.83	30	15	430

[a]Effective cost of borrowing. (See pages 205–206.)

From these three quotes, it is apparent that the longer the payback period, the more the finance charge. Also, the higher the rate charged, the more the finance charge will be.

You decide to accept the terms offered by lender 1. Once the necessary documentation is completed, the lender gives you $400, which you are free to use to buy the materials necessary to build the patio. He also gives you a loan book that consists of a cover page and twelve other pages, one for each payment you will make on the loan. Each page states the amount of the payment and the date on which it is due. Every month you will tear out the appropriate page, enclose it in an envelope with your payment, and mail it to the lender. On the stub remaining in the booklet, you record the amount paid and the date the payment was made. When there are no more payment pages in your loan book, your loan, plus the finance charge, will be paid off. By borrowing against your future income, you have gained the immediate use of a new patio.

The primary advantage of borrowing is that it permits people who lack the discipline or time to save money for cash purchases to acquire consumer goods. Therefore, borrowing forces a person to save after the fact, so to speak—he has spent his money before he has saved it. The principal disadvantage of borrowing is that, because it involves finance charges ranging from 8 to 35 percent a year, you will be paying more for the merchandise over the long run than you would if you had paid cash initially. Also, when borrowing money, you pay interest to the lender; when saving money, the interest is paid to you.

To Borrow or Not to Borrow

People often choose not to borrow. When this decision is based on emotional reactions to borrowing, it is less sound than when based on financial considerations.

A common reason for not borrowing is fear of personal insolvency, of not being able to honor debt obligations because of inadequate income. Application of the financial principles discussed in this text should help eliminate this danger.

Another reason often given is lack of confidence in the government's ability to keep the economy relatively stable and to prevent another Great Depression. In our opinion an economic debacle of that magnitude is very unlikely. We believe that government regulation of the securities markets and supervision of other sectors of our economy can forestall the speculative excesses that led to the crash of 1929 and the ensuing economic difficulties. We believe, however, that economic recessions and unemployment will occur from time to time. You must form your own opinions about the stability of our economy and your own ways of dealing with it.

Who Borrows Money?

Table 10-1 shows what percentage of families, by income level, have installment debt and in what amounts. As you can see, almost half of all families have some form of installment debt. In the $7500 to $14,999 levels of family income, the frequency of installment debt is highest. For family incomes of $5000 or more, those who borrow tend to carry at least $500 worth of debt.

Table 10-2 (p. 202) indicates what percentage of a family's disposable income (earnings less taxes), as calculated for 1969, was used to make debt payments. These percentages are presented according to both income

TABLE 10-1

PERCENTAGE OF FAMILIES, BY INCOME LEVEL, WITH INSTALLMENT DEBT

ANNUAL FAMILY INCOME	TOTAL WHO HAVE DEBT	AMOUNT OF DEBT OUTSTANDING				
		$1–199	$200–499	$500–999	$1,000–1,999	$2,000 or more
Less than $3000	19%	10%	5%	1%	2%	1%
$3000–4999	31	9	7	5	5	5
$5000–7499	52	10	10	12	11	9
$7500–9999	61	9	9	13	15	15
$10,000–14,999	65	9	10	10	17	19
$15,000 or more	49	4	6	8	11	20
All families	49	8	8	9	11	13

SOURCE: George Katona, Lewis Mandell, and Jay Schmiedeskamp, *1970 Survey of Consumer Finances* (Ann Arbor: University of Michigan, 1971), p. 23.

TABLE 10-2

PERCENTAGE OF DISPOSABLE INCOME USED FOR INSTALLMENT DEBT PAYMENTS

ANNUAL FAMILY INCOME	DISPOSABLE INCOME USED FOR DEBT PAYMENTS						
	No Debt	Less Than 5%	5–9%	10–19%	20–39%	40% or More	Not Ascertained
Less than $3000	81%	2%	5%	5%	4%	2%	1%
$3000–4999	69	5	7	9	7	2	1
$5000–7499	48	11	13	17	8	2	1
						less than	
$7500–9999	39	14	16	21	8	0.5	2
$10,000–14,999	35	17	24	18	3	1	2
$15,000 or more	51	17	18	10	1	11	2
AGE OF FAMILY HEAD							
Younger than 25	41	6	11	24	14	2	2
25–34	32	14	22	21	8	2	1
						less than	
35–44	37	19	22	15	5	0.5	2
45–54	44	17	17	15	2	2	3
55–64	64	9	13	9	2	1	2
65–74	87	3	4	3	1	1	1
					less than	less than	less than
75 or older	94	1	2	3	0.5	0.5	0.5
All Families	51	12	15	14	5	1	2

SOURCE: George Katona, Lewis Mandell, and Jay Schmiedeskamp, *1970 Survey of Consumer Finances* (Ann Arbor: University of Michigan, 1971), p. 25.

level and the age of the family's head-of-household. As the table shows, very few debt users spent more than 20 percent of their disposable income on installment debt payments. That is, most families kept their debt level under control. The table also indicates that families whose head was fifty-five or older used debt substantially less frequently than did families with younger heads. The younger the head of the family, the more likely the family was to be using 10 percent or more of its disposable income to resolve installment debts.

PROPER USE OF DEBT

If you have decided to accept borrowing in principle, you are ready to begin thinking about how much you should borrow and for what.

Setting Debt Limits

There is no one formula you can use in all instances to calculate debt limits for yourself. Generally, your debt limit at any one time is a product of two factors. The first factor is your need for borrowed money, which depends on both the stage of your life cycle and your income level. For example, if you buy a home and raise children during the early years of marriage, the financial requirements will probably be great relative to your income. As you grow older, these requirements will probably subside and your income will probably increase. The data in table 10-2 bear out these observations. The second factor involves the lender's estimation of your ability to repay a debt. For example, you may feel that you need $50,000 to meet your current financial needs whereas the lender may feel that you are able to repay only $15,000 at most. In this case, he would probably be unwilling to lend more than the latter amount. At any one time your debt limit will be determined by both your need to borrow money and your ability to do so, which is based on your ability to repay.

Each time you consider borrowing money you should ask yourself several questions. Do I want or need what I am going to buy with this borrowed money enough right now to justify remaining in debt for the loan period? Can another liability (a loan) be realistically added to my financial obligations without jeopardizing the soundness of my financial resources? Will I be able to repay this loan without taking money away from necessary expenditures (such as living expenses)? Your responses to these questions should indicate whether you are near your debt limit.

debt/equity ratio Commercial lenders generally agree that when a business's debts (liabilities) become equal to or greater than its equity (net worth), it is time to stop lending it money. You might also use this debt/equity ratio as an upper limit on your borrowing. It should be measured exclusive of the value of your home (an asset) and its mortgage (a liability). Therefore, if you find that all your other interest-bearing debt is as great as or greater than your net worth (minus your home and its financing), you should probably not take on more debt obligations.

This is just one possible measure and will not apply in all instances. As we indicated in chapter 2, the student who is heavily laden with educational loans may have a negative net worth, but he possesses income earning potential that may offset this otherwise bad economic position.

no more than 20 percent of disposable income Another way to measure your debt limit is to consider your ability to cover your debt payments out of your disposable income. If no more than 20 percent of your disposable income is used to make installment debt payments and other interest-bearing debt payments (exclusive of home mortgages), you probably will avoid misuse of debt.

You should not, however, try to keep your debt payments (not including mortgage payments) below 20 percent of your take-home pay by borrowing for longer periods. If you extend the maturities (time periods) of your debt arrangements, you reduce your monthly payments, but you also increase your total borrowing costs. If you rely on this tactic to keep your loan repayments manageable, you are probably misusing debt.

resolving debts every three years As a final way to set debt limits, you might try to resolve all your debt obligations, exclusive of home mortgages and educational loans, every three years. If you add new obligations to banks or lending companies before you pay off old ones or if you are frequently delinquent on payments, you are probably making too liberal and continuous use of debt.

When to Borrow?

You should borrow only if a loan is needed to finance an asset (home, car, education) or as part of an investment program. Consumer loans are generally used to buy expensive, fairly durable items such as a car or home furnishings. A mortgage loan to buy a house is not considered a consumer loan. Consumables (food, clothing, travel, entertainment) should come entirely out of your income. These quickly-used-up items should be a regular part of your budget. We advise that you limit the times you borrow money, but maximize the amounts borrowed.

Some people use loans to help consolidate many small debts into one lending arrangement. This consolidation often involves a longer repayment period so that the monthly payment can be brought down to an acceptable level. People are likely to find such consolidation attractive because the resulting monthly payment is smaller than the sum of the payments of the debts outstanding before consolidation. The ultimate effect, however, of borrowing over an extended period of time enough money to cover one's small debts is more total interest paid out. Therefore, if you can meet your current payments, it is almost always better to let them stand rather than consolidate.

TRUTH IN LENDING

The Consumer Credit Protection Act of 1968 has four main sections dealing with (1) the establishment of a consumer interest agency, (2) limitations on the activities of organized crime in the area of consumer credit, (3) wage garnishment, and (4) truth in lending. It is truth in lending that is of most interest here.

The act, which went into effect July 1, 1969, covers credit up to $25,000 extended to individuals for personal, family, household, and agricultural uses. However, all real estate credit extended to individuals is covered no matter what the amount. Compliance is required of any person or business that regularly extends or arranges for credit to individuals for personal, family, household, agricultural or real estate purposes. Most commonly this includes banks, savings and loan associations, department and retail stores, credit card companies, automobile dealers, credit unions, consumer finance companies, mortgage bankers, hospitals, doctors, home building and repair contractors, and the like. Credit exempted by the act includes business and commercial credit and securities and commodities credit as well as consumer credit in excess of $25,000 (real estate credit excepted).

The most significant requirement of this section of the act is that the terms of various credit transactions between lender and consumer be fully disclosed before the transaction is completed. The lender must identify the cash price, all other charges, the down payment, and the amount to be financed. This last amount must be equal to the cash price plus all other charges minus the down payment. The total cost of credit must also be expressed in terms of an annual percentage rate or an annual dollar amount. Whichever way it is expressed, this cost must be identified as the finance charge. This charge is not considered by this law as synonymous with interest rates. It is considered to include interest, investigation and finder's fees, service and carrying charges, and insurance and loan guarantee costs. The repayment schedule must be set out according to number of payments, amount of each payment, and either the final due date for all payments or the total length of time over which the payments must be made. Any items to be used as collateral for the transaction must be described and any default, delinquency, and late payment penalties disclosed. Your signature on the documents of the purchase agreement is considered proof that the lender or creditor has fulfilled his disclosure responsibilities. Therefore, you should make sure that he has complied with the disclosure requirements and that you understand what you are signing.

Enforcement responsibilities rest primarily with the Federal Trade Commission, although other federal agencies such as the Federal Reserve Board and Federal Home Loan Bank Board may also have jurisdiction. Because there are no severe financial penalties (the maximum is $1000) and the individual consumer may prove weak against a major creditor, more effective forms of enforcement and legal redress may yet have to be developed.

THE EFFECTIVE COST OF BORROWING

To demonstrate what the effective cost of borrowing is, we will use the following example. You ask to borrow $500 from a lender. He informs

you that the stated, or simple, interest rate is 6 percent. This implies a dollar cost of borrowing of $30 a year. Assume that you are to pay off this loan in twelve equal monthly installments beginning in thirty days. Therefore, you actually have use of the full $500 for only the first month of the lending period. If the balance outstanding at the end of the twelve-month period is zero, the average balance for the entire period is approximately $250. A $30 interest charge on an average outstanding balance of $250 is in reality costing you 12 percent a year. In this case, the effective cost of borrowing is twice as large as the stated rate.

Although most lending sources are required to let the borrower know the effective cost of borrowing before a borrowing contract is completed, you should be able to make this determination on your own. This will enable you to check the lender's honesty and to provide this information for yourself when you are not protected by legislation—in leasing arrangements, for example.

Determining the Cost of Borrowing

The following formula can be used to determine the effective annual rate of interest. This formula approximates the effective cost for short-term loans only.

$$\frac{200 \left(\begin{array}{c}\text{dollar credit} \\ \text{cost}\end{array}\right) \times \left(\begin{array}{c}\text{number of payments} \\ \text{per year}\end{array}\right)}{\left(\begin{array}{c}\text{amount} \\ \text{borrowed}\end{array}\right) \times \left(\begin{array}{c}\text{total number of payments} \\ \text{plus one}\end{array}\right)} = \begin{array}{l}\text{effective} \\ \text{annual rate} \\ \text{of interest}\end{array}$$

To demonstrate the use of this formula, let us assume that you make a $25 down payment on a $250 dishwasher and borrow $225 to pay off the rest. The dollar cost of credit as specified in the purchase agreement is $26.25. You are to pay off this debt in eighteen equal monthly installments. The number of yearly payments is twelve, and the total number of payments plus one is nineteen. These figures can be inserted in the formula as follows:

$$\frac{200 \,(\$26.25) \times 12}{225 \times 19} = \frac{63,000}{4275} = 14.7\% \begin{array}{l}\text{effective} \\ \text{annual rate} \\ \text{of interest}\end{array}$$

This method should be used when the payment schedule calls for regularly occurring payments of equal amounts. Computations involving deferred or irregular payments are more difficult, and you should seek professional help for determinations of this type.

Determining the Dollar Drain Due to Credit Buying

Suppose you were trying to decide whether to use credit to purchase a $2000 living room set or to wait for two years until you have saved the money to pay for it. The following procedure will help you determine the actual dollars you would lose if you bought the furniture on credit rather than saved for it by putting your money in a savings account.

1. *Determine the dollar credit cost* by using the following formula to check the information supplied by the lender or to determine it for yourself if he is not required to supply it.

$$\frac{\left(\begin{array}{c}\text{effective}\\\text{interest rate}\end{array}\right) \times \left(\begin{array}{c}\text{amount}\\\text{borrowed}\end{array}\right) \times \left(\begin{array}{c}\text{total number}\\\text{of payments plus one}\end{array}\right)}{200 \ \times \ \left(\begin{array}{c}\text{number of payments}\\\text{per year}\end{array}\right)} = \begin{array}{c}\text{dollar}\\\text{credit}\\\text{cost}\end{array}$$

   Assume that you could pay back the $2000 in monthly payments over a two-year period at a rate of 15 percent. Your collar credit cost would be as follows:

$$\frac{15 \times \$2000 \times 25}{200 \times 12} = \frac{\$750,000}{2400} = \$312.50 \text{ credit cost}$$

   Notice that in the formula you use the effective interest rate (15 percent) as a whole number, not as a decimal since the constant (200) is used.

2. *Determine how much interest you would receive in a savings account if you made regular deposits.* In the furniture example, assume that the savings and loan account yields 5 percent and that you put in $83.30 each month for a total of $1000 a year. During the first year you receive interest on an average balance of $500 and during the second year the average balance is $1500. The interest received for the first year is 5 percent of $500 or $25, and for the second year it is 5 percent of $1500 or $75. The total interest is $100.

3. *Add the amounts computed in steps 1 and 2 to arrive at the total dollar drain due to credit buying.* In our example, you would lose $412.50 of potential purchasing power if you bought the furniture on credit. Not only would you have to pay $312.50 in finance charges, but also you would lose $100 in earnings from a savings account. In other words, you are paying $412.50 for the privilege of having the furniture today rather than two years from now. You should decide whether the immediate use is worth the additional expense.

EFFECT OF INFLATION AND INCOME TAXES

Inflation and income taxes can reduce the effective cost of borrowing, and you should understand how these factors work.

Inflation

Inflation reduces the purchasing power of money. Assume that five years ago $1 could buy one widget. If it now takes $1.29 to buy that same widget, the cost of living (as reflected by the cost of widgets) has increased 29 percent in five years. Conversely, the purchasing power of the dollar has fallen to 77.5 percent of its original power (1.00 ÷ 1.29). This means that while $1 bought one widget five years ago, it now buys only 77.5 percent of a widget.

Let us apply this concept to the borrowing process in which a lump sum is obtained from a lender and installment payments are made until the debt is resolved. If the amount borrowed is spent immediately (perhaps for a car, home, or appliance), you have gained the current purchasing power of the dollars borrowed. Assume that inflation persists during the payback period. With each payment, you relinquish dollars of less and less purchasing power. The purchasing power you must give up (loan payments) to obtain immediate purchasing power (the loan) is less than if inflation did not exist. Remember, however, since lenders are aware of the effect of inflation on the value of money paid back, they adjust their rates as inflation grows or diminishes.

Income Taxes

Income taxes also reduce the cost of borrowing because interest may be taken as a type two deduction (p. 177). For example, assume that your taxable income without a type two deduction for loan interest is $14,000. If you are married and file a joint return, your tax is $2760. Now let us assume that you have interest charges of $500. This deductible expense reduces your taxable income to $13,500 and your tax liability to $2635, a tax savings of $125. You can also arrive at this figure by using the marginal tax rate of 25 percent (p. 189). Hence, your after-tax cost of borrowing would be $375 ($500 interest cost − $125 tax savings). These tax savings are available, however, only if you itemize your type two deductions.

An Example of the Effect of Inflation and Income Taxes

Figure 10-1 shows how a 3 percent annual rate of inflation and a 25 percent marginal tax rate affect the cost of borrowing $3000 at 10 percent to be paid back over a period of three years. The annual payment is

YEAR	AMOUNT PAID BACK			TAX SAVINGS (25% rate) ($)	REDUCTION IN PURCHASING POWER ($)	TOTAL COST SAVINGS ($)	NET COST OF BORROWING	
	Prin-cipal ($)	Inter-est ($)	Total ($)				($)	(%)
1	1000	300	1300	75	39[a]	114	186	6.2
2	1000	200	1200	50	72[b]	122	78	3.9
3	1000	100	1100	25	99[c]	124	(24)	

[a]3 percent of repayment
[b]6 percent of repayment
[c]9 percent of repayment

Fig. 10-1.
Effect of inflation
and tax savings on
cost of $3000 loan

$1000 plus interest on the outstanding balance. As you can see, in the third year the combined effect of tax savings and inflation (total cost savings) is so significant that the total repayment for that year (including interest) represents giving up less purchasing power than was received ($1000) when the money was borrowed. Although inflation and tax savings can substantially reduce the cost of borrowing, it would still cost $240 in today's after-tax dollars to borrow $3000 for three years.

Returning to our example of the dollar drain due to credit buying (p. 207), let us assume that the tax savings relative to interest cost were $78 (25% marginal tax rate × $312.50 interest cost). The reduction in purchasing power (3 percent annual inflation) would be computed in the following way. Your monthly payments each year would amount to $1156.25 ([$2000 + $312.50] ÷ 2). Therefore, the average amount paid back each year would be $578.125. In the first year of the payback period the reduction due to inflation would be $17.34 (3% × $578.125), and in the second year it would be $34.69 (6% × $578.125) for a total of $52.03 ($52 rounded). As a result, the after-tax-and-inflation effective cost of borrowing the $2000 for a living room set is $182.50 ($312.50 − $78 − $52). When the $100 lost in interest is added to this amount, your cost of immediate enjoyment is really $282.50. If you know in advance what this cost will be, you are better able to decide whether you want to incur it by using borrowed money.

PREPARING TO SHOP FOR A LOAN

Before you contact a lending source, you should do several things.

1. Decide on the exact amount of money you need. This will make it easier for you to identify the most appropriate loan source. A consumer finance company, for example, would be able to make loans only up to a certain amount. Furthermore, lenders often look more favorably on loan applicants who have a firm idea of how much money they need.

2. List the reasons why you want to take out a loan in this amount. Most likely one of your reasons will be that you do not have the cash you need for a particular purchase.
3. Note the use or uses to which the borrowed money will be put. You may, for example, want to use the money to buy new carpeting for your living room.
4. Locate your balance sheet and income statement so that you will be able to tell the lender about your financial resources—net worth, sources and amounts of income, and existing debts.
5. Be sure you can tell the lender about your financial responsibilities—number of dependents, amount and timing of existing debt repayments, and monthly living expenses (check your budget sheets).
6. Review your employment record so that you can describe any jobs you have had in the last five to ten years in addition to your present job. Be able to state how long you have been both in your current occupation and with your current employer.
7. Review your credit record so that you can accurately describe your borrowing experiences and the installment loans you have paid off on time. List your credit references such as credit cards, charge accounts, and banks.

SHOPPING FOR A LOAN

Investigate the loan possibilities at several sources such as banks, savings and loan associations, credit unions, and consumer finance companies. Collect the following information.

1. What is the exact amount of money that will be given to you?
2. How will the finance charges be treated? Will they be added to the principal, or will they be deducted from the principal and paid in advance? For example, lender A is willing to lend you $2000 at a finance charge of $200 that would be added to principal: you would get $2000 from him and pay back $2200. If you are to pay back the loan in one year, the charge would be 10 percent. If you go to lender B who uses discounted interest, and he will also charge $200 to loan you $2000, he will deduct the $200 in advance. You actually have use of only $1800, although you will pay back $2000, and the charge is slightly in excess of 11 percent.
3. What will be your effective annual rate of interest? The lender is required to provide you with this information, but you can check its accuracy by using the formula on page 206.
4. What is the repayment schedule?
5. Will there be a penalty if you decide to pay back the loan before it is due or if a payment is late? Lenders often discourage the bor-

rower from paying off a loan in advance. When the borrower does this, he denies the lender interest income he would have received had the loan been paid off on schedule. Admittedly, the lender can take the amount paid off in advance and lend it to someone else but probably not without losing interest while looking for another borrower. Therefore, the lender requires some compensation in the form of a prepayment penalty, usually a sliding percentage of the debt outstanding at the time of prepayment. Lenders also levy a penalty, usually 5 percent of the delinquent amount, for loan payments that are late. This penalty is intended to motivate the borrower to make his payments on time.

6. What collateral will be required? Often when a lender evaluates a prospective borrower, he looks for some assurance that the money he lends will in fact be repaid to him. One method of gaining this assurance is to ask the prospective borrower for collateral, or security, which can come in either of two forms. The first requires that you pledge an asset (chattel)—most likely the one to be purchased with the borrowed funds. If you default on the loan, the lender can take possession of the asset to compensate for the money he loaned you. (According to the Consumer Credit Protection Act, when a consumer loan is secured by a second mortgage on the consumer's home, he has the right to cancel the transaction within three days after signing the credit agreement if he changes his mind about the loan or about using the mortgage as security.) The second form of security is called a loan endorsement or guarantee. The prospective borrower has someone whose credit worthiness is stronger than his own promise to make the loan good (i.e., to repay it) if the borrower defaults on his payments. A secured loan has one of these two forms of security. An unsecured loan does not. Lenders with whom you have or have had successful borrowing relationships may require less collateral than other lenders.

Once you have collected this information from several sources, you should be able to identify which one offers you the best conditions and why.

Meeting the Lender

A lender usually evaluates three characteristics when deciding whether to extend credit: ability to repay, willingness to honor debt obligations, and the availability of collateral in the event of failure to repay. In particular he will want to know how much of your income is being used to repay other debts so that he can estimate whether you will be able to take on more debt. He will also want to know how regularly and faithfully you have paid off previous credit arrangements and what he can legally confiscate if you fail to repay him. If you have done your homework as we suggested, you will have all the necessary information ready to answer his questions and will probably make a favorable impression.

A personal information form is commonly used by lenders to get an initial picture of your financial situation. On this form you will be asked to list credit accounts and references (including your bank) and either your annual or monthly income. If you are a minor, an adult (usually your parent) may be asked to provide a guardian's guarantee.

An interview with the lender is often the second step. He will use this session to obtain information in addition to that found on the form you completed. Answer his questions truthfully. If you do not and the lender finds it out through his regular credit check, your credit rating will be very low.

A credit investigation will be conducted to check the accuracy of the information you gave on the form and during the interview. This investigation will cover your credit record with the local credit bureau or existing creditors, your employment history, and your character. If you pass all these checks, you qualify for a loan.

Disreputable Money Sources

When you look for an appropriate lending source, beware of those individuals or organizations known as loan sharks. They often may be identified if they do not display an official state lender's license, do not require you to qualify for a loan, attempt to predate a loan, urge you to sign loan papers before they are completely filled out, or refuse to give you a receipt or copies of the loan agreement.

Reputable lenders comply with the truth-in-lending provisions of the Consumer Credit Protection Act. These provisions are for your protection. If a lender refuses to comply with them, do not deal with him. Under no circumstances is dealing with disreputable lenders worth the cost and anxiety.

SOURCES OF CONSUMER LOANS

Sources of consumer loans include life insurance policies, credit unions, consumer finance companies, commercial banks, savings and loan associations, and pawnbrokers. Even second mortgages are in some ways similar to consumer loans. A second mortgage is a loan specifically secured by your equity (market value minus first mortgage balance) in your home. Admittedly, lenders of second mortgage money do not fall strictly in the category of sources of consumer loans. Nevertheless, because these cash loans are advertised and made for many of the same reasons as consumer loans, they deserve some treatment in this chapter. The specifics of first and second mortgages will be deferred until chapter 12. Figure 10-2 gives a general comparison of these sources.

Source	Who Is Eligible	Effective Annual Cost	Maximum Maturity	Maximum Loan Amount	Collateral Required	Credit Investigation
Life insurance policies	Policyholders	5 to 6 percent	Unlimited	Insurance policy's cash value	Insurance policy's cash value	No
Credit unions	Members	9 to 12 percent	5 years for unsecured loans 10 years for secured loans	$1000 to $2500 on unsecured loans; $2500 on secured loans	On secured loans only—cosigner or chattel mortgage	No
Consumer finance companies	Anyone meeting credit qualifications	12 to 36 percent	18 months to 5 years	$1000 to $5000	Signed promise to pay	Yes
Commercial banks	Anyone meeting credit qualifications	8 to 18 percent	Varies with circumstances of the loan	Varies with circumstances of the loan	On secured loans only	Yes
Savings and loan associations (consumer loans on passbook accounts only)	Savings or share account holders	1 to 1.5 percent above interest paid on savings deposits	1 to 3 years	90 to 100 percent of amount in savings account	Savings account	No
Pawnbrokers	Anyone with personal property	24 to 120 percent	1 year	50 to 60 percent of appraised value of personal property	Personal property	No
Second mortgage lenders	Anyone with equity in a home	15 percent and up	3 to 10 years	50 percent of home's equity	Home	Yes

Fig. 10-2.
Comparison of sources of consumer loans

Life Insurance Policies

The maximum loan amount available to you on a cash-value life insurance policy is usually limited to its accumulated cash value, plus dividends and interest. Loans on term life insurance policies are not available because such policies have no cash values.

There are several advantages to borrowing on the cash value of your policy. First, the interest rate is fixed and generally stated in the policy. In periods when interest rates are high, a policy written when rates were lower may offer a much lower loan charge. Second, interest is usually charged only on the balance of the loan outstanding and it may be paid with your regularly scheduled premium payments. Third, principal repayment schedules and periods are usually quite flexible and may not be specified at all. Although you may not be required to pay back the principal, the interest payments will probably be continuous as long as the debt is outstanding. Fourth, these loans can be obtained by simply writing the company for appropriate forms, filling them out, and returning them. Rarely does the life insurance company want to know your reasons for requesting a loan or ask for information such as your employment history. This is because you are, in reality, borrowing your own accumulated policy savings, not the company's money. Within a month you should have the amount you requested.

There are two disadvantages to using this type of borrowing despite its inherent attractiveness. First, the face value of your policy (its death benefit) is decreased by the amount borrowed. For example, if you had a $20,000 life insurance policy with an accumulated cash value of $6250 and you borrowed $5000 on the policy, the benefits your beneficiary would receive, if you died, would be only $15,000 ($20,000 face value minus $5000 loan outstanding). As you repaid the principal of this loan, however, the face value of the policy would increase. One way to avoid this reduction in death protection is to buy term insurance for the duration of the loan. Second, if the repayment schedule and period are not specified, you may put off resolving the debt and consequently continue to pay interest year after year. This disadvantage can be offset if you are disciplined enough to set your own schedule and stick to it.

Credit Unions

Sometimes a group of people with a common interest or activity join together to form credit unions that extend consumer loans to their members at rates lower than those they could obtain from commercial lenders. These rates are possible because credit unions do not seek a profit. They only provide financial services (emergency loans, credit counselling, insurance benefits, and the like) for their members. The primary requirement for membership usually is that a certain amount of savings be invested in the credit union. This limit is often expressed as a dollar amount. Some credit unions require as little as $5 or $10. Generally, maximum loan limits are determined by the policies of each credit union within the guidelines set down by appropriate government agencies.

The advantages of borrowing from a credit union can be quite attractive. First, interest costs are comparatively low—the lowest available for many people. One percent a month (12 percent annually) often is the maximum rate that the federal or state government regulating a credit union allows to be charged on the outstanding balance of unsecured loans. Secured loans may have monthly interest costs as low as three-fourths of 1 percent (9 percent a year). Second, security and endorsements are not required on small loans (up to $1000 for some of the larger credit unions). Third, as a borrower you can have confidence in the integrity of the lending organization because it consists of your associates.

One disadvantage is that, if you are not a member of a credit union, you cannot borrow from one. In other words, availability is limited. Another is that as a borrower you may hesitate to divulge your need for a loan to your associates. While they may employ a professionally trained person to handle the lending duties, he probably will be overseen by a committee composed of credit union members.

Consumer Finance (Small Loan) Companies

Consumer finance companies specialize in small loans. The maximum loan limit for unsecured loans is set by each state and ranges from $1000 to $5000. The maximum maturity is also set by each state and ranges from eighteen months to five years.

Both the advantages and the disadvantages of borrowing from consumer finance companies derive from their specializing in small loans with short and intermediate terms. These organizations are generally willing to write loans in smaller amounts than most other loan sources. However, a disadvantage is that they are limited in the amount they may lend and in the length of time over which the loan may be repaid. Qualification and security requirements are not as stringent as with some other sources. If you have a poor credit rating, finance companies may be your only loan source, but the disadvantage in this is that the interest charged is often higher than what other sources would charge if you qualified for a loan. (The higher rate is necessary to encourage consumer finance companies to grant these higher risk loans.) One last advantage is that interest is often charged only on the outstanding balance, not on the initial amount borrowed. Many people overlook the disadvantages of borrowing from small loan companies because they see these organizations as less formidable and imposing than banks. For this reason, the prospective borrower may feel more at ease at a consumer finance company.

Before the Consumer Credit Protection Act, only some states had guidelines regulating consumer finance companies. Regulation was often haphazard and inconsistent and provided insufficient protection for the consumer. In some instances, unscrupulous lending practices flourished. The new legislative act, combined with increasingly rigorous small loan state laws plus a better-educated consumer population, has done much to repair the reputation of this basically sound source of consumer loans.

Commercial Banks

The term *commercial banks* includes all institutions, except mutual savings banks, commonly referred to as banks. In general, commercial banks require that their customers have better credit records than consumer finance companies require. Because the risk of default is less for banks, their interest charges are lower than those levied by finance companies.

Banks offer consumer loan customers more extensive services than do most other lending institutions. Regarding installment loans, unsecured loans require only the borrower's signed promise to repay and are written generally for shorter periods and higher interest charges than are secured loans. Unsecured loans include regular loans, loans against a bank credit card, and loans that are automatically extended whenever a check is written for more money than is in a checking account. You must fulfill certain qualifications, however, before banks will allow you to use these unsecured loans. Since the costs of using them are relatively high, however, if you need money, it may be advisable to get it more cheaply with a secured loan.

Secured loans usually require some form of collateral. For automobile or home furnishing loans, the purchased item(s) can serve as security. A savings passbook loan uses your savings account as collateral; it may cost less for the short term than drawing down your savings just before interest is due, if interest is paid only on amounts held in the account for the full quarter. Real estate mortgage loans may be written for either home improvements or the purchase of a home, though only the former are, by definition, consumer loans. The maturity on these ranges from five to twenty-five years, and security is provided by the property itself.

Special payment or automatic transfer plans can direct the bank to deduct money from checking accounts to pay consumer loan and consumer credit repayments, and certain bills such as utilities, and insurance premiums. The authority to do this is granted in a written agreement.

There are definite advantages to borrowing from a commercial bank. First, because of strict federal regulations, the integrity of most banking institutions is rarely violated. Second, because of their credit requirements for applicants, borrowing costs are comparatively low. Third, successful borrowing and punctual repayment on your part will result in the establishment of a good credit rating that will make future loans less expensive and easier to obtain. This may be an advantage of dealing with any lender, but a good bank credit rating is of particular benefit.

The disadvantages are that it is difficult to obtain loans in small amounts, and the qualification and payback requirements are quite rigid.

Savings and Loan Associations

Savings and loan associations serve a dual purpose. As savings institutions, they offer returns slightly higher than commercial banks (see chapter 14). As lending institutions, they serve mainly the home mortgage market. In addition to mortgage loans, many savings and loan associations offer FHA insured home repair and modernization loans as well as consumer loans. In the past, these consumer loans were usually made solely against the value of savings held by a member (or depositor) of the institution granting the loan. The maximum loan limit was usually 90 percent of his savings investment for state chartered associations and 100 percent for federally chartered associations. In mid-1972 the federal government authorized a more extensive consumer lending program for savings and loan associations. Now these associations can make loans for such things as vacation and mobile homes as well as house improvements and household equipment (e.g., air conditioning systems).

With this type of loan no credit investigation is required. Over the very short term, such a loan may cost less than drawing down your savings account just before interest or dividends are to be paid, if interest is paid only on accounts held for the full quarter. Of course, such loans are available only to savings account holders. The cost is generally 1 to 1.5 percent above the return represented by your investments in savings and loan associations.

Pawnbrokers

Pawnbrokers most commonly serve as a lending source either in emergencies or when the applicant's credit is not accepted by other lenders. There is no need for a signed note because the personal property brought by the borrower serves as security. The pawnbroker rarely offers a loan exceeding 50 to 60 percent of the appraised market value of the property.

You may generally redeem your property within a year by paying a lump sum of principal plus interest, which may range from 24 to 120 percent annually. Installment payments are not used. If you fail to make the required payment, the pawnbroker has the right to auction your property, either publicly or privately, in order to retrieve his investment. Amounts in excess of his investment gained from the auction are rightfully yours. Instances of such surplus amounts are rare, however.

The chief advantages of pawnbrokers as a lending source are that transactions are quick and may be kept secret. Disadvantages are that interest rates are exceptionally high, and there is insufficient protection for the consumer because government regulations are often lax and vary from state to state.

Second Mortgages

The true costs of second mortgages are often obscured by their small monthly payments. In reality, the effective annual cost can be 15 percent or more because of a 10 to 12 percent annual interest charge plus fees that are attached at the beginning of the loan. The small monthly payments frequently represent little more than interest payments, with the amount of the loan itself coming due in one large payment at the end of the mortgage maturity. The danger in this form of borrowing is that you may be unable to make this large last payment and therefore have to refinance the loan at the continued high interest cost.

EDUCATION LOANS

Education loans are available in varying amounts and for varying terms through either government or private sources.

Government Sources

The National Defense Student Loan Program enables students at most colleges to borrow $1000 a year up to a total of $5000 while they are undergraduates. Repayment begins nine months after leaving school. The payback period is ten years and the annual interest rate on the outstanding balance is 3 percent. Service with the Peace Corps, Vista, or the military; attendance at a graduate school; or employment as a teacher can result in the deferment of the payback period (interest is not charged during deferral) or in reduction or cancellation of the amount owed. Eligibility requirements and applications for such loans are handled by the colleges themselves.

The Guaranteed Student Loan Program offers loans from private sources (banks, individuals, credit unions, and the like) which are guaranteed by the federal government. Up to $1500 is available each year not to exceed a total of $7500. Unlike the previous program, interest must be paid while the student is attending college; in certain instances this payment will be made by the federal government. The payback period, which begins nine months after graduation, varies in length from five to ten years and, as with the former program, repayment may be postponed for certain types of national service. Maximum interest rates are set at 7 percent. Because of the interest rate restriction, most lenders are reluctant to write these loans.

Private Sources

Private organizations, churches, colleges, unions, and service organizations occasionally have their own loan programs. Eligibility is more limited than with government loans, but terms are often quite favorable. Commercial lenders often grant installment loans, at market terms, to cover education expenses. In addition to traditional lenders, the following companies specialize in loans of this nature.

Education Funds, Inc., 36 South Wabash Avenue, Room 1000, Chicago, Illinois 60603

Funds for Education, 319 Lincoln Street, Manchester, New Hampshire 03103

Government Employees Financial Corporation, 41 East Colfax Avenue, Denver, Colorado 80202

Insured Tuition Payment Plan, 6 Saint James Avenue, Boston, Massachusetts 02116

The Tuition Plan, Inc., 575 Madison Avenue, New York, New York 10022

CONCLUSION

Borrowing is a means of increasing your immediate purchasing power. However, if you pay too much for the use of someone else's money or use it unwisely, borrowing can result in unnecessary drains on your financial resources. To ensure that this does not occur, use the measurement devices suggested in this chapter to determine what effect using consumer loans will have on your financial resources. Once you have done your homework, you will be prepared to check various sources of consumer loans and shop for the best deal.

VOCABULARY

balance outstanding
carrying cost
collateral
commerical bank
Consumer Credit Protection Act
creditor
credit union
discounted interest
effective cost

endorsement
finance charge
interest
maturity
prepayment penalty
secured loan
security
unsecured loan

QUESTIONS

1. Examine the validity of arguments used both for and against borrowing. Can it be morally right or wrong? Does it allow a person to live beyond his means? Can it lead to financial problems and, if so, how? Is it worth the cost and risks? Are you in favor of borrowing money? Do your reasons have a financial basis?
2. How do the two federal government college loan programs discussed in this chapter differ from each other?
3. Which source of consumer loans offers the most borrowing opportunities to the borrower with a good credit rating? Why?
4. What is the difference between a secured and an unsecured loan?
5. How do income level and position in the life cycle affect the use of borrowed money?
6. How does inflation affect the cost of borrowing?
7. Under what circumstances are there no tax savings associated with the cost of borrowing?
8. In what ways does borrowing resemble a forced savings plan?
9. How can you identify a disreputable lending source?
10. When shopping for a loan, what types of information should you collect?

CASE PROBLEM

Your best friend has come to you for advice about obtaining a loan. He needs at least $3000 to purchase kitchen and laundry appliances for his wife, and their budget will allow them to make monthly repayments of $125. He has already been out shopping in the money markets. His findings are given in figure 10-3. Based on this information, which alternative is most appropriate for your friend?

Source	Amount of Loan	Security	Annual Finance Charge	Payback Terms
Commercial bank A	$3000	None	11%[a] (interest added on)	90-day note[b]
Commercial bank B	$3500	Purchased goods	10%[a] (interest added on)	3-year amortized note
Consumer finance company	$3200	None	18%[c] (interest discounted)	Equal monthly installments over four years
Credit union	$4000	Purchased goods	9%[a] (interest added on)	Amortized over 5 years

Fig. 10-3.
Comparison of four consumer loans

[a]Effective rate of interest.
[b]This note is to be paid back at the end of the term in a lump sum plus interest; it may be renewed for three ninety-day periods.
[c]Stated rate of interest.

RECOMMENDED READING

BOOKS

Donaldson, Elvin, and Pfahl, John. *Personal Finance.* New York: Ronald Press, 1971.

> Chapter 4 discusses organizations offering consumer loans and how they work.

Katona, George; Mandell, Lewis; and Schmiedeskamp, Jay. *1970 Survey of Consumer Finances.* Ann Arbor: University of Michigan, 1971.

> Chapter 2 presents statistics concerning consumer use of installment credit.

MAGAZINES

"Personal Business." *Business Week,* July 24, 1971.

> A brief discussion of college loan alternatives.

"Where to Borrow Money for College." *Changing Times,* January 1971, pp. 15–17.

> A good treatment of this subject.

CHUCK AND NANCY ANDERSON

COMPUTING THE COST OF IMMEDIATE ENJOYMENT

Last year the Andersons took out a monthly payment installment loan of $4000 at an effective rate of 12 percent, with add-on interest, for three years in order to buy a car. Rather than borrow the money, they might have set aside a certain amount in their budget each month so that after three years they would have been able to purchase the car for cash.

QUESTIONS

1. Use the formula (p.207) to determine the total dollar cost the Andersons must bear for paying for their car with a loan.
2. What is the amount of each monthly payment (assuming level payments) that they must make on their car loan?
3. How much would they have had to invest in a 5 percent savings account at the end of each year for the three previous years in order to have $4000 with which they could pay cash for their car last year? (Use compound interest table B on page 500 to find the factor for three years at 5 percent.)

4. How much would the Andersons have had to set aside in their budget each month for those three years to allow for this investment?
5. Would this monthly amount represent a savings or an increased expense over what the Andersons are paying each month in loan repayments? How much?
6. What are the two ways the Andersons could compute the cost of immediate enjoyment of the car?

11
BORROWING: CONSUMER CREDIT

There are two types of lending that occur between the retailer and the consumer: open-ended credit and installment credit. Both are included here under the term *consumer credit.* In February, 1972, retailers were principally responsible for the over $26 billion of open-ended credit that was outstanding.[1] In addition, retailers were responsible for lending almost $15 billion of the $109 billion of installment debt outstanding.[2]

This chapter discusses how consumer credit works and how you can use it effectively. Being aware of what types of consumer credit there are and the ways in which you are protected by law should help you get the most out of income that is directed toward the use of consumer credit. We will also compare the costs of paying cash for a car, financing it, and leasing it.

HOW CONSUMER CREDIT WORKS

When you obtain credit, you obtain the use of someone else's money for a certain period of time, but no money changes hands. In exchange for the use of this money, you pay a fee called a *finance charge* (p. 199). However, as

1. Federal Reserve Board, *Federal Reserve Bulletin,* vol. 58, no. 4 (Washington, D.C.: April, 1972).
2. Ibid.

a sales incentive to customers, this fee may be omitted if the debt is paid off within a certain period, usually thirty days. For example, if you buy $5 worth of gasoline on credit, the oil company loans you the amount you need for the purchase at no extra cost (except that the company may charge generally higher prices in order to cover the cost of this service), and you agree to pay it back when you are billed.

With longer term credit, there is always a finance charge. For example, if you purchase a $200 dishwasher on a ten-month installment credit plan, you might pay $22 a month for a total of $220. The extra $20 represents the charge for the use of the appliance dealer's money over the ten-month period. If you borrow the same $200 on a twenty-month plan, you might have to pay $12 a month—a total of $240. Since you borrowed the money for a longer time, you had to pay $20 more in charges. In the end, your dishwasher cost you $40 more than if you had paid cash. As with consumer loans, the longer the payback period you choose for your debt, the more the total interest costs will be. Also, the higher the interest rate charged, the more the total interest cost will be.

OPEN-ENDED CREDIT

Charge accounts and credit cards are convenient, open-ended forms of consumer credit. Once you have qualified, you agree to pay for all items purchased on credit within a certain number of days either after you receive your bill or, sometimes, after you make your purchase.

The Consumer Credit Protection Act requires that issuers of open-ended credit disclose the period of time that may elapse before finance charges will be levied on outstanding balances (usually thirty or fifty-five days). They must also indentify the method they use to determine what the outstanding balance is. The most common method, the previous balance method, uses the amount outstanding at the end of the previous month to figure the finance charge for the current month. This method does not take into account payments made during the current month or the value of purchased items returned. The adjusted balance method takes these into account and is therefore more favorable to the consumer.

A non-card charge account is usually offered by an individual merchant for use at his store only. Credit cards are usually issued by manufacturers, such as oil companies, for use at local dealers or outlets. Credit cards may also be issued by banks or certain credit organizations to be used at affiliated places of business. Aside from this difference in scope, credit card accounts and charge accounts without cards serve many of the same purposes for consumers.

Open-ended consumer credit is an expense for the creditor because of bookkeeping, billing, collection, insurance, and bad debt losses. These costs generally cause prices to be higher for all customers who shop at a store that offers this type of credit. The cost of this service, however, should be distinguished from interest, which is the cost of using someone else's money.

How Much Open-Ended Credit Should You Use and For What?

There is a danger in open-ended credit that you will lose control of your expenditures. This loss of control would undermine the purpose of budgeting. You should use this form of spending only within the limits of your budget categories. To keep track of charge account or credit card purchases, enter them on your budget, as they are made, not when the bill arrives (p. 165). In this manner, you will be able to stop or reduce spending in certain categories when your monthly charges approach your monthly budgeted amounts.

Items purchased with credit cards and charge accounts usually are consumables, items that are quickly used up. By using this form of consumer credit to buy small priced, frequently purchased items such as food, gasoline, and entertainment, you can avoid having to carry a lot of cash. If you agree, however, that borrowing should be used only to accumulate assets, you should pay your charge account and credit card bills promptly to avoid the finance charge. The fact that the finance charge on this type of borrowing is commonly 18 percent annually should be all the motivation you need to pay these bills quickly. Do not let the convenience of charge accounts and credit cards cause you to lose control of your finances.

Types of Charge Accounts and Credit Cards

There are many types of charge accounts and credit cards (fig. 11-1, p. 226). Among the most common are thirty-day accounts, budget charge accounts, option charge accounts, revolving charge accounts, bank credit card accounts, and national credit cards.

thirty-day accounts Debts incurred on a thirty-day account must be paid within thirty days. There is no charge for the convenience of having such an account except as might be reflected in generally higher prices. Some means of identification (i.e., a card) may be required before credit is extended. One example of a thirty-day account is the monthly telephone bill.

budget charge accounts If you have a budget charge account, you are required to pay only a specified portion of your bill within the first thirty days. Although the remaining portion is usually paid regularly over a maximum of twelve months, you may pay off the balance earlier.

Type	Effective Cost	Conditions of Payment	Maximum Credit Limit	Maximum Payment Period
Thirty-day account	No charge for use of service	Debts must be resolved within 30 days of receipt of bill.	At individual creditor's discretion	30 days
Budget charge account	1.5% monthly, (18% annually) on the unpaid balance	Only a specific portion of the bill must be paid within 30 days (at no charge).	Set by creditor for each account	3 to 12 months
Option charge account	1.5% monthly (18% annually) on the unpaid balance	Consumer has the option of paying all or part of the debt within 30 days (at no charge).	At individual creditor's discretion	3 to 6 months
Revolving charge account	Refers to a feature of some budget and option charge accounts			
Bank credit card accounts	1.5% monthly (18% annually) on the unpaid balance up to $1000; lower rates for larger amounts	No charge for debts resolved within 25 days of the billing date. Commonly a fixed amount or percentage of debt outstanding is required to be paid monthly.	Set by creditor for each account	Determined by conditions of payments and maximum credit limit
National credit cards	1.5% monthly (18% annually) on unpaid balance; also, a fixed annual membership fee	No charge for debts resolved within 30 days of receipt of bill.	At discretion of credit card issuer	At discretion of credit card issuer

Fig. 11-1.
Types of charge accounts and credit cards

Fees or interest charges of 1.5 percent a month (18 percent a year) on the unpaid balance are commonly levied after the first month. This type of account is frequently offered by retailers such as department stores.

option charge accounts   With option charge accounts, you may pay all or part of the billed amount within thirty days at no charge. Any remaining amount is generally paid over three to six months. There is a usual fee of 1.5 percent a month (18 percent annually) on the unpaid balance. You may be required to pay a fixed dollar minimum or a fixed percentage of the bill outstanding each month. Many oil company credit cards are of this type, although they often allow fifty-five days before finance charges are levied.

revolving charge accounts   Revolving charge account is a name that can be applied to both budget and option accounts. The name simply emphasizes that you can continue to charge purchases on such an account (up to specified limits) without first paying off the old debts.

bank credit card accounts   Two notable examples of bank credit card accounts are BankAmericard and Master Charge. If you use either of these cards, you may make purchases at numerous locations and receive one monthly statement that covers all your purchases. The retailer who participates in this program pays the bank a small percentage of what he has sold to customers using the cards. In return, the bank assumes the burden of credit investigation, credit collection, and the risk of bad debts. Certain stores may levy a customer service charge for people using this program or they may pass this expense on to all customers through higher prices. This would be especially true where such programs do not appreciably increase the merchant's sales volume.

Usually no finance charges are levied if the total bill is paid within twenty-five days of the billing date. A minimum monthly payment of $10, or 5 percent of your bill if that amount would exceed $10, is commonly required. Hence, your total debt may never be entirely paid off. Finance charges of 1.5 percent a month (18 percent annually) generally are levied on the outstanding balance up to $1000. Above that amount the finance charge often is progressively reduced (1.2 percent, 1 percent, .7 percent, and so on). This type of credit often has a maximum limit based on the credit rating of each card user. The balance outstanding on the account must never exceed your limit.

national credit cards   National credit cards are issued by private credit organizations such as Diners Club, American Express, and Carte Blanche. They are similar to bank credit cards with the following exceptions. First, their credit qualifications are more rigid. Therefore, once you are accepted, your maximum credit limit may be higher. Second, in addition to the typical 1.5 percent monthly fee for bills older than thirty days, a flat annual fee is usually charged for membership in these organizations. Third, the cards are usually accepted only by certain types of merchants (travel associated, for example) rather than by the wide range of outlets available under bank programs.

INSTALLMENT CREDIT AND THE PURCHASE AGREEMENT

With installment credit, the retailer requires that periodic payments be made so that he can predict his cash inflow. Whereas credit cards and charge accounts are used for buying general merchandise, installment credit usually is limited to purchases of higher priced consumer durables such as appliances. The items purchased are used as collateral. Unlike open-ended credit, installment credit involves a down payment, and interest charges begin immediately.

Installment credit involves a purchase agreement that may be written either by the creditor himself, or for him by a bank or major finance company. The purchase agreement is made up of several components which include the sales contract, the note, and the credit life and/or disability insurance policy. The creditor selects the type of purchase agreement and includes those components that he feels offer him the greatest protection. As a consumer, you have little or no say in this matter. Therefore, make sure you read, understand, and are willing to accept all conditions specified in the documents associated with this agreement before you sign it. If you are not willing to accept all of them, shop elsewhere. (A sample purchase agreement is shown in figure 11-2.)

Sales Contract

The sales contract is one of the most common and significant components of any purchase agreement. This document is designed to protect the creditor against defaults on payments. The content and form of sales contracts is usually specified by state statute. The content commonly required includes the names and signatures of buyer and seller, the date of the transaction, address (residence or business) of buyer and seller, an adequate description of the goods subject to the contract, and services to be rendered. In regard to form, the document usually must be in writing (8-point type) with no large blank areas and represent the entire agreement between buyer and seller. A copy of the contract must be delivered to the buyer either upon delivery of the goods or shortly thereafter if so agreed.

There are other items that may be required by many states, and you should make sure which ones are specified in any contract you sign. These other items include cash sales price; amount of down payment; the difference between the down payment and the cash sales price;

DISCLOSURE STATEMENT
CREDIT SALE OF VEHICLE

The following disclosures are made pursuant to the Consumer Credit Protection Act by the Seller named herein (herein called Seller) to the Buyer(s) named herein (herein collectively called Buyer) in connection with the proposed credit sale of the vehicle together with equipment (herein called Vehicle) described below:

SELLER NAME AND ADDRESS _____

BUYER NAME(S) AND ADDRESS _____

New-Used	Year-Model I.D.	Make	Body Type	Serial or Engine No.	Key No.

Equipped With	☐ Automatic Transmission	☐ 3-4 Speed Trans.	☐ Radio	☐ Stereo	☐ Power Steering	☐ Power Brakes	☐ Power Windows	☐ Power Seats	☐ Air-Conditioning	Color

Other Equipment:

1. CASH PRICE (including sales tax only) $_____
2. DOWNPAYMENT
   CASH DOWNPAYMENT $_____
   TRADE-IN $_____
   Describe:_____
   TOTAL DOWNPAYMENT $_____
3. UNPAID BALANCE OF CASH PRICE (1 less 2) $_____
4. OTHER CHARGES INCLUDED IN AMOUNT FINANCED (Item 7) AND NOT PART OF FINANCE CHARGE (Item 8)
   (a) Official Fees
       License $_____
       Certificate of Title $_____
       Registration $_____
   (b) Insurance Premiums
       Credit Life $_____
       Credit Disability $_____
       Property $_____
       Liability $_____
                Total $_____
5. UNPAID BALANCE (3 plus 4) $_____
6. PREPAID FINANCE CHARGE $_____
7. AMOUNT FINANCED $_____
8. AMOUNTS INCLUDED IN FINANCE CHARGE
   (a) Time Price Differential $_____
   (b) Trailer Coach VSI (Conversion and Embezzlement) Insurance Premium $_____
   FINANCE CHARGE $_____

9. ANNUAL PERCENTAGE RATE   _____%
10. TOTAL OF PAYMENTS $_____
    Payable in_____payments as follows [Note: Identify any payment more than twice the amount of a regular equal payment as "Balloon Payment"]: _____equal successive _____ payments of $_____each on the_____day of _____commencing_____, 19____,
    _____
    _____
    _____
    _____
    _____
    _____, and a Balloon Payment of $_____on_____, 19____.
    Any Balloon Payment shown above will not be refinanced.
11. DEFERRED PAYMENT PRICE (1, 4 plus 8) $_____
12. DELINQUENCY CHARGE: A delinquency charge is payable on any payment in default for ten days or more in an amount equal to 5 % of such payment.
13. PREPAYMENT BEFORE MATURITY: Buyer may prepay the indebtedness in full at any time prior to maturity and obtain a refund credit of the unearned portion of the time price differential (Finance Charge), after first deducting therefrom $25.00, computed under the "Rule of 78's", provided, however, that no refund of less than $1.00 shall be made.
14. SECURITY: Indebtedness is to be secured by a conditional sale contract covering the Vehicle, and by an assignment of fire, theft, collision and comprehensive insurance policies thereon as required by Seller.

INSURANCE

ANY PROPERTY INSURANCE (meaning insurance against loss or damage to property) OR LIABILITY INSURANCE (meaning insurance against liability arising out of the ownership or use of property) TO BE WRITTEN IN CONNECTION WITH THE SALE MAY BE OBTAINED BY BUYER THROUGH ANY PERSON OF HIS CHOICE, provided, however, that Seller may, for reasonable cause, refuse to accept an insurer on any such insurance which is required by Seller. Such insurance may ☐ not be obtained from or through Seller ☐ be obtained through Seller at the estimated cost indicated:

INSURANCE COVERAGE	DEDUCTIBLE OR LIMITS	TERM IN MONTHS	ESTIMATED PREMIUM
Fire and Theft, ACV			
Comprehensive			
Combined Additional			
Collision			
Bodily Injury			
Property Damage			
Medical			

[Applicable if credit insurance may be written] CREDIT LIFE AND CREDIT DISABILITY INSURANCE ARE NOT REQUIRED IN CONNECTION WITH THE SALE. No charge is to be made for such insurance and none is to be provided unless Buyer to be insured thereunder signs and dates the statement below. If obtained through Seller, the cost of credit life insurance will be $_____ and of credit disability insurance will be $_____for the term of the credit.

I desire credit ☐ life and ☐ disability insurance.

_____ (DATE)   _____ (SIGNATURE)

* IMPORTANT NOTE: ASTERISK DENOTES THAT THE AMOUNT INDICATED IS AN ESTIMATE.

Buyer acknowledges reading and receiving a duplicate of this Disclosure Statement and that he has not entered into any agreement with Seller for the above credit sale. THIS IS NOT AN OFFER OR AN AGREEMENT TO SELL, OR TO PROVIDE INSURANCE.

_____ (DATE)   _____ (BUYER)   _____ (BUYER)

GBA-TL (CS)-1 (7-69)   ORIGINAL (BANK'S COPY)   DUPLICATE (BUYER'S COPY)   TRIPLICATE (SELLER'S COPY)

Fig. 11-2. Sample purchase agreement on an installment contract for a car

amount, cost, and type of insurance required; amount and type of official (local government) fees; balance owed (usually the sum of the previous three items); finance charges as an aggregate amount (in addition to the computations of annual amounts required by truth in lending); amount, number, and frequency of payments (amount will equal the sum of the balance owed and finance charges divided by the number of payments); and some indication of how much more the merchandise bought on credit will cost than if paid for in cash.

types of sales contracts   The *conditional sales contract* is the most common type of installment credit contract. This is the type you would probably sign if you purchased a new dishwasher on credit. Although you obtain immediate use of the dishwasher, the title of ownership remains with the owner of the store where you bought it until your payments are completed. If you fail to meet the payment schedule as specified in the purchase agreement, the dishwasher probably will be repossessed, and then it may be impossible to get back the down payment and monthly payments made so far. The store owner can maintain that these payments merely represent a deposit plus rent. Only if he resells the dishwasher for an amount great enough to cover his loss as well as the costs of repossession and resale (storage costs, collection fees, attorney's fees, and the like) can you get some of the money back. The chances that this will occur are not great since the store owner will have little motivation to resell a used dishwasher for the highest price. You have little or no legal means to require him to do so either. If the resale proceeds are not sufficient to cover the amount owed to the creditor plus the repossession and resale costs, you may be required to pay the difference.

The *chattel mortgage contract* is used for installment sales. Upon purchase, the title to the merchandise passes to the buyer. Title is then returned to the creditor to serve as collateral securing the sales contract, and the chattel mortgage is filed with the appropriate local government agency. By doing this the creditor can prevent the buyer from using the merchandise as collateral for other installment purchases. The chattel mortgage contract has the same power over the buyer (such as the creditor's right of repossession) as the conditional sales contract.

The *bailment lease* is a third and much less frequently used form of installment sales contract. Its main distinguishing feature is that the title to the purchased merchandise is retained by the creditor until final payment has been made. At this time, the buyer may purchase the title to his merchandise for a nominal amount.

oppressive clauses   These may be part of any of the above types of contracts. They are used to put the borrower at a legal disadvantage in relation to the lender. Although recent legislation in some states has made such practices more difficult for the creditor to justify, they do still exist. Here are some to watch out for: *wage assignment* (wage garnishment), whereby you assign to the creditor the right to attach a part of your wages in the event you default on your payments; *confession of judgment,* whereby you waive your right to an attorney or to judicial processes, thus allowing the creditor to make an admission of debt for you with legal authorities when default occurs; *repossession,* whereby you allow the creditor to take back the purchased goods if you fail to make your payments; *add-on clause,* whereby you allow the creditor to repossess items you have already purchased from him and paid for, if you default on your payments for additional items; *acceleration clause,* whereby the outstanding balance of payments becomes immediately due if you miss one (or more) payments; and *balloon clause,* whereby the payment schedule is structured in such a way that the final payment is substantially larger than the previous payments.

finance charges   These charges are another very important component of the sales contract. It is good to have the creditor itemize the various elements of these charges so that you will know exactly what you are paying for. Basically, finance charges consist of interest and carrying costs (bookkeeping, credit investigations, allowance for bad debts, credit life and/or disability insurance, and the like). In order to determine whether the annual finance charge percentage rate the creditor quotes you is accurate, use the formula given on page 206.

The Note

The note represents your written promise to resolve the debt you assumed through your purchase. In many instances, a conditional sales contract or a chattel mortgage is considered security for the note. The note specifies the amounts of your payments and when they are to be paid. Some notes enable the creditor, in the event of default on payments, not only to repossess the purchased goods but also to repossess enough additional property to cover the balance outstanding or to take legal action to obtain that amount if the proceeds from resale do not cover repossession and resale costs and the balance outstanding. There are three general types of notes with which you may be confronted: demand note, time note, and cognovit note.

The demand note has no maturity date. Usually the creditor retains the right to call in the note and receive full payment of the balance due whenever he desires. The time note has a specified date of maturity. It gives you a definite idea of when your final payments are due, as opposed to the demand note, which leaves you at the mercy of the creditor. Therefore, the time note is probably more attractive. The cognovit note allows the creditor to repossess the goods you purchased (if you have defaulted on your payments) without going through legal channels. Obviously, this is the least attractive type of note for you because it offers the least protection.

Credit Life and Disability Insurance

Often a creditor will require you to purchase term life insurance and possibly disability insurance to cover the outstanding balance on your installment credit purchases. Such insurance will pay off the unpaid balance if you die or become disabled. The cost of this creditor protection may be taken into account in the finance charges.

Credit insurance costs represent a potential area of abuse since the creditor receives sales commissions from the insurance company for the amount of coverage that he sells. He may be motivated to use those policies that have the most expensive premiums. Costs range from 37¢ to $1 annually for each $100 of life insurance coverage. An acceptable maximum is 60¢. If your creditor requires that you have credit insurance but offers only expensive coverage, obtain coverage elsewhere. A local insurance broker with a substantial business should be a less expensive source of coverage.

On car purchase contracts, auto insurance may also be required.

CONSIDERATIONS WHEN SHOPPING FOR CREDIT

1. Do you want to use consumer credit to pay many bills with a single check or to purchase an expensive item?
2. What type of credit can best be used to meet your requirements? If you want to buy gasoline, an oil company credit card would be appropriate. If you need a new appliance, then installment credit may be the answer. Once you know what type of credit you are looking for, you can begin to investigate the alternatives available.
3. How much additional money will it cost you to use consumer credit? Some forms of open-ended credit charge you nothing if you pay off the balance within thirty days. If you do not, you may be charged on the unpaid balance at a rate of 1.5 percent a month. Installment credit is different. It represents a rigid schedule of payments, and if you pay off the debt ahead of schedule you may be charged a prepayment penalty. Therefore, it is important to know how much more an installment credit contract will cost you than if you pay for items in cash. When you feel that the former is prohibitively expensive, you can plan for the purchase of the items for which the money was needed and avoid using consumer credit altogether.
4. Can you afford to pay the total amount represented by the price of the item to be purchased plus the credit costs?

5. What is the best schedule of payments offered? Remember that the longer the payback period, the more the total charges will be.
6. Can you meet the scheduled payments without straining your income unnecessarily? If your family had an emergency, such as a big dental bill, might your credit purchases have to be repossessed?
7. What is the reputation of the creditor you are considering borrowing from? Information about a creditor often may be found by contacting local credit counselling services or, in large metropolitan areas, a legal aid office.

Credit Counselling Services

If you are having credit problems that require more than the above sort of analysis, perhaps you should look for professional assistance. Several sources of advice are available. These include credit bureaus, credit unions, creditors, and family counselling services.

Credit bureaus serve as a link between creditors and people seeking credit. Their primary purpose is to gather information about the credit worthiness of applicants and provide it for creditors who are conducting investigations. Many credit bureaus, however, offer advice concerning both how to regain or retain a good credit rating and what a reasonable credit limit may be in a particular case. Credit unions often emphasize educating their members about consumer credit. Some of the larger ones employ full-time credit counsellors. Of course, you must be a member of a credit union to avail yourself of this service. Some creditors offer counselling services, but the quality of advice varies from creditor to creditor. Family counselling services, of which legal aid societies are usually a part, are likely to offer helpful, objective advice; these community-sponsored organizations may have licensed financial counselors.

CONSUMER CREDIT LEGISLATION

Between 1969 and 1971, two federal laws of major importance to the consumer were approved and put into effect. One limits the consumer's liability for unauthorized use of his credit cards. The other regulates more strictly the practices of credit bureaus.

Protection Against Lost or Stolen Credit Cards

Liability of credit card holders for unauthorized use of their credit cards was greatly restricted in 1971 by the federal government. As a result, you may be held liable only for up to $50 worth of unauthorized use of your lost, stolen, or misplaced cards. The issuer may hold you liable for this $50 only if he provided a self-addressed form to be used to notify him of the loss, theft, or disappearance of your card; if you accepted the card originally; if he adequately informed you of your potential liability; and if the unauthorized use in question occurred before you notified the issuer of your card's loss, theft, or disappearance.

Fair Credit Reporting Act

Credit bureaus sell information about the credit worthiness of consumers. The bureaus' customers are usually insurance companies, prospective employers, government agencies, creditors, and mailing list companies. A credit reporting system is an effective means of identifying poor credit risks in advance, and it makes it easy for most individuals with the right qualifications to obtain credit. In some instances, however, a good credit risk receives a poor rating because of misinformation. The chances that this might occur are greater than you might think, as you will realize when you examine the methods by which credit bureaus collect information about a credit applicant.

Three information sources are commonly used by credit bureaus: credit applications, public records, and hearsay reports. Each time you apply for credit, a copy of the application probably goes to the local credit bureau. Because of this, it behooves you to fill out a credit application accurately. Misleading information would have an adverse effect on the credit bureau's opinion of your integrity. Credit bureaus also employ individuals to check court cases, judgments, and so on to glean more information about consumers. By their own admission, the degree of accurate research and confirmation used by these investigators is often inadequate. An investigator also queries the consumer's neighbors, friends, and acquaintances about his morals, private life, reputation, and such. The accuracy of this information is highly exposed to human error, bias, and poor judgment. Because of this, there exists a real potential for misinformation to be collected about a consumer.

The Fair Credit Reporting Act that went into effect April 25, 1971, attempts, among other things, to regulate the actions of credit bureaus dispensing erroneous information about private citizens. You have some basic rights under this law. If you are rejected for credit, the prospective creditor must give you the name and address of the credit bureau that supplied the information causing your application to be rejected. This credit bureau must then disclose to you upon request the nature and substance of all information contained in your file (although they do not have to show you the actual file); the names of creditors who have received reports on you in the last six months; the names of potential employers who have received reports on you in the last two years; and the sources of all information in your file (credit applications, public records, and so on) with the exception of investigative hearsay reports.

If any of the information is found to be erroneous, inaccurate, or unverifiable, the credit bureau must promptly delete it and send notice of such deletion to creditors of the past six months and to potential employers of the last two years. If you and the credit bureau dispute the validity of certain information, you have the right to include in your file a one-hundred-word refutation of that information. This refutation will also be sent out to recent potential creditors and employers. The credit bureau may not charge you for any of their services in revealing the contents of your file in this case or for correcting false information.

If you have not been rejected for credit but want to see your file at the local credit bureau, these rights still hold. The only difference is that you may be charged a reasonable fee, which probably will not exceed $25 since the Federal Trade Commission has taken action against charges in excess of this amount. Adverse information more than seven years old may not be sent out—with the exception that information about bankruptcies has a fourteen-year limitation. Also, there is no limitation on the age of adverse information sent out for underwriter reports where the amount of proposed life insurance coverage is $50,000 or more, or for employer reports where the proposed salary is $20,000 or more. You may sue a credit bureau for false information that results from a malicious or willful intent to injure and for violations of the new law. However, it is still unclear how strictly this law can be enforced.

AUTO LEASING

The basic principle of auto leasing is that you (as lessee) agree to pay a monthly fee for a set period of time in exchange for the use of a car. At the end of that period, either the car or an equivalent dollar amount must be returned to the lessor. There are many ways of leasing cars and many types of leases, but the basic procedure is as follows.

Initially, you and the lessor negotiate the current value of the car (purchase price) and the residual value (projected trade-in value). The lessor determines the amount he is lending you by subtracting the residual value from the current value. The term *lending* is used here because the lessor purchases the car and lends it to you in return for lease payments. Your lease payments will include a charge (somewhat like interest) for the privilege of using the lessor's money (in the form of the leased car).

When you turn in the car at the end of the lease term (usually two or three years), the car's trade-in value must equal the initially projected residual value. If the car's trade-in value exceeds this amount, you will be refunded the excess amount. If it is less, you must make up the difference. Should you disagree with the lessor's appraised value of the car, you have the option of finding another person (car dealer or private individual) who will pay you more for it. In this case, you return to the lessor an amount of cash equal to the residual value. The lessor must receive remuneration equal to the residual value in the form of the leased car, the leased car plus cash, or just cash.

An Example

This example (fig. 11-3) embodies many of the financial considerations necessary in deciding whether it is better to pay cash for a car, finance it, or lease it. In each of these alternatives the total amount that must be paid for the car is $4200. The purchase price of the car is $4000, but the cash expenditure must also include $200 sales tax. The trade-in value after three years is $1600. If the car is bought with cash, the initial expenditure totals $4200 (cost of car plus sales tax). The trade-in value after three years is $1600, making the total cost of the car $2600.

If the car is financed, the initial outlay is $1000, which consists of a 20 percent down payment and a $200 sales tax. Subsequent outlays involve thirty-six monthly payments of $105 each or $3780 in total payments. Again the trade-in value is $1600, making the total cost $3180 ($1000 + $3780 − $1600). The inflation adjustment is computed as follows.

.03 × $630 (the average of the first year's payments)	= $ 19
.06 × $630 (the average of the second year's payments)	= 38
.09 × $630 (the average of the third year's payments)	= 56
Total inflation adjustment	113

The tax savings are derived from $580 credit costs ($3780 paid back on $3200 borrowed) times 25 percent marginal tax rate for a savings of $145. The tax savings and the inflation adjustment amounts are subtracted from the total cost of the car for a net cost of $2922 ($3180 − $145 − $133).

Costs and Adjustments	Paying Cash		Financing @ 12%		Leasing @ 12%
Initial Outlay	$4200		$1000		$ 186
Subsequent Outlays			3780		3162
TOTAL	4200		4780		3348
Trade-in Value	1600		1600		
TOTAL COST	2600		3180		3348
Inflation Adjustment		113		94	
Tax Savings		145			
TOTAL SAVINGS			258		94
Net Cost	$2600		$2922		$3254

Fig. 11-3.
Costs of paying cash for a car, financing it, and leasing it

If the car is leased, the initial outlay is made up of two months' payments of $93 each (roughly $88 plus $5 sales tax). There is a subsequent outlay of thirty-four monthly payments of $93 each. The trade-in value ($1600) is assumed to be equal to projected residual value. The inflation adjustment is as follows.

.03 × $513 (the average of the first year's eleven payments) = $15
.06 × $558 (the average of the second year's twelve payments) = 33
.09 × $513 (the average of the third year's eleven payments) = 46
Total inflation adjustment   94

Since no tax deduction is allowed for interest charges on a lease, the net cost is $3254 ([36 × $93] − $94).

Even after tax savings and inflation are taken into account, in this example the cash purchase of a car cost less than either short-term (three years or less) financing or leasing arrangements, where the terms are the same. Because their costs are generally high (10 percent a year or more), financing and leasing also are not attractive as investment strategies. Instead, they are usually an unnecessary drain on your income.

CONCLUSION

You should use consumer credit responsibly and effectively. First decide how much consumer credit you can afford and what you want to use it for. Then look for the most attractive source of credit. Several laws offer you safeguards in the area of consumer credit. Make sure that you are given full benefit of these laws in all your credit dealings.

VOCABULARY

acceleration clause
balloon clause
charge account
consumer credit
credit bureau
credit card
Fair Credit Reporting Act
installment credit

leasing
note
open-ended credit
oppressive clauses
purchase agreement
repossession
sales contract
trade-in value

QUESTIONS

1. What are the six oppressive clauses that may be found in sales contracts?
2. What are four typical items in the finance charge levied by a creditor?
3. Why is credit life and/or disability insurance a potential area of abuse from the consumer's point of view?

4. How are bank-issued credit cards different from those issued by national credit companies?
5. Under what financial circumstances can you justify using open-ended credit?
6. What is your liability for unauthorized use of a credit card that you have lost or had stolen?
7. What is a credit bureau required to do if you ask to see information from your file? When must you pay for this service? What is a reasonable fee?

CASE PROBLEM

Credit bureaus generally make it relatively easy for people whose finances are sound to obtain credit. They also enable creditors to avoid extending credit to individuals who probably would not be able to repay a debt. In order to make these judgments, credit bureaus must investigate people's financial circumstances and personal character. Certain of these activities are often considered an invasion of a prospective borrower's privacy. Furthermore, the methods credit bureaus use to gather information can result in the inclusion of inaccurate data in a person's file.

What is your position concerning credit bureaus? Which types of data, if any, do you think are valid for credit bureaus to gather? How would you improve their research efforts without violating personal privacy? What stand should the government take in this matter?

RECOMMENDED READING

MAGAZINES

"Interpretations of Regulation Z." *Consumer Finance News,* June 1969, p. 13.

A discussion of certain technical sections of truth in lending.

"New Rules to Protect Your Credit Rating." *Changing Times,* June 1969, pp. 25–28.

A brief discussion of the Fair Credit Reporting Act.

"The Santa Claus That Makes You Pay." *Business Week,* December 20, 1969, pp. 76–79.

Concerns phenomenal growth in use of credit cards, particularly those issued by banks.

"What is Truth in Lending?" *Consumer Finance News,* April 1969, p. 3.

> Questions and answers about truth in lending.

"What the New Truth-in-Lending Law Does for You." *Changing Times,* June 1969, pp. 7–12.

> A good explanation of the law.

"What to Do If Your Credit Goes Bad." *Consumer Reports,* April 1971, pp. 256–59.

> A good discussion of merits and weaknesses of the Fair Credit Reporting Act.

BOOKS

Changing Times Family Success Book, 1969. "How to Keep From Drowning in Debt."

> A discussion of practical family debt management.

National Retail Merchants Association. *Economic Characteristics of Department Store Credit.* 1969.

> A study showing that consumer credit is not profitable for the retailer and can be justified only as a selling tool.

CHUCK AND NANCY ANDERSON

ANALYZING THEIR DEBT STRUCTURE

Chuck and Nancy agree that borrowing money is most effective when it is used to purchase assets. They also think that they should borrow money only at rates lower than those they can achieve on their investment portfolio. Table 11-1 (p. 240) presents a comparison of their debt costs and their portfolio's return on investment—based on a combined (federal and state) marginal tax bracket of 25 percent and a rise in inflation of 3 percent a year.

TABLE 11-1

Comparison of the Andersons' Debt Costs and Investment Return

Debts	Gross Rate (%)	Tax Effect (%)	Effect of Inflation (%)	Net Rate (%)
Home	6	−1.5	−3	1.5
Car	12	−3	−3	6
Furniture	15	−3.75	−3	8.25
Margin Account	7	−1.75	−3	2.25
Investment Return	8	−1[a]	−3	4

[a]One-half of 25 percent marginal tax rate to reflect taxes on long-term capital gains.

The Andersons want to know which loans they should pay off. Which assets can they use to resolve these debts?

12

HOUSING

Your decisions about housing are among the most important you make as manager of your family's financial resources. They usually do not need to be made very often, but the size of the dollar investment required gives them special significance. If a hasty decision is made, the results may sap your income unnecessarily.

There are several questions to answer when considering housing. Should you rent or should you buy? How much should you pay for a house? Does the house suit your needs? Where is the house located?

TO RENT OR TO OWN

If you are a young person not yet ready to settle down in one place, a single adult, a couple without children, a holder of a job that requires frequent transfers, or an elderly person uninterested in the responsibilities of home maintenance, then renting may be appropriate for you. You may, however, find home ownership intrinsically more attractive than renting regardless of personal circumstances. Nevertheless, you should be aware of the advantages and disadvantages of both options.

Advantages and Disadvantages of Renting

Renting has several advantages. Initially, it involves no major capital outlay, such as a down payment. Despite the time constraints of a lease, changing accommodations is probably less expensive for a renter than for a homeowner. Some rental complexes offer swimming pools, game rooms, and health clubs. The homeowner would be hard pressed to duplicate these benefits as conveniently and economically on his own. Furthermore, rental units come in smaller sizes (e.g., studios and one-bedroom, one-bath units) than do most homes. The responsibilities for gardening, maintenance, and repair of rental units usually rest with the management.

The disadvantages of renting can be both financial and personal. As a renter, your entire rent payment is an expense item. You are building up no asset value. Also, you do not have the tax deductions for mortgage interest and property taxes that the homeowner does. You have little protection beyond the term of the lease against rent increases caused by inflation. If you rent an apartment of poor design and construction, your privacy may be sacrificed more than if you owned your own home.

You also have the burden of maintaining good relations with your landlord. Lack of communication can cause many difficulties between landlord and tenant. If you have problems with your rental unit, first try to work them out with your landlord. Problems that affect other tenants as well may be resolved by collective bargaining with the landlord. You may find, however, that he will try to evict you for seeking improvements in his services. Only California, Montana, North Dakota, Oklahoma, and South Dakota have laws requiring landlords to provide liveable accommodations for their tenants. If your rental quarters are inadequately maintained or if you face retaliatory eviction, the formation of a tenants' union may be appropriate. We suggest that you consult an attorney and find out the feelings of your fellow tenants before taking such action.

Advantages and Disadvantages of Owning

Many of the advantages of home ownership cannot be expressed in dollars and cents. One advantage is the feeling of permanence and security that can come with owning a home. Home ownership can also promote pride and a sense of responsibility in yourself and your spouse. Permanent residency can contribute to the quality of your children's lives.

From a financial viewpoint, once you have negotiated your mortgage, the amount of your loan payments should remain constant (although your property taxes may rise). If you rent, you cannot be as certain that your rental payments will remain constant after your lease has expired. This greater predictability of payments when buying a home makes it easier for you to project your housing expenditures. Furthermore, your mortgage payments represent a form of savings. With each payment, you own an increased percentage of your home. In addition, it is often less expensive over the long run to own rather than to rent.

The disadvantages that may offset these advantages are not many, but should be recognized. In many instances, owning a home for less than three years is more expensive than renting. Furthermore, a down payment is required as a minimum investment. This outlay could sap your financial resources and leave you vulnerable in financial emergencies. Once you have purchased a home, your ability to move without great cost is severely reduced. For this last reason, of course, you should buy a house only after careful planning, thought, and searching.

Comparing Costs

The costs of renting and buying are difficult to compare because the value (e.g., an apartment in the city) you receive for your rent or lease payment can be quite different than the value (e.g., a four-bedroom home in the suburbs) you receive for your mortgage payment. The costs of home ownership are also more numerous than just the mortgage payment. The only effective cost comparison must be made between renting a home and buying a home or between renting an apartment and buying a similar condominium unit.

In establishing the amount of the rent payment, the landlord makes sure he receives enough money to cover property taxes, maintenance, obsolescence, mortgage payment, a return on his investment plus a vacancy allowance and management costs. The costs of owning a home include all these expenses except the last two, since a vacant home does not deprive the owner of usual income and he does not have to engage a manager for his own home.

A cost you incur as a homeowner but not as a renter is the cost of selling your home when you move. This cost is made up of expenses such as real estate commission, termite inspection, title clearance, and advertising. It is a one-time expense that must be spread over several years of ownership before owning a home is more economical than renting one. Assume, for example, that your selling costs are $2000. Spread over two years of ownership, this would add $1000 annually to the cost of owning. If you owned your home for eight years, however, this additional cost of owning would average only $250 a year. The longer you own your home the less the cost (measured as an average annual expense) of selling it.

Maintenance costs tend to run higher in a rented home than in an owned home where a sense of responsibility and pride of ownership tend both to minimize the cost of upkeep and to keep things in continual good repair. Costs unique to renting such as the vacancy allowance and management fees gradually build up and make renting more expensive than owning a home after about three to five years. One factor that can hasten the profitability of home ownership is rapid appreciation in the value of the property. When this occurs, owning may become more economical than renting in two years or less.

An Example

To show how paying off a mortgage and taking deductions for mortgage interest and property taxes make owning a home less costly than renting it, we will use the example of a house that is bought with an $8000 down payment and annual mortgage payments of $2400 ($1800 interest, $600 principal). Let us assume that property taxes are $600 and maintenance and repairs cost $300, making the basic cost of the property $3300 a year. Figure 12-1 shows that for one year the net cost of buying a house is $1220 less than the net cost of renting a house. Of course, because of closing costs (p. 247) and selling costs (p. 243), an early sale can distort the expense figures in favor of renting unless significant price appreciation has occurred.

	Renter		Owner	
$3300	(basic cost)	$3300	(basic cost)
+ 300	(landlord profit)	− 720[a]	(tax savings on $1800 interest and $600 property taxes)
3600	(rent/year)		
− 400	(income @ 5 percent on $8000 not put out in down payment)	2580	(after-tax cost of ownership)
		− 600	(reduction of balance due on mortgage)
$3200	net cost	$1980	net cost

Fig. 12-1. Comparison of costs for renting and owning a home

[a]Calculated for a 30 percent tax bracket ($2400 reduction in taxable income).

Effects of Inflation

It is often said that home ownership is profitable because a house appreciates in value. If, however, all housing prices have risen equally because of inflation, any supposed profit on the sale of your old home will be lost because of the increased cost of your next home. Only by purchasing a smaller, less expensive house will you be able to retain some of the proceeds from your first sale. If your second home is similar to your first, logically it should cost you as much as your old one cost the person who bought it from you. A more valuable, larger home should cost you more than you received from the sale of your old home. The most likely way to profit from an increase in value is to sell at a time when your property has appreciated faster than most on the housing market. Deflated or declining housing values are similarly affected by the extent of price depreciation that has occurred and by the cost of the house you buy with the proceeds from the sale of another house.

Inflation and deflation affect rent and mortgage payments in that, during periods of inflation (or deflation), rents can be expected to rise (or fall) while mortgage payments remain fixed as specified in the sales contract. Therefore, inflation favors the home buyer while deflation favors the renter.

PREPARING TO RENT OR BUY

Before deciding to rent or buy a specific place of residence, you should do some careful thinking and research to ensure that the decision you make is a good one.

Determining Needs

Determining your needs is important whether you are considering renting an apartment or a house or buying a house or a condominium. By defining your needs, you will be able to identify appropriate apartments or homes. Whether you can afford them is another matter.

location What sort of location are you looking for? Do you want the closeness of nature in the country or the cultural variety of the city? (Tony and Angela Minelli, for example, prefer country living and have both a German shepherd and a kitten. They want to consider only suburban or rural locations so that they and their pets will have freedom of movement and open space.) You should also consider the proximity and adequacy of municipal transportation facilities, shopping facilities, recreational and medical facilities, schools and churches, and municipal fire and police facilities. If you work, do you want to live close enough to your job so that you can walk or ride a bike to work, or is easy access by car or public transportation a primary concern?

Once you have determined the characteristics of location that appeal to you, you should investigate those areas that offer these qualities. This search may take time, but, if done properly, can result in the selection of a well-situated home.

A certain location may now offer many of the qualities you seek in a neighborhood and a community, but this may not always be the case in the future. Urban use patterns are constantly changing. You should try to ensure that this process will not adversely affect the quality of your chosen location. For example, check the highway department's ten-year plan to make sure that a freeway is not planned to pass near the location you like.

Although strict zoning laws and building codes do not protect against all adverse changes, they control them somewhat. Look into the quality of these controls and the degree to which they are enforced. Officials of the local planning agency where you are considering moving can probably tell you about the zoning laws and possible changes in them. Talk with people, such as home contractors, who must comply with the building codes. They should be able to offer you some insight into the quality of construction being undertaken in your chosen area.

the apartment or house What characteristics of an apartment or a house are most appropriate for your needs? Because Tony and Angela plan to have children soon, they want to find a three-bedroom, two-bath house. When you determine your housing needs, make sure you consider not only your present needs, but your future needs as well.

Deciding what age apartment or home to rent or buy is another important consideration. Your choice of location may restrict the availability of new or old residences. Older apartment units, for example, are located almost exclusively in older sections of a community, whereas newer units may be found in almost any section. Be sure to compare the costs for both a new and an old apartment or home. A new apartment is likely to be more expensive than an old apartment since the former offers more amenities such as dishwashers, air conditioning, and recreational facilities. A new house is usually easier to sell in the short-term and easier to finance than an old house. The minimum down payment is smaller and the mortgage maturity is longer. As such, buying a new home may impose less of a financial strain on you.

An older home does have advantages, however. Generally you can buy a larger, older house for the same price as a smaller new house, although certain facilities such as the garage may be inadequate. Older homes may also have more landscaping and interior decorating than new homes. Property taxes can often be lower as well. Probably the most attractive aspects of an older home or apartment are its uniqueness and character. These qualities are not always available in the new, mass-produced house or apartment. Unlike new apartments, there are few large complexes of old apartment units.

Your Price Range

Once you have done some thinking about your needs, it is time to think about the costs involved.

the costs of renting How much can you afford to pay in rent for an apartment or house? A rough estimate can be made quickly by figuring out what 25 percent of your after-tax income is. The amount arrived at by this procedure should be taken not as an absolute upper limit on your rental expenditure, but as a guide to help you narrow your search realistically. Chances are that if you are willing to pay approximately one week's salary in rent a month, you will be able to find suitable accommodations and yet have enough money for other expenses.

the costs of buying   What you can afford to pay for a home must be accurately identified. If you have a firm idea of what you can afford, you will be better prepared to negotiate price with the seller and to control your emotions and, thus, to avoid buying a home that is completely outside your price range.

The annual recurring costs of home ownership, including mortgage payments, usually amount to 10 percent of the face value of the house. On the basis of national averages, this amount is also likely to equal 25 percent of the annual after-tax income of the homeowner. From these figures, it might seem reasonable to purchase a home valued at no more than two and one-half times your annual after-tax income. An example should make this clearer.

Let us say that the annual after-tax income for the Minellis is $12,000. They will probably spend approximately 25 percent of this income, or $3000, each year on housing costs. Since annual housing costs represent 10 percent of the market value of a house, the market value of a house that the Minellis can afford would probably be $30,000 (10 × $3000), which is also two and one-half times greater than the Minellis' annual after-tax income ($12,000).

Rather than simply using income as a means of finding an appropriate range of purchase prices, determine what you can afford by analyzing separately the various costs involved. Here you should make a distinction between those costs that occur only once and those that recur annually. The most significant *one-time cost*, of course, is the down payment. This represents the amount of cash you pay the seller to obtain use of the home. Other one-time costs are the closing costs, expenses that complete the sales transaction. Fees may be charged for credit reports; a conditional Federal Housing Authority (FHA) commitment to insure the mortgage; title search, examination, and insurance; loan origination; legal work including document preparation and recording plus an attorney's time; escrow duties; and property survey. (The Consumer Protection Act requires that these expenses not be considered part of the finance charge on a mortgage.) Local practices and negotiations usually determine whether the buyer or the seller covers these costs. As a buyer you may pay from $200 to over $2000 for closing costs. The sooner you know the number and amounts of these fees, the better prepared you will be to negotiate their payment with the seller.

To determine how much you can realistically afford to pay in one-time costs, you should consult your balance sheet. The amount should not be so large as to undermine the stability of your financial resources.

Nevertheless, there are several reasons why you may want to make this amount as large as possible. First, the more cash you are able to pay initially, the smaller the loan you will have to obtain. By minimizing the loan amount, you also minimize your total interest costs. Second, a larger down payment may preclude the need for a second mortgage, which can be very expensive. Third, often when a substantial down payment (25 percent of the purchase price) is made, the interest rate on the accompanying mortgage is 0.5 percent lower than if only a minimum down payment is made. Also, a larger down payment increases your chances of getting a mortgage.

Under some circumstances it may be best for you to make as small a down payment as possible and place your excess funds in an investment program. Generally, this is advisable only when the after-tax return on your investment consistently exceeds the after-tax costs of borrowing (i.e., interest) on your mortgage.

To determine how much you can afford to pay out in *annual recurring costs,* you should begin by identifying what these costs will be. Your real estate agent could be very helpful here. Generally these costs fall into five categories: loan repayments (both interest and principal), insurance (most likely property and liability), utilities (gas, electricity, water, and garbage disposal), maintenance, and property taxes.

Next, consult your income statement or budget to determine how much you have been paying for housing. These old costs, of course, would not be added to the new costs. If you find that the annual recurring costs associated with a purchase are greater than what you have been paying, you may choose to look for a less expensive house or to postpone the purchase until you can more reasonably afford it. Or you can reassess your budget limits and cut down in some categories so that more money can be used in the housing category. For example, the interest paid on mortgage and property taxes are type two deductions. The result can be a reduction in your income taxes. Therefore, you may not have to budget as much money to this category as you did before. This would leave more funds for housing expenditures.

You might also go back to your balance sheet to see if a larger down payment is possible. If so, the loan size could be reduced. An alternative to decreasing the loan size, however, is extending the payment period. Either approach can result in lower payments, although the latter approach will increase the total amount of interest paid in the long run. (See pages 257–58 to determine whether such a consideration is appropriate for you.)

RENTING

Before deciding what and where to rent, you should know what alternatives are available and what your signature on a lease agreement may require of you.

Rental Alternatives

Rental units consist primarily of single-family dwellings (houses) and multi-family dwellings (apartments). Some houses may be intended exclusively for rental use by their owners, whereas others may be available for rent only while the owners are away for long periods of time.

Apartments offer a wide variety of living accommodations. Garden apartments are usually clusters of small structures, each housing two to five rental units. They emphasize outdoor living. High rise apartments often resemble hotels in structure. Their chief attractions are spectacular views and proximity to urban centers.

As a result of the Housing and Urban Development Act passed by Congress in 1965, the federal government has become very active in providing livable quarters at below-market rental rates for economically disadvantaged individuals and families. Federal programs under this act provide what is known as Section 221 or Section 236 housing. In order to make below-market rental rates possible, the federal government does two things. It offers means for investor-landlords to obtain low cost mortgages, and it requires that these cost savings be passed on to the renter in the form of reduced rents. The federal government also provides rent supplements to qualified tenants.

To be eligible for the government's rent supplement program an applicant (individual or family) must have an adjusted annual income below limits set by the local FHA office for the community involved. The adjusted annual income is arrived at by determining the earnings of one or more of the adult members of the family and making deductions for eligible minor children. Other conditions that may qualify a family for rent supplement assistance include being displaced from one's original dwelling by government action or natural disaster, being handicapped, being sixty-two or older, living in a dwelling considered substandard by local housing authorities, or having no more than $2000 in assets ($5000, if sixty-five or over). Once admitted to the program, a tenant's eligibility must be recertified periodically, and he is expected to contribute 25 percent of his adjusted annual income on a monthly basis. Table 12-1 (p. 250) shows characteristics of households participating in the Section 236 program through December 1970. As you can see, subsidized households tend to be young families with gross annual incomes under $7000.

Lease Agreement

In many rental circumstances, you will be asked to sign a lease agreement—a legal document designed to protect the lessor (landlord) just as the sales contract (pp. 228–32) is designed to protect the creditor. Make sure you understand and approve the conditions of the lease before signing the agreement, since you are legally bound to pay rent for the entire term of the lease.

TABLE 12-1

CHARACTERISTICS OF HOUSEHOLDS
CERTIFIED FOR SUBSIDY IN SECTION 236 HOUSING
THROUGH DECEMBER 31, 1970

GROSS ANNUAL INCOME		AGE OF HEAD-OF-HOUSEHOLD		TOTAL NUMBER OF PERSONS	
Income	Percent distribution	Age	Percent distribution	Number	Percent distribution
Total	100.0	Total	100.0	Total	100.0
Under $3000	10.7	Under 24	7.5	1	13.6
$3000–3999	13.5	20–24	40.2	2	24.9
4000–4999	23.5	25–29	21.5	3	31.6
5000–5999	25.6	30–39	14.1	4	17.2
		40–49	6.3	5	7.9
6000–6999	17.6	50–59	3.0	6	3.2
7000–7999	6.6	60–69	3.7	7	1.1
8000–8999	1.9	70–79	2.9	8	0.4
9000–9999	0.4	80–89	0.7	9	0.1
10,000 and over	0.2	90 and over	0.1	10 and over	0.1
Median income $5089		Median age 25.5		Median number 3.36 Mean number 2.98	

SOURCE: U.S. Department of Housing and Urban Development.

rent   Rent is usually paid on a monthly basis. Make sure the amount due and the date on which it is due (e.g., first day of each month) are stated. Occasionally the landlord will require that you prepay not only the first month's rent but also the last month's to protect him if you move before the agreement has expired. There may also be a 5 percent penalty for late rent payments.

deposit   A deposit may be required in lieu of, or in addition to, the prepayment of the last month's rent. This amount is reserved by the landlord to repair and refurbish the apartment or house when you vacate. If you have maintained it reasonably well, a portion, or all, of this amount may be returned to you at the end of the lease agreement. (If there is any damage to the premises before you move in, be sure the details are noted in writing on the lease agreement before you sign lest your deposit be used to cover its repair.) However, a cleaning charge will probably be assessed against your deposit, regardless of the condition in which you leave the house or apartment. Final judgment on any amounts to be returned usually rests with the landlord, but substantial disagreement can often be reconciled satisfactorily in a small claims court. Lease terms are most commonly one year, although some may run as long as five years. This aspect can make a lease financially attractive for you since it means that your monthly payments will remain fixed for a certain time. The lease should also state what happens when it expires: if it becomes renewable on a month-to-month basis; if you may renew for an additional term at a renegotiated rental rate; or if it is automatically extended should you fail to inform the landlord of your intention to leave.

expenses   In addition to the rent, the lease should state who pays for utilities, repairs, replacements, insurance, and so on.

restrictions   Make sure the lease enumerates the landlord's policy on overnight guests; children; pets; use of piano, radio, television, and the like; subleasing; and alterations made by the tenant.

BUYING A HOUSE

Choose a real estate broker to help you make the proper purchase. A reputable broker will be licensed by the state in which he works. In some states, a broker license is granted only after the prospective real estate broker has a specified number of years of experience and has passed a state-administered battery of qualifying exams. Licenses to operate as a real estate agent may or may not require successful performance on qualifying exams and/or sponsorship by a licensed, practicing real estate broker. Because of the more exacting training and licensing requirements, it is generally preferable to deal with brokers. In either case, you should make sure that the realtor is active in the area where you wish to purchase.

Guard against brokers who use high pressure sales techniques, are inexperienced, have obviously overpriced listings, or have mostly listings that are offered by several real estate agencies. An "exclusive" listing is initially offered by only one realtor and is generally given to him because he is known to offer excellent services that enhance the possibilities of a sale. If you are suspicious of a broker, check out his reputation with local lending sources, the Better Business Bureau, and the local board of realtors.

A good broker will want to know what you are looking for and what you can afford. Discuss with him your housing needs and financial situation. With this information, he can search for the best available house for you. This task will be easier for him than for you because he is aware of what is for sale in your chosen location. You can expect ten days to two weeks of attention from your broker while he is deciding how serious you really are about buying. If, after this time, you have not demonstrated a serious intent to buy, he will probably turn his attention to other customers. He will not expect you to have bought a house within this time, but he will want some assurance that you are not still trying to decide in general whether to buy a house and that you have some definite ideas about the type of house you are looking for.

Condition of the Lot and House

When evaluating a lot, you will want to check the size and adequacy of yards and gardens; driveway access to and from the street; sewage facilities; noise from freeways, airports, railroads, or factories; and drainage configurations (to ensure safety of the house and garage in the event of flooding).

Checking the condition of a house is not always as easy. If it is a new house, you need an estimate of how well the house will hold up over the coming years. With an older home, this question has already been partly answered. What should concern you here is how much longer the various elements of the house will hold up before costly repairs are required.

Probably the best way to arrive at a reasonably accurate answer to these questions is to engage the services of a professional house inspector. By hiring an impartial builder, architect, or home appraiser (often for as little as $50 to $100) you can receive a good assessment of the condition of any prospective purchase. What you must be concerned with, however, is the quality of this assessment. You can judge the completeness of a professional inspection by comparing it with the items checked in figure 12-2. An appraisal that adequately covers these items should be fairly complete. If not, perhaps you should find a more competent inspector. In all cases, make sure a termite inspection is made. In some states, this is required by law.

An Offering Price

How much is your prospective house worth? Questions of valuation are always difficult to answer. Nevertheless, there are several things you can do to make sure your offer is reasonable. First, try to find out if a home with similar characteristics has been sold in the neighborhood recently and, if so, for how much. Second, find out what the asking price is for similar homes in similar locations that are also on the market. Third, ask a real estate lender for his appraisal of the home. From all these research efforts, you should be able to determine what your prospective house is worth in the current market. Make an offer for an amount less than this. Do not be alarmed if there is some disparity between the amount of your offer and the seller's asking price. It is customary in most areas for the seller and buyer to go through a series

	Basement and Foundation	Ceilings	Wiring	Walls	Exterior Siding	Fireplaces and Chimneys	Floors	Roof	Kitchen	General Floor Plan	Painted Surfaces	Plumbing	Temperature Control Mechanism
Structural soundness	✓	✓		✓	✓	✓	✓	✓					
Waterproof	✓	✓		✓	✓	✓	✓	✓			✓	✓	
Weather-proof			✓	✓	✓	✓	✓	✓			✓		
Durability	✓	✓		✓	✓	✓	✓	✓			✓	✓	
Safety			✓			✓			✓	✓	✓	✓	✓
Operational effectiveness			✓			✓			✓			✓	✓
Product guarantee			✓			✓			✓			✓	✓
Adequacy of layout	✓		✓			✓			✓	✓		✓	✓

Fig. 12-2.
Items that should be checked in a house inspection

of price, and possibly financing, negotiations, although the actual buying transaction may or may not begin with price negotiations. This depends on you, the seller, and, to a certain extent, on local real estate practice. In some cases, title clearance or delivery date for a property may be of primary concern to a buyer, and so negotiations would start with these rather than with price.

In the end, the value of the house will be the price agreed upon by a willing seller and a willing buyer. If you are not ready to raise your offer above a certain amount and the seller declines a lower selling price, you will have to shop elsewhere.

Deposit

After the purchase price has been settled, you will put up a deposit. Often called "earnest money," this deposit is evidence of your intention to buy and may be applied toward the down payment. If you change your mind and decide not to buy a house on which you have made a deposit, you will probably have to forfeit the money.

By mutual agreement between you and the seller, the deposit is sent to an escrow agent. Such an individual or organization acts as an impartial third party who judiciously guards all involved monies until the purchase agreement has been completed. With the deposit, you send instructions to the escrow agent to hold this money until you authorize its release to the seller.

Purchase Agreement

A purchase agreement is signed by you and the seller when the deposit is made. In some areas, this contract is confusingly termed a "deposit receipt." It is not a receipt, but a contract specifying all the conditions you and the seller have arrived at through negotiations and agreed to meet before the transaction is completed. You can cancel the agreement and thus obtain a refund of your deposit only if one or more of the terms in the agreement are not met. Therefore, be sure that you are satisfied with all points and "escape clauses" in the contract before you sign. Provisions appropriate to your particular situation can be included only at your request. Here is a partial list of the provisions that should be included in a purchase agreement.

- purchase price
- prohibition against raising the purchase price
- specification of amount of down payment and minimum acceptable financing
- date on which seller is required to deliver property
- hour and day of closing the sale

- delineation of builder's and/or seller's responsibility to complete plans and specifications after you move in
- prohibition of liability to you for seller's unpaid claims (such as property taxes up to the time of the new owner's occupancy)
- agreement as to who pays title search and insurance costs
- total number of square feet in structure and in lot
- mutual escape clauses, if any (to specify conditions under which buyer or seller may break contract)
- any appliances to be included
- seller's agreement to insure premises for an amount equal to the purchase price until the transaction is closed
- satisfactory passing of a house inspection
- disclosure of all existing easements (public or private) and zoning restrictions
- evidence that the property is not subject to any current or future condemnation proceedings

Figure 12-3 (p. 256) gives an example of a deposit receipt that might be used in simple transactions. Note the suggestion at the bottom of the form to consult an attorney. It is imperative that all important aspects of the purchase be enumerated in the agreement before you sign it. The assistance of a good attorney will be invaluable here.

Deed and Title

A deed is a legal document used to transfer or convey title (ownership interest) to property from one party (grantor) to another (grantee). Of course, there may be more than one grantor or grantee. Title can sometimes be difficult to determine legally. For example, a previous owner of a piece of property may have put a restriction on its use by retaining mineral rights or specifying that no building over two stories may be built on it. After several transfers of property, this restriction may have been temporarily lost and may not appear in the title until too late.

Several devices have been developed to offer title protection. First, a title abstract offers a history of the ownership of a piece of property. Second, a certificate of title gives an attorney's opinion as to the condition of the title of a piece of property. This includes a description of limiting restrictions placed on the title by past owners. Such a certificate often is used when the title abstract is lost or unavailable. Third, title insurance covers you against loss of your equity in the property if a flaw in the title is discovered later. Certain firms dealing solely in this type of insurance sell title insurance to cover the amount of the purchase price. These companies, of course, conduct a title search before they write their policy. In some states, title insurance companies also serve as escrow agents.

REAL ESTATE PURCHASE CONTRACT AND RECEIPT FOR DEPOSIT

CALIFORNIA REAL ESTATE ASSOCIATION STANDARD FORM

THIS IS MORE THAN A RECEIPT FOR MONEY. IT MAY BE A LEGALLY BINDING CONTRACT. READ IT CAREFULLY.

...., California,..., 19.............

Received from..

.... herein called Buyer,

the sum of...Dollars ($................................)

evidenced by cash ☐, personal check ☐, cashier's check ☐, or...

as deposit on account of purchase price of...Dollars ($................................)

for the purchase of property, situated in.. County of.. California, described as follows:

....

....

....

Buyer will deposit in escrow with..

the balance of purchase price as follows:..

....

....

....

1. Title is to be free of liens, encumbrances, easements, restrictions, rights and conditions of record or known to Seller, other than the following:...............

....

....

Seller shall furnish to Buyer at...expense a standard California Land Title Association policy insuring title in Buyer subject only to liens, encumbrances, easements, restrictions, rights and conditions of record as set forth above. If Seller fails to deliver title as herein provided, Buyer at his option may terminate this agreement and any deposit shall thereupon be returned to him.

2. Property taxes, premiums on insurance acceptable to Buyer, rents, interest, and..

....(Insert in blank any other items of income or expense to be prorated) shall be prorated as of (1) the date of recordation of deed or (2)...(Strike (1) if (2) is used). The amount of any bond or assessment which is a lien shall be paid/assumed (Strike one) by...Seller shall pay cost of revenue stamps on deed.

3. Possession shall be delivered to Buyer (Strike inapplicable alternatives) (a) on close of escrow, or (b) not later than.................days after closing escrow, or (c)...................

4. Escrow instructions signed by Buyer and Seller shall be delivered to the escrow holder within.................days from the Seller's acceptance hereof and shall provide for closing within.................days from the opening of escrow, subject to written extensions signed by Buyer and Seller.

5. Unless otherwise designated in the escrow instructions of Buyer, title shall vest as follows:...

....

....

(THE MANNER OF TAKING TITLE MAY HAVE SIGNIFICANT LEGAL AND TAX CONSEQUENCES. THEREFORE, GIVE THIS MATTER SERIOUS CONSIDERATION.)

6. If the improvements on the property are destroyed or materially damaged prior to close of escrow, then, on demand by Buyer, any deposit made by Buyer shall be returned to him and this contract thereupon shall terminate.

7. If Buyer fails to complete said purchase as herein provided by reason of any default of Buyer, Seller shall be released from his obligation to sell the property to Buyer and may proceed against Buyer upon any claim or remedy which he may have in law or equity; provided, however, that by placing their initials here (**Buyer**) (**Seller**) Buyer and Seller agree that it would be impractical or extremely difficult to fix actual damages in case of Buyer's default, that the amount of the deposit is a reasonable estimate of the damages, and that Seller shall retain the deposit as his sole right to damages.

8. Buyer's signature hereon constitutes an offer to Seller to purchase the real estate described above. Unless acceptance hereof is signed by Seller and the signed copy delivered to Buyer, either in person or by mail to the address shown below, within.................days hereof, this offer shall be deemed revoked and the deposit shall be returned to Buyer.

9. Other terms and conditions: (Set forth any terms and conditions of a factual nature applicable to this sale, such as financing, prior sale of other property, the matter of structural pest control inspection, repairs and personal property to be included in sale.)

....

....

....

....

10. Time is of the essence of this contract.

Real Estate Broker... **By**...

Address... **Telephone**...

The undersigned Buyer offers and agrees to buy the above described property on the terms and conditions above stated and acknowledges receipt of a copy hereof.

Dated:... ....

Address... ....

Telephone... **Buyer**...

ACCEPTANCE

The undersigned Seller accepts the foregoing offer and agrees to sell the property described thereon on the terms and conditions therein set forth.

The undersigned Seller has employed the Broker above named and for Broker's services agrees to pay Broker, as a commission, the sum of.................................. ....Dollars ($.................) payable as follows: (a) On recordation of the deed or other evidence of title, or (b) if completion of sale is prevented by default of Seller, upon Seller's default, or (c) if completion of sale is prevented by default of Buyer, only if and when Seller collects the damages from Buyer, by suit or otherwise, and then in an amount not to exceed one half that portion of the damages collected after first deducting title and escrow expenses and the expenses of collection, if any.

The undersigned acknowledges receipt of a copy hereof and authorizes Broker to deliver a signed copy of it to Buyer.

Dated:... ....

Address:... ....

Telephone:... **Seller**...

Broker consents to the foregoing.

Dated:... **Broker**...

A REAL ESTATE BROKER IS THE PERSON QUALIFIED TO ADVISE ON REAL ESTATE. IF YOU DESIRE LEGAL ADVICE CONSULT YOUR ATTORNEY.

THIS STANDARDIZED DOCUMENT FOR USE IN SIMPLE TRANSACTIONS HAS BEEN APPROVED BY THE CALIFORNIA REAL ESTATE ASSOCIATION AND THE STATE BAR OF CALIFORNIA IN FORM ONLY. NO REPRESENTATION IS MADE AS TO THE LEGAL VALIDITY OF ANY PROVISION OR THE ADEQUACY OF ANY PROVISION IN ANY SPECIFIC TRANSACTION. IT SHOULD NOT BE USED IN COMPLEX TRANSACTIONS OR WITH EXTENSIVE RIDERS OR ADDITIONS.

Copyright 1967 by California Real Estate Association

FORM NCR-D

Fig. 12-3.
Sample purchase
agreement

TABLE 12-2

Sales Price	One-Time Premium[a]
$20,000	$147.50
25,000	168.75
30,000	190.00
35,000	206.25
40,000	222.50
50,000	255.00

[a] Basic insurance rate taken from "Title Insurance Rates A-B-C-D,"
Title Insurance and Trust, 1971.

Table 12-2 offers examples of the costs of title insurance at various home sales prices for northern California. Rates vary for other regions of the country. Whether you or the seller pays for this insurance and how much is charged are usually determined by local real estate practices.

Once the purchase transaction has been completed, title is passed to the new owner. When mortgages are involved, title to the property is generally used as security. To be valid, a deed must be in writing and include date, identification of grantor and grantee, consideration clause, signatures of witnesses, and signature of grantor. It must also be delivered to the grantee, and title conveyance should be registered at the county recorder's office immediately after the sale.

There are several types of deeds. The safest type to have is a warranty deed since it guarantees that the title is conveyed free of any encumbrances—even those that may have been placed by prior parties. A special warranty deed guarantees only that the grantor has not placed any encumbrances on the title. A quitclaim deed extinguishes the grantor's title but does not transfer property or make any guarantee about the title. This type of deed is generally used when a grantor, such as an heir, gives up any claim he may have to property, thus removing doubt about the completeness of the grantee's claim. A deed of bargain and sale generally lacks the full title warranty coverage offered by the warranty deed but does carry with it an assertion that the grantor has an ownership interest in the property he is transferring.

An attorney should be able to advise you on how title to your new home should best be held and make sure this asset is included in your will if necessary. (See chapter 21 for a discussion of titles and wills.)

Down Payment

The down payment represents the initial amount of cash you put up to buy the property. How large should it be? Part of your concern should be to ensure that in addition to the down payment you will have enough cash to cover the expenses of moving, closing costs, and any initial remodeling or refurnishing that may be required to make the house more livable. These considerations may make a lower down payment and a larger mortgage preferable, especially if the borrowing costs on a mortgage would be less than those on a loan to cover the cost of home improvements or furnishings. You should also determine whether to use the entire amount of cash available for a down payment or only a portion of it and invest the remainder at a rate of return that would more than cover the cost of borrowing? Let us assume that you have $16,000 that you could use as a down payment on a $40,000 house. You are also able to spend as much as $2965 on mortgage payments each year. One way to finance the purchase of the house is to put the $16,000 down, take a mortgage of $24,000 at 8 percent for twenty-five years, and pay $2200 annually.

Another way is to put only $8000 down, take a mortgage of $32,000 at 8 percent for twenty-five years, and make annual payments of $2965. By the first method you would have $745 ($2965 − $2220) to invest each year for twenty-five years for a total investment of $18,625, whereas the second method permits you to have a lump sum of $8000 invested for the whole twenty-five years. Figure 12-4 shows the results of each of these methods at an average annual investment before-tax yield of 10 percent. A 30 percent marginal tax rate is assumed, and the approximate long-term capital gains tax is determined by multiplying the amount subject to tax by half this rate. This comparison shows that the second plan is more profitable than the first plan by $12,995.

As figure 12-4 shows, it is better to make a smaller down payment, take a larger mortgage at a long maturity period, and invest the difference between the two possible down payments as long as the after-tax return of the investment is greater than the after-tax cost of the mortgage. The increase in the amount earned from such an investment (in this case $12,995) depends on the amount to be financed, the tax bracket, and the rate of return on the investment.

Mortgage

The mortgage is the security offered by a borrower to a lender to obtain the loan necessary to buy a house. As in installment credit transactions, title to the property is conveyed to the lender. In the event of payment defaults, the lender may repossess the house and sell it to regain his investment. The interest rate on mortgage loans can vary according to market conditions, practices of the institution granting the loan, and changing conditions in the general economy.

amortized mortgage Amortization allows you to pay off a debt by making periodic payments of equal amounts. There are two ways in which this widely used loan repayment method may be used: direct reduction

Plan	A Before-Tax Value of Investment at Year 25 ($)	B Amount Subject to Capital Gains Tax ($)	Long-Term Capital Gains Tax ($)	C Net After-Tax Investment Value (A − B) ($)	Total Interest on Mortgage ($)	D Tax Savings ($)	Final Value (C + D) ($)
1	73,270	54,645 (73,270− 18,625) [a]	8197 (15% [b] × 54,645)	65,073 (73,270− 8197)	31,500 [(2220 × 25) −24,000] [c]	9450 (31,500 × 30%)	74,523 (65,073 + 9450)
2	86,680	78,680 (86,680− 8000) [a]	11,800 (15% [b] × 78,680)	74,880 (86,680− 11,800)	42,125 [(2965 × 25) −32,000] [c]	12,638 (42,125 × 30%)	87,518 (74,880 + 12,638)

[a] Cost basis of investments.
[b] One-half of 30 percent marginal tax bracket.
[c] Interest equals annual payment multiplied by number of years to maturity less the original amount borrowed.

Fig. 12-4.
Comparison of investment returns resulting from two different down payment plans for financing a house

plans and fund plans. Both plans involve payments of fixed amounts at regular intervals, but their payments are used differently. Under the *direct reduction plan*, each payment is used first to pay the interest due and then to reduce the amount of principal outstanding. With each payment the amount of interest due decreases because the principal is continually being reduced. Under the *fund plan*, the interest charges are paid first and the remaining amounts are put into a fund, usually a savings account at the institution from which the money was borrowed. When this fund plus interest equals the size of the loan, it is used to pay off the loan. Because the principal is not reduced until the end of the payment period, interest charges do not diminish as the payments are made. The interest earned on the amount of money held in the fund does not compensate for the cost of paying interest on the unreduced principal for the full term of the loan. Hence, the direct reduction plan is preferable.

Let us assume that Tony and Angela Minelli have decided on a mortgage of $20,000 for twenty years at 7 percent annual interest in order to buy a $30,000 house. Table 12-3 shows how much the Minellis will actually pay over twenty years by both the direct reduction and fund plans. Using the direct reduction plan, they would pay $20,000 in principal and $17,200 in interest for a total of $37,200. Using the fund plan, they would pay $13,330 in principal and $28,000 in interest for a total of $41,330. Obviously, the Minellis would be well advised to take out a mortgage that could be paid off through the direct reduction plan. By using this method they will save $4130 over the twenty-year period. At higher interest rates they would save even more money.

second mortgage If the down payment is small and the original lending source is not willing to write a mortgage for the balance of the purchase price, you will have to obtain a second mortgage. Second mortgages are generally more expensive (have a higher interest rate) than first mortgages since the house cannot be used as security. Therefore, they are usually written by lenders seeking more speculative investment returns. Occasionally, the second mortgage may be written by the seller himself. He would be motivated to do this if it expedited a sale at a price to his liking. Be careful that the seller's willingness to take back a second mortgage does not mean you will pay an unnecessarily high price for the home.

repayment period (maturity) Allowing for money market conditions and the age and condition of the house you buy, you have a choice of mortgage maturity periods ranging, generally, from ten to thirty years. The period should not be so short as to necessitate large annual payments that could put an undue financial burden on your budget. Nor should the period be so long that large aggregate interest costs are incurred— unless you can, and will, invest the extra money at a higher rate than

TABLE 12-3

COMPARISON OF DIRECT REDUCTION PLAN AND FUND PLAN
ON $20,000 MORTGAGE AT 7 PERCENT

DIRECT REDUCTION PLAN	YEAR						
	1	2	3	4	5	10	20
Annual payment	$ 1860	$ 1860	$ 1860	$ 1860	$ 1860	$ 1860	$ 1860
Interest portion	1380	1365	1345	1325	1300	1170	100
Principal reduction	480	495	515	535	560	690	1760
Outstanding principal	19,520	19,025	18,510	17,975	17,415	13,360	0
FUND PLAN							
Annual payment	$ 2067	$ 2067	$ 2067	$ 2067	$ 2067	$ 2067	$ 2067
Interest portion	1400	1400	1400	1400	1400	1400	1400
Principal payment	667	667	667	667	667	667	667
Amount in fund	680	1370	2100	2880	3690	8400	20,000

you are paying on the mortgage. Of course, the longer you take to repay the loan, the smaller your monthly payments are and the more expensive the house you can buy with the same income. However, the longer the repayment period, the slower the reduction in principal, making the interest on the principal greater in total. As a result, a twenty-year mortgage requires monthly payments that are more than half the amount of monthly payments on a ten-year mortgage (table 12-4, p. 262). In other words, the total amount of interest you pay on a loan is determined by both the interest rate and the length of the repayment period.

Why, then, might a wise money manager take out a mortgage loan that has a longer maturity than necessary? There are two possible reasons. First, taking a shorter mortgage might mean eliminating budgeted monthly savings and investment dollars. It may be more important to build up an emergency cash reserve than to keep interest costs down. Second, a longer mortgage maturity is attractive if the amount saved by not taking a short maturity is invested at a higher rate of return than the interest on the mortgage. (Chapters 13 through 19 will discuss rates of return for various types of investments.)

TABLE 12-4

Monthly Payments Necessary
to Amortize 7 Percent Mortgage Using
Direct Reduction Plan

Amount	Maturity (Years)				
	10	15	20	25	30
$10,000	$116	$ 90	$ 78	$ 71	$ 67
20,000	232	180	155	141	133
30,000	348	270	233	212	200

You should be certain that there will be no penalty for prepayment if you should later want to refinance the mortgage at a lower interest rate. You should also make sure that there is no clause that allows the lender arbitrarily to call back the loan or accelerate the payments.

Obtaining a Mortgage

The procedure for obtaining a mortgage is similar to that for obtaining consumer loans (pp. 210–12). Three types of mortgage loans are available for home purchases.

conventional mortgage   This type of loan involves a transaction solely between you and the lender. There is no government participation in terms of loan guarantees or insurance. Occasionally, these loans may be insured by a private loan insurance organization.

Typically, conventional mortgages are amortized, use the direct reduction plan, have no prepayment penalty, and mature in twenty-five years or more. The size of the loan usually ranges from 60 to 90 percent of the appraised (not market) value of the property. For example, if the lender's appraiser sets the value of the property at 80 percent of the market value, your loan at 60 to 90 percent of the appraised value would be for only 48 to 72 percent of the market value. Therefore, a sizeable down payment of from 28 to 52 percent of the purchase price may be required. Conventional loans can be written for up to 95 percent of the appraised value of a single-family dwelling only if the loan does not exceed $30,000 and 5 to 10 percent of it is guaranteed or insured by a private insurer approved by the federal government.

FHA loan   This type of loan is insured up to certain limits by the Federal Housing Administration (FHA), a division of the U.S. Department of Housing and Urban Development. The FHA was established by Congress in 1934 to provide mortgage and home improvement loan insurance to private lenders. It does not make loans; it only insures them. The FHA is self-supporting through insurance premiums and investment income. Currently its insurance reserves are over one billion dollars.

If you have FHA insurance, lenders generally do not require as large a down payment as would be necessary with a conventional loan. To qualify for insurance protection, the FHA requires that a 3 percent down payment be made on a house that costs up to $15,000, a 10 percent down payment on one costing between $15,000 and $25,000, and a 20 percent down payment on one valued above $25,000.

FHA offers insurance on many types of loans including those for property improvements, home purchase and improvements, second home purchases, multi-family-dwelling financing, and low-income-housing rehabilitation. Table 12-5 (p. 264) provides three examples of FHA insurable loans and the conditions that must be met before insurance coverage is granted. For a complete discussion of the types of loans that qualify for FHA insurance, contact the local FHA office or talk to a mortgage loan officer at a bank or savings and loan association.

Veterans Administration loan guarantee   The main purpose of this loan program is to ensure that a veteran will be able to obtain a loan to finance a home at reasonable interest rates. The Veterans Administration (VA) does not generally make loans. It offers a guarantee against loss to lending institutions and private lenders. The VA appraises property and offers a guarantee of no more than 60 percent of the appraised value of the home, with a maximum guarantee of $12,500. Originally, the loan guarantee dollar maximum was $4000; it was raised to $7500 before being increased to its current level.

To be eligible for a VA mortgage loan guarantee, the purchase price of the property must not exceed the VA's appraised value, the loan must have an interest rate of 8 percent or less, and the buyer must have served more than ninety days of active duty and been discharged for reasons other than dishonorable unless service-incurred injuries have resulted in an earlier discharge. This guarantee is available to a qualified veteran only once. If, however, a veteran used this guarantee when the dollar maximum was lower—at $4000, for example—then because of the subsequent increase in the maximum, he would now be eligible for a loan guarantee of $8500.

The GI Home Loan Law, which provides for VA mortgage loans, was altered by a bill that has been in effect since October, 1970. One major provision of the bill was the removal of all expiration dates on loan guarantee options available to World War II and Korean War veterans. The former group saw its options expire in July 1970, and members of the latter group were due to experience the same loss at varying times over the next several years. A second provision of significance was the

TABLE 12-5

EXAMPLE OF FHA INSURABLE LOANS AND CONDITIONS

Classification (Government)	Purpose	Maximum Amount Insured	Maximum Maturity on Loan (Years)	Maximum Finance Charge[a] (%)	Insurance Premium (%/year)	Payment Plan
Title I Class 1 (a)	Property improvement	$5000	7	5.5[b]	0.5 of amount advanced	Fund plan
Title II Section 203 (k)	Major home improvements	FHA valuation of structure	5 to 20	7	0.5 of balance outstanding	Direct reduction
Title II Section 203 (b)	Home purchase	$33,000	30	7	0.5 of balance outstanding	Direct reduction

SOURCE: Adapted from *Digest of Insurable Loans*, Federal Housing Administration, U.S. Department of Housing and Urban Development, HUD PG-4 (October 1966), pp. 2–5.

[a] As of October 1972.

[b] 5.5 percent discounted up to $2500; 4.5 percent discounted above $2500.

inclusion of mobile homes as an alternative for obtaining the $12,500 financing guarantee. If you are a WW II or Korean War veteran with unused guarantee benefits, you might find it attractive to take advantage of this provision by financing a mobile home as a retirement residence. If you are a younger veteran, you may initially use your benefits to finance a mobile home. Once it is paid for, you may reuse this benefit to buy a regular home. This sequence of financing may not be used in reverse, however (i.e., regular home paid for through VA benefits, then mobile home financing).

The maximum rate initially set on VA guaranteed loans for mobile homes is 10.75 percent. Since this rate approximates the 11 to 13 percent charged by lenders on conventional mobile home loans, you have a good chance of finding a lender who will offer VA guaranteed loans of this type. Maximum limits are $10,000 and twelve years for a straight mobile home loan. For loans that cover the purchase of a developed lot as well as the mobile home, maximum limits are $17,500 and fifteen years.

A special provision was also inserted for severely disabled veterans who are entitled to a specially adapted residence because of the nature of their disability. Until October, 1970, the VA would contribute one-half of the purchase price of such a residence up to a dollar maximum of $6250. Now the remainder of the purchase price can be borrowed directly from the VA.

points This is a term applied to a practice in the real estate mortgage market. This practice has developed because the federal government dictates the maximum interest levels for FHA and VA mortgages rather than allowing these rates to be determined by money market forces. If the rate on conventional mortgages were greater than the regulated rate on FHA/VA mortgages, lenders would find the former type of mortgage a more attractive investment instrument. Consequently, funds for FHA/VA mortgages would dry up.

To compensate for the lower yield from a government regulated mortgage, the lender generally requires that a lump-sum fee be paid at the start of the loan. The method of determining the amount of this fee is called *points*. One point equals one percent of the amount borrowed. Generally, two points are charged for each quarter of 1 percent difference between the rate available on conventional mortgages and the ceiling rate on FHA/VA mortgages. For example, let us assume that the conventional mortgage rate is 8 percent and the ceiling rate on government backed mortgages is 7 percent. On a loan of $20,000, one point is equal to $200. Hence, eight points, or $1600, will be charged on a government regulated mortgage since there are four quarters between the 8 percent conventionals and the 7 percent governmentals.

In addition, a fee called a *loan origination fee* or a *front-end load* may be charged on either conventional or governmental mortgage loans. It is also expressed in points and ranges from one to two points.

Sources of Mortgage Loans

The sources of mortgage loans also offer various consumer lending services (pp. 212–17). Savings and loan associations are the most prominent source of mortgage money. Mutual savings banks and private lenders also participate in this market. Mortgages written by commercial banks usually call for large down payments and short-term maturities. Occasionally life insurance companies write mortgages on expensive homes.

In addition to traditional commercial sources of home mortgages, there are several other alternatives for obtaining home financing. You may be able to obtain a first mortgage from the home's current owner. Often called a "purchase money" mortgage, its terms are similar to those of a conventional mortgage from a commercial source. Most likely, the owner will not charge you points or a loan origination fee, especially if the loan makes it easier for him to sell the house and the mortgage represents an attractive investment for him.

The seller may be willing to take back a second mortgage if your down payment and first mortgage do not fully cover the purchase price. Or you may be able to persuade him to deposit an amount equal to the second mortgage with the commercial lender granting the first mortgage. This would encourage the commercial lender to increase the size of the first mortgage to cover the entire difference between the purchase price and the down payment.

For example, assume that you make a $5000 down payment on a $35,000 house but cannot find a commercial lender willing to offer more than a $26,000 first mortgage. If the seller places the $4000 difference in escrow, the lender might be encouraged to increase the first mortgage to $30,000. The seller may be willing to do this to expedite the sale of the home and to earn interest on the $4000. The difficulty is in finding a seller with $4000.

Finally, you may be able to assume an existing mortgage. This would be most attractive to you where the interest rate on the assumable mortgage is less than that available from lenders and where the balance outstanding is still substantial. For example, a $10,000 mortgage on a $30,000 house would not be a good one to take over since it would require a down payment and probably a second mortgage totaling $20,000. Some recent mortgages have been written to discourage assuming or transferring an existing mortgage. If you are seriously considering taking either of these actions, we recommend that you seek legal assistance.

SELLING A HOUSE

Most of this chapter is devoted to the considerations involved in buying a home. Knowing how to sell one is also important. Once again, be sure to engage the services of a good realtor. His experience in the legal, financial, and sales aspects of this transaction will make him worth his 5 to 6 percent commission.

Before you put your home up for sale, you should clean it and make inexpensive but significant repairs. You might, for example, replace a damaged screen door, but you would probably not have new electrical wiring installed. Engage a qualified real estate appraiser if you find it difficult to establish an appropriate selling price. A good realtor should be able to offer this advice, too. If you plan to pay off your mortgage ahead of schedule, check to see that it has no penalty for prepayment. Decide whether you would be willing to take back a second to enhance the chances of either a quicker sale or one at a price more to your liking. If your present mortgage has an interest rate that is lower than those currently available on the market and the mortgage can be transferred to a new owner, be sure to use this fact as an attractive selling point. Find out what costs you will incur by closing the deal and moving. Make sure your property taxes are paid. Be prepared to wait for a willing buyer if your home is realistically priced. A buyer who senses that you cannot afford to wait will be in a favorable bargaining position. Consult an attorney to ensure that the purchase contract is in your best interests.

OTHER OWNERSHIP ALTERNATIVES

In recent years, with the costs of home ownership rising at a rapid rate, many people have been seeking to buy living accommodations other than the traditional house and lot. In many cases, these alternatives are attractive because they do not require a substantial outlay of money to purchase the land itself.

The Mobile Home

This type of housing resembles a good-sized apartment more than it does a trailer. Today, two large mobile homes can be combined to provide over 1000 square feet of living space. Prices range from $3000 to $15,000, with the average being about $8000. People with transient life styles such as college students, project engineers, construction workers, and military personnel find this form of housing quite convenient. Both young marrieds and senior citizens who need low cost, furnished housing requiring minimum upkeep may find the mobile home an attractive alternative. This form of housing can also serve very effectively as a recreational second home. You may obtain a mortgage-type loan (pp. 258–65) to buy a mobile home. Less money is required to initiate the purchase of a mobile home than is needed for a regular house and the monthly operating costs are lower. Over the longer term, however, there is a financial disadvantage. Mobile homes tend to depreciate in value and do not offer the inflationary hedge available with home ownership.

Cooperative Apartments

Membership in this housing alternative involves purchasing an ownership share proportionate to the living space you occupy in the entire dwelling complex. For example, if your apartment contains 5 percent of the living space of the entire building, then you purchase a 5 percent ownership share. Your right to the apartment is secured by a proprietary lease that lasts as long as you live.

As a member of the cooperative, you are subject to a monthly charge to cover maintenance, upkeep, debt retirement, taxes, insurance, and an emergency fund. In many instances, the costs of living in a cooperative apartment are less than renting because members of the cooperative, as owners, need not make a profit on their investment. Your equity build-up could also be advantageous if you are in a quality building that is well located.

Before signing your membership contract, make sure you are satisfied with the conditions of ownership. Otherwise, you may be adversely affected by policy decisions made by management and approved of by a majority of shareholders. For example, a plan to accelerate the payment of the mortgage would increase your assessment. There might also be restrictive policies concerning features such as subletting, entertaining, and resale.

Condominiums

Unlike cooperative apartments, in which you participate in the general ownership of an apartment building, condominium units are purchased outright. The purchase price usually includes, in addition to your living quarters, a proportionate interest in common areas such as lobbies, corridors, and grounds. Consequently, condominiums are often an attractive alternative to the homeowner who does not want the responsibility of caring for a yard. Also, the higher density land use, construction savings due to common walls, and the like make condominiums a lower cost alternative to owning a separate home and yard. Assessments for taxes, exterior building maintenance, gardening and so on are usually determined according to the circumstances of the specific accommodations. For this reason and because ownership of the unit itself is possible, condominiums are often easier to resell than cooperative apartments.

CONCLUSION

The decisions you make about housing represent substantial investments. Therefore, make your choices only after extensive investigation. Once this is accomplished, you should be able to use your financial resources in a constructive manner and avoid unnecessary drains on your income.

amortization
closing costs
condominium
cooperative apartment
deed
deposit
down payment
equity
escrow

Federal Housing Authority
lease agreement
mortgage
offering price
real estate agent
real estate broker
selling costs
title
Veterans Administration

1. What costs are exclusive to renting? To home ownership? Explain how they differ.
2. Under what circumstances can increased value in your home be of economic value to you?
3. When you buy a home, what services will an attorney perform? A house inspector? Realtor? Why is it important to obtain each of these services?
4. How do you determine whether a realtor is competent and honest?
5. Under what circumstances would you need a second mortgage?
6. What is the primary difference between FHA and VA mortgages?
7. Describe why points exist and how they work.
8. What is the difference between a direct reduction plan and a fund plan on an amortized mortgage?
9. Why is the deposit receipt, or purchase agreement, important?
10. What is the purpose of title insurance?

Terry and Andrea Carr are both twenty-five. They have been married for three years and have a one-year-old son. Terry's monthly salary is $1000, of which he actually brings home $750. The Carrs also have $27,000 in assets consisting of $4300 in a 5 percent savings account, $10,200 in a mutual fund earning 10 percent a year, $4500 in two cars, and $8000 in personal property. Their liabilities amount to $8000—$6500 for an educational loan and $1500 for a car loan. Their net worth is $19,000.

The Carrs have been shopping for a home and are seriously considering two prospects, as shown in figure 12-5. To make up the $8000 difference between the purchase price of the house and the first mortgage on it, they can either pay all cash or pay $4000 cash and assume from the seller a second mortgage of $4000 at 10 percent amortized over five years ($85 a month). The difference of $7500 between the purchase price of the condominium and the first mortgage on it can be made up entirely

Description	Selling Price	Mortgage	Finance Charge	Payback Terms	Closing Costs
Three-bedroom, two-bath home	$35,000	$27,000	7.5%	$199 a month for 25 years	$800
Two-bedroom, one-and-one-half bath condominium	$25,000	$19,000	8%	$159 a month for 20 years	$600

Fig. 12-5. Comparison of two housing prospects

with a cash down payment. The Carrs also have the option of assuming a $3000 second mortgage at 10 percent for five years ($64 a month). The Carrs realize that, irrespective of which housing prospect they choose, they will have to purchase an additional $2500 in furniture, drapes, carpets, and appliances. Property taxes, maintenance costs, and insurance are expected to average $70 a month for the house and $50 a month for the condominium.

Which housing prospect and which financing option seem most appropriate for the Carrs? Give your reasons for your choice and for discarding the other alternatives. What additional information would you need to make a better decision?

RECOMMENDED READING

MAGAZINES

"House Buying: The Costs of Closing the Deal." *Changing Times*, November 1971, pp. 15–17.

A good discussion and a nationwide survey of these costs.

"The How and Why of Taking Over a Mortgage." *Changing Times,* January 1970, pp. 21–23.

A good discussion of this subject.

Ingersoll, John H. "How to Finance a House in Today's Credit Crunch." *House Beautiful,* September 1970, p. 38.

A good discussion of less well known and less used methods of home financing.

"Is a Home Still a Good Investment?" *Better Homes and Gardens,* September 1969, p. 46.

An extensive discussion of reasons for and against renting and owning.

"A Mobile Home Vs a House: How the Costs Compare." *Changing Times,* January 1971, pp. 19–21.

A fair discussion of this subject.

"When Do You Need a Real Estate Agent?" *Better Homes and Gardens,* March 1970, p. 12.

> A good discussion of the services required when buying or selling a house.

BOOKS

Changing Times Family Success Book. 1969.

> One chapter offers a brief discussion of cooperatives and condominiums. Another discusses what tenants should look for in a lease.

Donaldson, Elvin, and Pfahl, John. *Personal Finance.* New York: Ronald

> Chapter 10 offers an extensive treatment of home ownership.

Smith, Carlton; Pratt, Richard Putnam; and the editors of Time-Life Books. *The Time-Life Book of Family Finance.* New York: Time-Life Books, 1969.

> Chapter 7 offers an excellent discussion of home ownership, especially in regard to selecting a house.

CHUCK AND NANCY ANDERSON

BUYING A NEW HOME

The Andersons have outgrown their house. Because of their reduced costs on insurance, taxes, and debt payments, they decide that they can afford to buy a new home. After much searching, they find a brand new house they can buy for $40,000. They can sell their present home for $35,000, with selling expenses of $2050. It has a mortgage of $14,500. Their best mortgage offer on the new house is $32,000 at 7.5 percent for twenty-nine years with monthly payments of $225.84. Closing costs plus initial furnishing and landscaping costs on the new home will amount to $2000.

QUESTIONS

1. What factors should the Andersons take into account when looking for a new home?
2. What information would you need to have to determine whether the Andersons are financially justified in buying another house?

3. By what percent will taxes and inflation affect the rate the Andersons must pay on their new mortgage? How does it compare with the net investment return they derived in chapter 11 (table 11-1)?
4. How are the costs of property taxes, utilities, property insurance, repairs, and gardening at the new house likely to compare with those at the old house?
5. Where will the funds for the $8000 down payment and the $2000 in related expenses (closing costs, furnishings, and landscaping) come from?
6. Does it appear that the Andersons can afford to buy the new house?

IV. INCREASING YOUR INCOME

Liquidity . . . maturity . . . straddle . . . proxy . . . no-par . . . OTC . . . To most people, these terms are part of a complex language spoken only by sophisticated investors. Often there is more than one term to describe the same thing. Not only are the terms confusing, but also the concepts they represent are unfamiliar. Therefore, most people find it hard to develop expertise in making investments. You should learn enough about various types of investments in chapters 13 through 19, so that you can begin to overcome these difficulties.

Unit two dealt with the strategy for protecting what you have. There you learned how to protect your financial resources against calamities by developing meaningful insurance programs at the lowest cost. In unit three, the strategy for getting the most out of your income was developed. You learned how to budget your money effectively and to eliminate unnecessary drains on financial resources. As a result of applying what you learned in those two units, you should have more money to invest.

In unit four the strategy for increasing your total gross income will be treated. Chapter 13 presents the basic concepts and principles of investing. The six chapters after that treat specific investment alternatives: time deposits, insurance and annuities, stocks and bonds, mutual funds, and real estate. When you have completed this unit, you should understand fundamental investment concepts as well as specific investment alternatives. You should also be able to decide intelligently which investment goals are appropriate for you and to identify accurately the investments that represent realistic strategies for achieving these goals.

13

INVESTMENT PRINCIPLES

It is possible to become a millionaire without having a rich uncle who names you in his will. Because of compounding on your investment, you could invest $10,000 today at an average return of 15 percent a year and have $1,000,000 in thirty-three years. Or you could invest $2000 each year at 15 percent and be a millionaire in thirty-one years. People have become rich using relatively small stakes and ordinary investment media such as the stock market or real estate. One such person put $10,000 down on a $42,000 piece of land in 1963 and sold it in 1972 for $400,000! Of course, he was extraordinarily fortunate; the return on his investment was approximately 80 percent annually.

You might argue that even 15 percent is a high rate of return, one that can be achieved only with considerable luck. Perhaps, but let us examine opportunities for such profit. If in 1960 you had randomly selected a broadly diversified portfolio on the New York Stock Exchange, reinvested all dividends, and sold the stocks for cash in 1968, you would have achieved a 15.6 percent compound return! Of course, in order to recognize that 1968 was a good time to sell, you would have needed to understand P/E ratios (p. 345) and other indicators of stock market trends. After selling the stocks, you might have been able to take further advantage of the economic situation by buying real estate if you had known that real estate is a good hedge against above-average inflation. Indeed, some real estate values rose in excess of 15 percent a year from 1968 through 1972.

Although these profits are possible, most American families do not make such investments. Table 13-1 shows how wealth is actually distributed among American families. Of families with $10,000 to $14,999 annual income, only 10 percent have more than $10,000 in savings and bonds, only 3 percent have over $35,000 worth of real estate other than their own homes; only 26 percent own common stock; and only 11 percent own mutual fund shares.

TABLE 13-1

PERCENT OF FAMILIES HOLDING VARIOUS INVESTMENT ASSETS IN 1970

ASSET	ALL FAMILIES (%)	FAMILY INCOME					
		Under $3000 (%)	$3000– 4999 (%)	$5000– 7499 (%)	$7500– 9999 (%)	$10,000– 14,999 (%)	$15,000 or more (%)
Savings accounts and bonds							
None	16	42	30	22	12	5	1
Under $10,000	72	53	58	67	81	85	74
Over $10,000	12	5	12	11	7	10	25
Real estate							
None	80	92	85	84	79	79	65
Under $35,000	17	6	12	14	15	16	23
Over $35,000	3		2	2	4	3	10
Common stock[a]	23	6	11	12	17	26	55
Mutual funds[a]	9	3	5	4	10	11	26
No stocks or funds	74	92	88	88	80	70	42

[a]Value of holdings not known. The majority of mutual fund owners also own stocks in individual corporations.

NOTE: Percents may not total 100 because of rounding or nonresponse.

SOURCE: George Katona, Lewis Mandell, and Jay Schmiedeskamp, *1970 Survey of Consumer Finances* (Ann Arbor: University of Michigan, 1971), pp. 101, 115, 129.

We do not believe that such statistics should cause you to set low goals. Being a millionaire may be an unrealistically high or even inappropriate objective for you. Nevertheless, the above-average income typically earned by a college graduate combined with the skills discussed in this unit, can help you achieve above-average investment objectives.

BUT I DON'T HAVE ANY MONEY TO INVEST

Before you can learn how to use investment alternatives to full advantage, you must have something to invest. If you have trouble saving money, you may be able to use one or more of the following five techniques for avoiding overspending.

Budget Your Savings

The budget techniques outlined in chapter 8 are probably the surest and most sophisticated means of regularly saving the amounts you need. If you have not given budgeting a try yet, go back and review that chapter. There is nothing better to help solve family financial woes than a good budgeting program.

Have Someone Else Help You

If even a flexible budget seems too constraining for you, you may at least be able to authorize your employer to withhold a certain percentage from your paycheck each month to be invested in the credit union, savings bonds, or company stock, if available. Or you may buy a cash-value insurance policy and have the insurance company force you to save through regular premium notices. You may overwithhold on your income taxes, and receive a refund each April to be invested or spent as your savings plan dictates. Remember, however, that the government pays no interest on withheld taxes! You could also consider one of the mutual fund savings accumulation plans discussed in chapter 18.

Spend Greenbacks Only

Many people save pennies until they have a jar full and then use them to make an addition to their savings account. It works, but it is a very slow way to save money. A more effective method is to put all loose change in a jar at the end of each day. In fact, if you never use change to help pay for purchases, but accumulate it all in a jar, you may be able to put $20 to $50 a month in your savings account! Some couples save as much as $75 each month by spending only greenbacks. Their paper money is their spending budget; their change is their savings budget.

Try a Frugality Month

A crash savings program can help you save money quickly. The key to this program's success is to ask yourself a question before you spend money for any reason: "Do I really need to make this purchase?" You will be surprised how often the answer is no and how rapidly your savings can mount. A period of frugality may also be beneficial in the long run.

Once you become used to spartan living you can add back only half of your previous expenses and perhaps discover that the other half really constituted unnecessary luxuries (such as a cafeteria lunch instead of a brown bag lunch). Your savings can then continue to grow.

Take Advantage of Windfalls

Everyone periodically discovers windfalls in his budget. Perhaps you are buying a car on the installment plan. After you make your last payment, continue writing a check for the same amount each month but use it to increase your savings and investments. Next time you buy a car you can pay cash for it and have money left over. Or, perhaps, you have received a $50 monthly raise. Last month you managed to get by on the previous paycheck; do it again this month and bank the raise. The general rule is: Do not let windfalls disappear into your daily expenses. Taking advantage of them is probably the most painless way to develop a regular savings habit.

RISK AND CERTAINTY

In unit two we discussed risks that can be covered by insurance. Now we will talk about investment risks, which generally are not insurable.

Risk is defined as the chance of loss in the future. In the absence of risk, there is certainty, or complete and perfect information about the future. The more information you have about what will happen in the future (i.e., the more certainty), the less the potential risk that something will cause you a loss. The measure of this relationship between risk and certainty is often termed the *degree of risk exposure*. That is, the degree of risk is simply a function of the amount of knowledge you have about future events. Although the relationship between risk and amount of knowledge is shown in a linear fashion in the graph, the line may be curved for different situations. The main idea, however, is that the more you know about the future, the less risk you must take.

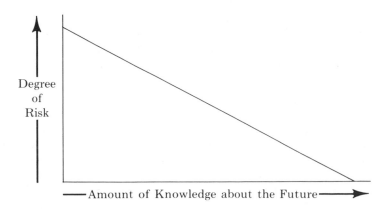

Relation of Risk and Certainty to Investments

If you invest in a U.S. savings bond, you can be certain that your principal and interest are guaranteed as fully as possible. You have virtually eliminated risk from your investment. If you invest in a growth common stock, there is a chance that you will make a 20 percent annual gain, considerably more than you would make on a savings bond. However, there is also a chance that the price of the stock will decline and you will lose money. If you invest in a small mining company, you might double or triple your money if the company strikes a big ore body. Conversely, the company may go bankrupt and you could lose your entire investment.

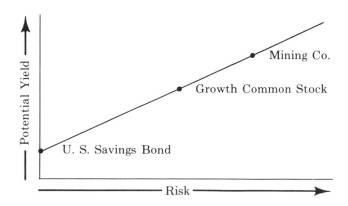

The higher the rate of return in an investment, the greater the risk assumed by an investor. A high degree of risk, however, does not necessarily indicate an expected high return. For example, a high risk investment such as a hamburger stand may offer a return no higher than that of an insured savings deposit.

Many investment advisers use other categories to describe risk. They speak of the following types of risk: interest rate risk (interest rates may change); purchasing power risk (inflation can reduce the real value of a bank account); market risk (stock prices fluctuate); psychological risk (one may be unable to control his emotions when investing). Although these are valid categories, we prefer to consider them as components of the total financial risk. As we proceed through the strategy of increasing your income, we will discuss these aspects of risk (and how to minimize or control them) as they pertain to each investment medium: time deposits, insurance, annuities, stocks, bonds, mutual funds, and real estate.

You Can Reduce Risk

Why are some people consistently successful in the stock market while others fail every time? Why do some people show a profit in such difficult trading arenas as commodities? We believe that it is largely because these people have more than average knowledge and expertise regarding their investment. They consciously strive to be very good at their kind of investing. They have learned much from their own experience and from history and are therefore better prepared to anticipate and understand the future. In our opinion, the most effective way to reduce risk in any investment medium is to gain as much knowledge and expertise as possible concerning that medium. Studying this unit on investing is a good first step toward increasing your knowledge.

INCOME AND GROWTH

The basic concept behind a financial investment is that you commit money today in the expectation of a return in the future. This return may be received both as *income from the principal* and as *growth of the principal.* Income from the principal may be obtained as interest, dividends, or rent payments. Growth of the principal is obtained as price appreciation (capital gains on property that is sold for more than was originally paid for it). For example, you may purchase 100 shares of a growth stock at $60 a share for a total cost of $6000. (We will ignore commissions in this example.) If during the year the company pays dividends totaling $1.40 on each share, your income from the principal would be $140 for the year. If you sold the shares at the end of the year for $70 a share, you would have a profit of $10 a share and your return due to the growth of the principal would be $1000 (capital gains). Your total return (income plus growth) would then be $1140.

Types of Investment Income

In order to understand the investment concepts introduced in later chapters, you should be thoroughly familiar with the various terms describing types of investment income: interest, dividend, rent, capital gain, and retirement payment.

interest   The payment you receive for allowing someone to use your money is called interest. For example, banks or savings and loan associations use the money you deposit with them to invest for their own gain. They, in turn, use some of the income from their investments to pay you interest for the use of your money. This interest is usually expressed in terms of an annual percentage rate.

dividend   A dividend is a distribution of corporate profits to shareholders. For example, if a major company makes $10,000,000 after taxes in an average year, it might pay stockholders $6,000,000 in dividends.

In this way, dividends represent income to the person who owns stock in the company. A company that has one or more unprofitable years or that needs to retain cash for growth may not pay any dividends. Corporate dividends are not assured. They depend both on the level of profits and on the way the company's management uses them. In the example above, the company decided to retain $4,000,000 of its profits for corporate growth.

rent Rent is the payment you receive for allowing someone to use your property. Rental agreements usually run from month to month. Lease payments are the same as rent, but leases involve agreements that bind both parties for the duration of the contract, usually at least a year.

capital gain A capital gain is income that you receive when you sell property or securities at a price above the total of the amount you paid for them plus what you paid in commissions and selling costs. If you do not make a profit on a sale of property or securities, you have a capital loss, even though you may have received rent or dividends.

retirement payments Retirement payments such as Social Security, pensions, life insurance benefits, and annuities represent a return of an original investment. Only to the extent that such payments include interest receipts above the original cost is there any investment income.

Compound Yield

Compound yield occurs when investment income—whether interest, dividends, or capital gains—is reinvested with the principal. For example, if you were to receive the interest from your savings account by check each quarter and not reinvest it, you would receive *simple interest,* not compound interest. If you were to leave the interest on deposit and get interest on interest, you would have compound interest, or a compound yield. Similarly, other types of investment income must be reinvested, rather than spent, if they are to achieve a compound yield. In the case of a common stock, the dividends received or capital gains realized should be reinvested in that stock (or a better stock opportunity) to achieve a compound yield on the investment.

We have included compound interest tables in this book (pp. 498–501). You should learn how to use these tables, since they will help you both to understand the chapters in this unit and to make sound investment decisions.

Compound interest table A illustrates the value of one dollar invested at various yields for up to thirty years. For example, assume that you invest $100 in a savings account with an annual yield of 5 percent. If

you let the interest compound, in ten years your $100 investment will be worth $160. If you request that the interest be paid to you each year, you will receive only $5 annual interest (simple interest) and in ten years your total investment will have brought you $150 ($100 + [10 × $5]). Another $10 could be earned, however, because of the compounding effect of interest on interest. Over longer periods of time, the actual dollar amounts that can be earned by compounding become more significant. Over thirty years, for example, $100 compounded at 5 percent would be worth $430, as opposed to the $250 it would be worth with simple interest ($100 + [30 × $5]).

Assume that you invest $1000 for twenty years in a mutual fund with an average rate of return of 10 percent a year. You could take your profits in cash, so that there would be only the original $1000 in the fund at the end of each year. You would receive an average of $100 simple return each year, and in twenty years the total amount received would be $3000 ($1000 + [20 × $100]). Or you could leave your investment income, including dividends and capital gains distributions (p. 413), in the fund to be reinvested in additional shares. In twenty years the $1000 would be worth $6727. This amount is more than twice what would have been achieved through a simple return. Table 13-2 demonstrates how annual compounding affects the size of an investment both over increasing periods of time and at higher rates of return.

TABLE 13-2

VALUE OF A $1000 INVESTMENT

YEARS	RETURN ON INVESTMENT (Compounded Annually)	
	5%	10%
0	$1,000	$ 1,000
10	1,629	2,594
20	2,653	6,727
30	4,322	17,449
40	7,040	45,259

The second compound interest table, Table B (p. 500), illustrates the value of investing one dollar each year at various compound interest rates and for various lengths of time. For example, if you invested $100 a year in a 5 percent savings account, after fifteen years you would have accumulated $2160.

INVESTMENT ALTERNATIVES

As we will see in chapters 14 through 19, there are many investments from which to choose: time deposits, annuities and insurance, stocks and bonds, mutual funds, and real estate. There are, however, basically only two ways to invest money: an investor can lend money at interest or he can own part of an income-producing asset.

Lending

There are four ways in which the average investor can loan money and receive interest. Through a savings account he can loan money to a bank, a savings and loan association, or a credit union. He can buy government or corporate bonds and thereby loan money to the government or to a business. He can buy mortgages (usually second mortgages or second deeds of trust) and thereby loan money to a homeowner. He can loan money to a life insurance company by buying cash-value life insurance.

Owning

There are seven ways an investor can obtain ownership of an asset in the hope of gaining a return on his money. He can buy common stock in a corporation; preferred stock in a corporation; mutual funds, which are an indirect means of investing in stocks; a partnership share in a small business; a share in an investment syndicate (usually involved in real estate); the deed to a piece of real estate; or personal property such as stamps, coins, and art works.

Effect of Inflation on Lending and Owning

As you can see from table 13-3 (p. 284), if you had put $2000 in your mattress in 1940, it would buy only $730 worth of 1940 goods in 1970 (compared to $2000 worth of goods in 1940). If you wanted your money to be worth as much today as it was thirty years ago, you would have had to average a 3 percent return on your money after taxes each year; this is because inflation, as measured by the consumer price index, has averaged 3 percent over the past three decades.

Let us compare the effects of inflation on lending and owning. Assume that you buy equal amounts of a car manufacturer's bonds and common stock and hold them twenty years. If in that time, the company does not grow in size and inflation causes the dollar to buy half as much as it does today, the sales volume of autos, the cost of wages, and so on will be double that today. The increased costs and their effect on the value of your stocks and bonds are hypothetically projected in figure 13-1 (p. 285). You can see from this example that in terms of purchasing power, stocks give you a chance to break even since the dividends paid by the company, the profitability of the company, and therefore the market value of the stock tend to rise with inflation. Bonds, however, have a fixed value. During inflation you lose purchasing power on them.

TABLE 13-3

Purchasing Power of the Dollar Since 1940
(1957–59 = $1)

Year	Value of the Dollar ($)	Approximate Annual Percentage Rate of Inflation (%)
1940–44	2.05 (1940)	4.0[a]
1945–49	1.60 (1945)	4.7[a]
1950	1.19	5.1
1951	1.11	8.0
1952	1.08	2.2
1953	1.07	0.8
1954	1.07	0.0
1955	1.07	0.0
1956	1.06	1.5
1957	1.02	3.5
1958	.99	2.7
1959	.98	0.8
1960	.97	1.5
1961	.96	1.1
1962	.95	1.1
1963	.94	1.3
1964	.92	1.6
1965	.91	1.8
1966	.88	3.0
1967	.86	2.3
1968	.82	4.6
1969	.77	6.0
1970	.73	5.5
1971	.71	3.4

Source: U.S. Dept. of Labor, Bureau of Labor Statistics, *Handbook of Labor Statistics 1971*, Bulletin 1705, p. 256.
[a]Annual average over five-year period.

If twenty years ago you bought a house for $20,000, today you probably could sell it for $40,000, even if you have made no permanent improvements in it. If you sell it, you will have only enough money to buy another house like it, but at least you will not have lost money. If twenty years ago you had put $20,000 in a mattress, today you could buy only half as much house as you could have bought then.

During periods of deflation (price decreases), such as the one the United States experienced in the depression of the 1930s, cash (lending) increases in value whereas real estate and common stocks (owning) fare poorly. Deflation seems to occur less frequently than inflation, as figure 13-2 (p. 286) shows.

Value of the Dollar	Today	In 20 Years
Amount needed to buy one car	$3,000	$6,000
The Company		
Autos sold	3,000,000	3,000,000
Price per car	3,000	6,000
Total sales	$9,000,000,000	$18,000,000,000
Labor and materials	8,000,000,000	16,000,000,000
Net profit	1,000,000,000	2,000,000,000[a]
Bonds		
Redemption value	$10,000	$10,000
Annual interest	700	700
Common Stock		
Average market value	$10,000	$20,000
Dividends paid	400	800

[a]It takes twice as many dollars to achieve the same profit level since the dollar is worth half as much as before.

Fig. 13-1. Common stock and bonds compared during a period of general inflation

CHARACTERISTICS OF INVESTMENT TYPES

All types of investments share certain characteristics in varying degrees. The seven most relevant characteristics that investors use to differentiate the alternatives available to them are degree of risk, average annual compound yield, liquidity, personal investment management required, maturity, protection against inflation, and tax aspects. Figure 13-3 (p. 287) compares these characteristics for the investment media to be discussed in chapters 14 through 19. You should refer to this figure as you read this unit and become better acquainted with these media.

Degree of Risk

The degree of risk involved in an investment is affected by several factors. A prime factor is price decline, which may occur at any time in the stock market. In real estate it may occur when the land next to yours is rezoned for junk yards. Another factor affecting the degree of risk is business failure. The company in which you buy stock may go broke, making your investment worthless. It is important to remember that when you invest, you risk losing money. Although risk cannot be measured, you will probably be able to estimate how much risk is involved in a specific investment on the basis of information about and insight into that investment.

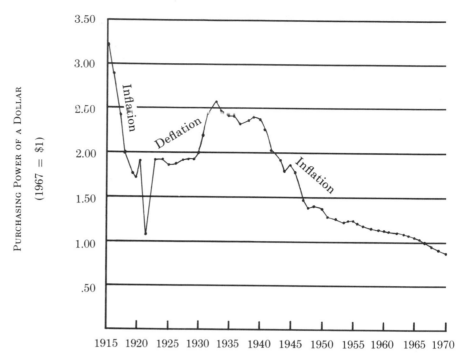

Fig. 13-2.
Trends in purchasing
power of the dollar
since 1915

SOURCE: Data taken from U. S. Dept. of Labor, Bureau of Labor Statistics, *Handbook of Labor Statistics 1971,* Bulletin 1705, p. 253.

Average Annual Compound Yield

The average annual compound yield is an average of the specific annual returns over a period of years. The yearly fluctuations you might expect in investment returns from various media will be explained in chapters 14 through 19.

Liquidity

Liquidity describes the ease with which an investment can be converted into cash. This characteristic can be important to investors who are likely to need money in a hurry for emergencies. Liquidity does not mean that you can always get back all of your original investment when you want it. Liquidity does mean that you can readily convert the current value of an investment into cash. For example, you may need to convert your common stock to cash at a time when the market price is lower than the price you paid.

Investment Type	Degree of Risk	Average Annual Compound Yield[a]	Liquidity (average time before conversion to cash)	Personal Investment Management Required	Maturity	Protection Against Inflation	Tax Aspects
Savings (time deposits)	None, if insured	2–6%	1 day (up to 90 days for some accounts)	None	90 days to 10 years, depending upon specific media	Almost none	Income taxes on interest (some are tax deferred)
Life Insurance and Annuities	None, if company is financially sound	2–4%	2 to 3 weeks	None	10 years to life, depending on specific media	None	Income taxes deferred to maturity
Common Stocks	Moderate to substantial	5–16%	1 week or more	Generally moderate to substantial	May be sold at any time	Variable, but generally good	Income taxes on dividends over $100 a year; capital gains taxes on sale
Corporate Bonds	Low to moderate	3–10%	1 week or more	Very little	Up to 30 years	None	Income taxes on interest; capital gains taxes on sale
Mutual Funds	Generally moderate (substantial in some funds)	5–14%	1 to 2 weeks	Very little	May be sold at any time	Variable, but generally good	Income taxes on dividends; capital gains taxes on sale
Real Estate (other than residence)	Moderate to substantial	5–20%	2 months to 2 years	Generally moderate to substantial	Depends on specific investment	Generally good	Some income sheltered by depreciation; capital gains taxes on sale
Syndicate Shares	Moderate to substantial	5–20%	Depends on specific investment	Very little	Depends on specific investment	Generally good	Same as above

[a]Range over last twenty years.

Fig. 13-3.
Investments compared by characteristics

Personal Investment Management Required

The amount of personal investment management required can be important to people who are busy or do not want to spend time watching over their investments. For example, it takes quite a bit of time to manage an apartment house or to play the stock market for short-term gains. If you do not want to spend the time, you can invest in a real estate syndicate or a mutual fund in which professionals do the investment management for you.

Maturity

Although the maturity of an investment usually refers to the dates on which certain types of investments may be redeemed at face value, in this section of the text we shall use the term to mean the minimum amount of time you must wait before you can realize the rate of return you expected when you made the investment. For example, you cannot buy a government savings bond today, sell it next week, and expect to be paid interest. You normally must hold the bond for at least a year.

Protection Against Inflation

The degree of protection against inflation can often be an important consideration in making investments. Because of the long-term effect of inflation, owning stocks or real estate offers at least a chance to stay even with inflation, while lending money through savings accounts, bonds, and life insurance offers only a chance to stay even with inflation if the after-tax interest yield is equal to the rate of inflation. This is because lending guarantees only a certain number of dollars, not what those dollars will buy. Owning guarantees a percentage share of ownership that will increase in dollar value during prolonged periods of inflation, provided that intrinsic value does not decline (i.e., the corporation grows smaller or the real estate deteriorates).

Tax Aspects

The higher the tax bracket an investor is in, the more important the tax aspects of an investment. A person in a 40 percent tax bracket might welcome the chance to invest for long-term capital gains, and have his gain taxed at the capital gains rate of 20 percent (one-half of his regular rate). Real estate depreciation is another way to reduce the effect of taxes on income. U.S. government savings bonds require no payment of taxes on the interest until you cash them in, and you may be in a lower tax bracket by that time. These and other tax considerations will be discussed in the following chapters.

ESTABLISHING INVESTMENT GOALS

Before making investments, you should think about why you want to invest and establish your investment goals. If you have a reason for investing, the chances that your efforts will result in the necessary financial resources are greatly improved.

Types of Investment Goals

A person may have several reasons for saving and investing money. He may wish to have emergency money in case he is disabled. He may wish to build up funds for a down payment on a house, for a summer vacation, or for retirement income. These goals can be classified as follows:

Type I Having an emergency fund of two to three months take-home pay

Type II-A Reaching specific goals of major importance

-B Reaching specific goals of minor importance

Type III-A Having a basic retirement income

-B Having extra retirement money for travel and other such goals

Type IV Building an estate

Once classified, these investment goals can be ranked in order of importance. The type I goal is usually considered first since it is very important to any family. The type IV goal is of little importance until the family has satisfied the first three types of goals. Thus, the importance of the goal types is generally in the order in which they are listed above.

This order may change, however. As you get older, having money for retirement and building an estate become more important, since your type I goal and many of your type II goals will have been satisfied. Also, as your investments accumulate, these early goals are likely to lose their importance for you. Eventually, as you acquire substantial funds, you may no longer be concerned about meeting any of the goals except building an estate for your heirs. At any one time your hierarchy of goals reflects both your stage in the life cycle and the status of your financial resources.

If you can separate your investment goals into these types, it will be much easier for you to know how much you will need at different times in your life and to enjoy the things you really want from your resources. Also, if you classify your goals, you will be better able to use the twelve-step procedure (pp. 291–96), in which you identify basic investment strategies.

An Example

At the age of twenty Richard Keller had only one investment goal: to build up at least $1000 to cover the costs of setting up a household (type II-A goal) before he married Deborah Levinson. Since this was a must goal for him, he did not want to risk his savings trying to get a high return. Therefore, he put $500 each year into a savings account and married Debbie two years later.

As soon as they were married, Rich and Debbie decided to put away $1000 as emergency money (type I). Since they wanted to make sure that the dollars would be available when they needed them, they kept the money in an insured savings investment yielding 5 percent a year.

Their next important goal was a down payment for a house (type II-A), and they decided to try to build up $3500 for this purpose. Since they had no specified date at which they had to have a house, they decided to try for a higher investment return (and thus assume greater investment risks) and attempt to build up the money as soon as possible. If they failed, the consequence would be a longer wait for their own home. Since Rich knew little about investing at this time, he invested $100 a month in a voluntary accumulation plan (p. 413) in a mutual fund. Within two years they had accumulated $2800. At this point, they decided not to risk this money any further since they were close to their goal, and so they put it in their 5 percent savings account.

Two years later, at the age of twenty-six, Rich and Debbie had $3500 in their savings account and a new baby. Because of the baby they decided that $2000 should now be their emergency reserve. They did not want to take on the financial risks of home ownership without an emergency cushion. Since this left only $1500 for the house down payment, they decided to put that money back into a mutual fund to try to build it up again. Four years later, after continued investments in the fund, they finally reached their goal of $3500 and made a down payment on a $31,000 home. They had used up all of their type II-A funds, but the value of these funds was now reflected in their equity in their new home.

As their next goal, Rich and Debbie wanted to start building up money for their child's college education (type II-A). This proceeded slowly at first, because they had to furnish their home. Rich finally built up an extra $1000 in their savings account and began to think about the college fund. At age thirty-four, Rich knew that their child would not be starting college for ten years. Thus, he had time to take some risk and seek a higher rate of return. In addition, he had to allow for the higher educational costs that inflation would bring.

By now he had learned something about investing in the stock market and had made friends with a good broker. If he could make 15 percent a year on this first $1000, it would be worth $4050 in ten years (see compound interest table A). He wanted at least that much. He made additional investments during the following years and had accumulated

$20,000 three years before their child would start college. He put $10,000 of this amount in their 5 percent account to make sure that at least that much would be available for initial college expenses. Once they had satisfied their type I and major type II goals, they could begin to think about type II-B and type III goals, such as building up a little retirement money to buy a cabin on a lake. They also wanted to have enough extra income to travel. These goals were less crucial and lay further in the future, and so they were willing to make high yield investments.

Since Rich paid for much of his child's education on a "pay as you go" basis, there was still $2500 left in the college fund after graduation. Rich decided to put this into a real estate syndicate. This investment offered from 10 to 20 percent return a year depending on its success. In addition, it offered some tax shelter because of depreciation. The tax aspects of investments were becoming more of a concern to Rich, since he was now in a higher tax bracket.

As the years progressed, Rich purchased his cabin on the lake (type II-B goal), built up $36,000 worth of stocks and mutual funds for additional retirement income purposes (type III-A goal), and built up $12,000 in real estate investments for an around-the-world cruise (type III-B goal). With these resources, the Kellers could allow their emergency reserves to dwindle to $2000, as they no longer needed to consider type I investments. Now that they had achieved their type I, II, and III goals, they could either spend their income as they pleased, or build an estate for their heirs (type IV goal).

As we look over Rich and Debbie's first thirty-five years of investing, several points are worth noting. First, because they planned ahead for the goals they wanted to reach, they improved their chances of getting many of the things they wanted. Second, by thinking about their goals in order of importance, they avoided confusing them and the timing of their investments to reach them. Third, this clear planning allowed them to assume higher risk investments with higher potential returns for long-term and low priority goals, without jeopardizing the family's financial stability. Because they had done these three things, they had plenty of resources with which to enjoy their later working and retirement years. And, in the interim, they had accumulated enough money to buy a home, send a child to college, buy a cabin for use as a second home, and take summer vacations. Results such as these show the importance of careful investment planning.

TWELVE-STEP PROCEDURE FOR PLANNING INVESTMENTS AND ACHIEVING GOALS

You have learned some fundamental investment concepts, as well as how your hierarchy of investment goals may change—especially if you make more money. You should now be ready to learn the twelve-step procedure for planning your investments and achieving your goals. If you never use such a procedure, you would have to be lucky to achieve your goals in the face of inflation, taxes, and the desire to spend your money today. You will not be able to apply this procedure fully until you have mastered the material in the remainder of this unit. However, a basic understanding of the procedure should make the entire unit more meaningful to you.

In figure 13-4 you will find the worksheet that Chuck and Nancy Anderson used for this twelve-step procedure. The blank spaces are part of the case problem at the end of this chapter.

Instructions

1 *Look at your balance sheet and enter the total amount of your investment assets, less a reserve for emergencies (type I goal) in the blank under column H showing the amount of money on hand.* Investment assets include all assets except personal property, home, and automobile.

The Andersons reviewed the investment assets they initially had on their balance sheet: $600 in a savings account, $1500 in savings bonds, $5600 (net of margin loan balance) in stocks, $1400 in mutual funds, $4800 in cash-value life insurance, and $18,450 (after subtracting commissions and mortgage loan balance) in equity from the sale of their home. From this total of $32,350 they subtracted the outlays they had already made with this money: down payment on the new house ($8000), moving costs and closing costs on the new house ($2000), auto loan balance paid off ($2850), furniture loan balance paid off ($1300), and emergency fund set aside ($2200). These uses amounted to $16,350, leaving them with $16,000 for investment goals.

2 *Look at your income statement and budget plan and estimate the amount you will have available each year for investment toward goals.* Enter this amount in the blank under column I showing the amount of money available.

The Andersons added together the annual savings they have realized as a result of their revised financial programs: $330 (recomputed income taxes), $224 (new auto insurance premium), $1600 (paid-off auto loan), $550 (paid-off furniture loan), $395 (revised health insurance program), $52 (new life insurance premium), and $1100 (one-time stock market loss). From this total of $4251, they subtracted $1090, the sum of the increased costs of some of their financial programs: $180 (annual housing costs on the new house), $910 (new mortgage payment level). The net of these adjustments is $3161, from which they then subtracted the negative amount ($1420) available on their earlier income statement and arrived at a projected annual cash surplus of $1741.

NAME(S) _Chuck and Nancy Anderson_

DATE _March 1973_

WORKSHEET FOR PLANNING INVESTMENTS AND ACHIEVING GOALS

A	B	C	D	E	F	G	H	I
Goal	Amount Needed	Years	Inflation Factor[a]	Adjusted Amount Needed (B × D)	Investment Medium	Average Yield (after tax)	Lump Sum Investment[a] ($6,000 on hand)	Annual Investment[b] ($1741 available)
Jim's college	$8000[c]	10	(5%)1.6	$12,800	mutual fund	8%	$5820	$533
Amount remaining							10,180	
Melora's college	8000[c]	13	(5%)		mutual fund	8%		
Amount remaining								
Furniture and carpets	3000	3	(3%)		corporate bond	6%		
Amount remaining								
Replace car	2000	4	(3%)1.12	2240	5½% savings account	4%		$533
Amount remaining								
Motorboat	5000	15	(3%)		common stock	(try for 10%)		
Amount remaining								
Retirement	(To be computed in chapter 20)	30	(3%)	(To be computed in chapter 20)	real estate	average 12%	$5000	
Amount remaining								

[a] Refer to compound interest table A.
[b] Refer to compound interest table B.
[c] $2000 minimum for each year. The other $500 in annual college expenses are to be covered each year out of current income at that time.

Fig. 13-4.
Sample worksheet for planning investments and achieving goals

3 *Decide which goals are important to you and your family and enter them in column A.* List them in order of your family's current priority of goals, starting with the most important goal.

Deciding which goals are really important is a step that too many people pass over lightly. If you do not sit down with your family and do some serious thinking about goals, several problems may arise. First, you may not adequately consider the emergency fund before you begin your investment program. Second, you may forget about a goal until it is too late to achieve the dollar amount required. Third, you may fail to understand the importance of the goal and therefore choose an inappropriate investment strategy for achieving it.

The Andersons decided that their goals, in order of importance, are college educations for the children, furniture and carpets for the new house, a new car to replace Nancy's, a motorboat, and retirement income.

4 *Estimate the amount of money needed (in today's dollars) to satisfy each goal, and enter the sums in the appropriate blanks of column B.* Do not try to estimate the retirement sums needed as they will be discussed in chapter 20.

The Andersons estimated what each of their goals would cost: $8000 for each of the children's college educations, $3000 for furniture and carpets, $2000 to replace one of their cars, and $5000 for a motorboat. (The amount needed for retirement will be computed in chapter 20.)

5 *Enter in column C the number of years you have to achieve each goal.*

The Andersons predicted that it would be ten years until they would need the money for Jim's college education, thirteen years until they would need it for Melissa's, three years until they would buy the furniture and carpets, four years until they would replace the car, fifteen years until they would buy a motorboat, and thirty years until they would retire.

6 *Estimate the rate at which inflation will probably affect your goal amount and select the appropriate factor from compound interest table A.* While inflation has averaged about 3 percent since 1945, it has ranged from 0 to 9 percent. Of course, not all costs rise at the same rate. For example, college tuitions have risen more than three times as fast as the price of automobiles. To keep abreast of price trends and outlooks for specific items, you should read the appropriate articles in the various news media.

The Andersons decided that a 3 percent rate would be appropriate for all their goals except the children's college education, which would probably increase at a rate of 5 percent. According to compound interest table A, the inflation factor for 5 percent over ten years (length of time until money is needed for Jim's college education) is 1.6; the factor for 3 percent over four years (length of time until money is needed to replace Nancy's car) is 1.12.

7 *Multiply the inflation factor times the original amount needed to arrive at your adjusted amount needed (column E).*

The Andersons' first goal of $8000 would cost $12,800 (1.6 × $8000) in ten years at a 5 percent inflation rate; their fourth goal of $2000 would cost $2240 (1.12 × $2000).

8 *Select an investment medium appropriate to both the importance of each goal and the amount of time you have to achieve it.* Write this in column F. Successful application of step 8 will become easier as you proceed through unit four and learn more about various types of investments.

The Andersons put down their initial selections, which may be revised as they learn more about investments. They chose mutual funds to provide money for the children's college educations, a corporate bond for the furniture and carpets, a 5.5 percent savings account for the car, common stocks for the motorboat, and a real estate investment for their retirement.

9 *Estimate an average total investment return (both income and capital gains) for each medium and enter this percentage yield in column G.* See figure 13-3 for ranges of returns you might expect from various investments. Use after-tax yields only. For example if you are in a 40 percent bracket, a 10 percent total yield on a mutual fund would be only 8 percent after tax, using capital gains tax rates. Obviously, your actual results will vary from your projections but, for now, some projection is more useful than none.

The Andersons projected an after-tax average yield of 8 percent for their mutual funds, 6 percent for the corporate bond, 4 percent for the 5.5 percent savings account, 10 percent for the common stocks, and 12 percent for the real estate investment.

10 *If you plan to use a lump-sum investment to satisfy a given goal, select the appropriate factor from compound interest table A.* For example, for ten years at 8 percent, the factor would be 2.2. Divide this factor into your adjusted need (column E) to arrive at the necessary lump sum. Enter this investment amount in column H and subtract it from the amount above it on your sheet of calculations (as in figure 13-4) to arrive at the lump-sum amount remaining for other purposes. Of course, this process is only an initial estimate. As time passes, you can see whether you are above or below your target and make adjustments.

The Andersons divided the $12,800 they would need for their son's college education by 2.2 and learned that if they invest a lump sum now to achieve their first goal in ten years, they would have to invest $5820.

11 *If you plan to use an annual investment of a regular amount, select the appropriate factor from compound interest table B.* Continue this procedure as in step 10. Of course, as you will learn, some investments are more suitable for small periodic investments than others.

The Andersons thought that they would make an annual investment toward replacing the car and therefore divided $2240 by 4.2 and got $533 as the amount they would have to invest each year.

12 *If you run out of investment funds (columns H and I) before your top priority goals are satisfied (and this will likely be the case if you are young), you have four alternatives: rearrange your budget to free up more money for investment purposes; look for higher yield investments on some goals; reduce the dollar amount for some goals; and increase the length of time allowed to achieve certain goals.* After you have made one or more of these adjustments, go over the procedure again to see if your revised plan will be successful in achieving your important goals.

Do not be dismayed if, as a young family, you discover that none of the options in step 12 enables you to achieve all of your top priority goals. You may yet have a fifth option. This extra option is that your family income or assets may increase in several ways. As your career progresses, you may qualify for promotional raises in pay, which may give you extra income for achieving goals. Or the family may add a second income source if your wife goes to work, perhaps when the children start school. This whole second income could be used for investment purposes. Of course, the decision concerning whether a wife should work to provide supplementary income requires thoughtful consideration. Figure 13-5 may be able to help you make certain you have taken into account the many aspects of this decision.

There is always the possibility that gifts or inheritances may increase your income. However, these should not be counted on, but should be considered windfalls and only allocated when actually received. As one or more of these items in the fifth option occurs, you can reapply the twelve-step procedure.

APPROPRIATENESS OF AN INVESTMENT MEDIUM

The appropriateness of an investment medium generally depends on three factors: your motives for saving and investing, your attitudes toward risk, and the actual advantages and disadvantages of each form of investment.

	POSSIBLE ADVANTAGES		POSSIBLE DISADVANTAGES	
	Monetary	Nonmonetary	Monetary	Nonmonetary
	Extra income	Fulfillment of need for diversion and personal growth	Expense of day care for small children	Burden of job added to housekeeping and child-raising
	Fringe benefits such as group insurance and pension income for retirement years	Enrichment through outside interests	Costs of commuting	Difference in family vacation schedules
	Extra retirement income from Social Security	Special family goals may be reached through use of wife's income	Clothes needed for job	
	Credit union membership		Increased income taxes and Social Security tax	
	Price discounts on items manufactured or sold by employer		Extra expenses of running household (convenience foods, eating out more often, extra laundry services)	

Fig. 13-5.
Aspects of deciding whether a wife should work to supplement a family's income

If you select a high risk, high return investment alternative to gain a much-needed goal and the investment goes bad, you may not reach your goal. Had you realized the importance of the goal, you might have invested the money in a lower risk investment. The opposite problem might arise if you invest your money at a low rate of return for a low-priority goal and thus divert too many dollars away from more important goals. Instead, you could invest fewer dollars at a higher rate of return. For example, you may be investing $600 a year in whole life insurance (at a 3 percent return) for your retirement thirty years hence, when you might invest only $200 in a mutual fund and achieve the same results. Even if the investment is slow or erratic in its early years, you would be able to use the remaining $400 a year to achieve goals that you current-ly consider more important.

Your values with regard to risk are something only you can decide. However, you should carefully consider the advantages and disadvan-tages of each form of investment. Consider how they pertain to your investment objectives before finally deciding on a particular investment. Only then will you know which investments suit your goals and what portion of your investment dollars should be put into each. You may decide that it is worth assuming a greater degree of risk to try for an annual rate of return of 10 to 12 percent.

The following three principles should be remembered whenever you try to select investment media to use to reach your goals.

1. The shorter the time you have to reach your goal, the higher the rate of return you must get to attain the goal or the greater the dollar amount you must invest.
2. The smaller your investments, the higher the rate of return you must get to reach your goals or the longer the time you must wait.
3. The higher the rate of return you seek, the greater the degree of risk you generally must assume.

CONCLUSION

There are several important concepts that you should understand before you leave this chapter. First, higher potential yields are usually associated with higher risk investments. Second, compounded rates of return can make small regular investments grow into sizeable sums. Be sure you know how to use the compound interest tables at the end of the book. Use them to help you formulate reasonable investment strategies. Third, know how to apply the twelve-step procedure for planning investments and achieving goals. Fourth, refer to figure 13-3 before you make any major investment decisions, in order to be sure that you select an invest-ment medium appropriate for your goal.

compound interest   liquidity

compound yield   maturity

dividend   principal

equity   rate of return

growth of the principal   rent

income from the principal   simple interest

interest   yield

1. What would a $3000 savings account with a 5 percent annual interest rate be worth in twelve years? What would $3000 be worth in twelve years if it were invested in a real estate syndicate with an average annual rate of return of 12 percent?
2. If you save $50 each month to invest at the end of each year in U.S. savings bonds that have a 5 percent return, how much will you have in ten years?
3. What is meant by *investment risk*? What affects it?
4. If the price of automobiles keeps rising at an annual rate of 3 percent, what will a $3000 automobile cost in twenty years?
5. How much would you have to invest each year in a 5 percent savings account in order to have $5000 (already adjusted for inflation) for a house down payment in five years?
6. From an investment point of view, why is lending less desirable than owning during long periods of inflation?
7. Assume that you have $2000 to invest toward a major goal. To achieve this goal, you need $3200 (allowing for inflation) in five years. According to compound interest table A (p. 498), you would have to get an average annual rate of return of 10 percent. However, because of the importance of the goal, you are unwilling to take such a high risk. Describe, in numerical detail, four alternative strategies for using a 6 percent investment to solve this problem.

Mike and Mary West were recently married. They are both working, so that they will have money to put toward their five financial goals: to maintain an emergency reserve ($1000); to take a trip to the Caribbean in two years ($1200); to buy a home in four years ($5000 down plus $1000 for basic furnishings), to begin a family in five years ($1500 initial medical costs); and to buy a camper trailer in seven years ($1800).

They plan to use a 5 percent savings account to achieve the first two goals and a mutual fund with a 10 percent annual average performance record for the other three goals. They have $1400 in savings, and they expect to save $2400 a year. They estimate that their marginal tax bracket will be 30 percent.

What inflation percentage do you think would be appropriate for each goal? Why? What is the resulting adjusted need for each goal? What must the Wests invest toward each goal in order to be able to achieve it if the investments do well? Can they satisfy all their goals with their present resources? If not, how can they revise their plans? (Base your answer to this question on numerical computations as much as possible.) If Mary were to quit her job when they start their family, what effect would this have on their overall strategy?

RECOMMENDED READING

Katona, George; Mandell, Lewis; and Schmiedeskamp, Jay. *1970 Survey of Consumer Finances*. Ann Arbor: University of Michigan, 1971.

Chapters 6 and 7 provide statistics about financial assets held by individuals.

Unger, Maurice, and Wolf, Harold. *Personal Finance*. Boston: Allyn and Bacon, 1972.

Pages 389 to 405 offer a somewhat different viewpoint on the fundamentals and risks of investments.

CHUCK AND NANCY ANDERSON

PLANNING INVESTMENTS AND ACHIEVING GOALS

You have seen how Chuck and Nancy used the twelve-step procedure to compute both the lump sum they must invest for their son's college education and the annual investment they must make to replace Nancy's car. Carry out the computations for their other goals except retirement. Assume that the Andersons make an annual investment for Melissa's college and lump-sum investments for the furniture and carpets and motorboat.

14

TIME DEPOSIT INVESTMENTS

Investment certificate . . . savings and loan account . . . savings bond . . . credit union share . . . passbook savings account . . . club account . . . savings certificate. These are all time deposits. They require that money be deposited for a specific period of time in order to earn an investment return.

More people use time deposits than any other investment instrument. According to Federal Reserve Board statistics, the total amount of money in such deposits in the United States was $516 billion in November, 1971.[1] Despite the widespread use of time deposits, however, people continue to be confused by the many alternatives available to them. This chapter will dwell chiefly on these alternatives and explain the more common technicalities with which you should be familiar.

INTEREST RATES

The interest rate on your time deposit determines the rate of return on your investment. Interest rates can be confusing unless a few common terms are understood.

1. Federal Reserve Board, *Federal Reserve Bulletin*, vol. 57, no. 12 (Washington, D.C.: December, 1971), p. A16.

Nominal Interest Rate and Effective Interest Rate

The nominal interest rate is the stated rate of interest. For example, a 5 percent passbook account has a nominal interest rate of 5 percent. The effective interest rate is the rate you actually receive on your invested savings. The amount of your effective interest rate depends upon how your interest is compounded. If your interest is compounded annually, your effective rate is equal to the nominal rate. If it is compounded in any term shorter than a year, your effective rate is higher than the stated rate. Obviously, the highest effective rate would be interest compounded daily, although the difference is not great. For example, a nominal 5 percent annual rate is actually worth 5.09 percent when compounded quarterly and 5.13 percent when compounded daily. Therefore, if other factors such as stated rate, security, and convenience are about the same, you should deposit your savings with the institution offering the shortest compounding period and, therefore, the highest effective rate.

an example Assume that Gene wants to invest $10,000 in a time deposit. He should first consider the stated, or nominal, interest rate. For example, he might invest his $10,000 in a 5 percent passbook account and pass up a chance for more interest income from a 6 percent investment certificate. (Both the savings account and the certificate are equally safe.) In the first year it would make a difference of $100 ($600 − $500). In succeeding years, this effect would be magnified by compounding, as table 14-1 shows. Gene would get $1619 more interest over ten years by investing his money at 6 percent than at 5 percent. (As you proceed through this unit on investing, you might question whether Gene should invest his whole $10,000 for such a long time at only 6 percent.)

TABLE 14-1

COMPARISON OF INTEREST RATES
($10,000 Investment, Compounded Annually)

Years	5%	6%
1	$ 500	$ 600
2	1025	1236
3	1576	1910
4	2155	2625
5	2763	3382
10	6289	7908

The second feature Gene should consider is how often interest is compounded. Suppose that he has his choice of two institutions: one offering 5 percent compounded annually and one offering 5 percent compounded quarterly. Table 14-2 shows what he would receive the first year both if the interest on his investment is compounded annually and if it is compounded quarterly. The extra $9.45 that he would receive with quarterly compounding represents the interest paid each quarter on the interest received in previous quarters. Therefore, he would probably be better off choosing the institution offering quarterly compounding.

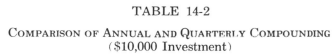

TABLE 14-2

COMPARISON OF ANNUAL AND QUARTERLY COMPOUNDING
($10,000 Investment)

| QUARTER | 5% INTEREST | |
	Annual Compounding	Quarterly Compounding
First	$125	$125.00
Second	125	126.56
Third	125	128.14
Fourth	125	129.75
Total	$500	$509.45

Computing Interest

Even though an institution may pay interest on sums held the full quarter, the actual interest paid can vary depending on the method of computation used: FIFO (first in, first out), LIFO (last in, first out), daily interest, or low balance.

Figure 14-1 shows the quarterly interest (4 percent annual rate) paid using each of these methods except low balance. If you deposit $1000 at the beginning of a quarter, another $1000 halfway through, and withdraw $1000 just before the end of the quarter, the FIFO method assumes that the $1000 you withdrew is the first $1000 you deposited. If interest

| WEEK | TRANSACTION | METHOD OF COMPUTING INTEREST | | |
		FIFO	LIFO	Daily
1	Deposit	+ $1000[a]	+ $1000	+ $1000
5	Deposit	+ 1000	+ 1000[a]	+ 1000[a]
8	Withdrawal	− 1000	− 1000	− 1000
13 Balance		1000	1000	1000
Interest paid[b]		$0.00	$10.00	$12.50

[a]Withdrawn in week 8.
[b]4 percent annual rate.

Fig. 14-1.
Comparison of
three methods of
computing interest

is paid only on sums held the full quarter, you would receive no interest that quarter, even though you had at least $1000 on deposit the whole time. The LIFO method assumes that the $1000 you withdrew was the second (or last) money you deposited, and so you would receive full interest on the initial $1000 deposited. The difference at a 5 percent rate would be $12.50 more interest than that computed by the FIFO method. The LIFO method yields the highest interest return on your money and, in any given quarter, can mean a difference of 50 percent or more over the FIFO method depending on your deposit and withdrawal patterns in that quarter.

Daily interest always yields the highest return and has no complications. Not only does daily interest yield a higher return, but also you do not have to leave your money in the account for the full quarter to get interest. You must keep your account open, however, to the end of the quarter, which usually means maintaining a $1 minimum balance. Interest is paid from the day of deposit to the day of withdrawal.

The low balance method pays interest on the lowest balance in your account during the quarter, regardless of how much was deposited. To compare this method of computing interest with the others, you would have to know the pattern of deposits and withdrawals. This method can, however, yield about as low a return as the FIFO method does.

Ask at savings institutions in your area to find out what method each uses in calculating interest. Then you will be able to choose among those that compute interest daily. If none do, consider those that use the LIFO method.

APPROPRIATENESS OF TIME DEPOSITS AS AN INVESTMENT

Before you decide that time deposits are right for you, you should consider your reasons for using them and their advantages and disadvantages compared to other forms of investments.

Reasons for Using Time Deposits

There are four major reasons why people invest their money in time deposits: for use in emergencies, for special goals, as a safe investment, and as a temporary investment.

emergency fund Having an emergency source of funds is one of the prime motives for investing in time deposits. The dollar amount of such an investment is guaranteed. If you have an emergency, the total amount you invested will be there since most time deposits are not subject to market-type fluctuations. In addition, you can readily withdraw the funds in an emergency. That is, they are liquid assets, as accessible as your cash or checking account. To be sure you understand the amounts and the appropriate uses of your emergency fund, review pages 42–43.

special goals   The advantages inherent in accumulating funds for special goals provide another motive for the use of time deposits. These goals may include a house down payment, Christmas holiday expenses, vacation funds, a college education, or a new car. For example, if you can regularly save the money you will need to buy a new car instead of financing it, you can add $500 or $600 to your purchasing power. These extra dollars are made up of saved finance charges and interest income earned on your savings.

safe investment   A safe investment with reasonably assured income is all the reason many people need for saving money in time deposits. They may have no definite reason for the investment when they make it. However, you should have a reason for each financial decision you make, including how to save money. You should use a savings account for your investment program because it is the best alternative for a given financial goal, not simply because it is convenient or because you are most familiar with that method.

temporary investment   You may wish to use a savings account to accumulate funds for another investment—perhaps, to build up $250 for a mutual fund. Or you may wish to put your stock market profits temporarily in a savings account where they will earn interest while the market goes through a period of declining prices. Or you may have achieved one of your investment goals a year or two ahead of time and wish to preserve your gain by liquidating your investment and putting the proceeds in a savings account until you spend them.

Advantages and Disadvantages of Time Deposits

One advantage of time deposits is that investment income is generally assured. The interest on all types of commercial bank time deposits is legally guaranteed. That is, your deposit with the bank represents a legal debt upon which the bank must pay interest as promised. However, the extent of the bank's responsibility may be subject to two considerations. First, there may be a certain minimum balance (from $5 to $100) on which no interest is paid (although there is no minimum dollar restriction on the amount deposited) because the cost of opening a small account does not make it worthwhile for the bank. Second, if there is excessive withdrawal activity, the bank may impose an interest penalty to compensate for the extra bookkeeping. Check with your bank to find out their ground rules.

In a few savings and loan associations and credit unions, your return on your investment comes in the form of dividends, which represent distributions of earnings. If the operations of these organizations are unprofitable and no earnings are generated, dividends cannot be paid. Failures to pay dividends occur rarely, however. Time deposits experience no price fluctuations such as those experienced by investments in the stock market or real estate. Your savings dollar is, in effect, guaranteed.

Another advantage of time deposits is that the federal government insures each account in a different name for up to $20,000. The $20,000 limit applies to the total of all types of accounts under the same name held by any one commercial bank, savings and loan association, or federally chartered credit union. Similar accounts in the same name in separate branches of the same institution do not qualify for separate insurance limits. All commercial bank deposits are insured by the Federal Deposit Insurance Corporation (FDIC). Almost three-fourths of all savings and loan associations (holding 96 percent of savings and loan assets) are insured by the Federal Savings and Loan Insurance Corporation (FSLIC). The other savings and loan associations are covered either by similar state insurance plans (Massachusetts, Ohio, Maryland) or not at all. The principal of U.S. savings bonds is also fully insured by the federal government.

In addition, there are no transaction costs such as brokerage fees or commissions involved in opening and closing your account. You may withdraw your funds immediately whenever they are needed, provided it is a business day. This feature makes savings-type investments appropriate for emergency funds. However, under certain circumstances the federal government can require thirty-day notice for withdrawing funds from a federally insured bank or savings and loan. This provision is designed to provide a cooling off period in the event there is a run on the banks. A savings institution would use the time to reduce the amount of new loans or mortgages being written so that inflowing loan or mortgage repayments could cover excessive deposit withdrawals. Instead of using this right, however, savings and loan associations usually turn to the Federal Home Loan Bank and banks turn to the Federal Reserve Bank to borrow funds (up to certain limits) whenever their withdrawals exceed their unloaned deposits. The right of notice before withdrawal of funds is also rarely exercised by mutual savings banks. With this type of bank, new deposits, earnings, and loan repayments more than make up for any withdrawal. A final advantage of time deposits is that they offer convenient alternatives. You may deal face-to-face with your local institution; you may use a payroll deduction plan; or you may deal with them through the mail.

Although there are only two disadvantages, each can have a significant impact, depending on your situation. First, you are likely to get a lower rate of return with time deposits than with higher risk investments such as mutual funds or real estate syndicates. Second, because time deposits are a fixed income investment, they offer poor protection against inflation. A 5 percent yield might give you an after-tax return of 3 to 4 percent. Since 1945, according to the consumer price index, inflation has affected the value of the dollar by an average of about 3 percent a year. During 1970, prices advanced at approximately 5.5 percent, resulting in a 0.5

percent net loss in the purchasing power of savings, not counting the loss due to income taxes! Thus, there is little margin for a reasonable rate of return on a time deposit investment. An example of the resulting purchasing power of your savings is shown in figure 14-2.

Items in Computation	Percentage Amounts	Dollar Amounts
Amount invested	100%	$2000
Annual yield	5%	100
Income taxes[a]	−1.5%	−30
After-tax yield	3.5%	70
Loss due to 3% inflation	−3.0%	−60
Net gain in purchasing power of your savings	0.5%	$ 10

[a]Assume 30 percent income tax bracket.

Fig. 14-2.
Inflation, taxes, and savings accounts

INSTITUTIONS OFFERING TIME DEPOSIT INVESTMENTS

If you own or are considering owning a time deposit investment you should carefully consider the various types offered by commercial banks, savings and loans, mutual savings banks, other thrift institutions, credit unions, and the federal government.

Commercial Banks

Commercial banks offer various kinds of accounts: regular passbook savings accounts, bonus savings accounts, and club accounts. They also offer certificates of deposit (CDs). CDs may pay interest at rates of up to two percentage points higher than passbook accounts, although they may have minimums as high as $100,000.

regular passbook savings accounts   These accounts may or may not have a savings passbook, since many banks are having their operations computerized. Your quarterly statement from the bank lists the latest interest credited and is all you need to prove how much money you have on deposit.

Among the various types of accounts you may open at any savings institution, the most common are an individual account, a joint tenancy account, a tenancy in common account, a trustee account, a minor's account, and a fiduciary account. (Since each account bears a different name or set of names, each would qualify for separate $20,000 insurance limits.) An individual account has one owner. A joint tenancy account is one to which each owner has access. A tenancy in common account requires that both owners sign any withdrawal slip before it will be honored. A trustee account is owned by an adult for his child who cannot withdraw money without the adult's signature. However, as owner, the adult must pay taxes on the interest income. A minor's account may be opened with permission of the parent when the child is old enough to sign his name. Unlike a trustee account, the minor is the owner and he must pay taxes, if any, on the interest. A fiduciary account may be opened in the name of an estate by an executor or in the name of a minor child or incompetent person by his guardian.

bonus savings accounts   These are generally passbook-type accounts that pay 0.25 to 0.5 percent higher rate. Depending on a bank's rules, this bonus is paid if a minimum required balance or a minimum holding period is maintained or if additional specified deposits are continually made. A bonus account reverts to a regular account if any of the conditions outlined by the bank is violated.

club accounts   These are special types of accounts developed by banks to boost their deposits, while enabling their customers to budget their savings for a specific goal, such as Christmas gifts or a vacation. These accounts help you acquire a regular (usually semimonthly) savings habit. The bank may even furnish a coupon book to help you make your deposits (from $2 to $40) on schedule. Often, however, there is little or no interest paid on such accounts because of the extra bookkeeping and the small balances involved. Even if the bank offers its regular rate, you may not receive the interest unless you keep your money on deposit until the end of the required period. Of course, once you have effectively set your budget in operation, you should not need such an account. If you do need the coupons of a club type of account to help you save, make your own coupon book for deposits to your regular passbook account rather than risk losing interest in a club account.

small-scale CDs   Sometimes called "savings certificates" or "bank bonds" or "guaranteed income bonds," small-scale certificates of deposit are issued in amounts ranging from $25 to $1000 and multiples thereof. The interest rate is guaranteed until the certificate reaches maturity, which can range from one to ten years. Interest may be paid to you (often quarterly), or it may accrue (be added) to the cash-in value of the bond. In the latter case, the bond is initially sold at a price discounted from the face value, and the interest may accrue at a fixed rate or at a rising rate. The cash-in value of the bond thus rises over time. These cash-in values may rise at a constant rate until the maturity date (the *fixed-interest-rate bond*) or at an increasing rate (the *rising-interest-rate bond*). The rising-interest-rate bond penalizes you, of course, if you cash in the bond before its maturity date, since the small rises in cash-in values in the early years represent a below average rate of return to you. These values, along with the relevant dates, are printed on the bond.

However, there is a possible tax advantage in the rising interest rate bond. Since the majority of the interest is accrued in the later years, you defer most of your income taxes on this investment until a time when you may be in a lower tax bracket. Therefore, you would receive more of your investment in actual after-tax dollars than you would have in your original tax bracket. A newer type of bond, the *deferred income bond*, offers the same tax advantage to an even greater degree. This bond pays all the interest in a lump sum at maturity, say, five or seven years later. These bonds and rising-interest-rate bonds are often purchased by older people who wish to defer investment income until retirement puts them in a lower tax bracket.

On all savings certificates you have to wait at least three months to withdraw your funds. Most bank certificates can be redeemed at any three-month anniversary (or within ten days of it). In an emergency, you can withdraw the funds at any time, but with an interest penalty and a little red tape.

large-scale CDs These have face amounts of $100,000 and up. They are negotiable, which means that they may be sold to a third party if you need the cash before the maturity date. They usually offer the highest interest rate currently available to bank savers.

Mutual Savings Banks

Mutual savings banks are located primarily in the eastern United States, but there are a few in the Northwest. Founded for the convenience and benefit of savers, they are organized as mutual associations with no capital stock. Dividends are paid out of earnings, but at an established rate, as banks and savings and loan associations do. The rate is somewhat higher than for banks since the dividends are not guaranteed. The principal and accumulated dividends, however, are generally insured by the federal government up to $20,000 for accounts in one name. There are limits on the total amount that may be invested in a mutual savings bank by one person. These vary according to state regulations.

Savings and Loan Associations

Savings and loan associations stimulate the home building industry by accumulating savings and investing them primarily in residential real estate mortgages. Dividends are paid to the savings account holders out of the association's earnings.

There are two types of savings and loan organizations: mutual and corporate. The mutual is the more widespread form. The savings account holders are the owners of the organization and are known legally as share owners. In a mutual savings and loan company you usually have one vote (for members of the board of directors) for each $100 deposited. Corporate savings and loan companies issue stock just as other corporations do. They are located primarily in California, Ohio, and Texas. Many corporate savings and loan companies pay interest instead of dividends.

About one-third of the original charters of savings and loan associations were granted by the federal government; the rest were granted by individual states.

Dividends paid out of profits by savings and loan associations are not guaranteed. In any given quarter, a savings and loan association may reduce the dividend payment because of profitability problems (although this is a very rare occurrence). At a bank, the depositor is a creditor and the interest is legally guaranteed, whether or not the bank makes a profit. If a savings and loan association pays interest instead of a dividend, the interest is guaranteed.

There are two major types of deposits in which you can invest: regular passbook accounts and bonus accounts. Regular passbook accounts are operated much the same as in a bank. Dividends or interest may be left in the account to compound, or they may be sent to you by check if regular income is desired. Bonus accounts, often in the form of investment certificates, are usually issued in multiples of $100 and may offer a 0.25 to 2.5 percent higher rate of return depending on the size of the deposit and current federal regulations. Minimum maturities may range from ninety days to two years. Withdrawal of funds before maturity usually results in an interest penalty.

Thrift Institutions

Thrift institutions are similar to small loan companies in that their primary purpose is to make small personal loans. Some of these institutions may be known as thrift and loan associations. Unless they specifically display the FSLIC or FDIC seals, which guarantee that deposits are insured, your savings dollars are probably not securely insured. The security of your investment is therefore dependent on the history, integrity, and business expertise of the owners and managers of these organizations. Because of this lower security, such institutions may offer dividends or interest at rates up to 7 or 8 percent.

Credit Unions

The purpose of credit unions is to provide low-cost consumer loans to members, who are individuals with a common interest such as having the same place of employment. The credit union pools the savings of its members for lending purposes.

You can invest in a credit union by purchasing shares (generally in $5 amounts). Most credit unions will immediately repurchase your shares at your request. Others may require a waiting period. Your maximum investment may be restricted to $5000 or $10,000 if the credit union is small. By enforcing a ceiling on individual investments, they avoid potential large withdrawals. Employee related credit unions often have payroll deduction plans for savings investment. Such a plan helps develop a thrift habit for those who could never save on their own. (There is no matching contribution by the employer.)

Dividend rates range from those of regular bank accounts to something in excess of that paid on savings and loan investment accounts. The actual dividend rate paid depends on the earnings of the credit union, after provision for expenses and bad-debt reserve. The federal government imposes a maximum rate of 6 percent, however, in order to prevent higher interest from being charged on loans granted by the union; for this would defeat the original purpose of the credit unions. Dividends may be sent to you or kept in your account, as you wish.

In addition to the high dividend yield and the payroll savings plans, most credit unions offer free term life insurance protection, matching one dollar of insurance for each dollar deposited up to a maximum of $1000 or $2000. Thus, a $2000 deposit could yield $4000 to your beneficiary if you died. After age fifty-five a declining scale applies for such coverage. Most credit unions also offer free loan protection insurance, which pays off any outstanding debt to the credit union in the event of your death or disability. Furthermore, members elect the board of directors to operate the credit union on a one-man, one-vote basis. As already mentioned in chapters 10 and 11, credit unions offer low-cost consumer loans to members with collateral; up to $2000 in unsecured loans may be taken out at a slightly higher rate; and financial counseling services may also be offered.

The disadvantages of credit unions fall into two categories: privacy and safety. Since your credit union is managed by your associates, a portion of your financial affairs is not strictly private. The security of your investment depends largely on whether the credit union has a federal or state charter. Since January 1, 1971, federally chartered credit unions automatically offer $20,000 federal deposit insurance. However, this automatic feature will expire on January 3, 1974, for credit unions that fail to meet federal government financial qualifications. The $20,000 federal deposit insurance is available for state chartered credit unions, provided they apply for it and qualify. So far, only a minority of credit unions have done so, because of the costs of joining the program. If you are depositing savings in a noninsured credit union, you are relying on their management ability to protect your funds. However, in some states, the rules of the charter and the periodic checks by state examiners have caused their record to be quite good. For example, in early 1972, the California Corporations Commissioner announced that in the three years ending December 31, 1970, twenty-eight out of 619 existing California chartered credit unions were liquidated for various reasons. Of these twenty-eight, twenty-three paid back 100 percent or more to their members. The other five, with 393 members, had a total loss of $12,697—or an average of about $33 per person. Of course, other states may not have rules as strict and, therefore, the record may be poorer.

U.S. Government Savings Bonds

The U.S. savings bond is one of the three major methods of financing the federal government. The other two are tax receipts and Treasury bonds (pp. 361–62).

There are two types of savings bonds currently being sold: Series E and Series H. Series E bonds are sold at three-fourths of face value to yield a 5.5 percent annual average rate if held to maturity (five years and ten months). Interest accumulates with the bond until you cash it in for its face value. If you cashed it in before the maturity date, you would get less than face value and your yield might be 5 percent or less because of graduated interest yields. The maximum size bond available is $1000, and $10,000 is the maximum total purchase a person can make in one year. Series H bonds are current income bonds. You buy the bond at its face value, and average interest of 5.5 percent is paid to you by check twice yearly until the bond matures in ten years. As with Series E bonds, interest is less than 5.5 percent in the early years but later rises above that point to make the ten-year average yield 5.5 percent.

Sixty days after buying a bond you may sell it back to the government at the face amount then applicable on the bond. Bonds are registered in your name and are nonnegotiable (nontransferable to a third party). Both series of bonds pay interest at an increasing scale. In order to make the 5 percent average annual yield, the actual yield of the bond in later years must be greater than 5 percent to compensate for the low yields in earlier years. Therefore, once you have held a Series E or Series H bond a few years, you would forfeit fairly good interest yields if you cashed it in before it matured. The average annual yield on U.S. savings bonds is illustrated in table 14-3.

U.S. savings bonds are a safe investment because the principal is fully insured and the interest is fully guaranteed by the federal government.

TABLE 14-3

AVERAGE ANNUAL YIELD ON SERIES E AND SERIES H BONDS

SERIES E BOND CASHED IN AFTER	AVERAGE ANNUAL YIELD (%)	SERIES H BOND CASHED IN AFTER	AVERAGE ANNUAL YIELD (%)
½ year	3.20	1 year	4.29
1 year	4.01	5 years	4.92
2 years	4.26	7 years	4.97
3 years	4.44	10 years	5.50
4 years	4.64		
5 years	4.84		
5 years 10 months	5.50		

The bonds can be replaced easily if they are lost or destroyed. They are also convenient since payroll savings plans are available at most companies. There are certain tax advantages in that no local or state income taxes are charged on the interest; you can defer the federal income tax on Series E bonds until you cash them in; you can get one or two ten-year extensions with interest accruing above face value, if you want to defer your taxes until your retirement years when you will be in a lower tax bracket; and you can exchange your Series E bonds for Series H bonds on a tax-free basis and pay taxes only on the interest from the H Bonds, thus deferring your taxes even further, perhaps permanently if you die before cashing them in.

There are two disadvantages of investing in savings bonds. One, you generally receive a somewhat lower rate of return than for some of the other time deposit investments. Two, the long maturity period results in some loss of flexibility in planning and managing your cash resources.

CONCLUSION

If you are looking for security and an assured return on your savings, time deposits may be a proper investment for you, although you should keep in mind that they offer practically no protection against inflation. Before you decide to use time deposits as your major investment, examine the other opportunities outlined in the remainder of this unit.

If you do decide to put some of your money (especially your emergency money or your accumulations for short-term goals) in time deposits, be sure you select a time deposit that offers the most appropriate liquidity and maturity, the greatest degree of security or insurance, a short compounding period, LIFO or daily interest (not FIFO or low balance), and the highest possible interest rate consistent with the foregoing considerations.

Once you have satisfied these five considerations, you can be confident that you are getting the most out of your time deposit investment.

VOCABULARY

bonus account
certificate of deposit
daily interest
effective rate
FDIC
FIFO
FSLIC
LIFO
low balance
nominal rate
passbook account
thrift institution
time deposit
U.S. savings bond

1. What are the four major reasons for having a savings account as part of your savings and investment program? Give examples of each.
2. Why should you not rely on a savings account as your only means of investing?
3. What are the principal differences between a savings account program offered by a bank and one offered by a savings and loan? Which, if any, are of significance to you, the investor?
4. If all local savings institutions offered the same stated rate of interest, but different methods of computing and compounding interest, what would be the optimum situation for your savings?
5. Assuming both paid the same stated yield, U.S. savings bonds would be preferable to passbook accounts under what circumstances?
6. Assume your checking account has a $300 minimum balance requirement, which you regularly violate, and it costs you an average of $2 a month in check charges. However, if your balance stayed above $300 continuously, there would be no charges. Should you leave your $1000 emergency fund entirely in your 5 percent (compounded annually) savings account, or keep $700 in savings and put $300 in the checking account? If you are in a 30 percent tax bracket, what is the dollar difference of the two alternatives for the next year?
7. Why is a U.S. savings bond a poor investment to use for achieving a two- or three-year goal?
8. Why may a credit union be the most advantageous place for a savings account? What are the key factors you should consider before opening an account with one?
9. Could you and your spouse qualify for more than $40,000 total deposit insurance at any one bank or savings and loan?
10. Assume that you have a $10,000 savings account that earned 6.2 percent last year. Inflation was at the rate of 3.4 percent as measured by the consumer price index. Your tax bracket is 32 percent, combined state and federal. What was your net gain in real purchasing power for the year?

Barbara is a sophomore at State University. The bank where she has her checking account offers free accounts to students who maintain a minimum $100 monthly balance. Her account rarely goes below $300, and she uses it mostly to make payments on her car. The bank also offers 4.5 percent passbook savings accounts, computed on a LIFO basis, and 5 percent bonus accounts on funds held the full ninety-day quarter. The savings and loan association nearby offers 5 percent passbook accounts, with interest from the date of deposit to the date of withdrawal, and 5.75 percent on one-year certificates of deposit.

Barbara's parents pay for her expenses during the summer when she lives with them as well as her tuition and room and board at the university. (Her father sends his $1000 check for her tuition and room and board about three weeks early each quarter to make sure she receives it in time.) Barbara is responsible for all other expenses. To cover these, she earns $400 (take-home pay) a month for two and one-half months' work during the summer and $120 (take-home pay) a month on a part-time job at school. Her summer savings usually are exhausted by the following June.

In what ways, if any, could Barbara make use of a savings account? Does she need an emergency fund? Why or why not? If Barbara were to put money aside in a time deposit, should she use an account at the bank, an account at the savings and loan, or U.S. savings bonds? What, approximately, is the maximum amount of dollars that Barbara could earn each year in interest (before taxes) if she took advantage of several opportunities peculiar to her situation?

RECOMMENDED READING

Donaldson, Elvin, and Pfahl, John. *Personal Finance.* New York: Ronald, 1971.

    Chapter 6 discusses types of savings instruments.

Meyer, Martin J., and McDaniel, Joseph M., Jr. *Don't Bank on It!* Lynbrook, N.Y.: Farnsworth, 1970.

    This book is a witty critique of the banking industry. Though not always accurate or up-to-date, the book does provide some interesting techniques for getting the largest possible yield out of your savings, provided you have the time and inclination to use them.

Smith, Carlton; Pratt, Richard P.; and editors of Time-Life. *The Time-Life Book of Family Finance.* New York: Time-Life Books, 1969.

    Chapter 11 explores the problems of saving money and gives numerical examples of the ways banks compute interest.

Unger, Maurice, and Wolf, Harold. *Personal Finance.* Boston: Allyn and Bacon, 1969.

    Chapter 12 provides information on the various types of savings investments.

CHUCK AND
NANCY ANDERSON

SELECTING THEIR SAVINGS INVESTMENTS

Chuck and Nancy have $2200 set aside in an emergency fund (chapter 3), and they need to put $533 a year in a savings investment that earns at least 5.5 percent in order to save for the car they plan to buy four years from now (chapter 13). They are trying to decide on the best type of savings investment for each of these, and so they gathered information on the minimum balance, maturity, stated annual rate, compounding interval, and safety of the following savings investments: passbook and bonus accounts at a bank, passbook and bonus accounts and certificates of deposit at a savings and loan, an account with the credit union where Nancy works (they also offer payroll deduction plans), and U.S. Series E savings bonds. This information is presented in table 14-4.

TABLE 14-4

Comparison of Several Time Deposits

Type of Investment	Minimum Balance	Maturity	Stated Annual Rate (%)	Compounding Interval	U.S. Government Insured
Bank					
passbook	$ 100.00	90 days	4.5	quarterly	yes
bonus	2000.00	1 year	5.25	quarterly	yes
Savings and Loan					
passbook	1.00	1 day	5.0	daily	yes
bonus	2000.00	1 year	5.5	daily	yes
certificate	5000.00	2 years	6.0	daily	yes
Credit Union	10.00	90 days	5.5	quarterly	no
Series E U.S. savings bonds	17.50	5 years, 10 months	5.5	annually	yes

QUESTIONS

1. Which of these savings investments would be best for the Andersons' emergency fund? Under what circumstances would one alternative be better than another?
2. Which of these savings investments would be best for the new car savings fund? Why? Under what circumstances would the credit union be the best alternative?

15

INSURANCE AND ANNUITIES AS INVESTMENTS

When life insurance was first sold, it offered only death benefit protection. At that time, a common objection to such insurance was that you had to die to collect benefits. To counter this objection, life insurance companies attached an investment program to some of their policies. Life insurance salesmen, therefore, have emphasized this more pleasant aspect of their product. They often tell you: "If you live a long life, there will be money for you." "You can borrow against the cash value or you can use it for retirement income." "By the time you are sixty-five, the total cost of your policy will be only $16,408, and you will have built up a retirement reserve of $24,652!"

With the exception of buying a home, life insurance probably represents the largest voluntary investment made by many families. In fact, the average family holds approximately $10,000 face amount of whole life insurance. This represents an average yearly investment ranging from $300 to $500 ($25 to $40 a month)—more than most families might save on their own, aside from the equity build-up of a home mortgage.

Life insurance as protection against dying too soon was discussed in chapter 7, when you learned how to provide your dependents with adequate insurance protection. If at age thirty you determine that your family will need $100,000 in the event of your death, you can buy $100,000 of five-year renewable term life insurance for $252 a year (the most competitive rate currently available). Such a policy has no investment feature, however.

The investment feature of life insurance will be critically analyzed in this chapter. The chapter will also cover annuities, which are a guaranteed monthly income investment also offered by insurance companies.

LIFE INSURANCE WITH CASH BENEFITS BEFORE DEATH

All forms of life insurance other than term insurance have some accumulation of cash values. As you learned in chapter 7, cash-value life insurance consists of decreasing term insurance protection and a systematic savings program. This savings aspect is the distinguishing feature of cash-value insurance. The relationship between protection and savings is shown in the diagram below—the amount of actual insurance protection decreases as your savings grow. In effect, you are providing self-insurance. The question to be dealt with in this chapter, then, is: "Is cash-value life insurance an efficient means of saving and investing money?" (For the rest of this chapter, unless otherwise noted, when we refer to life insurance, we will mean cash-value life insurance.)

PROTECTION AND SAVINGS IN A
CASH-VALUE POLICY

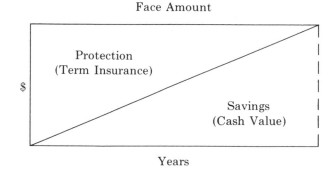

If you own life insurance, you should consider its cash value as part of your investment portfolio since you may either use it as collateral for a bank or insurance company loan or withdraw it. You should look at a proposed investment in life insurance with the same careful calculations of risk, return, convenience, and suitability that you apply to other investment decisions. Since you can buy all the death benefit protection you need with term insurance, cash-value insurance should be evaluated solely on its merits as an investment.

Making the Best Insurance Investment

As you learned in chapter 7, there are three general types of cash-value life insurance: straight life, limited payment, and endowment. Table 15-1 (p. 320) compares premiums and cash values for each of these types, including two examples of limited payment (life-paid-up-at-sixty-five and twenty-payment life) and three examples of endowment (twenty-year endowment, endowment at sixty-five, and retirement endowment at sixty-five). Figures are for rate-competitive insurance policies with $25,000 face amounts. (Policies with face amounts less than $25,000 normally cost more per $1000 of coverage.) All of the policies except retirement endowment at sixty-five offer $25,000 in death benefits at any time until cashed in. Retirement endowment at sixty-five offers $25,000 plus any cash value in excess of face amount as a death benefit.

To find the best investment, you should compare the difference between the total premiums paid and the cash value at maturity or at age sixty-five, whichever comes first. Those policies offering increasingly greater cash-value returns are likely to be better investments. As you can see in table 15-1, endowment policies tend to offer the greatest investment value (i.e., cash value in excess of premiums paid), even when bought fairly late in life. Since higher premiums are charged on such policies, a greater proportion of your premium dollar can go toward building up your cash value. Also, the shorter the maturity period of the policy, the greater the investment value. If you compare total premiums and cash values by age of the investor within any of the investment types, you will see that the younger you are when you invest in life insurance, the greater your investment value. Since younger people are less likely to die than older people, the portion of the premium that goes toward buying death benefit protection is relatively smaller. Table 15-1 also shows that if some of these policy types are bought at age forty or older, it may be impossible to build up the cash value in excess of premiums paid before the policy matures or the policyholder reaches age sixty-five.

When shopping for the best life insurance investment, you should shop for the best premium rate in relation to cash-value build-up, as scheduled in the policy (including projected dividends). Keep in mind also that you may get a quantity discount if you buy, for example, one $30,000 policy rather than two $15,000 policies.

Life Insurance Compared With Time Deposits and Mutual Funds: An Example

Jenny, a single woman of thirty-seven, has a well-paying career and hopes to maintain a comfortable standard of living after her retirement. Therefore, she feels that she ought to begin now to build up investments. Her fifty-eight-year-old mother lives with her and depends on her for living expenses. A life insurance agent has suggested that, for an annual

TABLE 15-1

Comparison of Six Cash-Value Life Insurance Policies

Age at Issue of Policy Fa	M	STRAIGHT LIFE Annual Premium	Total Premium to Age 65	Cash Value at Age 65	LIFE-PAID-UP-AT-65 Annual Premium	Total Premium to Age 65	Cash Value at Age 65	TWENTY-PAYMENT LIFE Annual Premium	Total Premium for 20 Years	Cash Value at Age 65
8	5	$186	$11,160	$14,961	$188	$11,280	$16,300	$311	$6,220	$16,299
23	20	214	9,630	14,034	275	12,375	16,300	426	8,520	16,299
28	25	253	10,120	13,589	328	13,120	16,300	485	9,700	16,299
33	30	306	10,710	13,016	402	14,070	16,300	557	11,140	16,299
38	35	374	11,220	12,267	503	15,090	16,300	643	12,860	16,299
43	40	465	11,625	(11,287)c	636	15,900	16,300	738	14,760	16,299
48	45	585	11,700	(10,012)c	856	17,120	(16,300)c	856	17,120	(16,299)c
53	50	750	11,250	(8,042)c	1200	18,000	(16,300)c	1031	20,620	(12,029)c
58	55	962	9,620	(5,761)c	1864	18,640	(16,300)c	1257	25,140	(7,775)c

Age at Issue of Policy Fa	M	TWENTY-YEAR ENDOWMENT Annual Premium	Total Premium for 20 years	Cash Value at Maturity b	ENDOWMENT AT 65 Annual Premium	Total Premium to Age 65	Cash Value at Age 65	RETIREMENT ENDOWMENT AT 65 Annual Premium	Total Premium to Age 65	Cash Value at Age 65
8	5	$1001	$20,020	$25,000	$215	$12,900	$25,000	$315	$18,900	$39,125
23	20	1024	20,480	25,000	342	15,390	25,000	508	22,860	39,125
28	25	1025	20,500	25,000	415	16,600	25,000	623	24,920	39,125
33	30	1031	20,620	25,000	516	18,060	25,000	775	27,125	39,125
38	35	1044	20,880	25,000	656	19,680	25,000	984	29,520	39,125
43	40	1063	21,260	25,000	826	20,650	25,000	1269	31,725	39,125
48	45	1102	22,040	25,000	1102	22,040	25,000	1676	33,520	39,125
53	50	1197	23,940	25,000	1599	23,985	25,000	2364	35,460	39,125
58	55	1343	26,860	(25,000)c	2569	25,690	(25,000)c	3747	37,470	39,125

Source: Rate tables for United Life and Accident Insurance Company, Concord, New Hampshire, 1972.

aPremium rates are different for a man and a woman of the same age because women have a slightly longer life expectancy than men.

bTwenty years from date of issue.

cNegative investment value (i.e., the accumulated guaranteed cash value is less than the total paid-in premiums).

premium of $563, Jenny could buy a $20,000 life-paid-up-at-sixty-five policy to cover her retirement needs and protect her mother. Although Jenny can afford this policy, she wants to examine a few alternatives before deciding what to do. During her investigation she finds that she can also purchase $20,000 of twenty-year mortgage (decreasing) term insurance for $104 annually. This policy offers an average of $1000 less in death benefits each year until it reaches zero in twenty years, when Jenny's mother would be seventy-eight years old. Jenny thinks that during those twenty years she could build up enough cash in another investment to make up for this decreasing amount of protection. The annual amount that she would have to invest by taking the term rather than the cash-value insurance would be $459 ($563 − $104).

According to projections of cash values and dividend accumulations made by Jenny's insurance agent, the life-paid-up-at-sixty-five policy would probably yield about $12,320 in twenty years. If she buys term insurance and invests the difference ($459 a year) in an insured time deposit yielding 5 percent, her total investment would be worth about $15,193 in twenty years. Even though the savings account would yield over $2900 more, Jenny is not sure that this investment is right for her since it would require her to make regular savings deposits. She feels that she would be more likely to pay life insurance premiums since she would be billed for them.

Another alternative would be to purchase term insurance and invest the difference in a long-term growth mutual fund recommended by a broker. The fund she is considering has achieved an average annual compound rate of growth of 12 percent since its founding fifteen years ago. To be conservative, Jenny figures the future value of her proposed investment at an annual rate of 10 percent compounded annually. This rate yields a total investment of approximately $26,300 and represents a larger possible investment value than either of the other two alternatives. As we shall see in succeeding chapters, this investment alternative carries significant risks (short-term price fluctuations) when compared to the guaranteed investments offered by the first two alternatives. However, Jenny is willing to live with these interim risks since she views this investment over a long period of time.

Jenny is still worried, however, that she might not make her investments on a regular basis, although she has generally been able to budget her money well for similar commitments or purchases. But her broker tells her that, if she enrolls in a voluntary savings accumulation plan (p. 413), the mutual fund will prod her with regular monthly statements. Jenny feels this would be all the encouragement she would need and she chooses the last alternative.

Jenny's three alternatives are compared in figure 15-1 (p. 322). The effect of the age of the investor upon these three alternatives is shown in figure 15-2 (p. 323). To make computations to fit your own situation and alternatives, refer to compound interest tables A and B (pp. 498–501).

| ALTERNATIVE | ANNUAL CASH OUTLAY | | | POSSIBLE VALUE IN TWENTY YEARS ($) | REMAINING LIFE INSURANCE BENEFIT (Face Amount Less Cash Value) ($) | INVESTMENT RISK | SAVING DISCIPLINE REQUIRED |
	Premium ($)	Cash Investment ($)	Total ($)				
Life-Paid-Up-at-65 (protection only)	563		563	12,320[a]	7680[b]	Very little	Premium notice forces her to save
Twenty-Year Decreasing Term and 5 Percent Savings Account	104	459	563	15,193		None, if insured by federal government	Requires considerable self-discipline
Twenty-Year Decreasing Term and Mutual Fund (10 percent total annual return)	104	459	563	26,301		Significant	Monthly statement will remind her

SOURCE: New York Life Insurance Company premium rates, cash values, and dividends for thirty-five-year-old male (approximately those for thirty-seven-year-old female) taken from *1972 Life Rates and Data* (Cincinnati: National Underwriter, 1972), pp. 324, 326.
[a]Includes guaranteed cash value and projected divided accumulations.
[b]If premiums continue to be paid after twenty years.

Fig. 15-1.
Comparison of insurance, savings account, and mutual fund as investments for a thirty-seven-year-old woman

Alternative	Age at Policy Purchase F[a]	M	Annual Cash Outlay Premium ($)	Cash Investment ($)	Total ($)	Possible Value in Ten Years ($)	Possible Value in Twenty Years ($)
Life-Paid-Up-at-65 (protection only)	27	25	379		379	3,361[b]	8,360[b]
	37	35	563		563	5,110[b]	12,320[b]
	48	45	892		892	8,069[b]	19,520[b]
Twenty-Year Decreasing Term and 5 Percent Savings Account	27	25	71	308	379	3,881	10,195
	37	35	104	459	563	5,783	15,193
	48	45	187	705	892	8,883	22,335
Twenty-Year Decreasing Term and Mutual Fund (10 percent total annual return)	27	25	71	308	379	4,897	17,648
	37	35	104	459	563	7,298	26,301
	48	45	187	705	892	11,209	40,396

SOURCE: New York Life Insurance Company premium rates, cash values, and dividends for males, taken from *1972 Life Rates and Data* (Cincinnati: National Underwriter, 1972), pp. 324, 326.

[a] Results for female approximate those for male two to three years younger.
[b] Includes guaranteed cash value and projected dividend accumulations.

Fig. 15-2.
Comparison of insurance, savings accounts, and mutual funds as investments for people of various ages

Settlement Options of Cash-Value Insurance

The settlement options applicable upon surrender of a cash-value policy are the same as those you may select for the beneficiary of your life insurance (pp. 143–44) except that you also have the nonforfeiture options of the extended term and paid-up insurance (p. 146). You can select whichever option you prefer for your beneficiary and then change it to what you want for yourself if you decide to surrender the policy for its cash value. We will examine these options from the viewpoint of choosing the one that will both provide retirement income and suit your particular needs. You have four basic alternatives from which to choose when you surrender your life insurance policy for its cash value.

lump sum   You may take the proceeds in a lump sum to spend and invest as you please. The advantages of lump-sum settlement were discussed in chapter 7 (pp. 143–44). In brief, the lump-sum option allows you to take your money and invest it at a rate of return higher than that available through insurance companies.

interest income   You may choose to receive interest income only. The size of the payment depends on your policy's cash value and the company's current rate of interest (usually guaranteed at a minimum rate, such as 2.5 percent). You retain ownership of the cash value of your policy and it will eventually become part of your estate, payable to the beneficiary of your choice. If you decide that the interest provides you with insufficient income, you may change your option and withdraw the cash as a lump sum.

installment payments   The installment payments option provides monthly income, consisting of both interest and principal, until the funds are exhausted. You may select either the *fixed period* or *fixed amount* option. With the fixed period option, the payee designates the number of years over which monthly payments will be received (usually from one to thirty), and the company declares the size of the payment, based on the amount of interest earned. Table 15-2 shows what these payments are likely to be for a $10,000 lump-sum value. In no case will the payments be less than the amounts printed in the table on the policy. With the fixed amount option, the payee chooses the monthly amount of benefits he wishes to receive, and the company makes payments of that amount until the money runs out, with interest credited to the principal at the current year's rate. (The rate is usually guaranteed at a certain minimum, often 2.5 percent.) In either case, if you die before the funds are exhausted, the remaining payments will be made to your beneficiary.

The advantage of the installment payments options over the lump-sum option is that you spread the taxable gain (ordinary income) on your

TABLE 15-2

INSTALLMENT PAYMENTS: FIXED PERIOD OPTION
($10,000 Initial Cash Value)

Period (Years)	Monthly Payment
1	$840
3	289
5	178
7	131
10	95
15	68
20	54
25	46
30	41

insurance investment over a number of years and, by not having to declare it all in one year, avoid the possibility of placing yourself in an unnecessarily high tax bracket.

annuity There are four standard annuity options available with most life insurance policies. All of them guarantee monthly benefits for life. As tables 15-3 and 15-4 show, the size of the monthly payment varies depending on the amounts left over for contingent beneficiaries.

Straight life annuity (also known as the life-income-without-refund annuity) offers monthly payments for life, regardless of how long the

TABLE 15-3

TYPICAL MONTHLY PAYMENTS FOR THREE ANNUITY OPTIONS
($10,000 Lump-Sum Annuity Value)

AGE OF PAYEE ON FIRST PAYMENT DATE		STRAIGHT LIFE ANNUITY	REFUND ANNUITY	CERTAIN AND CONTINUOUS ANNUITY[a]	
M	F			10 Years	20 Years
20	25	$29	$28	$29	$29
30	35	33	31	31	31
40	45	37	35	36	35
50	55	45	41	43	41
60	64	57	51	54	43
65	69	66	58	63	51
70	73	79	67	72	53

[a]Refund guaranteed to beneficiary if death occurs before ten years or twenty years, depending on option chosen.

TABLE 15-4

TYPICAL MONTHLY PAYMENTS FOR JOINT-AND-SURVIVORSHIP
ANNUITY WITH TWO-THIRDS TO SURVIVOR
($10,000 Lump-Sum Annuity Value)

Age at Start of Payments Female	Age at Start of Payments Male			
	55	60	65	70
55	$42	$44	$46	$47
60	47	50	53	57
65	50	54	58	63
70	54	59	64	70

NOTE: Here is an example that shows how to read this table. If at the start of benefits the man is age sixty-five and the woman is age sixty, the monthly benefit will be $53 while they are both alive. When one of them dies, the monthly benefit to the survivor will be two-thirds of that amount, or $35.50.

payee lives. If the payee dies young, the company keeps the remaining funds; if his life is unusually long, he collects not only more than he put in but also interest as well. The payment rate depends upon the interest the company earns on the money the payee invests; but it is guaranteed at the rate set in the table of the policy. Generally, under this option you must outlive normal life expectancy by as much as ten to twenty-five years to recoup your original investment plus interest.

Refund annuity offers income payments for the rest of the payee's life; but, if any funds remain upon the payee's death, they are paid to his beneficiaries. The minimum guaranteed payment rate set by the company for this type of annuity is somewhat lower than for the straight life annuity since the insurance company must ultimately pay back the entire investment. The only conditions under which you would wish to choose a refund-type annuity would be if you wished to leave an estate to your heirs and did not mind taking a lower monthly income for yourself, or if your family had a history of early deaths and you felt that you would not otherwise collect your full investment.

Certain and continuous annuity also offers income for life; if the payee dies within a specified period (usually five, ten, or twenty years), payments are made to his beneficiaries for the remainder of that period. Again, the monthly payments are lower than with the straight life annuity.

Joint-and-survivorship annuity offers a lifetime income for two persons, even if one outlives the other. The two recipients need not be related. If one of the payees dies, payments continue to the second payee at a specified rate—usually the same as, two-thirds of, or half of the amount of the payment made to both persons. The smaller the rate of payment chosen for the second payee alone, the larger the monthly payment will be for the two together. Again, the payment rate is set at a guaranteed minimum and may rise above that rate if a better interest return is earned by the insurance company on its investments.

The Advantages and Disadvantages of Life Insurance as an Investment

The advantages of life insurance as an investment are similar to those for time deposits: no price fluctuations, no transaction costs, no minimum dollar investment restrictions, immediate withdrawal (within two weeks, that is), and convenience.

An additional advantage is that insurance investments force you to save: if you do not pay your premiums within thirty days of the date they are due, your policy lapses and you must accept one of the nonforfeiture options (p. 146). If this happens and you later want to obtain a new policy, you may find it harder to qualify for good premium rates either medically or occupationally or both; also, because you will be older, your premiums for a similar program will be higher. This forced savings advantage is not peculiar to life insurance. Other such programs include annuities (pp. 328–33), front-end load contractual plans of mutual funds (p. 413), and all forms of installment credit and borrowing, such as the mortgage on your home or other real estate (chapters 10, 11, and 12). There are several alternatives to forced saving that also offer an incentive or a reminder to help you save on a regular basis. Among these are the budget (chapter 8), voluntary savings plans of mutual funds (p. 413), and other techniques such as the payroll savings plans discussed at the beginning of chapter 13 (pp. 277–78). If you feel that a more voluntary incentive plan is not sufficient for your needs, you should definitely consider cash-value insurance or an annuity.

Another important advantage is that income taxes are deferred until your policy is cashed in. There are no taxes payable while the policy is in force. If you are having your yearly dividends mailed to you by check, do not include them in your gross income for tax purposes since they represent merely a partial refund of the premium you paid. When you do surrender the policy for its cash value, you pay ordinary income taxes on any gain exceeding your total paid-in premiums (net premiums after dividends). If you cash in your policy after you retire, you can increase the after-tax return on your investment. (Of course, this advantage of postponing your tax liability until you retire and are probably in a lower tax bracket is available also with U.S. Series E savings bonds.) If you take the proceeds under one of the annuity options, the taxes are prorated over your expected life according to IRS tables. If you take the interest option, you are taxed only on the interest income at regular tax rates; taxes on the rest of your accumulated gains (cash value minus premiums) are deferred. The death benefit proceeds are subject only to estate taxes, unless the policyholder assigns all rights to the beneficiary. Then the policyholder pays only gift taxes on the cash value of the policy at the time it is given away.

In addition, the cash values of policies are guaranteed by the insurance companies themselves. Although there is no federal insurance backing life insurance policies, the only risk you run is that the company might

go out of business. However, because of the state regulation of insurance companies and their own conservative investment policies, mature insurance companies have an excellent record for staying in business and standing by their guarantees. Dividends are not guaranteed.

Some people may claim that the death benefit coverage included with your investment is also an advantage. For example, if you die before reaching your investment goal for your son's college education, the death benefit coverage will provide the rest of the money. However, this is not truly an investment consideration: you should always carry insurance coverage, regardless of cash values, if you wish to protect against contingencies arising from your death. If you do not need such protection, death benefit coverage only reduces the amount of your premium that goes into your cash investment. Therefore, the death benefit is not an investment advantage.

The disadvantages of a life insurance investment are also similar to those for time deposit investments: low rate of return and poor protection against inflation. Policies now average about 3.5 to 5 percent a year, compounded annually on the total cash in the policy (guaranteed cash, dividends, and interest on dividends). This rate of return is lower than that offered by insured time deposits. Furthermore, your guaranteed cash values are fixed in their dollar amount, and inflation reduces the purchasing power of these dollars. If your policy's cash value grows by 4.5 percent in one year, but inflation reduces the purchasing power of those dollars by 4 percent, your net gain in real value will be only 0.5 percent.

One disadvantage unique to life insurance as an investment is the possibility of diverting too many investment dollars toward protection by purchasing more death benefit coverage than you need. In such a case, the money spent on the extra insurance would be wasted. Therefore, if you are buying life insurance primarily as an investment, you should choose policies (such as endowment and retirement endowment) that rapidly accumulate cash values.

INVESTING IN ANNUITIES

An annuity is an investment program that provides monthly income for life. When you buy an annuity, you make an investment; there is no insurance coverage attached unless you request some. A company pension is one form of annuity; Social Security is another. In both cases, during your working years you build up a lifetime retirement income through an investment program. You can supplement these incomes with other annuities, which are usually purchased from insurance companies.

In selecting an annuity investment, you generally have two major alternatives: the fixed annuity and the variable annuity. Your *fixed annuity* choices are identical to the settlement options (lump sum, interest income, installment, and annuity) on your life insurance except that you can buy a fixed annuity without having to buy insurance protection as well. A *variable annuity* offers the same payment options except interest income, and the payment amounts vary from year to year according to the company's investment management expertise and stock market price fluctuations. Variable annuity funds are invested in common stocks, whereas fixed annuity funds are invested in mortgages and bonds. The payment schedule for fixed annuities can be projected and paid at a fixed rate. Only if the company's return is greater than some fixed amount (usually 2.5 percent) will the payments grow.

Variable annuities are a new field for insurance companies. They first were instituted in the early 1950s and began to expand in the 1960s as various states enacted legislation allowing their sale. Although such programs have previously been available only to groups, today many states have companies licensed to sell variable annuities to private individuals, and it may not be long before they are available in your state too, if they are not already.

Maturity Date

The maturity date of an annuity is the date selected by the contract holder as the time for monthly payments to begin. The *accumulation period* is the time before the maturity date, when the interest on fixed annuities and the dividends and capital gains on variable annuities accumulate either on the lump-sum payment or on the installments as they are being paid. If you die before the maturity date, the funds accumulated up to that time are paid to your designated beneficiary, just as they would be with any other investment.

The *distribution period* begins on the maturity date. At this time, whichever option (pp. 325–26) you have chosen goes into effect and cannot be changed. If you have chosen an annuity without refund and you die, the insurance company keeps the rest of the money. (Of course, you have been receiving the highest monthly benefit available.)

Also, on the maturity date and sometimes at other dates specified by the company, you have the option of withdrawing your investment in a lump sum rather than taking the monthly income payments from an installment or annuity option. You must carefully decide before the maturity date which settlement option you want for the rest of your life.

Extra Endorsements Sometimes Offered on Annuities

Many companies offer a choice of two extra endorsements (at additional cost) on an annuity purchase. The first is the disability waiver of premium endorsement, which calls for the company to finish paying your premiums in the event that you become disabled. In effect, this is a convenient way to add to your disability coverage. Costs of this protection vary from company to company. The second is the addition of term life insurance. In effect, the latter converts your annuity into an endowment insurance policy, and, when considering it, you should ask yourself whether you need this type of coverage.

Purchasing an Annuity

The only application requirement for purchasing an annuity is proof of age, such as a birth certificate. The older you are when monthly income payments begin, the higher will be your monthly income per premium dollar paid. No medical examination is required since annuities offer no death benefit. If you were to die before the maturity date, all your beneficiary would get would be the money you have invested.

Annuities are generally purchased from an insurance company under one of two plans. First, you may make a lump-sum investment, either with cash or with the settlement options of your life insurance policy. Annuities are available at the lowest possible cost through settlement options since they involve no sales commissions. Second, you may purchase an annuity with a series of installments (or premiums) much as you would purchase life insurance. Table 15-5 gives typical annual premium rates per $100 monthly income for life (with ten years certain and continuous option) starting at age sixty-five. (Add 10 percent to get the approximate rate for females.)

TABLE 15-5

ANNUAL PREMIUM PER $100 OF MONTHLY ANNUITY
BEGINNING AT AGE 65

PAYMENTS	INITIAL AGE (MALE)				
	30	35	40	45	50
Annual	$283	$357	$456	$610	$889
Semiannual	144	180	232	310	448
Quarterly	73	91	118	158	226

In some states you can buy an annuity that is part variable, part fixed. During the accumulation period your funds are invested in stocks, but during the distribution period your monthly payments remain fixed. Be careful not to buy this type of annuity if you are really looking for a variable annuity.

Since the value of a fixed annuity will not change after you buy it, you need not consider whether it is better to buy one with a lump-sum purchase at retirement or to begin much earlier by purchasing one with annual premiums. With variable annuities, however, the method of purchase is an important decision. You must consider both the flexibility you would have with a variable annuity and the short investment performance records of companies offering them. Although by using a regular premium accumulation plan, you will be reminded to save and you may benefit from deferred income taxes, you cannot change investments without a tax penalty if your variable annuity investment managers do poorly. There may be better investment returns available elsewhere if you are willing to work for higher yields and accept the accompanying higher risks and thus prepare to buy a variable annuity later with a lump sum. Since many life insurance companies have only recently entered the field of variable annuities, it may be difficult to compare their records and select a superior program, but you should select a variable annuity program much as you would select a mutual fund (pp. 421–22).

Fixed Annuity Compared with Time Deposits and Mutual Funds: An Example

Six years after buying a twenty-year decreasing term policy and investing in mutual funds, Jenny was earning a higher salary and wanted to begin an additional twenty-year investment program.This time she considered endowment policies, which have more investment value than the life-paid-up-at-sixty-five policy she thought about buying before. On a $20,000 twenty-year endowment policy, her $1010 annual premium would yield $25,520 in twenty years. However, according to the eleven-step procedure (pp. 126–33), Jenny did not need more death benefit protection because of both her increased monetary assets from the mutual fund and her mother's advancing age. Jenny began looking for an alternative investment.

She found out that an annuity at the same premium and yielding about 4 percent would return about $29,000 in twenty years. Given her circumstances, this appeared to be a more appropriate investment. Another alternative was to invest $1010 each year in a 6 percent insured time deposit. This would yield a little over $37,000 in twenty years, or about $8000 more than the annuity. Jenny's final alternative was to invest the $1010 each year in the mutual fund with a projected 10 percent return and maybe earn $58,000 in twenty years. Since she had done well with her voluntary program so far, she decided to continue it at the higher contribution rate. By now Jenny was convinced that for her cash-value insurance and annuities were appropriate investment choices only if she needed the premium notice to help her to save money.

The truth of this conclusion can be demonstrated with another example. If Jenny did need $20,000 extra death benefit protection and therefore bought a twenty-year endowment policy, her $1010 annual premium would yield $25,520 in twenty years. However, if she bought a twenty-year decreasing term policy and invested the difference in a 5 percent savings account, she would have $29,300 in twenty years. If she bought term insurance and invested in the mutual fund again, the yield would be about $50,500—almost twice as much as the yield from the endowment policy, although the investment risks would also be greater.

Investment Value of Fixed and Variable Annuities Compared

The oldest variable annuity still in effect was begun in 1952 and was offered to college professors through the College Retirement Equities Fund (CREF). CREF is managed by the same company that has managed the Teacher's Insurance and Annuity Association of America (TIAA), a fixed annuity dating back to 1918. Since CREF has the longest record for a variable annuity and the same management runs both funds, a comparison between the two seems appropriate.

TIAA offers a guaranteed minimum monthly income, with interest added as it is earned. CREF pays a monthly income that varies from year to year according to the current value of the fund. The annual payments resulting from a lump-sum investment of $12,500 in 1952 for a man age sixty-five are given in table 15-6.

TABLE 15-6

ANNUAL TIAA AND CREF PAYMENTS
ON $12,500 INVESTED IN 1952
BY A 65-YEAR-OLD MAN

YEAR	TIAA (Fixed)	CREF (Variable)	YEAR	TIAA (Fixed)	CREF (Variable)
1953	$1016	$1092	1962	$1073	$2866
1954	1014	1032	1963	1073	2852
1955	1012	1172	1964	1084	2476
1956	1018	1540	1965	1076	2891
1957	1019	2021	1966	1076	3080
1958	1030	1843	1967	1080	3322
1959	1030	1824	1967–68[a]	- - -	3192
1960	1039	2405	1968–69[a]	- - -	2990
1961	1073	2421	1969–70[a]	1100 (est.)	3250

[a] Reporting method changed from calendar year to fiscal year.

According to the consumer price index, $1 in 1953 was worth $.73 in 1969 purchasing power. Thus, while the annual payment of $1016 in 1953 may have been enough for the retiree who invested $12,500, the estimated $1100 received in 1969 was worth only $803 relative to the 1953 payment (.73 × $1100). The CREF payment of $3250 in 1969 was worth $2372 in 1953 dollars (.73 × $3250). The man in our example had actually been able to raise his standard of living during those years by investing in a variable annuity!

Advantages and Disadvantages of Buying an Annuity

Some of the advantages of an annuity are similar to those for cash-value life insurance: forced savings and tax deferral. People regard premium notices as bills, even though an insurance company cannot demand payment. If a premium is not paid, the contract lapses, leaving the holder with an annuity program worth only a portion of the cash value that would be present at maturity. To start such a program again, the investor would probably have to purchase a new annuity contract.

With annuities, you can build your investment on a tax-deferred basis during your working years. Taxes on both fixed and variable annuities are deferred until you begin taking out the principal and interest in monthly payments—probably in your retirement years when you will be in a lower tax bracket. Upon maturity, annuities are subject to ordinary income taxes on the same basis as other investments: total proceeds minus total costs equal taxable profits. However, the taxes are prorated over your expected lifetime for any of the lifetime annuity options or over the specified term for an installment annuity. With variable annuities you must pay regular income tax rates on the gains in your monthly receipts rather than the capital gains rate you would pay for a mutual fund investment.

A particular advantage of variable annuities is that you have a chance for above-average income growth. Variable annuities were designed to overcome the decline in purchasing power of a fixed monthly income, a disadvantage of the fixed annuity. Common stock investments are generally considered to offer good protection against inflation. New York Stock Exchange common stocks have grown by an average annual compound rate well above the average annual rate of inflation for the last forty-five years, as we shall see in chapter 16.

The disadvantages of an annuity depend on whether it is fixed or variable. Fixed annuities offer a lower yield (3.5 to 4.5 percent) than most other equally safe investments. Of course, the other investments would not offer the guaranteed life payment provision, which can take away much of the need for financial worry during retirement years. Also, fixed annuities offer no protection against inflation. The fixed monthly income will buy less and less each year during periods of inflation. The primary disadvantage of a variable annuity is the degree of risk exposure. No one can know for sure that stocks will not decline for several years at a time. The amount of your monthly payment is unpredictable and subject to normal stock market price fluctuations.

CONCLUSION

Cash-value life insurance and annuities should always be considered part of an investment portfolio. They are cash investments like stocks, mutual funds, and savings accounts. As investments, they have a special advantage: they "force" you to invest a regular amount each year.

If you examine your balance sheet and find that you have not met your savings and investment goals in the past, you should think seriously about investing in insurance or annuities. (If you have not tried any of the incentive savings programs mentioned earlier, you should also take a look at those.) However, almost any other investment, including a savings account, yields a higher return on your dollar than cash-value insurance or fixed annuities do. If you do decide to invest in life insurance, consider endowment policies since they have the most rapid cash-value build-up. Also, the shorter the premium period and/or the maturity period, the greater the policy's investment value. If you do not need death benefit coverage, buy an annuity.

VOCABULARY

accumulation period	joint-and-survivorship annuity
annuity	quantity discount
certain and continuous annuity	refund annuity
distribution period	straight life annuity
fixed annuity	variable annuity

QUESTIONS

1. Compare life insurance investments to savings account investments, with regard to yield, liquidity, taxability, and safety.
2. What is a special advantage of life insurance investments?
3. Rank the following policies according to their investment value for a thirty-year-old individual: ten-year endowment, straight life, twenty-payment life, twenty-year endowment.
4. What four options do you have in settling the cash value of your life insurance?
5. What would be the disadvantages to beginning a variable annuity investment program at age twenty-five, soon after you are married? What would be the advantage of beginning one at age fifty?
6. Henry is fifty-two years old and is in a 40 percent tax bracket. Which of the following low-risk investments would assure him of the greatest lump sum at age sixty-five if he invested the same amount in each: a 6 percent savings account, U.S. savings bonds bought through payroll deductions, or a thirteen-year fixed annuity accumulation?
7. What is the significance of the maturity date with any type of annuity program?
8. What is probably the biggest disadvantage of life insurance and fixed annuity investment programs?
9. How does a life insurance investment affect estate taxes?

Leonard and Ann are both twenty-six years old. They used the procedure for determining their life insurance needs (chapter 7) and found out that Leonard should carry $120,000. The family would need that much if Leonard were to die because they have a high standard of living, there are several young children, and Ann has low earning potential. Leonard and Ann want to pay as little as possible for this coverage because they are hoping to add approximately $4000 to their savings in the next two to three years so that they can buy a home. After shopping for rates, they narrowed their selection to two policies: (1) $120,000 straight life that would require an annual premium of $1405 and accumulate a cash value of $72,120 by age sixty-five and (2) $120,000 five-year guaranteed renewable term with a premium of $285 a year for the first five-year-period. Which policy suits their current needs? Why? Which policy would give them more flexibility in reducing coverage as the children grow older?

Walt and Pauline are both fifty years old. At the urging of their daughter Janet, they completed the procedure in chapter 7. It showed that they should carry $30,000 of life insurance on Walt's life. Janet drew up a balance sheet for her parents and noticed that their net worth was composed of equity in their home, personal property, equity in a site for a second home, and approximately $800 in savings. Walt and Pauline had always thought mostly about their current enjoyment of life and only now were beginning to wonder whether they would be able to retire comfortably.

Janet wanted to shop for rates for policies that would be appropriate for them. She presented them with two alternatives: (1) buy a $30,000 retirement endowment policy with an annual premium of $2980 and a cash value of $48,600 at retirement or (2) buy $30,000 of fifteen-year decreasing term at $280 a year and each year invest part of the $2700 difference in a mutual fund and the rest in a savings account. Judging by Walt and Pauline's financial goals and history of money management, which program would you recommend? Why? If they selected the second program, and regularly invested $1350 in a 5 percent savings account and $1350 in a mutual fund that averaged an annual 10 percent return, approximately how much would they have built up by age sixty-five?

Ken and Mary, both age forty-seven, have a $20,000 straight life policy. Its cash value is $6080, which will go up to $6460 during the next premium year. The annual premium is $250; there are no dividends. They are wondering whether it would be better to maintain the $20,000 of protection by buying a $14,000 fifteen-year decreasing term policy for $95 a year and investing the $6080 surrender value in U.S. savings bonds at 5.5 percent average yield. What should they do? How does the first-year return from the second program compare with the return from the first program during the next premium year? If Ken and Mary select the term insurance program, what should be their first step?

RECOMMENDED READING

Donaldson, Elvin, and Pfahl, John. *Personal Finance*. New York: Ronald, 1971.

> Chapter 7 gives facts and statistics about life insurance.

Institute of Life Insurance. *Life Insurance Fact Book 1971*. New York: Institute of Life Insurance. Published annually.

> This paperback contains statistics regarding the life insurance industry.

Reynolds, G. Scott. *The Mortality Merchants*. New York: McKay, 1968.

> This book convincingly attacks the notion of using life insurance as an investment program, although its biases are sometimes overdone.

Wolff, Thomas J. "Life Insurance—A 9% Investment?" Indianapolis: Research and Review Service of America, 1966.

> This brochure is commonly offered as an argument in favor of investing in life insurance. However, the author does not explain which ordinary life and term policies he uses for his illustration and whether or not the premium rates are competitive. Also, he does not take into account the taxes due eventually on a surrendered cash-value policy and the flexibility of term insurance.

CHUCK AND NANCY ANDERSON

INVESTING IN CASH-VALUE LIFE INSURANCE

The Andersons have recently adopted their orphaned niece, who is two years old, and therefore have decided that Chuck needs $20,000 more life insurance protection. They would also like to set up a sound long-range retirement investment program and keep the cost of the two programs under $45 a month, or $540 a year (an amount they think they can afford because of a surplus in their investment plan set up in chapter 13). Since they are now thirty-five years old, they need a thirty-year program.

Chuck has already compared a $20,000 life-paid-up-at-sixty-five policy with a twenty-year mortgage term policy. The premiums on the cash-value insurance ($534 a year) are payable for the thirty years until age sixty-five. Those on the term insurance ($107 a year) are due only for the first seventeen years of the thirty-year program. Therefore, under this second alternative, Chuck would have $427 to invest each year for the first seventeen years and $534 a year for the last thirteen years until he retires. He is considering investing these dollars in either a 6 percent savings account or a mutual fund earning an average of 10 percent a year.

Figure 15-3 is set up to show how these three alternatives compare. Computations for the first alternative are given. You will have to make the computations for the other two.

Alternative	Cash Value at Age 65	Dividends and Interest on Them	Investment Value (Savings Account or Mutual Fund) at Age 65 — Total	Average Annual Compound Yield (before taxes)	Total Payments	Before Tax Gain
$20,000 Life-Paid-Up-at-65 Policy ($534/year)	$14,900	$9,880	$24,780	2.9%	$16,020	$8,760
20-Year Mortgage Term Policy ($107/year for 17 years) and 6% Savings Account ($427/year for 17 years and $534/year for 13 years)	0	2,600			16,020	
20-Year Mortgage Term Policy ($107/year for 17 years) and Mutual Fund Earning 10% ($427/year for 17 years and $534/year for 13 years)	0	2,600			16,020	

Fig. 15-3.
Comparison of two insurance policies, savings account, and mutual fund as investments

QUESTIONS

1. Which of the three alternatives should Chuck and Nancy select if they are willing to assume some investment risk? If they are fairly conservative about taking risks? If they dislike taking investment risk and also know that they cannot save money on their own?
2. Knowing what you do about the Andersons, which of the three alternatives do you think best suits them?
3. What balance sheet and income statement entries have Chuck and Nancy changed, and in what ways?
4. Is it possible to have a blend of two or more of the alternatives? How?
5. What are the income tax consequences of each alternative?
6. What amount of financial protection would Chuck have at year thirty under each of the three alternatives? Would the Andersons be likely to need any life insurance for their niece at that time?

16

STOCKS AND BONDS

"September. This is one of the peculiarly dangerous months to speculate in stocks. Others are October, November, December, January, February, March, April, May, June, July, and August." Sam Clemens was one of America's unluckiest investors, and his attitude is typical of many people today who either are afraid to invest in the stock market or have done so once or twice and lost money.

The key word in the quotation is *speculate*. Speculation is an extreme form of risk taking—investing in the face of total uncertainty. Those who buy stocks on "hot tips" or on chance discoveries by fly-by-night companies are more likely to agree with Sam Clemens than are those who take a businesslike approach to investing in the stock market.

You might imagine that only the professional invests in the stock market. This is simply not true. Of the more than thirty million Americans who own stock, half have annual incomes of less than $13,500.[1] Millions more own shares in mutual funds. If you had bought a broadly diversified portfolio of common stock in 1926, you would have realized a 9 percent average annual compound rate of return up to 1960.[2] This period includes the crash of 1929 and the depression years of the 1930s and excludes the boom years of the 1960s. During much of the 1960s the market would have yielded an average rate of return close to 15 percent. Of course, some stocks go up and down fairly

1. *New York Stock Exchange 1971 Fact Book* (New York: New York Stock Exchange, 1971), p. 47.

2. Lawrence Fisher and James H. Lorie, "Rates of Return on Investments in Common Stock," *Journal of Business* (Chicago: University of Chicago, July, 1968).

regularly, others are doomed to prolonged downtrends, and still others continue to grow year after year.

Bonds are a different sort of investment. For the long-term investor, this investment can seem more like a savings account. For the trader, short-term price fluctuations in bonds can be just as unpredictable as stocks. The yield on bonds is generally only two or three percentage points, at most, above savings accounts. This is less than the long-run potential of common stocks, but bonds do offer less risk than stocks.

Chapters 16 and 17 should enable you to distinguish among the various types of stocks and bonds and gain some insight into why their prices move as they do. In addition, these chapters will help you understand the basic concepts involved in stock market investments, thereby enabling you to avoid making bad investments because of ignorance. Much of what separates success from failure in the stock market is knowledge and cool-headedness. You, too, can invest successfully in the stock market, if you equip yourself with the proper tools.

OPPORTUNITIES IN THE SECURITIES MARKETS: A GENERAL CLASSIFICATION

There are several types of securities: common stock, preferred stock, bonds, convertible bonds, and convertible preferred stock. These types may be compared according to their potential for capital gain or loss, the income they provide, their right to corporate income, the voting rights an owner may be entitled to, and the order of their claims on corporate assets if a company is liquidated. Figure 16-1 shows how these types of securities compare on the basis of these characteristics. You may want to refer to this figure as we treat each type of security in more detail.

Stock	Div.	Sales (hds)	High
APE Ind	2.40	19	44¾
Acme Clev.	.80	26	33 –
Ala Gas.	.20b	7	16⅝
Am Nuts	2.60	868	42⅜
Am Not	1.2a	35	
APPL Corp.	.07		
Arni Bltz	2.10		
Are To	.17b		
Bar			

COMMON STOCK

Common stock represents an ownership interest in a corporation. If you own 10 percent of a corporation's stock, you own 10 percent of the corporation. Common stock is also the foundation of corporate finance. A corporation must have stockholders with a monetary interest in it before a bank will loan it money or it can sell bonds to the public.

From a Stockholder's Point of View

For the stockholder, a publicly traded common stock provides an opportunity to own part of a profit-making enterprise that may or may not yield current income through dividend payments. It also offers a chance for capital gains income through price appreciation of the stock.

corporate income All profits, after bond interest and preferred stock dividends, are used to benefit the holders of common stock in one way

Security	Right to Corporate Income	Voting Rights	Current Income	Capital Gain/Loss Potential	Priority of Claim to Assets (if company is liquidated)[a]
Common stock	Yes	Yes	Dividends although not guaranteed	Yes	3
Preferred stock	Only to limit of fixed dividend	Generally none	Dividends usually paid if company is profitable	Same as for bonds	2
Bonds	None	None	Interest assured as long as company remains financially sound	Only if interest rates change or company's credit rating changes	1
Convertible bonds	(Same as for bonds until converted to common stock by investor. Security is lower since convertible bonds are generally subordinated to other bonds in their priority of claim to assets.)				
Convertible preferred stock	(Same as for preferred stock until converted to common stock by investor)				

[a] The higher the rank (e.g., 1), the lower the degree of risk of a total loss.

Fig. 16-1.
Comparison of types of securities

or another. Any dividends paid out of such profits must go to them. Profits not paid out in dividends are normally reinvested in the company to foster its growth. The common stock owner benefits in both cases because he gets either the dividend income or, because of reinvestment, the prospect of greater income and security from a larger business. Common stocks with strong prospects of future earnings are usually of greater value to investors than stocks with poor prospects. The right to corporate income, current and/or future, is the only sound financial reason that investors should have for buying common stock.

control of the company Stockholders may vote to elect the board of directors. The number of votes each stockholder has is proportionate to the number of shares he owns. The board of directors, in turn, both makes the major policy decisions and selects the principal operating officers of the company. The stockholders elect the board of directors at the company's annual meeting. If a stockholder cannot attend the meeting, he may vote by using the proxy that is supplied with the announcement of the meeting's place, date, and time. In reality, the average shareholder has relatively insignificant voting strength compared to that of officers or founders who hold large blocks of the company's stock.

Two classes (A and B) of common stock are sometimes used by a corporation. When current stockholders need to raise money for expansion but do not wish to give up their voting control of the corporation, they can issue common stock that has no voting rights. Sometimes this second class of common stock will pay a higher dividend to compensate for the lack of voting privileges. Commonly, the class A stock is the nonvoting stock.

claim to corporate assets If the company is liquidated, holders of common stock will be paid after all debt obligations and preferred stock claims have been met.

From the Company's Point of View

For the company issuing a publicly traded common stock, the stock, initially provides funds for working capital, growth, acquisitions, or debt payments. It also provides an established valuation of the company for borrowing purposes, mergers, and the like.

An Example: ABZ Corporation

In order to show you how and why stocks are issued, how dividends and retained earnings are used by a company, and how stock is traded between investors, we will use the example of a fictitious company. The

ABZ Corporation was founded for the purpose of manufacturing small pleasure boats. Since the company needed one million dollars to set up a plant and begin producing and marketing boats, it issued 100,000 shares of stock at $10 each.

Several years later, the company became profitable and earned $100,000 after taxes. For each $10 share of stock in the company that an investor held, he had the right to $1 of the earnings ($100,000 ÷ 100,000 shares). Future earnings were projected to reach $3 or $4 a share in five to ten years. Because the company was still rapidly growing, however, it needed to retain its earnings in order to finance the expansion of its production facilities and its sales force. Therefore, the board of directors declared no dividends. The stockholders had to forego their possible $1 a share in exchange for the prospect of greater earnings in the future.

Soon the company was making more money, had brighter earnings prospects, and was basically financially sound. It gained the attention of other investors. Many of them wanted to buy stock in the company, but ABZ Corporation had no need to raise funds by issuing more stock at this time. Hence, others could buy stock only from the original investors, some of whom agreed to sell their shares for $15 more than they had paid because they wanted compensation for the loss of future dividends. They chose to take their income as a capital gain of $15 a share.

Over the next few years, the stock continued to be sold from one person to another at prices ranging from $18 to $46 a share, depending on the current price mutually agreed upon by buyers and sellers. The price was based on the company's earnings, its prospects, and the effect of those prospects on the attitudes of both buyers and sellers. Eventually the company was making $500,000 a year after taxes and did not need all of its earnings for expansion purposes. As a result, the board of directors declared a dividend of $200,000 for that year ($2 for each of the 100,000 shares). The directors decided to pay the dividend in cash payments of 50¢ per share each quarter.

Several years later, ABZ Corporation decided to expand its operations into the manufacture of travel trailers, water skis, and, eventually, snow skis. However, in order to do this, it needed considerably more financing than could be obtained by retaining earnings or borrowing money. Therefore, it decided to issue more stock. This time the company sold 100,000 more shares at $50 each and raised $5,000,000. The company could get more than $10 a share on this second stock offering because it had become an established enterprise. Many of the people who purchased this new stock were already stockholders in the company; others were buying ABZ stock for the first time. After that sale there were 200,000 shares of ABZ stock outstanding.

The company became more and more successful. Annual sales were up to $24 million. The price of the stock went up to around $80 a share. However, it was difficult to buy or sell the stock efficiently because there was no central place where buyers and sellers could meet to trade it. Instead, a broker searched by phone to match buyers and sellers. In addition, the price varied substantially from person to person.

In order to eliminate this problem, the ABZ Corporation worked to meet the requirements for membership on the American Stock Exchange (pp. 374, 375) and finally got its stock listed on that exchange. From then on, its price was regularly established at a central location according to the supply and demand generated by the sellers and buyers of ABZ stock. Anyone could buy stock in the ABZ Corporation and hope that it would continue to grow, earn more money each year, and eventually pay higher dividends. The company may never again issue new stock, but it should continue to be possible to buy ABZ stock from someone willing to sell his shares, provided the price is right.

The Concept of Total Return

When investing in common stocks, some investors look only at the dividend yield. Others ignore dividends and try to estimate how much the price of the stocks will go up. Such investors fail to consider the total return on the proposed investment: *both the dividend yield and the potential capital gains.*

The dividend yield on a common stock is expressed as a percentage computed by dividing the dollar amount of the annual dividend by the current market price. For example, if ABZ stock is paying a $2 annual dividend per share and the stock is selling for $100 per share, the current dividend yield is 2 percent. An investment in ABZ stock will yield 2 percent a year based on the current dividend alone.

Table 16-1 shows that yields have been declining over recent decades. However, this decline is not due to lower dividend payments. On the contrary, dividend dollar payments have increased, but stock prices have risen even more rapidly. Hence, the average dividend yield has declined.

The capital gain potential of a common stock is entirely different from its dividend yield and depends on many factors. Suppose that you purchased ten shares of ABZ stock for a total cost of $1040 including commissions ([$100 × 10 shares] + $40 commission). One year later you sold the stock for $119 a share, and the commission was $50. Your total proceeds from the sale were $1140 ([119 × 10] − $50). Your net capital gain was $100 ($1140 − $1040), or $10 a share. Therefore, on your original purchase price of $100 a share you made a $10 profit, or a 10 percent capital gain yield. Your total return on the ABZ stock investment would be 12 percent (2% dividend yield + 10% capital gains yield). If you had realized a 10 percent capital loss on the sale of the stock, your total return would have been a minus 8 percent (2% − 10%).

TABLE 16-1

MEDIAN DIVIDEND YIELD
ON ALL DIVIDEND-PAYING COMMON STOCKS
LISTED ON THE NEW YORK STOCK EXCHANGE (1946–1971)

Year	Median Dividend Yield (%)	Year	Median Dividend Yield (%)	Year	Median Dividend Yield (%)
1946	4.8	1956	5.2	1966	4.1
1947	6.3	1957	6.1	1967	3.2
1948	7.8	1958	4.1	1968	2.6
1949	7.0	1959	3.8	1969	3.6
1950	6.7	1960	4.2	1970	3.7
1951	6.5	1961	3.3	1971	3.2
1952	6.0	1962	3.8		
1953	6.3	1963	3.6		
1954	4.7	1964	3.3		
1955	4.6	1965	3.2		

SOURCE: *New York Stock Exchange 1972 Fact Book,* p. 25.

Some Terms You Should Understand

Comprehension of the following terms is essential if one is to fully understand the concepts involved in investing in the stock market: earnings per share, P/E ratio, par value, cash dividends, stock dividends, stock splits, book value.

earnings per share (EPS)   This is the mathematical result of dividing the total after-tax earnings of the company by its total number of shares outstanding (in the hands of investors). For example, if after several more years the ABZ Corporation earns $3,400,000 after taxes, and there are 1,000,000 shares of its stock outstanding, the earnings per share for that year are $3.40 ($3,400,000 ÷ 1,000,000). This figure is usually computed by the company when it issues its earnings reports.

P/E ratio (P/E multiple)   This is the ratio of the price of stock to its earnings per share. For example, if the ABZ stock that offers $3.40 in annual earnings per share sells for $34 a share, it has a P/E ratio of ten ($34 ÷ $3.40). The normal P/E range for the stocks in the Dow Jones averages (table 16-2, p. 347) is from about ten to twenty. However, high growth stocks such as Xerox may have a P/E ratio as high as forty to sixty, since investors expect the earnings per share to continue to grow at substantial rates in future years. For example, a stock selling for $100 might have current earnings of $2 a share for a P/E multiple of fifty. However, in a few years the stock might be earning $4 a share and that price of $100 would then be only twenty-five times earnings. (The phrase "twenty-five times earnings" means the same as "a P/E ratio of twenty-five.")

The P/E ratio is one of the key figures that an investor examines in determining the worth of a potential investment. A decline in price does not necessarily mean that a stock is a good buy. The earnings might have declined even more. It is the ratio of price to earnings that investors should analyze. For example, the price may drop from $30 to $20, but if the earnings have dropped from $3 a share to $1, the P/E ratio will actually have risen from ten to twenty!

par value In the past this term was used to signify the level below which a company would not offer its shares to the public. However, it was often misunderstood to be a continued minimum price level guaranteed by the company. Today, the figure is of no significance to the investor, and much of the new stock is simply issued on a no par (zero par value) or a low par (usually $2) basis.

cash dividends These are simply a distribution of the company's earnings to its stockholders, in cash. The board of directors usually declares dividends on a quarterly basis (although, in accordance with the company's fiscal year, the quarters may end in months other than March, June, September, and December). Also, if it has had an especially good year, a company may occasionally declare special or bonus dividends in addition to the regular dividend. Or it may simply raise the level of the regular dividend, if the board of directors expects the higher level of earnings to continue. The term *dividend yield* refers to cash dividend divided by current price.

stock dividends These represent the issue of new stock certificates, not cash, on a basis proportional to the number of shares each investor owns. For example, if the board of directors declares a 10 percent stock dividend, each stockholder will receive one free share of stock for every ten shares he holds at the time. If an investor owns an odd number of shares, he will usually have the option of paying the extra amount for a whole share or taking his partial dividend share in cash.

Many investors think that stock dividends represent an increase in the value of their holdings. In reality, even though there may be a temporary rise in the price of the stock because of a stock dividend, there is no permanent benefit from such a distribution because the price of all shares normally goes down by the amount of that dividend within a few days. For example, assume that you own ten shares of ABZ stock selling for $100 a share before a stock dividend and that the earnings per share are $5. After a 10 percent stock dividend you would own eleven

TABLE 16-2

Dow Jones Industrial Averages

Year	Price Index at Year End	Approximate P/E Ratio at Year End	Approximate Annual Cash Dividend Yield
1929	$248	12.5	4.9%
32	60	d[a]	7.7
37	121	10.5	7.3
38	155	25.8	3.1
39	150	16.5	4.0
1940	131	12.0	5.4
41	111	9.5	6.8
42	119	12.9	5.4
43	136	14.0	4.6
44	152	15.1	4.3
1945	193	18.3	3.5
46	177	13.0	4.2
47	181	9.6	5.1
48	177	7.7	5.9
49	200	8.5	5.9
1950	235	7.7	6.6
51	269	10.1	5.7
52	292	11.8	5.2
53	281	10.3	5.4
54	404	14.4	4.2
1955	488	13.7	3.8
56	499	15.0	4.0
57	436	12.1	4.7
58	584	20.9	3.3
59	679	19.8	2.9
1960	616	19.1	3.3
61	731	22.9	2.9
62	652	17.9	3.4
63	763	18.5	3.0
64	874	18.8	2.9
1965	969	18.1	2.9
66	786	13.6	3.8
67	905	16.8	3.3
68	941	16.3	3.3
69	800	14.0	4.2
1970	839	16.1	3.7
71	889	16.9	3.5

[a]d = deficit earnings for the year

Items in Computation	Before 10% Dividend	After 10% Dividend
Number of shares outstanding	1,000,000	1,100,000
ABZ Corp. after-tax profits	$5,000,000	$5,000,000
Earnings per share	$5	$4.55[a]
Normal average P/E ratio	20	20
P/E ratio times earnings per share	$100	$91[a]
Value of ten shares	$1000 (10 × $100)	$1000[a] (11 × $91)

Fig. 16-2.
Comparison of value
of stocks before and
after stock dividend

[a] Figures not exact because of rounding

shares. Figure 16-2 shows that both before and after the stock dividend you hold $1000 worth of ABZ stock. There is no gain for you. In essence, the same pie has merely been divided into more pieces.

It may seem that if the cash dividend rate is kept the same, you will receive an extra share's worth of dividends. For example, if the old stock paid a $2 dividend per share, you would have received $20 in dividends a year. If the dividend rate per share remains unchanged after the stock dividend, you will receive $22 a year on your eleven shares. But do not construe this as an effect of the stock dividend. In effect, the directors simply raised the cash dividend payout by 10 percent to each stockholder. The directors might just as well have raised the cash dividend on the old stock to $2.20 and not offered the 10 percent stock dividend.

stock splits   For the investor, these are essentially the same as stock dividends, except on a bigger scale. (There are technical differences between stock splits and stock dividends, but the discussion of these is more appropriate to a corporate finance text.) A 100 percent stock dividend, in which the investor receives one new share for each share held, is equivalent to a two-for-one stock split. In either case, the investor has twice as many shares as he had before the declaration. On such a split, the company will also usually split the cash dividend. For example, on a two-for-one split a dividend of 50¢ per share would become 25¢ per share.

Stock splits often have real value to the investor. The split may broaden the market by making more shares available and may also bring the price down into what is generally considered the popular trading range—

$30 to $60 a share. These changes can arouse greater investor interest in the stock and permanently improve the P/E ratio for that stock. Consequently, stock splits are generally anticipated with greater enthusiasm by investors than are stock dividends.

book value   This is the dollar value of a company's assets minus its liabilities. It is comparable to a person's net worth on his balance sheet. This valuation for a company is generally used only if its assets are to be sold and its debts paid off—in other words, if the company is to be liquidated.

The *book value per share* is the book value of the company divided by the number of shares outstanding. To the investor, the book value per share is seldom a relevant consideration. A company may have a high book value; but if it is making very little profit, it would have little value as an investment, unless it is likely to earn more in the future. There is almost never any relationship between book value and the market price of a common stock.

Investor's Classification of Common Stocks

Although it is difficult, if not misleading, to classify every stock, certain groups of stocks have characteristics that are useful to keep in mind when you are reviewing a particular stock for a proposed investment.

blue chip stocks   These are the stocks of large companies that have demonstrated consistent earnings. These companies usually also have long-term growth potential and are fairly stable because of their above-average size (generally $500 million or more in annual sales). Although such companies may demonstrate fairly consistent earnings growth, this growth is usually not spectacular by market standards. Blue chip stocks often have a fairly high P/E ratio because investors are willing to pay more for the greater degree of certainty associated with them. Classic examples of such stocks are General Electric, Sears Roebuck, DuPont, and General Foods.

growth stocks   These are the stocks of corporations that have experienced several consecutive years of above-average growth in earnings (10 percent a year or better) and are expected to continue to do so in the future. Growth companies usually have annual sales volumes ranging from $100 million to $500 million. Below that range, the company may be unstable and speculative. Above that range, the company may become too big to continue a rapid rate of growth (although IBM has been an exception). These stocks usually sell at high P/E multiples because investors are looking forward to higher expected earnings in the future, generally over the next three to five years. Because these corporations are

growing rapidly, their stocks offer a relatively low dividend. The companies usually pay out less than 25 percent of their earnings in dividends; the rest is retained for growth.

Growth stocks are often called "glamour stocks." During the 1960s most computer-related companies were glamour stocks. However, some of them never achieved the earnings expected. A glamour stock may not necessarily be a growth stock.

income stocks In order to be considered an income stock, the company offering the stock must achieve fairly consistent profits year after year and pay out a high portion of them in dividends—as much as 50 percent or more. Common dividend yields range from 3 to 7 percent, depending on such factors as the stability and growth potential of the company, as well as the yields available on alternative investments. To an investor, the P/E ratio of an income stock is less important than its dividend yield. Many utility and blue chip stocks are considered income stocks.

speculative stocks These stocks are priced more on expectations about the future than on past records. Companies represented by such stocks may have recently experienced a dramatic jump in earnings for some special reason, and investors hope that the rise will continue. The price of such a stock may fluctuate rapidly up and down as good and bad news about the company's prospects are received. During periods of good news the P/E multiple of these stocks may be 100 or even higher. Sometimes the P/E multiple is infinite since, mathematically, division of a positive number (price) by a negative number (EPS) produces a quotient of infinity. This may occur, for example, when an oil company that has been losing money suddenly strikes a new oil field. Investors would drive up the price of such a stock in speculation about the size of the field and the effect its discovery will have on the company's future earnings. However, investors have no assurance that the company will ever really achieve the anticipated level of profits.

cyclical stocks These follow the ups and downs of cycles such as the general business cycle, in which the up phases are called *expansions* and the down phases *recessions*. Companies whose earnings follow these cycles are commonly found in industry groups such as automobiles, steel, textiles, and heavy machinery. When the economy appears to be entering a recession, cyclical stocks tend to fall somewhat in price, and vice versa. Many investors invest in such stocks whenever they expect an upward movement in a cycle to occur. Since the stock price cycles, however, run in advance of the actual profits cycles, smart investors should look ahead six to twelve months to make a profit on cyclical stocks.

defensive stock (counter-cyclical) The price of these stocks resists general market declines. Two common groups of stocks have this capability: those with a high dividend yield (income stocks) and those whose profits are little affected by recessions. The former stocks would not decline very far in price before their dividend yield became so attractive that no one would sell his stock. For example, a $100 stock paying a $6 dividend is unlikely to drop to a price near $50 because the dividend yield would then go up to 12 percent. This drop would occur only if the company's profit prospects were falling or if inflation had caused the yield on other investments to rise to around 12 percent as well. The second group of defensive stocks includes companies such as food packers, grocery retailers, and utilities since people must continue to eat and use power even during recessions.

Factors Determining the Price of a Stock

The major determinant of the price of a common stock is the law of supply and demand. If there are more investors who wish to buy ABZ stock than there are stockholders who wish to sell it, the supply and demand for ABZ stock is out of balance. If such an imbalance occurs when the price of ABZ is $20 a share, for example, the price may have to rise to $25 before those who hold the stock can be induced to sell it. As the price goes higher, the number of people who wish to buy the stock decreases, and so, at some level, there is a temporary balance in the supply of and the demand for a stock. Of course, this point varies from day to day as the company's prospects for growth and profitability change and investors respond to these changes.

How do investors decide when $20 is a good buy or when $25 is too expensive? The fundamental reason for investing in common stock should be to obtain the right to corporate earnings. Therefore, many investors view the price of a stock in relation to its earnings per share, and the law of supply and demand often tends to revolve around a stock's P/E ratio and what investors think of that ratio. If they feel it is low, they will buy and drive it up, and vice versa. Many investors think in terms not only of current earnings per share, but also of forecasted level of future earnings (hence the high P/E multiple on fast growth stocks). If a company has no current earnings, there is no current P/E ratio and the price of stock is based on some expected future earnings.

A wide array of factors affect the P/E ratio. They are often divided into two classes: fundamental and technical. Fundamental factors basically affect the company and its earnings. Technical factors affect only the actual trading of the stock.

fundamental factors Investors who analyze fundamental factors generally first ask the question: "What is the current situation at the company, and what is the outlook for its sales and earnings per share (EPS)?" If the answer is "above-average growth in earnings," they will tend to project earnings per share and stock prices into future years and be willing to pay higher current P/E ratios to buy such stocks (fig. 16-3). If the company is growing more slowly but has very stable earnings year after year, they may be willing to pay a higher than average P/E ratio simply for the stability of such stocks (fig. 16-3). If the stock is cyclical, the P/E ratio is often based on average earnings over the long run. Hence, the prices of cyclical stocks tend to anticipate profit trends by six months or more and to vary less than do the earnings (fig. 16-3).

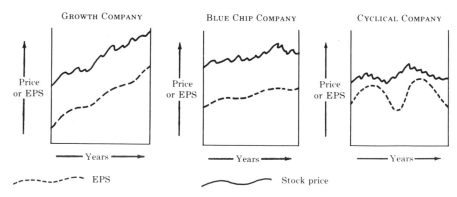

Fig. 16-3.
How type of company affects stock prices

Another factor that must be considered is the general business prospects for the industry in which the company is involved. The brighter the outlook for the industry, the more investors will be willing to pay in terms of P/E ratio. In fact, this effect often carries over to the stocks of companies (especially in the glamour industries) that have not yet themselves been able to cash in on a current industry boom. For example, during the 1960s the stock of companies involved in computers, anti-pollution equipment, or aerospace often sold for high P/E ratios, even though the company had yet to prove its management expertise or its ability to make a good profit. Conversely, if the industry outlook is gloomy, even a well-managed company's stock may be dragged down in price by a general negative reaction to the industry as a whole on the part of investors. The charts in figure 16-4 illustrate three different possible situations for companies with similar earnings characteristics.

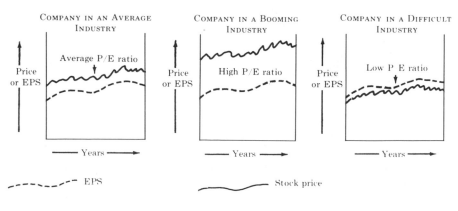

Fig. 16-4.
How business prospects for an industry affect stock prices within that industry

An especially significant factor that concerns slow growing, but stable, industries like utilities is the dividend yield. For example, although a company growing at 7 percent a year in earnings per share may not seem to be a particularly attractive investment, that growth rate becomes a potential 12 percent total return over the long run when a current 5 percent dividend yield is added to the average capital gains potential.

technical factors An analysis of technical factors takes into account prevailing market forces as evidenced by volume of shares traded, number of stocks that rose in price compared to those that declined, ratio of short sales to other sales, and many other statistics. Such technical items really belong in the realm of the professional market analyst or the expert stock trader. Their analysis involves too much time and expertise for the average investor. However, a brief discussion of the philosophy behind such analysis should help you both to understand the behavior of the stock market and to time the purchase and sale of your investments.

Investor psychology often plays an important role in temporarily overpricing or underpricing a stock. For example, when ABZ Corporation decided to enter the mobile home business, it attracted far more investors than before. As people began to buy in and the stock began rising, people became more and more enthusiastic about buying the stock. Temporarily, this enthusiasm drove the price and the P/E ratio well above any foreseeable trend in earnings per share. As enthusiasm reached a fever pitch, the more sophisticated and cool-headed investors began to take their profits; the resultant selling eventually outweighed the buying and the price began to retreat to a more reasonable level. Just the opposite effect often occurs near the bottom of a long price decline. Some smart investors invest in basically sound companies that are currently overly depressed, hoping to double or triple their investments when the company's profits go up again. Figure 16-5 illustrates how psychological overreactions typically result in unreasonably wide price swings for a stock.

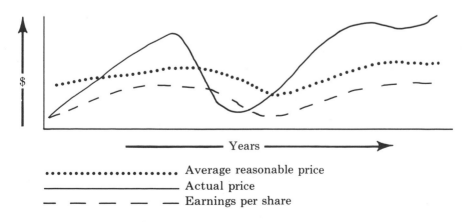

Fig. 16-5.
How investor
reactions affect stock
prices

The general market trend also affects the price of a stock. When sell orders exceed buy orders for the market as a whole, prices drop. If investor disenchantment or lack of enthusiasm continues, we have a declining market—a bear market. In such a psychological environment, only a few stocks can sustain uptrends in price, but strong stocks will drop less than weak stocks. The same kinds of overall price trends can be found in up markets (bull markets) as well. A more complete discussion of bull and bear markets is to be found in the next chapter.

How Appropriate Is a Common Stock for You?

There are several advantages and disadvantages in investing in common stocks. If you first acquire the knowledge and skills discussed in both this chapter and the following one, you should know exactly what benefits you might expect, as well as what problems you might encounter, before you decide whether to invest in the stock market at all or how much to invest.

advantages   Common stocks offer a high potential total return on your investment. You might expect an average annual rate of return of around 10 percent, if past trends continue. Common stocks also offer the chance for unusually big gains. For example, if you had bought IBM or Johnson and Johnson stock twelve years ago, you could have increased your investment 10 times. If you had bought Xerox, it would have returned you 100 times your invested dollars! Another advantage is that they offer a hedge against inflation. In the two decades ending December, 1971, for example, the average price of all stocks on the New York Stock Exchange rose about 280 percent, while the consumer price index rose only about 42 percent. Similarly, the average dividend paid by the blue chip stocks used in computing the Dow Jones averages has risen by over 100 percent.

There are also tax advantages to investing in common stocks. If you realize a capital gain on the sale of a stock that you have held for more than six months, your income on that gain is taxed at one-half of your regular tax rate, up to a limit of 25 percent of the amount of your capital gain. (Capital gains that exceed $50,000 in one year may be taxed as high as 35 percent, and short-term capital gains are taxed at regular rates.) Also, the first $100 ($200 on a joint return if the stock is jointly owned) of dividends can be received tax-free. One of the important reasons why Congress has put such tax advantages into law is to induce people to invest in corporations, thereby providing the capital needed for a fast growing economy for both wage earner and investor.

disadvantages   In exchange for the higher potential return offered by common stocks, you must accept a greater degree of risk and, in exchange for the chance for really big gains, there is also the chance for really big losses. The stock market often goes through significant periods of general price declines, as, for example, when the outlook for the economy changed in early 1969 and 1970. Stock prices fell in amounts ranging from 25 to 50 percent, depending on the type of stock. (Incidentally, that declining market was the worst since the crashes of 1929 and 1937.) If, for example, you had bought stock in Brunswick Corporation at its high of $74 in 1961 and held it, you would have held a stock worth as little as $6 a share in 1966. It has since risen well above that low point, though it is nowhere near $74. For another example, Memorex Corporation stock dropped 70 percent during a period of a few months in 1970.

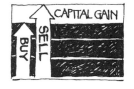

Common stocks offer a lower current income than might be obtained with other investments. Although some slower growing stocks offer a dividend yield of 6 or 7 percent, the average stock with growth potential has a dividend yield ranging from 0 to 4 percent. Therefore, the common stock investor usually sacrifices current dividend income for the prospect of longer term capital gains income.

Common stock investments require the constant attention of the investor. He must keep abreast of general business news, as well as specific news about companies whose stock he owns or plans to own. He must watch over his portfolio either to avoid big losses through price erosion or to take his gains after the stock has appreciated. Of course, if your account is big enough, you can get your broker or an investment adviser to take care of much of it and make decisions for you. However, hiring a professional does not ensure any better results than those you might obtain on your own. Not all professionals can necessarily make better investment decisions than an individual investor would make.

Stock market investing requires a certain amount of experience and expertise before you can expect that, more often than not, your investments will be successful. However, this does not mean that you must begin investing before you really know how. You can do considerable research and simulated investing on paper before you actually begin to invest. Even then, there is much that you will never learn until you have actually been investing for several years.

What Is the Right Price?

Stock market investing involves personal judgment. Whenever you buy or sell a stock, there is always someone on the other side of the transaction who feels differently about that stock! Always be sure, however, that you are investing in stocks for the right to corporate income and for no other reason. For example, consider a company whose earnings per share are growing at the rapid rate of 20 percent a year. If the current EPS is 50¢, it is difficult to justify paying $100 for this growth stock

since, at that rate, the projected EPS for three years from now is only 85¢. You would still be paying over 100 times future earnings for this high growth stock!

If you follow the precept of getting value for your investment, you will minimize your chances of behaving like the typical small investor whose enthusiasm causes him to buy when stocks are high and whose depression causes him to sell when stocks are low. This is no way to make money in the stock market. One rational approach to getting value for your investment in the stock market is to determine the right price for a given stock. To do this, compute the average P/E ratio for that stock (or for its industry group) over the past five or ten years. This method results in an average right price for the stock over a period of time—provided that there has been no change in the fundamental character of the company during that time.

You should also determine the typical high and low ends of the P/E ratio range over the past decade so that you can plan to buy the stock at below-average prices (within, say, 25 percent of the low end of the P/E ratio range) and sell the stock at above-average prices provided that the long-term fundamental outlook for the corporation's profits remains good. Such buying and selling opportunities occur for most stocks every two to five years. Such a strategy will definitely minimize your chances of losing amounts like those lost by many investors in the bear market crash of 1969–70. Instead, you should significantly increase your chances of making a profit over the long term.

Many other methods of securities management have been successfully applied. Further guidelines on investing in the stock market will be discussed in the next chapter.

PREFERRED STOCK

Like common stock, preferred stock represents an ownership interest in a corporation, but to a different degree. Holders of preferred stock do not generally participate in the profit growth of a company but do receive a high fixed dividend yield. Because preferred stock offers high cash dividends that must be paid out of after-tax profits, they are a more expensive way for a company to raise capital than either common stock or corporate bonds. Therefore, little new preferred stock is issued anymore. Quite a few old issues, however, are still being traded.

If you are considering buying a preferred stock, you should also look into preferred stock mutual funds (pp. 409, 412). These funds offer the same advantages without the accompanying risk of picking a bad stock.

Fixed Dividend Payment

Preferred stock offers a fixed dollar income (dividend) that must be paid before dividends can be paid on common stock, but only after the interest has been paid on outstanding bonds. Preferred stock dividends may be paid only if there are earnings, but interest on bonds must be paid in any case.

The fixed dividend may be a disadvantage for the owner of preferred stock. The value of your investment depends on current interest rates. If general interest rates are rising, the price of preferred stock will fall in order to keep the dividend yield in line with other interest rates available to investors. Conversely, if interest rates are falling, the price of preferred stock will go up. For example, if you hold a preferred stock that is worth $100 and pays a $5 dividend and comparable interest rates fall to 4 percent, the price of the stock may go up to $125.

Some companies issue two classes of preferred stock: *first preferred* and *second preferred*. Dividends are paid on the former before they are paid on the latter. In exchange for this preference, the dividend rate on first preferred may be somewhat lower than on second preferred.

A preferred stock may or may not have a *cumulative dividend* provision, which assures the stockholder that all dividends will be paid. A company that offers this provision and has no profits for a few years will keep track of the missed dividends and try to pay them off as soon as it regains profitability. However, some companies get so far behind in their dividends that they must negotiate a smaller settlement with their preferred stockholders.

If a preferred stock has a participating provision, or *bonus dividend,* the holders may receive a percentage of corporate earnings over a certain amount. This changes the stock into a hybrid composed of preferred and common stock.

Prior Claim to Corporate Assets

If a company goes bankrupt or is liquidated, the preferred stockholders must receive the full value of their shares before money can be paid to the holders of common stock. Of course, all corporate debts, including bonds, must be paid off before even the holders of preferred stock get any money. This feature may make preferred stock a more secure investment than common stock.

No Voting Rights

Preferred stocks generally offer no voting rights, except in specific situations. For example, a preferred stock may allow its holders to vote if the dividend goes unpaid for a certain number of years.

Call Feature

A preferred stock may or may not have a call feature whereby the company reserves the right to buy back outstanding preferred stock at its original issue price plus a premium of, say, 5 percent. A company will want to do this if it thinks it can issue a new preferred stock with a lower dividend rate or sell bonds at a lower rate of interest.

BONDS (LONG-TERM DEBT)

Bonds may be issued by corporations or by federal, state, or local governments to raise capital for various investment purposes.

Corporate Bonds

Bonds are an important source of long-term debt financing for corporations since banks generally do not like to loan money for longer than a few years. Corporate bonds usually have maturities ranging from twenty to thirty years although some are as short as five years. They offer a fixed dollar amount of interest and pay back the principal on the maturity date. They are usually issued in face amounts of $1000 each, but bond prices are quoted in terms of percentage of face value. A quote of 87, for example, means that the bond is selling for $870.

types of corporate bonds   The *mortgage bond* is generally the most secure type of bond because it has specific real estate assets (i.e., buildings) pledged as collateral. The *collateral trust bond* is similar to the mortgage bond except that it is secured by collateral other than real estate (i.e., common stock in other corporations, promissory notes, or accounts receivable). A *debenture* (ordinary bond) is a promissory note. The corporation simply promises to pay off its debt and, if it does not, the debenture holder has a right to all assets not pledged to mortgage or collateral trust bonds. A *subordinated debenture* is also a promissory note, but it has relatively low security (unless the corporation is financially strong) since holders of such bonds can claim assets only after other creditors and bonds and bank debts have been paid off. Generally, the security of a bond is indicated by its financial rating according to either Standard and Poor's or Moody's. The lower the degree of security, the higher the bond's interest yield.

fixed interest payment   By law, interest must be paid on all corporate bonds except income bonds whether or not a profit is made. On an *income bond* interest is paid only if the company earns sufficient profits to pay all, or part of, the interest due. Some of the older bonds are coupon bonds, which require the bond holder to clip off a coupon and send it to the company in order to collect his interest. There is potential for capital gains on bonds only if general interest rates decline, if the company's financial rating improves, or if you purchase a high quality bond that sells for less than face value, but is within a few years of maturity.

factors affecting bond prices The prices of corporate bonds change from day to day just as stock prices do. *As general interest rates in the economy rise, the market prices of bonds decline, and vice versa.* This is because the dollar payout is fixed for the life of the bond. For example, if a thirty-year maturity, $1000 corporate bond is purchased for $1000 and bears a stated interest of 6 percent, the company will pay the holder $60 in interest every year. If general money market interest rates rise to 9 percent for comparable debt issues, the market price of the bond will drop to about $667 ($60 ÷ 9% = $667). However, if you hold the bond to maturity, you will collect the original $1000 you invested, and in the meantime you will receive 6 percent a year. (Preferred stocks do not have this certainty of future redemption value, since they have no redemption date but may remain outstanding indefinitely.) Conversely, if interest rates fall, the price of the bond will rise, and you may wish to sell it through the bond market and take your profit in capital gains, rather than take the $60 a year. In these ways, investing in long-term bonds can be something like investing in the stock market.

Several factors affect bond prices relative to other bonds. The investment quality (or credit rating of the company) is very important. Standard and Poor's and Moody's publish bond ratings (fig. 16-6) based on the chances that companies will not be able to repay amounts borrowed on bonds (risk of default). The higher the rating, the greater the safety. The lower the investment quality, of course, the higher must be the yield on the bond to justify the assumption of greater risk by investors. An investor may have to wait twenty years to redeem a bond at maturity and, by then, a weak company may have gone out of business. The closer the bond is to its maturity date, the smaller will be the difference between

Meaning of Rating	Moody's	Standard and Poor's	
Investment quality	Aaa	AAA	
	Aa	AA	
	A	A	
	Baa	BBB	
		BB	
Speculative	Ba	B	
	B	CCC	
	Caa	CC	
	Ca	C	
Already in default	C	DDD	(Depends on
		DD	prospects for
		D	cash return
			on liquidation)

Fig. 16-6.
Bond ratings

the market price and the face (redemption) value of the bond. (Face value is also called *par value,* a term that should not be confused with the par value of stocks.)

If there is a *call feature* (usually five years and occasionally ten years from date of issue), the bond will offer a higher effective interest rate. A call feature allows the company to repurchase the bond at a set price after a specific date in the future. Because investors, via the call feature, may find their bonds called in before maturity, they often demand a slightly higher yield, the closer the call date is to the present. In fact, the very presence of a call price can keep the market price from going above that point even if interest rates drop, since there is the possibility that the company may call the bond for redemption at that price.

determining the effective yield on bonds   Although you can ask your broker to use his rate computation charts to compute a bond yield for you, it is useful to understand the procedure yourself. If a bond is selling at par, or maturity value (usually $1000), the effective yield is simply the annual interest yield. For example, on a bond selling for $1000 (quoted at 100) and paying $60 interest a year, the effective yield to maturity is 6 percent.

Bonds selling at a discount from par value require a three-step procedure for computing their yield. Let us take a hypothetical example of an ABZ bond selling for $900 (quoted at 90), paying $45 annual interest, and maturing in four years. (At maturity, the company will redeem the bond for the full $1000.)

1. Compute the effective current interest yield by dividing the annual interest by the current price.

$$\frac{\$45}{\$900} = 5\% \text{ effective interest yield}$$

2. Compute the effective capital gains yield by dividing the maturity value by the current price to get a factor that will be used in conjunction with compound interest table A.

$$\frac{\$1000}{\$900} = 1.11$$

Since the $900 is a lump-sum investment, compound interest table A can be used to find the percentage equivalent of the factor 1.11 for four years. This percentage equivalent, or the effective capital gains yield, is approximately 2.75 percent.

3. Add the results of steps 1 and 2. The total effective rate of return for this ABZ bond is 7.75 percent. This yield is slightly better than

a 7.75 percent savings account (if one were available) after tax since one-half of the $100 capital gain is tax-free. Of course, the risk is slightly higher; but bonds rated A, Aa, or Aaa have never gone bankrupt while holding those ratings.

advantages and disadvantages of corporate bonds   For the investor who has a financial goal he must achieve over the next three or four years or who is conservative but wants higher yields than those offered by savings accounts, corporate bonds may be the answer. There are four major advantages investors seek when buying corporate bonds: diversification of a common stock portfolio (spreading of risk); guaranteed return of principal if held to maturity; assured income through fixed interest payments; security, especially if the bond is issued by a substantial company; and low cost of purchase (the standard broker's fee is $2.50 per $1000 bond).

There are two disadvantages to keep in mind before you decide to invest in bonds. First, small changes in interest rates can produce large fluctuations in the value of your principal, especially on bonds with maturities ten to twenty years away. Second, bonds are not a hedge against inflation, since inflation causes all costs to rise, including interest rates (at least temporarily), thus forcing bond prices down. Besides, the face value of bonds cannot grow with inflation.

U.S. Government Securities

The United States government finances much of the federal debt, as well as its working capital needs, through the issue of Treasury bills, notes, and bonds. (Treasury bonds are different from U.S. savings bonds.) These securities are similar to corporate bonds, except that interest is paid by selling them at a discount from face value; no actual interest payments are made. As with Series E savings bonds, this discount produces an interest yield when the bond is held to maturity, at which time the government redeems it at face value. New issues of bonds are sold weekly to the highest bidder. These bidders are individuals and investment houses, who may or may not resell them on the open market to other investors. Figure 16-7 shows the basic differences in maturities and minimum face amounts for the three types of securities.

Type of Government Security	Maturity	Minimum Face Amount
Treasury bills	3 to 6 months	$10,000 (sometimes $1000)
Treasury notes	1 to 5 years	$1000
Treasury bonds	More than 5 years	$1000

Fig. 16-7.
Basic features of U.S. government securities

The market price of these securities varies, of course, with general market conditions, just as the market price on corporate bonds does. The closer the securities are to maturity, the closer the market price is to its redemption value. Also, the shorter the maturity at issue, the more the interest yield tends to vary according to current interest rate conditions. The primary advantage of federal securities is their safety. However, they also offer the lowest current yields available on bond-type investments.

Municipal Bonds

State and municipal governments and special districts such as school or irrigation districts issue bonds to help finance their operations. These may be bought at a discount and accrue interest, or they may be bought at face value and pay interest. The primary advantage of municipal bonds is that the interest is exempt from federal income taxes. They may also be exempt from state income taxes in the state in which they are issued. They are generally more appropriate than corporate bonds for investors in the 35 percent tax bracket and up. For example, to a married couple reporting $24,000 to $28,000 taxable income (36 percent tax bracket), a 5 percent municipal is as desirable as a corporate bond offering a 7.6 percent interest yield. Although municipal bond interest is tax-free, capital gains on the sale of a bond are taxable.

Invest only in *general obligation bonds* that are rated A or better by Moody's or Standard and Poor's. Such bonds are backed by the full faith, credit, and unlimited taxing power of a financially sound municipality, county, or state. *Revenue bonds* have limited taxing ability (e.g., tolls from toll roads) and do not offer the safety of general obligation bonds.

We recommend state bonds over city bonds. In the depression of the 30s, only one state (Arkansas) defaulted on its bonds, while over 4500 local governments failed to meet their obligations. Most of these defaults did not involve major cities. If you are a resident of a state that has income taxes you should buy only bonds issued by your state or one of its governmental subdivisions. In this way, you avoid paying both federal income taxes and state income taxes on the bonds. Otherwise, you must pay your state's income tax on out-of-state bonds.

Since marketability of some bonds is a problem and therefore reduces liquidity, we recommend buying only well known, actively traded issues.

Guidelines for Investing in Bonds

Investors in high tax brackets who are seeking tax advantages should consider municipal bonds, since their interest is tax-free. Investors in more moderate tax brackets who want maximum marketability should consider U.S. government bonds or major corporate bonds. Although U.S.

government bonds, bills, and notes offer the lowest risk, they also offer the lowest yields.

You should always buy corporate bonds issued by stable companies rather than assume a greater risk on your investment just to obtain a slightly higher interest payment. Bank trust departments usually stick to bonds rated Baa (Moody's), BBB (Standard and Poor's), or better to assure quality.

If you want to avoid extreme price fluctuations in your corporate bond investments, restrict yourself to bonds with a maturity of five years or less. If you get longer term bonds, try to get them with call protection in order to assure that high yield for as long as possible. Everything else being equal, you should select the bond offering the highest current yield (although the differences may not be very large).

You should shop around for brokerage houses offering the lowest commissions on bond transactions. Some houses charge significantly higher fees than others for buying and selling bonds.

CONVERTIBLE BONDS AND CONVERTIBLE PREFERRED STOCKS

Convertible securities allow the investor to convert his holdings into a fixed number of shares of common stock. Such investments offer the investor some of the security of a preferred stock or a bond and some of the capital gains potential of common stock. However, in exchange for these features, there is usually a lower dividend or interest rate.

Nearly all convertibles have a call feature, which gives the company the right to redeem the securities on or after a stated date in exchange for a stated amount in cash, usually a few points above the issue price. The company would want to exercise this feature and force conversion to reduce the amount of money they have to pay in interest. The possibility of a call increases as the price of the common stock rises above the conversion price.

Convertible bonds are like regular bonds, except for the conversion feature. Therefore, convertible bond prices tend to be related more to the price of the common stock than to the interest yield.

The number of convertible preferred stock issues has more than doubled in the past few years since they offer the chance for corporations who have reached their debt capacity limit to get more financing through lower-than-normal-cost preferred stock. Assume that you have bought convertible preferred that pays a $4 dividend and may be converted into ten shares of the company's common stock at any time. The common stock is currently selling for $8 a share. If the price of the common goes to $12, the price of your preferred will go to $120 and you can make the conversion at no loss to you. If the price of the common stock falls to $5 a share, the price of the preferred may not drop to $50 a share unless comparable preferred stocks are also yielding 8 percent ($4 ÷ $50).

Convertible securities may sound like they offer the best of both worlds. However, you should ask yourself two questions when considering such investments. First, how sound is the issuing corporation? This consideration is just as important for investors in convertibles as it is for investors in straight bonds and preferreds. Second, what are the prospects for the common stock? Since you would probably consider buying a convertible for its appreciation prospects, this is a very important question. Why buy the convertible bond of a company whose earnings outlook is poor? If the prospects for the common stock are very good, you may pay a large speculative premium for the conversion privilege. That is, the price of the bond may be 20 or 30 percent higher than the total current price of the number of converted shares. In such a case you may be better off investing in the common stock only.

CONCLUSION

There are three basic types of investments you can make in the securities markets: you can buy common stock, preferred stock, or bonds. You can also sometimes purchase convertible bonds and convertible preferred stock, which you may subsequently convert into a fixed number of shares of common stock.

The basic reason for investing in common stock is to obtain the right to corporate income. The more money the company earns, the more income you receive from your common stock investment as dividends or capital gains. The price of the common stock depends to a great degree upon the earnings history and earnings prospects of the company. Therefore, the price-to-earnings ratio (P/E ratio) is commonly used by investors to determine whether a stock is over-priced or under-priced.

Some important advantages of investing in common stocks include possible above-average return on investments, long-term hedge against inflation, and capital gains taxes at one-half the ordinary income tax rate. Major disadvantages are possible above-average loss on your investment and the amount of investment management required.

Most investors classify common stocks into the following categories: blue chip, growth, income, speculative, cyclical, and defensive. The type of stock in which you invest depends on your investment objectives. You should understand the differences between the various classifications, and know how to identify the type of stock investment you wish to make.

Bonds have fixed interest rates. They can be of value to the investor who is very safety conscious or has a very important goal to achieve in the next few years and does not want to lose money. To minimize price fluctuations due to interest rate changes, the investor should consider bonds that mature in five years or less.

blue chip

book value

bond

call feature

class "A" and "B" stock

common stock

convertible bond

convertible preferred stock

coupon bond

debenture

dividend (cash)

dividend yield

earnings per share (EPS)

growth stock

municipal bond

par value (of a bond)

par value (of a stock)

P/E ratio

preferred stock

proxy

stock dividend

stock split

subordinated debenture

Treasury bond

1. What is the most important right held by the average common stock investor?
2. What is the primary reason why corporations issue common stock?
3. Explain the difference between a cash dividend, a stock dividend, and a stock split. Which is most attractive to an investor?
4. ABZ common stock is selling for $90 per share. The cash dividend is $1.80. The EPS are $4 for the most recent twelve-month period and are projected to be $4.50 for the next twelve months. The par value is $10; the book value is $45. There are 2,000,000 shares outstanding.
   a) What is the current P/E ratio on ABZ common?
   b) How many dollars after taxes is the company expected to earn next year?
   c) What is the current dividend yield?
   d) If ABZ stock were split 3 for 1, what would be the current EPS?
   e) At first glance, would you call this an income stock or a growth stock?
5. Assume that you purchased ten shares of XYZ common stock for $100 a share, held it for one year, and then sold it at $108. During that year you received $26 in cash dividends and a 10 percent stock dividend. Your commissions for both buying and selling totaled $25. What is your total percentage rate of return before taxes for the year?
6. What is the difference between a blue chip stock whose EPS is growing at an average of 10 percent a year and ABZ Corporation stock, whose earnings are growing at a similar rate?
7. Why should an investor analyze both the fundamental outlook for a company and its P/E ratio before buying or selling a common stock?
8. When are corporate bonds an appropriate investment?
9. The QQZ Corporation bond (Aa rated) is selling for $850 and matures in five years. The annual interest payment is $30. What is the total average yield to maturity?

The case at the end of chapter 17 is intended to cover the concepts in both chapters 16 and 17.

RECOMMENDED READING

Please see listing at the end of chapter 17.

CHUCK AND NANCY ANDERSON

USING LONG-TERM STOCK CHARTS

Chuck and Nancy want you to help them select the best two stocks out of six through which they might reach their goal of buying a motorboat fourteen years from now. (Keep in mind Chuck's moderately aggressive, growth-oriented stance regarding stocks.) Use the long-term charts of common stock prices and earnings trends on pages 366–67 to answer the questions before coming to your conclusions.

The long-term stock charts are constructed on a logarithmic grid, and so a percentage change at a low price shows up the same size as an equal percentage change at a high price. Also, whenever the price and EPS lines are at the same point, the P/E ratio is 16. When the price is above the EPS, the P/E ratio is greater than 16, and vice versa. As a result, you can visualize from these charts the changes in P/E ratio values over the past decade. Of course, these changes may be due to a variety of factors such as overall market conditions and fundamental outlook for the company.

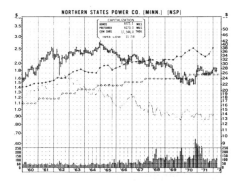

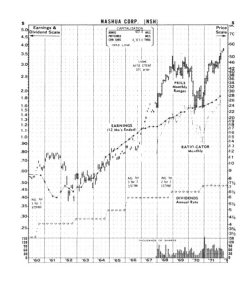

SOURCE: Securities Research, *3-Trend Cycli-Graphs*, March ed. (Boston: Securities Research, 1972). This book may be available at a broker's office or a library, or it may be subscribed to (Securities Research Company, 208 Newbury Street, Boston, Massachusetts 02116) for $27 a year (quarterly editions).

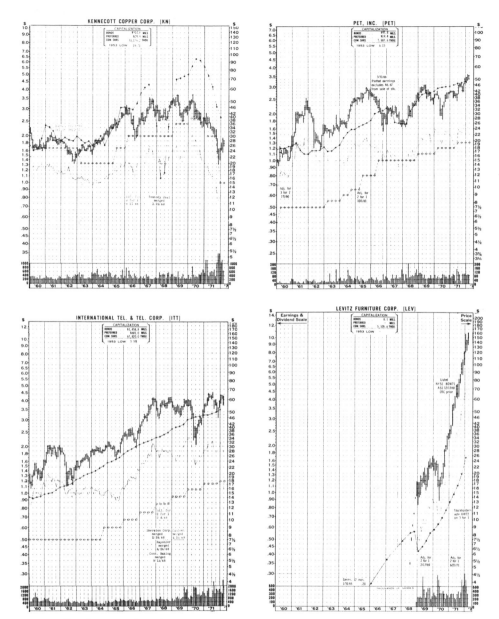

Earnings per share for most recent twelve months. (Read values from left-hand scale.) For example, IT&T's earnings at the end of 1971 were approximately $3.50 per share.

Dividend rate per share for most recent twelve months. (Read values from left-hand scale.) For example, IT&T's dividends per share beginning in 1972 were $1.20.

Monthly price range per share of stock. The cross bar on each vertical range bar indicates closing price for the month. (Read values from right-hand scale.) For example, IT&T's price range for March, 1972 was $63 (high), $55 (low), and $57 (close).

QUESTIONS

1. Which stock, on the basis of past performance, seems to offer a small potential gain and a high degree of risk?
2. Which stock has a short but impressive earnings history and seems likely to make investors enthusiastic about its future?
3. Which stock warrants further study of industry and corporate prospects because it seems underpriced and the recent earnings trend looks uncertain?
4. General interest rates have risen significantly since 1965 because of inflation. The price of which stock appears to be related more to interest rates than to the stock's past P/E ratios? What is the current dividend yield on this stock?
5. Which two stocks appear to be reasonably priced growth stocks?
6. Now that you have made a superficial screening of these stocks, which two or three do you believe to be appropriate for Chuck and Nancy? Why?

17

BUYING AND SELLING STOCKS AND BONDS

Now that you understand common stock, preferred stock, and bonds, you are about half-way to understanding the fundamentals of stock market investing. You must still learn how to buy and sell these securities on the various markets. You will need to be able to use stock price tables and market averages both to help you decide on an investment before you make it and to follow its progress afterwards. You will also need to know what to look for when choosing a stockbroker.

SECURITIES MARKETS

As you recall from the ABZ Corporation example (pp. 342–44), common stocks are first sold by the company to the public. After this initial sale, the stocks are sold back and forth among investors. The original sale by the company involves the use of primary markets to distribute the shares to the investor public. The second type of sale, stock trading among investors, involves the use of secondary markets. Secondary markets include organized exchanges as well as over-the-counter markets. Figure 17-1 (p. 370) shows how stocks or bonds move in each of these types of markets.

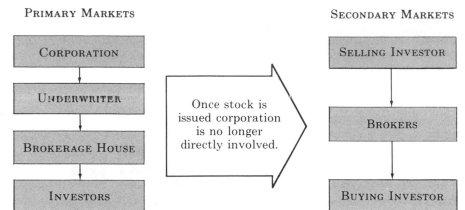

PRIMARY MARKETS   SECONDARY MARKETS

CORPORATION   SELLING INVESTOR

UNDERWRITER   Once stock is issued corporation is no longer directly involved.   BROKERS

BROKERAGE HOUSE

INVESTORS   BUYING INVESTOR

Fig. 17–1.
Flow of stocks and bonds on primary and secondary markets

Primary Markets

Investment bankers handle all the transactions of the primary markets. They may work for stock brokerage houses that deal with the public or for organizations that specialize in investment banking. Investment banking primarily involves raising money for corporations. This task is called *underwriting.*

To demonstrate how underwriting works, let us return to the example of the ABZ Corporation. Assume that the company did not have the time and contacts required to sell the 100,000 shares in the initial offering. Therefore, they engaged Funstun Brothers & Query, an investment banking house in New York City, to handle this task. One of the first things to be done was to establish the price per share at which the stock would be offered to the public. In the judgment of Reginald I. Query, the appropriate price would be $10 per share. Next, the company and the investment bankers had to agree on a discounted price that would determine the net proceeds per share to the company, i.e., the price the investment banker would pay ABZ Corporation for each share of stock. Generally, the greater the risk that the underwriters will not be able to sell all of the issue, the larger the discount they want. Funston Brothers & Query arrived at a discounted price of $8.50 for the ABZ stock.

Once the price was decided, the investment banking house purchased the 100,000 shares from the ABZ Corporation for $850,000. The investment banker then made a public announcement in the various financial journals that the primary offering of 100,000 shares of ABZ Corporation common stock at $10 per share would occur on a certain date. Assuming all 100,000 shares are sold at $10 each, the proceeds to Funstun Brothers & Query would be $150,000 ($1,000,000 − $850,000).

The procedure by which these shares are sold to the public involves several sales levels. Funstun Brothers & Query sell portions of the stock to many different brokerage houses, usually at a discount. (For example, the other brokerage houses may pay $9.50 a share to Funstun Brothers & Query and keep the 50¢ difference as their commission for selling the stock to the public. If Funstun farms out all of the ABZ stock, it would keep only $100,000 as its underwriting fee—$950,000 − $850,000.) The brokerage houses then distribute the shares to their various branches. Thus, each branch has only a few hundred or a few thousand shares to sell. Prior to the day when shares go on sale, the brokers at the branch offices contact some of their preferred customers (those who have large accounts). If any shares are left after these first contacts, the general public may buy them on a first-come, first-served basis. However, as a general rule, if the preferred investors do not buy all of a primary offering, it probably is not a good investment.

Ideally, before buying, everyone should examine the prospectus that must be issued by the company in accordance with government regulations. This publication describes the characteristics of the stock and the company. Often, all the stock is committed for sale by the time the first sale day arrives. If you wait until then you will probably find the stock sold out if it is a good investment, and you will have to buy it at the current market price, plus commissions, on the secondary markets. Investors buying stock on the primary markets pay no cash commission, although there is $1.50 per share commission in the ABZ example, buried in the several layers of underwriter's and broker's fees.

rights The bylaws of some companies require that any new offerings of common stocks (or bonds) be first offered to existing shareholders. They are considered to have a preemptive right to maintain their proportionate ownership in the company if they so desire. Let us return to the example of the ABZ Corporation in which each of 100 stockholders initially held 1000 shares. Each man held 1 percent of the company. If the company wished to issue 10,000 new shares, it could have issued stock purchase rights to the existing shareholders at the rate of one right for each ten shares of stock already owned. That is, each right would allow a stockholder to purchase one share of the new issue. If a stockholder exercised his option and purchased his 100 shares, he would own 1100 shares of stock, exactly 1 percent of the 110,000 shares outstanding, the same proportion of the company that he owned before the second issue.

A right is issued as a certificate to the stockholder; it has the number of shares he is allowed to purchase printed on it, along with the date by which he must exercise his right (usually about a month from the date of issue). If the stockholder does not wish to purchase the extra stock (or does not have the money to do so), he may sell the right to someone else. These rights are traded on the same stock exchange as the parent company's stock and are valued at the price spread between the regular stock and the new issue stock. For example, if ABZ stock sold for $10 a share, and the new issue was set at $9 a share, the price spread would be $1. The rights would be traded at $1 each. When the term of the rights expires, any unsold shares are sold to the general public, still at the issue price of $9. However, the chances of acquiring these few remaining $9 shares are very slim.

Companies increasingly try to avoid having rights offerings because of the expense involved and because such an offering tends to limit the breadth of stockholder ownership. Some states, however, require that corporations chartered in them use rights offerings for all new issues.

warrants   Warrants are functionally the same as rights to the investor trading in them. A warrant gives you the right to purchase a specified number of shares of a stock at a specified price within a specified time. If the market price of the stock goes above the price specified in the warrant, the warrant becomes an asset of value. For example, if a stock's market price goes to $55 and the warrant's specified price is $50, the warrant has a value of $5. Warrants are generally issued to enhance the sale of new bond issues, to finance mergers, and so on.

There are four possible differences between rights and warrants. First, rights are issued to finance an immediate and specific corporate need, whereas warrants are issued for both present and future financing needs. Second, rights generally involve a shorter option period than do warrants. Third, the new issue price exercisable by the right is generally below the current market price of the stock, whereas the new issue price exercisable by the warrant is generally above or at the current market price of the stock. Fourth, the new issue price exercisable by the right is fixed, whereas the new issue price exercisable by the warrant may vary.

Secondary Markets

Secondary markets are simply trading forums where investors can buy and sell securities among themselves. For little known companies, or companies whose stock is infrequently traded, this may be nothing more than a single brokerage house that matches buy and sell orders for its customers. This is the rudimentary form of the over-the-counter (OTC) market. The more active OTC stocks have their prices quoted on a central computer for nationally competitive trading among investors at different brokerage houses.

For actively traded securities of well established companies, organized secondary markets such as the New York Stock Exchange enable buyers and sellers to complete their transactions via brokers and telephones at a central location. Exchange specialists match orders to buy at a certain price with orders to sell at a certain price. No sale occurs until there is a match. Therefore, if there is very little trading activity in a stock, a transaction request will be recorded on a specialist's books to await a counter-transaction request. This may take several hours or even days. Normally, your broker can have a buy or sell order transacted within a few minutes. He simply telephones the order to his company's trader in New York; he, in turn, contacts the company's broker on the floor of the exchange, who takes the order to the specialist coordinating transactions in that stock. As soon as the trade is made, the floor broker returns the phone call and explains the details of the transaction. Figure 17-2 shows the movement of such a transaction.

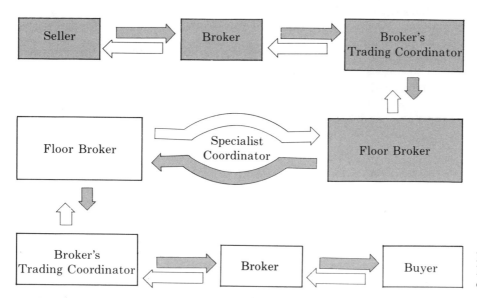

Fig. 17-2
Flow of orders on an organized exchange

organized exchanges   Each of the organized exchanges has a central trading floor. In order for a company to have its stock traded on an organized exchange, it must meet certain requirements (fig. 17-3, p. 374). These requirements ensure that the exchange will not get a bad reputation by selling stocks issued by fly-by-night companies. One of the listing requirements of all exchanges is that the company must file audited annual reports with the exchange, so that the potential investor will get accurate information concerning the company's finances. A company's stock may be delisted if it fails to meet the exchange's listing requirements at any time. The most stringent listing requirements are those of the New York Stock Exchange.

The *New York Stock Exchange* (NYSE) was founded in 1792 as a federation of about a dozen securities traders. Today, it is the largest stock exchange in the world. Ninety percent of the market value of all outstanding stockholdings in the United States is listed on this exchange. Currently, there are about 1300 companies listed on the NYSE. They are, by and large, the industrial giants of America, accounting for over 60 percent of our country's total output of goods and services and offering over 1700 different stocks and 1200 different bonds. (Bonds are listed on the New York Bond Exchange.) There are more than twenty-four

Requirement	Exchange			
	New York	American	Midwest	Pacific
Shareholders				
Total number		900	1000	750
Minimum number holding at least 100 shares each	2000	600		
Shares				
Total number outstanding			250,000	250,000
Number held by public (as opposed to company officers and their families)	1,000,000	300,000		
Valuation				
Total market value of shares outstanding	$16,000,000	$2,000,000		$1,000,000
Minimum price per share		$5		$2
Earnings				
Before income taxes	$2,500,000	$500,000		
After income taxes		$300,000	$100,000	$100,000
Net Assets	$16,000,000	$3,000,000	$2,000,000	$1,000,000

Fig. 17-3.
Requirements for listing companies on four major exchanges

million shareholders of NYSE stocks. About one-fifth of the shares are held by institutions such as mutual funds and life insurance companies.

Only members of the NYSE are permitted to transact trades on the floor of the exchange. Membership in the exchange is limited to regulated stock brokerage houses and other highly qualified individuals who are able to purchase a seat on the exchange at the going price, which currently ranges from $200,000 to $500,000 depending on such things as market conditions. Houses that do considerable trading in securities may own several seats on the exchange.

The board of governors for the exchange sets up the principles, practices, and code of ethics for exchange members. (The board must abide by the rulings of the U.S. Securities and Exchange Commission and cooperate in its investigations.) The governors also set up the requirements a company must meet in order to have its stock listed on the exchange. In addition to the basic requirements about shareholders, shares, valuation, earnings, and net assets (fig. 17-3), the company's character, stability, quality of markets, degree of national (as opposed to local) interest, and the like must all be approved by the board of governors before they will grant listing on the exchange.

The *American Stock Exchange*, also located in New York City, is the second largest stock exchange in the world. It was unofficially begun in 1849 on a corner of Wall Street by a group of dealers in unlisted securities. This street corner soon became a regular trading spot known as the Outdoor Curb Exchange. In 1921, the renamed New York Curb Exchange moved to an indoor location and then, in 1931, into its present building. This exchange continued its upward climb in status when, in 1952, it discontinued trading on Saturdays. Although the name was finally changed to the American Stock Exchange (ASE or Amex) in 1953, it is still referred to by many investors as "the Curb." Today, the American Stock Exchange has over 1000 listed stocks and over 150 listed bonds. Their requirements for membership and stock listings (fig. 17-3) are somewhat less stringent than those of the NYSE.

The *Pacific Coast Stock Exchange* (PCSE) is one of several regional stock exchanges in the United States. It has trading floors in Los Angeles and San Francisco. There are over 700 listed stocks, many of which are also listed on the NYSE or Amex. The PCSE is usually open two hours longer than are the major exchanges in order to generate extra volume from late trading after the New York City exchanges are closed for the day. Listing requirements (fig. 17-3) are less rigorous for this exchange.

The *Midwest Stock Exchange* is the other major regional exchange in the United States. Its trading floor is located in Chicago.

There are other stock exchanges throughout North America, but, as table 17-1 shows, most of these do a fairly small amount of trading compared to NYSE and Amex. If you are interested in trading in special types of stocks, one of the smaller exchanges may merit consideration. For example, most Canadian mining stocks can be bought on the Toronto or Montreal exchanges.

TABLE 17-1

TOTAL VALUE OF TRADING
ON NORTH AMERICAN STOCK EXCHANGES IN 1969

Stock Exchange	Total Value (Billions)	Stock Exchange	Total Value (Billions)
New York	$130.0	Detroit	.2
American	35.0	National	.2
Midwest	6.0	Calgary	.08
Toronto	5.8	Pittsburgh	.05
Pacific Coast	5.4	Cincinnati	.02
Philadelphia–Baltimore–		Salt Lake City	.02
Washington	2.6	Spokane	.01
Montreal	1.5	Honolulu	.01
Boston	1.2	Winnepeg	.006
Vancouver	.6	Richmond	.002

SOURCE: *1969 Trading Records of Stock Exchanges in North America.*

over-the-counter markets (OTC) The over-the-counter market is not an organized central stock exchange. It is the mechanism by which brokers negotiate trades between each other for the benefit of their clients. For example, if you wanted to buy ABZ stock before it was listed on the American Stock Exchange, your broker would have called other brokers until he found one who represented an ABZ shareholder willing to sell some of his stock for the price you were willing to pay.

OTC stocks consist of all those publicly traded stocks that are not listed on one of the organized stock exchanges. Some of these stocks are traded as actively as many of the listed stocks. Certain brokers specialize in making a market in one or more of these active stocks: they clear so many trades per day that they have a good idea of what the going market price is and can build a reputation among other brokers as market-makers in these OTC stocks. Your broker may know exactly whom to call to execute a particular stock purchase immediately at a price very close to a realistic market price. Brokers who make markets in a stock actually keep an inventory of it on hand so that they can readily sell stock or buy it back at the going prices.

Two prices are always quoted for OTC stocks: the bid price and the asked price. The *bid price* is the price at which a broker would be willing to buy a stock from you—the price he is willing to bid for your stock. The *asked price* is the price at which a broker would be willing to sell a stock to you—the price he is asking for the stock. The difference between the two current prices is part of the broker's commission. He will also generally charge the standard brokerage commission (p. 384). Of course, the bid price is always lower than the asked price.

Current prices of OTC stocks are sometimes difficult to obtain. Local newspapers usually list only the prices for the OTC stocks of companies likely to interest local readers because of their location, type, and so forth. The *Wall Street Journal* has the most extensive daily listing of OTC prices. On Mondays it adds a supplement for OTC stocks that are less actively traded. As an alternative, you can call your broker to get the latest prices. If the stock is only infrequently traded, even he may have trouble getting a firm quote. In fact, sometimes you can call two different brokers and get quotes up to 10 percent apart for the same stock. When this happens, you should, of course, buy the stock at the lower price.

As of February 8, 1971, price discrepancies have been eliminated for most actively traded OTC stocks. On that date the National Association of Securities Dealers Automated Quotation system (NASDAQ) came into being. The system involves a central computer with live terminals at the more than 400 brokerage firms that are members. These houses regularly supply to the central computer their current quotes on OTC stocks in which they make a market. As a result of this, your broker can obtain for you the best quotes on more than 3000 OTC stocks, and place your order through the appropriate house. With everybody's quotes out in the open, the OTC market for NASDAQ stocks is behaving much like the organized exchanges. On NASDAQ stocks, you can rely on getting a current fair market quote from your broker through the computer terminal in his office. Eventually, NASDAQ hopes to cover 20,000 stocks.

Regulation of the Securities Markets

The fraud, manipulation, and concealed information of the 1920s brought about the passage of the Securities Exchange Acts of 1933 and 1934. These acts created the Securities Exchange Commission (SEC) to administer the newly established regulations of the organized securities exchanges. Because of the activities of the SEC, the small investor can now avail himself of a complete and current disclosure of information and thus is much less likely to be abused by swindlers or by unethical big investors and brokers. The following is a list of the SEC's powers.

- To regulate and register the exchanges
- To register all securities listed on an exchange
- To regulate investment advisers and all dealers and brokers who are members of an organized exchange
- To require that audited and reasonably current financial reports be filed and that most of this information be made available in reports to the stockholders
- To require that the trading of major stock holdings by officers and directors be disclosed
- To require that proxies and proxy statements be mailed to all stockholders so that they can vote in absentia at annual meetings
- To regulate and review all advertising by brokers and by companies (in their prospectuses), thereby eliminating false promises and exaggerated claims
- To control credit on both broker-to-client and broker-to-broker loans by setting margin requirements (minimums are set by the Federal Reserve Board) and requiring that all finance charges on margin accounts be disclosed to holders at least every three months
- To prohibit all forms of stock price manipulation

The state governments have also set up organizations to regulate the issue of new stocks by both new and established corporations. Such regulations may, for example, prevent the sale of stock in financially shaky corporations to uninformed investors.

The National Association of Securities Dealers (NASD) regulates the over-the-counter markets and NASDAQ. This self-regulatory body works to preserve the integrity of the OTC market by monitoring the ethics of brokers who deal in OTC stocks.

The exchanges themselves have set up governing bodies to police their activities and maintain their public integrity.

SOURCES OF INVESTMENT INFORMATION

Even though most investors lack the time and the contacts necessary to conduct their own in-depth research on a particular investment opportunity, such research is necessary before one can make intelligent investment decisions. In addition, an investor must be able to get a perspective on the general economy and make comparisons between one industry and another.

Investor demand for a way to overcome this handicap has fostered the development of daily, weekly, monthly, quarterly, and annual publications that offer insights into specific companies and industries and into business conditions in general. In fact, there are so many publications to choose from (including numerous "Get Rich Quick" paperbacks) that we have compiled a list (pp. 401–403) of the more commonly used and generally available publications. Some of the materials may be bought at the local newsstand or bookstore, some are available at libraries, and some may be used at stockbroker offices.

If you are a novice in stock market investments, perhaps you should first read some of the publications that offer general information about investing in the stock market. Other sources on the list can help you keep abreast of general business news and learn about specific stocks and bonds. You should always consult the latter sources before you make a final investment decision. Do not rely on hearsay; do your own research to make sure that your information is complete and correct.

Information on Stocks and the Stock Market in the Newspapers

Nearly every major newspaper in the country lists the daily prices of stocks on the major stock exchanges. In addition to the prices of individual stocks, the newspapers report on the general trend of market prices by giving market indices such as the Dow Jones averages, Standard and Poor's averages, the New York Stock Exchange Index, and the American Stock Exchange Index. Investors follow these averages to acquire a feel for general market trends, for aid in timing their purchases and sales, and to have a means of measuring their investment performance.

listings of individual stocks The individual stock listings are most easily understood through the following example (fig. 17-4). Your local paper may omit some of the items to save space. The first two columns in the stock listing give the high and low prices of the stock for the

Fig. 17-4.
Individual stock
listing

| 1972 | | STOCKS | DIV. | SALES IN 100s | P/E | HIGH | LOW | CLOSE | NET CHG. |
HIGH	LOW								
94½	60¼	M Hse	2.60	481	21	76¼	74	76	+1¼

year. If a split or a stock dividend of 25 percent or more has been paid, this range is shown for the new stock only. In figure 17-4, Mill House common stock has sold for as high as 94½ and as low as 60¼ a share in the current calendar year. However, for the first few months of the subsequent year, this column will give the 1972–73 high and low prices, and the heading will be 1972–73. The next entry is the name of the stock, in this case Mill House common stock. An entry for a preferred stock might be written, for example, "M Hse pf," and this should be read "Mill House preferred stock."

Under the "div." heading and printed right after the name of the stock is the current annual dividend paid. The current annual dividend amount is based on the amount of the last quarterly or semiannual declaration. Therefore, if a company has been paying a dividend of 20¢ per share each quarter, the rate listed in the table would be 80¢, the annual rate. If that company raised the regular quarterly rate to 25¢ at the next director's meeting, the rate in the table would be changed to $1 as soon as the first payment was made at the new rate. If a split or stock dividend of 25 percent or more is paid, the dividend is shown for the new stock only. In this case, Mill House common pays a dividend of $2.60 per share per year, although you may receive it in quarterly amounts. If a stock dividend is also regularly paid, a footnote will notify you of that fact.

The next column, sales in 100s, reports the actual number of shares of stock that changed hands during the day. In this case, there were 48,100 shares of Mill House stock traded that day. The next column indicates the stock's P/E ratio computed using today's price and the earnings per share for the most recently reported twelve-month period. In this case, Mill House is selling at twenty-one times earnings. (Some papers use this column to report the opening price for the stock on that date rather than the P/E ratio.) The next three columns report various significant prices at which Mill House stock was traded during the day: the highest price at which it was traded (high); the lowest price (low); and the price at which the last sale was made before the exchange was closed (close). In this case, Mill House stock was traded during the day at prices ranging from $74 to $76.25 per share.

The last column, "net chg.," reports the difference between today's closing price and yesterday's closing price. In this case, the figure of 1¼ indicates that today's closing price of $76 is $1.25 higher than yesterday's close, which must have been $74.75.

Although the stock price tables in the newspaper give most of the basic current data about a security, there are many qualifying remarks for which there is no room in the actual tables. Therefore, there are always explanatory notes, or footnotes, at the end of the listings. Since these notes are not always easily understood, we have explained them more fully in figure 17-5 (pp. 380–81). Footnotes "a" through "x" apply to special or extra dividends or payments that are not regular. The other footnotes usually refer to factors other than dividends.

z   Sales in full   Some stocks are sold in 10- or 25-share round lots instead of the usual 100-share round lots. In this case, the figures given are the total actual sales for the day; you do not have to add the usual double zero to the sales figure.

a   Also extra or extras   The company paid an extra dividend, over and above the regular rate, sometime in the past year.

b   Annual rate plus stock dividend   In addition to the regular cash dividend, the company paid a stock dividend.

c   Liquidating dividend   This is the amount of money being paid to stockholders as a consequence of the liquidation of all or part of the company.

d   Declared or paid in the current, plus stock dividend   The company has yet to establish a regular annual dividend pattern. This would occur if it had just begun paying dividends or had a history of irregular dividend payments.

e   Paid last year   The dollar amount paid in the last calendar year. The dividend rate for this year is still uncertain.

f   Payable in stock during the current year, estimated value on ex-dividend or ex-distribution date   The amount of the stock dividend expressed in dollars. For example, if a 10 percent stock dividend is payable in a few months and the stock generally sells for around $10, the estimated value of the stock dividend (in dollars) is claimed to be $1.

g   Declared or paid so far this year   The actual cash dividend paid, or declared payable by the directors, so far this year. Dividends for the rest of the year remain uncertain.

h   Declared or paid after stock dividend or split up   The total amount paid since a recent stock dividend or stock split.

k   Declared or paid this year, an accumulative issue with dividends in arrears   A cumulative preferred stock that still owes back dividends, even though it has so far this year paid the amount stated under "div" in the listing.

n   A new issue   This is a newly issued common stock that has yet to establish a dividend pattern.

p   Paid this year, dividend omitted, deferred, or no action taken last meeting   Although the company has paid a dividend in the amount printed, for some reason there was no positive action taken on continuing the preceding dividend rate.

r   Declared or paid in the previous year plus stock dividend   The cash amount paid to stockholders last year, along with a stock dividend. So far this year, no dividend has been declared.

Fig. 17-5.
Explanations of
footnotes found in
stock price tables

t   Paid in stock during the previous year, estimated cash value on ex-dividend or ex-distribution date   The same as footnote f, except it was paid last year. There have been no dividends declared so far this year.

Cld   Called   The issue, perhaps a convertible preferred, has been called by the company and will soon be delisted, as the security will no longer exist.

x   Ex-dividend   All persons who own the securities on this date will receive the current dividend payment. If you buy the security after this date, you must wait until the next dividend payment. Theoretically, the stock would decline in price by the amount of the dividend on that date; this is indicated in the "net change" figure for that security. For example, if a stock is paying a $1 quarterly dividend and the previous day's closing price for the stock was $105, the net change column would show $+1$ if the stock closed at $105 the day it went ex-dividend.

y   Ex-dividend and sales in full   A combination of the z and x footnotes.

x-dis   Ex-distribution   Similar to the x footnote, except that in this case the note refers to stock dividends.

xr   Ex-rights   Rights equivalent of the ex-dividend notation (x). In order to claim the rights currently being distributed to all stockholders, you must have owned the security on that day.

xw   Without warrants   This stock is being traded without the warrants that were issued in conjunction with the stock. The former stockholder apparently retained ownership in the warrants when he sold the stock.

ww   With warrants   The opposite of xw.

wi   When issued   A security has not yet been issued, but rights to the stock have. Therefore, investors are essentially trading the rights at this time, before the stock itself is actually issued.

wt   Warrant   The security listed is a warrant.

nd   Next day delivery   Normal delivery time on a stock is five days. Certain securities or certain special sales sometimes have one-day special delivery schedules. If you buy such a stock, it is a cash trade; that is, you must pay for the security the very next day when the stock is delivered.

vj   In bankruptcy or receivership or being reorganized under the Bankruptcy Act, or securities assumed by such companies   If you buy this stock you may only be buying assets in the process of liquidation, not those of an income-producing corporation.

fn   Foreign securities subject to interest equalization tax   In order to keep foreign interest rates no more attractive than those offered in the United States, the federal government levies this tax on foreign securities owned by Americans.

Fig. 17-5. *(cont.)*

Dow Jones Averages

The Dow Jones averages are not actual dollar averages of current market prices; they are instead an index value of the average price of a specific group of stocks. Many investors use these indices as general indicators of market trends. The Dow Jones Company computes price indices for (1) thirty industrial stocks, (2) twenty transportation stocks, (3) fifteen utility stocks, and (4) a composite of all sixty-five of the stocks. These stocks are hand-picked to represent a cross section of the market leaders, not of all stocks on the New York Stock Exchange (which are used in computing the NYSE Index). Substitutions are made from time to time in the list of stocks used in the averages in order to ensure that the list represents the personal interest of a broad spectrum of the investing public. Sometimes such substitution decisions have a major effect on the averages. For example, in 1939 the Dow Jones Company decided to remove International Business Machines from the list of Dow industrials. If IBM had been left on the list, the peak of the average in 1968 would have been over 1500 instead of at 998! The sixty-five stocks currently used in the averages are listed every Monday in the *Wall Street Journal*. The movements of the actual indices are charted on a daily basis by the *Journal* and sometimes by local papers, too.

The Dow Jones averages are sometimes criticized because they measure the price changes of the blue chips rather than the general market. However, these averages do often follow the general trend of the markets, and they are part of the everyday language of stock market investors.

Standard and Poor's Averages

Standard and Poor's computes indices for 425 industrial stocks, 50 utilities, and 24 railroads, and all 500 stocks taken together. The Standard and Poor's index, like the Dow, hand-picks stocks from the NYSE to use in their sample, but it is generally regarded as a better measure of the overall trend of the market because it uses a greater number of different types of stocks. Standard and Poor's averages are reported daily in the *Wall Street Journal* and are sometimes charted daily in the financial sections of local newspapers.

New York Stock Exchange Index

This index records the average price and net change of all common stocks listed on the New York Stock Exchange. The computation of this index was made possible by the use of high-speed computers. Although it is fairly new, it has acquired widespread usage because of the precision with which it measures the price movement of the general market. In addition to the general (composite) common stock index, the exchange publishes indices for industrial, transportation, finance, and utility stocks.

American Stock Exchange Index

This index is similar to the NYSE Index. The ASE Index is also new, but it is gaining widespread usage among investors. It is the only index of any significance publicly published for ASE stocks.

BROKERS AND BROKERAGE HOUSES

A broker is licensed to buy and sell securities for clients, as well as for himself. These securities include common stocks (both listed and unlisted), preferred stocks, bonds, and mutual fund shares. Other terms commonly used in place of the word *broker* include *customer's broker, registered representative,* and *account executive.* The brokers of nearly all major public brokerage houses go through a training and apprenticeship period before they become full-fledged brokers.

Brokerage houses are the companies that stockbrokers represent. Some brokerage houses are partnerships; others are corporations. Some are local; others have regional or nationwide networks of branch offices.

Types of Brokerage Houses

Most investors are familiar with *general brokerage houses.* Some of these houses require a minimum-sized account, perhaps ranging from $1000 to $10,000. Others welcome even the smallest investor and offer nearly all of their services to him, even if he purchases only a few hundred dollars worth of stock each year.

Specialty brokerage houses usually deal only with persons who have substantial accounts, generally ranging from $50,000 to $100,000 and up. These houses offer personal consultation and special portfolio research and management as a regular service. The general houses may perform such services as well, but only on a selective basis. Some busy investors with substantial funds simply turn the management of their portfolios over to a broker in a specialty house and have him make the buy and sell decisions on his own.

Brokerage House Regulations and Ethics

In general, brokerage houses do their best to stay within the law and to maintain a high standard of ethics. This, of course, helps them maintain the good public reputation that keeps them in business.

All brokerage houses that are members of organized exchanges (and most are) are regulated by the SEC. One of the most significant regulations, as far as the investor is concerned, is the prohibition of untrue or overstated advertising. The houses must clearly state what is fact and what is opinion with regard to any investment recommendations they make.

In addition to the regulations, there are certain ethics common to most houses. First, the names and financial circumstances of all customers are kept in strict confidence. Second, brokers do not try to persuade you to make a stock transaction that you really do not want to make. Third, all orders are executed faithfully for you by your broker. If he makes a mistake, it will be corrected at no cost to you.

Brokerage Commissions and Other Fees

On every buy and sell transaction your broker executes for you, he receives a commission for his services. For stocks traded on the NYSE or Amex, most member firms charge the minimum commission allowed by that exchange. This commission usually ranges from 6 percent (on very small transactions) to 0.1 percent (on very large transactions). Because of the way commissions are graduated, it generally makes economic sense to buy or sell at least $1000 worth of stock per trade. This keeps your percentage cost per transaction to around 1 or 2 percent. If your transaction is not in 100-share multiples, there is an additional charge of 12½ cents per share. This is known as the odd lot commission.

For stocks changing hands in New York State (any stock traded on the NYSE or Amex), there is a small tax amounting to about one-half of 1 percent of the value of the sale (less for non-New York residents). Certain other states may also charge such a tax. Another fee is the federal registration fee on securities. This relatively insignificant charge is levied against the registration of the stock in your name when you buy it.

Typical Brokerage House Services

In addition to the trading service for which a commission is charged, many houses offer extra free services designed to encourage investors to do business with them. Most of these services involve supplying information. Many brokerage houses send monthly statements of your account balance, dividends received, and the like. Written analyses of individual stocks and special industry reports are often printed by brokerage houses and are available upon request. Sometimes your broker will mail them to you if he thinks you might be interested. If there is urgent news about a stock, some houses print newswire bulletins for distribution by brokers to their clients who hold that stock. Stock price quotations are supplied over the telephone at your request.

Some brokerage houses also have available in their offices ticker tape, newswire, quote board, and, often, telequote machines for their customers' use. If your broker has a telequote machine available for his clients, have him show you how to use it. It can be very useful, for example, when you stop by your stockbroker's office just for a few price quotes. A general reference library is often available to the clients of a brokerage house (and sometimes even to passersby). Such a library will usually contain Standard and Poor's stock sheets, house publications, copies of the *Wall Street Journal, Barron's,* and similar publications.

You can get the house's recommendations regarding a certain stock upon inquiry. Most houses have a full-time staff of research analysts who continually review stocks and make recommendations as to whether you should buy, sell, or hold a given security. Of course, this is only their opinion and you may choose to do differently.

Safe-keeping of your securities is another useful service offered by most houses. A brokerage house that holds securities in their safe for a client is said to hold them "in street name." This service is usually convenient and safe for the clients. If the broker holds your securities in street name, you do not have to keep track of the certificates, sign them over when you sell them, transfer them in and out of your own safety deposit box, and so on. It is easier to compound your investment by reinvesting all of your dividends. The dividends are paid to your account, not sent to you by check, and so you avoid spending dividend payments on daily expenses. However, you must request that your broker send you any credit balances in your account because of sale of stock. Otherwise your funds will be held in your brokerage account and not receive interest.

The house keeps securities in its vault, and they are insured by the federal government through the newly formed Securities Investor Protection Corporation (SIPC). This corporation provides up to $50,000 insurance ($20,000 for cash not currently invested in securities) per account in case of brokerage house failure. However, this provides only for the return of your actual securities, not for the return of their dollar value at the time of the house's failure. Early experience with the program suggests that it may take the SIPC weeks or months to clear up the accounts of bankrupt houses. Hence, your stocks may be tied up and may decline in price while you are unable to sell them. If you keep your stocks yourself, however, and you lose the certificates, you will have to replace them at a penalty.

Brokerage House Research

Most brokerage houses do not consistently excel in all areas of their investment research because of three practices. First, each researcher may be assigned to research a certain industry group. While this may make him a specialist in that group, it also may cause him to recommend purchasing the best stocks in his industry when, in comparison with other industries, none of these stocks is currently a good buy. Second, most brokerage houses do not research all industries. Third, many brokerage houses that handle the primary offering of a stock and are committed to its success recommend it even when it has become overpriced.

Within brokerage houses or research organizations there are people who turn out high quality research, in spite of these three practices. The task, then, is to identify these people and gain access to their research. Here are a few guidelines to help you in your search. Researchers who do their own leg work (i.e., visit the actual company) usually develop the most cogent analyses. Since the two major considerations in most stock investment situations are (1) the competitive position of the company due to its technological sophistication and (2) the competence of its management team, the best research should come from the researcher who has direct access to top management and working knowledge of the technology in question. A background of research experience in both prolonged bear as well as bull markets is also helpful. Without this perspective, it is difficult for the researcher to relate a specific stock opportunity to general market conditions.

Identifying reliable researchers probably can be accomplished only by doing your own reading of research reports, investigating, and interviewing. If you find a person whose research you would like to have and this person works for a pure research organization, you may have to pay a subscription fee. If the person does research for a brokerage house, you may have to open an account there.

One way around the problem of finding good research is to identify brokerage houses that not only do good research in certain areas, but also honestly admit to using competent outside sources in areas where they are weak. This is the type of organization to use. In any case, the larger your account, the more leverage you have in obtaining good research very quickly.

Selecting a Broker and Opening an Account

Your relationship with your broker is very important. You should select your broker and house as carefully as you would select a doctor or a lawyer. Talk to your banker and your friends, read the ads and brochures, and talk to representatives in several different houses before you select the house that you feel best suits your objectives and your situation.

It is important when choosing a particular broker within a brokerage house that his investment attitude be similar to yours. Since a broker is trading in the market for himself as well as for his client, he is going to know more about stocks and trading techniques that suit his goals than about those attractive to someone with a different investment philosophy. If you wish to invest for long-term growth, make sure you do not select a broker who is interested in trading for short-term gains, and vice versa. If, after you have been with a broker for a while, you find that he does not suit your needs, you may request a change or even transfer your account to another house.

One way to distinguish the broker who is interested only in generating commissions from the broker interested in providing good long-term service is to ask this question early in your initial interview: "What stocks do you recommend for making money in the market?" If the broker begins immediately to explain his favorite stocks, he may well be primarily a securities salesman. If he responds by asking about your objectives and your financial situation, you can be more certain that he will be able to give responsible advice.

Once you have decided on a broker, it is simple to open an account. You fill out a few forms, and you are ready for your first stock purchase. At first you may rely heavily on your broker's recommendations and advice. Once he understands your investment objectives, he can be quite helpful. Of course, as time goes on, you should acquire more and more expertise in the market and be able to do much of your own research and decision-making.

THE CONDITION OF THE MARKET: BULLS AND BEARS

When the stock market is in an uptrend, as measured by the stock market averages, investors refer to it as a *bull market*. If the market is in a downtrend, it is referred to as a *bear market*. Among the factors that can initiate a bull market are investor optimism that the economy will improve over the next six months or so, and economically stimulating government actions—such as a tax cut or deficit spending. Of course, to maintain a bull market for a long time there must be continued economic growth (as measured by the quarterly Gross National Product), continued government actions that are not intended to restrain the economy, and, most important, continued growth in corporate profits.

Bear markets are usually initiated by one or both of the following factors: widespread pessimism among investors, and an unusually high rate of inflation. The latter can result in temporary restraining government actions, such as cutting back on the budget or raising taxes. Any minor decline (correction) in stock market prices can grow into a major bear market if the following occur: the GNP growth rate slows to well below normal; the government continues to work on restraining an unusually difficult siege of inflation; or, especially, corporate profits go into a period of decline. There have been times (1966, for example) when pessimism about the future of the stock market has actually brought about bear markets, even though the economy did not slow down. Bear markets are usually short-lived. Over the long run, stock prices have generally tended to rise, as figure 17-6 (p. 388) shows.

Regardless of the condition of the general market, investors can be bullish about certain well-selected stocks. For example, Proctor and Gamble stock rose 29 percent in 1969, when the NYSE Index dropped about 15 percent (a bear market). The converse can also be true. In the bull market of 1965 (up 15 percent), General Portland Cement stock dropped 37 percent because of considerable overcapacity in the cement industry.

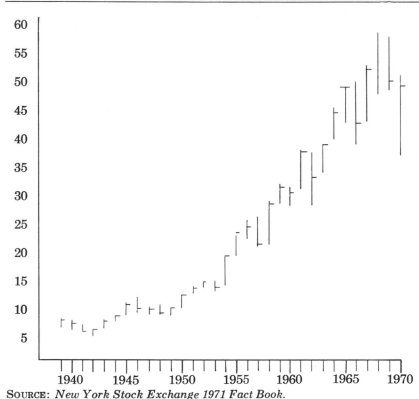

THE NEW YORK STOCK EXCHANGE COMMON STOCK INDEX:
ANNUAL DATA FOR THE YEARS BEGINNING WITH 1939
(The NYSE index was set at 50.0 on 12/31/65.)

SOURCE: *New York Stock Exchange 1971 Fact Book.*

Fig. 17-6.
The rising trend
in stock prices

NOTE: The vertical lines for each year plot the extent of the high and low readings for the index. The horizontal tick marks the closing price of the index for the year. For example, in 1965 the market closed at 50. During 1966 the average price of all stocks plunged to as low as about 37 (bear market), but eventually closed that year at about 43. The index was not calculated for the years prior to 1939.

Trading Techniques for the Long-Term Investor

The basic trading technique with regard to bull markets or growth stocks is simply to buy long—to buy a stock and hold it for price appreciation. With regard to bear markets or stocks with poor prospects, however, this technique is not very successful. Many long-term investors simply wait out short-term price erosion (decline), which may happen even to stocks with good prospects. You must be aware of both bull and bear market trends in order to time your trades to best advantage. You would want to buy stock whenever the market or an individual stock has undergone a sustained bearish trend, because the stock would probably be relatively cheap (provided that you have reason to believe that the stock will rise again). Conversely, you would want to sell a stock and take your profits in cash whenever the market had sustained a long bullish trend and a bear market seemed imminent. Later, you could use those cash profits (which were not affected by the bear market) and reinvest them in the same, or different, stocks at a much lower price.

When you ask your broker to buy or sell a stock, you will in all likelihood give him either a market order, a limit order, or a stop order. Any of these orders can be used with odd lots (fewer than 100 shares of stock) or round lots (multiples of 100 shares). For the investor who does not have time to follow every turn of the market, dollar cost averaging is a useful investment technique, as is also the Monthly Investment Plan offered by the NYSE.

market order　A market order is an order to your broker to buy or sell a stock for you at the best price he can obtain at that time. Since you probably know what the current price of a stock is before you buy (or sell) it, you simply tell your broker to buy (or sell) as many shares of the stock as you want at the market. He will attempt to complete the order for you within a few minutes after you place it with him.

limit order　A limit order is an order to buy a stock at the best possible price, but not above a specified limit price. For example, you might tell your broker to buy 100 shares of ABZ stock at a price of $18 per share or lower—a "limit" of $18. He would then immediately forward this order to the specialist on the floor of the exchange. If the price dropped to 17⅞, your order may be activated. If there were other limit orders on the specialist's books ahead of yours, they might buy up all ABZ stock offered at that low price before your order could be executed. In that case supply and demand would force the market price back above 18, and you would have missed your opportunity to have your limit order executed. If you really thought that ABZ stock represented a good investment opportunity, your limit order might have been unwise; it cost you the chance to buy ABZ stock simply because you wanted to save 25¢ per share. Later when the stock sold for $29 per share, your unwillingness to pay a little over $18 per share would probably seem foolish.

Only when the market for a given stock is undergoing rapid and extreme price fluctuations does a limit order make sense. Limit orders, unlike market orders, prevent you from buying a stock at a price higher than desired and let you get a good price on your purchase without sitting by the ticker tape waiting for the time when exactly the right price is available. Of course, that time may not come, and so periodically the specialist clears his books of unexecuted limit orders.

stop order　A stop order, also called a "stop-loss order," is an order to sell stock at the market when it reaches or goes below a certain price.

The stop order is useful if you become nervous about a stock you own and want to make sure that your loss is no greater than a certain amount, in case the stock really goes into a nose dive.

Assume, for example, that you purchased ABZ stock at $18 per share. Since that time there has been some discouraging news about the company's earnings, and the price of the stock has gradually dropped to $14 per share. You are unsure whether or not the next earnings report will indicate a resumption in the earnings growth of the company, and you decide not to sell until you can see the report. As time goes on, you become a little more nervous about the prospects for the stock and decide that you do not want to take a loss of more than 33 percent. Therefore, you give your broker a stop order on ABZ stock at $12. This means that if the stock goes to $12 or lower, the floor specialist will sell it at the best price he can get for you.

The next report from the company indicates that the earnings decline will be a long-term problem. The price of the stock drops rapidly to $12, and your order goes into effect. However, by the time the specialist on the exchange matches your order to a buy order, the price of the stock is $11.50. Over the next six months the price of ABZ stock ranges between $6 and $9 per share and the stop-loss order has proved its usefulness to you. This order would have been especially useful if the stock had dropped all the way to $9 per share in one day. You might not have learned of the price drop until you read about it in the papers the next day, when it would have been too late to sell the stock at a higher price.

Of course, that $11.50 price you sold for may have been the low point for the stock—a point at which you might not have sold if the stop order had not been in effect. For example, you may have been following ABZ stock closely and had news, as its price neared $11.50, that caused you to feel that the stock would not go much lower. In that case, you would not have decided to sell; but, if you had had a stop order in, you would have had no choice. If you had not placed the stop order, however, or if you had removed it in time, you would have still been holding the stock when the price turned around. You can see that limit orders and stop orders should not be used indiscriminately.

odd lot transactions All trading on the organized exchanges occurs in round lots. If you want to buy or sell 263 shares of ABZ stock, for example, 200 shares would be treated as a round lot and sold in a direct floor trade. Your order on the other 63 shares would go to one of the two large odd lot brokerage houses that maintain an inventory of all stocks. As soon as the odd lot broker gets your order, he checks the very next price for a round lot trade in that stock on the floor. Then, he completes the transaction out of his own inventory at that price, plus a small commission. If your order is a buy order, and the broker does not have sufficient inventory of that stock, he will buy a round lot for himself at the next floor trade and resell part of that lot to you.

The commission you pay the odd lot broker is collected both when you buy and when you sell stock in odd lots. This fee amounts to an extra one-eighth of a point per share. For example, if you have your broker order fifteen shares of ABZ stock for you and the next price on the ticker tape is $19, your statement from your broker would show a purchase price of 19⅛ per share. In addition to the odd lot commission, you would pay the regular commission to your broker.

dollar cost averaging   Dollar cost averaging simply involves investing the same *fixed dollar amount* in the *same long-term growth stock* at *regular intervals* over a *long period of time*. All four of these variables must be observed for this investment method to succeed. The principle is that fewer shares are bought when the price is high than when the price is low.

Assume that you select ABZ Corporation, a long-term growth stock, and decide to buy as many shares as you can with $500 every six months for five years. The results of this program are shown in table 17-2. As you can see, the $6916 value of the portfolio after five years represents a total return, on paper, of about 39.8 percent. Of course, you might claim that that was an easy accomplishment, regardless of the technique used, since the price of the stock advanced from $10 to $14 a share over that period—a rise of 40 percent.

TABLE 17-2

RESULTS OF INVESTING $500
EVERY SIX MONTHS FOR FIVE YEARS

Year	Price[a]	Shares	Cost	Total Shares	Total Value	Cumulative Total Cost
1	$10	50	$500	50	$ 500	$ 500
	12	41	492	91	1092	992
2	7	71	497	162	1134	1489
	6	83	498	245	1470	1987
3	9	55	495	300	2700	2482
	13	38	494	338	4394	2976
4	15	33	495	371	5565	3471
	10	50	500	421	4210	3971
5	13	38	494	459	5967	4465
	14	35	490	494	6916	4955

NOTE: $4955 ÷ 494 = $10.03 average price paid per share.
[a]Commissions included.

To see whether another method would have been as effective, let us assume that you bought fifty shares every six months. As table 17-3 shows, the $1550 paper profits resulting from this method amount to only a 28.4 percent gain on an investment that is $495 larger than that for the dollar cost averaging method. With the fixed number of shares method, you bought fifty shares each time, no matter how high the price. With the fixed dollar amount method, you bought fewer shares when they were high priced, more shares when they were low priced. Therefore, the average price paid per share using the fixed amount method was $10.03, compared with $10.90 using the other method. Dollar cost averaging gave you a profit even when the stock was worth only $9 a share (in the third year). The other technique, however, showed a loss. There would be an even greater contrast if the two programs were carried out for a longer time and for ever-increasing stock prices.

TABLE 17-3

RESULTS OF BUYING FIFTY SHARES
EVERY SIX MONTHS FOR FIVE YEARS

Year	Price[a]	Shares	Cost	Total Shares	Total Value	Cumulative Total Cost
1	$10	50	$500	50	$ 500	$ 500
	12	50	600	100	1200	1100
2	7	50	350	150	1050	1450
	6	50	300	200	1200	1750
3	9	50	450	250	2050	2200
	13	50	650	300	3900	2850
4	15	50	750	350	5250	3600
	10	50	500	400	4000	4100
5	13	50	650	450	5850	4750
	14	50	700	500	7000	5450

NOTE: $5450 ÷ 500 = $10.90 average price paid per share.
[a]Commissions included.

New York Stock Exchange Monthly Investment Plan   In order to offer even the small investor a chance to participate in stock market opportunities, the New York Stock Exchange initiated the Monthly Investment Plan (MIP) in 1954. This plan allows you to purchase NYSE stocks with a regular monthly or quarterly investment of $40 or more. There is no penalty if you fail to meet one of your regular investment payments. Any dividends received are automatically reinvested in more shares of stock, ensuring that your investment will grow at a compound rate. Your broker can arrange all details. The MIP is used by some corporations as a means of allowing their employees to buy shares in their company on a regular payroll deduction basis.

To the small investor, the primary advantage of this plan is the opportunity to purchase a few stocks without first having to save several hundred dollars. This plan also fosters a regular habit of saving and investing. Another important benefit of the MIP is that it enables the investor to utilize the fairly successful technique of dollar cost averaging. By investing the same dollar amount in the same long-term growth stock at regular intervals over a long period of time, you will buy fewer shares when the price is high than when the price is low, and your average price for the shares that you hold will be lower than the average price paid on each investment. This technique also helps you control the urge to buy lots of stock when it is doing well and therefore pay too much for the stock.

With each purchase, you are credited with whole and fractional shares to the fourth decimal point. For example, assume that you decided to invest $50 each month in ABZ stock. On your first investment, you purchased the stock for $15 a share. After deducting a $4 commission, you could buy $46 worth of stock. Your account would therefore be credited with 3.0667 shares of ABZ stock.

The biggest disadvantage to MIP is the proportionately high commissions because of the small size of the trade. Since commissions are proportionally less on purchases over $100, many MIP customers let their monthly savings accumulate and invest them on a quarterly basis. For example, if you let $50 a month accumulate, you can invest $150 each quarter, and the commission on that investment would be only $6.

Trading Techniques for the Trader

The trader (short-term investor) likes to try to make money in both bull and bear markets. In order to take full advantage of bear market opportunities, he tries to anticipate the beginning stages of a market downtrend. He looks at the leading general economic indicators computed by various federal agencies because the stock market often begins a downturn several months before an economic recession is really in evidence. He also observes the mood of Wall Street. General attitudes about the future course of the market often are printed in the *Wall Street Journal.* Among the trading techniques he uses are short sales, margin buying, and puts and calls.

selling short   A short sale is the opposite of the usual stock market transaction. When you sell short, you sell the stock and later buy it back, hopefully at a lower price. To do this, you borrow the stock from your broker. Then you sell that stock at the market. Later, you buy the stock back at the market and return to your broker the number of shares that you previously borrowed from him. Only listed stocks can be sold short.

Perhaps an example will help you understand short selling and how a trader can profit from such a transaction. Assume that the common stock of the ABZ Corporation has risen in price from $18 to $33 in the past six months because of continued growth in the company's profitability. However, you believe that the company will suffer because of a newly emerging competitor and an impending recession. In fact, the market itself has begun to decline in anticipation of lower profits. Therefore, you feel that the stock could easily drop back down to $18, and you decide to sell it short.

You telephone your broker and ask him to sell 100 shares of ABZ for you at the current price of $30. Your broker loans you the shares, if available, to make the sale and then completes the transaction for you. (These shares are borrowed from an investor who is holding them in his margin account. The only cost of borrowing them is that you must pay the owner any dividends they would normally earn.) The broker will also require you to put up a cash deposit equal to no less than the Federal Reserve Board's current margin requirements on the value of the borrowed stock. For example, if the current margin requirements are 80 percent, he will require a cash deposit of $2400 ($3000 × 0.80). If, a few months later, ABZ stock is selling for around $19, you can buy back those 100 shares you sold and make a sizable profit on the deal. If those 100 shares cost you $1900, and your commissions both ways amounted to $100, you would have made $1000 ($3000 − $2000) on your short sale. In the event that the stock does not drop in price, but rises instead, you could lose money. In fact, you might later decide that your losses had run far enough and buy back the 100 shares at, perhaps, $41 each, returning them to your broker at a loss of $1200 ($1100 loss plus $100 in commissions).

With short selling you are going against the long-term uptrend of the stock market, although traders do use the short-sale technique even in bull markets, when their industry or stock research uncovers a prime prospect for a price decline. It is possible to lose more money on a bad short sale than on a bad decision when you are buying long. If that $30 stock rose to a price of $70, you would lose $40 a share on a short sale—more than the stock was worth when you initiated the deal. If you bought the stock long at $30, the most you could lose would be the $30 you invested if the company went broke. Of course, you should be careful not to let your losses become excessive.

Furthermore, your broker could require you to increase your cash margin deposit if the price of ABZ stock went very far above the original $30 price. If you did not have the extra reserve cash, you would have to use the cash in your account to buy back the stock right away to cover your short position and pay off your debt to the broker. You can see that selling short has greater risks and requires more expertise than buying long.

buying stocks with borrowed money   Borrowing money from your broker to buy stock is called *buying on margin.* If you went to a bank to borrow money to buy stock, they would probably not loan you any more than about 20 to 30 percent of the face value of securities you already own. However, your broker will loan you 20 to 45 percent of the face value of the stock you intend to purchase, depending on the current requirements of the Federal Reserve Board. In addition, you would pay interest on the loan from your broker at about the lowest possible rate, usually about 0.5 to 1 percent above the rate the brokerage house must pay to the bank (usually close to the prime rate).

In order to open a margin account, you must make at least a $2000 cash down payment and agree to let your shares be loaned to short sellers. Otherwise, the down payment must be at least equal to the current margin requirements set down by the Federal Reserve Board. For example, if the requirements were set at 70 percent, and you wished to buy 100 shares of a $40 stock, you would have to put up a $2800 down payment ($4000 $\times$ 0.70). Your broker would lend you the rest of the money ($1200) at his current annual interest charge. This technique lets you buy more stock than you otherwise could with the same amount of money, thereby raising your potential return on your investment. However, your potential loss is exaggerated because of the interest you must pay on the margin loan, regardless of whether the stock goes up or down. You cannot purchase any over-the-counter stocks on margin.

Assume that you have $7000 to invest in one stock for one year. Rather than invest only your own money, you decide to buy on margin when the margin requirements are set at 70 percent. This means that on a $10,000 stock purchase (100 shares at $100 a share) you can borrow $3000. One year later you sell the stock at $140 a share. As figure 17-7 (p. 396) shows, buying on margin has increased your rate of return by 13.7 percentage points over what it would have been if you had invested only your $7000. If, however, you had sold the stock at $60 a share, your rate of loss would have been 20.6 percentage points greater than if you had not used borrowed money. Because of the possibility of greater loss, margin buying is generally used only by sophisticated market traders who are willing to take such risks.

The New York Stock Exchange requires you to put up extra money if the stock price falls to the point where your equity (total share value minus the amount of the loan) is 25 percent or less of the total market value of your shares. For example, if that $100 stock dropped to $40 a share, the total value of the 100 shares would be $4000. If you were to sell the stock at this time, you would have only $1000 left over after

Transaction	Without Margin	With 70% Margin
Original purchase ($100/share)		
Number of shares	70	100
Dollar amount	$7000	$10,000
Loan from broker		$3,000
Profit ($140/share sale price)		
Dollar receipts	$9800	$14,000
Interest (8%) on loan		$240
Original cost	$7000	$10,000
Net profit (before commissions)	$2800	$3,760
Rate of return on $7000	40%	53.7%
Loss ($60/share sale price)		
Dollar receipts	$4200	$6,000
Interest (8%) on loan		$240
Original cost	$7000	$10,000
Net loss (before commissions)	($2800)	($4,240)
Rate of loss on $7000	(40%)	(60.6%)

Fig. 17-7. Comparison of a profit and a loss when buying on margin and without margin

you paid back the $3000 loaned by your broker. This $1000 is exactly 25 percent of the current value of the stock ($4000). If the stock's price were to drop any further, your broker would call for more margin (more cash on deposit). Your broker's house margin requirements may be even higher than the minimum set by the NYSE.

using puts and calls An investor can buy a put or a call on most listed stocks through any of more than twenty dealers who specialize in this business. If he buys a put, he buys the *right to sell*, within a given period of time at the price specified in the contract, 100 shares of a specified stock to the person who wrote the put. A call is the *right to buy*—from the person who wrote the call—100 shares of a stock at a stated price.

For example, you may buy a thirty-day call costing $200 that gives you the option of buying stock for $30 a share, its current price. If the stock rises to $35 within that time, you would want to exercise your call option and take your profit. You could buy the 100 shares from the put-and-call dealer for $30 each, or a total cost of $3000. You would then sell those 100 shares on the market for $35 each, or $3500 total. The $500 gain, minus the $200 cost of the call, gives you a net profit of $300. On the $200 investment, this gives you a return of 150 percent in one month! Of course, if the stock had not gone above $32 (your break-even price is $30 + [$200 ÷ 100]), you could not have exercised your call profitably, and you would have realized a 100 percent loss on your $200 investment.

Sometimes a speculator may buy both a put and a call on the same stock. If the price goes up or down he can take advantage of it. This is called a *straddle*. Of course, if both options are bought, a $500 gain will be cut by $400 ($200 for each option), and your profit will be only 25 percent on the $400 investment. If the stock did not go up or down, you would show a 100 percent loss on the whole $400. These examples show why puts and calls are appropriate only for sophisticated investors.

The terms of put and call options are fairly well standardized. Common options run for thirty, sixty, or ninety days, with some running as long as six months or a year. The longer the period, the higher the price you pay for the option, because you stand a greater chance of being able to exercise it to your advantage.

Puts and calls are not traded on any exchange. You may buy one by having your broker arrange the deal. This costs you nothing extra since your broker gets his compensation from the put-and-call dealer.

Puts and calls may be used for purposes other than speculation. For example, you may buy a put on a stock to protect your paper profit in it if you wish to delay the cash profits until the next taxable year. For a more complete discussion of such concepts, refer to one of the basic texts listed at the end of this chapter.

GUIDELINES FOR STOCK MARKET INVESTORS

Carefully study these ten guidelines for investing in the stock market. Investors who follow such rules usually do much better over the long run in their securities investments. Take the list to your stock broker sometime. He should be able to tell you of several experiences confirming each of the guidelines.

1. *Investigate before you invest.* This time-honored Wall Street maxim is the best preventive for the plague of the "hot tip."
2. *Buy low; sell high.* This may seem obvious, but too many investors let their emotions tell them to buy when the stock is riding high and to sell when the stock is overly depressed.
3. *Do not buy too many different stocks.* The average investor does not have time to watch over a portfolio of more than four or five different stocks. If you want diversification, buy a mutual fund.
4. *Begin with quality.* There are too many special kinds of risks for the average beginning investor to deal with when investing in small company, over-the-counter stocks.
5. *Do not be afraid to take your profits.* If you see one of your stocks selling near its all-time high P/E ratio and you see little reason for it to rise much higher, sell and take your profit before it goes down. A buy-and-hold philosophy will only result in the average of the up-and-down cycles.

6. *Do not be afraid to take a loss.* If your stock is down, and its prospects for recovery are poor, sell it and put the proceeds into something that has a good outlook. There is no such thing as being "locked in."

7. *Do not sell just for tax-loss write-offs.* If your stock is down, but the prospects for a recovery seem good, keep it!

8. *Wait for the right deal.* If you think stocks are currently high priced and you cannot find a suitable investment, keep your money in a savings account and wait for lower prices. That was a winning strategy in 1968.

9. *Accumulate dividends for reinvestment.* This will enable you to achieve the full effect of compounding on your investment dollars (as long as you do not need the current income of the dividends).

10. *Do not use short-selling, buying on margin, or puts and calls—* unless you really know what you are doing.

CONCLUSION

This chapter has presented a general overview of the securities markets, sources of information, brokerage houses, and trading techniques. Even if you have time only to buy long, you should at least understand the basic types of orders you can place with your broker, as well as the effects of bull and bear markets.

VOCABULARY

Amex
asked price
at-the-market
bear market
bid price
broker
bull market
buy long
call
commission
dollar cost averaging
Dow Jones averages
investment banker
limit order
margin buying

NYSE
odd lot
over-the-counter (OTC)
primary offering
prospectus
put
right
round lot
SEC
secondary offering
short sale
specialist
stop order
underwrite
warrant

1. How is the issuing corporation involved in a primary offering of its stock? How is it involved in the sale of its stock in the secondary market?

2. Why does the average over-the-counter stock have a greater chance of going broke than the average American Stock Exchange stock?

3. What is the most important factor to consider in selecting a broker? Why?

4. Recently ABZ stock has been fluctuating weekly between $31 and $39 a share. If you believe that the stock is a good buy, but do not wish to pay more than $3300 for 100 shares (before commissions), what order would you give your broker? What would he do with the order?

5. Compare the usefulness of the Dow Jones averages with that of the New York Stock Exchange Index.

6. What qualifications should an investor have before he engages in such activities as selling short or buying on margin? Under what circumstances would it make sense for him to sell short? To buy on margin?

7. One should always use a stop order at 10 to 20 percent below current market price. Comment on this statement.

8. Assume that your 100 shares of ABZ stock are worth $50 a share, and you paid $100 a share for them ten months ago. Your marginal tax bracket is 40 percent. You believe that the stock has an excellent chance to recover to at least $70 a share during the next six months. Should you sell for the tax write-off or hold the stock? What would be the after-tax dollar loss between selling now and selling at $70 in six months?

9. What advantage does dollar cost averaging have for the investor who tends to become emotionally involved in his stock holdings? What possible disadvantage is there for such a person?

10. Where could you find out quickly and easily the corporate history and P/E ratio ranges for a listed stock? (Refer to pages 401–403.)

This case is designed to utilize what you have learned from chapters 16 and 17. Assume that your father inherited a $45,200 portfolio of common stocks. Because he knew little about the stock market and wanted to provide a good educational experience for you, he asked you to evaluate the portfolio and advise him on when to buy and sell the stocks. Your father's investment objective is to obtain long-term growth of capital for his retirement without taking speculative risks. He has no need for current income from the stocks, and so any dividends he receives can be reinvested in the market. As compensation to you, he plans to pay you 1 percent of the total market value of the portfolio each December 31. You will be performing this job in your spare time.

Figure 17-8 shows the stocks he inherited. Each company is expected to continue its past five-year trend. The following questions should help you develop your initial portfolio review.

| NUMBER OF SHARES | ISSUE | CURRENT STATE | | | | AVERAGE ANNUAL EPS GROWTH (Past 5 years) | FIVE YEAR P/E RANGE |
		Price	EPS	Divi-dends per Share	Total Sales for Company		
10	Multitron	$240	$2.40	$ .10	$ 32,000,000	+15%	30–105
100	City Bank	36	3.00	1.00	150,000,000	+ 9%	10–16
50	Q. Gas & Electric	18	1.50	1.00	180,000,000	+ 4%	11–14
300	Busy Stores	80	4.00	.80	165,000,000	+12%	16–30
100	Z. Gas & Electric	25	2.00	1.30	263,000,000	+ 8%	11–16
300	State Airlines	11	.50	.10	290,000,000	+ 8%	15–22
100	Bolt Textiles	60	3.00	2.50	15,000,000	− 2%	10–21
20	N.Y. Mfg.	210	7.00	2.00	194,000,000	+12%	25–57
200	Dyno-research	8	.04	0.00	1,500,000	+10%	180–300

Fig. 17-8.
Facts about stocks in the portfolio

1. What would be an appropriate number of stocks for the portfolio? What should be the proportionate size of each holding?
2. What is the current P/E ratio and dividend yield for each of the stocks?
3. Describe the typical stock that you feel belongs in the portfolio. What is its P/E ratio, dividend yield, average annual EPS growth for the past five years, five-year P/E range? How much do the company's current sales amount to?
4. Judging by the information in figure 17-8, which stocks would you sell? Hold? Buy more of? List your reasons for each recommendation.
5. Is the dividend yield an important consideration with regard to any of the stocks?
6. Are the company's total sales an important consideration with regard to any of the stocks?
7. Would it ever make sense to hold cash temporarily in the portfolio?
8. What kind of brokerage house and individual broker should you select to help you with this account?

9. What sources could you consult for up-to-date information on each company?
10. Under what circumstances might you want to use limit orders or stop orders for this portfolio?
11. Are there circumstances under which you would use margin buying, short selling, or the Monthly Investment Plan for this portfolio?

GENERAL INFORMATION ABOUT INVESTING IN THE STOCK MARKET

Crane, Burton. *The Sophisticated Investor.* Revision by Sylvia Crane. New York: Simon and Schuster, 1964.

> This paperback offers an in-depth discussion of the psychology of investing. It takes the viewpoint of the short- to medium-term trader and emphasizes the timing of transactions, charting, technical signals, and the like.

Engel, Louis. *How to Buy Stocks.* 5th ed. Boston: Little Brown, 1971.

> This popular book is written simply, but covers every important aspect of stock market investing. It is almost a must for anyone beginning a stock market investment program.

Fisher, Philip A. *Common Stocks and Uncommon Profits.* Rev. ed. New York: Harper, 1960.

> The author offers his version of what thorough stock analysis should be.

Graham, Benjamin. *The Intelligent Investor: A Book of Practical Counsel.* New York: Harper, 1965.

> A thorough discussion of sound investment principles and individual stock analysis (extracted from a popular and time-tested textbook for college and business school students).

Loeb, Gerald M. *The Battle for Stock Market Profit.* New York: Simon and Schuster, 1971.

> This book contains the somewhat unusual strategy followed by a man who has made millions in the stock market during the last few decades.

UNITED STATES ECONOMY, THE STOCK EXCHANGES,
AND SPECIFIC INDUSTRIES

Barron's National Business and Financial Weekly.

> This weekly tabloid offers information written expressly with the investor's viewpoint in mind.

Brokerage house special reports.

> Your broker may occasionally have available special industry or general economic reports that have been prepared by his company.

Business Week.

> The "Business Outlook" section (two-page weekly summary) in this magazine is very useful for the busy investor. This magazine also has frequent reports on various industries.

Financial sections in major daily newspapers.

> Papers such as the *New York Times, Chicago Tribune,* and *Los Angeles Times* have especially good business and financial sections.

Fortune Magazine.

> The "Business Roundup" section offers substantial monthly summaries for businessmen and investors.

New York Stock Exchange Fact Book. Published annually by the NYSE.

> This book is crammed with historical facts about the exchange: sales volumes, prices, dividend yields, numbers of shareholders, and so on. A similar publication is published by the American Stock Exchange.

Private agency reports.

> Publications such as *F. W. Dodge Construction Surveys* and *Best Insurance Surveys* provide up-to-date statistics on various industries.

Standard and Poor's Outlook.

> This publication offers market analyses.

Trade association publications and trade journals.

> These provide in-depth reports on specific industries, although the information may often be beyond the scope of the investor's needs. Examples include *Oil and Gas Journal, Advertising Age, American Banker,* and the *Engineering and Mining Journal.*

Value Line Investment Survey.

> This weekly advisory service often runs special analyses of industry groups.

Wall Street Journal.

> This daily newspaper is the last word in news for the serious investor. The "Outlook" column in the Monday edition gives in-depth analyses of various aspects of the general economy. The column "Keeping Abreast of the Market" offers useful analyses of the stock market. The paper also provides daily market averages and the like.

Companies themselves.

A company publishes a certain amount of information for the benefit of its stockholders and prospective investors. Such publications include the annual report and quarterly reports, which show the company's income statement and balance sheet. Also, whenever the company issues new stock, it must publish a prospectus describing the new stock and the company.

Monthly Stock Digest. Published by Data Digest.

This publication is similar to the *Standard and Poor's Stock Guide,* though smaller. It may be available from your broker.

Moody's Handbook. Published annually.

This publication provides special survey updates as well as good summary information concerning most major industries.

Standard and Poor's Stock Guide. Published monthly.

This excellent summary of almost all publicly traded stocks provides much of the basic information that an investor needs prior to making an in-depth survey of a stock. This information includes prices, dividends, P/E ratios, earnings, and the Standard and Poor's ranking from A through C on the stability and growth of earnings and dividends. It is generally available from your broker.

Value Line Investment Survey.

This weekly advisory service gives excellent, up-to-date statistical summaries on individual stocks.

CHUCK AND NANCY ANDERSON

THEIR SECURITIES TRADING ACCOUNT

As we saw in chapter 13, Chuck and Nancy selected common stocks as the investment medium for their low priority goal—the motorboat. They favored mutual funds for their other goals because of their limited time and expertise.

The Andersons have a margin account and have borrowed $1500 from their broker. Although they sometimes ask him for his opinion, they usually find a couple of hours once or twice a month for research and stock selection on their own, and then they plan the timing of purchases and sales.

QUESTIONS

1. Should the Andersons maintain the loan in their margin account? Why or why not?
2. Should they do any short selling? Why or why not?
3. Should the Andersons try mostly for long-term or short-term trading gains? Why do you think so?
4. Should they invest in two to four stocks or five to seven stocks at the beginning of their boat investment program? Why do you think so?

18

MUTUAL FUNDS

The fifth-floor staff at the Automatic Tractor Company often talked about the stock market during their lunch hour. One of them, Bernie, was regarded as the expert since he had achieved a 15 to 20 percent return each of the three years that he had been active in the stock market. Although Bernie spent a lot of time researching and investing in the market, he was frustrated that he currently had only about $3000 for investment purposes and had to pay so much in commissions on small trades.

One noon hour, Harry and Tony were talking with Bernie about the market. Neither Harry nor Tony had ever been much involved in investing. As Tony put it: "I just don't have time to fool with all those charts, pamphlets, and notebooks that you spend so much time on, Bernie. Besides, I'd rather invest for long-term gains, but I have only enough to buy stock in one or two companies. And, if any of those stocks turn out to be a lemon—brother, I just can't live with that kind of risk!"

"Well, then," Harry interjected, "what we need to do is pool our money somehow and pay Bernie some percentage of the assets to manage the money for us. Then we would have three advantages. One, we'd have our expert taking care of the investment chores and responsibilities. Two, we could minimize our commission costs by buying bigger blocks of stock. And three, we would have enough money to buy several different stocks and, if one turned out to be a real loser, we wouldn't get hurt so badly because our risk would be spread."

"That's a great idea!" exclaimed Bernie and Tony. With that, the three of them wrote up an agreement and tried to get other fifth-floor staffers to join their Fifth-Floor Mutual Investment Fund.

Ten people joined the group. Each invested $1000 and received one hundred $10 shares in return. At the end of one year, Bernie's efforts showed some real success. The fund had achieved a 14 percent growth in portfolio value. The original $10,000 was now worth $11,400. The stocks owned by the fund also earned dividends amounting to $274. After Bernie's fee of 1 percent ($114) of the portfolio value was subtracted, $160 in dividends was distributed to the ten fund shareholders—$16 each. In addition, each of their shares was worth $11.40. That is, the net asset value per share had risen from $10 to $11.40. The Fifth-Floor Mutual Investment Fund was indeed proud of its first year's record.

WHAT ARE MUTUAL FUNDS?

The concept of a mutual fund is fairly simple. An investment company sells its mutual fund shares to individual investors, pools the dollars gained from the sale of such shares, and invests them in common stocks of publicly held companies, in preferred stocks, and in corporate and government bonds. The company continues to buy and sell investments on a regular basis as it finds appropriate opportunities to do so.

The mutual fund industry began as a public business in this country in the early 1920s, but its main development came after World War II. Today, we have over 600 of them, with assets of from a few million dollars to over a billion dollars. All these mutual funds together control over $50,000,000,000 in total assets. Out of every $20 worth of stock on the New York Stock Exchange, more than $1 is held by mutual funds.[1] There are over nine million shareholder accounts outstanding. The average size of each account is between $5000 and $6000, but accounts may be as low as $100.[2] In spite of the seeming popularity of mutual funds, according to a study sponsored by the Investment Company Institute in 1971 only 30 percent of American adults say they "know something about" mutual funds.[3]

---

1. Investment Company Institute, *Mutual Fund Fact Book* (Washington, D.C.: Investment Company Institute, 1971).

2. Investment Company Institute, "The Mutual Fund Shareholder—A Comprehensive Study" (Washington, D.C.: Investment Company Institute, 1966).

3. *FundScope,* ed. Allen Silver (Los Angeles: December 1971), p. 16.

An Investment Company Grows: Fifth-Floor Mutual Investment Fund

Once the news of the success of the Fifth-Floor Mutual Investment Fund spread around the office, many people who had been skeptical of the fund wanted to invest with it. The ten original investors held a meeting to decide what to do.

Tony was the first to speak as Bernie opened the floor for discussion. "I think we ought to let well enough alone. We have 1000 shares outstanding and this seems to be about right. Let's not let a good thing get out of hand! Only if somebody wants to leave the fund should anyone else be allowed in. The newcomer can buy the shares from the person who is leaving."

Harry felt differently. "I don't see anything wrong with bigger size. The more the merrier! Besides, one of the current shareholders might want to increase his investment in the fund. Why not print share certificates for anyone who wants to buy them?" Kathy then said, "Also, we ought to provide a way for someone to leave the fund. Calvin is to be transferred to West Lockport in a month and he ought to be able to sell his shares back to the fund, rather than having to find someone else to buy them. He should be able to cash in his shares and collect the net asset value per share as of that date."

The ten members voted in favor of the last two proposals.

Types of Investment Companies

There are two basic types of investment companies: closed-end and open-end. Neither of these allows the stockholder to participate in stock voting rights. The fund management votes as it sees fit the common stock shares that the fund holds. However, the mutual fund shareholder does have voting rights on some fund business, such as fund share splits. Both types of investment companies customarily take their management fees as a percentage of net assets. A single group of managers may manage more than one investment company; such groups are known as families of funds. All publicly held investment companies are regulated in one way or another by the SEC.

closed-end companies   These companies issue a fixed number of shares that are traded like common stocks either on organized exchanges or over the counter. The cost of buying and selling such shares is the standard broker's commission for stock transactions. Closed-end companies account for less than 10 percent of total investment company assets. In our example of the Fifth-Floor Mutual Investment Fund, the fund would have become a closed-end company if the fund holders had decided not to issue any new shares.

open-end companies These companies (popularly called mutual funds, although the term really applies to both types) continually sell and redeem their shares to meet investor demand, with no limit on the total number to be sold. The price is equal to the *net asset value per share* of the fund. This value is computed at the end of each business day, when liabilities are subtracted from the market value of the fund's assets, and the resulting figure is divided by the number of shares outstanding. For example, at the end of a business day a fund might have net assets consisting of $98,000,000 in common stock, $4,000,000 in cash holdings, and $500,000 in cash from the sale of new shares that day. From this total of $102,500,000 the fund subtracts its liabilities and bills due, which might amount to $300,000. This leaves $102,200,000 in net assets. If the fund had 9,950,000 fund shares outstanding yesterday and sold 50,000 new shares today, the total shares outstanding would be 10,000,000. Therefore, the net asset value per share at the close of business that day would be $10.22 ($102,200,000 ÷ 10,000,000). This would be the price at which shares would be redeemed by the fund the next day (the bid price). In our example of the Fifth-Floor Mutual Investment Fund, the fund holders' decision to issue new shares caused the fund to become an open-end company.

A sales charge, called a *load*, may be added when the fund sells its shares. *Load funds* (those with a sales charge) sell their shares through regular stock brokers and/or salesmen employed by one or more investment companies. Sales commissions are charged only on purchases you make; you can sell your shares back to the company without charge. The bid price of a load fund share is its net asset value; the asked price is equal to the net asset value plus the sales commission. A listing may read, for example, "N Fund $11.12–$12.15". You could buy shares that day at $12.15 each and sell them back at $11.12 each (the net asset value). Commissions usually average 7.5 to 9 percent of the net asset price of the stock. For sizeable purchases, around $25,000 or more, the commission rate is usually reduced. Some of these funds can be purchased through payroll deduction plans. Under these circumstances the load charge is often 1 to 3 percent.

No-load funds charge no sales commissions because there are no salesmen. Shares are bought and sold directly from the company, either through the mail or over the phone. The bid and asked prices quoted in the newspaper are the same and, therefore, equal to the net asset value. However, a few no-load funds charge a 1 or 2 percent commission to redeem shares.

The sales commission should not be the deciding factor in buying a load or no-load fund. It is not wise to buy a no-load fund simply to save the sales charge. A poorly managed no-load fund may yield a poorer return on your investment than a well-managed load fund. Always check a fund's past record to get an idea of its management quality. However, everything else being equal, you should avoid the 8 or 9 percent commission of a load fund, if possible.

MUTUAL FUNDS CLASSIFIED BY PORTFOLIO AND INVESTMENT OBJECTIVE

A mutual fund's investment holdings (portfolio) may include primarily common stocks, bonds, preferred stocks, or even mutual funds; or it may include both stocks and bonds. Those funds that concentrate on common stocks may also specialize in particular stock types such as blue chip or growth stocks. Figure 18-1 shows how the portfolio typically relates to the investment objectives for each type of fund. The investment company's prospectus outlines the objectives of the fund.

Type of Fund	Type of Portfolio	Investment Objectives
Diversified Common Stock	Blue chip stock	Income; stability; long-term growth
	Growth stock	Long-term growth with some income
	Speculative stock	Above-average returns
	Specially selected stocks	Unusual price appreciation
	Specialization in an industry or related industries	Varies
Bond	Corporate and government bonds (some solely in tax-exempt state and municipal bonds)	Safe but relatively low rate of return
Preferred Stock	Preferred stock	Good fixed rate of return
Mutual Fund	Selected mutual funds	Wide diversification; long-term growth
Balanced (bond-stock)	Common and preferred stocks; corporate and government bonds	Relatively safe fixed return from bonds and chance for growth through capital gains from stock investment

Fig. 18-1. Types of mutual funds

Closed- and open-end diversified common stock funds have together, more total assets than all the other types of funds combined. By and large, the best long-term capital gains records are to be found in growth funds. Figure 18-2 shows a typical portfolio for a growth fund: risks are spread over a variety of growth stocks. Many of the newer funds that invest in speculative stocks (the so-called "go-go" funds and hedge funds) often use trading techniques such as short selling, margin buying, and puts and calls. The record to date of most funds using these techniques is generally below the average for common stock mutual funds.

A few closed-end diversified common stock funds are structured in such a way that the investor can choose *income shares* or *capital gains shares*. (The investment objective of these *dual funds* depends on the securities that are invested in.) Income shares receive the income from the entire fund portfolio, but no capital gains or losses. Thus, the income-share owner has income from twice his investment. If the dividend yield on the entire portfolio is 3 percent, the yield to the income shares is 6 percent. Capital gains shares get the entire capital gains (or losses) but receive no dividend income. The holders of these shares receive the same doubling effect for the capital gains and losses. The record of dual funds to date is spotty.

Fig. 18-2.
Typical portfolio of a diversified common stock fund seeking long-term growth

Number of Shares	Market Value	Number of Shares	Market Value
AIRLINES (2%)		COSMETICS (3%)	
75,000 American	$2,600,000	33,000 Avon Products	$4,500,000
50,000 Eastern	1,400,000	36,000 Chesebrough-P	1,500,000
	$4,000,000		$6,000,000
AEROSPACE (1.5%)		DRUGS (7%)	
62,000 Boeing	$3,000,000	90,000 Becton-Dickin.	$6,000,000
	$3,000,000	55,000 Merck	5,000,000
AMUSEMENT AND		45,000 Syntex	3,000,000
RECREATION (3%)			$14,000,000
70,000 Walt Disney	$5,000,000	ELECTRONICS (10.5%)	
22,000 Cox Broadcast	1,000,000	125,000 AMP	$ 5,000,000
	$6,000,000	230,000 Ampex	9,000,000
CHEMICALS (3.5%)		50,000 General Elec.	4,000,000
90,000 FMC	$3,000,000	25,000 Litton Ind.	
20,000 Hercules	1,000,000	Conv. Pfd.	2,000,000
38,000 Monsanto	2,000,000	10,000 Motorola	1,000,000
25,000 Tex. Gulf.			$21,000,000
Sulfur	1,000,000		
	$7,000,000		

Number of Shares	Market Value	Number of Shares	Market Value
FINANCIAL SERVICES (6%)		**PHOTOGRAPHIC PRODUCTS (5.5%)**	
40,000 Union Bancorp	$ 2,000,000	110,000 Eastman Kodak	8,000,000
120,000 Franklin Life	3,000,000	25,000 Polaroid	3,000,000
60,000 Conn. General	5,000,000		$11,000,000
60,000 NLT	2,000,000	**PUBLIC UTILITIES (4%)**	
	$12,000,000	30,000 Florida Pow. & Lt.	$ 2,000,000
FOOD PRODUCTS (5%)		80,000 Continental Tele.	2,000,000
190,000 Del Monte	$ 4,000,000	75,000 Houston Light	3,000,000
180,000 Gen. Foods	6,000,000	40,000 Sierra Pacific Pow.	1,000,000
	$10,000,000		$ 8,000,000
HOUSING (4.5%)		**TOBACCO (2%)**	
100,000 Larwin	$3,000,000	70,000 Philip Morris	4,000,000
80,000 Jim Walter	2,400,000	**MISCELLANEOUS (7.5%)**	
90,000 Weyerhauser	3,600,000	11,000 Corning Glass	3,000,000
	$9,000,000	20,000 Ford Motor	1,000,000
OFFICE EQUIPMENT (14%)		125,000 McCulloch Oil	5,000,000
8,000 Burroughs	$ 2,000,000	65,000 Minn. Mng. & Mfg.	5,500,000
110,000 Dennison Mfg.	5,000,000	5,000 Pinkerton's	500,000
60,000 IBM	18,000,000		$15,000,000
20,000 Sperry Rand	1,000,000	**CASH AND EQUIVALENT (9%)**	
8,000 Xerox	2,000,000	Corporate bonds	$ 5,500,000
	$28,000,000	Government Securities	6,500,000
PETROLEUM (12%)		Certificates of Deposit	3,000,000
30,000 Atl. Richfield (conv. pfd.)	6,000,000	Net Cash	3,000,000
60,000 Kerr-McGee	7,000,000		$18,000,000
100,000 Occidental Petroleum	4,000,000		
20,000 Sinclair	3,000,000	**TOTAL ASSETS (100%)**	$200,000,000
40,000 Texaco	4,000,000		
	$24,000,000		

NOTE: Figures rounded for convenience.

Fig. 18-2. (*cont.*)

Since preferred stock funds lack the appeal of common stock funds, relatively few remain today. Bond funds are similarly few in number. Mutual fund funds are a special new breed, and their growth performance is still not described by any past record. They spread the risk over the many stocks of many mutual funds. Such a fund is allowed to charge only a 1 to 3 percent load commission. Otherwise, the investor might have to pay an 8 percent load plus a 1 percent management fee on top of the 4 to 5 percent commission paid by the fund when it makes purchases of other mutual fund shares. In general, the multi-layered fee structure tends to argue against owning shares of this type of fund.

With balanced funds, the proportion of money invested in bonds and stocks varies. When stocks become high-priced, the fund gradually transfers its investment into bonds (vice versa when stocks have experienced a long decline in price). The bonds offer protection against recessions, and the stocks offer protection against inflation. Although risk is thus minimized, so is the chance for above-average investment return.

SPECIAL FEATURES OF OPEN-END MUTUAL FUNDS

All funds in the mutual fund listings in your newspaper are of the open-end variety. You may buy and sell shares at net asset value from the company at any time. There may or may not be a sales commission, depending on whether it is a load or no-load fund.

If you buy into an open-end mutual fund on an irregular basis, the minimum purchase each time may range from $100 to $1000. Most funds allow you to purchase a straight dollar amount, regardless of the price per share. For example, if you buy $300 worth of a fund (after commissions) whose net asset value is $22 per share, your account would be credited with 300/22, or 13.636 shares. If you wish to buy a mutual fund in smaller amounts than their normal minimum investments, you may use their savings accumulation plan.

Savings Accumulation Plan

A savings accumulation plan is often very much like the Monthly Investment Plan of the New York Stock Exchange, in which you agree to invest fixed amounts at regular intervals. Such a regular-dollar-amount investment follows the principle of dollar cost averaging. Also, the regular monthly notice you receive helps foster a program of regular savings and investment.

The initial investment required to open such a plan typically ranges from $25 to $500. Regular monthly or quarterly investment minimums generally range from $25 to $100. This fixed amount is only a minimum and you may invest more if you wish. The plans offered include contractual and voluntary accumulation plans. Contractual plans are offered only by load funds; voluntary plans are offered by all mutual funds.

Under *contractual accumulation plans,* the investor agrees to invest a specified amount over a specified number of years—for example, $10,000 over ten years. A *contractual plan with penalty* has a front-end load; that is, up to 100 percent of the total contract commissions may be taken out of your invested dollar during the first few years (generally, the first two). If you are unable to make payments after that time and are forced to drop out of the program, you suffer a penalty in that your dollars have not bought as many shares as they would have under a different type of contract.

Some people claim that such a plan forces regular saving on people who would not otherwise develop this habit. However, there has been so much criticism of these contracts that the SEC is hoping to spread the front-end commission paying period over four years instead of two. Many funds have begun doing this on their own to promote sales. Because of state laws, front-end load contracts cannot be offered in California, Illinois, New Hampshire, Ohio, and Wisconsin.

Under the *contractual plan without penalty,* commissions are paid on the shares only as they are purchased. There is no penalty for not making a payment. However, if several payments are missed, the investor may be taken off the contractual plan and put on an irregular purchase account, which requires no regular contributions.

The *voluntary accumulation plan* has no fixed total dollar amount or number of years of payments. The investor simply invests a certain minimum amount on specified dates, usually monthly or quarterly, when a reminder comes from the company. There is no penalty for not making a payment. If you do not maintain a regular investment habit, eventually the company will remove you from the plan, however, and put you on a normal irregular purchase account. On such an account, your minimum required investment per payment will probably be higher.

Automatic Reinvestment Plan

Automatic reinvestment plans are offered by mutual funds to enable the investor to reinvest his earnings at no extra commission, thereby automatically compounding his investment. This plan may be for just dividends or for both dividends and capital gains distributions. Most voluntary plans require automatic reinvestment of dividends and capital gains distributions into fund shares at no extra sales commission.

Dividends represent the dividends and interest received by the fund from its investments, less management fees and operating costs. These dividends are taxed as a part of your ordinary gross income, whether they are reinvested or not. The dividends may be reinvested automatically in whole and fractional shares of the fund at no extra charge if you so request or if required by your voluntary plan.

Capital gains distributions represent the capital gains that the fund has realized through the profitable sale of some of its stock holdings.

Since the fund distributes such gains directly to the shareholders, they can avoid paying income taxes on these gains (no double taxation). Only the investor must pay a capital gains tax on the amount received in any given year. Such distributions may also be reinvested automatically in whole and fractional shares of the fund at no extra charge if you request it, or if required by your plan.

Figure 18-3 shows the effect of automatic reinvestment of capital gains distributions earned on a $10,000 investment in a fictitious mutual fund that seeks long-term growth by investing in a diversified portfolio of common stocks. This fund represents a composite of several large funds with above-average performance. Some funds have done better; many have done worse. Nevertheless, at the end of 1971, the value of the original shares was $26,300 and the cumulative value of the reinvested capital gains distributions was $18,800.

What would have happened to the $10,000 investment if all dividends and capital gains distributions had been taken in cash or if they had been reinvested? What would have happened if the $10,000 had been invested in average common stocks or in a savings account? Figure 18-4 (p. 416) shows how compounding affects the total return from the mutual fund investment when greater and greater portions of the investment income are reinvested. The value of the savings account would be much lower than that for any of the other investments. The stock investment should be compared solely with the mutual fund plan that reinvests only capital gains. In this case, the mutual fund underperformed the stock market by about $4000. This difference probably reflects either the management fee or the fund's management expertise or both.

Systematic Withdrawal Plans

All open-end mutual funds offer one or more types of systematic withdrawal plans provided you have at least $10,000 worth of shares when you start the plan. These allow you to draw income from your investment as you need it, leaving the rest invested to continue growing. You simply authorize the fund to send a check each period for a specified amount until you authorize a change or until the money runs out. There are four types of plans based on the type of withdrawal made: fixed dollar amount, fixed number of shares, percentage of asset growth, and dividends and capital gains distributions only.

Under the fixed dollar amount plan, the investment company pays you a fixed amount each month, or quarter, as you designate. There is usually a minimum withdrawal of $50 a period. Each payment is mailed directly to you. The company redeems only enough shares to meet the payment. If the net asset value is $20, two and one-half shares will be redeemed to make a $50 payment.

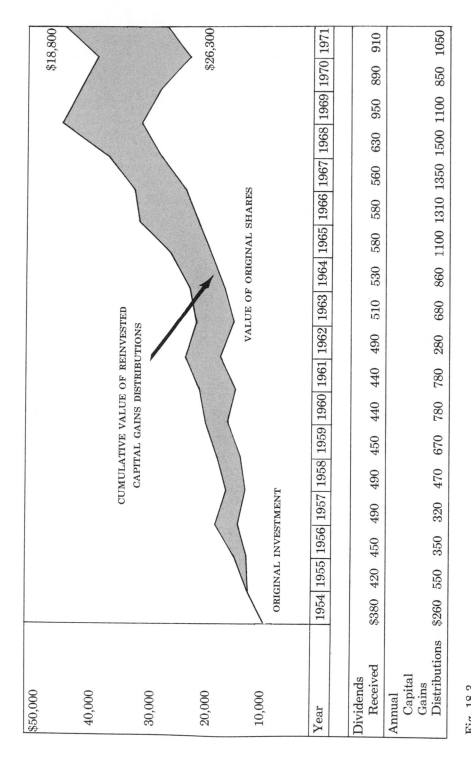

Year	1954	1955	1956	1957	1958	1959	1960	1961	1962	1963	1964	1965	1966	1967	1968	1969	1970	1971
Dividends Received	$380	420	450	490	490	450	440	440	490	510	530	580	580	560	630	950	890	910
Annual Capital Gains Distributions	$260	550	350	320	470	670	780	780	280	680	860	1100	1310	1350	1500	1100	850	1050

Fig. 18-3.
Effect of reinvesting capital gains
distributions earned on a $10,000 investment

Investment Alternative	Initial Investment (1954)	Share Asset Value (December 1971)	Dividends Not Reinvested	Capital Gains Distributions Not Reinvested	Total Value
Mutual Fund					
Dividends and capital gains taken in cash	$10,000	$26,300	$ 7,800	$9,900	$44,000
Capital gains reinvested	10,000	45,100	10,390		55,490
Capital gains and dividends reinvested	10,000	67,400			67,400
Common Stocks (dividends taken in cash)	10,000				59,200[a]
Savings Account (Dividends left to compound)	10,000				20,140[b]

NOTE: No adjustments have been made for taxes on dividends, interest, or capital gains.

[a] Assumes a rate of growth equal to the NYSE composite index and dividends equal to the median dividend yield.

[b] Assumes an average annual interest rate available in the United States from 1954 through 1971.

Fig. 18-4. Comparison of investment alternatives

The fixed number of shares plan offers a variable payment, depending on the current asset value. The monthly or quarterly minimum is usually $50. Under this plan, you avoid excessive draw down of your investment during periods of low stock prices. You have to be willing to accept lower monthly payments, but in periods of high stock prices, your payments are higher. Thus, as your mutual fund asset value grows, your monthly payments grow, keeping pace with inflation. Of course, you own only a fixed number of shares (plus those from any automatic reinvestment plans) and eventually your fund will run out.

The percentage of assets growth plan assures that your investment will never be depleted. Say, for example, you authorize 80 percent of the asset growth to be paid to you each quarter. If there is no growth in that quarter, you get no payment. Your original investment remains protected because of the condition placed on payments to you.

Under the dividends and capital gains distributions plan, the principal is never touched, but is allowed to accumulate toward your estate or other goals. Only dividends and capital gains distributions are sent to you. As you can see from figures 18-3 and 18-4, such a plan offers a good chance to stay ahead of inflation. In 1954, total dividends and capital gains distributions from a $10,000 investment were $640. By 1971 your total income would have been $1960 and your original $10,000 investment would still have grown to $26,300. Your choice of any of these plans depends on several factors: how much other income you have, how much you want to leave to your wife or children, and how long you want your mutual fund income to last.

None of these plans must be permanent. At any time, you can change your mind and choose a different option or take out all the money.

During the past decade, the income of many funds has been such that you could take a monthly check of $50 (income and possible principal) for each $10,000 invested and still realize some long-term growth. Larger amounts may be withdrawn, but eventually your investment may be exhausted (unless the investment company is unusually successful). Two guidelines for withdrawing from diversified growth stock funds are to take out no more than $150 a year per $1000 investment if you want your investment to yield regular payments for at least ten years, and to take out no more than $105 a year per $1000 invested if you want your funds to last at least twenty years.

Insurance Against Loss

Since 1969, it has been possible to get insurance against loss of value in several of the mutual funds. The Harleysville Mutual Insurance Company was licensed by Pennsylvania to insure investments (minimum $3000) in a restricted list of open-end, growth-type mutual funds, provided that all dividends and capital gains distributions are reinvested. Under their plan, you can buy insured shares, guaranteeing that at the end of ten, twelve and one-half, or fifteen years (terms selected by the fund) you will suffer no dollar loss on your investment. This insurance costs 6 percent of the total investment spread over the term of the coverage. Shares must be held the full term of the plan. If you quit the plan early, you have no more insurance, and you owe no more payments.

It is our opinion that such plans generally are not worthwhile expenses. First of all, you lose investment flexibility for ten to fifteen years. Second, there have been very few instances when any claims would have been paid had such a program been in force, and those losses would have been small. In fact, for the past two decades an average mutual fund would have shown a profit in any five-year period, as shown in table 18-1 (p. 418). Chances are, that any insurance fees you pay will only reduce the total return on your investment by 6 percent.

TABLE 18-1

AVERAGE MUTUAL FUND RESULTS
FOR FIVE-YEAR PERIODS
SINCE 1950

(All Distributions Reinvested)

Period	Liquidating Value of $10,000 Initial Investment
1950–54	$21,241
1951–55	20,492
1952–56	19,155
1953–57	15,396
1954–58	21,377
1955–59	16,438
1956–60	14,353
1957–61	16,534
1958–62	16,503
1959–63	14,258
1960–64	14,387
1961–65	16,473
1962–66	12,516[a]
1963–67	19,302
1964–68	19,023
1965–69	14,341
1966–70	11,350[a]
1967–71	14,328

SOURCE: Adapted from *FundScope,* ed. Allen Silver (Los Angeles: May 1972), p. 106.

[a]Investing $10,000 in a 5 percent savings account (compounded quarterly) would result in $12,820 in five years.

Retirement Plans

Approved retirement plans for the self-employed are offered by many open-end mutual funds. Contributions to a Keogh Act plan (pp. 460–61) can be invested in mutual fund shares.

SPECIAL FEATURES OF CLOSED-END FUNDS

The market price of the shares of closed-end funds is generally different from the net asset value. Since closed-end funds issue a fixed number of shares, investors may place a special value on the prospects of the fund or the market, on the absence of a load charge, or on the dividend yield. As with common stocks, the law of supply and demand determines the market price. While most closed-end shares sell at a discount from their net asset value, a few sometimes sell at a premium above this value.

If you buy a closed-end fund at a discount, you will probably sell it at a discount. However, there may be an advantage to this. The amount of the dividend is generally related to the net asset value. When you can buy a closed-end fund at an amount below net asset value, your effective yield may be higher than it would be on an open-end fund purchased at the same price. This is because, in the case of the closed-end fund, the cash dividend yield is computed on a smaller per-share price.

Another possible advantage is related to the restriction on the total number of shares outstanding. When an open-end fund is very successful, many new investors may buy shares, hoping to take advantage of the success. This phenomenon may easily triple the size of the assets of a smaller fund in less than a year. The fund may temporarily become too unwieldy for the existing management and go into a slump or be unable to sustain its previous growth rate. Closed-end funds, however, have only one means of growth in the size of their total assets: the increase in value of the investments held by these funds. This is distinctly different than increasing the size of total assets by selling more shares. Thus, a closed-end fund avoids the possibility of becoming too large too quickly.

Although no savings accumulation plan is provided by closed-end funds, you may use the Monthly Investment Plan (MIP) for those stocks listed on the New York Stock Exchange. This plan operates in much the same way as the savings accumulation plans offered by open-end funds, except that NYSE commissions are more expensive. Also, to reinvest the dividends you receive, you must pay the regular broker's commission, and there is no systematic withdrawal plan. You may purchase a closed-end fund through your broker just as you would purchase a common stock.

TAX ASPECTS OF MUTUAL FUNDS

The investment company, if it is highly specialized and nondiversified, receives the same tax treatment as any other corporation. Diversified investment companies (which include most closed-end and open-end funds) pay no federal income taxes, provided certain restrictions are met. In other words, the profits from your investment in a mutual fund flow directly to you: you are the only one who must pay taxes.

In order to be considered a diversified investment company by the SEC and, therefore, avoid paying federal corporate income taxes on that portion of income paid to the shareholders, the investment company (1) must have 90 percent of its gross income derived from interest, dividends, and securities profits, and (2) have at least 75 percent of its assets diversified, so that no single holding is greater than 5 percent of the fund's assets and no holding in a particular corporation is equal to 10 percent or more of that company's voting stock.

Each year, the mutual fund shareholder must pay ordinary income taxes on dividends received, and capital gains taxes on capital gains distributions and on gains resulting from the sale of fund shares held for more than six months. Some states, such as California, treat capital gains distributions as ordinary income for state income tax purposes.

ADVANTAGES AND DISADVANTAGES OF MUTUAL FUNDS
AS AN INVESTMENT

Perhaps the two most important advantages of investing in mutual funds are diversification and professional management. Your investment may be spread over 40 to 100 stocks, thus minimizing risk. You could never do this on your own because of the time and effort involved in managing a large portfolio. In terms of personal time and effort, with mutual funds there is no portfolio management required of you. Professionals do the worrying about when and what to buy and sell. Only if you become discontented with their results must you consider changing your investment.

In addition, there is potential for an above-average rate of return on well-selected funds. Over the past ten to twenty years, many funds looking for long-term growth have averaged 10 to 15 percent total return to the investor, compounded annually. Some have done better; many have done worse. As you can see from table 18-1, even an average mutual fund would have outperformed a 5 percent savings account in all but two five-year periods since 1950.

Also, a regular savings habit may be achieved with one of the accumulation plans. Quick dissipation of your built up investment is avoided by using a systematic withdrawal plan. There is also the advantage of capital gains tax rates. And, finally, you have the relative ease of matching your goals with the investment. A fund's prospectus states its investment goals in plain language. (The fund is required to show you a prospectus before you buy.)

The primary dangers to be aware of are selecting a poorly managed mutual fund, and investing for only a short period of time during which the stock market declines. In either case, you could lose money. If a fund is broadly diversified, there is generally little or no chance for abnormally high gains in the market. Also, good results are not assured, even with professional management. For example, an extensive study made in 1962 by the Wharton School of Finance and Commerce for the SEC showed that the balanced funds (stock-bond) performed no better on average than an unmanaged portfolio would have![1] Of course, this does

---

1. Report of the Committee on Interstate and Foreign Commerce, prepared by the Wharton School of Finance and Commerce, University of Pennsylvania, House report no. 2274 (Washington, D.C.: Government Printing Office, 1962).

not mean that all funds were average or that management has not improved since 1962. In addition, other types of funds may do better or worse. However, another study that was reported during 1966 showed that even the average common stock funds tended to perform 0.5 to 1 percent worse than the stock market averages.[1] This is probably due to the management fee. Thus, the bulk of mutual fund managers do no better and no worse than the market in general over the long term. Individual management, however, can range from excellent to poor. Even among the large, growth-oriented mutual funds (1971 assets over $300,000,000) performance for the ten years ended December 31, 1971, ranged from +55 percent to +174 percent.[2] The former is equal to a 4.6 percent annual compound gain. Thus, even among established firms, the performance can be worse than holding funds in a 6 percent account.

Short-term fluctuations must also be expected. Like common stocks, mutual funds are a long-term investment. If you invest for a short time only, you may have to sell during bear market conditions.

GUIDELINES FOR BUYING A MUTUAL FUND

The following points of consideration should help you choose between the hundreds of mutual funds available.

Do the investment goals of the fund match your own? The fund's prospectus (which you should always examine before you invest) outlines the objectives of the fund's management.

How much is the sales commission, if there is one? This can range from nothing (for a no-load fund) to 8 percent of the amount of each purchase. The management fees, which may range from 0.5 to 1 percent a year for all funds, are of little consequence.

Do you want the size restrictions of a closed-end fund? If so, do you want to give up the various accumulation, reinvestment, and withdrawal plans available with open-end funds? Remember, you will also have the cost of standard brokerage commissions and the problems of a market price that may fluctuate more than the asset value of the stocks held by the fund.

Past record should be the most important consideration. Most prospectuses give you the full details of a fund's record. In addition, the information sources listed at the end of the chapter can be useful in comparing the records of several funds. However, you should always check the prospectus to make sure that the management of the fund has not recently changed hands!

---

1. William F. Sharpe, "Mutual Fund Performance," *Journal of Business* (January, 1966), pp. 119–35.

2. *Investment Companies* (New York: Wiesenberger Services, 1971).

In addition, we discourage investing in small mutual funds (less than $25,000,000 in assets) if they have recently shown a spectacular performance. Such a record usually attracts a flood of investor dollars and, almost overnight, the fund becomes a major-sized fund. The management that was expert at investing a small flexible fund is suddenly in a very different situation, and the results can be disastrous. For example, the O'Neil Fund was the number one fund in 1967, with a growth rate of 115.6 percent and total net assets of $9.2 million. In 1968, a great influx of new investor dollars made the fund five times larger (total net assets of $48.7 million), and O'Neil wound up near the bottom of mutual fund ratings with a gain of only 3.8 percent in the bull market of 1968.

Mutual funds are continually starting up. Generally, the younger the fund, the less experienced the management and the shorter the record that you have to look at. One year in a bull market would not be representative. However, if a new fund is simply a new addition to an old family, you may have an excellent blend of experience and flexibility. The size of the fund may also increase with age, since an open-end fund usually continues to acquire new shareholders. Figure 18-5 may help you decide what size mutual fund (diversified common stock) to buy, assuming that size correlates with experience and age.

If you have decided to purchase a closed-end fund, see your stockbroker both for information about the company and to purchase the shares. For open-end load funds, contact your broker or respond to an advertisement in the newspaper. Your broker may be an authorized and commissioned representative for the fund you wish to buy. Otherwise, a fund salesman will call on you. In either case you should realize that both the broker and the fund salesman will want to make a sale and take a commission.

Range of Fund's Net Assets (approximate)	Possible Characteristics
Less than $25 million	Low experience or security (unless new fund in old family) Generally high price fluctuations Flexibility to take advantage of opportunities Possible "go–go" growth
$25–$300 million	Blend of experience, stability, and flexibility Possible above-average growth
Over $300 million	Security, stability, and experience Limited flexibility to take advantage of opportunities Fund growth may approximate that of the general market

Fig. 18-5.
Characteristics of
mutual funds based
on size

With open-end no-load funds, you must write to the company for information and a prospectus. All dealings will be directly with them. You can get addresses from ads in the newspaper, from your broker, and from other information sources. Here is a list of some major funds with above-average records.

Funds stressing long-term growth

David L. Babson Investment Fund, Inc., 301 West Eleventh Street, Kansas City, Missouri 64105

Beacon Hill Mutual Fund, Inc., 75 Federal Street, Boston, Massachusetts 02110

deVegh Mutual Fund, 20 Exchange Place, New York, New York 10005

Drexel Equity Fund, 1500 Walnut Street, Philadelphia, Pennsylvania 19101

Growth Industry Shares, Inc., 135 South LaSalle Street, Chicago, Illinois 60603

Guardian Mutual Fund, Inc., 120 Broadway Street, New York, New York 10005

Johnston Mutual Fund, 460 Park Avenue, New York, New York 10022

Loomis-Sales Mutual Fund, Inc., 225 Franklin Street, Boston, Massachusetts 02110

The One William Street Fund, Inc., One William Street, New York, New York 10004

Penn Square Mutual Fund, 451 Penn Square, Reading, Pennsylvania 19601

Pine Street Fund, Inc., 20 Exchange Place, New York, New York 10005

T. Rowe Price Growth Stock Fund, One Charles Center, Baltimore, Maryland 21201

Steadman Associated Fund, Inc., 919 Eighteenth Street N.W., Washington, D.C. 20006

Stein Roe & Farnham Balanced Fund, Inc., 150 South Wacker Drive, Chicago, Illinois 60606

Stein Roe & Farnham Stock Fund, Inc., 150 South Wacker Drive, Chicago, Illinois 60606

Funds stressing performance (often highly volatile)

Hedberg and Gordon Fund, One Station Square, Paoli, Pennsylvania 19301

Ivy Fund, 155 Berkeley Street, Boston, Massachusetts 02116

Loomis-Sales Capital Development Fund, 225 Franklin Street, Boston, Massachusetts 02110

Mathers Fund, One First National Plaza, Chicago, Illinois 60607

Naess & Thomas Special Fund, Inc., 201 North Charles Street, Baltimore, Maryland 21201

Rowe Price New Horizons Fund, Inc., One Charles Center, Baltimore, Maryland 21201

Scudder Special Fund, 10 Post Office Square, Boston, Massachusetts 02109

CONCLUSION

Mutual funds provide the average investor with a way to invest in the stock market without either risking money on just a few stocks or spending a lot of time watching over his investments. The only task left him is to choose an appropriate fund, a task that we hope this chapter has made less burdensome. However, since a mutual fund investment is spread over many stocks, the chances of making an extraordinary profit are reduced.

VOCABULARY

balanced fund
capital gains distribution
closed-end fund
contractual savings plan
dual fund
investment company
load
load fund

net asset value
no-load fund
open-end fund
prospectus
savings accumulation plan
systematic withdrawal plan
voluntary accumulation plan

QUESTIONS

1. What is the difference, if any, in commissions and management fees charged by load funds and no-load funds?
2. Describe the kind of investor for whom mutual funds are an appropriate investment.
3. Why may your stockbroker not be an appropriate source of information regarding the selection of mutual funds? What would be a good source?
4. What special advantages do mutual funds have over individual stock market investments? Describe at least four.
5. What should a person check for before signing a contractual investment plan with a mutual fund?

6. How might the size of a mutual fund be a factor in your investment decision?
7. What is the most important factor in selecting a mutual fund?
8. Why are closed-end investment companies much like common stocks?
9. Using the information provided in figure 18-3, determine the years during which your investment would have shown a loss had you bought shares at the first of the year.
10. Why might it be better to invest in a mutual fund that was consistently above average over the past decade than in a new fund that was the leading growth performer last year?

CASE PROBLEM

Two months ago Jay graduated from college and started a well-paying job. Since, as a student, he had become accustomed to living on a part-time income, he was able to save about $200 a month from his salary. His job and his personal life kept him busy, and so he decided to keep his investments simple by selecting a mutual fund. Having neither dependents nor high priority investment objectives as yet, he was willing to take a certain amount of risk in exchange for a potentially high return.

In order to find a good aggressive growth mutual fund, Jay read the prospectuses on eight mutual funds that were recommended by a business professor of his. Figure 18-6 (p. 426) shows how these funds compare in objective, age, size, and performance history.

1. What is the average compound return for each of these funds since its inception? Does Jay's professor seem to have selected an above-average group of funds?
2. Which of these funds appears to be most appropriate for Jay in objective, size, and management performance? Give several reasons for your choice.
3. If Jay wanted to look at other funds and make a quick comparison of performance over comparable time periods, what should he do?
4. What would you recommend to Jay if the fund you selected had a $1000 minimum investment requirement, with a $50 monthly minimum thereafter, while the other funds required an initial minimum of $400? (Assume that Jay has saved $400 from his salary for his first two months' work.)

Fund	Management Company	Investment Growth Objective	Age (Years)	Size (Millions)	Performance History			1972 Value of $10,000 Investment[a]
					1970	1971	1972	
1	Smith & Co.	Long term	20	$400	Down	Up	Down	$105,000
2	Black & Co.	Aggressive	10	520	Down	Up	Up	29,000
3	Black & Co.	Aggressive	2	45	–	Up	Even	15,000
4	J. Jones, Inc.	Long term	20	460	Even	Up	Up	137,000
5	J. Jones, Inc.	Aggressive	3	105	Down	Up	Up	16,000
6	W. W. Wilson	Aggressive	2	20	–	Up	Up	16,000
7	P. Green Co.	Long term	18	90	Down	Up	Even	79,000
8	P. Green Co.	Long term	4	60	Even	Up	Up	15,000

[a]Invested at fund's inception and all dividends and capital gains distributions reinvested.

Fig. 18-6.
Comparison of eight
mutual funds
(fictitious)

The following sources should help you compare and select mutual funds. Most are expensive, but they are available at major libraries and brokerage houses.

Forbes (60 Fifth Avenue, New York, New York 10011).

> This business magazine is published twice a month and costs $7.50 a year. Each year the August fifteenth issue presents a survey of fund performance and rates mutual funds according to its own evaluation system.

FundScope (1900 Avenue of the Stars, Los Angeles, California 90067).

> This monthly publication is devoted entirely to mutual funds. It costs $60 a year. The annual guide (April edition) is available separately for $20, and ranks all funds for the past ten years. Other issues rank fund performance for the past one- and five-year periods and for special periods such as those characterized by important advances or declines or by bull or bear markets.

Investment Companies (Wiesenberger Services, One New York Plaza, New York, New York 10004).

> This annual publication costs $45, which includes the cost of quarterly supplements on leading funds. This book is a large and complete reference source, now in its thirty-first edition. It gives general information about mutual funds and provides facts and figures on individual funds.

Johnson's Investment Company Charts (Rand Building, Buffalo, New York 14203).

> This annual publication costs $40. It presents readily comparable data on 177 mutual funds through full-page graphs that show the results of a $10,000 investment made ten years ago. The book also provides data on more than 300 funds.

CHUCK AND NANCY ANDERSON

COMPUTING THE EFFECTIVE RETURN ON A MUTUAL FUND

Chuck and Nancy have decided that mutual funds are an appropriate investment for some of their goals. Now they must decide which funds to invest in. After reading several prospectuses, Chuck decided that Growth Fund and Dynamic Fund have objectives that match his. They also offer the voluntary accumulation plan he wants, and each fund is under the same management as when it started. Both funds are fairly large. On closer inspection of the prospectuses for these two funds, Chuck and Nancy find the following statements:

(Growth Fund) Assume a $10,000 investment in March 1958. If all dividends and capital gains were received as cash, the value of your shares today would be $21,370. If only capital gains were reinvested, the value of your shares would be $39,625. If both dividends and capital gains were reinvested, your $10,000 investment would have grown to $48,512 as of March 31, 1972.

(Dynamic Fund) Assume a $10,000 investment in June 1955. If all dividends and capital gains were received as cash, the value of your shares today would be $34,420. If only capital gains were reinvested, the value of your shares would be $48,122. If both dividends and capital gains were reinvested, your $10,000 investment would have grown to $53,260 as of June 30, 1972.

QUESTIONS

1. Which figure in these quotes is the appropriate one to compare for each fund?
2. What is the effective compound rate of return for each fund?
3. Which fund should Chuck select?
4. If Chuck read the prospectus of the Dynagrowth Fund, founded in 1966, would he probably be able to make a fair comparison of the three funds? Why or why not?
5. What source could Chuck use if he needed information that would help him compare funds with widely disparate founding dates?

19

REAL ESTATE

"Real estate never wears out; it never goes out of style."

"Money in land isn't spent—it's saved."

"The supply of land is fixed; you can't manufacture more of it. Yet the demand inevitably grows with the population."

"You don't wait to invest in real estate; you invest and then wait."

Nearly everyone hears such ideas at some time and seriously considers investing in real estate. Fortunes have been made in real estate because of these simple premises; but thousands of unsophisticated real estate investors have lost money because they were unaware of the risks involved or how to avoid them.

This chapter will deal with several phases of real estate investing: investing in a site for a second home, investing in trust deeds, and investing in professional trusts and syndicates. We will not discuss investing in and managing real estate on your own since that would require another complete text, at the very least.

A SECOND HOME IN THE COUNTRY

Because of increased affluence and the deterioration of the urban environment, more and more Americans want land in the country—somewhere to build a weekend home. If this ever becomes one of your goals, you should know how to reach that goal without incurring unnecessary expenses.

The Current Situation

The demand for recreational lots has grown so large that the business has become profitable for major land developers. In California, this demand put the developers into a full-fledged boom. According to the California State Treasurer's office, at the present rate of construction only two-thirds of the 300,000 available lots will have been built on by the year 2025.[1] As a consequence, there are more pieces of land available than there are people wanting to buy them—especially at developers' prices. For example, in the late 1960s the Board of Supervisors of El Dorado County (which includes the south shore of Lake Tahoe) commissioned a three-year study to determine the investment quality of recreational subdivision lots. Their results showed that of 255 lots resold by original purchasers, 251 were sold for less than their purchase price!

Guidelines for the Buyer

If you are shopping for country property in order to build a cabin or second home (not for investment, which is highly speculative and requires a complicated analysis), use the following guidelines to minimize both expense and frustration.

1. Try to buy a lot from an individual rather than a developer. Otherwise, you could spend more money than necessary.
2. Do not buy without visiting the property—it may be swampy or undesirable in some other equally important way. While you are there, check with other realtors to compare prices on similar lots.
3. Before you buy find out what your utilities, sewer or septic tank, water well, and the like will cost so that you know whether you can afford them.
4. Get bids on the potential building cost before committing yourself to buy a lot.
5. Before you buy a lot, visit the assessor's office to determine what the property taxes will be after the purchase. They may be raised a significant amount.
6. Check with the state commissioner's office to see what protection, if any, you have under state laws. In California, for example, a 1971 law provides that a buyer can change his mind without cause and

---

1. David Jensen, "Recreation Land Developers Controlled Under New Law." *Palo Alto Times*, November 17, 1971, p. 24.

without penalty up to fourteen days after signing a contract with a developer. The law also provides that subdivisions of more than fifty lots cannot be sold unless the state real estate commissioner has issued a report on the project and the report has been issued to the prospective buyer.

HIGH INTEREST ON YOUR MONEY: MORTGAGES AND DEEDS OF TRUST

Mortgages and deeds of trust are two slightly different legal mechanisms for borrowing money against a piece of real estate. Unlike a mortgage, a deed of trust is held by an independent party (trustee) until the debt is paid off. Usage of one or the other varies from state to state.

First mortgages, or first deeds of trust, (commonly known as *firsts*) have first claim against a property in the event of a default in loan payments; second mortgages, or second deeds of trust, (*seconds*) have claim to the equity remaining after the first holder's claim has been settled. For example, a $40,000 home may have a $30,000 first and a $5000 second; the owner of the home has only $5000 of his own money in the property. The rest is borrowed from the first and second lender.

In the event of a default on either loan, the lenders would begin foreclosure proceedings. That is, they would go through the state legal process to put the home up for sale in order to recoup their loans. If there were any money left after the first and second lenders have been paid off and the legal expenses paid, it would go to the homeowner. (Often such legal expenses can run to as much as 5 to 10 percent of the sale price of the property.)

First Mortgages (or First Deeds of Trust)

Firsts are usually issued by banks, savings and loan associations, and similar institutional investors. However, sometimes such investments are available to private investors through mortgage pools. For example, a savings and loan, having run out of loanable funds and unable to satisfy its customers' demands for mortgage loans, may pool several mortgages and offer investment shares in the pool to the public for perhaps $5000 each. Such shares may carry interest rates one or two percentage points above those allowed on federally insured deposits. In this case, your insurance is the security offered by the mortgages or deeds of trust themselves. Since such loans usually amount to no more than 80 or 90 percent of the market value of the property, they are fairly safe investments for the lender.

If you are considering such an investment but are unsure about the reputation of the savings and loan or about the soundness of the security offered, check with your lawyer. Such investments can offer a fairly low-risk, high-yield opportunity.

Second Mortgages (or Second Deeds of Trust)

A second mortgage is usually issued to finance the portion of the purchase price on a piece of property that is not covered by the down payment and the first mortgage. In the event of default, a second has a claim to the property but only after the balance on the first has been settled. Hence, there is less protection for the investor in second mortgages. In exchange for this higher risk, seconds usually offer a return that is several percentage points above the rates on firsts. For an investment of $3000 to $5000, for example, the investor usually receives a 10 to 11 percent yield in interest income.

In general, second trust deeds are used by borrowers to reduce the down payment on the purchase of a home, to provide capital to start a business or for some other investment, or to consolidate higher interest cost debts into one lower cost package. Terms are flexible, with maturities ranging from three to ten years. Ten percent interest is generally the maximum allowed by state law, but the lender may also charge an extra nine to fifteen points to write the loan, as well as six to twelve months' interest as a prepayment penalty. Therefore, a borrower's annual effective interest cost often exceeds 15 percent. Other sources of loans are usually much less expensive.

advantages of seconds for the investor As figure 19-1 shows, for the lender, second deeds of trust have a significant advantage over second mortgages in that there are standard procedures for the trustee to follow in the event of default on a trust deed. He merely executes and records a notice of default. On a second mortgage, however, title is held by the borrower, and so it is necessary to have an attorney initiate foreclosure proceedings. Then it may take six to twelve months to force the sale of the mortgaged property so that the lender can recover his money. On a second deed of trust the lender is likely to have to wait only four to six months. The shorter the period, the better because during these months the holder of a second must use his own money to make the payments on the first in order to protect his investment.

Both second mortgages and second deeds of trust are advantageous because they offer high interest yields. Since the lender who originates the loan retains the front-end points, the return available to the investor who purchases the loan is the 10 percent interest allowed by law. This return generally averages out to 11 percent total yield over many second deeds of trust because the investor usually shares in the prepayment penalties, and sometimes there are also late payment penalties.

The regular income, generally monthly or quarterly, from seconds is especially attractive to retired persons or others seeking to supplement their ordinary income. And, finally, there are no management duties required of the investor if the deed is handled by a full-service loan broker.

Type of Loan	Holder of Title to Property	Average Foreclosure Period	Investor Action Needed for Foreclosure
Second Deed of Trust	Third party trustee	4 to 6 months	Have trustee execute and record notice of default
Second Mortgage	Borrower	6 to 12 months	Have attorney initiate foreclosure proceedings

Fig. 19-1. Comparison of second deed of trust and second mortgage

disadvantages of seconds for the investor Some people lose money in poorly written seconds. If you have to foreclose, you may find that you cannot sell the house for enough to pay off the first and the broker's fee, and still recover your investment. In order to minimize this possibility, you should deal only with reputable loan brokers. They will generally loan only up to 50 percent of the available equity value (market price less the first's balance due) based on a conservative appraisal. This is your best guarantee of investment security. In any case, foreclosures generally occur in only about 3 percent of all loans.

There is a long holding period generally required on seconds—three to five years. Of course, if it is an amortized loan with no balloon payment, you will get your money back earlier because of installments. It is also possible to sell seconds that are several years old but not yet at maturity through loan brokers to other investors if you need the funds early. However, this may require a small discount from the face value.

There is no inflation protection with seconds because the face value and the interest rate remain the same, regardless of how the cost of living changes. Of course, when compared with other interest-bearing investments, 10 percent is a favorable return.

This investment is not for conservative investors. If you feel uneasy about foreclosures or would worry if a payment came a few weeks late, perhaps for your own peace of mind you would be better off taking a lower rate of return on short-maturity corporate bonds.

sources of seconds The primary source of seconds for the investor is a loan broker. He appraises the property, makes the loan, and collects the points as his fee. He will then sell the loan certificate to the investor, who collects the interest and principal payments. The broker makes collections and provides other services such as managing delinquent loans or initiating foreclosure proceedings.

In selecting the proper loan broker, you should examine his foreclosure and loss record. Some large and/or well-managed firms have yet to lose money for their clients. You should also look for the following features in the loans he writes: request for notices of default and sale, acceleration clause, penalty on late payments, and prepayment penalties.

The *request for notices of default and sale* requires second and first lenders to let each other know when a loan is in default. This prohibits foreclosure by one lender without the knowledge of the other. The result is that the first lender will generally go to the second lender for his monthly payments rather than foreclose and sell at a low bid (enough only for the first mortgage) and wipe out the second lender's security. The second lender must then handle the foreclosure to protect his investment in the mortgage as well as the first lender's investment.

An *acceleration clause* prevents the borrower from assigning his debt to any other person without the permission of the lender. For example, if you sell your house to a poor risk as far as the second lender is concerned, he will ask for full payment from you, rather than carry a high-risk second. In such a situation, the lender can demand full and immediate payment of the loan balance or else start foreclosure proceedings. Once started, these proceedings cannot be stopped legally without full payment of the second loan balance due.

A small *penalty on late payments*—usually 10 percent on the monthly amount—may be levied. This penalty increases the likelihood that payments will be made on time. It also makes it possible that a 10 percent interest yield will become a 13 to 16 percent total annual yield if borrowers frequently pay late. In addition, when loans are paid off early, there may be a small *prepayment penalty*—usually four to six months' interest on the outstanding debt—to compensate the lender for the trouble of getting his money reinvested. This penalty often provides an extra margin of profit for the lender.

OWNING THE PROPERTY, NOT JUST THE MORTGAGE

If you have several thousand dollars that you know will not be needed for several years and are willing to take the time to learn about selecting and managing real estate, you may wish to consider investing in real estate on your own. If you do not feel competent to select and manage your own real estate but still want to take advantage of such investments, you should consider investing in real estate investment trusts, companies, or syndicates.

Real Estate Investment Trust (REIT)

A real estate investment trust is an unincorporated association that invests in mortgages (a mortgage trust) or real property (an equity trust). Investment trusts spread their risk over many different properties. Mortgage trusts, for example, do not necessarily invest their funds in first and second mortgages. Many of the mortgages are construction loans to builders at high rates of interest (9 to 18 percent annually) for short periods of time. Such trusts are capable of adapting to economic conditions. In fact, during the inflationary period of 1970–71, they offered as much as a 9 to 10 percent annual dividend yield. Equity trusts invest in properties such as apartments and office buildings and thus obtain most of their income from rents, less expenses. This income tends to be a smaller annual amount than that for mortgage trusts. However, the capital gains potential and inflationary hedge due to possible price appreciation are definitely compensating factors.

There are over a hundred investment trusts whose shares are traded on the open market just like common stock. Since they are traded like stocks, their value is not always equal to the asset value of the holdings, but fluctuates with changing market conditions. These shares can usually be bought for $10 to $20 each, and may be sold fairly easily in an emergency. Many trusts are listed on major stock exchanges. To minimize investment risks in the highly competitive REIT industry, stick with the major listed trusts. Your stockbroker can identify most of them for you. In addition, he may have reports on REITs in general. You should evaluate REITs much as you would common stocks.

Investment trusts are a direct result of the Real Estate Investment Trust Act of 1960, which was designed to provide an opportunity for small investors to invest in real estate. They are exempted from corporate income taxes provided they conform to certain rules. Among the rules are that at least 90 percent of a trust's income must be distributed to the shareholders; the trust must have at least 100 shareholders; three-fourths of its income and assets must be related to real estate investments, either ownership or mortgages; capital gains income is limited to 30 percent of its gross income (to minimize wild stock or land speculation that might offer more risk to the shareholder than he expected when he made his investment); a trust cannot directly manage any property it owns (to prevent the investor from being victimized by sophisticated trust managers who may extract many different, and often hidden, management fees).

The income received by the stockholder is taxed only to him, not to the trust, and he pays capital gains rates on the capital gains portion of this income. Other portions of the income may be tax-free because of depreciation shelter provisions in the tax law regarding equity trusts.

Real Estate Investment Company

A real estate investment company is similar to a trust except that it must pay a corporate income tax. Therefore, you can be taxed twice on the same real estate income—first at the corporate level and then at the individual level when any income such as dividends is distributed.

The advantage in this sort of company is that it can retain its earnings and grow faster than a trust can; the investor thus benefits from the capital growth of his shares. This type of investment is simply another common stock investment.

Limited Partnerships: The Real Estate Syndicate

A real estate investment syndicate is a group of people (partnership) joined together under one management (general partner) to buy and manage property—usually a single piece of property, but sometimes as many as five or ten pieces. Most syndicates are limited partnerships, in which nonmanaging investors (limited partners) assume a risk up to the limit of their original investment (as little as $2500). Syndicate shares are usually sold in multiples of $500 or $1000.

Two forms of syndicates are offered in many states: single property and blind pool. The single property syndicator simply purchases, for a small percentage sum, an option to buy one apartment house, mobile home park, or office building, and then offers shares in the project to prospective investors in order to raise the rest of the money needed to close the deal. With the blind pool type of investment, the syndicator first raises perhaps a million dollars or more (based only on the strength of his reputation as a syndicator) and then decides on purchases of several properties in different areas, thus diversifying the investor's risk.

In a single property syndicate, a group of sixty investors might decide to purchase a $1,000,000 apartment complex by putting $300,000 down ($5000 each). A blind pool would involve more properties and require more money from a greater number of limited partners. The syndicate management, usually a real estate brokerage or finance firm, would take a small percentage of the income as its fee and distribute the rest of the income to the investors. The management usually takes fees in other forms, such as property management, as well.

total yield Investors in real estate syndicates should look at four aspects of return on the investment in order to get the true picture of their anticipated total yield: cash flow distribution, equity build-up, price appreciation, and tax shelter benefits.

The *cash flow distribution* is the actual cash distributed to all investors out of the cash income (rental revenues) of the property. For example, an annual operating statement might look like this:

Rent revenues (at 95 percent occupancy)		$480,000
Operating and management expenses	$176,000	
Mortgage payment	210,000	
Reserve for repairs (5 percent)	24,000	
Emergency reserve	10,000	
Total	420,000	
Cash flow to partners		$ 60,000

If the investors had invested $800,000, this cash flow would amount to 7.5 percent a year. Because of the depreciation provisions of the tax law, most, if not all, of that distribution is tax-free to investors. Annual cash flow generally ranges from 5 to 8 percent of an investment each year for average properties under normal conditions. On one hand, in hard economic times or with poor cash control management, the cash flow may be zero or negative. On the other, if a property is purchased cheaply during difficult economic situations, later cash flow rates may rise as high as 30 percent annually!

The *equity build-up* is the amount by which the investor's equity investment grows each year as mortgage balances are reduced by the monthly payments made from revenues. Such equity build-up can add 4 to 7 percent each year to the total return, provided the property does not decline in price. If at least part of the mortgage loan is paid off, the eventual sale of the property should result in more cash to the investor.

Price appreciation may occur if the property is bought for a good price, well maintained, and well managed for growing profits. Negotiating a good purchase price for the investor is a difficult job that not all syndicators do well. If it is done well, however, an annual price appreciation of 3 to 5 percent is not uncommon (but by no means guaranteed).

Tax shelter benefits are also available. Often, a portion of the original investment can be written off against other taxable income because of tax deductions for prepaid interest (second year's interest paid ahead of time) and certain partnership formation expenses. In addition, during the first few years, there may be excess tax shelter benefits (depreciation losses) over and above the cash flow amounts, which you can also apply against income and thereby reduce your income taxes.

potential risks   There are four broad categories of risk that you should be aware of before investing in a real estate syndicate.

1. *Will there be price appreciation or depreciation?* This problem can often be solved by making sure you are not paying too much for the property. (You must realize that the syndicator is probably taking a commission related to the dollar amount of the purchase price.) In general, there are two guidelines for estimating the right price. One is the gross income multiplier (G.M.), and the other is the capitalization rate (cap rate).

   The *gross income multiplier* is computed by dividing the total price (all monies paid to close the deal, including mortgages) by the projected gross rents. For example, a $1,200,000 purchase projecting rent revenues—gross income—of $200,000 (assuming no vacancies) would have a G.M. of 6. Such a figure may or may not be good, depending on the local rate. Check with several local realtors to determine the average gross income multiplier for the area. Generally, it is very difficult to justify a gross income multiplier in excess of 7.

The *capitalization rate* is derived by dividing the net operating income (after expenses but before depreciation and loan payments) by the total purchase price. For example, a $1,000,000 property with net income of $100,000 would have a cap rate of 10 percent. That is, if you paid full cash for the building, you would have a 10 percent cash yield each year, as long as the building was 95 percent full. The minimum acceptable cap rate for any income property should be 8.5 to 10 percent depending upon the risk involved and current cap rates for comparable properties.

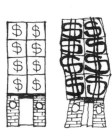

2. *Will the building stay fully rented at the proposed rents?* Although you cannot know the future for a building that is new, you can at least check with a few realtors to see if the proposed rents are realistic for that type of property. Check also to see whether there are unusual vacancy problems in similar properties around town. For an existing building, check the syndicators' projections by asking the present manager what the rent is and how many units are vacant. Even if the tax consequences on your property are straightforward, an investment may be highly speculative because a property has a small down payment and a sizeable mortgage. The mortgage payments may be so high that the property could tolerate only a slight vacancy problem before foreclosure would be likely.

3. *Will the IRS challenge your right to some of the proposed tax deductions?* Syndicators sometimes try to squeeze more than the last drop of tax loss out of a property. Check with a tax attorney or C.P.A. to see if your proposed investment may have trouble getting by the IRS. You should be especially suspicious of any syndicator who promises more than a 50 percent write-off in the first year of your original investment (e.g., a $5000 tax loss on a $10,000 investment).

4. *Will the general partner stay solvent and stand behind the investment?* If the general partner goes bankrupt, property management often declines in quality or becomes nonexistent while the limited partners try to decide whom to sue and whom to get for a new manager. The consequences often result in default on the properties and foreclosure by the lender. Therefore, you should seek out established general partners who have a strong balance sheet (positive net worth with a good proportion of liquid assets) and a history of profitability. Established general partners have been known to stand behind a property that was having temporary financial difficulty by waiving their management fee and/or extending low-interest loans to the partnership. A financially weak general partner could not do this.

advantages and disadvantages of a syndicate investment The major advantages that attract investors to real estate syndicates are high

total yield, no management required of the investor, and economies of scale. It is not uncommon for total return on an investment in a real estate syndicate to range between 12 and 24 percent a year, depending on the investor's tax bracket, the syndicator's expertise, and local real estate conditions. Furthermore, in order to retain limited partner status (and, therefore, limited liability status), the investor is not allowed to participate in management functions except to vote on disbandment of the partnership and on replacement of the general partner/manager. Economies of scale—such as management overhead, advertising, grounds maintenance, and supplies and equipment purchasing—begin to occur with apartment houses of about 100 or more units. An investor with only $5000 could not obtain these economies on his own. In addition, the new blind pools offer diversification over several large properties, something that would be even more impossible for the small investor. However, the usual advantages of real estate investing (tax benefits and price appreciation, for example) are available to the investor just as they would be if he were investing on his own.

As with all real estate investments, the investor should consider syndicates as a long-term investment. It usually takes at least six or seven years before the accelerated depreciation declines to the point at which it may be advantageous to sell because there are no further excess tax shelter benefits. Selling your share to someone else at a profit before the actual building is sold is almost impossible, no matter what the syndicator says, and this holding period could be a disadvantage for some investors. Because of the lack of liquidity, an investor should never invest more than 50 percent of his investment dollars either in real estate syndicates or in speculative real estate on his own.

Another disadvantage of investing in real estate syndicates is the many risks associated with them. As we stated in chapter 13, high potential yields on an investment usually indicate high risks. In this case, your investment could suffer from too many vacancies and, therefore, have insufficient cash to meet the mortgage payments. Or the syndicator may have paid so much for the property that there will be loss when it is sold. Of course, proven management can minimize these risks.

The $2500 to $10,000 minimum investment required may be a disadvantage if you do not have that much money for a long-term investment. In that case, you should consider REITs (trusts) instead of syndications. Or maybe you have that much money but do not meet minimum state financial qualifications. In California, for example, you must have $20,000 gross income and $20,000 assets. For single property syndicates, the requirements are stiffer. These regulations are designed to screen out unsophisticated investors. Even if you are willing to invest without meeting the qualifications, the syndicator will prevent you from signing if he finds out that your financial situation does not qualify. He does not want to risk losing his license from the state.

locating and making the syndicate investment   To locate real estate syndicates, you can search the ads on the financial pages of the newspaper (many such firms hold seminars on real estate that are really only sales promotions to solicit syndicate investors); ask large local real estate brokerage firms whether they put together syndicates; and consult national directories and other such sources for complete listings of syndicate management groups. One such directory is the *National Real Estate Investor*, available for $5 from Communication Channels (132 W. Thirty-First Street, New York, New York 10001). This directory is published annually.

Before making a final decision on a syndicate investment, you should do three things. First, check with the local Better Business Bureau, Chamber of Commerce, and real estate boards to make sure that the management's practices are fair and honest. Second, check with your attorney as to the legality of the syndicate's partnership agreement and whether it includes restrictions on selling shares after they are bought or any other undesirable restrictions. Third, apply to the proposed investment the twelve points for evaluation outlined below. This analysis could take you an hour or two, but it might also keep you out of one of the many bad deals being offered.

1. *Ignore the tax shelter gimmicks.* Depending on the amount of prepaid interest and front-end management fees involved and how small the down payment is, your initial tax write-off could range from 10 to 80 percent of your original investment. Look past these tax shelter gimmicks to see if you are getting an investment that is sound on the basis of its own merits. Tax shelter selling is often a cover-up for an otherwise bad deal that a syndicator is trying to push for his own gain. This is very likely to be the case when write-offs greater than 50 percent are promised.

2. *What is the syndicator's record?* Does he have at least several years of experience in real estate syndicates? If not, is he experienced in real estate, particularly the financial and managerial aspects, or has he been involved in real estate merely as a broker? Brokers know how to sell properties, not necessarily how to manage them or structure financial agreements.

3. *Look for public deals only.* These are syndicates that have been registered with the state commissioner or SEC. Although some private deals offer above-average potential for friends of the syndicator or small groups of large investors, too many of them are loaded with excessive and hidden fees for the syndicator.

4. *Are you paying a fair price for the property?* The simplest way to determine this is to apply the gross income multiplier, a figure similar to the stock market P/E ratio. If your figure is too high compared to local gross income multipliers, the syndicator is ap-

parently too anxious to put together a deal. Look for a lower priced syndicate. In general, any property priced at more than seven times gross income is probably too expensive.

5. *Is the financing about right?* The proposed project should have a 20 to 30 percent down payment, and the total annual debt service (principal and interest) should not exceed 50 to 52 percent of the project's gross income after a 5 percent vacancy allowance. Also, note when the second mortgage balloon payment is due. If the maturity is less than ten years, will the cash be there to pay it off, or will your cash income payment for several years be wiped out to pay off the mortgage? Do not count on being able to refinance the second at favorable terms.

6. *Does the property have any reserves?* Roughly 5 percent of the partners' total contributed capital should be set aside in a reserve fund for such things as new carpets and water heaters. If not, you can probably bet that the cash flow projections for the first year or two will not be achieved.

7. *Be wary of appreciation factors.* To boost their yield projections, some syndicators automatically plug in an annual price appreciation factor of about 4 percent. Appreciation is not automatic. It can be achieved only if the building is worth more upon resale (income has grown faster than expenses); and only at that time can you know what the price will be. Compare your alternatives without the appreciation factors.

8. *Are vacancy allowances realistic?* You might think that if a syndicator plugs in a 2 percent vacancy allowance he is being conservative. On the contrary, 2 percent is the minimum economic vacancy rate. A 5 percent rate is more realistic. Even more preferable is to compare the projected rate with current vacancy rates in that project as well as in others in the surrounding area. A local realtor can often help you here.

9. *Is the syndicate diversified or one building only?* An investor in a diversified syndicate can take advantage of the spreading of some overhead costs and the spreading of risks even if he has only $5000 or $10,000 to invest. Since, in this case he is buying the syndicator's management expertise, however, he is unable to evaluate the individual properties. Diversified syndicates buy properties only as they raise the funds—over a period of six to twelve months. Of course, if the syndicator's record is good, diversified syndicates may be a wise investment.

10. *Is your liability limited?* Check to see whether there is a clause providing for assessments if additional money is needed. If so, be

sure that it is limited to 3 or 5 percent or else you may not be able to pay assessments and may have to forfeit profits. Also, be sure you are investing only as a limited partner and not as a general partner or a participant in joint venture, in which cases your liability would be unlimited.

11. *Are there any potential conflicts of interest?* Avoid investments where, according to the prospectus, the syndicator may purchase a property for the partnership from one of his subsidiaries. He may be making a substantial markup over cost. Also, be careful if any remodeling, repair, or other services can be provided by the syndicators' firm without requiring competitive bids.

12. *What does the syndicator get?* Typical fees can include up to 6 percent real estate brokerage commissions on property purchases and sales; 5 percent of rentals for on-site property management; about 1 percent of gross income for partnership management; and 2 to 10 percent of profits, usually payable only after the limited partners receive a 100 percent payback of their investment. Try to avoid syndicates that take more than this, especially if there are sales commission charges of 8 or 9 percent paid by the investor in addition to the real estate brokerage commissions or if the syndicator takes more than 6 percent of the gross income for combined property and partnership management fees. Such excessive fees serve only to reduce your potential return.

CONCLUSION

Second-home sites should be purchased only to build on for your own use, not for speculation unless you are thoroughly familiar with local economics. Keep in mind that you often will pay more for a lot from a developer than if you buy a lot from an individual.

Second deeds of trust, when properly screened and managed by professionals, can offer relatively secure fixed income and high yield. They are especially appropriate for retired persons or others who are in low tax brackets and do not need additional long-term capital gains.

Equity investments in carefully selected, professionally managed real estate trust or syndicates can provide high yield with both tax advantages through depreciation deductions and a hedge against inflation.

This chapter should in no way be construed as offering insights into real estate analysis, acquisition, and management on your own.

cash flow
deed of trust
depreciation
foreclosure
general partner

limited partner
mortgage
prepaid interest
real estate syndicate
real estate investment trust (REIT)

1. What are the potential pitfalls in investing in recreational lots?
2. What risks must you assume in exchange for the 10 percent yields offered by second deeds of trust?
3. What are the income tax consequences of investing in second deeds?
4. Why is it good for the investor to have an acceleration clause in a second trust deed?
5. What is the difference between a mortgage REIT and an equity REIT?
6. Under what circumstances would an equity REIT be a more appropriate investment than a real estate syndicate?
7. Compare blind pool and single property syndicates.
8. As a syndicate investor, what three types of financial items should you keep a record of if you wish to compute your total return on your investment?
9. Name three potential risks that you face when you invest in real estate limited partnerships.

In June, Bob and Kay Winkelmann graduated from college, and in August each started a well-paying job. They had no investments but wanted to start some, and so by the next June they had accumulated $5000 to use in this way. They expected that by the end of the year they would have $7000 to $8000 in addition to their emergency fund. Since they had that much money for investments and their $20,000 joint taxable income would be taxed in a combined state and federal marginal tax bracket of 30 percent, they decided to consider investing in real estate. This investment might provide them with not only long-term growth and a hedge against inflation but also tax savings. Figure 19-2 (p. 444) compares the five alternatives they had to choose from.

Investment	Projected Income Yield (%)	Minimum Investment Amount	Income Tax Aspects
Second deeds of trust	10 (interest)	$2000	Interest fully taxable
Mortgage trust (REIT)	9 (dividend)	$20 per share	Dividend fully taxable; long-term capital gains taxed at one-half
Equity trust (REIT)	8 (dividend)	$20 per share	75% of dividend tax-free; remainder as in mortgage trust
Single property syndicate	6 (cash flow)	$5000	Cash flow tax-free in early years; 40% of initial investment tax deductible in year committed
Blind pool syndicate	6 (cash flow)	$5000	Same as single property syndicate

Fig. 19-2. Characteristics of various types of real estate investments

1. Which of these five alternatives would probably be best for the Winkelmanns? Why? What is a major reason for not selecting each of the other four? (Give one reason for each alternative.)
2. What will be the tax effect this year if the Winkelmanns invest $5000 in a real estate syndicate?
3. Should they invest $2000, $5000, or $8000 in the alternative you have selected for them? Is liquidity an issue?
4. Should they consider investments other than those related to real estate? Why or why not?

RECOMMENDED READING

Beaton, William R. *Real Estate Investment.* Englewood Cliffs, N.J.: Prentice-Hall, 1971.

   A good basic text.

Crabtree, David, and Glaser, Barney. *Second Deeds of Trust.* Mill Valley, Cal.: Balboa, 1969.

   A useful treatment of this subject.

Other publications of interest to the investor are published by the Real Estate Research Corporation. You can write them for a catalog at 73 West Monroe Street, Chicago, Illinois 60603.

CHUCK AND NANCY ANDERSON

THEIR REAL ESTATE INVESTMENT PROGRAM

As you recall from the investment plan Chuck and Nancy outlined in chapter 13, they allotted $5000 to investing in real estate as a long-term program of building up funds for their retirement.

QUESTIONS

1. Which of the three real estate investment types—recreational lots, second trust deeds, or REITs and syndicates—seems most appropriate for the Andersons? Why? Why would you reject the other two alternatives?
2. If you selected recreational lots, find out what the current prices are in local land developments and what consumer protection the local state laws provide.
3. If you selected second trust deeds, check the yellow pages for local mortgage brokers and ask them about investments available in your region.
4. If Chuck and Nancy were choosing only between REITs and syndicates, which should they probably select? Is liquidity (with accompanying price fluctuations) an important consideration for the Andersons? If they were to select an REIT, should it be a mortgage or an equity trust? Why? If they selected a syndicate, would a single property or blind pool type be more appropriate? Why?

V. PLANNING FOR RETIREMENT AND ESTATE TRANSFER

Perhaps, back in the first chapter of this book you established as one of your financial goals being able to enjoy a comfortable retirement. Since then you have learned how to protect your resources, how to get the most out of your income, and how to increase your income. In chapter 20 you will learn how to use these strategies to prepare for retirement.

By using the skills and strategies you have learned in this book, you will probably not only assure having an enjoyable retirement but also build an estate. It does not matter whether your estate is large or small. Having worked to assemble your financial resources, you should take precautions to see that they are not dissipated through senseless investments and undue taxation after your death. Chapter 21 is presented to help you avoid these problems.

20

RETIREMENT

Retirement is eagerly anticipated by many people as a time for leisure and relaxation after the long span of productive years. It is a time to enjoy grandchildren and to pursue the interests and hobbies there was never time for while working.

The financial aspect of retirement may be less pleasant to consider because, when you retire, you may have to relinquish your personal earning power. The annual wage or salary income that resulted from your work ceases. Ideally, you will have acquired enough income-producing financial resources during your working years to compensate for this loss of annual income. However, in reality, this is not always true.

In the late 1960s the Special Committee on Aging reported to the U.S. Senate that 25 percent of the nation's retired people have incomes that are at or near poverty level. The report described several financial problems that commonly occur during retirement. First, a great majority of retired individuals live on fixed incomes. Inflation, especially since World War II, has been continually eroding the purchasing power of these incomes. Second, people are retiring earlier and living longer. As a result, greater amounts of financial resources are required to provide adequate incomes for retired people. Finally, retired individuals have become accustomed to the higher and higher living standards produced by our continued national economic growth. Because of the effects of inflation on their fixed incomes and their longer retirements, however, they are finding it difficult to maintain their expected standards of living.

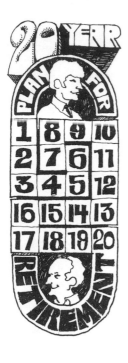

To avoid these problems, you must both think about what your financial goals will be when you retire and consider the financial means available to achieve these goals, including what you can expect from the federal government and your company as well as the programs you can use to supplement payments from these sources.

THE IMPORTANCE OF PLANNING

Advance planning is your best guarantee that you will be able to afford retirement. As we discussed in chapter 13, retirement is a type III goal. Once you have put your investment programs into effect and are achieving your type II goals, it is time to turn your attention to retirement planning. We recommend that you begin your planning and investing at least twenty years before you expect to retire. These years of preparation should give you enough time to reach your financial retirement goals, and allow for the effects of inflation as well. Hand-in-hand with advance planning goes frequent plan assessment. Then, if circumstances change or your strategies do not turn out as expected, you can adapt your plans as necessary.

Your Stage in the Life Cycle When You Retire

Before you can start to think intelligently about your retirement goals and what it will cost to achieve them, you must identify fairly accurately what your position in the life cycle will be at that time. It seems reasonable to assume, for example, that most people will have neither dependent children nor dependent parents to support if they retire rather late in their own lives. The younger you retire, however, the more likely these possibilities become.

For example, John and Martha Shipstead are both forty-five and are considering retiring in five years. At that time, their youngest child will be entering college and both of Mrs. Shipstead's parents (whom the Shipsteads are supporting) will be seventy years old. Obviously, when planning his own retirement, John must make allowances for the expenses of these dependents.

If you are married, it is best to assume that both you and your spouse will be living when you retire. If you are single and marriage seems unlikely, your life cycle considerations are going to be different.

Retirement Goals

At a minimum, you will want to be assured that you will always have the basic necessities: food, shelter, clothing, and health care. Your first point of planning should be to ensure that these needs will be fulfilled. Only after you have satisfactorily provided for them should you consider your other retirement goals such as traveling, pursuing hobbies and interests, spending time with your family and grandchildren, and increasing the size of your financial estate. Achieving these goals can transform retirement from merely a secure existence into an enjoyable experience.

COMPUTING YOUR TOTAL RETIREMENT NEEDS

The farther away from retirement you are, the more difficult it is to estimate what it will cost. Nevertheless, the earlier you begin planning and making estimates of the costs, the easier it will be to make adjustments for changes in living expense needs or in projected income as your retirement draws nearer. To compute your total financial needs for retirement, use the following procedure. Figure 20-1 (p. 452) shows how the Shipsteads used it to determine their retirement needs. You may want to make a similar form on which to record the figures you arrive at as you compute your needs. Completion of this procedure should give you a reasonably accurate estimate of what your retirement will cost, and you will then be ready to consider how to finance it.

Instructions

1   *Age at Retirement. Decide at what age you plan to retire.*
    John and Martha Shipstead decide to defer their retirement to age sixty-five when they will probably have no dependents.

2   *Basic Living Expenses. Consider what your life style during retirement is likely to be and how much it will cost.* Your basic living expenses for food, housing, clothing, and health care will be prescribed by your life style. The U.S. Labor Department's Bureau of Labor Statistics reported that in 1969 a moderate annual retirement living standard for two was from $3900 to $4700, depending on where the couple lived. Table 20-1 (p. 453) indicates how these expenses vary for different urban areas of our country. The most expensive places to retire are on the East and West coasts (New York–New Jersey, Los Angeles–Long Beach, and Seattle) while the most inexpensive are in the south (Dallas and Atlanta). The level of spending increases by area for all categories except medical care costs. They remain in the $335 to $360 range for all budget levels and areas except Los Angeles–Long Beach, where they are slightly higher. (These rather constant costs can probably be attributed to Social Security's Medicare program, which makes low-cost health care available to most citizens of age sixty-five and older.) Only in the high budget levels are personal income taxes incurred. At the low and medium levels, a retired couple's $3000 in exemptions, the retirement income credit (p. 460), and the standard deduction eliminate any tax liability.

NAME(S) _John and Martha Shijatani_

DATE _March 1973_

RETIREMENT LIVING EXPENSE NEEDS

1 Age at Retirement

Husband	65
Wife	65

2 Basic Living Expenses

	Month	Year
Housing	$25	$300
Utilities		
Repairs		
Insurance		
Taxes		
Other		
Rent or mortgage payments	200	2400
Food	125	1500
Clothing, personal care		
Medical		
Doctor		160
Dentist		80
Medicines		100
Insurance		60
Taxes (personal income)		500
TOTAL		7700

3 Recurrent Extra Expenses

	Month	Year
Him		300
Her		600
Gifts, contributions		500
Gardening		100
Travel		200
Other _entertainment_		500
TOTAL		800

Transportation

	Month	Year
Gas	25	300
Repairs	13	156
Licenses	5	60
Insurance	10	120
Auto payments or purchase	47	564

4 Total Annual Living Expenses		$8500
5 Expected Number of Years of Retirement		20
6 Total Living Expenses During Retirement		$170,000
7 One-Time Costs		$4000
8 Total Funds Needed at Retirement		$174,000
9 Years to Retirement		20
10 Inflation Factor		1.81
11 Total Inflated Living Expenses at Retirement		$314,940

Fig. 20-1.
Sample computation of retirement living expense needs

TABLE 20-1

ANNUAL BUDGET COSTS FOR A RETIRED COUPLE
Spring 1969

Area	Budget Level	Total Costs[a]	Food	Housing	Transpor-tation	Clothing/Personal Care	Medical Care	Gifts and Contribu-tions	Miscella-neous
New York and Northeastern New Jersey	Low	$3080	$ 919	$1239	$ 34	$249	$353	$133	$153
	Medium	4689	1277	1835	269	412	355	282	259
	High ($499)[b]	7690	1543	2858	685	617	357	568	563
Chicago and Northwestern Indiana	Low	2906	884	1109	60	250	335	125	143
	Medium	4309	1135	1546	384	404	338	259	243
	High ($296)[b]	6820	1400	2418	704	626	340	521	515
Atlanta	Low	2690	791	815	238	235	341	116	154
	Medium	3923	1069	1202	434	386	343	236	253
	High ($192)[b]	6148	1316	1968	738	593	347	482	512
Dallas	Low	2745	777	888	245	227	347	118	143
	Medium	4000	1052	1302	442	378	349	241	236
	High ($251)[b]	6542	1322	2212	783	584	352	505	533
Los Angeles–Long Beach	Low	3069	841	1063	258	246	381	132	148
	Medium	4374	1095	1519	458	406	385	263	248
	High ($340)[b]	7077	1367	2522	803	602	387	536	520
Seattle–Everett	Low	3221	922	1141	261	260	352	139	146
	Medium	4623	1201	1656	466	418	354	278	250
	High ($336)[b]	7049	1485	2396	805	616	357	534	520

SOURCE: U.S. Dept. of Labor, Bureau of Labor Statistics, *1971 Handbook of Labor Statistics*, Bulletin 1705.

[a]Includes cost of personal income taxes for couples with high-level budgets.

[b]Portion of high-level budget total used to pay personal income taxes.

CHOOSING AN EASY-UPKEEP LIFE-STYLE

To get an idea of how much your retirement life style is going to cost, consult your budget records. They should indicate what it is costing to maintain your present life style. If your current life style is substantially different than what you envision for retirement, this should be taken into consideration in your projections. For example, at present you may need a larger home than you will after retirement. Therefore, housing expenses will be considerably less in those later years. If you do plan to continue living in your present home, make sure that your mortgage is paid off in advance. This will ensure that the burden of mortgage payments does not drain your retirement income. Also, current living expenses may include the expenses of dependent children or parents. These might not be a consideration when you retire. Review Medicare benefits and costs (chapter 6) to make sure that your health insurance program will not duplicate the coverage offered by Medicare and that your retirement health needs will be adequately covered. Note that the medical insurance portion of Medicare is optional and must be applied for by age sixty-eight if it is desired. Under Medicare the federal government pays half the premium, thus offering very low cost protection. Be sure to take these changes in your living expenses into account when developing your cost estimates.

On the basis of their current expenses, the Shipsteads estimated what their basic living expenses would be during retirement. They also took into consideration that they would probably be living near New York and that their life style would probably require a high level of budget expenditures. They expect to pay off the mortgage on their home, sell it, and move to an apartment. Of course, if the Shipsteads decided not to sell their home, they would not include a $200 a month rental cost in the original living expense estimates for their retirement years, but would include enough to cover property taxes, insurance, and upkeep. A major expense will probably be maintaining a car. They expect to receive Medicare benefits and so are not allotting much for health care.

3 *Recurrent Extra Expenses. Determine how much you are likely to spend each year fulfilling retirement goals other than meeting basic needs.*

The Shipsteads want to pursue their interest in gardening and also have money each year to visit their children and grandchildren at Christmas and during the summer. The annual cost of these two recurring expenses and entertainment comes to $800.

4 *Total Annual Living Expenses. Add the totals for annual basic living expenses (step 2) and your annual recurrent extra expenses (step 3).*

The Shipsteads have a total of $8500 in annual living expenses.

5 *Expected Number of Years of Retirement. Use the estimates in table 20-2 to determine how many years your retirement is likely to last.* In the table find your average life expectancy upon reaching retirement. If there is reason to believe that you or your wife will live longer than average (due to good health and/or the experience of other members of the family), add an appropriate estimate to the longest figure. To be conservative, do not use a shorter estimate than that given in the table.

TABLE 20-2

AVERAGE FUTURE LIFETIME IN THE UNITED STATES

AGE INTERVAL	AVERAGE REMAINING LIFETIME (YEARS)	
	Male	Female
50–55	23	29
55–60	19	24
60–65	16	20
at 65	15	18
65–70	13	16
70–75	10	13

SOURCE: U.S. Department of Health, Education, and Welfare; National Center for Health Statistics, 1968 data.

John Shipstead can expect to live approximately fifteen years after he retires, and his wife about eighteen years. To be conservative, they estimated that their retirement will last about twenty years (two years longer than her expected remaining lifetime).

6 *Total Living Expenses During Retirement. Multiply your total annual living expenses (step 4) by your expected number of years of retirement (step 5).*

The Shipsteads estimate that their total annual living expenses during retirement will be $170,000.

7 *One-Time Costs. Add the lump sum cost of reaching goals that can be expected to occur only once or twice.*

The Shipsteads want to have $4000 for an around-the-world cruise sometime during their retirement.

8 *Total Funds Needed at Retirement. Add your total one-time costs (step 7) to your total living expenses during retirement (step 6).*

The Shipsteads have a total of $174,000 that they will need at retirement.

9 *Years to Retirement. Subtract your age now from your age at retirement.*

Since the Shipsteads are both now forty-five and plan to retire when they are sixty-five, it will be twenty years before they retire.

10   *Inflation Factor. Use compound interest table A to find the infla-
      tion factor that accords with both the most likely annual rate
      of inflation and the number of years from now until you retire.*
      Since World War II, inflation has averaged roughly 3 percent a
      year, but the rising rate in recent years suggests that this average
      may be higher in the future.

      The Shipsteads find that for a 3 percent annual rate of inflation
      and the twenty years until they retire, the inflation factor is 1.81.

11   *Total Inflated Living Expenses at Retirement. Multiply the infla-
      tion factor (step 10) times your total funds needed at retirement
      (step 8).* This will indicate how much money you will need upon
      retirement to offset the effect of inflation up to that time. Al-
      though inflation will continue to affect your cost of living during
      retirement, the investments made for retirement purposes should
      continue to grow and to offer higher income during those years.
      For example, assume that you need $20,000 in investments to begin
      retirement and will spend $1000 of that amount each year. At
      the end of the first year, that principal would amount to only
      $19,000. However, if the money is in a 4 percent savings account,
      the principal plus interest would be worth at least $19,780. (The
      $780 represents 4 percent on an average balance of $19,500 in the
      account for that year.) That extra amount is more than would
      be needed to offset a 3 percent rate of inflation. Based on past
      Congressional action, it seems reasonable to assume that Social
      Security benefits will increase enough to meet rises in the cost
      of living over the long run. The effect of inflation after retirement
      has begun is important only if all your investment money is tied
      up in a fixed annuity such as a pension plan that offers only fixed
      monthly payments for life. The important thing is to prepare
      properly before your retirement by selecting investments with an
      inflationary hedge.

      The Shipsteads figure that they will need $314,940 to cover living
      expenses after they retire.

SOURCES OF RETIREMENT INCOME

Very few people must depend solely on investment programs developed
through their own initiative to provide for their retirement years. Some
of the most common programs offered by other sources are Social Security
and pension funds. Among the investment alternatives you might use
to supplement your retirement income are certificates of deposit, certain
common stocks, and some bonds.

Social Security

The fundamental concept upon which Social Security is based is that
when earnings stop or are reduced because the worker retires, dies, or

becomes disabled, monthly cash benefits are paid to replace part of the earnings the family has lost. These benefits are paid out of a pool of Social Security contributions made by employees, employers, and self-employed people. Four types of payments are made: disability payments, Medicare, survivor's benefits, and retirement payments.

Retirement benefits are generally available to individuals when they reach age sixty-five. Benefits at a reduced level may be available as early as age sixty-two. There are several special considerations concerning divorcees, nonworking wives, and certain dependents. Contact your local Social Security office if you feel you might be eligible under any of these special circumstances.

Working while receiving retirement benefits is subject to certain limitations. Full benefits are available if you earn less than $2100 annually in wages or salaries. One dollar of benefits is forfeited for every two dollars earned between $2100 and $2880. One dollar of benefits is forfeited for each dollar earned above $2880. For example, if you normally receive $3420 a year from Social Security but this year you earned $3000, your benefit payments would be affected in the following ways: you would receive the first $2100 of those earnings without any reduction in Social Security payments; the next $780 of earnings ($2880 – $2100) reduces your Social Security payments by $390; the last $120 ($3000 – $2880) reduces your Social Security benefits by $120. You could have received that $120 from Social Security rather than working for it. Your total Social Security benefits for the year would amount to $2910 ($3420 − $510).

There are loopholes in this regulation. First, not all income is considered earnings for Social Security purposes. Among excludable items are private pension payments, dividends from stocks, rents and royalties, profits on securities transactions, and interest on savings deposits. Second, you may collect full benefits for any month in which you earn $175 or less. Therefore, you might earn substantially more than $2100 in a short-term job and still collect benefits for the remainder of the year. For example, as a school crossing guard, you may not work at all during the summer and therefore be eligible for full benefits in those months. Your payments may be reduced or stop if a marriage or divorce changes your status, children grow out of being qualified dependents, or you die.

Benefit payments are not automatic. An application must be filed before they can begin. We recommend that you get in touch with the local Social Security office within the six months before retirement.

Pension Funds

Pension funds are available to employees of most companies and to employees of federal, state, and local government organizations, including the armed services. If you are a member of such a program, use this discussion as a guideline for evaluating it so that you will know how best to supplement pension benefits with your own investments.

financing   Pension funds may be financed in two ways. "Pay-as-you-go" financing involves no advance build-up of funds. The organization involved merely draws checks on its bank account as benefits come due. This type of pension fund financing offers its members or beneficiaries no assurance that benefits would continue if the organization were dissolved or went out of business. As a consequence, it is not satisfactory and, fortunately, it is not very common.

The second form of financing involves advance funding. With this method, organizations contribute funds annually to a managed investment fund. These contributions will be made to cover benefits earned but not yet payable, benefits currently being earned, or a combination of both. With this form of financing, the faster the funds are contributed, the more secure future benefits are—as long as the funds are not mismanaged. As the benefits earned become payable, disbursements are made from the pension fund.

Contributions to finance a pension plan can be obtained through three methods. First, the sponsoring organization might provide all the funds. Second, the organization's members or employees might be required to provide part of the funds. Third, the members or employees might have the option of voluntarily providing additional funds. In the latter case, a person who contributes voluntarily usually receives additional benefits in proportion to his contributions.

Management of pension funds that use advance funding can be conducted by two types of management groups—an insurance company or a trustee. In the first case, as funds are contributed they are turned over to an insurance company and used to buy either cash-value life insurance or deferred annuities. If cash-value insurance is bought and you die before retirement, your survivors receive a death benefit; if you live to retirement, the cash-value life insurance may be converted into an annuity payment program. If deferred annuities are purchased with the contributed funds, you receive an annuity upon retirement. To provide death coverage during your working years, term insurance can be carried on you, in effect, converting your deferred annuity program into a cash-value insurance program.

In the second case, the fund is managed by a trustee, which might be a bank or a group of the organization's executives. The funds may be invested in annuities, preferred stocks, bonds, or another investment medium depending on the policies of the fund's trustee. This is the most common form of pension fund management. When you retire, money is withdrawn from the fund either to purchase an annuity for you or to provide you with regular benefits. These programs are often supplemented with some form of life insurance.

eligibility requirements   Find out how long you must be a member of an organization before you are eligible for its pension fund program.

Some programs offer eligibility from the beginning of service or employment. Others require a minimum number of years of service or employment (often two to three years) or a minimum age level (often twenty-five) before admitting someone to the program. Also find out how old you can be and still be admitted to a pension fund program. Do not wait too long to join or you may be left out.

Some programs require that members belong for a certain length of time before they are eligible to receive benefits. Check the program's required retirement age to make sure that there are enough years of employment before retirement to make you eligible for pension payments. In some instances, organizations allow you to continue your membership or employment past the required retirement age so that you can be eligible for pension benefits.

retirement date   Pension programs usually specify the date on which an employee may retire—June 1 of the year in which he turns sixty-five, for example. Many pension funds make reduced retirement payments to employees who retire before this date. Be sure to take these stipulations into consideration when making your retirement plans.

If you leave a company before retirement, the amount of pension payments you can look forward to will depend on the pension fund's rules and the circumstances under which you leave. At a very minimum, any amount that you have contributed to the fund, plus interest, should be returned to you. You also might have the option of leaving your contributions in the program to provide a future retirement benefit.

If you are vested with, or given, rights to pension benefits based on contributions made by your employer, you will receive partial pension benefits based on those contributions even if you leave the company before retirement. Usually, to receive this right, you must leave any contributions you have made in the fund. The more progressive programs often vest you with an interest in pension rights that increases in proportion to the length of time you participate in their program. Most of them require that you either work for a certain number of years or until you reach a certain age (or both) before the vesting procedure begins. For example, you might become vested with a 50 percent right to pension benefits after ten years in the program. Each succeeding year, you would be vested with an additional 10 percent. After fifteen years, you would be 100 percent vested. This means, whether you left the company before retirement or not, you would be entitled to a full retirement benefit based on the company's contributions.

receiving pension payments   Pension payments may be taken in any of several forms, depending upon the options offered by the organization. The most common option is straight life annuity. However, there are several variations on this basic form. A refund annuity will provide a smaller monthly payment so that a lump-sum payment may be made to your beneficiary upon your death. A certain and continuous annuity makes monthly payments for life or for a specified period of time, whichever is greater. Should you die before this period expires, the payments will be continued to a designated beneficiary to the end of the period. The joint-and-survivorship annuity pays an annuity to you and to another person. Upon the death of one of the annuitants, the remaining portion is paid in annuities to the survivor. A Social Security annuity is designed for individuals who retire before they are eligible for Social Security retirement benefits. In this instance, you would receive large monthly payments until you begin to receive Social Security benefits, at which time your annuity payments would be reduced.

tax treatment of pension payments   Social Security, railroad retirement, and veterans' pension benefits are tax-free. Military retirement benefits and lump-sum distributions of Keogh plan funds (pp. 460–61) are all fully taxable. If you belong to a pension program to which you make contributions during your working years, part of your benefit payments will be tax-free. This portion represents a return of your original contribution. For example, if your contributions equalled 25 percent of the value of your benefits, then theoretically 25 percent of each benefit payment would be tax-free. In practice, the computation required by the IRS to determine the tax-free portion may be much more complex.

The retirement income credit represents a tax break for taxpayers sixty-five and older who receive little, if any, tax-free pension benefits. If your retirement income comes mainly from dividends, interest, rent, taxable pensions, and the like, this credit can benefit you. You can receive a credit for 15 percent of taxable income up to $1524. For a single person this means a maximum credit of $228.60 and for a couple, $457.20

deferred profit sharing   Usually a company that offers deferred profit sharing sets aside a small fixed percentage of profits in a trust fund. Each employee is credited with a portion of this fund according to his wage or salary level and/or length of employment. Such a program is often used as a supplement to, or a substitute for, a pension fund. It does not offer guaranteed retirement benefits. The amount of benefits available to the retiring employee is based on the profit performance of the company. Thus, such a program provides the employee with an incentive to make the operations of the company as profitable as possible. Generally these benefits may be taken in a lump sum or used to purchase an annuity.

A Retirement Plan for Self-Employed Persons

In 1962, Congress passed the Keogh Act, which allows self-employed individuals to set up their own retirement funds. The act applies to professional people such as lawyers, doctors, artists, accountants, and architects as well as farmers, business partners, and sole proprietors of their own businesses. All these people receive income that is not subject to withholding for income tax purposes. Generally, any income of this nature may be diverted in part to a retirement fund.

For such a fund to fall under the guidelines of this act, it must fulfill the following qualifications. First, the retirement benefits to be derived from the fund cannot be initiated before the individual is fifty-nine and one-half years old. However, they must be initiated before he reaches the age of seventy and one-half. Second, if the person setting up the plan has people working for him, he must also set up retirement funds for all full-time employees who have worked for him for at least three years. In this case, he must make the same percentage of salary contribution for each qualified employee that he makes for himself. Third, contributions to the retirement plan must be invested in an approved manner. Eligible investment plans include trusts administered by a bank or trust company, annuities and endowment life insurance, and mutual funds. Most mutual funds and insurance companies have plans that have received official approval from appropriate government agencies. If a trust arrangement is desired because of specific considerations not covered by the more generalized plans, official sanction is required before the plan may be put into effect.

There are two tax advantages to such plans. First, plan contributions of up to 10 percent of income gained from self-employment (up to a dollar maximum of $2500) may be deducted from annual gross income for federal income tax purposes. Second, income earned from the fund, plus any capital appreciation that occurs, is not subject to federal taxation until the retirement benefits have begun to be paid. The tax rate that applies during retirement years will probably be less than the rate that would have applied during the working years when the fund was growing. When similar treatment is accorded by state income tax regulations, the value of these two tax advantages is increased.

Selling Your Home

There is a significant tax break attached to selling your home when you retire. The tax law provides a once-in-a-lifetime exclusion for persons sixty-five and older on certain portions of the gain realized on the sale of a home. All of the gain attributable to the initial $20,000 of the selling price may be excluded. Above that amount only portions of the gain are excludable. To be eligible, you must have occupied your home as your principal place of residence for five of the last eight years. You may need to consult a tax authority to determine the application of this law to your circumstances.

Once you have sold your home, there are numerous things that can be done with the money. You might make an investment that will provide

a monthly payment to cover the expense of renting an apartment and possibly a portion of other living expenses. You might buy a mobile home or a membership in a retirement community with part of the proceeds. The remaining proceeds might then be invested to help provide for monthly living expenses (including the rental of a mobile home site).

Investment Strategies

Probably your most important investment consideration during retirement is current income. Appropriate investment vehicles offering regular income include income bonds such as U.S. Series H bonds and corporate bonds; certificates of deposit or savings certificates that pay interest in cash; fixed and variable annuities; certain types of common stocks such as utilities; mutual funds (systematic withdrawal plans); and income-producing real estate. The first three types of investment offer the greatest certainty of continued future income, while the last three offer a possible hedge against inflation. Other investment income sources such as dividends from a growth stock are less appropriate because of their low or irregular income payout (unless you plan to sell off a portion of your investment regularly and realize capital gains income also).

If you want the security of a guaranteed income for life, consider annuities. If you invest only in fixed annuities, start with an annuity income well above your initial needs. Inflation will gradually erode the purchasing power of the payments and you may eventually find it difficult to cover your expenses. If possible, try to put some of your money into a variable annuity. In any case, you would be better off to consider spreading your investments to include those that offer some protection against inflation.

ACHIEVING YOUR RETIREMENT GOALS

Earlier in this chapter, we showed you how to estimate what retirement will cost. Here is a procedure to use for planning how to meet these expenses. Achieving a successful and comfortable retirement is not as difficult as it may seem.

The planning procedure is illustrated with financial data for the Shipsteads (fig. 20-2).

Instructions

1 *Age at Retirement. Decide the age at which you plan to retire.* This may affect the amount of Social Security benefits as well as your pension payments.

   The Shipsteads still plan to retire at age sixty-five.

2 *Monthly Social Security Benefits. Use the Social Security Addendum on pages 493–97 to determine these.* Estimating your retire-

NAME(S) *John and Martha Shipstead*

DATE *March 1973*

RETIREMENT INVESTMENT NEEDS

1 *Age at Retirement*
    Husband   65
    Wife   65

2 *Monthly Social Security Benefits*
    Worker at 65 $219
    Spouse at 65   109
    TOTAL   328

3 *Annual Income from Social Security* $3936

4 *Inflation Factor*   1.81

5 *Inflated Annual Income
       from Social Security* $7125

6 *Annual Pension Benefits*
    Worker $3000
    Spouse   1500
    TOTAL $4500

7 *Total Estimated Annual Income from
       Social Security and Pension* $11,625

8 *Expected Number of Years of Retirement*   20

9 *Total Estimated Retirement Income from
       Social Security and Pension* $232,500

10 *Total Inflated Living Expenses* $314,940

11 *Investment Needed at Retirement* $82,440

12 *Profit from Sale of Home* (after taxes and selling costs) $40,600
    Current market value of home $35,000
    Inflation factor   1.49
    Market value at retirement $52,150

13 *Adjusted Total Investment Needed at Retirement* $42,440

14 *Investment Strategy Needed*
    Amount to be invested yearly $ 1150
    After-tax interest   6%

Fig. 20-2.
Sample computation
of retirement
investment needs

ment benefits in terms of monthly payments is a somewhat inaccurate procedure. To be completely accurate, you would have to wait until you retired and applied for benefits. At that time, the Social Security Administration would make the computations for you. Nevertheless, attempt to estimate what these benefits will be. Without some idea of the amounts involved, projections concerning Social Security's contributions to your retirement goals will be useless.

The Shipsteads estimated that at age sixty-five he would be eligible to receive $219 a month in Social Security benefits and she would be eligible to receive $109—a total of $328.

3 *Annual Income from Social Security. Multiply the total monthly Social Security benefits (step 2) by twelve.*

The Shipsteads can expect to receive $3936 from Social Security in yearly retirement payments.

4 *Inflation Factor. Use the figure derived in step 10 of the procedure for computing retirement needs.* (We have assumed that Social Security benefits will roughly increase with the rate of inflation in the general economy.)

The Shipsteads find that, for a 3 percent annual rate of inflation and the twenty years until they retire, the inflation factor is 1.81.

5 *Inflated Annual Income from Social Security. Multiply annual income from Social Security (step 3) by the appropriate inflation factor (step 4).*

The inflated value of the Shipsteads' annual Social Security benefits is $7125.

6 *Annual Pension Benefits. Find out the method used by your employer to compute pension benefits and use it to compute yours.* The amount of your pension benefits depends upon your organization's computation method. One method adds a specific dollar amount to the size of your monthly pension payment for each year of eligible membership or employment completed. A second method adds a dollar amount to the size of your monthly pension payment based on a fixed percentage of your annual wage or salary. A third method computes a fixed percentage of your average annual earnings over the duration of your membership or employment and pays this amount to you. These three basic methods offer fixed monthly payments during retirement. However, some pension funds may try to offset the effect of inflation by investing part of their funds in variable annuities, thereby increasing the size of monthly retirement payments as the cost of living increases.

The Shipsteads' employers use the third method of computing pension benefits. Mrs. Shipstead's pension benefit is lower because

Pension Recipient	Length of Employment to Age 65	Average Annual Salary	Pension Payment Factor	Annual Value of Pension
Mr. Shipstead	30 years	$10,000	30%	$3000
Mrs. Shipstead	15 years	$10,000	15%	$1500

her length of eligible employment is less. The Shipsteads have no assurance that their pension plan will be able to offset the effect of inflation.

7 *Total Estimated Annual Income from Social Security and Pension. Add inflated annual income from Social Security (step 5) and total annual pension benefits (step 6).*

The Shipsteads expect to have a total annual income of $11,625.

8 *Expected Number of Years of Retirement. Use the figure derived in step 5 of the procedure for computing retirement needs.* You need not be concerned that you might live well beyond your estimate. Your Social Security and pension benefits will continue; and, with careful planning, your investments should continue to grow faster than the rate of inflation and thus provide funds for those later years.

The Shipsteads expect their retirement to last twenty years.

9 *Total Estimated Retirement Income from Social Security and Pension. Multiply total estimated annual income from Social Security and pension (step 7) by the expected number of years of retirement (step 8).*

The Shipsteads expect to have a total income of $232,500.

10 *Total Investment Needed at Retirement. Subtract total inflated living expenses (step 10) from total estimated income (step 9).*

The Shipsteads will need $314,940 at retirement.

11 *Total Investment Needed at Retirement. Subtract total inflated living expenses (step 10) from total estimated income (step 9).*

The Shipsteads will need $82,440 at retirement.

12 *Profit from Sale of Home. Multiply the current market value of your home by an appropriate appreciation factor to determine market value at retirement and then subtract probable taxes and selling costs.* If you do not plan to sell your house or if for some reason you think a profit would not result from the sale, you cannot count on this financial resource to reduce the amount that must be invested in preparation for retirement.

The market value of the Shipsteads' home is $35,000. To be conservative, they assume that their home will appreciate in value about 2 percent a year between now and retirement. According to compound interest table A, the factor for 2 percent for twenty years is 1.49. At this rate, the house and property would be worth $52,150 ($35,000 × 1.49) when they retire. They estimate that $40,000 would be left after all taxes and selling costs have been paid.

13 *Adjusted Total Investment Needed at Retirement. Subtract profit from sale of home (step 12) from total investment needed at retirement (step 11).*

The $40,000 received from the sale of the Shipsteads' home would result in an adjusted total investment need of $42,440.

14 *Investment Strategy Needed. Use compound interest table B to determine how much you must invest each year until you retire and at what rate of return in order to reach the figure derived in step 13.*

To reach $42,440 the Shipsteads need to invest approximately $1150 a year ($96 a month) for the next twenty years at interest averaging 6 percent after taxes.

Because of the sale of their house and retirement investments, the Shipsteads expect to have $82,440 by age sixty-five. If they then purchase a $40,000 joint and two-thirds survivorship annuity, they will receive monthly income of $230 from it. If they purchase $42,000 worth of two mutual funds, they can reasonably expect to take out a total of $315 a month for the rest of their lives without seriously depleting the original capital. Their annual investment income would be $6540 before taxes. This more than makes up for the difference between their annual inflated living expenses ($314,940 ÷ 20 = $15,747) and their income from Social Security and their pension plans ($11,625). Of course, the annuity portion of the $6540 is fixed at $2760 annually and will not rise with the cost of living.

CONCLUSION

The key to a successful and pleasant retirement is to plan for it in advance. In this chapter, we have provided a framework to guide your planning. We have also indicated what you might expect from the more common retirement programs and what you can do for yourself. With this background, you must take the initiative in planning for and achieving your retirement goals.

deferred profit sharing
Keogh Act
pension fund

retirement income credit
vesting

1. Why do retired individuals with incomes below $6000 seldom need to pay any personal income taxes?
2. How would you compute the effect of 3 percent annual inflation for twenty-five years on a $10,000 current living standard?
3. Under what circumstances is it possible to work during retirement and not forfeit Social Security retirement benefits?
4. How does vesting work in relation to pension plan benefits? Why is it important to consider this retirement income source?
5. What is the difference between a straight life annuity and a joint-and-survivorship annuity?
6. What are the tax advantages of selling your home after you have reached age sixty-five?
7. Why are fixed annuities a poor hedge against inflation? What types of investments offer an effective hedge?
8. What is the most important consideration for a successful retirement as far as financial resources are concerned?
9. What is the purpose of the retirement income credit? What is the dollar maximum of this credit available to a retired couple?

Wayne and Janet Meyers are both sixty-five. They are in good health and have jobs that allow them to work to age seventy. They are eligible for combined Social Security retirement benefits of $4800 annually, and from pensions they can expect to receive an additional $2000 a year. They also receive an average of 6 percent a year from the $50,000 they have in bank savings accounts and good quality corporate bonds. They estimate that their annual retirement needs will cost $10,000, but realize that inflation is likely to increase this amount by 3 percent each of the twenty years that they expect to live.

If they were both to retire today, is there enough in their investment portfolio (earning 3 percent a year after inflation) to make up the difference between the $6800 they would receive annually from Social Security and pensions and the $10,000 they need to cover their annual retirement living expenses? Will they probably have to pay income taxes on their investment income? How would their retirement planning be affected if they were to retire at age seventy? How would their income situation change?

RECOMMENDED READING

"Can You Retire on $4100 a Year?" *Changing Times,* April 1969, pp. 39–42.

> Gives insight into the basic living expenses of retirement both in dollar amounts and percentages.

"The Forces Reshaping Social Security." *Business Week,* July 15, 1972, pp. 54–60.

> A complete treatment of the current status of Social Security programs.

"For Women: Advice on Social Security." *Changing Times,* November 1969, pp. 37–38.

> A good treatment of benefits available to women, especially widows, single women, and divorcees.

"How Good Is Your Company's Pension Plan?" *Changing Times,* March 1969, pp. 6–10.

> A good discussion of the fundamentals.

"Tax Angles on Pensions and Annuities." *Changing Times,* March 1972, pp. 30–31.

> A brief overview of tax treatment of various forms of pension programs.

"Tax Information on Pensions and Annuities."

> Federal government booklet free at local IRS offices.

U.S. Department of Health, Education, and Welfare. "Your Social Security." SSI-351 May 1970.

> A complete treatment of Social Security in layman's terms.

CHUCK AND NANCY ANDERSON

PLANNING FOR RETIREMENT

Although retirement is thirty years away for Chuck and Nancy, they feel it is necessary to begin planning for it now. By the time they reach age sixty-five, their children will be grown and self-supporting. Therefore, the Andersons will have no dependents to support.

They have made a careful analysis of their current living expense patterns and have thought a lot about the hobbies and interests they wish to pursue during retirement. They estimate that, in current dollars, they will need $12,000 annually to achieve their desired retirement life style.

Now they must figure out the total amount they can expect to receive from Social Security in retirement benefits and from the pension fund where Chuck works. They anticipate that Chuck's average annual earnings creditable for Social Security will be $7200. Chuck's conservative estimate of what he can expect from his firm's pension fund upon retirement is $5000 a year. The Andersons feel that it is reasonable to expect Social Security benefits to rise with inflation, but they doubt that this will happen with the pension benefits.

QUESTIONS

1. How long can the Andersons reasonably expect to live after reaching age sixty-five?
2. What would be an appropriate inflation factor for them to use for the next thirty years?
3. What aggregate amount will Chuck and Nancy need upon retiring?
4. How did they arrive at their estimate of Chuck's average annual earnings creditable for Social Security?
5. What will be the amount of their annual retirement Social Security benefits?
6. What is the annual amount represented by Social Security (with the inflation adjustment) and pension fund benefits?
7. What is the aggregate value of these retirement income sources?
8. Does this exceed or fall short of the Andersons' total retirement living expense needs?
9. What investment strategies would help Chuck and Nancy make up any difference there might be?

21
TRANSFERRING YOUR ESTATE

For a family, the financial implications of the death of their breadwinner can be twofold. They will probably lose not only part or all of their earning power, but also their primary money manager. In chapter 7 you determined what your family's income needs would be if you, as breadwinner, were to die. In reading this book, you have since learned how to obtain life insurance and income-producing assets to fulfill these needs. Now that the problem of finding sources of adequate income has been dealt with, it is time to consider the problems that might arise if another family member has to take over management of your financial resources.

The transfer of an estate is not automatic. Nor can there be any assurance that transfer of management responsibilities will be smooth and efficient unless certain steps have been taken while the primary breadwinner and money manager is still alive. The first step is to make sure that you and your family know exactly what your financial resources are. Many people have only a vague idea about what assets they own, how much their assets are worth, or even where they are. The second step is to keep the family members apprised of your money management activities. Too often family estates are quickly wasted because the heirs have little knowledge or ability concerning the management of these assets. The third step—a

THE ESTATE

very important one—is to keep accurate, up-to-date records of your family's financial activities.

This chapter deals with many of the legal and financial considerations that will affect a family's financial resources upon the death of their head-of-household. Read it now, even though death may seem remote. It is never too early to lay the foundation for a smooth transfer of your estate—assets such as cash, personal property, life insurance policies, marketable securities, savings, real estate (including your home), and ownership interests in ongoing businesses. We will discuss first the legal aspects of transferring an estate and then the financial aspects of such a transfer, including ways to reduce the cost of the probate fees and taxes.

LEGAL ASPECTS OF ESTATE TRANSFER

To transfer your estate means to transfer to another (or others) those assets in which you have the legal rights of ownership, or title. If the legal right of ownership of a portion or all of your family's assets is vested in you, then you must make arrangements for the transfer of these rights according to your wishes upon your death. The most common means of accomplishing this is to make a will. In the absence of a valid will declaring how your estate should be settled, the state in which you are a legal resident will normally settle it.

Ownership Rights

There is an important distrinction to understand about property rights; it is the difference between *source* and *form*. There are essentially two sources, or derivations, of property rights: separate property and community property. The sources of property rights vary according to state statute. These statutes may be roughly divided into community property and non-community property statutes. There are only eight states with community property laws. They are Arizona, California, Idaho, Louisiana, Nevada, New Mexico, Texas, and Washington. The other states have no community laws as such.

Property rights in a community state are derived from two sources. *Community property* represents that property earned by a husband and wife during their marriage, irrespective of which one is the breadwinner. *Separate property* represents that property which was acquired by an individual prior to marriage or which the individual specifically inherited or received via gift during the marriage.

Title to property in noncommunity states is derived solely as separate property. However, these states have passed specific laws that generally create the same end result for title to property earned by the joint efforts of a married couple. What this means is that one spouse has a marital right to a portion of property acquired by the other spouse during marriage.

The *forms of title* are basically (1) separate property, (2) community property, and (3) joint ownership. The important thing to note is that the form in which you hold title does not necessarily have to parallel its source. For example, separately derived property might be held as community property or in some form of joint ownership. Where this occurs, there are usually important tax and legal considerations. We recommend that you seek legal advice before deciding what form of title in which to hold any substantial portion of your assets.

Joint ownership can take the form of *joint tenancy, tenancy by the entirety,* or *tenancy in common.* In joint tenancy, there may be two or more owners, each of whom owns a percentage, but not a specific piece of the property. Each may dispose of his share without the permission of the other owners. Upon the death of one owner, his share passes to the surviving owners. Tenancy by the entirety is available only to husbands and wives, neither of whom can dispose of his share without the permission of the other (while both are living). Upon the death of one spouse, entire ownership of the property becomes vested in the surviving spouse. Tenancy in common may have two or more owners, each of whom may dispose of his share without the permission of the other owners. Upon the death of one owner, his share goes to his heirs, who may not necessarily be the other owner or owners.

Your Will

A will is a written, legal document that expresses the manner in which you desire to have your estate disposed of upon your death. In most states, anyone of sound mind and legal age (eighteen or twenty-one) can make one. The following elements are essential to a will: opening recitation, disposition clauses, administration clauses, testamonium clause, and attestation clause. The opening recitation usually describes you, your place of residence, any previous will(s) to be revoked, and the procedure to be followed for settling the debts of your estate and resolving funeral expenses. The disposition clauses indicate what elements of your estate are to be distributed and to whom. The administration clauses indicate how the instructions of your will are to be carried out. The testamonium clause contains your signature of approval. The attestation clause contains a recitation of the circumstances under which the signing of the will was witnessed and the signatures of the witnesses.

Before writing your will, discuss possible instructions with your spouse and maybe with other members of your family. Determine just what you want to accomplish in your will. A will can be used to designate your choice of an executor; to itemize what property is to be distributed, to whom, and in what manner; to create trusts (legal contracts whereby

you deposit certain assets with a trustee who will control and manage them); and to designate guardians for children who are minors.

choosing an executor An executor (executrix) is charged with the responsibility of administering the disposition of your estate. he should be trustworthy, responsible, and capable of handling the adminsitrative matters related to the probate process (that process which attempts to settle your estate according to your wishes). If you choose a friend, you will ensure that a personal interest will bo taken in the disposition of your estate. (In this case, an alternative executor should be named in case your designated executor dies before you do or while your will is in probate.) If you are not sure how capable a friend would be in administering your estate, you might choose a professional trust company as executor. This organization will probalby still be in business when you die, although they may take little or no personal interest in the disposition of your estate. Some people try to gain the best features of both alternatives by appointing a personal friend and a professional trust company as coexecutors.

distributing your property If you want to eliminate a possible source of family quarrels after your death, you should try to distribute your property evenly among family members of equal status. For example, you may want your spouse to receive the largest percentage of your property. However, the remaining property might most wisely be distributed equally among your children. Be sure you correctly identify each beneficiary by using his complete name and current address. You should also state whether inheritance taxes are to be paid initially out of your estate or individually by each beneficiary. The former method may be preferable since it may facilitiate disposition of the estate. For example, it might be difficult for a beneficiary to pay estate taxes on a house without having to sell it.

You should include instructions as to the disposition of your estate if you and your primary beneficiary were to die simultaneously—as in an automobile accident, for example. You should also take precautions to avoid an excessively long and expensive probate on your property if your primary beneficiary were to die shortly after you do. To accomplish this, many people include a conditional survival clause in their wills. This clause states that beneficiaries must survive the deceased by a certain period of time, say 120 days, to qualify as heirs. (For estate tax purposes, conditional survival is limited by law to six months or less.)

creating trusts As grantor, or trustor, you may deposit certain assets with a trustee who will be responsible for the control and management of these assets. The individuals who are to receive the income from the management of these assets are known as *beneficiaries*. Those who are to receive the assets in the trust upon its termination are known as *remaindermen*. For example, Lee Fong owns $75,000 worth of securities, which pay annual dividends of $4500. He put these securities in a trust with directions that the annual dividends are to be paid to his son Lou and the securities are to become the property of Lee's grandchildren when the trust agreement expires. Lou is the beneficiary and Mr. Fong's grandchildren are the remaindermen.

A trustee has two primary duties: (1) to preserve the principal and invest it so that the beneficiaries receive a reasonable return and, (2) to execute his fiduciary responsibility prudently and in good faith at all times. If your beneficiaries are dissatisfied with your trustee's performance, they may petition the appropriate state court for a change in the trust agreement, a change of trustees, or similar help.

Therefore, the trustees charged with the responsibility of managing the assets you put in trust must be chosen very carefully. You can select either individuals—such as friends, relatives, or associates—or professional trust companies. An individual whom you know well and respect for his integrity will probably take a personal interest in managing your trust for the sake of your beneficiaries. A professional trust company, however, can offer investment competence and management continuity for the life of the trust as well as integrity. If your heirs have shown a tendency to squander your financial resources or if you fear that the management of your estate will be too difficult for them after your death, the prospects offered by the professional investment management of a trust may be quite attractive.

You would be well-advised to make the trust agreement as flexible as possible. First, you should ensure that your trustee is given the ability to deal effectively with changing economic and business conditions, changing styles of prudent investing, and changing statutes governing trust administration. (For example, it might be unwise to restrict your trustee to fixed principal investments during times of inflation.) Second, you could provide power of appointment as a legal means whereby a surviving beneficiary would be given the power to determine how the income and proceeds of the trust shall be distributed upon his death. This would eliminate the possibility that you might leave out deserving beneficiaries (often unborn grandchildren).

writing your will   Once you have done this background work on your will, you will be ready to engage the services of an attorney to help you write it. It is a good idea to have your spouse meet your attorney so that she will feel comfortable when she has to deal with him after your death. You should discuss with him any bequests you have in mind so that he can advise you as to whether they are legally defensible. Most states have homestead laws that prevent you from disinheriting your

spouse and that protect your heirs against creditors. To a certain extent, they also set limitations on the duration of trusts. Your attorney should also be invaluable in helping you to write your will according to the accepted wording in your state. By using words whose meanings have been clearly established, a potential source of confusion can be avoided.

Revising your will is as important as its initial writing. Changes in your will should be made as the composition of your estate changes and/or the number of beneficiaries increases or decreases. Most revisions can be made by means of a codicil, a legal instrument that enables you to revise your will without completely rewriting it. If you move your principal residence to another state, be sure your will is valid in the new state.

The best place of safekeeping for your will is probably with your attorney or in your safety deposit box. A copy of your will should be kept in your general file at home.

Letter of Last Instructions

Often the letter of last instructions is a more appropriate place than your will for instructions concerning the details of your burial. This document should also indicate where all your records, as well as your will, are located. This letter is normally kept at home where it will be readily available in time of need. Be sure your executor knows where it is located.

The Probate Process

Before your will can be put into effect, a determination must be made as to its authenticity and legality. First and most important, your will should be in writing. Second, your signature must appear in ink immediately after the last sentence. It is preferable that you sign your will with exactly the same name as that appearing in the body of the will. Third, there usually must be at least two witnesses who have signed your will. It is never advisable to have your spouse or any prospective beneficiaries witness your will. By performing this function, they will probably invalidate their claims to your estate. The best witnesses are individuals of legal age but younger than yourself, who are not your heirs, and who could testify in court when the will is probated.

Once the appropriate state court has satisfied itself as to the legality and authenticity of your will, it will direct a qualified executor (usually the one appointed in the will) to administer the settlement of your estate. This direction is provided through the issuance of what are termed *letters testamentary*. When this point is reached, the primary burden of responsibility for the estate will be shifted to the executor. He must, however, keep detailed records of all transactions and periodically account for his actions to the court officials.

duties of the executor   The executor must first assemble and preserve all the deeds and certificates of ownership to property in which you had an interest upon death, as well as all records of outstanding debts. This job will be much easier for him if you have kept complete and orderly records of your financial affairs.

He must also safeguard and manage your financial interests. This can be a very demanding task, particularly if you had an extensive investment portfolio. For example, rents might have to be collected, securities managed, life insurance proceeds collected, and small businesses operated. While you are alive and as your investments become more extensive and complex, you should ensure that professional investment management will be retained or continued during the probating of your estate.

Resolving claims by creditors against your estate is another task for your executor. You may have owed $3000 for an around-the-world trip completed shortly before your death. This would be an enforceable claim that would have to be resolved before your estate could be distributed to your heirs. Creditors are usually notified through a legal announcement in the newspapers that they must submit their claims within four to nine months from the beginning date of the settlement period. Any claims that are submitted after this time are usually declared invalid.

Payment of taxes is yet another duty of your executor. He must first see that a final income tax return and payment is filed for you. He must also file income tax returns for income earned by your estate between the time of your death and the final distribution of its assets to your heirs. Taxes based on the final value of your estate must also be paid. These taxes come in two forms: estate taxes and inheritance taxes. The federal government and some states levy an estate tax on the transfer of property. This tax is based on the taxable value of your entire estate and is paid by the estate. States commonly levy an inheritance tax on the right to receive property. This tax is based on the value of property received by each heir and can be paid either out of the estate or by the heir—whichever way you have designated in your will.

The last duties of the executor are the distribution of your estate according to your will and a final accounting to the probate authorities.

Partially Bypassing the Probate Process

You may use gifts, joint ownership, or trusts to have certain pieces of property in your estate bypass the probate process. This does not mean, however, that you may necessarily avoid the entire process.

gifts   The most obvious and easy way to have part of your estate bypass the probate process is to give it away before your death. In this way, you will reduce both the size of your estate and the amount of estate taxes that will have to be paid. Of course, any gifts you make may be subject to the federal gift tax. To make the transfer valid, you must divest yourself of all ownership interests in the property given away. Many people find it emotionally difficult to relinquish control of their hard-earned financial resources.

joint ownership   When you die, all property held as joint tenancy automatically goes to the surviving joint owner, usually your spouse, without having to go through probate. Property held as tenancy by the entirety would also pass automatically to your spouse. Since this transfer cannot be affected by your will, the property passes outside the probate process. Therefore, a certain degree of the expense and effort associated with the probate process is avoided. Property held as tenancy in common goes to the deceased joint owner's designated heirs. Therefore, it is included in the deceased's estate and must pass through probate.

The advantages of joint ownership lie chiefly in the time- and cost-saving features related to probate. In addition, a jointly owned home is protected against the claims of creditors in some states. The disadvantages are several. First, no one joint owner has complete control. Second, selling the property can pose a problem. Under one form of joint ownership, one owner can sell his share without obtaining the approval of the other owner(s). Under another form, one owner cannot sell his share without obtaining the approval of the other owner(s). Third, joint ownership does not offer the flexibility to adjust to changing circumstances that a will does (through revision). Fourth, some states allow jointly owned property to be seized to satisfy claims against one of the joint owners of that property.

trusts   There are two primary forms of trusts. The first is termed a *living* (or intervivos) trust because it is put into effect during the lifetime of the trustor. The second is termed a *testamentary* trust because it is set up in the trustor's will and does not go into effect until his death.

There are three categories of living trusts: revocable, irrevocable, and a hybrid of the two called reversionary or short-term. In the revocable trust the trust agreement may be cancelled by the trustor at any time. The assets transferred to the trust are still considered part of the trustor's estate. Life insurance trusts are one of the most popular forms of revocable trusts. They are usually recommended, however, only where substantial amounts of life insurance are involved. Proceeds from the trust are paid to the beneficiaries as an annuity, which may include a return on investment or a return of part of the principal plus an investment return. The most significant advantage of a living revocable trust is that all assets in the trust pass outside probate. In addition, this type of trust can be coordinated very effectively with any testamentary trust provisions.

In the irrevocable trust, the trust agreement can never be cancelled once it has been put into effect. Because of the complete loss of control over the assets involved, this type of trust is used mostly as a protection against senility, investment incompetence, or mental instability, but it can also be a convenient way to reduce the size of one's taxable estate.

The reversionary (or short-term) trust is a hybrid of the revocable and the irrevocable trust. It must be irrevocable for ten years or more or until the occurrence of an event specified in the trust agreement, such as the marriage of a daughter who is the beneficiary. This event must not normally be expected to occur within a ten-year period. (Life expectancy forecasts are not relevant to this consideration.) The income from such a trust must be accumulated for the benefit of, or distributed to, a beneficiary other than the trustor. This type of trust represents a gift of income, not principal, as the principal returns to the trustor upon termination of the trust agreement. Therefore, estate taxes are not avoided. A gift tax on a partial value of the assets put into trust will be levied. There are definite income tax advantages in such trusts. For example, a taxpayer in a high income tax bracket may transfer income to a taxpayer in a lower tax bracket by placing certain income-producing assets in a reversionary trust. The effect is to reduce the total amount of taxes paid and so increase the total amount of income retained.

The attractive feature of a testamentary trust is that, during his lifetime, the trustor does not have to relinquish control of the property to be put in trust, and yet his beneficiaries will be protected from unscrupulous individuals or their own investment incompetence after his death. However, these trusts do not avoid the federal estate tax.

The period for which all but charitable trusts (which may continue indefinitely) are allowed to remain in effect is determined by state law. The most common maximum period allowed ends twenty-one years and nine months after the death of all living individuals named specifically in the trust agreement. This makes it possible for grandchildren not born when the trust was created to be included as beneficiaries and remaindermen.

Intestacy

The absence of a valid will declaring how your estate should be settled upon your death is termed *intestacy*. The state in which you are a legal resident will normally settle your estate if you die intestate. The guidelines for this type of settlement are set down in state law. Since they are designed for general situations, you have little assurance that considerations unique to your estate will be taken into account or that your estate will be disposed of according to your wishes or in the best interests of your survivors. For example, Mr. J. B. Jones died leaving no known living relatives and no will. He had long been very interested and active in the Boy Scouts and had intended to leave his estate for the benefit of this organization. Because he never made a will, his wishes were not fulfilled and his property went to the state in which he resided.

FINANCIAL ASPECTS OF ESTATE TRANSFER

There are essentially two types of costs of estate transfer with which you should be concerned: (1) probate and administrative fees and (2) taxes. The fees include court costs, accountant's fees, appraisal fees, legal fees, and executor's fees and expenses. They are generally levied as a percentage of the gross estate, less debts. (The percentage for particular estate sizes is determined in many cases by statute and may bear little or no correlation to the cost of services rendered to probate an estate.) On an estate of $100,000 the fees might be over $8000. This expense should not be taken lightly. Any of the means you can use to bypass the probate process should help save some of this expense.

The second type of expense is taxes, which may be both federal estate taxes and federal gift taxes. We will treat these tax costs in more detail.

Federal Estate Tax

The estate tax return (Form 706) must be filed within nine months of the date of death, if the deceased's gross estate exceeds $60,000. In cases where the probate process is unduly long and complicated, time extensions may be granted.

computation procedure As was demonstrated in the chapter on income taxes, gross income and taxable income are usually two very different amounts; the same is true of your gross estate and your taxable estate. Figure 21-1 shows how the net estate tax is derived from your taxable estate, which is based on your gross estate.

Your gross estate includes both separate property and one-half the value of all community property in which you had an ownership interest upon your death. Either of these might include the following assets:

- cash
- personal property
- real estate
- stocks and bonds
- tax-exempt state and municipal securities
- federal securities
- joint ownership interests (to the extent of the contributions of the decedent)
- gifts made in contemplation of death (those made within three years of death, unless it can be proven to the satisfaction of the court that the intent of the gift was not to avoid estate taxes)
- transferred property on which certain ownership rights were retained by the transferor (such as reversionary or revocable trusts)
- life insurance where the deceased retained any of the ownership rights
- any portion of an annuity that a beneficiary, designated by the deceased, may receive

Begin with	GROSS ESTATE
Subtract	TYPE ONE DEDUCTIONS
To Arrive at	ADJUSTED GROSS ESTATE
Subtract	MARITAL DEDUCTION
	TYPE TWO DEDUCTIONS
To Arrive at	ESTATE BEFORE EXEMPTION
Subtract	$60,000 EXEMPTION
To Arrive at	TAXABLE ESTATE
Compute	GROSS ESTATE TAX
Subtract	CREDITS
To Arrive at	NET ESTATE TAX

Fig. 21-1.
Framework for
computing estate tax

While this list is not complete, it does include some of the major items. We recommend that you consult a tax authority if you have questions about specific treatment of these items or about items not listed here.

Type one deductions are subtracted from your gross estate to arrive at your *adjusted gross estate.* Although we are using the same term as we used in chapter 9 to indicate how adjusted gross estate is derived from gross estate, the type one deductions used for estate tax purposes are not necessarily the same as those used for income tax purposes.

There are five major categories of expenses that qualify as type one deductions for estate tax purposes. These are: (1) funeral expenses paid out of the estate's proceeds; (2) administration expenses incurred in the collection of an estate's assets, the payment of its debts, and the distribution of the estate to its beneficiaries; (3) expenses incurred in the administration of the estate's assets not subject to the probate process (e.g., trusts, joint ownership interest); (4) enforceable claims (debts, mortgages, and taxes) against the estate; and (5) losses occurring during the administration of the estate to the extent that they are not covered by insurance.

The *marital deduction* allows you to transfer 50 percent of your adjusted gross estate to your spouse free of federal estate taxation. This deduction has the same effect as community property statutes. Not all states have enacted community property laws, nor is all property necessarily subject to these statutes where they exist. The marital deduction is directed toward those instances where the concept of community property does not apply.

This deduction is not allowed in certain instances. If, for example, property deducted from your estate in this manner would not be subject to taxation in your spouse's estate upon his or her death, then the marital deduction would not be allowed. (You might leave $100,000 worth of stocks in trust for your son with the income to go to your wife for the rest of her life. When your son is twenty-one, ownership of the stock will be vested in him, though the income derived from the stock will

not be his until his mother dies. Since this $100,000 bequest never becomes part of your wife's estate—even though she has rights to the income—you cannot include this amount in any marital deduction computations for your estate.)

Let us see what happens when the marital deduction is allowed because the property transferred will become part of the taxable estate of your wife at her death. You leave $100,000 worth of stocks outright to your wife. Whatever is left upon her death is fully included in her estate for taxation since the marital deduction allowed 50 percent of it, or $50,000, to go untaxed in your estate. However, estate taxes on the $100,000 portion would be avoided entirely if your wife were to spend or give away this sum during her lifetime.

Your *estate before exemption* is derived by subtracting any marital deduction allowed plus qualified charitable deductions from your adjusted gross estate. *Type two deductions* represent our designation for charitable deductions. Such transfer of property may be made either during your lifetime or upon your death and still be deductible. Qualified type two deductions are allowed for contributions to the following types of charitable organizations: corporations operating exclusively for charitable, educational, literary, religious, or scientific purposes; any federal or state political subdivision exclusively pursuing public purposes; and any Congressionally approved veteran's organization.

The next step is to take the $60,000 exemption available to all U.S. resident and nonresident citizens. Your *taxable estate* is what remains after taking this exemption. Obviously, if your estate before exemption is less than $60,000, you will not be liable for federal estate taxes. This might very well occur even though your gross estate was in excess of $60,000 and you were required to file Form 706.

Your *gross estate tax* is based on the amount of your taxable estate. A partial table of tax rates that apply to this text is given in table 21-1. These figures are not necessarily the exact amounts of tax you will have to pay because several credits are allowed against your gross estate tax. The four categories of credits are state death taxes, certain gift taxes, certain estate taxes paid on an earlier estate, and foreign death taxes. You should be certain to consult an attorney to determine which of these credits are available for your estate.

Your *net estate tax* is derived by subtracting any available credits from your gross estate tax. Note that they are deducted not from your taxable estate, but directly from the tax computed on this amount.

an example Let us assume that Lee Fong dies leaving a gross estate of $325,000. His executor must pay the expenses that qualify as type one deductions. After the funeral expenses ($5000), administration expenses ($15,000), and claims against the estate ($35,000) are deducted, Mr. Fong's adjusted gross estate is $270,000. Since Mr. Fong lived in

TABLE 21-1

Federal Estate Tax Rates

A		B	C
TAXABLE ESTATE		TAX ON AMOUNT IN COLUMN A	RATE OF TAX ON EXCESS OVER AMOUNT IN COLUMN A
Equal to or More Than	But Less Than		
$ 0	$ 5,000	$ 0	3%
5,000	10,000	150	7
10,000	20,000	500	11
20,000	30,000	1,600	14
30,000	40,000	3,000	18
40,000	50,000	4,800	22
50,000	60,000	7,000	25
60,000	100,000	9,500	28
100,000	250,000	20,700	30
250,000	500,000	65,700	32
500,000	750,000	145,700	35
750,000	1,000,000	233,200	37
1,000,000	1,250,000	325,700	39
1,250,000	1,500,000	423,200	42
1,500,000	2,000,000	528,200	45
2,000,000	2,500,000	753,000	49
2,500,000	3,000,000	998,200	53
3,000,000	3,500,000	1,263,200	56
3,500,000	4,000,000	1,543,200	59
4,000,000	5,000,000	1,838,200	63
5,000,000	6,000,000	2,468,200	67
6,000,000	7,000,000	3,138,200	70
7,000,000	8,000,000	3,838,200	73
8,000,000	10,000,000	4,568,200	76
10,000,000	– – –	6,088,200	77

a state that does not have community property laws and he acquired his entire estate after his marriage, Mrs. Fong may receive tax-free 50 percent of her husband's adjusted gross estate ($135,000). Mr. Fong also directed through his will that a certain university be given a bequest (type two deduction) of $35,000. Therefore, Mr. Fong's estate before exemption is $100,000. From this amount the $60,000 exemption is taken, making Mr. Fong's taxable estate $40,000. His gross estate tax on this amount (as derived from table 21-1) is $4800. Against this amount, Mr. Fong has credits for state death taxes ($200), estate taxes paid on prior transfers of property ($500), and foreign death taxes ($1000) he pays as a citizen of Taiwan. Mr. Fong's net estate tax is $3100.

Federal Gift Tax

This tax is imposed on the transfer of property between individuals. The amount of the tax is based upon the value of the transferred property.

The filing of gift tax returns and the payment of the tax is done on a quarterly basis. Form 709 and the tax due must be filed by the fifteenth of the second month following the end of the calendar quarter in which the gift was made. For example, if you made a gift in August, both Form 709 and your tax payment are due by November fifteenth of that year since the calendar quarter ends September thirtieth.

annual exclusion   Every year you and your spouse are each allowed to exclude from federal gift taxation the first $3000 worth of gifts that you make to each donee for that year. Conceivably, if you had ten children, you could give $30,000 away tax-free each year by giving each child no more than $3000 worth of gifts. In addition, your spouse could also give away $30,000 each year tax-free to the same ten children. If you and your spouse give away property in which each of you own a half interest, then the exclusion limit for each donee would be $6000 (the sum of the $3000 exclusions available to you and your spouse).

one lifetime exemption   In addition to annual exclusions, you and your spouse are each entitled to one lifetime exemption of $30,000. You may take advantage of this exemption all in one year or spread it over several years. If you and your spouse give property in which each of you has a half interest, then the exemption would be $60,000. The lifetime exemption is available only once. If you desire, you may divide it among several children. However, remember that the exclusion is $30,000 *per donor,* not $30,000 per donee.

deductions   The *marital deduction* has the same effect on federal gift taxes as it does on estate taxes. Where community property is not a consideration, you may transfer property that you own separately to your spouse with only one-half of the value of this gift being subject to taxation. All charitable contributions are free of gift taxes, no matter how large they might be. (However, you should note that charitable contributions may only be deducted from your income for income tax purposes up to 50 percent of your adjusted gross income each year.)

the gift tax's cumulative structure   With income taxes, the tax bracket you are in varies annually, depending on the amount of money you earn each year. This is not true for gift taxes. After your one lifetime exemption, annual exclusions, and allowable deductions are taken, *the gifts you made during the year are added to the gifts you paid taxes on in previous years* in determining the amount of tax you must pay.

An example should help make this clear. J. Paul Wetherhill's total amount of taxable gifts, including this year's and all previous years' taxable gifts, is $60,000. As can be seen from table 21-2, the tax on this amount is $7125. Mr. Wetherhill's taxable gifts previous to the current year amounted to $50,000. The tax he has paid on this amount in past years (as seen in table 21-2) is $5250. Therefore, the gift tax he must pay for his current taxable gifts of $10,000 is $1875 ($7125 –$5250). Admittedly, this is a rather simple explanation of what can be a complex computation. We suggest that you consult a tax attorney to determine accurately your gift tax liability.

Now let us consider the same example and its effect on Mr. Wetherhill's estate taxes. Assume that before the $60,000 in gifts, Mr. Wetherhill's taxable estate was $260,000. On this amount he would have to pay $68,900 in federal estate taxes. However, after the $60,000 was given away, he owed federal estate taxes of only $50,700 on his $200,000 taxable estate. His estate tax savings amounted to $18,200. When you compare this savings with the total gift taxes of $7125 he must pay, you can see the dramatic effect of taking money off the top of the estate tax brackets and taxing it at the low end of the gift tax rates. The net tax savings in this example is $11,075, one-sixth of his total gifts!

One warning should be issued, however. Gifts made within three years of death will be included in your gross estate unless it can be proved to the court that the intent of the gifts was not to avoid estate taxes. Such intent can usually be proven when, for example, the giver was in good health and had a life expectancy of more than three years at the time he made the gifts.

TABLE 21-2

FEDERAL GIFT TAX RATES

A		B	C
TOTAL AMOUNT OF TAXABLE GIFTS		TAX ON AMOUNT IN COLUMN A	RATE OF TAX ON EXCESS OVER AMOUNT IN COLUMN A
Equal to or More Than	But Less Than		
$ 0	$ 5,000	$ 0	2.25%
5,000	10,000	112.50	5.25
10,000	20,000	375.00	8.25
20,000	30,000	1,200.00	10.50
30,000	40,000	2,250.00	13.50
40,000	50,000	3,600.00	16.50
50,000	60,000	5,250.00	18.75
60,000	100,000	7,125.00	21.00
100,000	250,000	15,525.00	22.50
250,000	500,000	49,275,00	24.00
500,000	750,000	109,275.00	26.25

Effect of Gifts, Joint Ownership, and Trusts on Taxes

Now we will look at what the tax treatment would most likely be for each means of bypassing probate. Any tax savings would be in addition to savings from reduced probate and administrative fees.

gifts   The tax advantages of transferring your estate by making gifts are that (1) the gift tax rate is only 75 percent of the estate tax rate for similar taxable amounts; (2) the first gifts are removed from taxation in the highest estate tax brackets and are taxed in the lowest gift tax brackets; and (3) the gift's recipient is likely to pay less in income taxes on the income from the gift than the donor would have had to pay because the recipient is often in a lower tax bracket. The principal disadvantage of making gifts is that the donor loses both the income-producing value of the gift and any funds used to pay his gift tax liability.

If, while still alive, you give away your life insurance policy and all its rights of ownership, your policy will not be considered part of your estate, and you will avoid paying estate taxes on it. These rights include borrowing against the cash value; owning the policy; changing the beneficiaries; retaining any economic benefit from the policy; using proceeds upon your death for the benefit of your estate; and surrendering and cancelling the policy. Although you avoid estate taxation, you subject your policy to the gift tax. The tax will be paid on the existing cash value. This procedure may also be used in certain instances with annuity contracts and qualified employee benefit plans. Once again, we recommend that you consult your attorney about proper application and implementation.

joint ownership   The tax considerations here are threefold. First, in the case of property that is held in tenancy in common, when one joint owner dies, for estate tax purposes the IRS treats the entire property as if it were owned by the deceased. This is a particularly important consideration when the joint owners are not husband and wife. If they are husband and wife, the marital deduction rules would apply. If you are a joint owner of property that is held in tenancy in common and you want to ensure that the property belonging to the other joint owner(s) is not taxed in your estate, the surviving owner(s) must be able to document that he (they) contributed to the purchase of the subject property. Otherwise, upon your death the entire value of the property might- be taxed in your estate; and when the surviving joint owner dies, the entire property may be subject to estate taxation again.

Second, joint ownership permits the splitting of income and capital gains among the joint owners proportionate to their interest. This could be beneficial for husbands and wives filing separate income tax returns. Third, a gift tax could be levied if one joint owner pays for the entire property, allowing the other joint owner to acquire an ownership interest without making any contribution. This tax would be assessed on the value of the portion the noncontributing joint owner received.

trusts There are three possible tax advantages that might be derived from transferring some of your estate through trusts. First, the gift tax levied when irrevocable living trusts are established could be less than the estate tax that would eventually have to be paid if the assets were left in your estate until your death. Second, if you are in a high income tax bracket and place certain income-producing assets in a reversionary trust with income going to someone (e.g., a child) who is in a lower tax bracket, that income would be taxed at a lower rate. Third, a trust's ultimate effect on your estate would be to divert, to other persons, income that otherwise might contribute to the size of your estate and therefore increase your estate taxes. Figure 21-2 summarizes these tax advantages.

An example should help to show you the value of such tax advantages. In order to let their two children enjoy the income from some of their estate, Mr. and Mrs. Fong put $72,000 worth of stock into two irrevocable trusts that would go to the children at age twenty-one. The Fongs paid no gift taxes on this amount since each claimed his lifetime exemption of $30,000 and an annual exclusion of $3000. The dividend income from these stocks averaged about $3300 a year. Since Mr. Fong was in a 30 percent tax bracket, his taxes on this amount would be $990 a year. The taxes to each child would be approximately $130 a year (assuming no other taxable income), for a total of $260 a year. In the ten years until Mr. Fong's death, this amounted to $7300 ([$990 − $260] × 10) in tax savings. At his death, these stocks were worth $98,000; they had grown about 3 percent a year. This meant that Mr. Fong would have a gross estate worth $227,000 instead of $325,000. His estate after all deductions but before the $60,000 exemption would be $55,000. His net

Type of Trust	Gift Tax Incurred	Estate Tax Reduced	Probate Fees Reduced	Control Lost	Income Taxed to
Living					
Revocable	No	No	Yes	No	Grantor
Irrevocable	Yes	Yes	Yes	Yes	Beneficiary
Reversionary	Yes[1]	No	No	Temporarily[2]	Beneficiary
Testamentary	No	No	No	No	

[1]Gift taxes are paid, subject to standard exclusions, on approximately 44 percent of the value of the assets placed in trust for ten years. For periods longer than this, the percentage will increase.

[2]Must be irrevocable for at least ten years.

Fig. 21-2. Effect of trusts on taxes

estate tax would be zero instead of $3100, giving him a net estate tax savings of $3100. His total tax savings achieved by simply setting up two trusts amounted to $10,400 ($7300 + $3100). Also, because he had made this gift before death, probate and administrative fees, possibly as high as $6500, would probably be saved. These total savings of $16,900 must be offset against trust administration and investment advisory fees, which would probably amount to $5000 for the ten-year period. Thus, a net savings of $11,900 would be possible.

In any event, where tax savings are a consideration, you must weigh the savings gained against the control lost. In order for trust agreements to be valid and affect any estate tax savings, they often must be binding for life. If you would find this loss of flexibility a definite hindrance, it may be worth it to you to pay higher taxes and maintain control over your property.

CONCLUSION

There is no substitute for careful and thoughtful planning involving estate transfer. Be sure to include your family in this process. Because of the often complex nature of these transactions, enlist the assistance of good professionals. They will ensure that the means you use to make the transfer efficient and economical are also in the best interest of you and your survivors.

VOCABULARY

beneficiary
bequest
estate
estate tax
executor (executrix)
gift tax
heir
inheritance tax

intestacy
joint ownership
probate process
remaindermen
trust
trustee
trustor
will

QUESTIONS

1. What types of property may be included in a person's gross estate?
2. What does it mean to die "intestate"? What are its consequences?
3. What can a will be used to accomplish?
4. How does the probate process work? What role does the executor play in this process?
5. What are the two major costs of estate transfer? How do the methods of determining their amount differ?

6. Under what circumstances might you be required to file Form 706 and yet have to pay no federal estate taxes?
7. What is the difference between an estate tax and an inheritance tax?
8. How do the three types of living trusts differ in the way they are treated for federal estate tax purposes?
9. What are the three forms of joint ownership and how do they differ from one another?
10. What must you do to ensure that life insurance death benefits are not included in your estate?
11. Under what circumstances might it be financially advantageous to leave property in your estate rather than to make a gift of it?

CASE PROBLEM

Whitney Cragge's taxable estate is $150,000. Disregarding any credits, what would be the estate tax on this amount if he were to die today? What would be the gift tax effect of giving $60,000 to his aging brother or $20,000 to each of his brother's three adult children? What would either of these strategies do to Whitney's estate tax liability? At what point would it no longer be beneficial to make gifts rather than leave assets in his estate? (Assume that Whitney has not made any gifts up to this time.)

RECOMMENDED READING

MAGAZINES

"Could Most Wives Take Over the Family Finances?" *Better Homes and Gardens,* February 1970.

> Offers a checklist to test a wife's knowledge of her family's finances and guidelines for improving her ability to assume responsibility if her husband dies.

"If You're Asked to Be an Executor." *Changing Times,* October 1970, pp. 37–39.

> A survey discussion of the complex and demanding tasks that must be performed by an executor.

"Joint Ownership Isn't Always Smart." *Changing Times,* August 1968, pp. 7–10.

> A good discussion of joint ownership.

"Personal Business." *Business Week,* December 13, 1969, p. 97.

> A comparison of custodial gifts and gifts in trust for minors.

BOOKS

Donaldson, Elvin, and Pfahl, John. *Personal Finance.* New York: Ronald, 1971.

> Chapter 19 provides a good discussion of estate planning, wills, trusts, and taxes.

Smith, Carlton; Pratt, Richard R.; and editors of *Time-Life. The Time-Life Book of Family Finance.* New York: Time-Life Books, 1969.

> Chapter 13 discusses the basic issues of estate transfer.

CHUCK AND NANCY ANDERSON

COMPUTING CHUCK'S NET ESTATE TAX

Let us assume we are twenty-five years in the future and Chuck Anderson has just died unexpectedly at the age of sixty. Nancy has asked you to assist her with her duties as executor of Chuck's estate. One of the pieces of information she would like you to determine roughly is the net estate tax liability to the federal government.

Below are all the items you need to make this determination. Your task is to assemble the information properly and make two sets of computations. In making the first set, assume that, at the time of Chuck's death, the Andersons resided in a noncommunity property state and that the value of all assets is initially included in Chuck's gross estate. In making the second set of computations, assume that the Andersons resided in a community property state and that the nature of all their assets is community property.

Cash	$5,000
State inheritance tax	500
Probate and administration fees	15,000
Charitable bequest	5,000
Home mortgage balance	1,500
Funeral expenses	3,500
Securities value	35,000
Home value	65,000
Mutual fund value	43,500
Cars	8,500
Real estate loan	15,000
Personal property	25,000
Real estate investment value	37,500

SOCIAL SECURITY
ADDENDUM
AND
COMPOUND INTEREST
TABLES

HOW TO QUALIFY FOR SOCIAL SECURITY

To qualify for Social Security benefits, you must meet the length of service requirements; that is, you must have worked for a certain length of time in an occupation covered by Social Security. The type of benefits (retirement, survivors, disability, or Medicare) available to you depends on the number of quarters of credit you have accumulated, i.e., the length of time you have worked. The amount of benefits depends on your average annual earnings during the time you worked.

Nine out of every ten people who work are covered by Social Security.[1] The only workers not covered are state and local government employees (including teachers), railroad workers, some household and farm workers, and persons with less than $400 a year in net earnings from self-employment. If you are among these, check with your local Social Security Administration office for further details about the rulings.

Quarters of Credit

To receive credits that go to satisfy the length of service requirements, you must earn at least $50 of nonfarm income in a calendar quarter. If you earn $50 or more during each of four consecutive three-month periods, you accumulate one full year of credit. The minimum service requirement that must be met before any benefits will be paid is one and one-half years (six quarters). Figure 1 (p. 494) shows how many years of credit must be accumulated to qualify for various types of retirement, survivors, disability, and Medicare benefits.

Average Annual Earnings and Monthly Benefits

To determine the amount of monthly benefits you may be eligible to receive, you must first determine your average annual earnings. You can do this by using the following procedure. We have used the example of Chuck Anderson and his family to illustrate this procedure.

Instructions

1 *Find the initial year you must use in figuring the number of years you must count.* If you were born before 1930, start counting with the year 1956. If you were born in the year 1930 or thereafter, begin counting with the year in which you reached your twenty-

---

1. U.S. Department of Health, Education, and Welfare, "Your Social Security," Publication No. (SSA) 72-10035 (Washington, D.C.: Government Printing Office, October 1971), p. 5.

Type of Benefits	Payable to	Minimum Years of Work Under Social Security
Retirement	You, your wife, child Dependent husband 62 or over	10 years (fully insured status)
Survivors[1]		
Full	Widow 00 or over Disabled widow 50–59 Widow if caring for child 18 years or younger Dependent children Dependent widower 62 or over Disabled dependent widower 50–61 Dependent parent at 62	10 years (fully insured status)
Current	Widow caring for child 18 years or younger Dependent children	1½ years of last three years before death (currently insured status)
Disability	You and your dependents	If under age 24, you need 1½ years of work in the three years prior to disablement. If between ages 24 and 31, you need to work half the time between when you turned 21 and your date of disablement. If age 31 or older, you must have worked ten years, five of which must have occurred during the ten years prior to disablement.
Medicare		
Hospitalization (automatic benefits)	Anyone 65 or over	If you turn 65 after 1975, you need ten years of work experience. If you turn 65 before 1975, consult your local Social Security Administration office.
Medical expense (voluntary benefits)	Anyone 65 or over who pays monthly premiums	No prior work under Social Security is required.

Fig. 1.
Length of service requirements for Social Security benefits

SOURCE: Data taken from U.S. Department of Health, Education, and Welfare, "Your Social Security." Publication No. (SSA) 72-10035 (Washington, D.C.: Government Printing Office, October 1971), pp. 14, 18.

[1]A lump-sum death benefit no greater than $255 is also granted to dependents of those either fully or currently insured.

seventh birthday. At least two years of earnings must be used to figure disability or survivor benefits and at least five years to figure retirement benefits.

Chuck was born in 1938 and is thirty-five years old. Since he was born after 1930, he must begin counting with 1965, the year in which he reached age twenty-seven.

2   *Subtract this initial year (step 1) from the present year to obtain the number of years you must count.* A man sixty-five years old or older would count only the years until he reached age sixty-five. A woman sixty-two years old or older would count only until the year of her sixty-second birthday.

Chuck must count eight years of earnings (1965 through 1972).

3   *List your earnings for all years beginning with 1951.* Do not count more than $3600 of earnings for any one year 1951 through 1954, $4200 for any one year 1955 through 1958, $4800 for any one year 1959 through 1965, $6600 for any one year 1966 through 1967, $7800 for any one year 1968 through 1971, and $9000 for the year 1972 and thereafter.

Chuck listed his earnings for 1951 through 1972.

4   *Cross off your list the years of lowest earnings until the number remaining is the same as the number derived in step 2.* If the number derived in step 3 is less than that derived in step 2, you will have to include years in which you had no earnings.

Since Chuck need count only the eight years of highest earnings and has earned more and more each year, he counted his earnings only for each year back to and including 1965. He earned $3800 that year. Each year since then he has earned more than the allowable maximum. He was allowed to count only $6600 of his wages in 1966 and 1967, $7800 in 1968 through 1971, and $9000 in 1972.

5   *Total your earnings for all the years remaining on your list and divide by the number of years you were to count (step 2).* The result is your average annual earnings.

Chuck's average earnings were $7400 ($57,200 ÷ 8).

6   *Use the tables in figure 2 to determine the size of benefits you and your dependents can expect from Social Security.*

By looking at the tables of benefits in figure 2 (p. 496), Chuck saw that he and his family (Nancy, Jim, and Melissa) would begin receiving approximately $560 a month if he became disabled or died. If Chuck were sixty-five, retired, and still had dependents, he would also be able to receive that amount in retirement benefits.

Type of Benefits	Average Yearly Benefits Since 1951						
	$923 or Less	$3000	$4200	$5400	$6600	$7800	$9000
Retirement							
Retired worker 65 or older	$ 84	$175	$213	$251	$288	$331	$354
Wife 65 or older	42	87	107	125	144	165	177
Retired worker at 62	68	140	171	200	231	265	284
Wife at 62, no child	32	66	80	94	108	124	133
Wife under 65, one child[a]	42	92	157	217	234	248	266
One child of retired worker	42	87	107	125	144	165	177
Survivors[b]							
Widow at 60, no child	73	125	153	179	206	237	253
Widow or widower at 62 or older	84	144	176	207	238	273	292
Widow under 62, one child	127	262	320	377	433	497	532
Widow under 62, two children	127	267	371	468	522	579	620
One surviving child	84	131	160	188	216	248	266
Disability							
Disabled worker under 65[c]	84	175	213	251	288	331	354
Wife at 62, no child	32	66	80	94	108	124	133
Wife under 65, one child[a]	42	92	157	217	234	248	266
One child of disabled worker	42	87	107	125	144	165	177
Maximum Family Payment for Each Type	127	267	371	468	522	579	620

SOURCE: U.S. Department of Health, Education, and Welfare, "Higher Social Security Payments," DHEW Publication No. (SSA) 73-10324, July 1972.

NOTE: The amounts of benefits have been rounded to the nearest dollar.

[a]Under age eighteen.

[b]The lump-sum death benefit is ordinarily three times the amount of the deceased's monthly retirement benefit at age 65, or $255, whichever is less.

[c]A person who becomes disabled receives no extra benefit payment for his wife unless she is at least sixty-two years old or they have children.

Fig. 2.
Amounts of Social Security retirement, survivors, and disability benefits

Applying for Social Security Benefits

No benefits begin unless you file a valid claim. Figure 3 shows the proof necessary to satisfy the Social Security Administration that a claim is valid. To file a claim for benefits, contact your local Social Security Administration office. They will provide the necessary forms. Once your application is approved, monthly checks will be mailed to you by the U.S. Treasury Department shortly after the close of the month.

Type of Benefits	Necessary Proof of Qualification
Retirement	
Insured worker	Age
Wife of insured worker	Age
Husband of insured worker	Age, marriage, and support
Child of insured worker	Age, relationship, dependency; evidence of full-time school attendance if over 18 and under 22
Mother (under 62) of insured, child in care	Marriage, relationship to child, and responsibility for child's care
Survivors	
Widow of insured	Marriage, death of worker, age of beneficiary if without child in care
Divorced, child of deceased in care	Support, marriage, death of worker, relationship of child, and responsibility for child's care
Divorced after 20 or more years of marriage, no children	Age, marriage, and half support or substantial contribution from former husband under written agreement or court order
Husband of insured	Age, marriage, support, and death of worker
Widow (over 60) or widower (over 62) who remarries and makes a claim on the record of first spouse	Age, marriage of first spouse, Social Security number of first spouse
Child of insured	Age, relationship, dependency; evidence of full-time school attendance if over 18 and under 22
Mother (under 62), child in care	Marriage, death of worker, relationship to child, and responsiblity for child's care
Parents of deceased worker	Age, relationship, support, no remarriage of parent since death of the worker
Any person who paid funeral expenses if there is no widow or widower	Itemized and receipted bill from undertaker
Disability	
Insured worker	Disability

Fig. 3.
Type of proof required for Social Security retirement, survivors, and disability benefits

SOURCE: U.S. Department of Health, Education, and Welfare, "Your Social Security," Publication No. (SSA) 72-10035 (Washington, D.C.: Government Printing Office, October 1971), pp. 14, 18.

COMPOUND INTEREST TABLE A

For Lump-Sum Investments

Length of Investment (Years)	\multicolumn{12}{c}{Percentage Rate of Return or of Inflation}

Length of Investment (Years)	2%	3%	4%	5%	6%	8%	10%	12%	14%	16%	18%	20%
1	1.02	1.03	1.04	1.0	1.1	1.1	1.1	1.1	1.1	1.2	1.2	1.2
2	1.04	1.06	1.08	1.1	1.1	1.2	1.2	1.2	1.3	1.3	1.4	1.4
3	1.06	1.09	1.12	1.2	1.2	1.3	1.3	1.4	1.5	1.6	1.6	1.7
4	1.08	1.12	1.17	1.2	1.3	1.4	1.5	1.6	1.7	1.8	1.9	2.1
5	1.10	1.16	1.22	1.3	1.3	1.5	1.6	1.8	1.9	2.1	2.3	2.5
6	1.13	1.19	1.26	1.3	1.4	1.6	1.8	2.0	2.2	2.4	2.7	3.0
7	1.15	1.23	1.32	1.4	1.5	1.7	2.0	2.2	2.5	2.8	3.2	3.6
8	1.17	1.27	1.37	1.5	1.6	1.8	2.1	2.5	2.8	3.3	3.8	4.3
9	1.20	1.30	1.42	1.6	1.7	2.0	2.4	2.8	3.2	3.8	4.4	5.2
10	1.22	1.34	1.48	1.6	1.8	2.2	2.6	3.1	3.7	4.4	5.2	6.2
11	1.24	1.38	1.54	1.7	1.9	2.3	2.8	3.5	4.2	5.1	6.2	7.4
12	1.27	1.42	1.60	1.8	2.0	2.5	3.1	3.9	4.8	5.9	7.3	8.9
13	1.29	1.47	1.66	1.9	2.1	2.7	3.4	4.4	5.5	6.9	8.6	10.7
14	1.32	1.51	1.73	2.0	2.3	2.9	3.8	4.9	6.3	8.0	10.1	12.8
15	1.34	1.56	1.80	2.1	2.4	3.2	4.2	5.5	7.1	9.3	12.0	15.4
16	1.37	1.60	1.87	2.2	2.5	3.4	4.6	6.1	8.1	10.7	14.1	18.5
17	1.40	1.65	1.95	2.3	2.7	3.7	5.0	6.8	9.3	12.5	16.7	22.2
18	1.43	1.70	2.02	2.4	2.8	4.0	5.6	7.7	10.5	14.7	19.6	26.6
19	1.46	1.75	2.11	2.5	3.0	4.3	6.1	8.6	12.0	16.7	23.2	31.9
20	1.48	1.81	2.19	2.6	3.2	4.7	6.7	9.6	13.7	19.6	27.0	38.3
21	1.52	1.86	2.28	2.8	3.4	5.0	7.4	10.7	15.6			
22	1.55	1.91	2.37	2.9	3.6	5.4	8.1	11.9	17.8			
23	1.58	1.97	2.46	3.1	3.8	5.9	8.9	13.4	20.3			
24	1.61	2.03	2.56	3.2	4.0	6.3	9.8	15.0	23.1			
25	1.64	2.09	2.66	3.4	4.3	6.8	10.8	17.0	26.4			
26	1.67	2.16	2.77	3.6	4.5	7.4	11.9	19.2	30.1			
27	1.71	2.22	2.88	3.7	4.8	8.0	13.1	21.6	34.3			
28	1.74	2.29	3.00	3.9	5.1	8.6	14.4	24.2	39.1			
29	1.78	2.36	3.12	4.1	5.4	9.3	15.9	27.1	44.6			
30	1.81	2.43	3.24	4.3	5.7	10.1	17.4	30.1	50.8			

NOTE: The numbers at the end of the last columns are not supplied because they are not needed for financial planning. It would be unrealistic to expect such high returns over long periods of time.

Instructions for use of compound interest table A

1. To find the future value of a lump-sum investment after a specific number of years, multiply the amount of the investment by the factor derived as follows: find the line representing the number of years the money will be invested and read across it until you reach the column representing the rate of return you expect to receive on the investment. For example, if you put $1000 in a 5 percent savings account and allowed the interest to compound for ten years, the factor would be 1.6 and the total in the account would be $1600.

2. To find the inflated future cost of a goal after a specific number of years, multiply today's price by the factor derived as follows: find the line representing the number of years within which you want to achieve the goal and read across it until you reach the column representing the expected percentage rate of inflation. For example, if inflation is expected to rise at an average rate of 4 percent a year, a car that cost $3000 today would sell for $3660 ($3000 × 1.22) in five years.

3. To find the lump-sum amount you must invest today to achieve a goal within a specific number of years, divide the inflated future cost of the goal (the second use of table A) by the factor derived as follows: find the line representing the number of years within which you plan to achieve the goal and read across it until you reach the column representing the rate of return you expect to receive on your investment. For example, if you plan to invest in a mutual fund with an average annual growth (percentage rate of return) of 8 percent so that in five years you will have enough money to buy a car you have calculated will cost $3660, you would have to invest $2440 ($3660 ÷ 1.5).

4. To find the percentage rate of return you need to receive on an initial investment in order to reach a certain goal within a certain length of time, divide the goal amount by the investment amount and use the resulting factor as follows: find the line for the year when the total amount of money will be needed for the goal and read across it until you find the factor you derived, which will be in the column for the appropriate percentage rate of return. For example, if you will need $4400 in ten years and you have $2000 to invest initially, the factor is 2.2 (4400 ÷ 2000), and the rate of return you need is 8 percent.

5. To find the number of years required to achieve an investment goal by investing a lump sum at a certain rate of return, divide the goal amount by the investment amount and use the resulting factor as follows: find the column representing the highest rate of return you feel comfortable striving for and read down it until you find the factor you derived, which will be opposite the number of years required to reach the goal. For example, if you have $2000 to invest at 8 percent to reach an investment goal of $4400, the factor is 2.2 (4400 ÷ 2000), and ten years will be required to reach the goal.

COMPOUND INTEREST TABLE B

For Investments Made at the End of Each Year

Number of Years	Percentage Rate of Return										
	3%	4%	5%	6%	8%	10%	12%	14%	16%	18%	20%
1	1.0	1.0	1.0	1.0	1.0	1.0	1.0	1.0	1.0	1.0	1.0
2	2.0	2.0	2.0	2.1	2.1	2.1	2.1	2.1	2.2	2.2	2.2
3	3.1	3.1	3.2	3.2	3.2	3.3	3.4	3.4	3.5	3.6	3.6
4	4.2	4.2	4.3	4.4	4.5	4.6	4.8	4.9	5.1	5.2	5.4
5	5.3	5.4	5.5	5.6	5.9	6.1	6.4	6.6	6.9	7.2	7.4
6	6.5	6.6	6.8	7.0	7.3	7.7	8.1	8.5	9.0	9.4	9.9
7	7.7	7.9	8.1	8.4	8.9	9.5	10.1	10.7	11.4	12.1	12.9
8	8.9	9.2	9.5	9.9	10.6	11.4	12.3	13.2	14.2	15.3	16.5
9	10.2	10.6	11.0	11.5	12.5	13.6	14.8	16.1	17.5	19.1	20.8
10	11.5	12.0	12.6	13.2	14.5	15.9	17.5	19.3	21.3	23.5	26.0
11	12.8	13.5	14.2	15.0	16.6	18.5	20.6	23.0	25.7	28.8	32.2
12	14.2	15.0	15.9	16.9	19.0	21.4	24.1	27.3	30.8	34.9	39.6
13	15.6	16.6	17.7	18.9	21.5	24.5	28.0	32.1	36.8	42.2	48.5
14	17.1	18.3	19.6	21.0	24.2	28.0	32.4	37.6	43.7	50.8	59.2
15	18.6	20.0	21.6	23.3	27.2	31.8	37.3	43.8	51.6	61.0	72.0
16	20.2	21.8	23.6	25.7	30.3	35.9	42.7	50.9	60.8	73.0	87.4
17	21.8	23.7	25.8	28.2	33.8	40.5	48.9	59.1	71.6	87.1	105.9
18	23.4	25.6	28.1	30.9	37.4	45.6	55.7	68.3	84.0	103.8	128.1
19	25.1	27.7	30.5	33.8	41.4	51.2	63.4	78.9	98.5	123.5	154.7
20	26.9	29.8	33.1	36.8	45.8	57.3	72.0	90.9	115.2	146.7	186.7
21	28.7	32.0	35.7	40.0	50.4	64.0	81.7				
22	30.5	34.2	38.5	43.4	55.5	71.4	92.5				
23	32.4	36.6	41.4	47.0	60.9	79.5	104.6				
24	34.4	39.1	44.5	50.8	66.8	88.5	118.2				
25	36.4	41.6	47.7	54.9	73.1	98.3	133.3				
26	38.5	44.3	51.1	59.2	79.9	109.0	150.3				
27	40.7	47.1	54.7	63.7	87.4	121.0	169.4				
28	42.9	50.0	58.4	68.5	95.3	134.0	190.7				
29	45.2	53.0	62.3	73.6	104.0	149.0	214.6				
30	47.6	56.1	66.4	79.0	113.0	164.0	241.3				

NOTE: The numbers at the end of the last columns are not supplied because they are not needed for financial planning. It would be unrealistic to expect such high returns over long periods of time.

Instructions for use of compound interest table B

1. To find the future value of a regular annual investment, multiply the amount of the investment by the factor derived as follows: find the line representing the number of years over which the investment will be made and read across it until you reach the column representing the percentage rate of return you expect to receive. For example, if you invested $1000 each year for fifteen years in a mutual fund with an average annual growth (percentage rate of return) of 8 percent, at the end of that time you would have $27,200 ($1000 × 27.2).

2. To find the amount of the regular annual investment you must make to achieve a goal within a specified number of years, divide the inflated value of the goal (derived by using compound interest table A) by the factor derived as follows: find the line representing the number of years within which you plan to achieve the goal and read across it until you reach the column representing the percentage rate of return you can expect to receive on your investment. For example, if you want to make regular annual investments for a period of five years at a rate of 5 percent in order to buy a car that will cost $3660, the amount of your regular annual investment must be $665 ($3660 ÷ 5.5).

3. To find the percentage rate of return you need in order to achieve a goal by investing a certain amount annually for a certain number of years, divide the goal amount by the investment amount and use the resulting factor as follows: find the line for the total number of years of the investment and read across it until you reach the factor you derived, which will be in the column for the appropriate percentage rate of return. For example, if you invest $1000 annually in order to have $14,500 in ten years, the factor is 14.5 (14,500 ÷ 1000), and the percentage rate of return you need is 8 percent.

4. To find the number of years required to achieve a goal by investing a certain amount annually at a certain rate of return, divide the goal amount by the investment amount and use the resulting factor as follows: find the column representing the percentage rate of return you feel comfortable striving for and read down it until you come to the factor you derived, which will be opposite the number of years required to reach the goal. For example, if you invest $1000 a year at a rate of 8 percent in order to have $14,500, the factor is 14.5 (14,500 ÷ 1000), and ten years will be required to reach the goal.

GLOSSARY

acceleration clause   An oppressive clause often found in installment sales contracts whereby all or part of the outstanding balance of payments becomes immediately due if the borrower defaults on any of his payments.

account executive   See "registered representative."

accumulated cash value   The amount of money to which a policyholder is entitled if he discontinues his cash-value life insurance. It is made up of portions of life insurance premiums not used to buy protection but held by the insurance company as savings of the insured.

accumulation period   For an annuity, the period of time prior to the maturity date.

acts of God   Natural phenomena (such as lightning and floods) that are considered impossible to prevent or control and are usually insurable because they are impersonal in nature.

actuary   A mathematician who uses probability theory to calculate degrees of risk for use in insurance rate-making.

additional living expenses   The amount of money that an insurance company may pay a policyholder to cover what it costs to live elsewhere while his home is being restored or repaired after some calamity that it is insured against. All homeowner policies contain a provision for additional living expenses.

add-on clause   An oppressive clause often found in installment sales contracts whereby the creditor may repossess items already purchased from him and paid for, if the borrower defaults on payments for additional items.

adjusted gross estate   For federal estate tax purposes, the value of the deceased's estate after deductions have been taken from the amount of the gross estate for funeral expenses; expenses in collection of the estate's assets, payment of its debts, and its distribution to the beneficiaries; expenses incurred in administration of assets not subject to probate; payment of enforceable claims; expenses of uninsured losses occurring during administration of the estate; and probate fees.

adjusted gross income   For federal income tax purposes, the amount of an individual's annual income that results from subtracting business (type one) deductions from gross income.

administrator   A person appointed by a probate court to settle the affairs of an estate whose owner did not leave a valid will.

agent   Typically, one who sells and services insurance policies or who sells real estate. In insurance, an exclusive agent usually represents only one company; an independent agent may represent several. In real estate, an agent is usually a salesman who works for a fully licensed real estate broker. (See also "transfer agent," "health/life agent," and "property/casualty agent.")

all-risk coverage Insurance protection against all perils or hazards that might jeopardize what is being insured—with the exception of perils that are specifically excluded in the insurance contract.

American Stock Exchange (Amex or ASE) Second largest stock exchange in the world.

amortize To resolve a debt, usually through periodic payments of equal amounts.

ancillary charges Charges (although not specifically finance charges) that may arise in an installment sales contract.

annual exclusion The amount ($3000 per donee each year) not subject to federal gift taxation by the donor.

annual report Yearly publication by a business such as a corporation or a mutual fund depicting its current financial situation and outlining recent financial results and other relevant information about the company for the preceding year.

annuitant An individual who receives monthly annuity benefit payments.

annuity A guaranteed income for life, with payments received at regular intervals; a type of investment offered by insurance companies.

apportionment clause This clause states that the maximum extended coverage for any peril covered by a fire insurance policy is equal to the ratio of (1) that policy's fire coverage to the total fire coverage on the same property by both that policy and all other policies or (2) the non-fire coverage to the total non-fire coverage on the same property. This clause may be appended to dwelling, dwelling contents, and homeowners insurance policies.

appraisal An impartial determination of property value.

appraiser An expert in establishing current market value for property such as a house, jewelry, or antiques, depending on his specialty.

appreciation Increase in the dollar value of an asset over time.

asked price The price at which a broker is willing to sell a security to a customer.

assets In financial usage, all forms of property owned by a person or a business. (See also "fixed assets" and "monetary assets.")

asset value See "net asset value."

at the market A term used to describe orders to buy or sell securities at the best price currently available in the market.

audit Formal or official examination to verify accuracy of figures and statements in an account book or on a tax return.

authorized stock The total number of shares of stock that a company's articles of incorporation allow it to issue; any additional authorization requires approval of stockholders representing a majority of the stock outstanding.

automatic reinvestment plan An optional plan offered by most open-end mutual funds whereby an investor instructs the fund to reinvest in additional fund shares all cash dividends and capital gains distributions that otherwise would be sent to him by check.

avoidance Legal reduction (i.e., by using exclusions and deductions) of the amount of income tax that must be paid. (See "evasion.")

bailment lease Seldom used form of installment sales contract whereby title to purchased merchandise is retained by the creditor until the final payment has been made, at which time the buyer may purchase title from the creditor for a nominal fee.

balanced fund A mutual fund with a portfolio consisting of stocks and bonds and offering prospects for both capital growth and income; the proportion of money invested in stocks or bonds varies according to the condition of the market.

balance outstanding The amount of unpaid principal on a loan.

balance sheet A financial form that lists, as of a specific date, the financial assets and liabilities of a person, family, or business and shows the difference between the two (net worth); also known as a statement of financial condition.

balloon payment A final loan payment that is substantially larger than any previous payments.

bank bond See "certificate of deposit."

bankruptcy A state of insolvency. (State law usually allows a bankrupt person's creditors to have his estate, with the exception of property protected by homestead rights, administered for their benefit in settling his debts to the fullest extent possible.)

basic form A type of homeowners insurance policy (often called HO-1) that covers property against losses due to perils such as fire, windstorm, explosion, smoke, vandalism, and theft.

bear market A securities market characterized by generally declining prices over a period of several months.

bearer bond See "coupon bond."

beneficiary The recipient of the death benefits of a life insurance policy. (See also "primary beneficiary" and "contingent beneficiary.") Also, the person named in a will or trust agreement to receive rights to property or income from an estate or a trust.

benefits The amount of money to be paid to an insured or to his beneficiary by an insurer according to the terms of the insurance contract.

bequeath To give or leave property by means of a will.

bequest A gift of personal property made while alive. Also, property transferred through a will.

bid price The price at which a broker is willing to buy a security from a customer.

blanket coverage Insurance protection provided by a single policy that covers all types of property to the same degree.

blue chip stock Common stock of large, fairly stable companies that have demonstrated consistent earnings and, usually, have long-term growth potential.

board of directors A stockholder-elected committee responsible for ensuring that a company is managed according to the best interests of its stockholders.

book value The dollar value of a company's assets minus its liabilities. Book value per share is the company's book value divided by the number of its common stock shares outstanding.

bond An interest-bearing certificate of public or private indebtedness.

bonus account A passbook-type savings account paying .25 to 0.5 percent higher rate than a regular passbook account provided that a minimum required balance or a minimum holding period is maintained or that additional specified deposits are made regularly.

broad form A type of homeowners insurance policy (often called HO-2) that covers property against nearly all perils except landslide, flood, and earthquake.

broker One who acts as a selling and/or buying middleman for securities, insurance, or real estate. (See also "registered representative.")

bull market A securities market characterized by generally rising prices over a period of several months.

buy long To invest in securities with the hope of selling them at a higher price in the future.

buy on margin To buy securities with a partial payment and borrow the rest of the required cash from one's brokerage house.

calendar year The twelve-month period beginning January 1 and ending December 31.

call A purchased option to buy, within a certain period of time at a price that has been agreed upon, 100 shares of a specified stock from the person who wrote the call.

call feature A clause whereby a corporation reserves the right to buy back outstanding preferred stock or bonds, often at the issue price plus a specified premium.

cancellation   The termination of an insurance contract by either the insurer or the insured according to provisions set down within the contract.

capital   Cash or cash equivalents.

capital asset   For federal income tax purposes, any property other than that used in a trade or business; includes stocks, bonds, residences, personal automobiles, household furnishings, and jewelry.

capital gain   A gain derived from the sale or exchange of a capital asset.

capital gains distribution   A distribution to shareholders of all net capital gains realized by a mutual fund during its business year.

capital gains tax   The tax levied on capital gains made on sales or exchanges of capital assets held for more than six months.

capital improvements   For federal income tax purposes, improvements to a piece of real property that increase its value or materially prolong its useful life. (Expenses that are not capital improvements can be deducted in the year they are paid; deductions for capital improvements must be spread over the expected useful life of the improvement as directed by specific IRS regulations.)

capital loss   A loss incurred on the sale or exchange of a capital asset.

carrying costs   The part of the finance cost that is charged by most creditors to cover costs incurred by loaning money or extending credit—billing fees, administrative expenses, and bad debt losses.

cash flow   The cash surplus generated from an investment irrespective of the amount of taxable profit involved.

cash surrender value   See "accumulated cash value."

cash value   See "accumulated cash value."

cash-value life insurance   A type of life insurance policy, such as whole life or endowment, that offers a combination of decreasing term insurance and accumulation of cash savings.

casualty insurance   See "liability insurance."

ceiling rate   The maximum tax rate that may be levied on specified taxable transactions. Also, the maximum interest cost for certain types of consumer credit. Also, the maximum interest rate payable on some types of savings accounts.

certain and continuous annuity   An annuity payout option in which payments are guaranteed to the annuitant for life or to his beneficiary for the balance of a specified period of time—often five, ten, or twenty years—if the annuitant dies within that time.

certificate of deposit (CD)   In normal usage, a time deposit requiring a larger investment and yielding a higher return than a normal savings account. A small-scale CD is generally known as a bank bond, guaranteed income bond, or savings certificate.

certificate of title   A document giving an attorney's opinion as to the condition of the title of a piece of property and including a description of limiting restrictions placed on the title by past owners.

certified public accountant (CPA)   An accountant who has fulfilled local, state, and federal requirements and is therefore allowed to represent himself to the public as a certified accountant.

charitable trust   A trust whose beneficiary is a qualified charity.

chattel   An item of real or tangible property other than real estate.

chattel mortgage contract   A form of installment sales contract in which the title to purchased goods passes to the buyer and is then returned to the creditor to serve as collateral securing the sales contract.

claim   A policyholder's demand for benefits in accordance with his insurance contract or another person's contract.

class A stock   Common stock with income rights but not voting rights.

class B stock   Common stock with both income and voting rights.

closed-end fund   A mutual fund with a fixed number of shares to be bought and sold, like common stocks, over the counter or through organized exchanges.

closed-end plan   A plan offered by health expense associations whereby the insured is covered for treatment only at specific contracted hospitals. (See also "open-end plans.")

closing costs   The costs of transactions necessary to complete a real estate sale; these include credit reports, title search, and escrow duties.

club account   A special type of savings account developed by banks to enable customers to budget their savings for specific goals such as buying Christmas gifts.

codicil   A legal document used to revise parts of a will without rewriting the entire will.

coexecutor   One of two or more executors of a will.

cognovit note   A written promise to repay a debt, signed by the borrower, allowing a creditor to repossess purchased goods without going through legal channels if the borrower defaults on his payments.

coinsurance clause   For property insurance, a provision informing the insured that he must buy insurance coverage for at least 80 percent of the value of the property being insured in order to receive full payment of claims up to the face amount of the policy. For health insurance (usually major medical policies), a provision requiring the insured to share with his insurance company expenses arising from a claim.

collateral   Security provided by the borrower for a creditor's loan in the form of either pledged assets or endorsement by a cosigner; if the debtor defaults on his payments, the assets may be taken or, if there is a cosigner, he must complete the payments.

commercial bank   All institutions (except mutual savings banks) that are commonly referred to as banks.

commission   A fee paid to an agent or employee for transacting some business or performing a service, usually a percentage of the money involved in the transaction.

commodities futures   Contracts for future delivery of economic goods, such as agricultural and mining products, at a predetermined price; these contracts are traded on commodities exchanges.

common stock   Securities representing an ownership interest in a corporation.

community property   Property held jointly by husband and wife; according to community property laws in some states, property accumulated during marriage (except through inheritance or gift) belongs equally to each spouse.

compound interest   Interest earned on interest already paid on the invested principal when it is left to accumulate with the principal.

compound yield   The income realized on reinvested income from an investment.

comprehensive coverage   Physical damage coverage that protects an automobile against loss due to every possible peril except collision damage.

comprehensive form   A type of homeowners property insurance policy that is basically all-risk coverage.

conditional sales contract   A written document conveying to a lender title to purchased goods until the debt associated with them has been resolved by the borrower.

confession of judgment   An oppressive clause often found in installment sales contracts whereby the borrower waives in advance his right to representation by an attorney or to judicial processes if he defaults on his payments.

consumer price index (CPI)   An economic index prepared by the U.S. Department of Labor to indicate the relative change in the prices of a selected group of consumer goods.

contingent beneficiary   An individual or entity who receives death proceeds from a life insurance policy if the primary beneficiary dies prior to receiving the full amount of the proceeds.

contributions   For federal income tax purposes, monetary and non-monetary gifts made to qualified charities but not to private individuals.

convertibles   Various types of securities that can be exchanged for other forms of securities at a predetermined conversion ratio; convertible bonds and convertible preferred stock often may be converted into common stock.

conveyance   A written document by means of which title to real estate is transferred from one individual to another.

cosigner   An individual with a good credit rating who provides security for another person's loan through his endorsement. Also, an individual who signs a note jointly with one or more other borrowers.

coupon bond   A debt obligation on which the bond holder collects interest by regularly sending a coupon to the bond issuer who then makes the interest payment. (See "registered bond.")

coverage provisions   Clauses within an insurance contract stating the conditions under which the insurer will make benefit payments, how much they may be, and how long they will continue.

credit life insurance   A life insurance contract on a borrower in which the death benefit always equals the balance outstanding on his debt and which is used to resolve the debt if he dies.

creditor   One who extends credit.

credit rating   A measure used by credit bureaus to determine an individual's ability or willingness to pay his debts; based on the individual's history of resolving debts and his current financial position.

credit union   An organization composed of members with a common interest who bind together to offer loans to each other at rates lower than they might be able to obtain otherwise.

cumulative dividends   Unpaid back dividends that must be paid to holders of preferred stock before any dividends are paid to holders of common stock.

current assets   Cash, marketable securities, receivables, and inventories.

current liabilities   Accounts payable, unpaid taxes, and other debts due within one year.

custodial gift   A gift to a minor child from an adult who retains control over the gift, or grants such control to another adult, until the child reaches majority and can legally accept responsibility for the gift.

customer's broker   See "registered representative."

cyclical stock   A common stock whose fluctuations in price and earnings per share typically show a rough correlation with some other economic cycle—commonly the three-to-five-year cycle of business expansion and recession.

daily interest   Interest that is computed daily on the balance of a savings account.

death benefits See "benefits."

death tax Any tax paid because of a death-related occurrence; this tax is usually imposed by states. Examples are inheritance tax, legacy tax, and succession tax.

debenture A corporate bond or debt obligation on which the corporation promises that, if it fails to pay off its debt, the debenture holder has a right to all assets not pledged to mortgage or collateral trust bonds.

decedent A deceased person.

declarations Information given by the insured regarding characteristics such as age, sex, and marital status; these guide the insurance company in rate-making.

decreasing term insurance A type of life insurance whose face amount, or death proceeds payable, decreases each year the policy is in force. As a term policy it offers no cash-value build-up, simply protection if the insured dies. The face amount may decrease an equal amount each year (uniform decreasing term) or just a small amount during the first few years the policy is in force and an increasingly larger amount in the later years (mortgage term).

deductible clause A provision in a property, auto, or health insurance contract that directs the insured to pay the amount of any loss up to a certain limit above which the insurance company will pay the balance.

deductions Expenditures that, as expressly provided by tax law and/or IRS regulations, can be deducted from gross income, gross estate, adjusted gross income, or adjusted gross estate, when computing taxes.

deed A legal document used to transfer title (ownership interest) to property from one party to another.

deed of trust Security offered by a borrower to a lender in order to obtain a loan on real property. The deed is held by an independent third party (trustee) until the debt has been paid.

default Failure to fulfill the conditions of a contract (most commonly, by not making the scheduled payments on a debt).

defensive stock A common stock whose price and earnings per share typically remain relatively constant throughout economic recessions.

deferred income bond A type of bond on which interest income is not payable until several years in the future.

deferred profit sharing A program whereby a company sets aside a small fixed percentage of its profits in a trust fund and each employee is credited with a portion of the fund according to his wage or salary level and/or length of employment; often used as a supplement to, or a substitute for, a pension fund.

deflation A decline in the general level of prices.

degree of risk exposure A measure of the total potential monetary loss one might incur. (See also "risk.")

dependent For federal income tax purposes, an individual who is recognized as a dependent by law (as are most close relatives and adopted or foster children), derives more than 50 percent of his support from a taxpayer, and has a gross annual income lower than the level at which he would be required to file a return. A child under nineteen or a full-time student (no age limit) may also be considered dependent, no matter what his gross income, as long as the other two conditions are met.

deposit Money pledged to show the sincerity of one's intention to buy. Also, the money a person places in a savings account or checking account.

depreciation Decline in the dollar value of an asset over time and through use. For tax purposes, the dollar amount of annual depreciation may be computed differently from the actual decline in value.

devise To give real estate (not personal property) through a will.

devisee A recipient of real estate (not personal property) from a will.

disability, partial For disability insurance purposes, a condition brought about by an accident or illness that prevents a person from performing all of his usual job duties, although he may be able to do other types of work or perform a portion of his previous job.

disability, permanent For disability insurance purposes, a disabled condition that will last for the rest of one's life.

disability, temporary For disability insurance purposes, a disabled condition that a person can expect to recover from within a certain length of time.

disability, total For disability insurance purposes, a condition brought about by an accident or illness that prevents a person from working at any job either temporarily or permanently.

disability waiver of premium endorsement An endorsement stating that the insurance company will pay a policyholder's premiums if he becomes disabled and is unable to work.

disclosure statement A printed document, in standard form and type, citing the various terms and conditions of consumer credit contracts as required by truth in lending.

discounted interest A deduction from principal for finance charges at the time a loan is made. The remaining amount is repaid through installment payments.

discounted price The price of a security (usually bonds) that has a market price less than its face value and accrues interest until it reaches its face value.

dismemberment For insurance purposes, loss, or loss of use, of an arm or leg, part of an arm or leg, or one or both eyes.

distribution period For an annuity, the period of time following the maturity date during which the annuitant receives regular (usually monthly) payments.

dividend A share of profits distributed in cash to stockholders. (See also "stock dividend.") Also, a share of surplus revenues allocated to the holder of a participating insurance policy; in reality, this is a refund of premium. (See also "nonparticipating policy.")

dividend clause A provision in a participating insurance policy to indicate to the policyholder the various ways in which annual dividends (returns of capital) may be paid: in cash, in credit to reduce premiums, in payments for paid-up additions or term additions, or in deposits left with the insurance company.

dividend yield For stocks, the annual cash dividend divided by the current market price of a security and expressed as a percentage. For savings accounts that pay dividends rather than interest, the same as the effective rate of interest.

dollar cost averaging A method of buying stocks in installments by investing the same fixed dollar amount in the same long-term growth stock at regular intervals over a long period of time, making the average cost per share less than the average price paid per share.

domicile Legal place of residence.

donee Recipient of a gift.

Dow Jones averages Numerical indicators of the movements of prices of certain groups of securities (utilities, industrials, transportation, and composite) on the NYSE. These averages are computed by Dow Jones Company, a provider of statistical information services.

down payment The initial amount of the purchase price of an item bought on credit that the purchaser pays in cash.

double indemnity A clause in a life or accident insurance policy that pays the insured double the ordinary insurance benefit payments if accidental death or dismemberment occurs in some specified way.

earnings per share (EPS) The mathematical result of dividing the total after-tax earnings of a corporation by the total number of its shares outstanding.

effective interest cost See "effective rate."

effective rate The percentage figure representing the true cost of credit, based on the average outstanding amount of credit throughout the scheduled life of a credit contract. Also, the real or actual return one receives on an investment (on a savings account it may be higher than the nominal rate if the interest is compounded more frequently than annually).

effective yield See second definition of "effective rate."

election   An option whereby the taxpayer may choose among two or more alternatives in certain areas of tax treatment.

emergency cash reserve   See "emergency fund."

emergency fund   An amount of money placed in a liquid investment medium as a reserve to handle possible financial calamities; also called emergency cash reserve.

encumbrance   A liability or claim placed against property.

endorsement   A change in or an addition to an insurance or annuity contract, made in writing and attached to the policy itself. Also, the signature of a person (cosigner) with a good credit rating who agrees to complete payment on a secured loan if the borrower defaults on the loan.

endowment policy   A type of cash-value life insurance in which savings accumulate more rapidly than in other types of similar insurance.

equity   The amount of one's investment in an ownership position. In regard to real property, it is calculated as the market value minus claims against the property, such as a first mortgage balance.

escape clauses   Clauses inserted in contracts to enable either or both parties to declare the contract null and void if certain conditions are not met.

escrow   A deed, bond, money, or piece of property placed in the safekeeping of a third party until the first and second parties to a transaction have successfully completed it.

estate   One's ownership interest in all forms of property. Also, the financial resources and personal assets left upon death.

estate tax   A tax levied on the transfer of rights to property in an estate.

estimated tax   Amount of income tax (paid in quarterly installments) on current income not subject to withholding.

exchange   An organized market for trading securities. Also, the giving or taking of property for remuneration other than money and/or debt obligations.

excludable items   Income items that are not included in gross income for tax purposes.

exclusion   For insurance purposes, a condition under which insurance protection is not provided. Also, for federal income tax purposes, an income item that has no tax liability.

exclusive listing   Real estate offered for sale through only one realtor.

exculpatory clause   A clause included in a trust or will absolving trustees and executors of blame for mistakes (usually of omission) that have minor consequences.

ex-dividend   Without dividend. A buyer of a stock with this notation cannot receive the current dividend. However, he will receive the next declared dividend.

executor (executrix)   Individual appointed in a will and approved by a probate court to administer the disposition of an estate according to directions in the will.

exemption   For income tax purposes, the amount a taxpayer is allowed to deduct—for himself and for each of his dependents and for certain special circumstances such as the blindness of a spouse—the total of which is deducted from income to determine taxable income. Also, for federal estate tax purposes, the $60,000 subtracted from an estate before exemption to arrive at taxable estate. And, for federal gift tax purposes, the $30,000 (lifetime exemption) in gifts that may be exempted once by an individual.

expansion   A period of economic growth characterized by increases in employment, productivity, incomes, profits, and general prosperity.

extended coverage   A clause providing protection against additional perils; it is appended to normal fire insurance contracts. (See "apportionment clause.")

evasion   Unlawful failure to pay all or part of one's income taxes.

face amount   See "face value."

face value   For insurance, the dollar value that expresses coverage limits; it appears on the front of the policy. For a bond, the value at which it can be redeemed at maturity. (See also "par value.")

fair market price   The amount of money a buyer is willing to offer and a seller willing to accept (assuming both are fully informed and act voluntarily and intelligently).

Federal Deposit Insurance Corporation (FDIC)   A governmental agency insuring savings deposits of Federal Reserve member banks and of other banks that seek their protection.

Federal Housing Administration (FHA)   A division of the U.S. Department of Housing and Urban Development established by Congress to provide mortgage and home improvement loan insurance to private lenders. It insures loans but does not make them.

Federal Insurance Contribution Act (FICA)   An act that combined Social Security old age, survivors, disability, and hospital insurance taxes into a single tax.

Federal Reserve Bank   The official U.S. central banking organization.

Federal Reserve Board   The federal organization responsible for regulating credit and the money supply in the economy.

Federal Savings and Loan Insurance Corporation (FSLIC)   This organization offers the same deposit insurance programs for savings and loan associations as the FDIC does for banks.

Federal Trade Commission (FTC)   The federal regulatory agency charged with responsibility for policing unfair trade practices.

Federal Unemployment Tax Act (FUTA)   This act created the Social Security unemployment insurance tax.

fiduciary responsibility   Responsibility entrusted to a third party by a first party to be carried out according to the wishes of the first, for the benefit of the second; trust responsibility.

finance charge   The fee, consisting of both interest and charges for carrying costs, that is paid by a borrower for the privilege of using credit.

financial responsibility laws   State laws requiring that the operator or owner of a motor vehicle give evidence of his ability to pay, by means of either insurance or his own financial assets, claims made against him arising from the operation of that vehicle. Requirements of these laws differ from state to state but normally apply only to drivers who have had a previous accident requiring them to pay damage or injury claims in excess of certain minimums.

first-in, first-out (FIFO)   A technique used by savings institutions to compute the interest they owe on the balance in a savings account. (The first money deposited is considered to be the first money withdrawn.)

first mortgage   The senior security (in the form of real property) offered by a borrower to a lender to obtain a loan on a piece of property.

fixed amount option   An annuity payout option in which the monthly benefit level is selected by the annuitant; payments are made by the insurance company to the annuitant or his beneficiary until the principal and accrued interest are exhausted.

fixed annuity   Guaranteed income, received at regular intervals, for which the basic amount of each payment has been fixed in advance; there may be minor variations due to interest rate changes.

fixed assets   Property not easily convertible into cash—i.e., furniture, clothes, cars, and real estate. (See also "monetary assets.")

fixed expenses   Expenses, such as monthly rent or mortgage payments, that must be paid at regular intervals and in fairly set amounts.

fixed income investment   A type of investment in which the dividend, interest, or rental income is contractually fixed, either until maturity or in perpetuity.

fixed period option   An annuity payout option in which the annuitant selects the period of time for which he wishes to receive benefits; the insurance company computes the monthly benefit amount by calculating the interest expected to accrue over the life of the declining principal balance; also known as the "installment refund option."

floater An insurance policy covering property not only while it is in one's home but also wherever it may be transported.

foreclosure The legal process by which a lender, in case of a mortgage payment default by the owner of mortgaged property, can force the sale of that property in order to recover the money he lent on it.

Form 1040 Standard federal income tax return form used by individuals to file separate or joint returns.

front-end load Commission and other costs deducted from the amount placed in an investment such as mutual funds, real estate syndicates, or oil and gas drilling funds.

general partner Member of a general partnership. Each member is fully responsible for all partnership debts.

gift tax Tax levied by federal, state, and foreign governments on the transfer of financial assets as gifts.

glamour stock Securities that are relatively high priced because of their attractive growth potential, but not necessarily because of their past growth record.

grace period The length of time an insurance policy remains in force past its expiration date before a premium must be paid.

grantee One who receives something.

grantor One who gives something. See also "trustor."

gross estate An individual's net worth plus existing life insurance proceeds and any portion of an annuity that a beneficiary may receive. For federal estate tax purposes, the amount from which type one deductions are taken to find the amount of one's adjusted gross estate.

gross estate tax For federal estate tax purposes, the tax computed on the amount of one's taxable estate before the amount allowed for any credits (state death taxes paid or to be paid, certain gift taxes, certain estate taxes paid on an earlier estate, and foreign death taxes) is subtracted to find the amount of the net estate tax.

gross income All income in the form of money, property, and services that is not, by law, expressly exempt from tax.

Gross National Product (GNP) The total production of the nation in terms of goods and services for an expressed period of time, usually one year, as measured by their current market prices.

group insurance Insurance (either health, life, auto, liability, or property) written for a specific group of people. A master policy is issued by the insurance company covering the whole group; members of the group are issued joinder agreements that tie them to the master policy. Reduced administration costs and savings due to favorable loss experience for the group as a whole generally make these policies less expensive than individually written policies.

growth stock The stock of a small to medium-sized company that has experienced several years of above-average growth in earnings and appears likely to continue such growth.

guarantee A signed promise obtained by a prospective borrower from someone whose credit worthiness is stronger than his to make good a debt obligation if he defaults on it.

guaranteed cash value See "accumulated cash value."

guaranteed income bond See "certificate of deposit."

guaranteed renewable provision A clause (found primarily in annual renewable term life insurance contracts and health insurance contracts) that prohibits the insurance company from refusing to renew coverage for the next coverage period until the insured reaches a certain specified age.

guardian An individual appointed in a will or by court order to care for minor children or for an incompetent adult.

head-of-household An individual, not necessarily married, who provides more than 50 percent of the support for at least one qualified dependent.

health expense association A nonprofit organization that dispenses medical treatment and charges members a monthly, quarterly, or annual fee.

health/life agent An insurance representative who sells health and life insurance policies.

hedge To protect oneself against a potential investment loss by making a counterbalancing transaction.

hedge fund A mutual fund that invests in speculative stocks and uses many sophisticated trading techniques in an attempt to achieve an above-average return on investment in both bull and bear markets.

heir One who inherits or is entitled to inherit property.

holographic will A will written entirely in the handwriting of the individual making it.

homestead laws Legislative acts passed in most states generally to (1) permit a family head to declare that his house and land are his family's homestead and therefore exempt from the claims of creditors and lawsuits and (2) protect the home for the benefit of his spouse and minor children upon his death.

homestead rights Rights granted to citizens under homestead laws.

incidents of ownership See "rights of ownership."

includable items For federal income tax purposes, items considered as part of gross income.

income averaging   A means whereby taxpayers who experience radical fluctuations in their incomes from year to year are allowed to spread their income evenly over a period of five years and avoid having to pay exceptionally high taxes in high income years.

income before exemptions   For federal income tax purposes, the amount of income remaining after all deductions have been taken.

income splitting   A technique used to shift income from an individual in a higher tax bracket to someone in a lower one in order to take advantage of lower tax rates.

income statement   A financial form that serves as a record of all income and expense transactions occurring over a specific period of time, usually one year.

income stock   A common stock whose high dividend yield and historical consistency in meeting its cash dividend payments make it attractive for investors seeking a high rate of steady income from their investment.

indemnity   Security against loss; insurance policies are contracts of indemnity because they ensure that a policyholder will not suffer a financial loss.

index   In economics, a numerical figure that describes relative changes in some quantity. Examples are the consumer price index and the New York Stock Exchange Index.

inflation   A rise in the general level of prices.

inflation guard policy   A property insurance policy that automatically raises the coverage limits each year by 3 to 4 percent supposedly to allow for rising costs.

inheritance tax   A tax based on the value of property received by an heir; it can be paid either out of the estate or by the heir.

installment debt   A debt resolved in two or more payments made at regular intervals over a period of time.

insurable risk   A potential financial calamity that insurance companies deem profitable to insure; normally, such a risk will not be associated with a possible widespread disaster such as an earthquake, and the amount of the potential loss must be easily measurable.

insuring clause   A provision in an insurance contract designating the benefit to be paid and the perils insured against.

interest   A charge made for allowing someone else to use one's money, usually a percentage of the amount being used. Specifically, for a borrower, the cost of borrowing money; for an investor, the payment received from a bank or similar institution for lending money to it.

intestacy   Absence of a valid will.

Internal Revenue Service (IRS)   Official U.S. government agency that directs the collection of federal taxes.

investment company   A mutual fund. Also, a real estate investment management company.

investment profit   The amount of money an insurance company or other financial institution may earn from the investment of their cash reserves in excess of their investment expenses.

issued stock   Capital stock issued in exchange for money, claims to money, or other considerations.

jacket provisions   The clauses within an insurance contract that state what the insured must do to qualify for insurance benefits.

joint-and-survivorship annuity   An annuity payout option that specifies a certain payout level for two joint annuitants while alive and, usually, a lower payout level for the surviving annuitant after the death of the other.

joint owners   Two or more individuals possessing ownership interests in the same property. (See also "joint tenants," "tenants by the entirety," and "tenants in common.")

joint return   A method of reporting federal income tax whereby a husband and wife file on the same form.

joint tenants   Two or more persons each of whom owns a percentage, but not a specific piece, of some form of property; each may dispose of his share without the permission of the other(s).

joint venture   A business agreement between two or more individuals or corporations to set up and operate a jointly owned business enterprise.

Keogh Act   The federal Self-Employed Individuals Tax Retirement Act of 1963. It enables self-employed persons to make tax-deferred retirement investments.

last in, first out (LIFO)   One of the techniques used by banks for computing the interest they owe on the balance in a savings account. (The last money deposited is considered to be the first money withdrawn.)

legacy   A gift of personal (not real) property made in a will.

leasehold clause   A clause covering a renter for damages to any leasehold improvements he may have made. For example, if you have just repainted, at your own expense, an apartment that you rent, you can be reimbursed for that expense if fire or a similar peril destroys your apartment.

legatee   A recipient of a gift of personal (not real) property made in a will.

letter of last instructions   The means by which an individual can give his survivors important information after his death (i.e., the circumstances he has arranged for his burial and the whereabouts of his will and personal records). It is not a substitute for a will.

letters testamentary Probate court's certification of the legality of a will and approval of the qualifications of the executor(s).

level term insurance A form of life insurance that has no cash value; the face amount remains level over the entire policy period.

leverage The use of borrowed money to get a higher rate of return provided that the interest rate on the loan is lower than the rate of return on the investment.

liability The extent to which one may be subject to punishment under the law for interference with another person's rights as recognized in the Bill of Rights. Also, an obligation to pay one's current debts—i.e., bills, loans, balances due on charge accounts, or mortgages on a home.

liability insurance A form of coverage that protects a policyholder against claims derived from any sort of negligence on his part.

lien A legal claim to property in the event of payment default.

limited partnership A partnership in which members are liable for partnership debts only to the extent of their contributed capital. (See "general partnership.")

limited payment life insurance A form of cash-value life insurance that spreads the cost of the policy over a fixed number of years rather than over the entire life of the policy; such a policy is used to restrict premium payments to the policyholder's earning years.

limit order An order for a broker to buy a stock at the best possible price, provided that it does not exceed a certain amount.

liquid assets See "monetary assets."

liquidation The procedure by which a business (often bankrupt) sells its assets, uses the money from the sale to pay off its debts, and distributes what is left to the stockholders.

liquidity The ease with which an investment can be converted to cash.

load See "loading charge."

load fund A mutual fund in which part of the purchase price of a share represents a sales commission.

loading charge Sales commission plus certain distribution fees imposed on shares in certain mutual funds. Also known as load.

loan clause A provision (found only in cash-value life insurance policies) that explains how the policyholder can borrow up to the total accumulated cash values from his policy.

long term For federal income tax purposes, more than six months between buy and sell transactions. As an investment phrase, a period of six months or longer.

low balance method A method of computing quarterly interest on a savings account; it applies the percentage rate against the lowest balance in the account for the quarter.

low income allowance A dollar amount ($1300) that may be used as the standard deduction by federal income taxpayers with incomes of less than $10,000.

margin account A stock brokerage account that allows an investor to buy on margin (borrow investment funds from his broker) at the investor's discretion; subject to margin deposit requirements set by the Federal Reserve Board.

marginal tax bracket The tax bracket into which the highest portion of one's taxable income falls.

margin deposit requirements Minimum down payment levels, expressed in percentages, for the purchase of stocks and bonds; they are set down by the Federal Reserve Board and changed periodically depending on FRB policy.

margin loan A loan from a stock brokerage house, with purchased securities held as collateral.

marital deduction For federal estate and gift taxation purposes, this deduction allows one to transfer, free of taxation, to his spouse 50 percent of his adjusted gross estate.

marketable securities Securities that have been cleared by the SEC and/or the appropriate state authority for sale on public securities markets.

market maker In the over-the-counter markets, a brokerage house that carries an inventory of a certain stock and stands ready to buy or sell that stock at its specified prices.

market value The dollar value one could realize on property if he were to sell it.

maturity The period of time for which credit, an insurance contract, or a mortgage loan is written. Also, the minimum amount of time one must hold an investment in order to realize the rate of return anticipated when the investment was made.

money market Colloquial term for the large pools of lendable funds that exist in the economy.

monetary assets All property, owned by a person or a business, that can easily be converted into cash at a readily determinable fair market price—e.g., savings accounts, stocks and bonds, cash-value life insurance; also called liquid assets. (See also "fixed assets.")

Monthly Investment Plan (MIP) A means of purchasing NYSE shares through regular monthly or quarterly investments of $40 or more.

mortality table　A set of statistics indicating how many people per thousand die at various ages. It can be used to determine one's life expectancy at any age.

mortgage　The security offered by a borrower to a lender in order to obtain a loan on real property. (See also "first mortgage" and "second mortgage.")

mortgage bond　A debt obligation, issued by a corporation, that has specific real estate assets pledged as collateral.

mortgage clause　A provision in a property insurance contract that defines the obligations and powers of the mortgagor if there is a mortgage outstanding on the insured properties.

mortgage term policy　See "decreasing term insurance."

multiple line insurance　A policy covering more than one type of insurance need (e.g., liability and property insurance) together in one policy.

multiple listing　Real estate offered for sale through more than one realtor.

municipal bond　A debt obligation issued by a state or local governmental agency. Such bonds are exempt from federal income taxes.

mutual fund　An investment company that uses the proceeds from the public sale of its shares in order to invest in various securities for the benefit of its public shareholders. Also, the popular name for an open-end investment company.

mutual insurance company　An insurance company owned by its policyholders. (See "stock insurance company.")

mutual savings bank　An association of savings account holders formed for the purpose of paying out all operating profits to account holders in the form of dividends rather than interest.

negligence　For liability insurance purposes, any careless act on the part of the insured for which he may be subject to punishment under the law. For federal income tax purposes, intentional disregard of tax regulations without intent to defraud.

negotiable investment　An investment that can be sold.

net asset value　The total value of an investment company's liabilities subtracted from the total of its cash plus the market value of its securities. Also, the listed bid price of a load fund.

net asset value per share　Net asset value of an investment company divided by the number of its shares outstanding.

net estate tax　The amount resulting from subtracting certain allowable credits (state death taxes paid or to be paid, certain gift taxes, certain gift taxes paid on an earlier estate, and foreign death taxes) from the gross estate tax.

net income Revenues minus expenses, taxes, interest paid, and depreciation.

net income per share See "earnings per share."

net worth The difference between assets and liabilities for a person, family, or business. If the dollar value of assets is greater than that of liabilities, there is a positive net worth. In a business, net worth may also be known as "partnership share" or "owner's equity."

New York Stock Exchange (NYSE) The largest stock exchange in the world.

no-load fund A mutual fund that charges no sales commission on the purchase of its shares because the fund itself buys and sells its shares to the public without salesmen.

nominal rate Rate of interest stated for an investment. See "effective rate."

nonforfeiture option An option that gives a life insurance policyholder who has allowed his policy to lapse the right to take the cash value of his policy in either cash, extended term insurance, or reduced paid-up life insurance.

nonparticipating policy An insurance contract that pays no dividends.

non-waiver agreement A provision in an insurance policy stating that the insurance company can investigate a claim without invalidating the terms of the contract.

no-par stock A stock issued with no assigned face value.

note A signed promise to resolve a debt.

nuncupative will A will made orally.

occupational disease A disease caused by the nature of one's job.

odd lot A block of shares smaller in number than a round lot, which is the amount (a multiple of 100) usually traded at one time.

open-ended credit Charge accounts and credit cards.

open-end fund A mutual fund that continually sells and redeems its shares according to investor demand and has no limits on the total number of shares to be bought or sold.

open-end plan A plan offered by health expense associations whereby the insured may receive treatment at any hospital. (See also "closed-end plan.")

oppressive clauses Conditions set forth in a sales contract that can give a lender an unfair advantage over the borrower in default circumstances.

ordinary life See "straight life."

other insurance clause A clause stating that when more than one insurance company covers the same loss, each pays a share of the expense in proportion to its share of the total insurance coverage for the loss. Also called "pro rata clause" in some types of policies and is one of prorating clauses in disability income policies.

outstanding balance See "balance outstanding."

overinsurance Insurance in an amount that exceeds the amount of potential loss.

over-the-counter (OTC) A means of trading shares of a company not listed on an organized stock exchange.

package policy An insurance contract (normally property) that combines several types of coverage. A homeowners policy, for example, combines property coverage with liability and medical coverage.

paid-up addition An amount of prepaid cash-value life insurance coverage that can be purchased with one policy dividend.

paid-up insurance Life insurance on which no further premium payments are due.

paper profit Profit yet to be realized on held securities because no buying or selling transaction has taken place.

par value The face value assigned and printed on a security certificate. It originally signified the price level below which a company would not offer its shares to the public. Also, the value of a bond at maturity.

participating policy An insurance policy that returns a portion of the premium, in the form of dividends, to the policyholder at the end of the policy period.

partnership A legal relationship between two or more individuals acting together as owners of an enterprise. (See also "limited partnership" and "general partnership.")

passbook account The standard savings account offered by a bank or savings and loan association; it usually offers the lowest interest rates of the various types of available accounts.

pension fund The amount of financial resources set aside to provide income benefits at a future date, usually upon retirement.

percentage standard deduction The amount specified as a fixed percentage of adjusted gross income, up to a specified dollar maximum, that may be deducted from adjusted gross income if business (type two) deductions are not itemized.

personal loss experience A record of the total amount of money an individual has had to pay because of damage or loss due to perils that have occurred.

P/E ratio   The ratio (expressed as a multiple) of the price of a share of stock to the company's earnings per share.

point   In regard to a mortgage loan, an extra service charge initially deducted from it in addition to the regular interest cost; one point is equal to a front-end service charge of 1 percent of the loan amount. In regard to stocks and other securities, a unit used in quoting their price changes. For insurance companies' safe driver plans, values allocated to certain types of auto traffic violations; the number of points a motorist accumulates over a specified period of years is one factor used to determine his premium rate.

portfolio   The investments held by an individual or by an organization such as a mutual fund.

power of attorney   Written authorization from a person enabling someone else to perform binding legal acts on his behalf.

power of appointment   A legal means whereby a surviving beneficiary is given the power to determine how the income and proceeds of a trust shall be distributed upon his death.

precomputation   Procedure by which a borrower receives the principal amount in full and pays back an amount equal to the principal plus finance charges.

preferred risk   An individual whose loss experience is good; a situation that has a low degree of risk exposure.

preferred stock   A stock featuring a fixed dollar income and, if the company has any earnings, a claim to earnings and assets before the claim of common stock, but after that of bonds.

premises   A specific location (i.e., land and the buildings thereon) identified in an insurance contract.

premium   Money paid for insurance protection or to buy an annuity.

premium payment clause   A provision in all insurance contracts stating that premiums may be paid annually, semiannually, quarterly, or monthly.

prepaid interest   Interest paid in advance of the due date. Up to two years' mortgage interest may be deducted from taxable income in the year of purchase, provided that such interest is actually paid then.

prepayment penalty   A fee levied by a lender on loans paid off before maturity to reimburse himself for interest lost.

price earnings ratio   See "P/E ratio."

primary beneficiary   An individual or entity entitled to receive the benefits of an insurance policy or annuity upon the death of the insured. (See also "contingent beneficiary.")

primary offering   The sale of previously unissued stock by the issuing company, through investment bankers and brokerage houses, to the investor.

primary market   The means whereby new common stock is offered for sale to the public and the net proceeds go to the issuing corporation.

prime rate   The lowest loan interest rate charged by all banks at any given time. It is usually available to special customers.

principal   The total amount originally invested, including equity and borrowed portions. Also, a major owner of a business enterprise. Also, the face amount of a mortgage loan.

probate process   The judicial procedure for establishing the validity of a will and ensuring that it is fully and properly executed.

progressive tax rates   The system whereby an increasing tax rate is levied on each successive bracket or amount of taxable income. (See also "regressive tax.")

promissory note   A written promise to resolve a debt obligation.

proof of loss   A written statement of a loss submitted as a claim to an insurer.

property/casualty agent   An insurance representative who sells property and casualty insurance policies.

pro rata clause   See "other insurance clauses."

prospectus   A publication issued by a company to describe the securities to be offered for public sale and under what conditions they will be offered, as well as the prospects for company performance.

protection period   The length of time over which insurance benefits may be given.

proxy   The means by which a stockholder authorizes others to exercise his voting rights in his absence, according to his direction.

purchase agreement   A written document between a buyer and seller giving the terms of a sale transaction. It consists of a sales contract, note, and credit life and/or disability insurance policy.

put   A purchased option to sell to the person who wrote the put 100 shares of a specified stock within a certain period of time at the price specified in the contract.

rate-making   Establishing prices of insurance contracts.

rate of return   Measurement of the profitability of invested resources; it is usually expressed as a percentage rate of gain or loss per year on the amount invested; also known as "return on investment" or as the "yield."

real estate investment trust (REIT)   An unincorporated association that invests in real property or mortgages and sells its shares to the general public.

real property   Land and anything permanently fixed thereon.

recession   A period of reduced economic activity during which unemployment rises, productive capacity becomes increasingly idle, and income profitability and general prosperity lag.

reciprocal   An organization offering insurance protection to its members, who pay a proportionate share of any loss that befalls them. Instead of charging premiums based on expected loss, as is typical of insurance companies, reciprocals prorate the actual loss over their members.

refinance a mortgage   To take out a new mortgage on a mortgaged piece of property, often at a lower rate of interest than on the old mortgage, and use the proceeds to pay off the old mortgage.

refund annuity   An annuity payout option that returns to a beneficiary the principal balance remaining at the death of an annuitant.

registered bond   The most commonly issued bond, in which the company automatically mails interest payments to the bond's current owner. (See also "coupon bond.")

regressive tax   A tax that is the same rate regardless of one's level of taxable income. (See also "progressive tax rates.")

remaindermen   Individuals who are to receive the assets of a trust upon its termination.

renewable term insurance   A life insurance policy that has no cash value and may be renewed by the policyholder at the end of the policy period for another policy period of the same duration; a five-year renewable term policy, for example, would have to be renewed every five years.

rent   Payment one receives for allowing someone else to use his property.

replacement cost   See "replacement value."

replacement value   The amount of money that would have to be paid today to replace an object with a new one; this value is acceptable to property insurers only when used to determine the amount of insurance needed for physical structures such as the home. Also called replacement cost.

repossession   Procedure by which a creditor takes back purchased goods when the buyer defaults on his payments.

retained earnings   Corporate profits that are not paid out in cash dividends, but are reinvested in the company to foster its growth.

retirement income credit   A beneficial federal tax treatment of certain forms of retirement income such as annuities, pensions, interest, rent, and dividends.

return on investment See "rate of return."

rider An attachment to an insurance policy amending or extending the policy's coverage.

rights In regard to a piece of property, the ownership interest one has in it (e.g., mineral rights). In regard to securities, negotiable certificates evidencing the privilege given to stockholders to subscribe to a new issue at a predetermined cost that is generally below market price.

rights of ownership Benefits available to the owner of an asset; also called incidents of ownership.

risk The possibility of loss now or in the future. With regard to insurable risk, it is the chance of financial loss from perils named in the insurance contract. With regard to investment risk, it is the chance for financial loss due to uncertainty about the future. With regard to general economic risk, it is the chance of financial loss due to recessions, unemployment, inflation, and so on.

round lot A block of shares, usually in multiples of 100, for trading on the exchanges.

royalties Income, typically on a per unit basis, from the sale of certain rights—usually publishing rights to a book.

sales charge See "commission."

sales contract The portion of a purchase agreement designed to protect a creditor against defaults on payments. (See also "conditional sales contract," "chattel mortgage contract," and "bailment lease.")

sales tax A general tax levied (usually by state or local governments) on sales transactions.

savings accumulation plan A means of investing in a mutual fund at regularly scheduled intervals. In a contractual plan with penalty, all commission costs are levied during the initial payment periods. In a voluntary payment plan or a contractual plan without penalty, commission costs, if any, are levied only on the amount of each payment over the entire life of the investment program.

savings bond A savings certificate offered by the U.S. government; it is sold at a certain percent of its face value and interest accumulates with it for a specified period of time until it can be cashed in for face value. It may also be offered by commercial banks.

savings certificate See "certificate of deposit."

schedule A statement of supplementary details appended to Form 1040. Also, a written or printed list, catalog, or inventory, such as that which may be used in an insurance policy.

scheduled floater A type of inland marine property insurance coverage that protects such specific, highly valued items as are described on the face of the policy.

scheduled property Personal property that is described and given an appropriate value, article by article, on the face of an insurance policy rather than lumped together under general property coverage.

secondary distribution Marketing of large blocks of already issued shares of stock in the same manner as new issues are handled; also called secondary offering.

second deed of trust Similar to a second mortgage except that foreclosure proceedings in the event of a borrower's default are easier to initiate and take less time.

second mortgage A loan specifically secured by one's equity in real property, which is subordinated to the equity interests of any first mortgage holder.

secured loan A loan on which title to property is conveyed to the lender as security in the event of default.

Securities Exchange Commission (SEC) An agency charged with the responsibility of regulating the securities markets and all publicly held investment companies.

securities market A mechanism for the buying and selling of securities between investors; examples are the over-the-counter markets, New York Stock Exchange, and American Stock Exchange.

security Property given, deposited, or pledged in a credit agreement to make certain the repayment of a debt. Also, an evidence of debt or of property (as a bond or stock certificate).

self-employment tax A form of Social Security tax that is levied on self-employed individuals.

self-insurance A personal emergency fund used to cover one's own losses instead of buying insurance.

selling costs The expenses of selling an asset, such as a house; in the determination of capital gains, these may be added to the cost basis of the asset.

separate return A method of reporting income of one spouse separately from that of the other spouse.

settlement options The ways that a life insurance or annuity policyholder or beneficiary may choose to have policy proceeds paid.

short sale A trading technique in which an investor borrows shares of a security from a broker in the hope of selling them on the market when the price of the stock is high, buying them back when the price has dropped, and returning them to the broker after having made a profit.

short term For federal income tax purposes, a period of six months or less between buy and sell transactions.

simple interest Interest that is calculated only on the original amount of a loan outstanding, not on the average amount outstanding over the term of the loan.

single-limit liability An auto insurance policy that combines bodily injury liability and property damage liability and pays up to the maximum limit on a per occurrence basis; it does away with the per person limit on bodily injury coverage, thereby expanding the protection offered.

special form A type of homeowners insurance policy that covers basically all risks to a house but not to personal property.

specialist One who works on the floor of a stock exchange to coordinate buy and sell transactions in a particular stock.

special warranty deed A deed guaranteeing that the grantor has not placed any encumbrances on the title.

speculate To make an investment despite great uncertainty in the hope of achieving a substantial return.

standard deduction For federal income tax purposes, the amount that may be deducted from one's adjusted gross income in lieu of itemizing type two deductions. See "low income allowance" and "percentage standard deduction."

statement of financial condition See "balance sheet."

stock Ownership interest (divided into shares) in the assets, earnings, and direction of a corporation.

stock dividend The issue by a corporation of new stock certificates to current stockholders on a basis proportional to the number of shares each investor owns. These do not represent a distribution of earnings.

stockholder One who owns part of a corporation as represented by the shares he holds.

stock insurance company An insurance company owned by stockholders. (See "mutual insurance company.")

stock outstanding Shares of a company's stock that are held by the public; does not include any issued stock held in the company treasury. (See "treasury stock.")

stock price tables Tables in the *Wall Street Journal* and other newspapers that give daily prices and other information on common stocks.

stock right See the second definition of "rights."

stock split The division of outstanding shares of stock into a greater number of shares; essentially the same to the investor as a stock dividend except on a larger scale.

stop order An order to one's broker to sell a stock at the market when it reaches or goes below a certain price. Also called a stop-loss order.

straddle A trading technique whereby a speculator buys both a put and a call on the same stock in order to be able to take advantage of any change in the price of that stock on the market.

straight life A cash-value life insurance policy for which one pays premiums either for life or until the policy is surrendered; also called ordinary life or whole life.

straight life annuity An annuity payout option offering the highest monthly payout level. Upon the death of an annuitant, however, any remaining principal balance is claimed by the insurance company; there are no benefits to a beneficiary.

subordinated debenture A corporate bond that has relatively low security in that holders of such bonds can claim assets only after other creditors and bonds and bank debts have been paid.

surcharge See "surtax."

surtax A tax in addition to the normal income tax; it can be either graduated rates for brackets of taxable income or a flat rate; also called surcharge.

syndicate A combination of individuals or organizations to accomplish an investment goal of mutual interest.

systematic withdrawal plan A mutual fund payout option whereby an investor may draw regular cash payments from his investment by authorizing the fund to send a check for a specified amount at regular intervals until he authorizes a change or the money runs out.

taxable estate For federal estate tax purposes, the amount on which gross estate tax is levied; it consists of the gross estate less the total of type one deductions, the marital deduction, type two deductions, and the $60,000 exemption.

taxable income For federal income tax purposes, the amount of income, less exemptions, on which income tax is determined.

tax bracket For federal income tax purposes, a segment of taxable income that is subject to a certain percentage of taxation (tax rate).

tax court A court system created by the Constitution to rule on tax disputes.

tax credit For federal income or estate tax purposes, an amount that may be subtracted directly from one's tax because of a previous tax overpayment or a payment for another type of tax.

tax deferred investment An investment on which the payment of income tax owed is postponed.

tax exempt Not subject to federal and/or state income tax.

Taxpayer Identification number   For an individual, the same as his Social Security number. For corporations, trusts, or partnerships, this is a specially issued number.

Tax Rate Schedules   Tables listing federal income tax rates for individuals who (1) have incomes of more than $10,000 or (2) have incomes of $10,000 or less and itemize their deductions.

tax shelter   An investment that offers certain income tax advantages.

tax tables   Rate tables used by individuals to compute their federal income tax if they have incomes of $10,000 or less and take the standard deduction.

tax write-off   An investment loss that can be offset against one's gross income when determining adjusted gross income.

telequote machine   An instrument that provides current market prices and other data for listed securities. It is usually available for investor use in broker offices.

tenants by the entirety   Joint owners of an asset who are husband and wife.

tenants in common   Two or more owners of an asset for which transactions are not legal unless all the owners give their signed permission.

term   The period of time for which an insurance policy is to be in effect.

term insurance   A type of life insurance that offers death benefit protection, but no investment cash value, for the duration of the contract.

testator (testatrix)   A person who leaves a will in force at his (her) death.

third-party insurance   Insurance that pays benefits to someone other than the insured (i.e., liability insurance).

thrift institution   Usually, a savings institution specializing in small personal loans. Savings accounts are not insured by a federal agency.

ticker tape   A continuous and instantaneous teletype printout indicating the price and volume of all transactions that occur on an organized exchange during trading hours.

tight money   Colloquial term used by the financial community to describe the scarcity of loanable funds. This scarcity contributes to high borrowing costs.

time deposit   An investment on which interest is earned according to the length of the investment. The principal is always fixed.

title   Ownership interest in property.

title clearance   Notification that title to a particular asset is free of encumbrances that would block its sale or use.

title insurance   Coverage against loss of one's equity investment in real property if a flaw in the property's title is found.

title search Inquiry into the nature of title to a piece of property and the status of any encumbrances on the title.

trader An investor who takes advantage of short-term (usually daily or weekly) fluctuations in the prices of stocks.

transfer agent An institution, typically a bank, authorized by a corporation to administer and record the transfer of its stocks or bonds between investors.

transfer tax A tax levied by some states and the federal government on the transfer of securities.

Treasury bill See "Treasury bond."

Treasury bond A negotiable debt obligation issued by the federal government with a minimum face amount of $1000 and a maturity greater than five years. Treasury bills and Treasury notes are similar except that they have shorter maturities.

Treasury note See "Treasury bond."

treasury stock Corporate stock that was originally issued to the public and has since been reacquired by the corporation to be either cancelled or reissued at a later date.

true interest See the first definition of "effective rate."

trust company An organization offering professional expertise in trust management and estate administration.

trust A legal contract for the management and control of certain assets held by one person for the benefit of another.

trustee An individual or organization legally responsible for managing a trust. Also, the person who holds deeds of trust on properties until they are paid for.

trust fund Financial resources put in the custody of an individual (trustee) by someone (trustor) for the benefit of someone else (beneficiaries and remaindermen); one person may fill more than one role, depending on the type of trust.

trustor Individual who provides the assets that are set up in a trust.

type one deductions For federal income tax purposes, the expenses that may be deducted from gross income to arrive at adjusted gross income. For federal estate tax purposes, the expenses that may be deducted from the gross estate to arrive at the adjusted gross estate.

type two deductions For federal income tax purposes, itemized deductions (or the standard deduction) that may be subtracted from adjusted gross income to determine income before exemptions. These deductions may be itemized, or the standard deduction may be used. For federal estate purposes, charitable deductions that may be subtracted, along with the marital deduction, from adjusted gross estate to determine the amount of the estate before the $60,000 exemption.

umbrella policy   A type of liability insurance contract that extends sizable dollar amounts of coverage over many types of liability exposures, not just one.

underwriter   A person or firm who assumes the risk of selling a stock issue to the public. Also, an insurance agent qualified to write insurance agreements.

uniform decreasing term insurance   See "decreasing term insurance."

unlisted stock   Stocks that are not listed on a national or regional stock exchange.

U.S. savings bond   See "savings bond."

unoccupied   For property insurance purposes, the condition of a building when the contents remain but the tenant is gone. (See also "vacant.")

unsecured loan   A loan on which the only collateral is the signed guarantee of the borrower.

utilities   Stock classification that includes all electricity, gas, telephone, and water companies.

vacancy allowance   The portion of rental fees that is used to offset any loss of revenue due to vacancies.

vacant   For property insurance purposes, the condition of a dwelling when both the contents and the tenants are gone. (See "unoccupied.")

variable annuity   A regular lifetime monthly payment, the amount of which varies according to the performance of the securities held in the annuity company's portfolio.

variable expenses   Expenses that vary from month to month or year to year and allow a person some control over their amount and timing. (See also "fixed expenses.")

vesting   The process whereby an employee receives increasingly greater rights (usually as his length of employment increases) to retirement benefits based on contributions made to a retirement fund by his employer.

Veterans Administration (VA)   The federal agency charged with administering government sponsored military veterans programs; one function is to guarantee lenders against losses due to default on VA approved home mortgages taken out by veterans.

volume   For stock exchange purposes, the total number of shares of all companies traded on an organized exchange during a certain period of time such as an hour, day, or week.

W-2 Form   Record received by an employee from his employer showing the amount of income earned and the amount withheld from his earnings during the year for income and Social Security tax purposes.

wage assignment clause   The means whereby a creditor is granted the right to have a borrower's employer withhold a portion of the borrower's wages if he defaults on payments on a loan or an installment purchase; generally such action must be cleared by court order, but occasionally such a clause may be part of a sales contract. Also known as wage garnishment.

waiting period   On a disability income insurance policy, the length of time between the date of disability and the time when income benefits begin.

waiver   The voluntary surrender of a known right, claim, or privilege.

warrant   An instrument issued by a corporation giving to the holder an option to purchase a security at a predetermined price, usually within a specified but long-term period.

warranty deed   A deed guaranteeing that title to property is conveyed free of encumbrances.

when issued   A term used to describe transactions involving securities that have been authorized for issuance but have not yet been issued and delivered to the public.

whole life   See "straight life."

will   A written, legal document through which a person expresses the manner in which his estate is to be disposed of upon his death.

withholding   For federal income tax and Social Security tax purposes, the procedure whereby an employer pays a specified part of his employee's wages to the government to be applied against these taxes.

working capital   Investable funds that are not currently tied up in long-term assets; it is equal to current assets minus current liabilities.

yield   See "rate of return."

zoning   Legal ordinances used to restrict the uses to which specific pieces of property may be put.

INDEX

mortgage bond, 358
mortgage clause, 68
multiple-line insurance, 63
municipal bond, 362
mutual funds
  advantages and disadvantages of
    investing in, 420–21
  automatic reinvestment plan,
    413–14
  capital gains distribution, 413–14
  closed-end, 407–409, 418–19
  compared to alternatives, 287, 416
  definition of, 406
  dividends, 413
  dual fund, 410
  growth fund, 410
  guidelines for investing in, 421–24
  hedge fund, 410
  insurance against loss on, 417
  investment objectives of, 409
  Keogh Plan, 418, 460–61
  load fund, 408–409
  net asset value, 408
  no-load, 408–409
    selected addresses of, 423–24
  open-end, 407–409, 412–18
  portfolio, example of, 410–11
  savings plans, 412–13
    contractual and voluntary
      plans, 413
  size of, 422
  tax aspects of, 419–20
  types of, 409–12
  withdrawal plans, 414–17
mutual insurance company, 38–39,
  144–45
  compared to stock company, 39
mutual savings bank, 309

NASDAQ, 376–77
negligence and liability, 74–75
net asset value (mutual funds), 408
net estate tax, 482
net income
  on personal income statement,
    17–19
  for corporation, 340

net income per share. *See* earnings
  per share
net worth, definition of, 22
New York Stock Exchange
  average price history, 339
  common stock index, 382, 388
  description of, 373–74
  listing on, qualifications for, 374
no-fault insurance, 94–95
nominal rate, compared to effective
  rate, 205–206, 302
no-load fund, 408–409. *See also*
  mutual funds
  selected addresses of, 423–24
nonforfeiture options, 146
nonparticipating policy, 38
no-par stock, 346

odd lot, 390–91
open-ended credit, 224–28
open-end fund, 407–409. *See also*
  mutual funds
ordinary life insurance, 138, 141
other insurance clause, 68
over-the-counter market, 376–77
owning a house. *See* house,
  ownership of
ownership positions. *See* investments

paid-up addition, 145
paid-up insurance, 145
pain and suffering multiplier, 93
par value (stock), 346
participating policy, 38–39, 144–45
partnership. *See* limited partnership
passbook savings account, 307–308,
  310
pawnbrokers, 217–18
P/E ratio. *See* common stock
penalties. *See* federal income tax;
  loans
pensions
  availability of, 457
  contributions to, 458
  deferred profit sharing, 460
  eligibility requirements for, 458–59
  financing, methods of, 458

regressive tax, 178–79
REIT. *See* real estate
remaindermen (trust), 475
rent, as type of investment income, 281
renting
    advantages and disadvantages of, 241–42
    costs of, 246–47
    federal housing programs, 249
    lease agreement, 249–51
    property insurance needs, in relation to, 58, 65, 66–68
    rental alternatives, 246, 248
replacement cost
    on home, 56
    market value, compared to, 57–58
repossession, 231
research, on stocks. *See* common stock
retirement. *See also* investments; pensions; Social Security
    annuities, 459–60, 466
    house, sale of, 461–62, 465
    investments for, 462, 466
    Keogh Act, 460–61
    life expectancy table, 455
    Medicare, 115, 116, 454
    pension funds, 457–61
    retirement expenses, 451–56
        effect of inflation on, 456
    retirement goals, achieving, 462–66
    retirement income
        sources of, 456–62
        effect of inflation on, 449, 464
    retirement income credit, 460
    retirement needs, determining, 451–55
    Social Security retirement benefits, 456–67, 496
        applying for, 457, 496–97
        qualifying for, 457, 493–97
retirement income credit, 460
return on investment. *See* rate of return
rider (insurance), 113
rights (common stock), 371–72
risk (insurance). *See also* insurable risk; investment risk

definition of, 33–34
minimizing, 34–35
retaining, 35–36
transferring, 36–37
risk exposure. *See* insurable risk; investment risk; risk
round lot, 390–91

safe driver plans, 87–89
sales contract. *See* consumer credit
saving and investing money, techniques for, 277–78, 327
savings accounts. *See* time deposits
savings accumulation plan, 412–13
savings and loan associations
    as loan sources, 217
    as savings institutions, 309–10
savings bond, 312–13
scheduled property (insurance), 65, 66
schedules, 181. *See also* Tax Rate Schedules
secondary offering (secondary markets), 372–77
Securities Exchange Commission (SEC), 377, 383
Securities Investor Protection Corp. (SIPC), 385
self-employment tax, 188
Self-Employment Tax Act (SETA), 188
self-insurance, 35–36, 85, 101, 105, 111, 135, 136
selling a house. *See* house, sale of
separate property, 472, 473
separate tax return, 180
settlement options. *See* life insurance
short sale, 393–95
small loan companies. *See* loans
Social Security (FICA)
    death benefits, 130, 134–45, 496
    eligibility, required proof of, 497
    health benefits, 108, 114–16, 496
    retirement benefits, 456–57, 496
    tables of benefits, 494, 496
    taxes, 187–88
specialist (stock exchange), 372–73

ABOUT THE AUTHORS

Thomas E. Bailard, David L. Biehl, and Ronald W. Kaiser are principals in the firm Bailard, Biehl & Kaiser, Inc., registered investment counsel in Menlo Park, California. All three received their bachelor's degrees and master's degrees (business administration) from Stanford University. The authors began their careers by developing and teaching courses in personal financial development to groups of executives in large corporations in the San Francisco Bay Area. After a year's experience with corporate executives, they began to offer their classes to the public—the sole purpose being to teach people how to manage their money better and relate to the ever increasing variety of available financial services. These classes were so popular that Stanford University videotaped them and continues to broadcast them to employees in major corporations in the area as well as to students as a part of its continuing education program.

A few years ago Bailard, Biehl, and Kaiser began to shift their emphasis away from teaching people how to manage their money to actually managing their money for them. Because of their success in this area—attributable to the firm's comprehensiveness, objectivity, and research capability—Bailard, Biehl & Kaiser, Inc. now devotes nearly all of its efforts to this activity. The authors are active in the management of the firm as well as in consulting. Occasionally they find time to lecture to professional groups throughout the country.

This textbook is a product of their practical involvement in managing large sums of money as well as their experience in communicating, in a classroom environment, the skills and information people need to get the most from their incomes.

This book was set
in 10-point Century Schoolbook
with display lines in Blippo Modern Medium,
composed by Continental Data Graphics, Culver City, California,
and printed by Kingsport Press, Kingsport, Tennessee.
The paper is 50# publishers white Finch Textbook Offset, vellum finish.

The Century Schoolbook typeface was designed in 1890
by Lynn Boyd Benton for use in *Century Magazine*.
Since that time, it has become widely used
and appreciated for its readability
and versatility.

Project Editor   Gretchen Hargis
Designer   Naomi Takigawa
Illustrator   Ralph Mapson
Sponsoring Editors   Paul Kelly and Osborne Bethea, Jr.